#6

HOLT

Western World

PEOPLE, PLACES, AND CHANGE

An Introduction to World Studies

HOLT, RINEHART AND WINSTON
A Harcourt Education Company
Austin • Orlando • Chicago • New York • Toronto • London • San Diego

THE AUTHORS

Prof. Robert J. Sager is Chair of Earth Sciences at Pierce College in Lakewood, Washington. Prof. Sager received his B.S. in geology and geography and M.S. in geography from the University of Wisconsin and holds a J.D. in international law from Western State University College of Law. He is the coauthor of several geography and earth science textbooks and has written many articles and educational media programs on the geography of the Pacific. Prof. Sager has received several National Science Foundation study grants and has twice been a recipient of the University of Texas NISOD National Teaching Excellence Award. He is a founding member of the Southern California Geographic Alliance and former president of the Association of Washington Geographers.

Prof. David M. Helgren is Director of the Center for Geographic Education at San Jose State University in California, where he is also Chair of the Department of Geography. Prof. Helgren received his Ph.D. in geography from the University of Chicago. He is the coauthor of several geography textbooks and has written many articles on the geography of Africa. Awards from the National Geographic Society, the National Science Foundation, and the L. S. B. Leakey Foundation have supported his many field research projects. Prof. Helgren is a former president of the California Geographical Society and a founder of the Northern California Geographic Alliance.

Prof. Alison S. Brooks is Professor of Anthropology at George Washington University and a Research Associate in Anthropology at the Smithsonian Institution. She received her A.B., M.A., and Ph.D. in Anthropology from Harvard University. Since 1964, she has carried out ethnological and archaeological research in Africa, Europe, and Asia and is the author of more than 300 scholarly and popular publications. She has served as a consultant to Smithsonian exhibits and to National Geographic, Public Broadcasting, the Discovery Channel, and other public media. In addition, she is a founder and editor of *Anthro Notes: The National Museum of Natural History Bulletin for Teachers* and has received numerous grants and awards to develop and lead in-service training institutes for teachers in grades 5–12. She served as the American Anthropological Association's representative to the NCSS task force on developing Scope and Sequence guidelines for Social Studies Education in grade K–12.

While the details of the young people's stories in the chapter openers are real, their identities have been changed to protect their privacy.

Cover and Title Page Photo Credits: (child image) AlaskaStock Images; (bkgd) Image Copyright © 2003 PhotoDisc, Inc./HRW

For acknowledgments, see page R37, which is an extension of the copyright page.

Printed in the United States of America

ISBN 0-03-053607-3

2 3 4 5 6 7 8 9 032 05 04 03

CONTENT REVIEWERS

Robin Datel
Instructor in Geography
California State University, Sacramento

David Dickason
Professor of Geography
Western Michigan University

Dennis Dingemans
Professor of Geography
University of California, Davis

Robert Gabler
Professor of Geography
Western Illinois University

Jeffrey Gritzner
Professor of Geography
University of Montana

W. A. Douglas Jackson
Professor of Geography, Emeritus
University of Washington

Robert B. Kent
Professor of Geography and Planning
University of Akron

Kwadwo Konadu-Agyemang
Professor of Geography and Planning
University of Akron

Nancy Lewis
Professor of Geography
University of Hawaii

Bill Takizawa
Professor of Geography
San Jose State University

EDUCATIONAL REVIEWERS

Patricia Britt
Durant Middle School
Durant, Oklahoma

Marcia Caldwell
Lamar Middle School
Austin, Texas

Marcia Clevenger
Roosevelt Junior High School
Charleston, West Virginia

James Corley
Durant Middle School
Durant, Oklahoma

Maureen Dempsey
Spring Creek Middle School
Spring Creek, Nevada

Jean Eldredge
Teague Middle School
Altamonte, Florida

Cindy Herring
Old Town Elementary School
Round Rock, Texas

Lois Jordan
Pearl/Cohn Comprehensive High School
Nashville, Tennessee

Kay A. Knowles
Montross Middle School
Montross, Virginia

Wendy Mason
Corbett Junior High School
Schertz, Texas

Rebecca Minnear
Burkholder Middle School
Las Vegas, Nevada

Jane Palmer
District Supervisor for Social Studies
Sanford, Florida

Sandra Rojas
Adams City Middle School
Commerce City, Colorado

JoAnn Sadler
Curriculum Supervisor
Buffalo City Schools
Buffalo, New York

Celeste Smith
Crockett High School
Austin, Texas

Frank Thomas
Crockett High School
Austin, Texas

Susan Walker
Beaufort County School District
Beaufort, South Carolina

Field Test Teachers

Ricky A. Blackman
Rawlinson Road Middle School
Rock Hill, South Carolina

Lisa Klien
Daniels Middle School
Raleigh, North Carolina

Deborah D. Larry
Garland V. Stewart Middle School
Tampa, Florida

Linda P. Moore
Cramerton Middle School
Cramerton, North Carolina

Earl F. Sease
Portage Area School District
Portage, Pennsylvania

Christi Sherrill
Grier Middle School
Gastonia, North Carolina

John W. Watkins, Jr.
Clark Middle School
East St. Louis, Illinois

Editorial
Sue Miller, *Director*
Robert Wehnke, *Managing Editor*
Diana Holman Walker, *Senior Editor*
Holly Norman, *Project Editor*
Daniel M. Quinn, *Senior Editor*
Sue Minkler, *Assistant Editorial Coordinator*
Gina Rogers, *Administrative Assistant*

Pupil's Edition
Andrew Miles, *Editor*
Jarred Prejean, *Associate Editor*

Teacher's Edition
Lissa B. Anderson, *Editor*
Suzanne Hurley, *Senior Editor*

Technology Resources
Annette Saunders, *Editor*

Fact Checking
Bob Fullilove, *Editor*
Jenny Rose, *Associate Editor*

Copy Editing
Julie Beckman, *Senior Copy Editor*

Text Permissions
Ann B. Farrar, *Senior Permissions Editor*

Art, Design and Photo
Book Design
Diane Motz, *Senior Design Director*
Candace Moore, *Senior Designer*
Mercedes Newman, *Designer*

Image Acquisitions
Joe London, *Director*
Tim Taylor, *Photo Research Supervisor*
Stephanie Morris, *Photo Researcher*
Michelle Rumpf, *Art Buyer Supervisor*
Coco Weir, *Art Buyer*
Julie Kelly, *Art Buyer*

Design Implementation
The GTS Companies

Design New Media
Susan Michael, *Design Director*
Kimberly Cammaerata, *Design Manager*
Grant Davidson, *Designer*

Media Design
Curtis Riker, *Design Director*

Cover Design
Jason Wilson, *Designer*

Pre-press and Manufacturing
Gene Rumann, *Production Manager*
Nancy Hargis, *Production Supervisor*
Vivian Hess, *Administrative Assistant*
Clary Knapp, *Production Coordinator*
Rhonda Farris, *Inventory Planner*
Kim Harrison, *Manufacturing Coordinator, Media*

HOLT

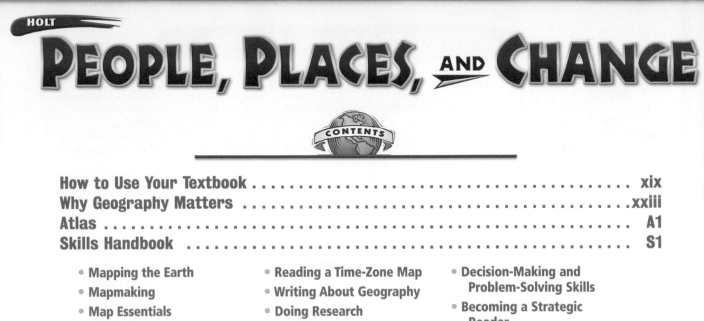

PEOPLE, PLACES, AND CHANGE

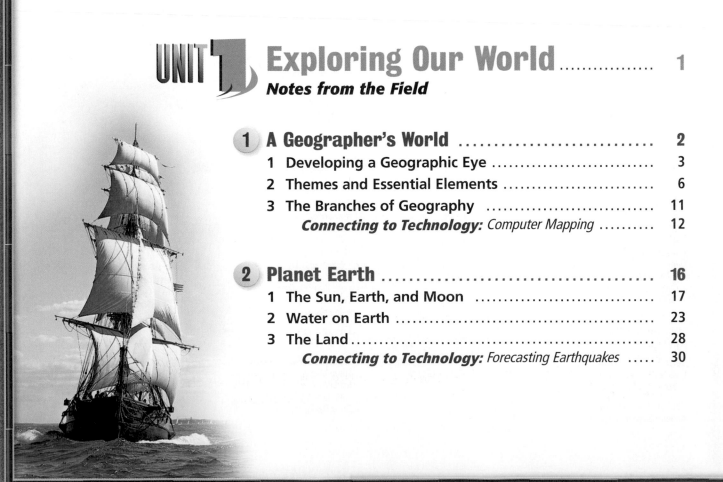

CONTENTS

UNIT 3

United States and Canada 206

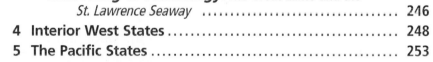

OUI
ui
et ça devient possible

UNIT 4 Middle and South America

Title	HOLT PEOPLE, PLACES, AND CHANGE:
Condition	Very Good
Location	Aisle 21 Bay 2 Shelf 5 Item 182
Description	Book is in very good condition. There is no writing or highlighting, spine is tight and the pages are uncreased. We ship within 1 business day. Big Hearted Books shares its profits with schools, churches and non-profit groups throughout New England. Thank you for your support! This item is listed as very good and contains all suplementary materials and is free of writing and highlighting. May have standard light shelfwear but all pages are clean, uncreased and the binding is tight.
Source	July
SKU	34FD10000E65
ASIN	0030536073
Code	9780030536076
Employee	kristeng
Date Added	7/21/2016 9:42:01 AM

REFERENCE SECTION

FEATURES

Connecting to Art

Connecting to History

Connecting to Literature

Connecting to Math

Connecting to Science

Connecting to Technology

CASE STUDY

FOCUS ON

FEATURES

Geo Skills

BUILDING SKILLS FOR LIFE:

Hands On Geography

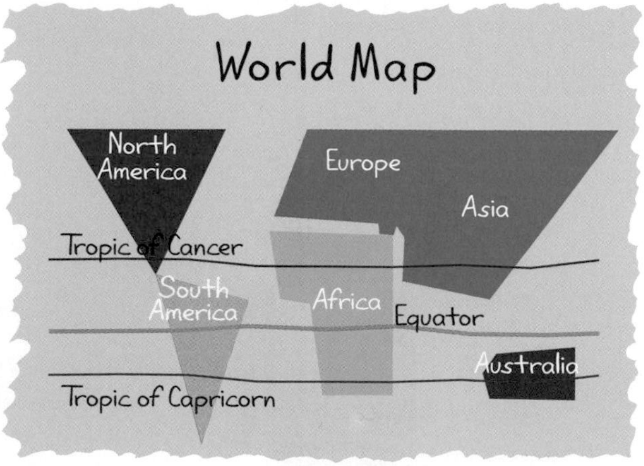

World Map
North America
Europe
Asia
Tropic of Cancer
South America
Africa
Equator
Australia
Tropic of Capricorn

MAPS

FEATURES

DIAGRAMS, CHARTS, and TABLES

FEATURES

DIAGRAMS, CHARTS, and TABLES *continued*

How To Use Your Textbook

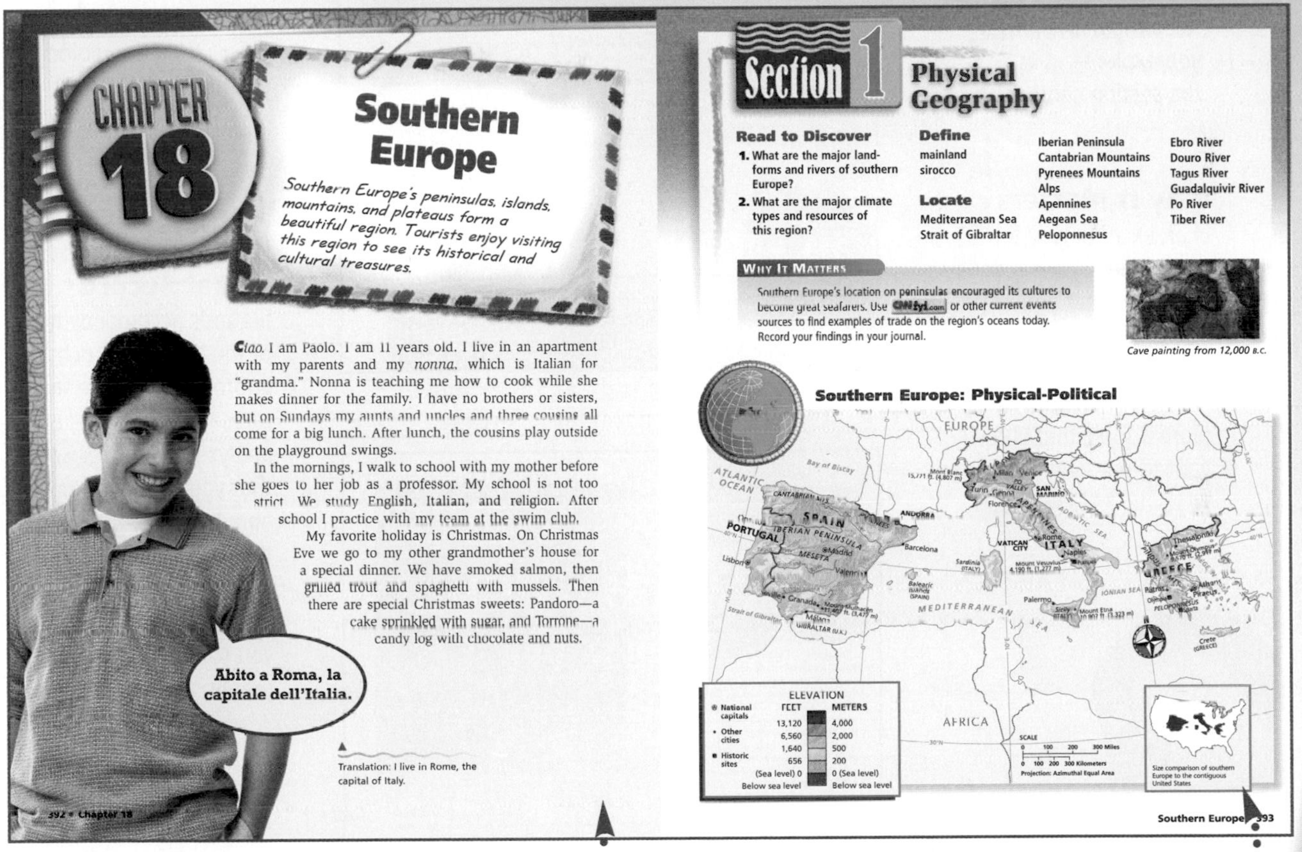
CHAPTER 18
Southern Europe
Southern Europe's peninsulas, islands, mountains, and plateaus form a beautiful region. Tourists enjoy visiting this region to see its historical and cultural treasures.
Ciao. I am Paolo. I am 11 years old. I live in an apartment with my parents and my *nonna*, which is Italian for "grandma." Nonna is teaching me how to cook while she makes dinner for the family. I have no brothers or sisters, but on Sundays my aunts and uncles and three cousins all come for a big lunch. After lunch, the cousins play outside on the playground swings.
In the mornings, I walk to school with my mother before she goes to her job as a professor. My school is not too strict. We study English, Italian, and religion. After school I practice with my team at the swim club.
My favorite holiday is Christmas. On Christmas Eve we go to my other grandmother's house for a special dinner. We have smoked salmon, then grilled trout and spaghetti with mussels. Then there are special Christmas sweets: Pandoro—a cake sprinkled with sugar, and Torrone—a candy log with chocolate and nuts.
Abito a Roma, la capitale dell'Italia.
Translation: I live in Rome, the capital of Italy.
392 • Chapter 18
Section 1 Physical Geography
Read to Discover
1. What are the major landforms and rivers of southern Europe?
2. What are the major climate types and resources of this region?
Define
mainland
sirocco
Locate
Mediterranean Sea
Strait of Gibraltar
Iberian Peninsula
Cantabrian Mountains
Pyrenees Mountains
Alps
Apennines
Aegean Sea
Peloponnesus
Ebro River
Douro River
Tagus River
Guadalquivir River
Po River
Tiber River
WHY IT MATTERS
Southern Europe's location on peninsulas encouraged its cultures to become great seafarers. Use CNNfyi.com or other current events sources to find examples of trade on the region's oceans today. Record your findings in your journal.
Cave painting from 12,000 B.C.
Southern Europe: Physical-Political
EUROPE
ATLANTIC OCEAN
SPAIN
PORTUGAL
ITALY
GREECE
MEDITERRANEAN SEA
AFRICA
ELEVATION
Southern Europe 393

An interview with a student begins each regional chapter. These interviews give you a glimpse of what life is like for some people in the region you are about to study.

Chapter Map The map at the beginning of Section 1 in regional chapters shows you the countries you will read about. You can use this map to identify country names and capitals and to locate physical features. These chapter maps will also help you create sketch maps in section reviews.

Use these built-in tools to read for understanding.

Read to Discover questions begin each section of *Holt People, Places, and Change.* These questions serve as your guide as you read through the section. Keep them in mind as you explore the section content.

Why It Matters is an exciting way for you to make connections between what you are reading in your geography textbook and the world around you. Explore a topic that is relevant to our lives today by using CNNfyi.com.

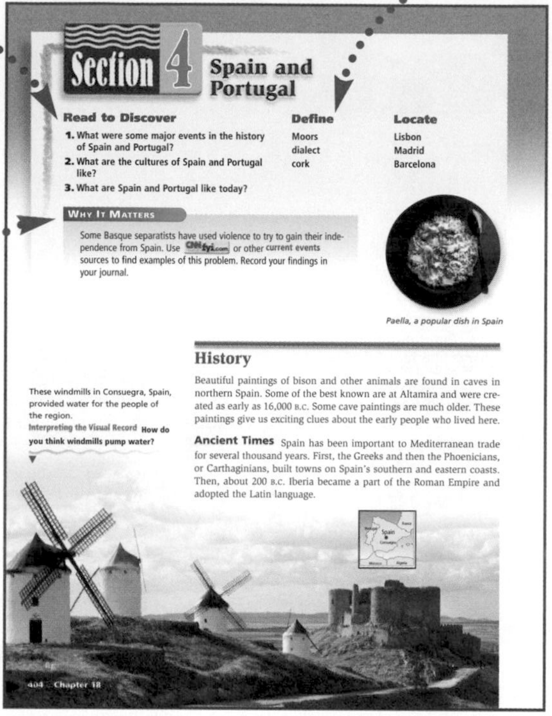

Section 4 Spain and Portugal

Read to Discover
1. What were some major events in the history of Spain and Portugal?
2. What are the cultures of Spain and Portugal like?
3. What are Spain and Portugal like today?

Define
Moors
dialect
cork

Locate
Lisbon
Madrid
Barcelona

Why It Matters
Some Basque separatists have used violence to try to gain their independence from Spain. Use CNNfyi.com or other current events sources to find examples of this problem. Record your findings in your journal.

Paella, a popular dish in Spain

History
Beautiful paintings of bison and other animals are found in caves in northern Spain. Some of the best known are at Altamira and were created as early as 16,000 B.C. Some cave paintings are much older. These paintings give us exciting clues about the early people who lived here.

Ancient Times Spain has been important to Mediterranean trade for several thousand years. First, the Greeks and then the Phoenicians, or Carthaginians, built towns on Spain's southern and eastern coasts. Then, about 200 B.C. Iberia became a part of the Roman Empire and adopted the Latin language.

These windmills in Consuegra, Spain, provided water for the people of the region.
Interpreting the Visual Record How do you think windmills pump water?

404 Chapter 18

Define and Locate terms are introduced at the beginning of each section. The Define terms include terms important to the study of geography and to the region you are studying. The Locate terms are important physical features or places from the region you are studying.

Interpreting the Visual Record features accompany many of the textbook's rich photographs. These features invite you to analyze the images so that you can learn more about their content and their links to what you are studying in the section. Other captions ask you to interpret maps, graphs, and charts.

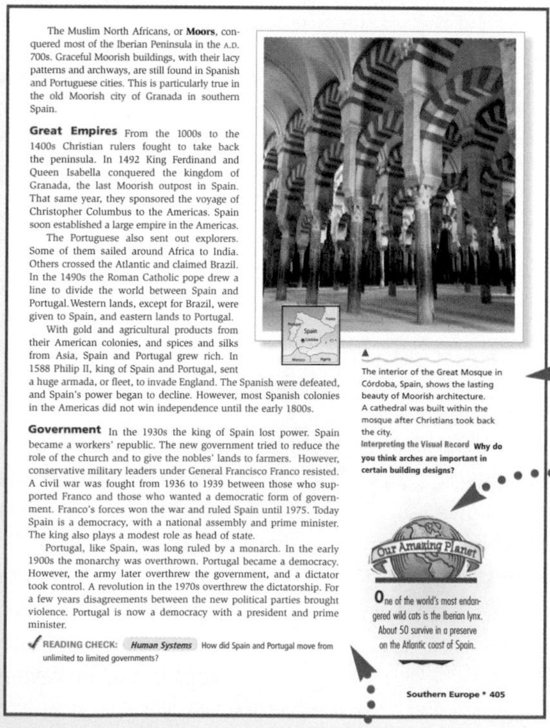

The Muslim North Africans, or **Moors**, conquered most of the Iberian Peninsula in the A.D. 700s. Graceful Moorish buildings, with their lacy patterns and archways, are still found in Spanish and Portuguese cities. This is particularly true in the old Moorish city of Granada in southern Spain.

Great Empires From the 1000s to the 1400s Christian rulers fought to take back the peninsula. In 1492 King Ferdinand and Queen Isabella conquered the kingdom of Granada, the last Moorish outpost in Spain. That same year, they sponsored the voyage of Christopher Columbus to the Americas. Spain soon established a large empire in the Americas.

The Portuguese also sent out explorers. Some of them sailed around Africa to India. Others crossed the Atlantic and claimed Brazil. In the 1490s the Roman Catholic pope drew a line to divide the world between Spain and Portugal. Western lands, except for Brazil, were given to Spain, and eastern lands to Portugal.

With gold and agricultural products from their American colonies, and spices and silks from Asia, Spain and Portugal grew rich. In 1588 Philip II, king of Spain and Portugal, sent a huge armada, or fleet, to invade England. The Spanish were defeated, and Spain's power began to decline. However, most Spanish colonies in the Americas did not win independence until the early 1800s.

Government In the 1930s the king of Spain lost power. Spain became a workers' republic. The new government tried to reduce the role of the church and to give the nobles' lands to farmers. However, conservative military leaders under General Francisco Franco resisted. A civil war was fought from 1936 to 1939 between those who supported Franco and those who wanted a democratic form of government. Franco's forces won the war and ruled Spain until 1975. Today Spain is a democracy, with a national assembly and prime minister. The king also plays a modest role as head of state.

Portugal, like Spain, was long ruled by a monarch. In the early 1900s the monarchy was overthrown. Portugal became a democracy. However, the army later overthrew the government, and a dictator took control. A revolution in the 1970s overthrew the dictatorship. For a few years disagreements between the new political parties brought violence. Portugal is now a democracy with a president and prime minister.

✓ READING CHECK: *Human Systems* How did Spain and Portugal move from unlimited to limited governments?

The interior of the Great Mosque in Córdoba, Spain, shows the lasting beauty of Moorish architecture. A cathedral was built within the mosque after Christians took back the city.
Interpreting the Visual Record Why do you think arches are important in certain building designs?

Our Amazing Planet
One of the world's most endangered wild cats is the Iberian lynx. About 50 survive in a preserve on the Atlantic coast of Spain.

Southern Europe • 405

Our Amazing Planet features provide interesting facts about the region you are studying. Here you will learn about the origins of place-names and fascinating tidbits like the size of South America's rain forests.

Reading Check questions appear often throughout the textbook to allow you to check your comprehension. As you read, pause for a moment to consider each Reading Check. If you have trouble answering the question, review the material that you just read.

Use these tools to pull together all of the information you have learned.

Critical Thinking activities in section and chapter reviews allow you to explore a topic in greater depth and to build your skills.

Homework Practice Online lets you log on to the HRW Go site to complete an interactive self-check of the material covered.

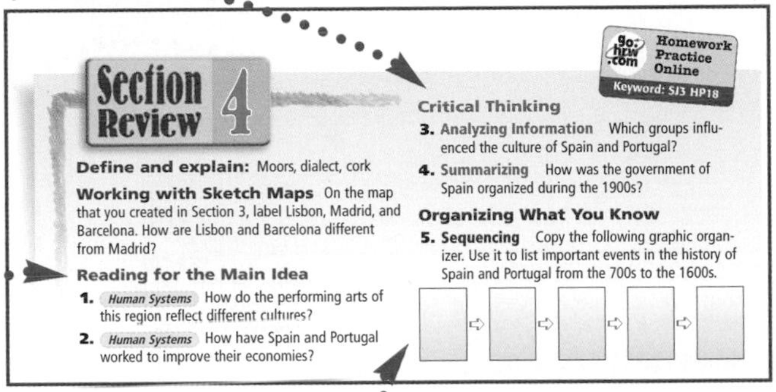

Section 4 Review

go.hrw.com Homework Practice Online Keyword: SJ3 HP18

Define and explain: Moors, dialect, cork

Working with Sketch Maps On the map that you created in Section 3, label Lisbon, Madrid, and Barcelona. How are Lisbon and Barcelona different from Madrid?

Reading for the Main Idea

1. *Human Systems* How do the performing arts of this region reflect different cultures?
2. *Human Systems* How have Spain and Portugal worked to improve their economies?

Critical Thinking

3. **Analyzing Information** Which groups influenced the culture of Spain and Portugal?
4. **Summarizing** How was the government of Spain organized during the 1900s?

Organizing What You Know

5. **Sequencing** Copy the following graphic organizer. Use it to list important events in the history of Spain and Portugal from the 700s to the 1600s.

Reading for the Main Idea questions help review the main points you have studied in the section.

Graphic Organizers will help you pull together important information from the section.

Building Social Studies Skills activities help you develop the mapping and writing skills you need to study geography.

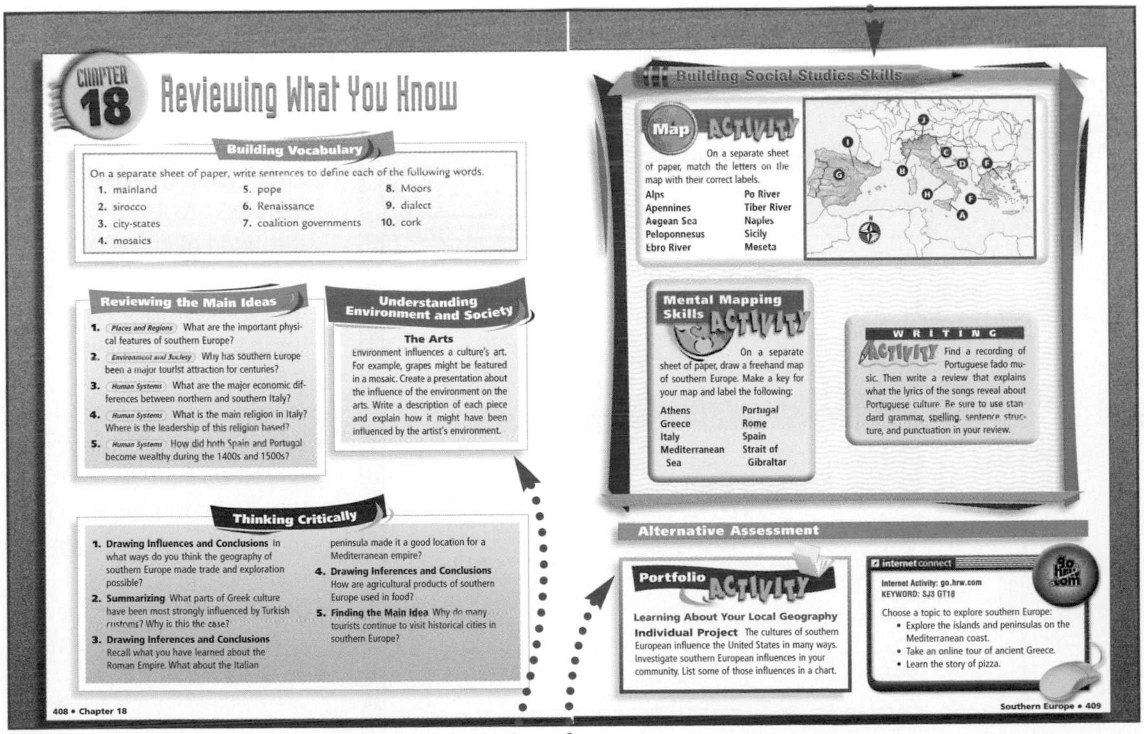

Chapter 18 Reviewing What You Know

Building Vocabulary

On a separate sheet of paper, write sentences to define each of the following words.

1. mainland
2. sirocco
3. city-states
4. mosaics
5. pope
6. Renaissance
7. coalition governments
8. Moors
9. dialect
10. cork

Reviewing the Main Ideas

1. *Places and Regions* What are the important physical features of southern Europe?
2. *Environment and Society* Why has southern Europe been a major tourist attraction for centuries?
3. *Human Systems* What are the major economic differences between northern and southern Italy?
4. *Human Systems* What is the main religion in Italy? Where is the leadership of this religion based?
5. *Human Systems* How did both Spain and Portugal become wealthy during the 1400s and 1500s?

Understanding Environment and Society

The Arts

Environment influences a culture's art. For example, grapes might be featured in a mosaic. Create a presentation about the influence of the environment on the arts. Write a description of each piece and explain how it might have been influenced by the artist's environment.

Thinking Critically

1. **Drawing Influences and Conclusions** In what ways do you think the geography of southern Europe made trade and exploration possible?
2. **Summarizing** What parts of Greek culture have been most strongly influenced by Turkish customs? Why is this the case?
3. **Drawing Inferences and Conclusions** Recall what you have learned about the Roman Empire. What about the Italian peninsula made it a good location for a Mediterranean empire?
4. **Drawing Inferences and Conclusions** How are agricultural products of southern Europe used in food?
5. **Finding the Main Idea** Why do many tourists continue to visit historical cities in southern Europe?

408 • Chapter 18

Building Social Studies Skills

Map Activity

On a separate sheet of paper, match the letters on the map with their correct labels.

Alps	Po River
Apennines	Tiber River
Aegean Sea	Naples
Peloponnesus	Sicily
Ebro River	Meseta

Mental Mapping Skills Activity

On a separate sheet of paper, draw a freehand map of southern Europe. Make a key for your map and label the following:

Athens	Portugal
Greece	Rome
Italy	Spain
Mediterranean Sea	Strait of Gibraltar

Writing Activity

Find a recording of Portuguese fado music. Then write a review that explains what the lyrics of the songs reveal about Portuguese culture. Be sure to use standard grammar, spelling, sentence structure, and punctuation in your review.

Alternative Assessment

Portfolio Activity

Learning About Your Local Geography

Individual Project The cultures of southern European influence the United States in many ways. Investigate southern European influences in your community. List some of those influences in a chart.

internet connect

Internet Activity: go.hrw.com
KEYWORD: SJ3 GT18

Choose a topic to explore southern Europe:
- Explore the islands and peninsulas on the Mediterranean coast.
- Take an online tour of ancient Greece.
- Learn the story of pizza.

Southern Europe • 409

Understanding Environment and Society activities ask you to research and create a presentation expanding on an issue you have read about in the chapter.

Portfolio Activities are exciting and creative ways to explore your local geography and to make connections to the region you are studying.

Use these online tools to review and complete online activities.

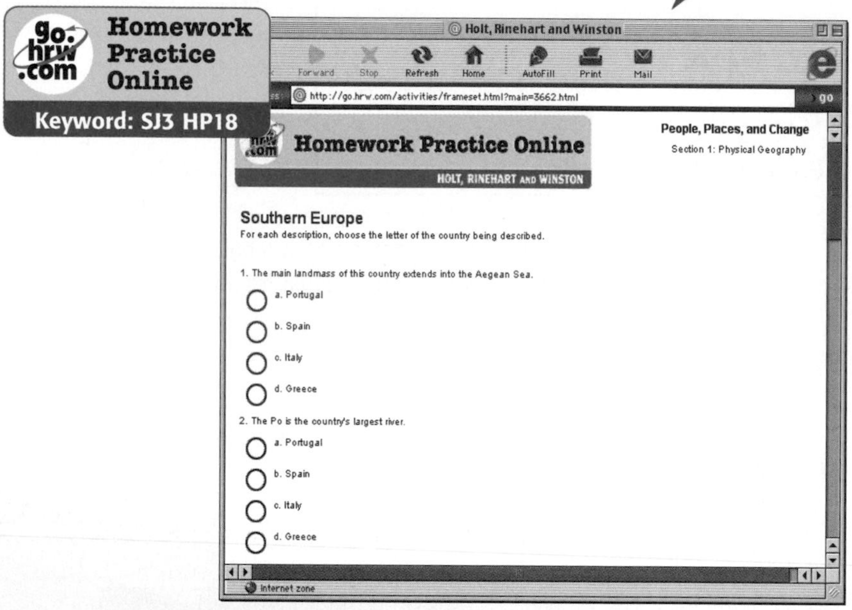

go.hrw.com
Homework Practice Online
Keyword: SJ3 HP18
Holt, Rinehart and Winston
Forward
Stop
Refresh
Home
AutoFill
Print
Mail
http://go.hrw.com/activities/frameset.html?main=3662.html
Homework Practice Online
HOLT, RINEHART AND WINSTON
People, Places, and Change
Section 1: Physical Geography
Southern Europe
For each description, choose the letter of the country being described.
1. The main landmass of this country extends into the Aegean Sea.
a. Portugal
b. Spain
c. Italy
d. Greece
2. The Po is the country's largest river.
a. Portugal
b. Spain
c. Italy
d. Greece
Internet zone

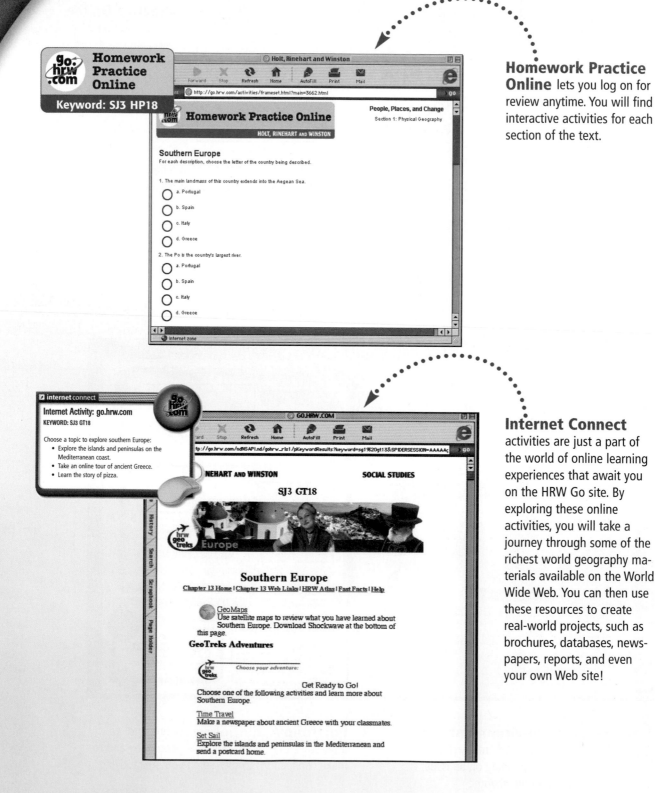

Homework Practice Online lets you log on for review anytime. You will find interactive activities for each section of the text.

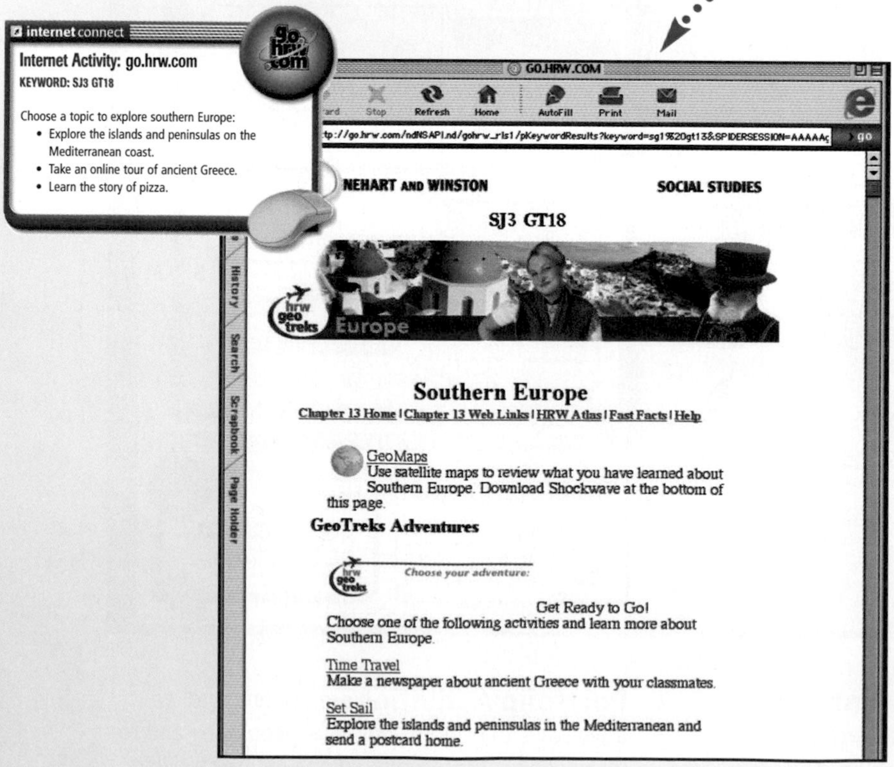

internet connect
Internet Activity: go.hrw.com
KEYWORD: SJ3 GT18
Choose a topic to explore southern Europe:
• Explore the islands and peninsulas on the Mediterranean coast.
• Take an online tour of ancient Greece.
• Learn the story of pizza.
GO.HRW.COM
Stop
Refresh
Home
AutoFill
Print
Mail
NEHART AND WINSTON
SOCIAL STUDIES
SJ3 GT18
Europe
Southern Europe
Chapter 13 Home | Chapter 13 Web Links | HRW Atlas | Fast Facts | Help
GeoMaps
Use satellite maps to review what you have learned about Southern Europe. Download Shockwave at the bottom of this page.
GeoTreks Adventures
Choose your adventure:
Get Ready to Go!
Choose one of the following activities and learn more about Southern Europe.
Time Travel
Make a newspaper about ancient Greece with your classmates.
Set Sail
Explore the islands and peninsulas in the Mediterranean and send a postcard home.
History
Search
Scrapbook
Page Holder

Internet Connect activities are just a part of the world of online learning experiences that await you on the HRW Go site. By exploring these online activities, you will take a journey through some of the richest world geography materials available on the World Wide Web. You can then use these resources to create real-world projects, such as brochures, databases, newspapers, reports, and even your own Web site!

Why Geography Matters

Have you ever wondered. . .

why some places are deserts while other places get so much rain? What makes certain times of the year cooler than others? Why do some rivers run dry?

cnn_fav_ref.mov
CNNfyi.com
JANA JACOBS
CNN STUDENT BUREAU
CNN.com
Blind children share with sighted
CNN Student Bureau's Jana Jacobs reports on a program in Alanta that brings sighted and blind children together (August 7)

CNNfyi.com
CNNfyi.com >News for students, resources for teachers
Harcourt
Riverdeep
Weekly Activities
Mosquitoes harbor more than West Nile
New object deemed largest minor planet
U.S. investigators to probe Aaliyah crash
U.S. fines citizens for travel to Cuba
Helms says he won't seek re-election
THE ALL-PURPOSE SCHOOL
FEATURED LINK
More Stories/Lesson Plans:
WORLD EVENTS / GEOGRAPHY
EXTRA EXTRA EXTRA

The CNNfyi.com Web site

Maybe you live near mountains and wonder what processes created them. Do you know why the loss of huge forest areas in one part of the world can affect areas far away? Why does the United States have many different kinds of churches and other places of worship? Perhaps you are curious why Americans and people from other countries have such different points of view on many issues. The key to understanding questions and issues like these lies in the study of geography.

Geography and Your World

All you need to do is watch or read the news to see the importance of geography. You have probably seen news stories about the effects of floods, volcanic eruptions, and other natural events on people and places. You likely have also seen how conflict and cooperation shape the relations between peoples and countries around the world. The Why It Matters feature beginning every section of *Holt People, Places, and Change* uses the vast resources of CNNfyi.com or other current events sources to examine the importance of geography. Through this feature you will be able to draw connections between what you are studying in your geography textbook and events and conditions found around the world today.

My fall semester project, growing a garden

Geography and Making Connections

When you think of the word *geography,* what comes to mind? Perhaps you simply picture people memorizing names of countries and capitals. Maybe you think of people studying maps to identify features like deserts, mountains, oceans, and rivers. These things are important, but the study of geography includes much more. Geography involves asking questions and solving problems. It focuses on looking at people and their ways of life as well as studying physical features like mountains, oceans, and rivers. Studying geography also means looking at why things are where they are and at the relationships between human and physical features of Earth.

The study of geography helps us make connections between what was, what is, and what may be. It helps us understand the processes that have shaped the features we observe around us today, as well as the ways those features may be different tomorrow. In short, geography helps us understand the processes that have created a world that is home to more than 6 billion people and countless billions of other creatures.

Geography and You

Anyone can influence the geography of our world. For example, the actions of individuals affect local environments. Some individual actions might pollute the environment. Other actions might contribute to efforts to keep the environment clean and healthy. Various other things also influence geography. For example, governments create political divisions, such as countries and states. The borders between these divisions influence the human geography of regions by separating peoples, legal systems, and human activities.

Governments and businesses also plan and build structures like dams, railroads, and airports, which change the physical characteristics of places. As you might expect, some actions influence Earth's geography in negative ways, others in positive ways. Understanding geography helps us evaluate the consequences of our actions.

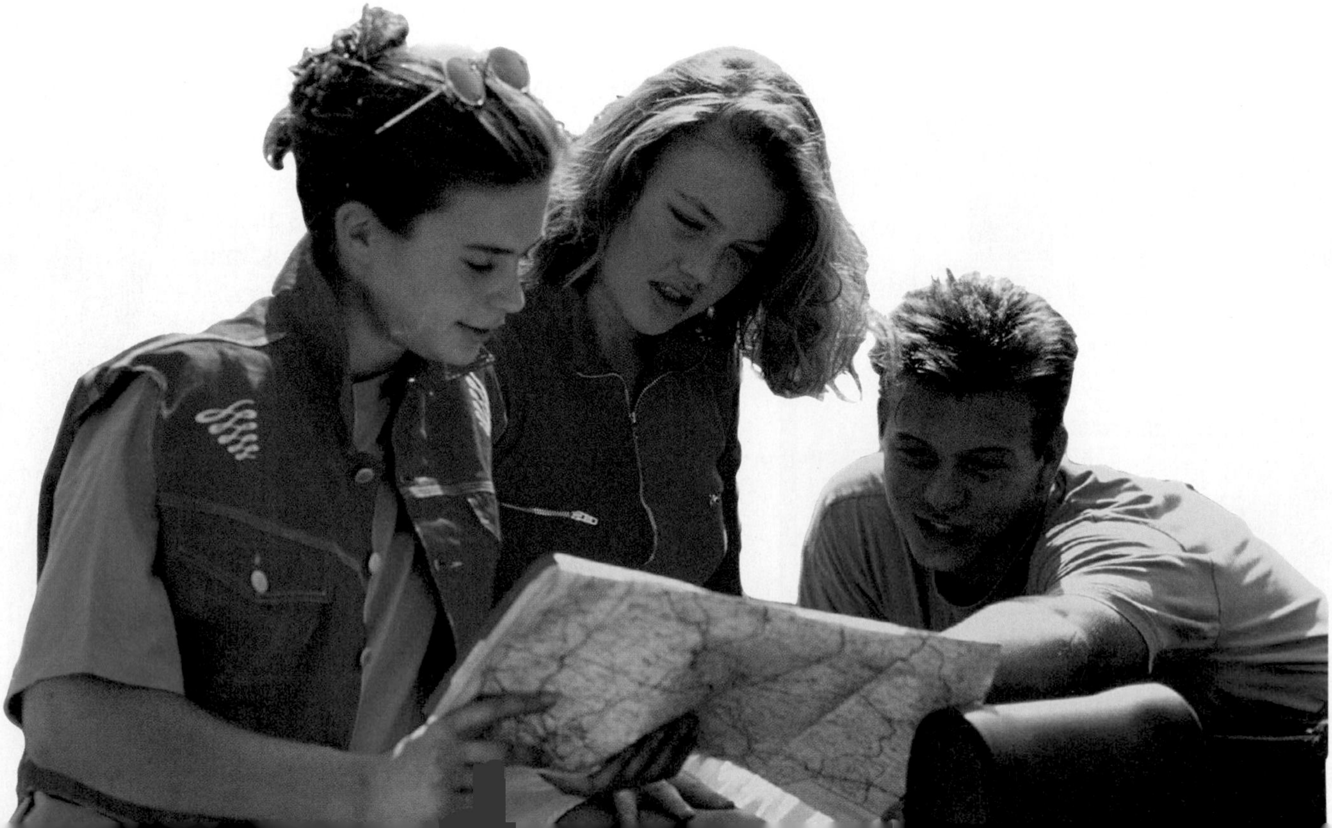

ATLAS

CONTENTS

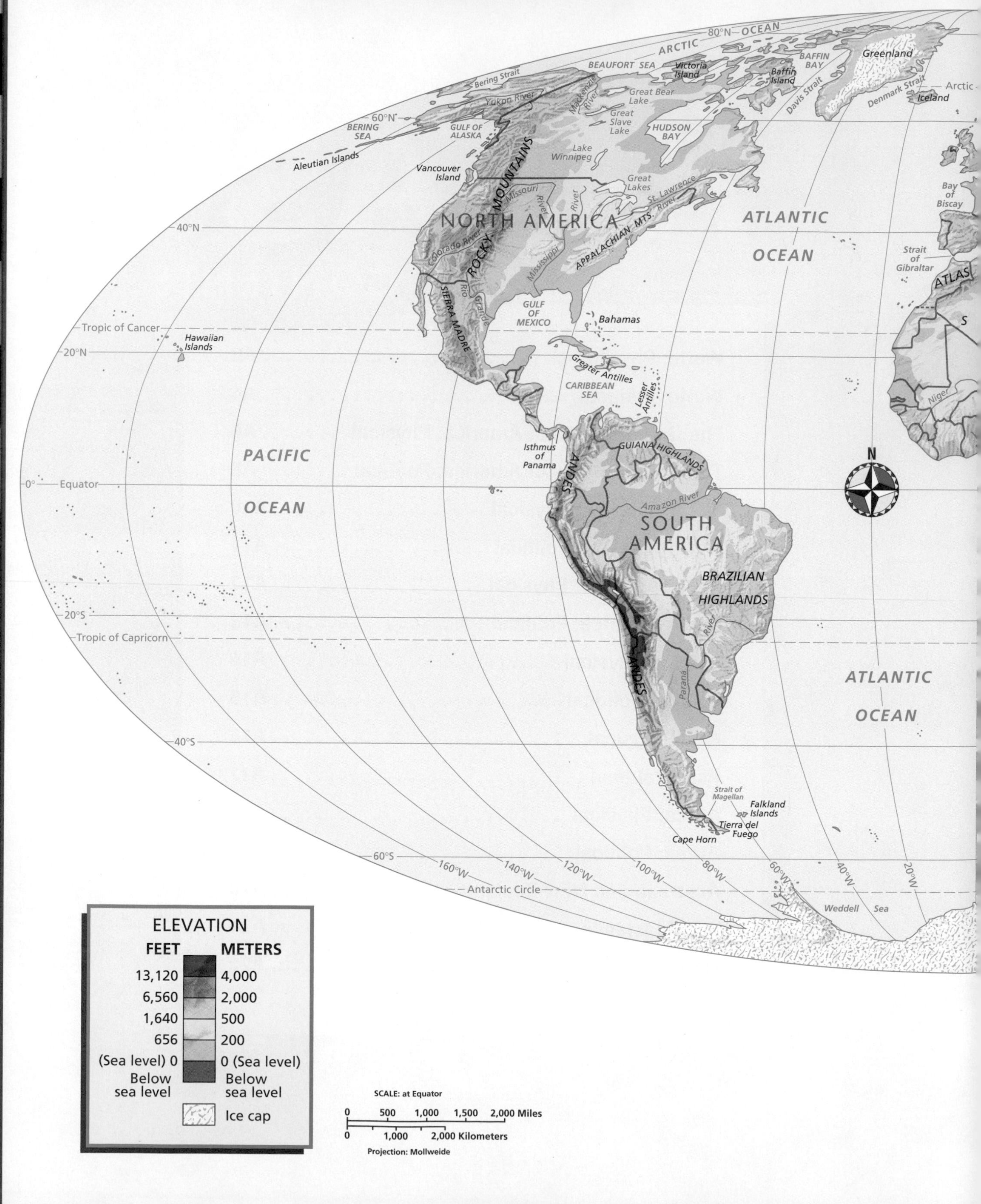
ARCTIC OCEAN
BEAUFORT SEA
Victoria Island
Baffin Island
BAFFIN BAY
Greenland
Bering Strait
Yukon River
Mackenzie River
Great Bear Lake
Great Slave Lake
HUDSON BAY
Davis Strait
Denmark Strait
Iceland
BERING SEA
GULF OF ALASKA
Aleutian Islands
Lake Winnipeg
Vancouver Island
ROCKY MOUNTAINS
Missouri River
Great Lakes
St. Lawrence River
NORTH AMERICA
APPALACHIAN MTS.
Colorado River
Mississippi River
Rio Grande
SIERRA MADRE
GULF OF MEXICO
Bahamas
Hawaiian Islands
Tropic of Cancer
Greater Antilles
CARIBBEAN SEA
Lesser Antilles
ATLANTIC OCEAN
Bay of Biscay
Strait of Gibraltar
ATLAS
Niger
PACIFIC OCEAN
Isthmus of Panama
ANDES
GUIANA HIGHLANDS
Equator
Amazon River
SOUTH AMERICA
BRAZILIAN HIGHLANDS
Paraná River
Tropic of Capricorn
Strait of Magellan
Falkland Islands
Tierra del Fuego
Cape Horn
Antarctic Circle
Weddell Sea
80°N
60°N
40°N
20°N
0°
20°S
40°S
60°S
160°W
140°W
120°W
100°W
80°W
60°W
40°W
20°W
N
ELEVATION
FEET
METERS
13,120
6,560
1,640
656
(Sea level) 0
Below sea level
4,000
2,000
500
200
0 (Sea level)
Below sea level
Ice cap
SCALE: at Equator
0
500
1,000
1,500
2,000 Miles
0
1,000
2,000 Kilometers
Projection: Mollweide

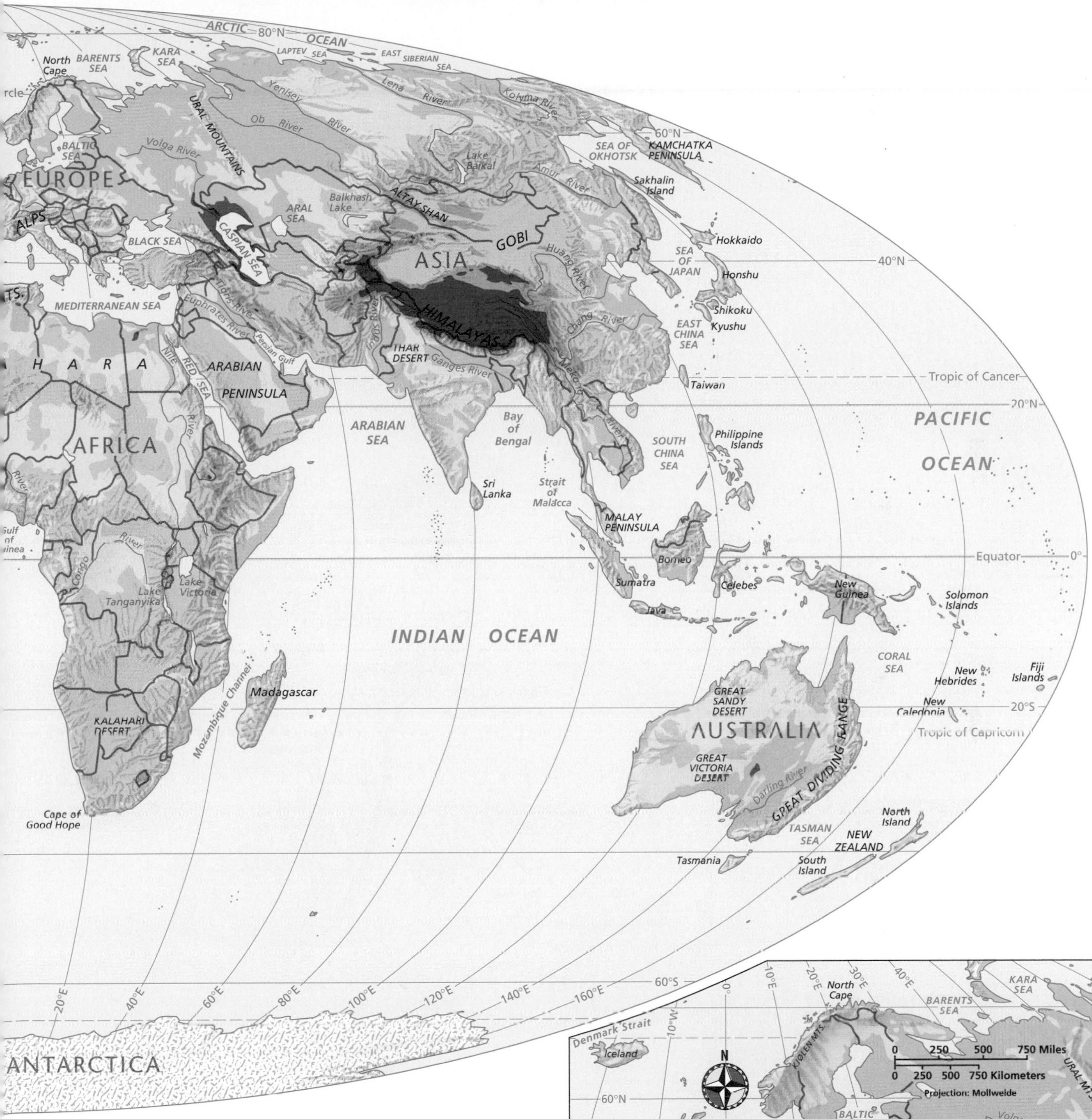

ARCTIC OCEAN
80°N
North Cape
BARENTS SEA
KARA SEA
LAPTEV SEA
EAST SIBERIAN SEA
Lena River
Yenisey River
Kolyma River
Ob River
URAL MOUNTAINS
BALTIC SEA
Volga River
60°N
SEA OF OKHOTSK
KAMCHATKA PENINSULA
Lake Baikal
Amur River
EUROPE
Sakhalin Island
Balkhash Lake
ARAL SEA
ALTAY SHAN
ALPS
CASPIAN SEA
BLACK SEA
GOBI
Hokkaido
ASIA
SEA OF JAPAN
40°N
Honshu
Huang River
MEDITERRANEAN SEA
Euphrates River
Tigris River
HIMALAYAS
Shikoku
Kyushu
EAST CHINA SEA
Chang River
Indus River
Persian Gulf
Nile
RED SEA
ARABIAN
PENINSULA
THAR DESERT
Ganges River
H A R A
Taiwan
Tropic of Cancer
20°N
ARABIAN SEA
Bay of Bengal
SOUTH CHINA SEA
Philippine Islands
PACIFIC
OCEAN
AFRICA
Sri Lanka
Strait of Malacca
MALAY PENINSULA
Borneo
Equator
0°
Sumatra
Celebes
New Guinea
Solomon Islands
Lake Victoria
Lake Tanganyika
Congo
Java
INDIAN OCEAN
CORAL SEA
New Hebrides
Fiji Islands
Madagascar
Mozambique Channel
GREAT SANDY DESERT
New Caledonia
20°S
KALAHARI DESERT
AUSTRALIA
Tropic of Capricorn
GREAT VICTORIA DESERT
GREAT DIVIDING RANGE
Darling River
Cape of Good Hope
North Island
TASMAN SEA
NEW ZEALAND
Tasmania
South Island
60°S
20°E
40°E
60°E
80°E
100°E
120°E
140°E
160°E
ANTARCTICA

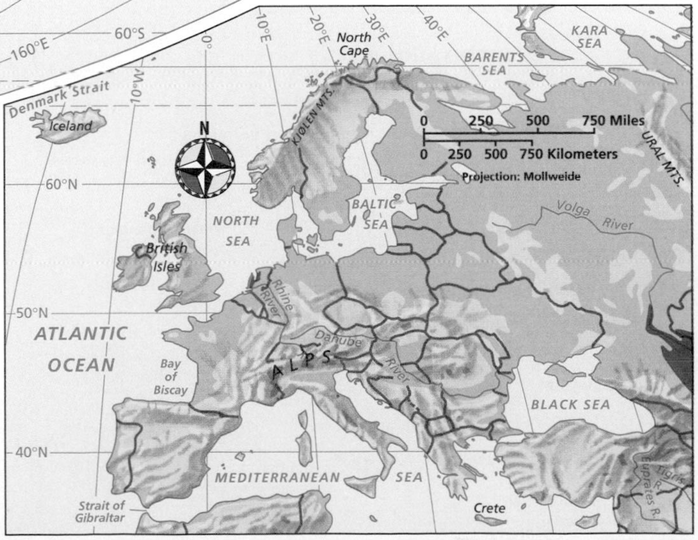

KARA SEA
BARENTS SEA
North Cape
Denmark Strait
Iceland
KJOLEN MTS.
URAL MTS.
0 250 500 750 Miles
0 250 500 750 Kilometers
Projection: Mollweide
N
60°N
NORTH SEA
BALTIC SEA
Volga River
British Isles
50°N
Rhine River
ATLANTIC OCEAN
Danube
ALPS
Bay of Biscay
BLACK SEA
40°N
MEDITERRANEAN SEA
Strait of Gibraltar
Crete
10°W
0°
10°E
20°E
30°E
40°E

WORLD: POLITICAL

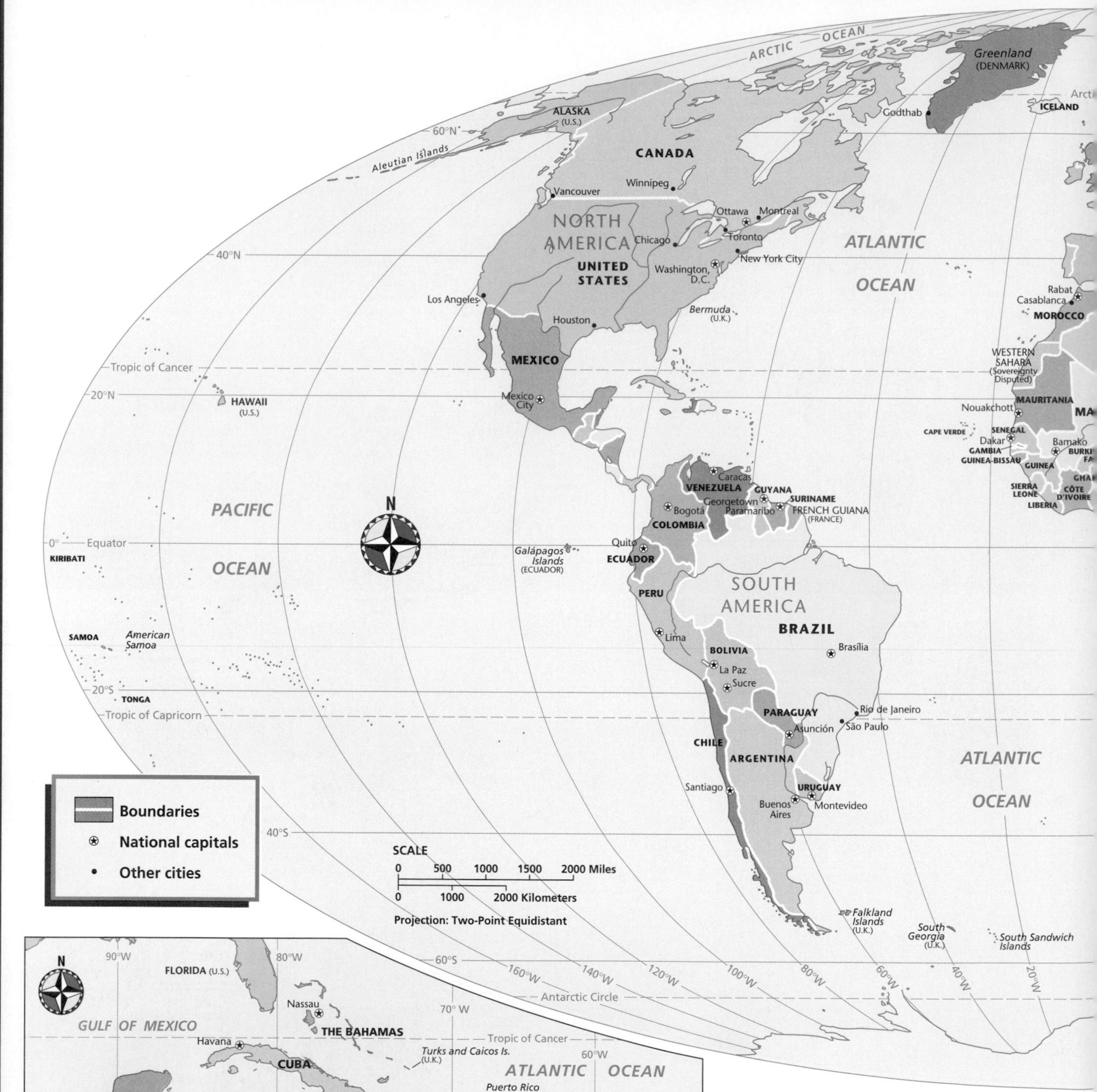

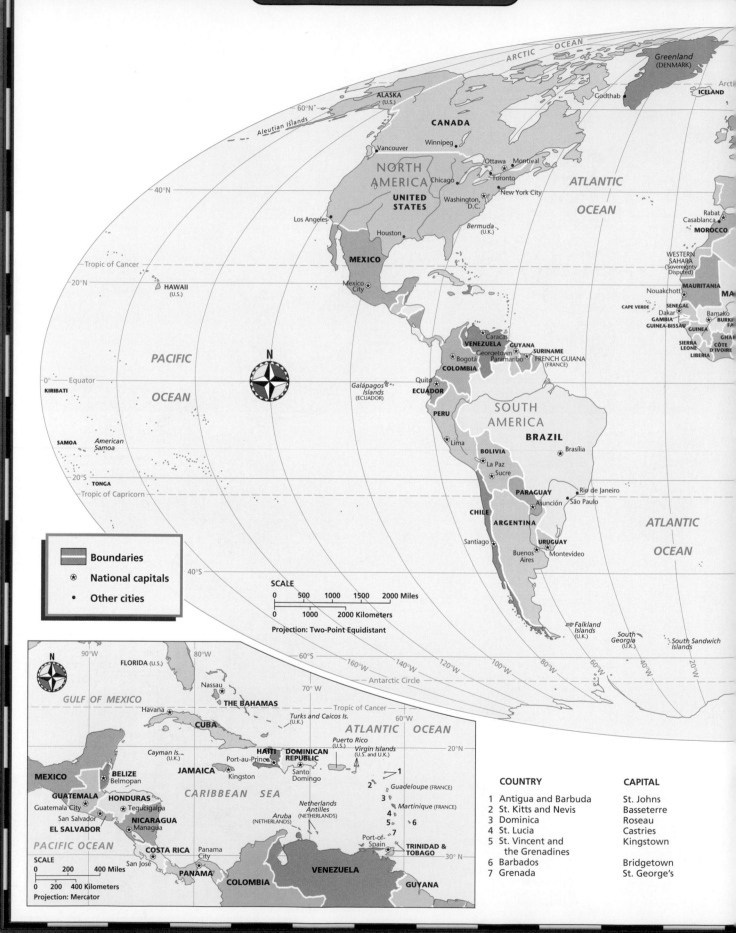

ARCTIC OCEAN
Greenland (DENMARK)
ICELAND
Godthab
ALASKA (U.S.)
60°N
Aleutian Islands
CANADA
Winnipeg
Vancouver
Ottawa
Montreal
Toronto
NORTH AMERICA
Chicago
UNITED STATES
Washington, D.C.
New York City
40°N
ATLANTIC OCEAN
Los Angeles
Houston
Bermuda (U.K.)
Rabat
Casablanca
MOROCCO
WESTERN SAHARA (Sovereignty Disputed)
Tropic of Cancer
MEXICO
20°N
HAWAII (U.S.)
Mexico City
MAURITANIA
Nouakchott
CAPE VERDE
SENEGAL
Dakar
GAMBIA
GUINEA-BISSAU
GUINEA
Bamako
SIERRA LEONE
LIBERIA
CÔTE D'IVOIRE
Caracas
VENEZUELA
GUYANA
Georgetown
SURINAME
Paramaribo
FRENCH GUIANA (FRANCE)
Bogotá
COLOMBIA
PACIFIC OCEAN
0° Equator
KIRIBATI
Quito
ECUADOR
Galápagos Islands (ECUADOR)
SOUTH AMERICA
PERU
BRAZIL
Lima
Brasília
SAMOA
American Samoa
BOLIVIA
La Paz
Sucre
20°S
TONGA
Tropic of Capricorn
PARAGUAY
Asunción
Rio de Janeiro
São Paulo
CHILE
ARGENTINA
ATLANTIC OCEAN
Santiago
URUGUAY
Buenos Aires
Montevideo
40°S
Boundaries
National capitals
Other cities
SCALE
0 500 1000 1500 2000 Miles
0 1000 2000 Kilometers
Projection: Two-Point Equidistant
Falkland Islands (U.K.)
South Georgia (U.K.)
South Sandwich Islands
60°S
160°W
140°W
120°W
100°W
80°W
60°W
40°W
20°W
Antarctic Circle

90°W
80°W
FLORIDA (U.S.)
Nassau
THE BAHAMAS
70°W
GULF OF MEXICO
Tropic of Cancer
Havana
CUBA
Turks and Caicos Is. (U.K.)
60°W
ATLANTIC OCEAN
Cayman Is. (U.K.)
HAITI
DOMINICAN REPUBLIC
Port-au-Prince
Puerto Rico (U.S.)
Virgin Islands (U.S. and U.K.)
20°N
JAMAICA
Kingston
Santo Domingo
MEXICO
BELIZE
Belmopan
1
2
Guadeloupe (FRANCE)
GUATEMALA
HONDURAS
CARIBBEAN SEA
3
Guatemala City
Tegucigalpa
Martinique (FRANCE)
Netherlands Antilles (NETHERLANDS)
Aruba (NETHERLANDS)
4
5
6
San Salvador
NICARAGUA
EL SALVADOR
Managua
7
Port-of-Spain
PACIFIC OCEAN
COSTA RICA
Panama City
TRINIDAD & TOBAGO
30°N
SCALE
0 200 400 Miles
0 200 400 Kilometers
San José
PANAMA
VENEZUELA
COLOMBIA
GUYANA
Projection: Mercator

COUNTRY	CAPITAL
1 Antigua and Barbuda	St. Johns
2 St. Kitts and Nevis	Basseterre
3 Dominica	Roseau
4 St. Lucia	Castries
5 St. Vincent and the Grenadines	Kingstown
6 Barbados	Bridgetown
7 Grenada	St. George's

ARCTIC OCEAN
RUSSIA
Moscow
EUROPE
Astana
KAZAKHSTAN
Ulaanbaatar
MONGOLIA
Harbin
GEORGIA
Almaty
ASIA
UZBEKISTAN
Tashkent
KYRGYZSTAN
Istanbul
Baku
Ankara
ARMENIA
TURKMENISTAN
TURKEY
AZERBAIJAN
Ashgabat
TAJIKISTAN
CHINA
Beijing
Tianjin
NORTH KOREA
P'yŏngyang
Seoul
SOUTH KOREA
Pusan
JAPAN
Tokyo
Nagoya
Yokohama
Osaka
60°N
40°N
TUNISIA
Tripoli
Nicosia
CYPRUS
SYRIA
Beirut
LEBANON
Damascus
Jerusalem
ISRAEL
Amman
JORDAN
Tehran
Baghdad
IRAQ
IRAN
Kabul
AFGHANISTAN
Islamabad
Cairo
KUWAIT
BAHRAIN
QATAR
OMAN
PAKISTAN
Delhi
New Delhi
NEPAL
Kathmandu
BHUTAN
Wuhan
Chongqing
Shanghai
LIBYA
EGYPT
SAUDI ARABIA
Riyadh
Karachi
Masqat (Muscat)
UNITED ARAB EMIRATES
INDIA
Dhaka
BANGLADESH
Kolkata (Calcutta)
MYANMAR (BURMA)
Guangzhou
Hong Kong
Taipei
TAIWAN
Tropic of Cancer
AFRICA
20°N
NIGER
CHAD
Khartoum
ERITREA
Asmara
YEMEN
Sanaa
Mumbai (Bombay)
Yangon (Rangoon)
LAOS
Hanoi
THAILAND
VIETNAM
Bangkok
CAMBODIA
Phnom Penh
Ho Chi Minh City
Manila
PHILIPPINES
Northern Marianas (U.S.)
PACIFIC OCEAN
Guam (U.S.)
MARSHALL ISLANDS
N'Djamena
NIGERIA
Abuja
SUDAN
DJIBOUTI
Addis Ababa
ETHIOPIA
Chennai (Madras)
SRI LANKA
Colombo
PALAU
BRUNEI
FEDERATED STATES OF MICRONESIA
CENTRAL AFRICAN REPUBLIC
CAMEROON
EQUATORIAL GUINEA
GABON
REP. OF THE CONGO
UGANDA
KENYA
SOMALIA
MALDIVES
Kuala Lumpur
MALAYSIA
Singapore
SINGAPORE
Equator
0°
NAURU
KIRIBATI
RWANDA
BURUNDI
Nairobi
DEMOCRATIC REP. OF THE CONGO
Kinshasa
TANZANIA
Dar es Salaam
SEYCHELLES
INDONESIA
Jakarta
Surabaya
PAPUA NEW GUINEA
Port Moresby
SOLOMON ISLANDS
TUVALU
Luanda
ANGOLA
MALAWI
COMOROS
INDIAN OCEAN
ZAMBIA
Lusaka
MOZAMBIQUE
Harare
ZIMBABWE
MADAGASCAR
Antananarivo
VANUATU
FIJI
NAMIBIA
MAURITIUS
Réunion (FRANCE)
New Caledonia (FRANCE)
20°S
Windhoek
BOTSWANA
Gaborone
Pretoria
Maputo
SWAZILAND
AUSTRALIA
Tropic of Capricorn
Johannesburg
LESOTHO
SOUTH AFRICA
Cape Town
Sydney
Canberra
Melbourne
NEW ZEALAND
Wellington
Tasmania
60°S
20°E
40°E
60°E
80°E
100°E
120°E
140°E
160°E
ANTARCTICA

COUNTRY	CAPITAL
1 Czech Republic	Prague
2 Slovakia	Bratislava
3 Slovenia	Ljubljana
4 Croatia	Zagreb
5 Bosnia and Herzegovina	Sarajevo
6 Macedonia	Skopje
7 Yugoslavia (Serbia and Montenegro)	Belgrade
8 Lithuania	Vilnius
9 Latvia	Riga
10 Estonia	Tallinn

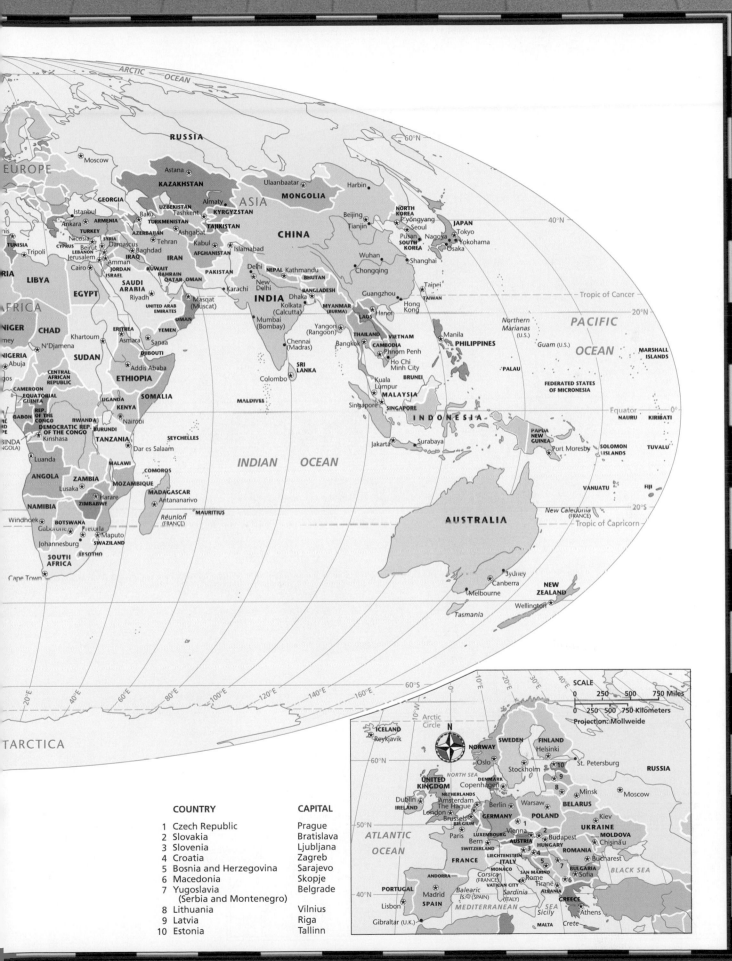

SCALE
0 250 500 750 Miles
0 250 500 750 Kilometers
Projection: Mollweide
10°W
0°
10°E
20°E
30°E
40°E
Arctic Circle
ICELAND
Reykjavik
N
NORWAY
SWEDEN
FINLAND
Helsinki
Oslo
Stockholm
St. Petersburg
RUSSIA
60°N
NORTH SEA
DENMARK
Copenhagen
UNITED KINGDOM
Minsk
Moscow
Dublin
IRELAND
NETHERLANDS
Amsterdam
The Hague
London
Berlin
Warsaw
BELARUS
Brussels
BELGIUM
GERMANY
POLAND
Kiev
50°N
UKRAINE
ATLANTIC OCEAN
Paris
LUXEMBOURG
Vienna
Bern
AUSTRIA
Budapest
MOLDOVA
Chişinău
SWITZERLAND
HUNGARY
ROMANIA
LIECHTENSTEIN
FRANCE
ITALY
Bucharest
MONACO
SAN MARINO
BULGARIA
Sofia
ANDORRA
Corsica (FRANCE)
Rome
BLACK SEA
VATICAN CITY
Tiranë
ALBANIA
PORTUGAL
Madrid
Balearic Is. (SPAIN)
Sardinia (ITALY)
40°N
Lisbon
SPAIN
GREECE
MEDITERRANEAN SEA
Sicily
Athens
Gibraltar (U.K.)
MALTA
Crete

THE UNITED STATES OF AMERICA: PHYSICAL

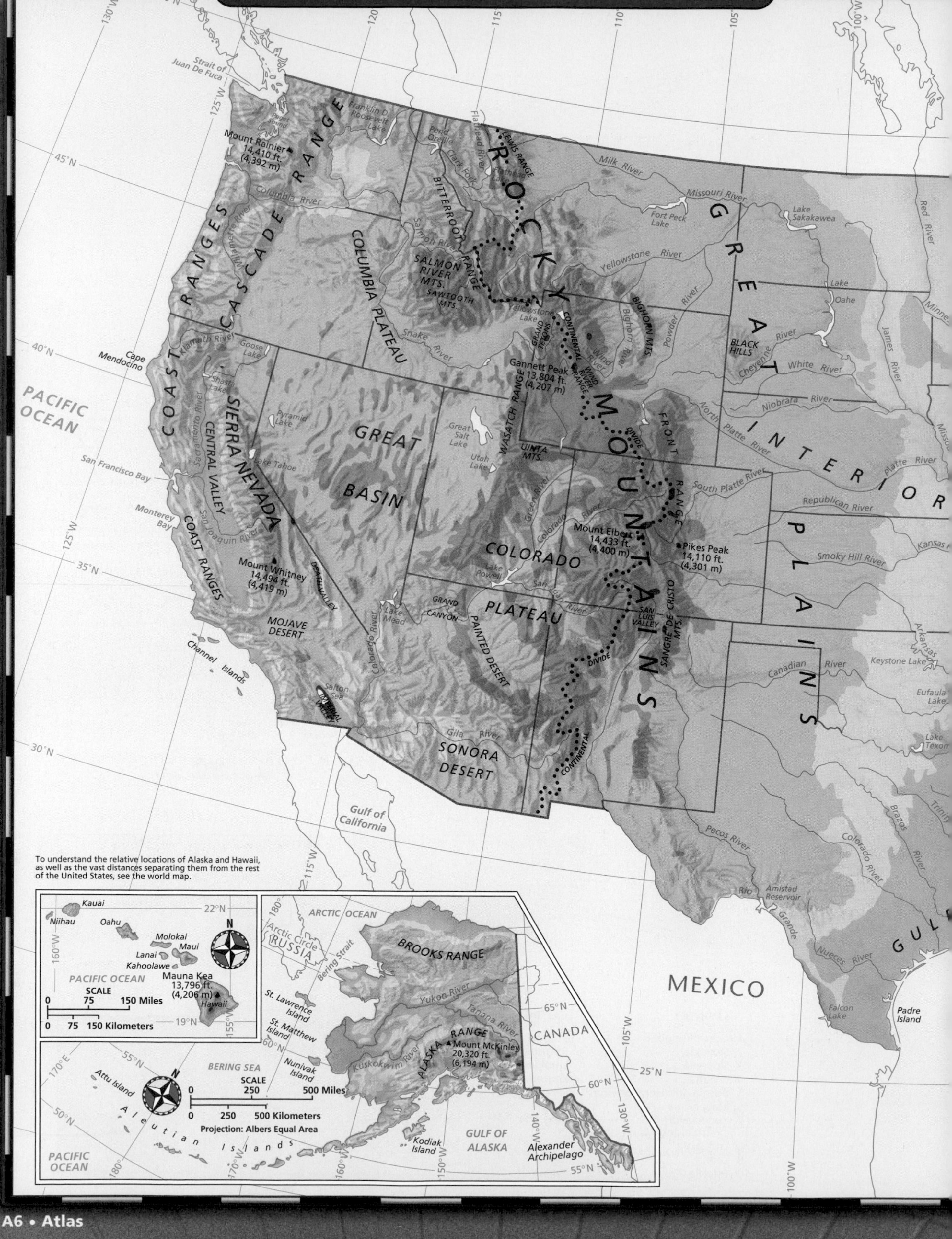

PACIFIC OCEAN
Strait of Juan De Fuca
Puget Sound
Mount Rainier 14,410 ft. (4,392 m)
COAST RANGES
CASCADE RANGE
Columbia River
Willamette River
Franklin D. Roosevelt Lake
Pend Oreille Lake
Flathead River
Flathead Lake
Clark Fork
LEWIS RANGE
BITTERROOT RANGE
Salmon River
SALMON RIVER MTS.
SAWTOOTH MTS.
COLUMBIA PLATEAU
Snake River
ROCKY MOUNTAINS
Milk River
Missouri River
Fort Peck Lake
Lake Sakakawea
Yellowstone River
Yellowstone Lake
GRAND TETONS
CONTINENTAL DIVIDE
BIGHORN MTS.
Bighorn River
Wind River
WIND RIVER RANGE
Powder River
Gannett Peak 13,804 ft. (4,207 m)
Lake Oahe
BLACK HILLS
Cheyenne River
White River
James River
Red River
Niobrara River
North Platte River
Platte River
South Platte River
Republican River
Smoky Hill River
Kansas River
GREAT PLAINS
GREAT INTERIOR PLAINS
Cape Mendocino
Klamath River
Goose Lake
Shasta Lake
Sacramento River
CENTRAL VALLEY
SIERRA NEVADA
Pyramid Lake
Lake Tahoe
San Francisco Bay
Monterey Bay
San Joaquin River
GREAT BASIN
Great Salt Lake
Utah Lake
WASATCH RANGE
UINTA MTS.
Green River
Colorado River
FRONT RANGE
Mount Elbert 14,433 ft. (4,400 m)
Pikes Peak 14,110 ft. (4,301 m)
Mount Whitney 14,494 ft. (4,419 m)
DEATH VALLEY
COLORADO PLATEAU
Lake Powell
San Juan River
GRAND CANYON
Lake Mead
PAINTED DESERT
SAN LUIS VALLEY
SANGRE DE CRISTO MTS.
MOJAVE DESERT
Channel Islands
Salton Sea
IMPERIAL VALLEY
Gila River
SONORA DESERT
Arkansas River
Canadian River
Keystone Lake
Eufaula Lake
Lake Texoma
Trinity River
Brazos River
Colorado River
Pecos River
Amistad Reservoir
Rio Grande
Nueces River
Falcon Lake
Padre Island
Gulf of California
MEXICO
GULF
50°N
45°N
40°N
35°N
30°N
25°N
130°W
125°W
120°
115°
110°
105°
100°W
To understand the relative locations of Alaska and Hawaii, as well as the vast distances separating them from the rest of the United States, see the world map.
Kauai
Niihau
Oahu
Molokai
Maui
Lanai
Kahoolawe
Hawaii
Mauna Kea 13,796 ft. (4,206 m)
PACIFIC OCEAN
SCALE
0 75 150 Miles
0 75 150 Kilometers
22°N
19°N
160°W
155°W
N
ARCTIC OCEAN
Arctic Circle
RUSSIA
Bering Strait
BROOKS RANGE
St. Lawrence Island
St. Matthew Island
Nunivak Island
Yukon River
Tanana River
Kuskokwim River
ALASKA RANGE
Mount McKinley 20,320 ft. (6,194 m)
CANADA
BERING SEA
Attu Island
Aleutian Islands
SCALE
0 250 500 Miles
0 250 500 Kilometers
Projection: Albers Equal Area
Kodiak Island
GULF OF ALASKA
Alexander Archipelago
PACIFIC OCEAN
65°N
60°N
55°N
50°N
180°
170°E
170°W
160°
150°W
140°W
130°W

CANADA
MESABI RANGE
Isle Royale
Lake Superior
Lake Huron
Lake Michigan
Lake Ontario
Lake Erie
Mississippi River
Wisconsin River
Des Moines River
Illinois River
Wabash River
Ohio River
Scioto River
St. Lawrence River
St. Lawrence Seaway
St. John River
Penobscot River
LONGFELLOW MTS.
WHITE MTS.
GREEN MTS.
Lake Champlain
ADIRONDACK MTS.
Finger Lakes
CATSKILL MTS.
Hudson R.
Connecticut River
Cape Cod
Long Island Sound
Long Island
Allegheny River
Susquehanna River
Delaware R.
PLATEAU
APPALACHIAN MOUNTAINS
ALLEGHENY
Monongahela R.
Potomac River
Delaware Bay
ATLANTIC OCEAN
Chesapeake Bay
James River
Kanawha River
CUMBERLAND PLATEAU
BLUE RIDGE MOUNTAINS
GREAT SMOKY MTS.
PIEDMONT
Roanoke River
ATLANTIC COASTAL PLAIN
Pamlico Sound
Cape Hatteras
PLAINS
Lake of the Ozarks
PLATEAU
Lake Barkley
Kentucky Lake
Cumberland River
White River
River
ACHITA MTS.
Mississippi River
Tennessee River
Tombigbee River
Coosa River
Savannah River
Oconee River
Red
Sea Islands
Altamaha River
Alabama R.
Pearl River
Chattahoochee River
Toledo Bend Reservoir
COASTAL PLAIN
Okefenokee Swamp
Chandeleur Islands
Mississippi Delta
FLORIDA PENINSULA
Cape Canaveral
GULF OF MEXICO
Lake Okeechobee
THE BAHAMAS
The Everglades
Cape Sable
Florida Key
Straits of Florida
CUBA
N
ELEVATION
FEET
METERS
13,120
4,000
6,560
2,000
1,640
500
656
200
(Sea level) 0
0 (Sea level)
Below sea level
Below sea level
Ice cap
SCALE
0
250
500 Miles
0
250
500 Kilometers
Projection: Albers Equal Area
90°W
85°W
80°W
75°W
70°W
65°W
60°W
50°N
45°N
40°N
35°N
30°N
25°N
20°N

PACIFIC OCEAN
Strait of Juan de Fuca
Puget Sound
Seattle
Tacoma
Olympia
Spokane
Franklin D. Roosevelt Lake
WASHINGTON
Portland
Columbia River
Salem
Eugene
OREGON
IDAHO
Boise
Snake River
Pocatello
Pend Oreille
Flathead Lake
Helena
MONTANA
Missouri River
Fort Peck Lake
Yellowstone River
Billings
Lake Sakakawea
NORTH DAKOTA
Bismarck
Fargo
Red River
Lake Oahe
SOUTH DAKOTA
Pierre
Sioux Falls
Yellowstone Lake
WYOMING
Casper
Cheyenne
NEBRASKA
Platte River
Omaha
Lincoln
Goose Lake
Cape Mendocino
Shasta Lake
Sacramento River
Pyramid Lake
Reno
Carson City
Lake Tahoe
NEVADA
Oakland
San Francisco
San Francisco Bay
Sacramento
Stockton
Modesto
San Jose
Monterey Bay
San Joaquin R.
Fresno
CALIFORNIA
Bakersfield
Las Vegas
Lake Mead
Great Salt Lake
Salt Lake City
Utah Lake
Provo
UTAH
Green River
Lake Powell
Denver
COLORADO
Colorado Springs
Topeka
KANSAS
Arkansas River
Wichita
Los Angeles
Long Beach
Channel Islands
Anaheim
Santa Ana
Salton Sea
San Diego
Colorado River
ARIZONA
Phoenix
Gila River
Tucson
Santa Fe
Albuquerque
NEW MEXICO
Canadian River
Keystone Lake
Tulsa
OKLAHOMA
Oklahoma City
Eufaula Lake
Amarillo
Lake Texoma
Lubbock
Fort Worth
Dallas
Abilene
Odessa
El Paso
TEXAS
Brazos River
Colorado River
Waco
Pecos River
Austin
Houston
Rio Grande
Amistad Reservoir
San Antonio
Corpus Christi
Laredo
Padre Island
Gulf of California
MEXICO
Minnesota
Missouri River
50°N
45°N
40°N
35°N
30°N
25°N
130°W
125°W
115°W
110°W
105°W
100°W
115°W
To understand the relative locations of Alaska and Hawaii as well as the vast distances separating them from the rest of the United States, see the world map.
Kauai
Niihau
Oahu
Honolulu
Molokai
HAWAII
Lanai
Kahoolawe
Maui
Hawaii
PACIFIC OCEAN
22°N
19°N
160°W
155°W
SCALE
0 75 150 Miles
0 75 150 Kilometers
N
ARCTIC OCEAN
Arctic Circle
RUSSIA
Bering Strait
Nome
Yukon River
St. Lawrence Island
St. Matthew Island
Fairbanks
ALASKA
CANADA
Nunivak Island
BERING SEA
Anchorage
Attu Island
Aleutian Islands
Kodiak Island
GULF OF ALASKA
Juneau
Alexander Archipelago
PACIFIC OCEAN
SCALE
0 250 500 Miles
0 250 500 Kilometers
Projection: Albers Equal Area
180°
170°E
170°W
160°W
150°W
140°W
130°W
65°N
60°N
55°N
50°N

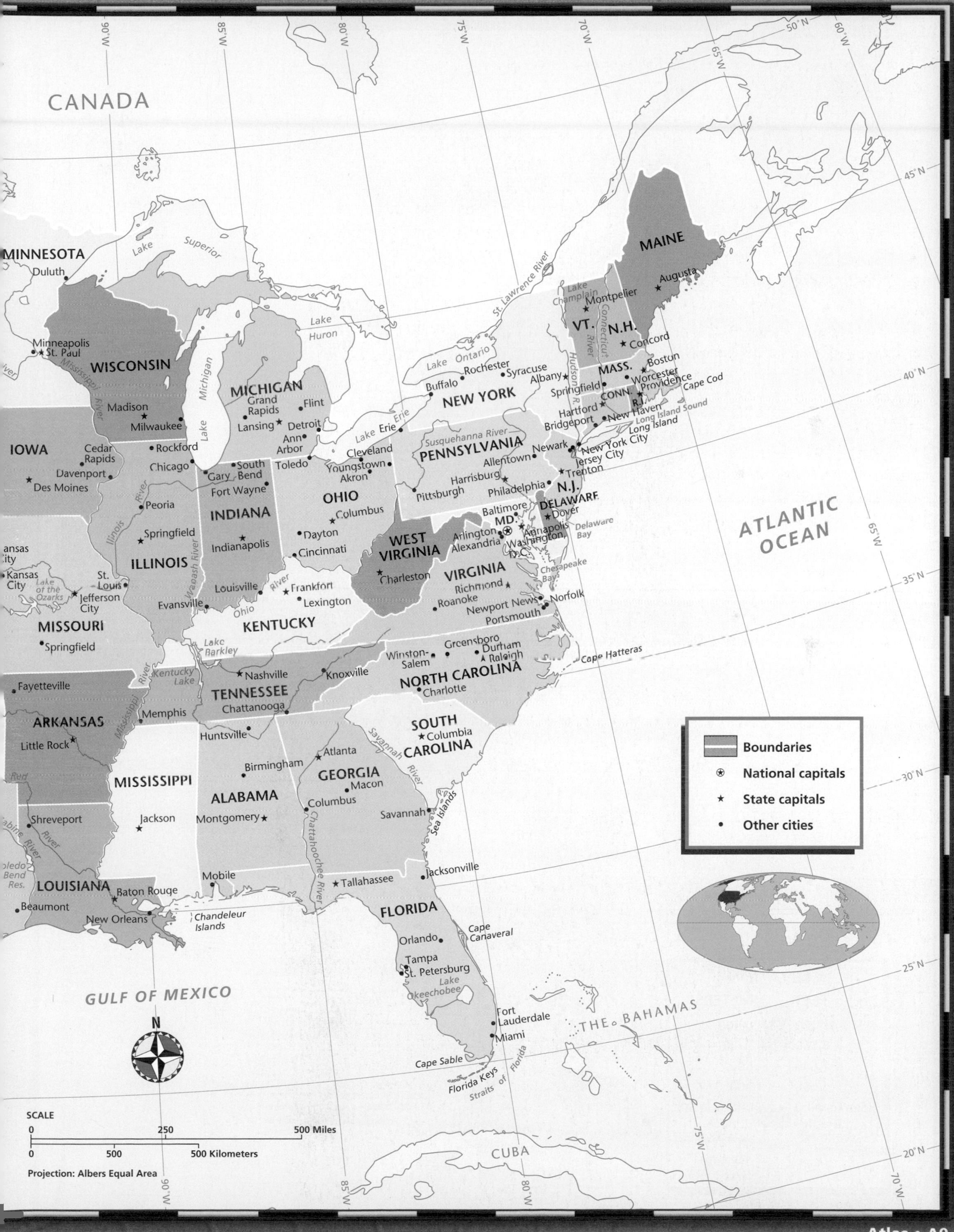

CANADA
ATLANTIC OCEAN
GULF OF MEXICO
THE BAHAMAS
CUBA
MINNESOTA
WISCONSIN
MICHIGAN
IOWA
ILLINOIS
INDIANA
OHIO
MISSOURI
KENTUCKY
TENNESSEE
ARKANSAS
MISSISSIPPI
ALABAMA
GEORGIA
LOUISIANA
FLORIDA
SOUTH CAROLINA
NORTH CAROLINA
VIRGINIA
WEST VIRGINIA
PENNSYLVANIA
NEW YORK
MAINE
VT.
N.H.
MASS.
CONN.
R.I.
N.J.
DELAWARE
MD.
Lake Superior
Lake Michigan
Lake Huron
Lake Ontario
Lake Erie
Lake Champlain
St. Lawrence River
Mississippi River
Illinois River
Wabash River
Ohio River
Savannah River
Chattahoochee River
Susquehanna River
Hudson R.
Connecticut River
Red River
Sabine River
Toledo Bend Res.
Lake of the Ozarks
Lake Barkley
Kentucky Lake
Lake Okeechobee
Chesapeake Bay
Delaware Bay
Long Island Sound
Long Island
Cape Cod
Cape Hatteras
Cape Canaveral
Cape Sable
Florida Keys
Straits of Florida
Sea Islands
Chandeleur Islands
Duluth
Minneapolis
St. Paul
Madison
Milwaukee
Grand Rapids
Lansing
Flint
Detroit
Ann Arbor
Cedar Rapids
Rockford
Chicago
Davenport
Des Moines
South Bend
Gary
Fort Wayne
Toledo
Cleveland
Youngstown
Akron
Columbus
Dayton
Cincinnati
Peoria
Springfield
Indianapolis
Kansas City
St. Louis
Jefferson City
Louisville
Frankfort
Lexington
Evansville
Springfield
Nashville
Knoxville
Memphis
Chattanooga
Fayetteville
Little Rock
Huntsville
Birmingham
Atlanta
Macon
Columbus
Montgomery
Jackson
Shreveport
Mobile
Baton Rouge
New Orleans
Beaumont
Tallahassee
Jacksonville
Savannah
Orlando
Tampa
St. Petersburg
Fort Lauderdale
Miami
Columbia
Charlotte
Winston-Salem
Greensboro
Durham
Raleigh
Charleston
Roanoke
Richmond
Newport News
Portsmouth
Norfolk
Arlington
Alexandria
Washington, D.C.
Baltimore
Annapolis
Dover
Pittsburgh
Harrisburg
Philadelphia
Allentown
Trenton
Newark
Jersey City
New York City
Buffalo
Rochester
Syracuse
Albany
Erie
Bridgeport
New Haven
Hartford
Springfield
Providence
Worcester
Boston
Concord
Montpelier
Augusta
Boundaries
National capitals
State capitals
Other cities
SCALE
0
250
500 Miles
0
500
500 Kilometers
Projection: Albers Equal Area
N
90°W
85°W
80°W
75°W
70°W
65°W
60°W
50°N
45°N
40°N
35°N
30°N
25°N
20°N

NORTH AMERICA: PHYSICAL

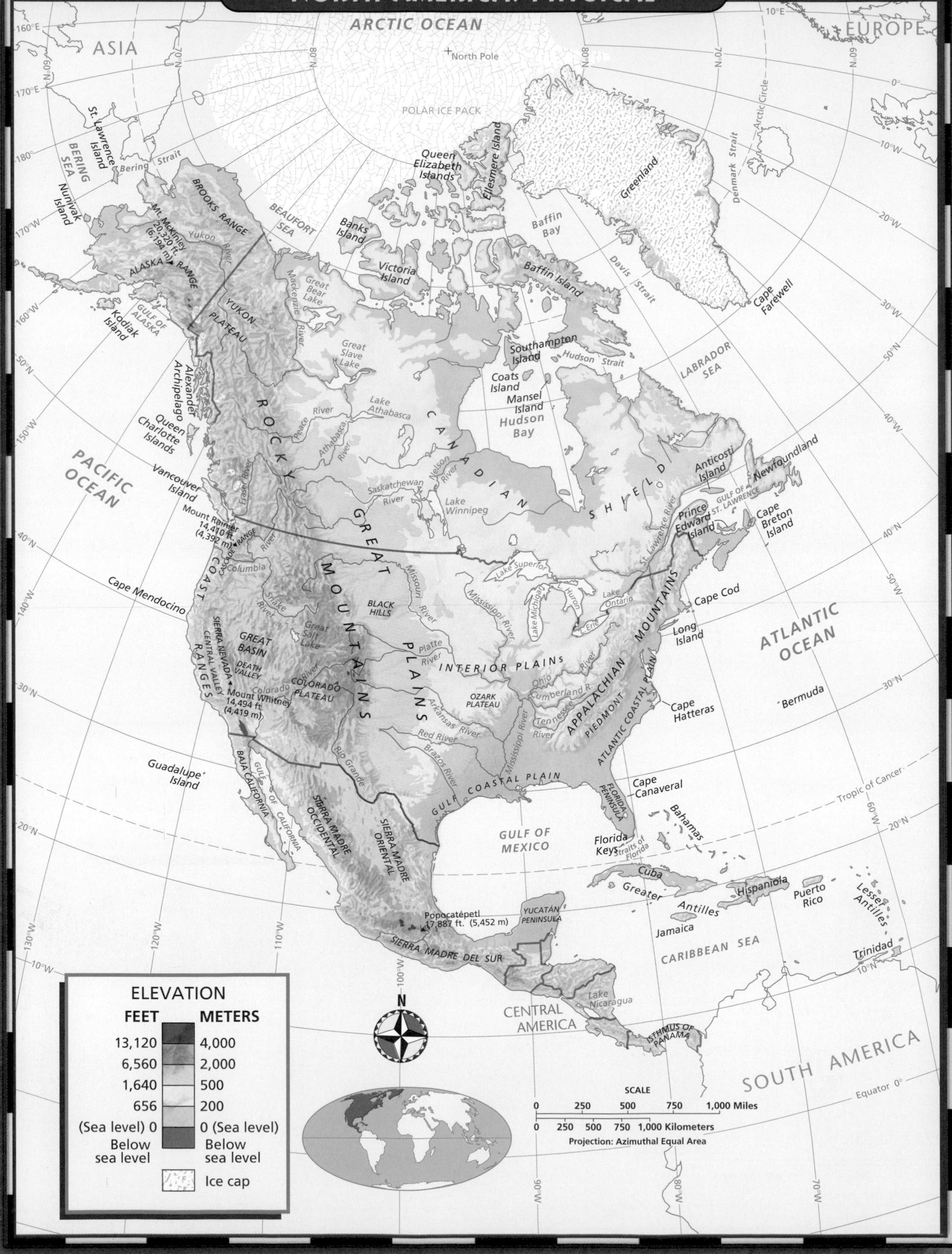
ARCTIC OCEAN
North Pole
POLAR ICE PACK
ASIA
EUROPE
BERING SEA
Bering Strait
St. Lawrence Island
Nunivak Island
BROOKS RANGE
Mt. McKinley 20,320 ft. (6,194 m)
Yukon River
ALASKA RANGE
GULF OF ALASKA
Kodiak Island
BEAUFORT SEA
Queen Elizabeth Islands
Ellesmere Island
Greenland
Banks Island
Victoria Island
Baffin Bay
Baffin Island
Davis Strait
Denmark Strait
Arctic Circle
Cape Farewell
YUKON PLATEAU
Mackenzie River
Great Bear Lake
Great Slave Lake
Southampton Island
Coats Island
Mansel Island
Hudson Strait
Hudson Bay
LABRADOR SEA
Alexander Archipelago
Queen Charlotte Islands
ROCKY MOUNTAINS
Peace River
Lake Athabasca
Athabasca River
CANADIAN SHIELD
Nelson River
Saskatchewan River
Lake Winnipeg
Anticosti Island
Newfoundland
GULF OF ST. LAWRENCE
Prince Edward Island
Cape Breton Island
St. Lawrence River
PACIFIC OCEAN
Vancouver Island
Fraser River
Mount Rainier 14,410 ft. (4,392 m)
CASCADE RANGE
Columbia River
COAST RANGES
Cape Mendocino
GREAT PLAINS
Missouri River
BLACK HILLS
Lake Superior
Lake Michigan
Lake Huron
Lake Ontario
Lake Erie
Mississippi River
Cape Cod
Long Island
APPALACHIAN MOUNTAINS
ATLANTIC OCEAN
Snake River
Great Salt Lake
GREAT BASIN
SIERRA NEVADA
CENTRAL VALLEY
DEATH VALLEY
Platte River
INTERIOR PLAINS
Ohio River
Cumberland R.
Tennessee River
Colorado River
COLORADO PLATEAU
Mount Whitney 14,494 ft. (4,419 m)
OZARK PLATEAU
Arkansas River
Red River
Brazos River
PIEDMONT
ATLANTIC COASTAL PLAIN
Cape Hatteras
Bermuda
Guadalupe Island
BAJA CALIFORNIA
GULF OF CALIFORNIA
Rio Grande
GULF COASTAL PLAIN
FLORIDA PENINSULA
Cape Canaveral
Tropic of Cancer
SIERRA MADRE OCCIDENTAL
SIERRA MADRE ORIENTAL
GULF OF MEXICO
Florida Keys
Straits of Florida
Bahamas
Cuba
Greater Antilles
Hispaniola
Puerto Rico
Lesser Antilles
Jamaica
Popocatépetl 17,887 ft. (5,452 m)
YUCATÁN PENINSULA
SIERRA MADRE DEL SUR
CARIBBEAN SEA
Trinidad
Lake Nicaragua
CENTRAL AMERICA
ISTHMUS OF PANAMA
SOUTH AMERICA
Equator 0°
N
ELEVATION
FEET
METERS
13,120
4,000
6,560
2,000
1,640
500
656
200
(Sea level) 0
0 (Sea level)
Below sea level
Below sea level
Ice cap
SCALE
0 250 500 750 1,000 Miles
0 250 500 750 1,000 Kilometers
Projection: Azimuthal Equal Area

NORTH AMERICA: POLITICAL

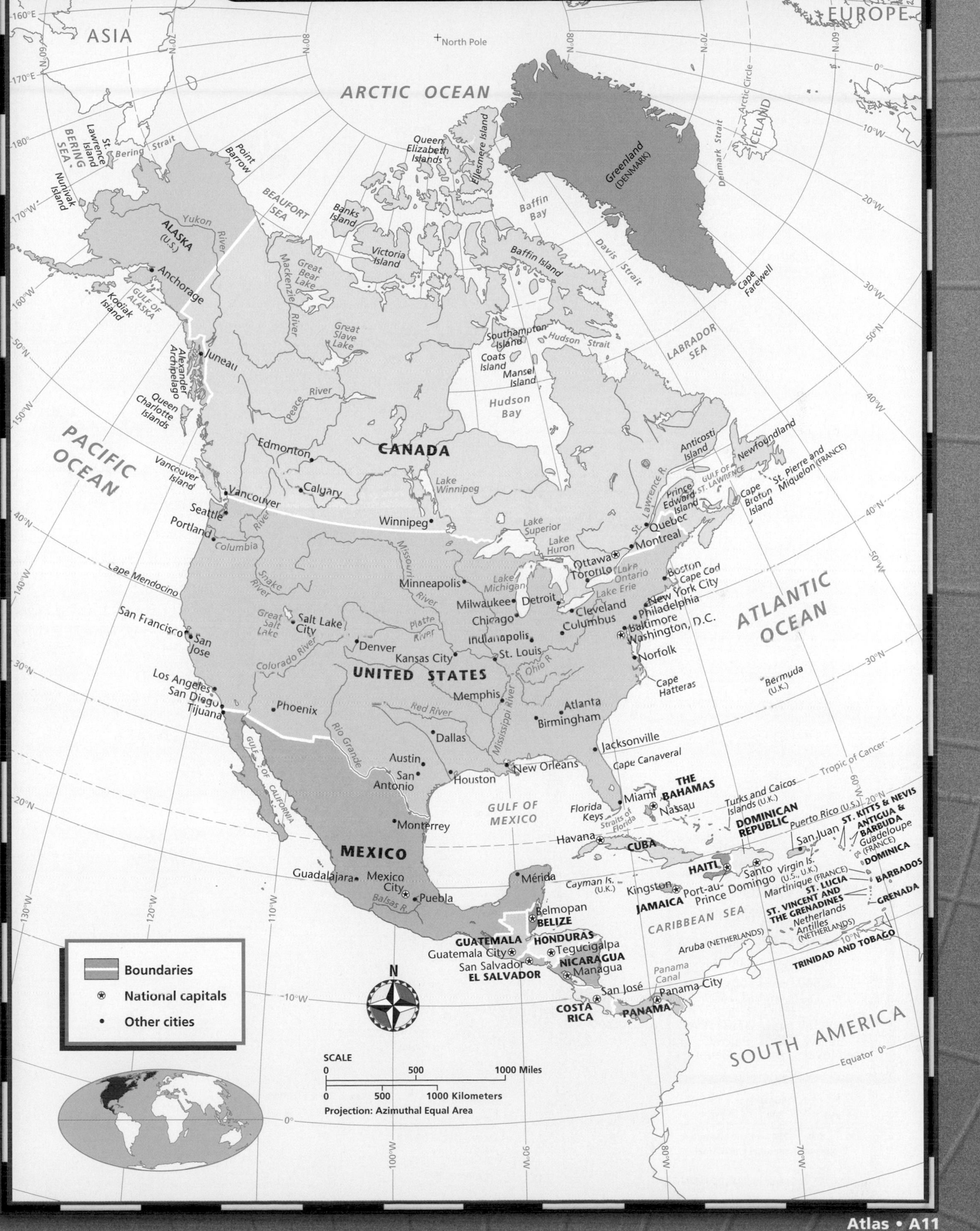

ASIA
EUROPE
North Pole
ARCTIC OCEAN
PACIFIC OCEAN
ATLANTIC OCEAN
SOUTH AMERICA
BERING SEA
Bering Strait
St. Lawrence Island
Nunivak Island
Point Barrow
BEAUFORT SEA
Queen Elizabeth Islands
Ellesmere Island
Greenland (DENMARK)
ICELAND
Denmark Strait
Arctic Circle
Baffin Bay
Banks Island
Victoria Island
Baffin Island
Davis Strait
Cape Farewell
ALASKA (U.S.)
Yukon River
Anchorage
GULF OF ALASKA
Kodiak Island
Great Bear Lake
Mackenzie River
Great Slave Lake
Southampton Island
Hudson Strait
Coats Island
Mansel Island
LABRADOR SEA
Juneau
Alexander Archipelago
Queen Charlotte Islands
Peace River
Hudson Bay
CANADA
Edmonton
Calgary
Lake Winnipeg
Anticosti Island
Newfoundland
GULF OF ST. LAWRENCE
St. Pierre and Miquelon (FRANCE)
Prince Edward Island
Cape Breton Island
St. Lawrence R.
Vancouver Island
Vancouver
Seattle
Portland
Winnipeg
Lake Superior
Lake Huron
Quebec
Montreal
Ottawa
Toronto
Lake Ontario
Lake Erie
Lake Michigan
Boston
Cape Cod
New York City
Philadelphia
Baltimore
Washington, D.C.
Norfolk
Cape Hatteras
Bermuda (U.K.)
Columbia River
Snake River
Missouri River
Cape Mendocino
Minneapolis
Milwaukee
Detroit
Cleveland
Chicago
Columbus
Indianapolis
St. Louis
Ohio R.
San Francisco
San Jose
Great Salt Lake
Salt Lake City
Platte River
Denver
Kansas City
Colorado River
UNITED STATES
Los Angeles
San Diego
Tijuana
Phoenix
Memphis
Atlanta
Birmingham
Mississippi River
Red River
Dallas
Rio Grande
Jacksonville
Austin
San Antonio
Houston
New Orleans
Cape Canaveral
GULF OF CALIFORNIA
GULF OF MEXICO
Monterrey
Florida Keys
Straits of Florida
Miami
THE BAHAMAS
Nassau
Turks and Caicos Islands (U.K.)
Tropic of Cancer
DOMINICAN REPUBLIC
Puerto Rico (U.S.)
San Juan
ST. KITTS & NEVIS
ANTIGUA & BARBUDA
Guadeloupe (FRANCE)
DOMINICA
Havana
CUBA
HAITI
Santo Domingo
Virgin Is. (U.S., U.K.)
Martinique (FRANCE)
ST. LUCIA
BARBADOS
MEXICO
Guadalajara
Mexico City
Puebla
Balsas R.
Mérida
Cayman Is. (U.K.)
Kingston
Port-au-Prince
JAMAICA
ST. VINCENT AND THE GRENADINES
GRENADA
Netherlands Antilles (NETHERLANDS)
CARIBBEAN SEA
Belmopan
BELIZE
GUATEMALA
HONDURAS
Guatemala City
Tegucigalpa
San Salvador
NICARAGUA
EL SALVADOR
Managua
Aruba (NETHERLANDS)
TRINIDAD AND TOBAGO
Panama Canal
San José
Panama City
COSTA RICA
PANAMA
Equator 0°
Boundaries
National capitals
Other cities
N
SCALE
0 500 1000 Miles
0 500 1000 Kilometers
Projection: Azimuthal Equal Area
160°E
170°E
180°
170°W
160°W
150°W
140°W
130°W
120°W
110°W
100°W
90°W
80°W
70°W
60°W
50°W
40°W
30°W
20°W
10°W
0°
10°E
60°N
50°N
40°N
30°N
20°N
10°N

SOUTH AMERICA: PHYSICAL

CENTRAL AMERICA
CARIBBEAN SEA
Margarita Island
Tobago
Trinidad
Panama Canal
Lake Maracaibo
Orinoco River Delta
GULF OF PANAMA
LLANOS
Orinoco River
Meta River
Angel Falls
GUIANA
HIGHLANDS
ATLANTIC OCEAN
Devil's Island
Cape Orange
Cauca River
Magdalena River
Mount Tolima 18,425 ft. (5,616 m)
Malpelo Island
Orinoco River
Amazon River Delta
Caquetá River
Rio Negro
Equator 0°
Mount Chimborazo 20,561 ft. (6,267 m)
Japurá River
AMAZON BASIN
Amazon River
Galápagos Islands
GULF OF GUAYAQUIL
Marañón River
Juruá River
Tapajós River
Xingu River
Tocantins River
Parnaíba River
ANDES
Ucayali River
Purus River
Madeira River
Mount Huascarán 22,205 ft. (6,768 m)
Beni River
Mamoré River
Araguaia River
São Francisco River
BRAZILIAN HIGHLANDS
MATO GROSSO PLATEAU
PACIFIC OCEAN
Lake Titicaca
Ancohuma Peak 20,958 ft. (6,388 m)
Lake Poopó
Pilcomayo River
ATACAMA DESERT
CHACO
BRAZILIAN PLATEAU
Paraguay River
Tropic of Capricorn
San Ambrosio Island
San Félix Island
Salado River
Paraná River
Uruguay River
Mount Aconcagua 22,834 ft. (6,960 m)
Juan Fernández Islands
Salado River
PAMPAS
Río de la Plata
ATLANTIC OCEAN
Colorado River
GULF OF SAN MATÍAS
Chiloé Island
CHONOS ARCHIPELAGO
PATAGONIA
GULF OF SAN JORGE
Cape Tres Puntas
Bahía Grande
Strait of Magellan
Falkland Islands
TIERRA DEL FUEGO
CAPE HORN
South Georgia Islands
20°N
10°N
10°S
20°S
30°S
40°S
50°S
90°W
80°W
70°W
60°W
50°W
40°W
30°W
20°W
100°W
ELEVATION
FEET METERS
13,120 4,000
6,560 2,000
1,640 500
656 200
(Sea level) 0 0 (Sea level)
Below sea level Below sea level
SCALE
0 250 500 750 1,000 Miles
0 250 500 750 1,000 Kilometers
Projection: Azimuthal Equal Area
N

SOUTH AMERICA: POLITICAL

CARIBBEAN SEA
CENTRAL AMERICA
ATLANTIC OCEAN
PACIFIC OCEAN
VENEZUELA
Caracas
Lake Maracaibo
Orinoco River
GUYANA
Georgetown
SURINAME
Paramaribo
FRENCH GUIANA (FRANCE)
Cayenne
COLOMBIA
Barranquilla
Cartagena
Medellín
Bogotá
Cali
Malpelo Island (COLOMBIA)
ECUADOR
Quito
Guayaquil
Galápagos Islands (ECUADOR)
Rio Negro
Amazon River
Belém
BRAZIL
Recife
Salvador
São Francisco River
Brasília
Belo Horizonte
Campinas
São Paulo
Rio de Janeiro
Curitiba
Pôrto Alegre
PERU
Marañón River
Ucayali River
Trujillo
Callao
Lima
Arequipa
Lake Titicaca
BOLIVIA
La Paz
Lake Poopó
Sucre
PARAGUAY
Asunción
Paraguay River
Paraná River
Uruguay River
URUGUAY
Montevideo
Río de la Plata
CHILE
Valparaíso
Santiago
San Félix Island (CHILE)
San Ambrosio Island (CHILE)
Juan Fernández Islands (CHILE)
ARGENTINA
Córdoba
Rosario
Buenos Aires
Strait of Magellan
Tierra del Fuego
Falkland Islands (U.K.)
South Georgia Island (U.K.)
Equator 0°
Tropic of Capricorn
20°N
10°N
10°S
20°S
30°S
40°S
50°S
100°W
90°W
80°W
70°W
60°W
50°W
40°W
30°W
20°W
N
Boundaries
National capitals
Other cities
SCALE
0 250 500 750 1000 Miles
0 250 500 250 1000 Kilometers
Projection: Azimuthal Equal Area

EUROPE: PHYSICAL

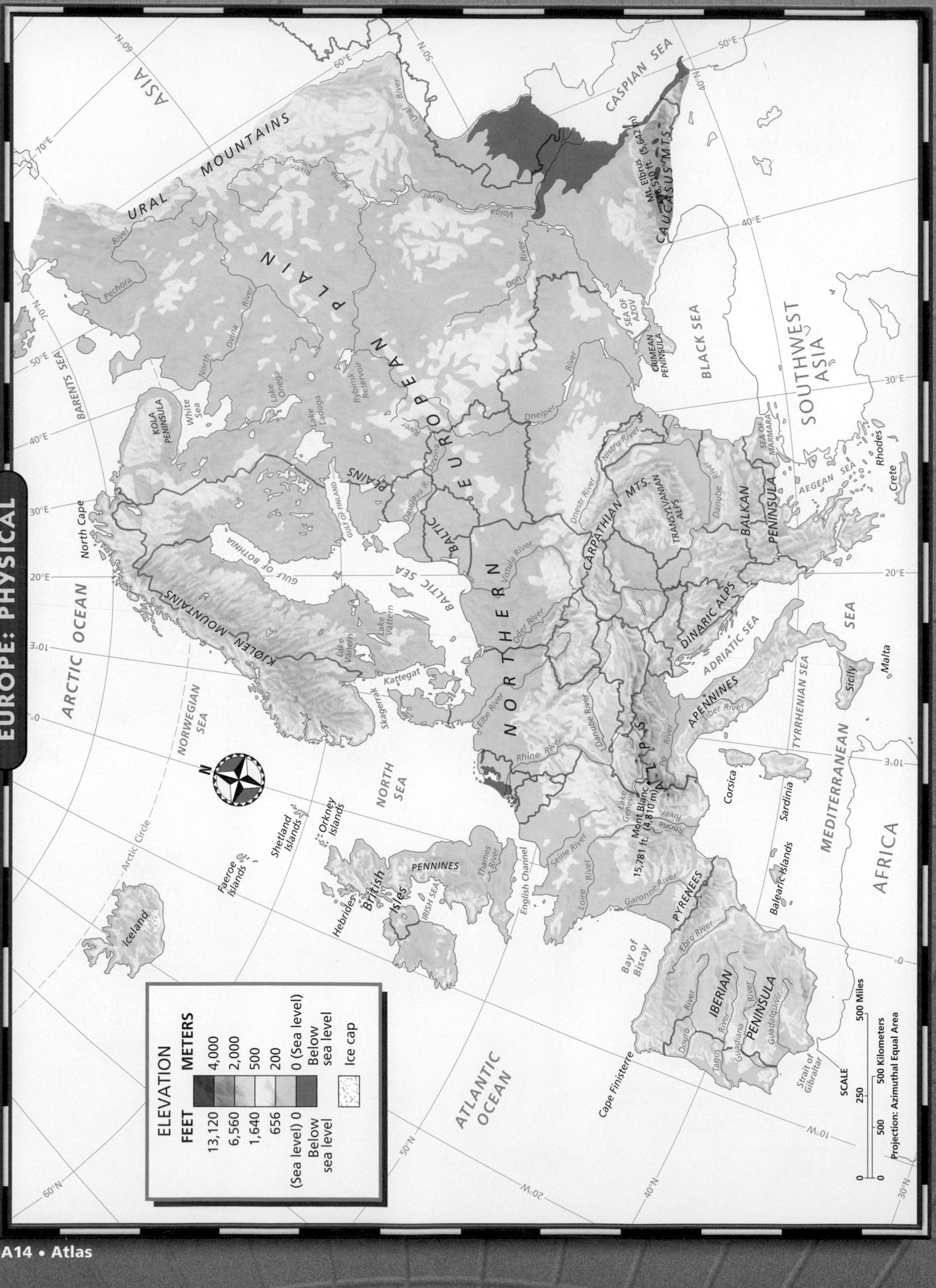

ASIA
URAL MOUNTAINS
CASPIAN SEA
Ural River
Kama River
Volga River
Mt. Elbrus (5,642 m) 18,510 ft.
CAUCASUS MTS.
Pechora River
PLAIN
EUROPEAN
NORTHERN
North Dvina River
Don River
SEA OF AZOV
CRIMEAN PENINSULA
BLACK SEA
SOUTHWEST ASIA
BARENTS SEA
KOLA PENINSULA
White Sea
Lake Onega
Lake Ladoga
Rybinsk Reservoir
Dnieper River
Nistru River
Dnestr River
Dvina River
Daugava R.
BALTIC PLAINS
GULF OF FINLAND
GULF OF BOTHNIA
BALTIC SEA
North Cape
ARCTIC OCEAN
KJØLEN MOUNTAINS
Lake Vänern
Lake Vättern
Kattegat
Skagerrak
NORWEGIAN SEA
NORTH SEA
Vistula River
Oder River
Elbe River
Rhine River
Danube River
CARPATHIAN MTS.
TRANSYLVANIAN ALPS
BALKAN PENINSULA
SEA OF MARMARA
AEGEAN SEA
Rhodes
Crete
DINARIC ALPS
ADRIATIC SEA
APENNINES
Tiber River
Po River
ALPS
Sicily
Malta
TYRRHENIAN SEA
MEDITERRANEAN SEA
Corsica
Sardinia
Balearic Islands
AFRICA
Lake Geneva
Mont Blanc 15,781 ft. (4,810 m)
Rhone River
Seine River
Loire River
Garonne River
PYRENEES
Ebro River
IBERIAN PENINSULA
Douro River
Tagus River
Guadiana River
Guadalquivir River
Strait of Gibraltar
Bay of Biscay
Cape Finisterre
ATLANTIC OCEAN
English Channel
Thames River
PENNINES
British Isles
IRISH SEA
Hebrides
Shetland Islands
Orkney Islands
Faeroe Islands
Iceland
Arctic Circle
ELEVATION
FEET METERS
13,120 4,000
6,560 2,000
1,640 500
656 200
(Sea level) 0 0 (Sea level)
Below sea level Below sea level
Ice cap
SCALE
0 250 500 Miles
0 500 Kilometers
Projection: Azimuthal Equal Area

EUROPE: POLITICAL

ARCTIC OCEAN
ATLANTIC OCEAN
NORTH SEA
BALTIC SEA
BARENTS SEA
WHITE SEA
BLACK SEA
CASPIAN SEA
MEDITERRANEAN SEA
ADRIATIC SEA
AEGEAN SEA
GULF OF BOTHNIA
GULF OF FINLAND
Bay of Biscay
English Channel
Strait of Gibraltar
Arctic Circle
URAL MOUNTAINS
PYRENEES
ALPS
ASIA
SOUTHWEST ASIA
AFRICA
Boundaries
National capitals
Other cities
N
ICELAND
Reykjavik
Faeroe Islands (DENMARK)
Shetland Islands
British Isles
Channel Islands (U.K.)
NORWAY
Bergen
Oslo
SWEDEN
Stockholm
Göteborg
FINLAND
Helsinki
North Cape
RUSSIA
St. Petersburg
Moscow
Nizhny Novgorod
ESTONIA
Tallinn
LATVIA
Riga
LITHUANIA
Vilnius
BELARUS
Minsk
UKRAINE
Kiev
MOLDOVA
Chişinău
ROMANIA
Bucharest
BULGARIA
Sofia
POLAND
Warsaw
Krakow
CZECH REPUBLIC
Prague
SLOVAKIA
Bratislava
HUNGARY
Budapest
AUSTRIA
Vienna
SLOVENIA
Ljubljana
CROATIA
Zagreb
BOSNIA & HERZEGOVINA
Sarajevo
YUGOSLAVIA
SERBIA
Belgrade
MONTENEGRO
MACEDONIA
Skopje
ALBANIA
Tiranë
GREECE
Athens
Rhodes
Crete
DENMARK
Copenhagen
GERMANY
Berlin
Hamburg
Dresden
Munich
Cologne
Bonn
THE NETHERLANDS
Amsterdam
The Hague
BELGIUM
Brussels
LUXEMBOURG
Luxembourg
FRANCE
Paris
Lyons
Marseille
MONACO
Monaco
SWITZERLAND
Bern
LIECHTENSTEIN
Vaduz
ITALY
Milan
Rome
Naples
SAN MARINO
San Marino
VATICAN CITY
Corsica (FRANCE)
Sardinia (ITALY)
Sicily
MALTA
Valletta
UNITED KINGDOM
SCOTLAND
Edinburgh
ENGLAND
London
Liverpool
WALES
NORTHERN IRELAND
Belfast
IRELAND
Dublin
SPAIN
Madrid
Barcelona
Valencia
Seville
Gibraltar (U.K.)
Balearic Islands (SPAIN)
ANDORRA
Andorra la Vella
PORTUGAL
Lisbon
Thames R.
Seine River
Loire River
Rhine River
Rhone River
Elbe River
Danube River
Po River
Tagus River
Dnieper River
Don River
Volga River
Ural River
Lake Geneva
0°
10°E
20°E
30°E
40°E
50°E
10°W
20°W
40°N
50°N
70°N
SCALE
0
250
500 Miles
500 Kilometers
Projection: Azimuthal Equal Area

ASIA: PHYSICAL

ELEVATION
FEET METERS
13,120 4,000
6,560 2,000
1,640 500
656 200
(Sea level) 0 0 (Sea level)
Below sea level Below sea level
Ice cap
NORTH AMERICA
BERING SEA
Aleutian Islands
KAMCHATKA PENINSULA
CENTRAL RANGE
SEA OF OKHOTSK
Kuril Islands
Sakhalin Island
Hokkaido
Honshu
Shikoku
Kyushu
SEA OF JAPAN
Korea Strait
Okinawa
Ryukyu Islands
EAST CHINA SEA
YELLOW SEA
Taiwan
Luzon Strait
Luzon
Philippines
Mindanao
PACIFIC OCEAN
Tropic of Cancer
Equator
New Guinea
MAOKE MOUNTAINS
ARAFURA SEA
AUSTRALIA
Moluccas
BANDA SEA
Celebes
CELEBES SEA
Borneo
JAVA SEA
Java
SOUTH CHINA SEA
Hainan
BOHEA HILLS
GULF OF TONKIN
INDOCHINA PENINSULA
Mekong River
GULF OF THAILAND
Chao Phraya River
MALAY PENINSULA
Strait of Malacca
Sumatra
Bangka
Mentawai Islands
ANDAMAN SEA
Irrawaddy River
Hong River
Xi River
Chang River
Huang River
QIN LING
NORTH CHINA PLAIN
GREAT WALL OF CHINA
GREATER KHINGAN RANGE
Amur River
STANOVOY MOUNTAINS
YABLONOVY RANGE
Shilka River
Lake Baikal
MONGOLIAN PLATEAU
GOBI
KOLYMA MTS.
CHERSKIY RANGE
VERKHOYANSKIY RANGE
Aldan River
Lena River
Wrangel Island
New Siberian Islands
LAPTEV SEA
SIBERIA
CENTRAL SIBERIAN PLATEAU
Lower Tunguska River
Angara River
North Land
TAYMYR PENINSULA
Yenisey River
SAYAN MOUNTAINS
ALTAI SHAN
Franz Josef Land
KARA SEA
Novaya Zemlya
BARENTS SEA
WEST SIBERIAN PLAIN
Ob River
Irtysh River
Ishim River
URAL MOUNTAINS
Ural River
KAZAKH UPLANDS
Lake Balkhash
TIAN SHAN
TARIM BASIN
TAKLIMAKAN DESERT
KUNLUN MOUNTAINS
PLATEAU OF TIBET
Mount Everest 29,035 ft. (8,850 m)
HIMALAYAS
Brahmaputra River
INDO-GANGETIC PLAIN
Ganges River
HINDU KUSH
Indus River
Sutlej River
THAR DESERT
DECCAN PLATEAU
Godavari River
EASTERN GHATS
WESTERN GHATS
Sri Lanka
Bay of Bengal
Andaman Islands
Nicobar Islands
INDIAN OCEAN
Maldives
Lakshadweep Islands
ARABIAN SEA
Syr Darya
KYZYL KUM
TURAN LOWLAND
ARAL SEA
Amu Darya
KARA-KUM
USTYURT PLATEAU
CASPIAN SEA
CAUCASUS MTS.
SEA OF AZOV
BLACK SEA
Bosporus
Mount Ararat 16,945 ft. (5,165 m)
ANATOLIAN PLATEAU
Tigris River
Euphrates River
ZAGROS MTS.
GREAT SALT DESERT
GULF OF OMAN
Strait of Hormuz
PERSIAN GULF
SYRIAN DESERT
AN-NAFUD
RUB' AL-KHALI
Cyprus
SINAI PENINSULA
RED SEA
GULF OF ADEN
Socotra Island
MEDITERRANEAN SEA
EUROPE
AFRICA
Arctic Circle
SCALE
0 500 1,000 Miles
0 500 1,000 Kilometers
Projection: Modified Oblique Conic
N

ASIA: POLITICAL

Boundaries
National capitals
Other cities
SCALE
0 500 1000 Miles
0 500 1000 Kilometers
Projection: Two-Point Equidistant
EUROPE
AFRICA
AUSTRALIA
PACIFIC OCEAN
INDIAN OCEAN
RUSSIA
KAZAKHSTAN
MONGOLIA
CHINA
INDIA
PAKISTAN
AFGHANISTAN
IRAN
IRAQ
TURKEY
SYRIA
JORDAN
LEBANON
ISRAEL
CYPRUS
GEORGIA
ARMENIA
AZERBAIJAN
TURKMENISTAN
UZBEKISTAN
KYRGYZSTAN
TAJIKISTAN
SAUDI ARABIA
KUWAIT
BAHRAIN
QATAR
UNITED ARAB EMIRATES
OMAN
YEMEN
NEPAL
BHUTAN
BANGLADESH
MYANMAR (BURMA)
LAOS
THAILAND
CAMBODIA
VIETNAM
MALAYSIA
SINGAPORE
BRUNEI
INDONESIA
PHILIPPINES
TAIWAN
NORTH KOREA
SOUTH KOREA
JAPAN
SRI LANKA
MALDIVES
EAST TIMOR
IRIAN JAYA
MEDITERRANEAN SEA
BLACK SEA
CASPIAN SEA
ARAL SEA
RED SEA
PERSIAN GULF
GULF OF ADEN
ARABIAN SEA
Bay of Bengal
ANDAMAN SEA
GULF OF THAILAND
SOUTH CHINA SEA
JAVA SEA
CELEBES SEA
ARAFURA SEA
EAST CHINA SEA
YELLOW SEA
SEA OF JAPAN
SEA OF OKHOTSK
BERING SEA
BARENTS SEA
KARA SEA
LAPTEV SEA
Lake Balkhash
Lake Baykal
URAL MOUNTAINS
Ural River
Ob River
Irtysh River
Yenisey River
Angara River
Lena River
Amur River
Huang River
Chang River
Nu River
Brahmaputra River
Ganges River
Indus River
Irrawaddy River
Mekong River
Tigris River
Euphrates River
Great Wall of China
Sakhalin Island
Kuril Islands (RUSSIA)
Aleutian Islands
Ryukyu Islands (JAPAN)
Hainan (CHINA)
Socotra (YEMEN)
Lakshadweep Islands (INDIA)
Andaman Islands (INDIA)
Nicobar Islands (INDIA)
Luzon Strait
Tropic of Cancer
Arctic Circle
Equator
Moscow
Yekaterinburg
Chelyabinsk
Omsk
Novosibirsk
Irkutsk
Yakutsk
Vladivostok
Astana
Almaty
Bishkek
Tashkent
Dushanbe
Ashgabat
Kabul
Islamabad
Lahore
Faisalabad
Karachi
Istanbul
Izmir
Ankara
Nicosia
Beirut
Tel Aviv
Jerusalem
Amman
Damascus
Aleppo
T'bilisi
Yerevan
Baku
Tabriz
Mosul
Baghdad
Basra
Tehran
Mashhad
Isfahan
Shiraz
Kuwait City
Manama
Doha
Riyadh
Abu Dhabi
Masqat (Muscat)
Jidda
Mecca
Sanaa
Delhi
New Delhi
Jaipur
Ahmadabad
Bhopal
Nagpur
Mumbai (Bombay)
Hyderabad
Bangalore
Chennai (Madras)
Kolkata (Calcutta)
Kathmandu
Thimphu
Dhaka
Chittagong
Colombo
Male
Mandalay
Yangon (Rangoon)
Bangkok
Vientiane
Hanoi
Phnom Penh
Ho Chi Minh City
Kuala Lumpur
Singapore
Medan
Bandar Seri Begawan
Manila
Jakarta
Bandung
Semarang
Surabaya
Ujung Pandang
Ulaanbaatar
Beijing
Harbin
Changchun
Fushun
Dalian
Qingdao
Xi'an
Chengdu
Chongqing
Wuhan
Nanjing
Shanghai
Guangzhou
Hong Kong
Macao
Taipei
P'yongyang
Seoul
Pusan
Sapporo
Tokyo
Yokohama
Nagoya
Kyoto
Osaka
Hiroshima
Nagasaki

AFRICA: PHYSICAL

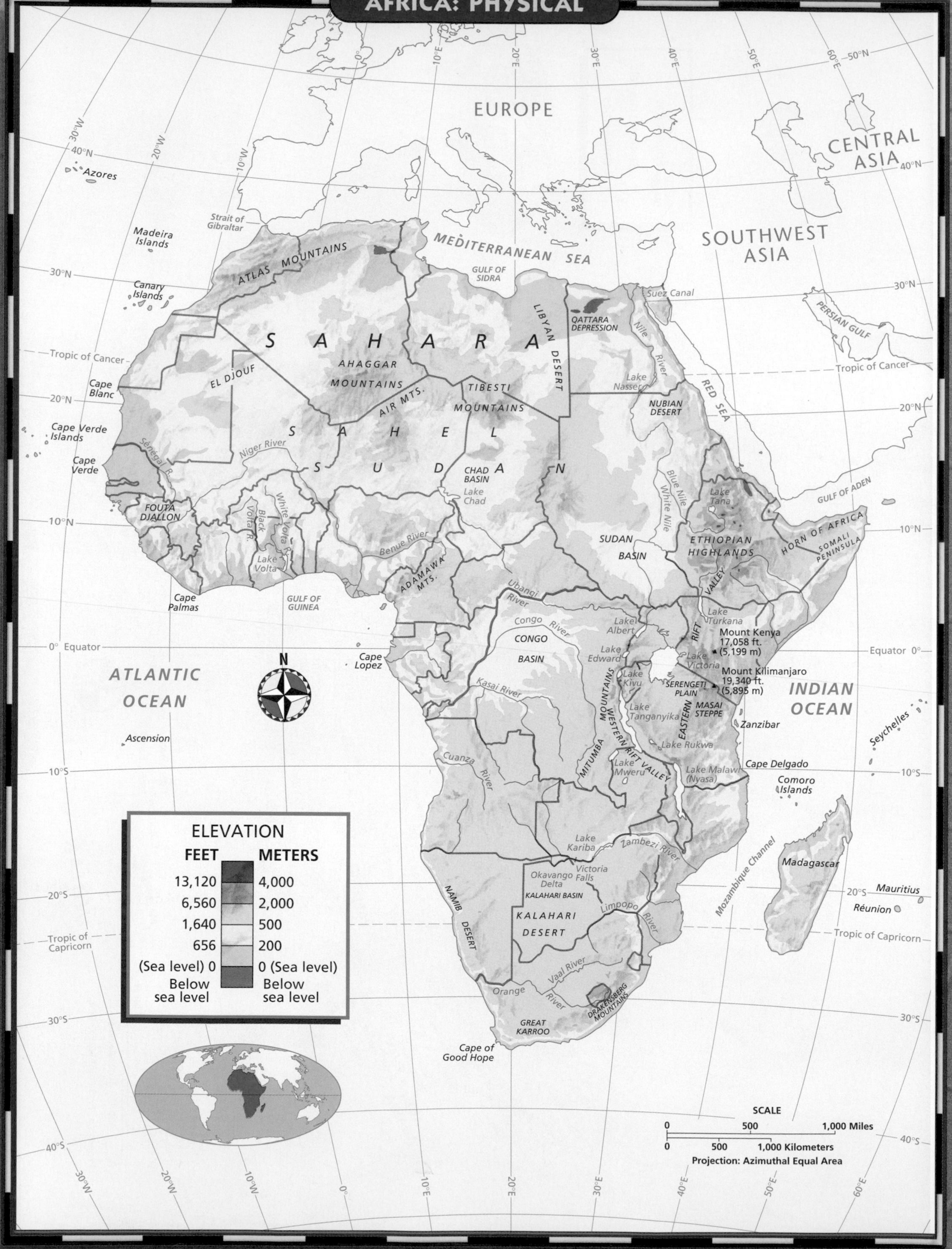
EUROPE
CENTRAL ASIA
SOUTHWEST ASIA
Azores
Madeira Islands
Strait of Gibraltar
Canary Islands
MEDITERRANEAN SEA
GULF OF SIDRA
ATLAS MOUNTAINS
S A H A R A
AHAGGAR MOUNTAINS
LIBYAN DESERT
QATTARA DEPRESSION
Suez Canal
PERSIAN GULF
Nile River
Lake Nasser
NUBIAN DESERT
RED SEA
Tropic of Cancer
EL DJOUF
AIR MTS.
TIBESTI MOUNTAINS
S A H E L
S U D A N
Cape Blanc
Cape Verde Islands
Cape Verde
Senegal R.
Niger River
CHAD BASIN
Lake Chad
Blue Nile
White Nile
Lake Tana
GULF OF ADEN
ETHIOPIAN HIGHLANDS
HORN OF AFRICA
SOMALI PENINSULA
SUDAN BASIN
FOUTA DJALLON
Black Volta R.
White Volta R.
Lake Volta
Benue River
ADAMAWA MTS.
Cape Palmas
GULF OF GUINEA
Ubangi River
Congo River
CONGO BASIN
Lake Albert
Lake Turkana
RIFT VALLEY
Mount Kenya 17,058 ft. (5,199 m)
Lake Edward
Lake Victoria
Mount Kilimanjaro 19,340 ft. (5,895 m)
Lake Kivu
SERENGETI PLAIN
MASAI STEPPE
Equator
Cape Lopez
ATLANTIC OCEAN
INDIAN OCEAN
N
Kasai River
MITUMBA MOUNTAINS
WESTERN RIFT VALLEY
EASTERN
Lake Tanganyika
Zanzibar
Seychelles
Ascension
Lake Rukwa
Cape Delgado
Lake Mweru
Lake Malawi (Nyasa)
Comoro Islands
Cuanza River
Lake Kariba
Zambezi River
Mozambique Channel
Madagascar
Victoria Falls
Okavango Delta
KALAHARI BASIN
KALAHARI DESERT
NAMIB DESERT
Limpopo River
Mauritius
Réunion
Tropic of Capricorn
Vaal River
Orange River
DRAKENSBERG MOUNTAINS
GREAT KARROO
Cape of Good Hope
ELEVATION
FEET
METERS
13,120
4,000
6,560
2,000
1,640
500
656
200
(Sea level) 0
0 (Sea level)
Below sea level
Below sea level
SCALE
0 500 1,000 Miles
0 500 1,000 Kilometers
Projection: Azimuthal Equal Area
50°N
40°N
30°N
20°N
10°N
0°
10°S
20°S
30°S
40°S
30°W
20°W
10°W
10°E
20°E
30°E
40°E
50°E
60°E

AFRICA: POLITICAL

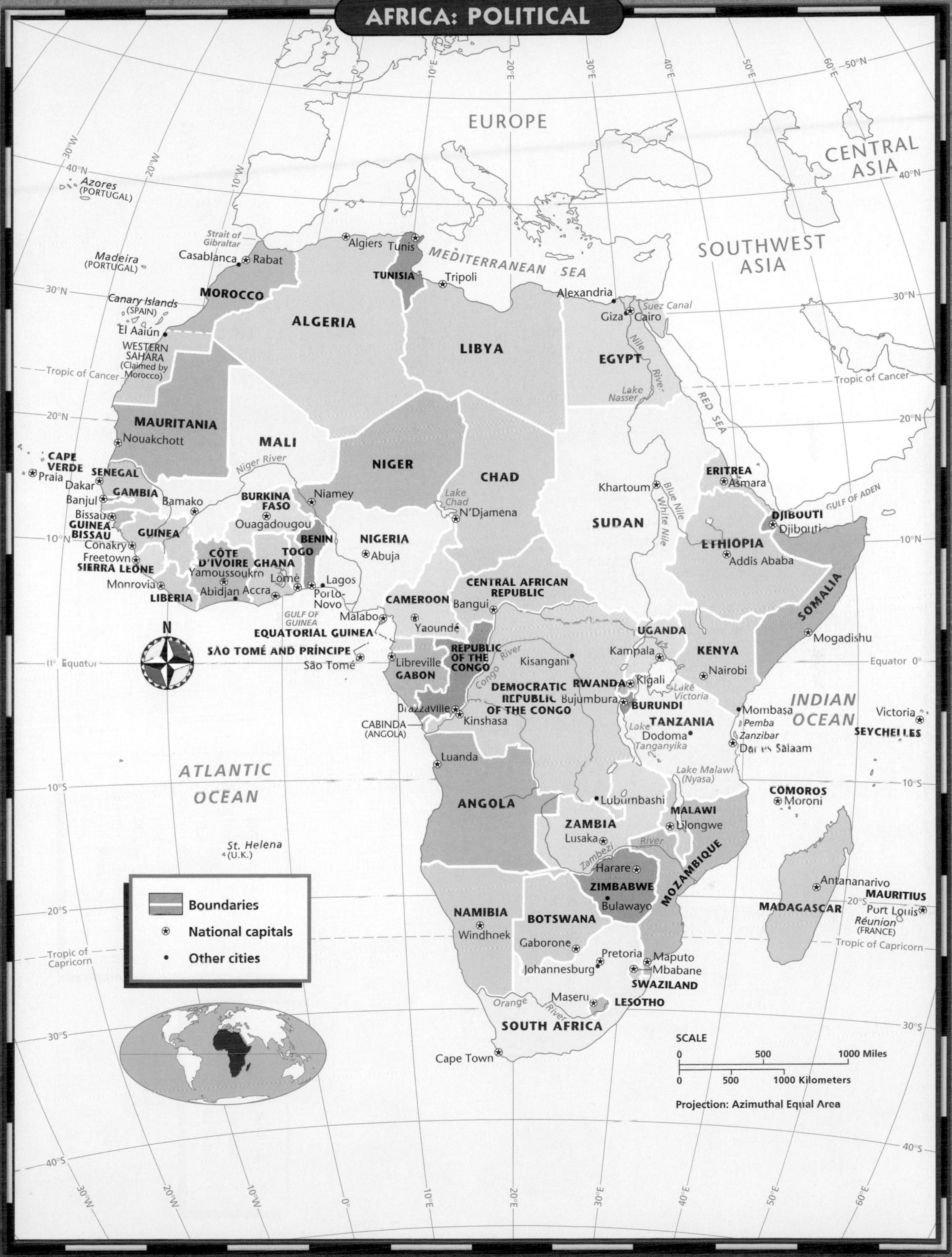
EUROPE
CENTRAL ASIA
SOUTHWEST ASIA
MEDITERRANEAN SEA
RED SEA
GULF OF ADEN
INDIAN OCEAN
ATLANTIC OCEAN
GULF OF GUINEA
Azores (PORTUGAL)
Madeira (PORTUGAL)
Canary Islands (SPAIN)
Strait of Gibraltar
Casablanca
Rabat
MOROCCO
El Aaiún
WESTERN SAHARA (Claimed by Morocco)
Algiers
Tunis
TUNISIA
Tripoli
ALGERIA
LIBYA
Alexandria
Giza
Cairo
Suez Canal
EGYPT
Nile River
Lake Nasser
MAURITANIA
Nouakchott
MALI
Niger River
NIGER
CHAD
Lake Chad
SUDAN
Khartoum
Blue Nile
White Nile
ERITREA
Asmara
DJIBOUTI
Djibouti
ETHIOPIA
Addis Ababa
SOMALIA
Mogadishu
CAPE VERDE
Praia
SENEGAL
Dakar
GAMBIA
Banjul
Bissau
GUINEA-BISSAU
GUINEA
Conakry
Freetown
SIERRA LEONE
Monrovia
LIBERIA
Bamako
BURKINA FASO
Ouagadougou
Niamey
BENIN
TOGO
NIGERIA
Abuja
CÔTE D'IVOIRE
Yamoussoukro
Abidjan
GHANA
Accra
Lomé
Lagos
Porto-Novo
N'Djamena
CENTRAL AFRICAN REPUBLIC
Bangui
CAMEROON
Yaoundé
Malabo
EQUATORIAL GUINEA
SÃO TOMÉ AND PRÍNCIPE
São Tomé
Libreville
GABON
REPUBLIC OF THE CONGO
Congo River
Brazzaville
Kinshasa
CABINDA (ANGOLA)
DEMOCRATIC REPUBLIC OF THE CONGO
Kisangani
UGANDA
Kampala
KENYA
Nairobi
RWANDA
Kigali
BURUNDI
Bujumbura
Lake Victoria
TANZANIA
Dodoma
Lake Tanganyika
Mombasa
Pemba
Zanzibar
Dar es Salaam
SEYCHELLES
Victoria
Lake Malawi (Nyasa)
COMOROS
Moroni
Luanda
ANGOLA
Lubumbashi
ZAMBIA
Lusaka
MALAWI
Lilongwe
Zambezi River
Harare
ZIMBABWE
Bulawayo
MOZAMBIQUE
Antananarivo
MADAGASCAR
MAURITIUS
Port Louis
Réunion (FRANCE)
NAMIBIA
Windhoek
BOTSWANA
Gaborone
Pretoria
Johannesburg
Maputo
Mbabane
SWAZILAND
Maseru
LESOTHO
Orange River
SOUTH AFRICA
Cape Town
St. Helena (U.K.)
N
Equator 0°
Tropic of Cancer
Tropic of Capricorn
50°N
40°N
30°N
20°N
10°N
10°S
20°S
30°S
40°S
30°W
20°W
10°W
0°
10°E
20°E
30°E
40°E
50°E
60°E
Boundaries
National capitals
Other cities
SCALE
0
500
1000 Miles
0
500
1000 Kilometers
Projection: Azimuthal Equal Area

AUSTRALIA AND NEW ZEALAND

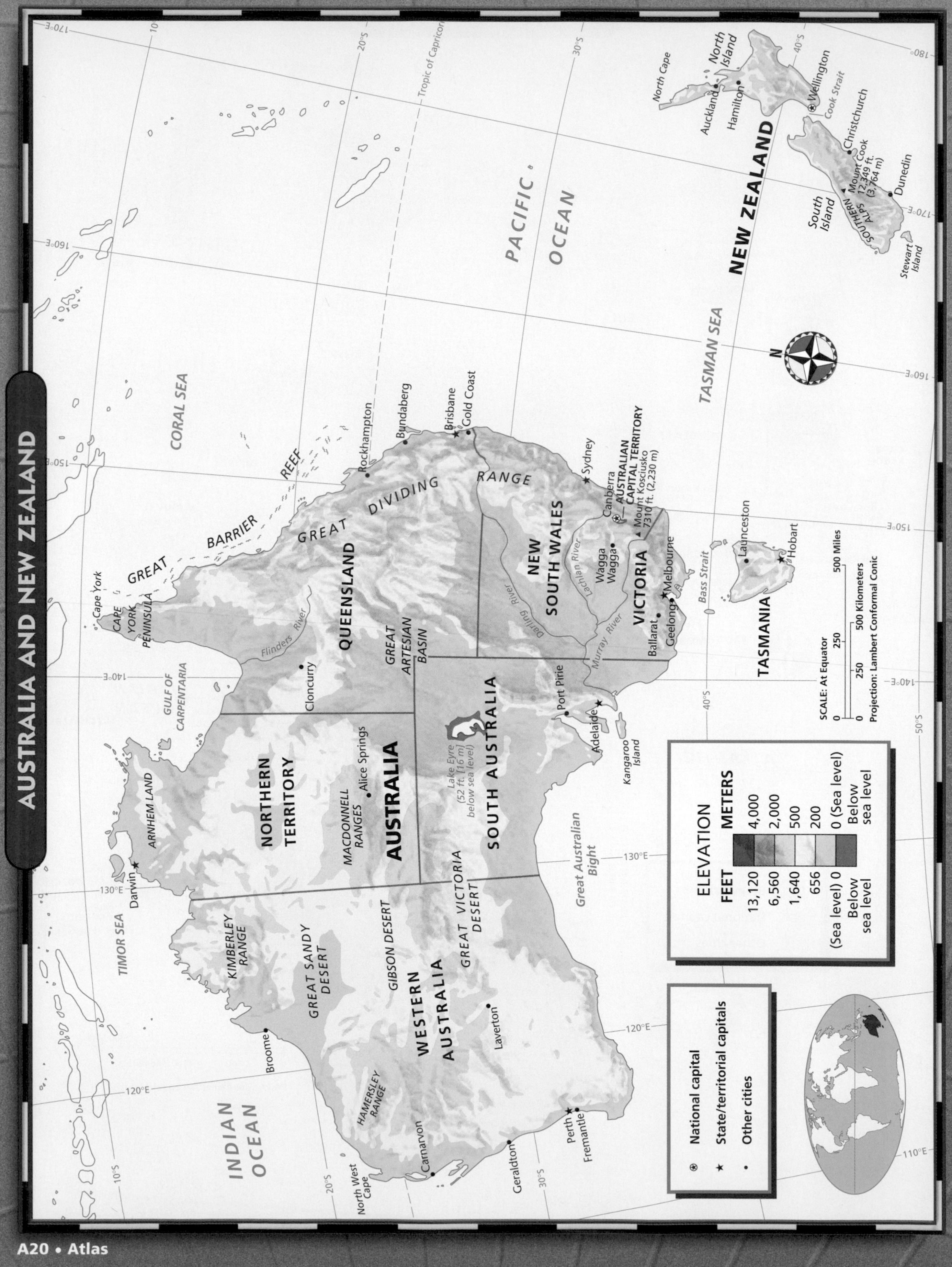

INDIAN OCEAN
PACIFIC OCEAN
CORAL SEA
TASMAN SEA
TIMOR SEA
GULF OF CARPENTARIA
Great Australian Bight
Bass Strait
Cook Strait
GREAT BARRIER REEF
GREAT DIVIDING RANGE
GREAT ARTESIAN BASIN
CAPE YORK PENINSULA
Cape York
ARNHEM LAND
KIMBERLEY RANGE
HAMERSLEY RANGE
MACDONNELL RANGES
GREAT SANDY DESERT
GIBSON DESERT
GREAT VICTORIA DESERT
Lake Eyre (52 ft. [16 m] below sea level)
Flinders River
Darling River
Lachlan River
Murray River
AUSTRALIA
WESTERN AUSTRALIA
NORTHERN TERRITORY
SOUTH AUSTRALIA
QUEENSLAND
NEW SOUTH WALES
VICTORIA
TASMANIA
AUSTRALIAN CAPITAL TERRITORY
Mount Kosciusko 7310 ft. (2,230 m)
Darwin
Broome
Carnarvon
North West Cape
Geraldton
Perth
Fremantle
Laverton
Alice Springs
Cloncurry
Port Pirie
Adelaide
Kangaroo Island
Ballarat
Geelong
Melbourne
Wagga Wagga
Canberra
Sydney
Brisbane
Gold Coast
Bundaberg
Rockhampton
Launceston
Hobart
NEW ZEALAND
North Island
South Island
Stewart Island
North Cape
Auckland
Hamilton
Wellington
Christchurch
Dunedin
SOUTHERN ALPS
Mount Cook 12,349 ft. (3,764 m)
Tropic of Capricorn
10°S
20°S
30°S
40°S
50°S
110°E
120°E
130°E
140°E
150°E
160°E
170°E
180°
N
ELEVATION
FEET
METERS
13,120
6,560
1,640
656
(Sea level) 0
Below sea level
4,000
2,000
500
200
0 (Sea level)
Below sea level
National capital
State/territorial capitals
Other cities
SCALE: At Equator
0
250
500 Miles
500 Kilometers
Projection: Lambert Conformal Conic

PACIFIC ISLANDS

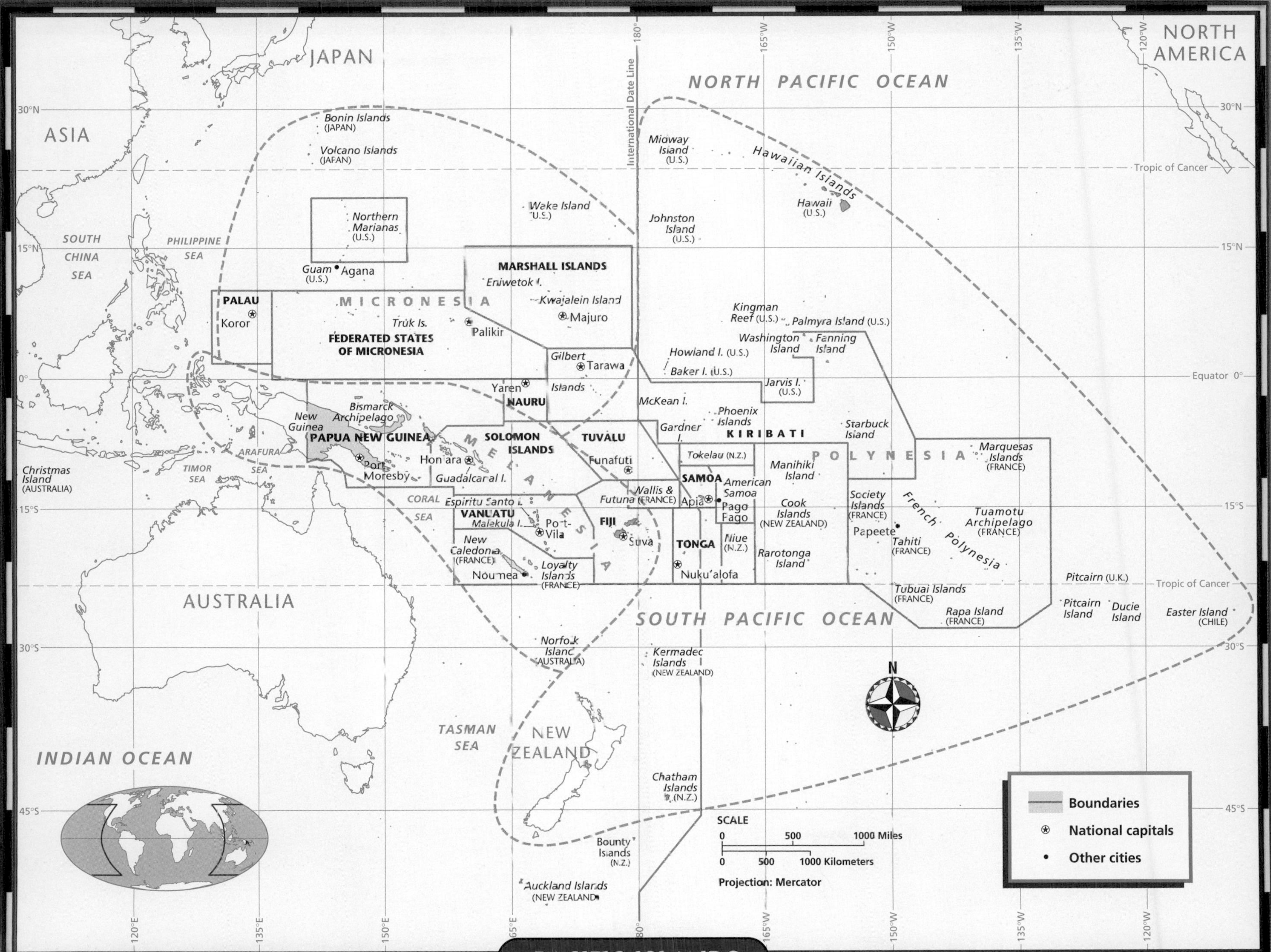
NORTH AMERICA
NORTH PACIFIC OCEAN
SOUTH PACIFIC OCEAN
INDIAN OCEAN
ASIA
JAPAN
AUSTRALIA
NEW ZEALAND
SOUTH CHINA SEA
PHILIPPINE SEA
CORAL SEA
TASMAN SEA
TIMOR SEA
ARAFURA SEA
MICRONESIA
MELANESIA
POLYNESIA
International Date Line
Tropic of Cancer
Equator 0°
30°N
15°N
15°S
30°S
45°S
120°E
135°E
150°E
165°E
180°
165°W
150°W
135°W
120°W
Bonin Islands (JAPAN)
Volcano Islands (JAPAN)
Northern Marianas (U.S.)
Guam (U.S.)
Agana
Wake Island (U.S.)
Midway Island (U.S.)
Johnston Island (U.S.)
Hawaiian Islands
Hawaii (U.S.)
PALAU
Koror
FEDERATED STATES OF MICRONESIA
Truk Is.
Palikir
MARSHALL ISLANDS
Eniwetok I.
Kwajalein Island
Majuro
Gilbert Islands
Tarawa
Yaren
NAURU
Kingman Reef (U.S.)
Palmyra Island (U.S.)
Washington Island
Fanning Island
Howland I. (U.S.)
Baker I. (U.S.)
Jarvis I. (U.S.)
McKean I.
Phoenix Islands
Gardner I.
KIRIBATI
Starbuck Island
New Guinea
Bismarck Archipelago
PAPUA NEW GUINEA
Port Moresby
SOLOMON ISLANDS
Honiara
Guadalcanal I.
TUVALU
Funafuti
Tokelau (N.Z.)
SAMOA
Apia
American Samoa
Pago Pago
Wallis & Futuna (FRANCE)
Espiritu Santo I.
VANUATU
Malekula I.
Port-Vila
New Caledonia (FRANCE)
Noumea
Loyalty Islands (FRANCE)
FIJI
Suva
TONGA
Nuku'alofa
Niue (N.Z.)
Manihiki Island
Cook Islands (NEW ZEALAND)
Rarotonga Island
Society Islands (FRANCE)
Papeete
Tahiti (FRANCE)
French Polynesia
Marquesas Islands (FRANCE)
Tuamotu Archipelago (FRANCE)
Tubuai Islands (FRANCE)
Rapa Island (FRANCE)
Pitcairn (U.K.)
Pitcairn Island
Ducie Island
Easter Island (CHILE)
Christmas Island (AUSTRALIA)
Norfolk Island (AUSTRALIA)
Kermadec Islands (NEW ZEALAND)
Chatham Islands (N.Z.)
Bounty Islands (N.Z.)
Auckland Islands (NEW ZEALAND)
N
Boundaries
National capitals
Other cities
SCALE
0
500
1000 Miles
0
500
1000 Kilometers
Projection: Mercator

NORTH POLE

EUROPE
BARENTS SEA
KARA SEA
NORWEGIAN SEA
ASIA
LAPTEV SEA
GREENLAND SEA
Iceland
ARCTIC OCEAN
ATLANTIC OCEAN
NORTH POLE
Greenland (DENMARK)
International Date Line
Arctic Circle
PACK ICE
Queen Elizabeth Islands
NORTH MAGNETIC POLE
Baffin Bay
Baffin Island
BERING SEA
BEAUFORT SEA
NORTH AMERICA
PACIFIC OCEAN
150°E
30°W
90°E
60°E
30°E
0°
80°N
70°N
60°N
50°N
180°
150°W
120°W
90°W
60°W
SCALE
0 250 500 750 Miles
0 250 500 750 Kilometers
Projection: Polar Azimuthal Equidistant

SOUTH POLE

PACIFIC OCEAN
SOUTH AMERICA
AMUNDSEN SEA
BELLINGSHAUSEN SEA
PACK ICE
ROSS SEA
MARIE BYRD LAND
ELLSWORTH LAND
ANTARCTIC PENINSULA
International Date Line
Vinson Massif 16,066 ft. (4,897 m)
ROSS ICE SHELF
RONNE ICE SHELF
EDITH RONNE LAND
WEDDELL SEA
FILCHNER ICE SHELF
QUEEN MAUD MOUNTAINS
POLAR PLATEAU
Mount Markham over 14,275 ft. (over 4,351 m)
SOUTH POLE
COATS LAND
ATLANTIC OCEAN
ADELIE LAND
SOUTH MAGNETIC POLE
ANTARCTICA
WILKES LAND
ICE CAP
QUEEN MAUD LAND
Antarctic Circle
SHACKLETON ICE SHELF
AMERICAN HIGHLAND
ENDERBY LAND
INDIAN OCEAN
180°
150°W
120°W
90°W
60°W
30°W
0°
150°E
120°E
90°E
60°E
30°E
70°S
60°S
50°S
SCALE
0 250 500 750 Miles
0 250 500 750 Kilometers
Projection: Polar Azimuthal Equidistant

SKILLS HANDBOOK

Studying geography requires the ability to understand and use various tools. This Skills Handbook explains how to use maps, charts, and other graphics to help you learn about geography and the various regions of the world. Throughout this textbook, you will have the opportunity to improve these skills and build upon them.

CONTENTS

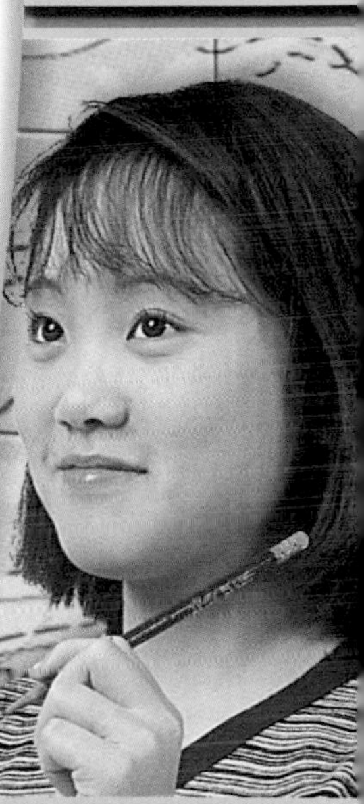

GEOGRAPHIC Dictionary

- globe
- grid
- latitude
- equator
- parallels
- degrees
- minutes
- longitude
- prime meridian
- meridians
- hemispheres
- continents
- islands
- ocean
- map
- map projections
- compass rose
- scale
- legend

MAPPING
THE EARTH

The Globe

A **globe** is a scale model of Earth. It is useful for looking at the entire Earth or at large areas of Earth's surface.

The pattern of lines that circle the globe in east-west and north-south directions is called a **grid**. The intersection of these imaginary lines helps us find places on Earth.

The east-west lines in the grid are lines of **latitude**. These imaginary lines measure distance north and south of the **equator**. The equator is an imaginary line that circles the globe halfway between the North and South Poles. Lines of latitude are called **parallels** because they are always parallel to the equator. Parallels measure distance from the equator in **degrees**. The symbol for degrees is °. Degrees are further divided into **minutes**. The symbol for minutes is ′. There are 60 minutes in a degree. Parallels north of the equator are labeled with an *N*. Those south of the equator are labeled with an *S*.

The north-south lines are lines of **longitude**. These imaginary lines pass through the Poles. They measure distance east and west of the **prime meridian**. The prime meridian is an imaginary line that runs through Greenwich, England. It represents 0° longitude. Lines of longitude are called **meridians**.

Lines of latitude range from 0°, for locations on the equator, to 90°N or 90°S, for locations at the Poles. See **Figure 1**. Lines of longitude range from 0° on the prime meridian to 180° on a meridian in the mid-Pacific Ocean. Meridians west of the prime meridian to 180° are labeled with a *W*. Those east of the prime meridian to 180° are labeled with an *E*. See **Figure 2**.

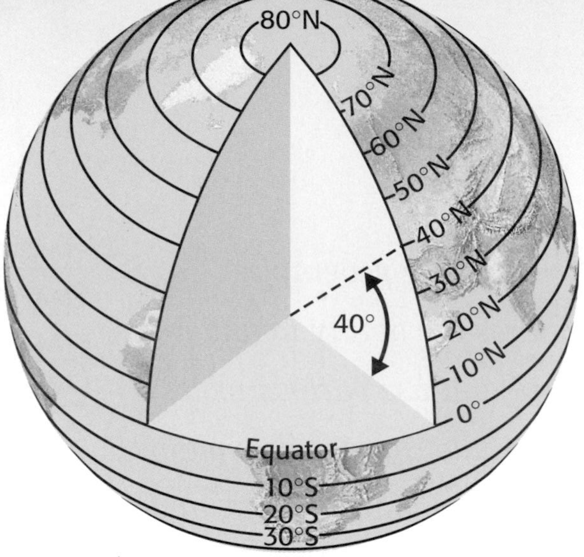
80°N
70°N
60°N
50°N
40°N
30°N
20°N
10°N
0°
40°
Equator
10°S
20°S
30°S

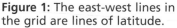

Figure 1: The east-west lines in the grid are lines of latitude.

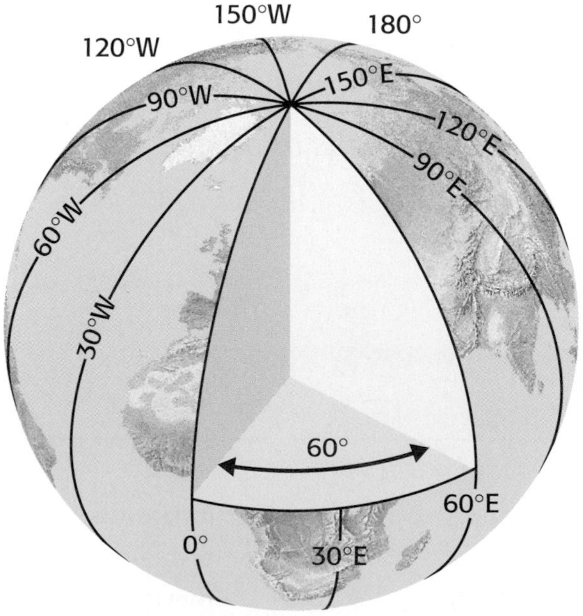
150°W
180°
120°W
90°W
150°E
120°E
90°E
60°W
30°W
60°
60°E
0°
30°E

Figure 2: The north-south lines are lines of longitude.

Figure 3: The hemispheres

NORTHERN HEMISPHERE

INDIAN OCEAN
ASIA
EUROPE
AFRICA
ARCTIC OCEAN
North Pole
PACIFIC OCEAN
ATLANTIC OCEAN
Equator
NORTH AMERICA

SOUTHERN HEMISPHERE

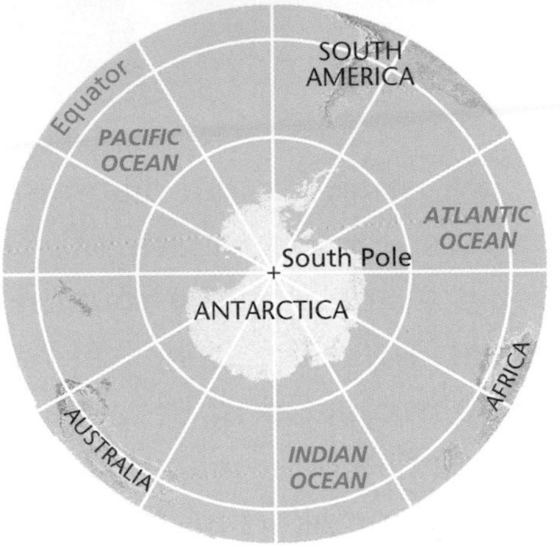

SOUTH AMERICA
Equator
PACIFIC OCEAN
ATLANTIC OCEAN
South Pole
ANTARCTICA
AFRICA
AUSTRALIA
INDIAN OCEAN

The equator divides the globe into two halves, called **hemispheres**. See **Figure 3**. The half north of the equator is the Northern Hemisphere. The southern half is the Southern Hemisphere. The prime meridian and the 180° meridian divide the world into the Eastern Hemisphere and the Western Hemisphere. The prime meridian separates parts of Europe and Africa into two different hemispheres. To prevent this, some mapmakers divide the Eastern and Western hemispheres at 20° W. This places all of Europe and Africa in the Eastern Hemisphere.

Our planet's land surface is organized into seven large landmasses, called **continents**. They are identified in **Figure 3**. Landmasses smaller than continents and completely surrounded by water are called **islands**. Geographers also organize Earth's water surface into parts. The largest is the world **ocean**. Geographers divide the world ocean into the Pacific Ocean, the Atlantic Ocean, the Indian Ocean, and the Arctic Ocean. Lakes and seas are smaller bodies of water.

EASTERN HEMISPHERE

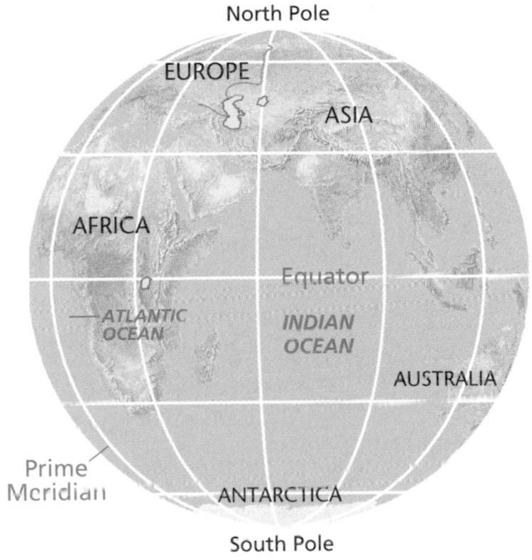

North Pole
EUROPE
ASIA
AFRICA
Equator
ATLANTIC OCEAN
INDIAN OCEAN
AUSTRALIA
Prime Meridian
ANTARCTICA
South Pole

WESTERN HEMISPHERE

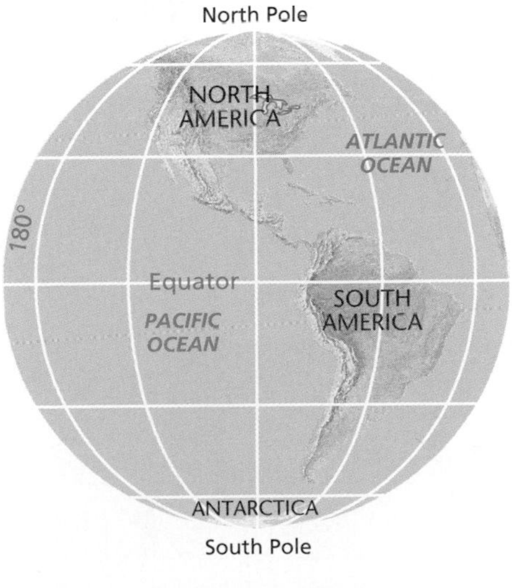

North Pole
NORTH AMERICA
ATLANTIC OCEAN
180°
Equator
PACIFIC OCEAN
SOUTH AMERICA
ANTARCTICA
South Pole

YOUR TURN

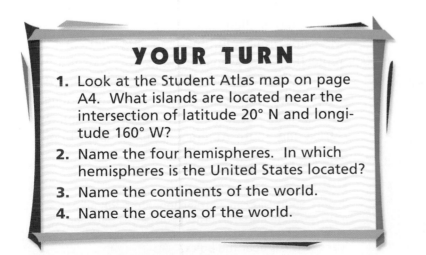

1. Look at the Student Atlas map on page A4. What islands are located near the intersection of latitude 20° N and longitude 160° W?
2. Name the four hemispheres. In which hemispheres is the United States located?
3. Name the continents of the world.
4. Name the oceans of the world.

MAPMAKING

A **map** is a flat diagram of all or part of Earth's surface. Mapmakers have different ways of showing our round Earth on flat maps. These different ways are called **map projections**. Because our planet is round, all flat maps lose some accuracy. Mapmakers must choose the type of map projection that is best for their purposes. Many map projections are one of three kinds: cylindrical, conic, or flat-plane.

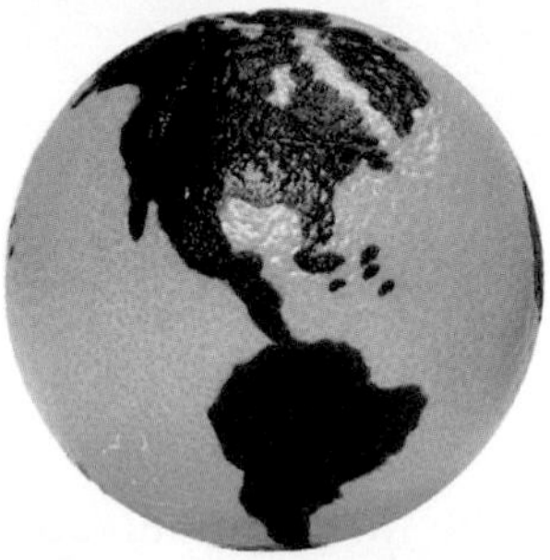

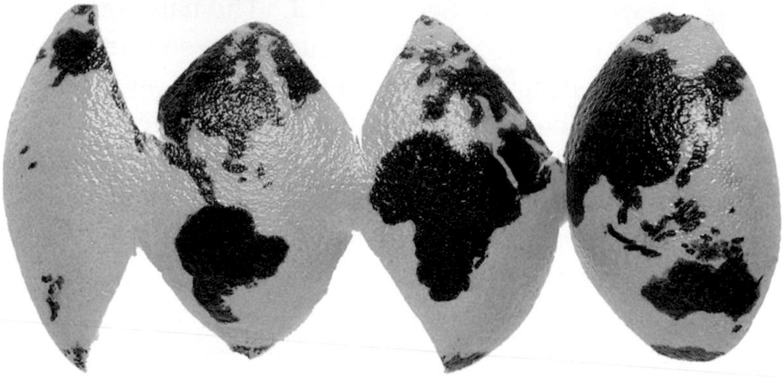

Figure 4: If you remove the peel from the orange and flatten the peel, it will stretch and tear. The larger the piece of peel, the more its shape is distorted as it is flattened. Also distorted are the distances between points on the peel.

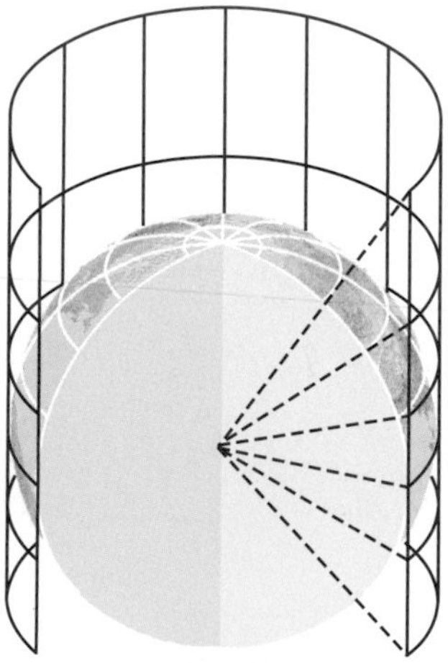

Figure 5A: Paper cylinder

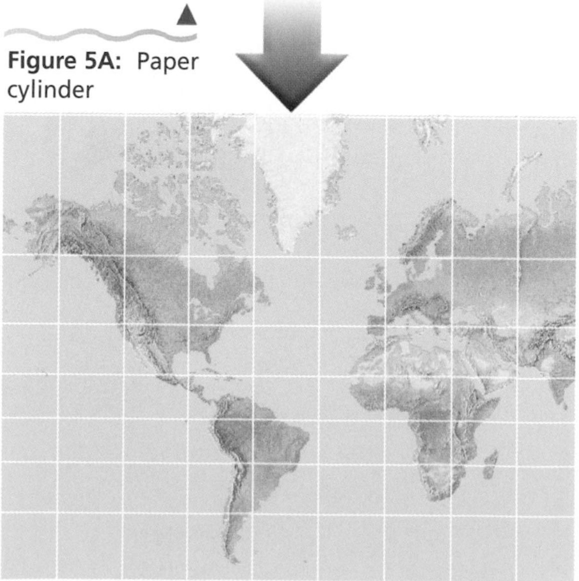

Cylindrical projections are designed from a cylinder wrapped around the globe. See **Figure 5A**. The cylinder touches the globe only at the equator. The meridians are pulled apart and are parallel to each other instead of meeting at the Poles. This causes landmasses near the Poles to appear larger than they really are. **Figure 5B** is a Mercator projection, one type of cylindrical projection. The Mercator projection is useful for navigators because it shows true direction and shape. The Mercator projection for world maps, however, emphasizes the Northern Hemisphere. Africa and South America appear smaller than they really are.

Figure 5B: A Mercator projection, although accurate near the equator, distorts distances between regions of land. This projection also distorts the sizes of areas near the poles.

Conic projections are designed from a cone placed over the globe. See **Figure 6A**. A conic projection is most accurate along the lines of latitude where it touches the globe. It retains almost true shape and size. Conic projections are most useful for areas that have long east-west dimensions, such as the United States. See the map in **Figure 6B**.

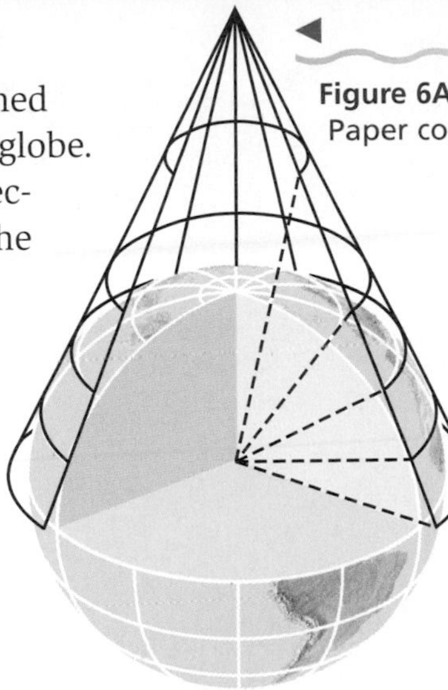

Figure 6A: Paper cone

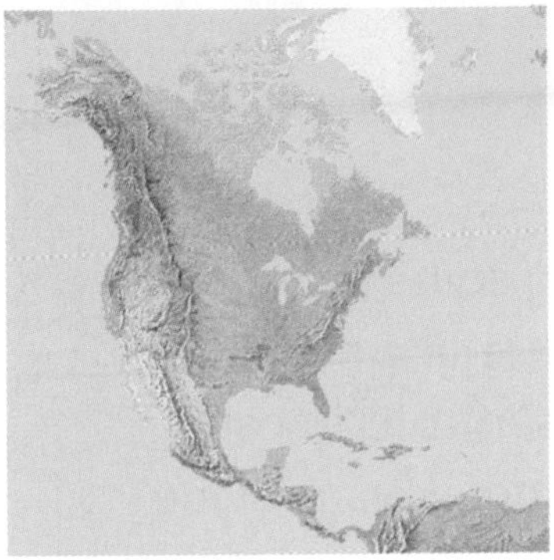

Figure 6B: Conic projection

Flat-plane projections are designed from a plane touching the globe at one point, such as at the North Pole or South Pole. See **Figures 7A** and **7B**. A flat-plane projection is useful for showing true direction for airplane pilots and ship navigators. It also shows true area. However, it distorts true shape.

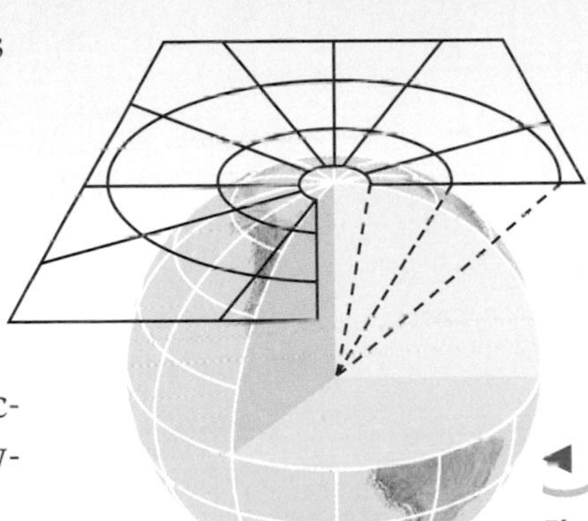

Figure 7A: Flat plane

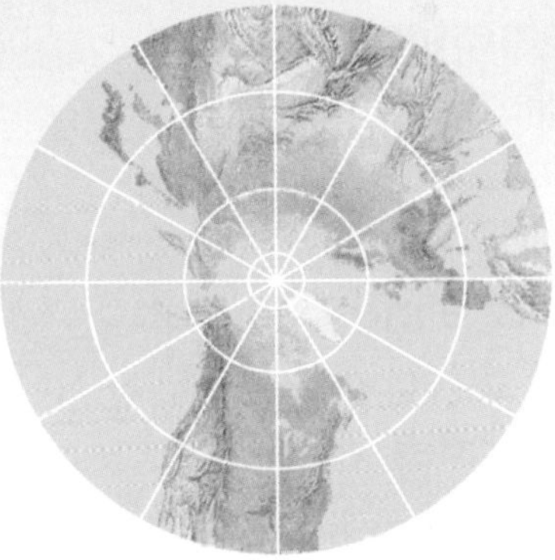

Figure 7B: Flat-plane projection

The Robinson projection is a compromise between size and shape distortions. It often is used for world maps, such as the map on page 76. The minor distortions in size at high latitudes on Robinson projections are balanced by realistic shapes at the middle and low latitudes.

YOUR TURN

1. What are three major kinds of map projections?
2. Why is a Robinson projection often used for world maps?
3. What kind of projection is a Mercator map?
4. When would a mapmaker choose to use a conic projection?

MAP ESSENTIALS

In some ways, maps are like messages sent out in code. Mapmakers provide certain elements that help us translate these codes. These elements help us understand the message they are presenting about a particular part of the world. Of these elements, almost all maps have directional indicators, scales, and legends, or keys. **Figure 8**, a map of East Asia, has all three elements.

MONGOLIA
MONGOLIAN PLATEAU
GOBI
TIAN SHAN
TAKLIMAKAN DESERT
KUNLUN MOUNTAINS
PLATEAU OF TIBET
HIMALAYAS
CHINA
QIN LING
Huang (Yellow R.)
NORTH CHINA PLAIN
SICHUAN PLAIN
Chang (Yangtze) River
Brahmaputra River
Tropic of Cancer
SOUTH ASIA
MANCHURIAN PLAIN
NORTH KOREA
SOUTH KOREA
SEA OF JAPAN
Honshu
JAPAN
Shikoku
Kyushu
YELLOW SEA
EAST CHINA SEA
Okinawa
Ryukyu Islands (JAPAN)
TAIWAN
20°N
MYANMAR (BURMA)
Irrawaddy River
Hong (Red) River
LAOS
Mekong R.
Hainan (CHINA)
Luzon
PHILIPPINE SEA
Bay of Bengal
Chao Phraya River
THAILAND
VIETNAM
SOUTH CHINA SEA
PHILIPPINES
CAMBODIA
Tonle Sap
10°N
GULF OF THAILAND
Mindanao
N
1
BRUNEI
Strait of Malacca
MALAYSIA
Equator
Sumatra
SINGAPORE
Borneo
Sulawesi (Celebes)
Moluccas
INDIAN OCEAN
2
INDONESIA
SCALE
0 500 1000 Miles
0 500 1000 Kilometers
Projection: Two-Point Equidistant
10°S
Java
Timor

Figure 8: East and Southeast Asia—Physical

A directional indicator shows which directions are north, south, east, and west. Some mapmakers use a "north arrow," which points toward the North Pole. Remember, "north" is not always at the top of a map. The way a map is drawn and the location of directions on that map depend on the perspective of the mapmaker. Maps in this textbook indicate direction by using a **compass rose** (1). A compass rose has arrows that point to all four principal directions, as shown in **Figure 8**.

Mapmakers use scales to represent distances between points on a map. Scales may appear on maps in several different forms. The maps in this textbook provide a line **scale** (2). Scales give distances in miles and kilometers (km).

To find the distance between two points on the map in **Figure 8**, place a piece of paper so that the edge connects the two points. Mark the location of each point on the paper with a line or dot. Then, compare the distance between the two dots with the map's line scale. The number on the top of the scale gives the distance in miles. The number on the bottom gives the distance in kilometers. Because the distances are given in intervals, you will have to approximate the actual distance on the scale.

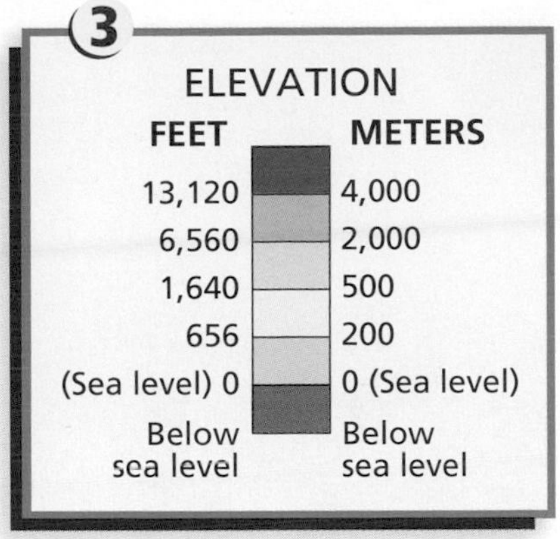
3
ELEVATION
FEET
METERS
13,120
4,000
6,560
2,000
1,640
500
656
200
(Sea level) 0
0 (Sea level)
Below sea level
Below sea level

The **legend** (3), or key, explains what the symbols on the map represent. Point symbols are used to specify the location of things, such as cities, that do not take up much space on a large-scale map. Some legends, such as the one in **Figure 8**, show which colors represent certain elevations. Other maps might have legends with symbols or colors that represent things such as roads. Legends can also show economic resources, land use, population density, and climate.

4
Size comparison of Canada to the contiguous United States

Physical maps at the beginning of each unit have size comparison maps (4). An outline of the mainland United States (not including Alaska and Hawaii) is compared to the area under study in that chapter. These size comparison maps help you understand the size of the areas you are studying in relation to the size of the United States.

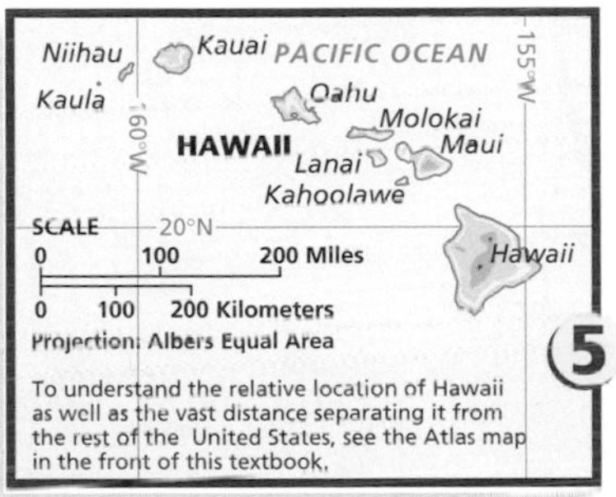
Niihau
Kauai
PACIFIC OCEAN
155°W
Kaula
Oahu
160°W
Molokai
HAWAII
Maui
Lanai
Kahoolawe
SCALE
20°N
0
100
200 Miles
Hawaii
0
100
200 Kilometers
Projection: Albers Equal Area
5
To understand the relative location of Hawaii as well as the vast distance separating it from the rest of the United States, see the Atlas map in the front of this textbook.

Inset maps are sometimes used to show a small part of a larger map. Mapmakers also use inset maps to show areas that are far away from the areas shown on the main map. Maps of the United States, for example, often include inset maps of Alaska and Hawaii (5). Those two states are too far from the other 48 states to accurately represent the true distance on the main map. Subject areas in inset maps can be drawn to a scale different from the scale used on the main map.

YOUR TURN

Look at the Student Atlas map on pages A4 and A5.

1. Locate the compass rose. What country is directly west of Madagascar in Africa?
2. What island country is located southeast of India?
3. Locate the distance scale. Using the inset map, find the approximate distance in miles and kilometers from Oslo, Norway, to Stockholm, Sweden.
4. What is the capital of Brazil? What other cities are shown in Brazil?

WORKING WITH MAPS

The Atlas at the front of this textbook includes two kinds of maps: physical and political. At the beginning of most units in this textbook, you will find five kinds of maps. These physical, political, climate, population, and land use and resources maps provide different kinds of information about the region you will study in that unit. These maps are accompanied by questions. Some questions ask you to show how the information on each of the maps might be related.

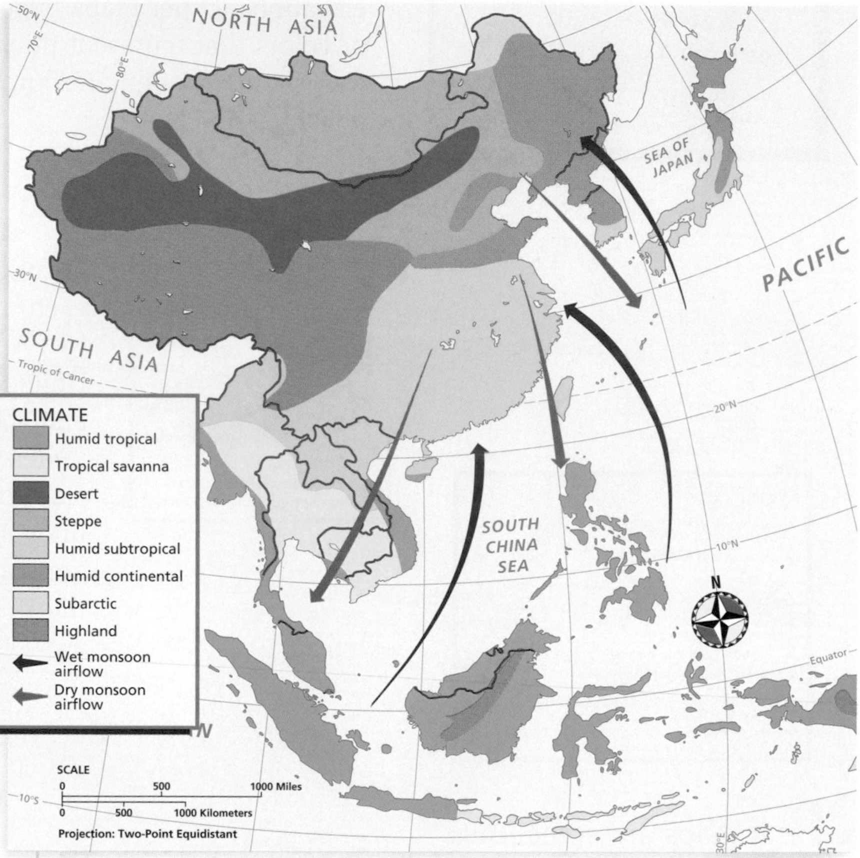

NORTH ASIA
SEA OF JAPAN
PACIFIC
SOUTH ASIA
Tropic of Cancer
SOUTH CHINA SEA
Equator
N
CLIMATE
Humid tropical
Tropical savanna
Desert
Steppe
Humid subtropical
Humid continental
Subarctic
Highland
Wet monsoon airflow
Dry monsoon airflow
SCALE
0 500 1000 Miles
0 500 1000 Kilometers
Projection: Two-Point Equidistant

Figure 9: East and Southeast Asia—Climate

Mapmakers often combine physical and political features into one map. Physical maps, such as the one in **Figure 8** on page S6, show important physical features in a region, including major mountains and mountain ranges, rivers, oceans and other bodies of water, deserts, and plains. Physical-political maps also show important political features, such as national borders, state and provincial boundaries, and capitals and other important cities. You will find a physical-political map at the beginning of most chapters.

Mapmakers use climate maps to show the most important weather patterns in certain areas. Climate maps throughout this textbook use color to show the various climate regions of the world. See **Figure 9**. Colors that identify climate types are found in a legend with each map. Boundaries between climate regions do not indicate an immediate change in the main weather conditions between two climate regions. Instead, boundaries show the general areas of gradual change between climate regions.

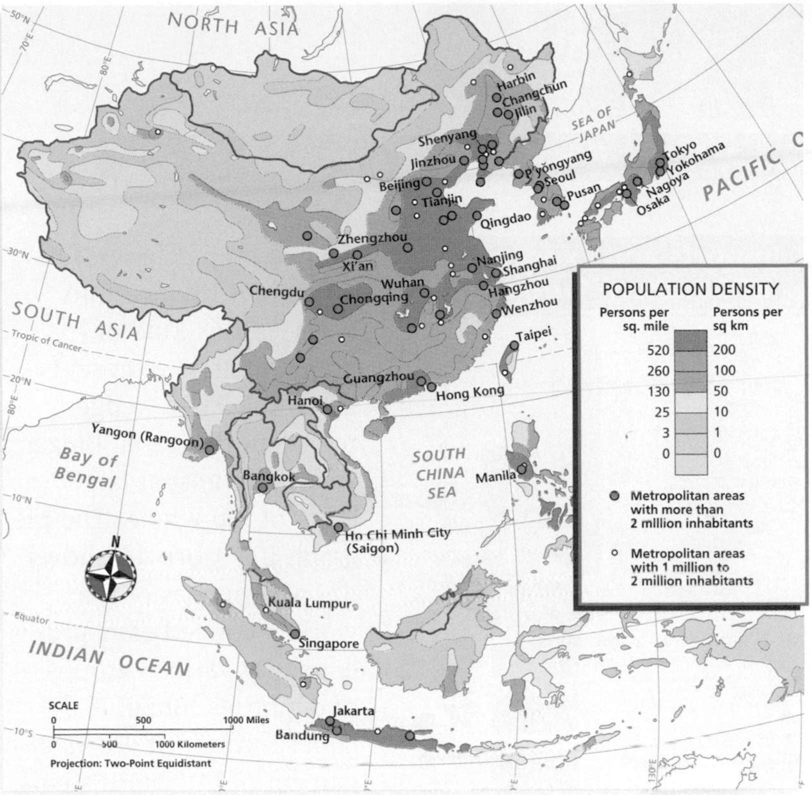

NORTH ASIA
SOUTH ASIA
Tropic of Cancer
Equator
INDIAN OCEAN
Bay of Bengal
SOUTH CHINA SEA
SEA OF JAPAN
PACIFIC
Harbin
Changchun
Jilin
Shenyang
Jinzhou
P'yŏngyang
Seoul
Pusan
Tokyo
Yokohama
Nagoya
Osaka
Beijing
Tianjin
Qingdao
Zhengzhou
Xi'an
Nanjing
Shanghai
Wuhan
Hangzhou
Chengdu
Chongqing
Wenzhou
Taipei
Guangzhou
Hong Kong
Hanoi
Yangon (Rangoon)
Bangkok
Manila
Ho Chi Minh City (Saigon)
Kuala Lumpur
Singapore
Jakarta
Bandung
POPULATION DENSITY
Persons per sq. mile
Persons per sq km
520 200
260 100
130 50
25 10
3 1
0 0
Metropolitan areas with more than 2 million inhabitants
Metropolitan areas with 1 million to 2 million inhabitants
SCALE
0 500 1000 Miles
0 500 1000 Kilometers
Projection: Two-Point Equidistant

Figure 10: East and Southeast Asia—Population

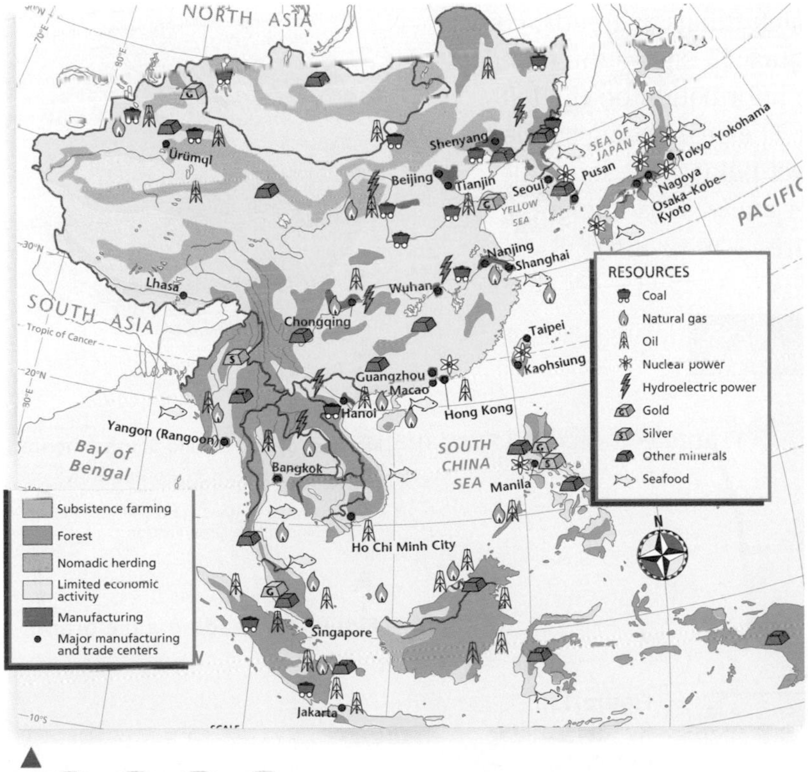

NORTH ASIA
SOUTH ASIA
Tropic of Cancer
Bay of Bengal
SOUTH CHINA SEA
SEA OF JAPAN
YELLOW SEA
PACIFIC
Ürümqi
Shenyang
Beijing
Tianjin
Seoul
Pusan
Tokyo-Yokohama
Nagoya
Osaka-Kobe-Kyoto
Nanjing
Shanghai
Lhasa
Wuhan
Chongqing
Taipei
Kaohsiung
Guangzhou
Macao
Hanoi
Hong Kong
Yangon (Rangoon)
Bangkok
Manila
Ho Chi Minh City
Singapore
Jakarta
RESOURCES
Coal
Natural gas
Oil
Nuclear power
Hydroelectric power
Gold
Silver
Other minerals
Seafood
Subsistence farming
Forest
Nomadic herding
Limited economic activity
Manufacturing
Major manufacturing and trade centers

Figure 11: East and Southeast Asia—Land Use and Resources

Population maps show where people live in a particular region. They also show how crowded, or densely populated, regions are. Population maps throughout this textbook use color to show population density. See **Figure 10**. Each color represents a certain number of people living within a square mile or square kilometer. Population maps also use symbols to show metropolitan areas with populations of a particular size. These symbols and colors are shown in a legend.

Land Use and Resources maps show the important resources of a region. See **Figure 11**. Symbols and colors are used to show information about economic development, such as where industry is located or where farming is most common. The meanings of each symbol and color are shown in a legend.

YOUR TURN

1. What is the purpose of a climate map?
2. Look at the population map. What is the population density of the area around Qingdao in northern China?
3. What energy resource is found near Ho Chi Minh City?

USING

GRAPHS, DIAGRAMS, CHARTS, AND TABLES

Bar graphs are a visual way to present information. The bar graph in **Figure 12** shows the imports and exports of the countries of southern Europe. The amount of imports and exports in billions of dollars is listed on the left side of the graph. Along the bottom of the graph are the names of the countries of southern Europe. Above each country or group of countries is a vertical bar. The top of the bar corresponds to a number along the left side of the graph. For example, Italy imports $200 billion worth of goods.

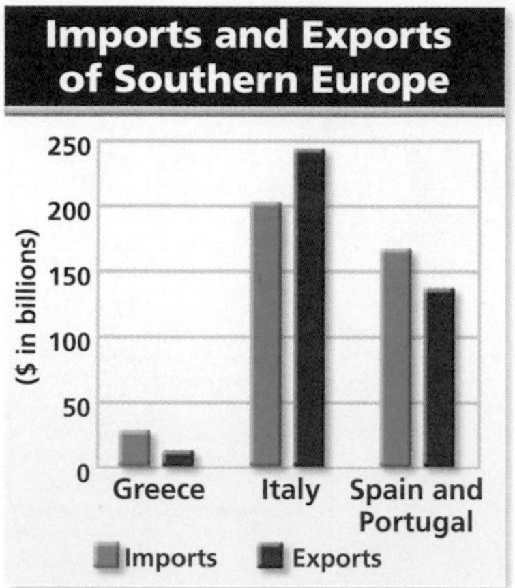

Imports and Exports of Southern Europe
250
200
150
100
50
0
($ in billions)
Greece
Italy
Spain and Portugal
Imports
Exports

Figure 12: Reading a bar graph

Often, line graphs are used to show such things as trends, comparisons, and size. The line graph in **Figure 13** shows the population growth of the world over time. The information on the left shows the number of people in billions. The years being studied are listed along the bottom. Lines connect points that show the population in billions at each year under study. This line graph projects population growth into the future.

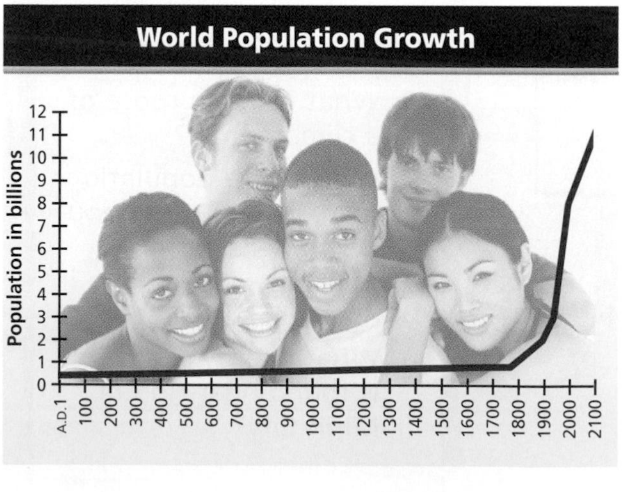

World Population Growth
Population in billions
12
11
10
9
8
7
6
5
4
3
2
1
0
A.D.1
100
200
300
400
500
600
700
800
900
1000
1100
1200
1300
1400
1500
1600
1700
1800
1900
2000
2100

Figure 13: Reading a line graph

A pie graph shows how a whole is divided into parts. In this kind of graph, a circle represents the whole. The wedges represent the parts. Bigger wedges represent larger parts of the whole. The pie graph in **Figure 14** shows the percentages of the world's coffee beans produced by various groups of countries. Brazil is the largest grower. It grows 25 percent of the world's coffee beans.

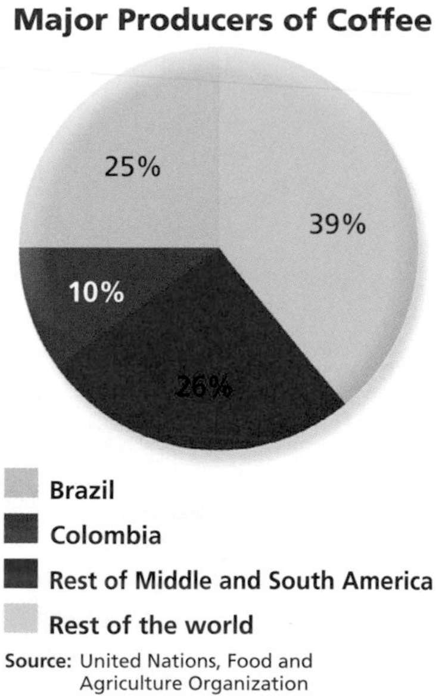

Major Producers of Coffee
25%
39%
10%
26%
Brazil
Colombia
Rest of Middle and South America
Rest of the world
Source: United Nations, Food and Agriculture Organization

Figure 14: Reading a pie graph

Age structure diagrams show the number of males and females by age group. These diagrams are split into two sides, one for male and one for female. Along the bottom are numbers that show the number of males or females in the age groups. The age groups are listed on the side of the diagram. The wider the base of a country's diagram, the younger the population of that country. The wider the top of a country's diagram, the older the population.

Some countries have so many younger people that their age structure diagrams are shaped like pyramids. For this reason, these diagrams are sometimes called population pyramids. However, in some countries the population is more evenly distributed by age group. For example, see the age structure diagram for Germany in **Figure 15**. Germany's population is older. It is not growing as fast as countries with younger populations.

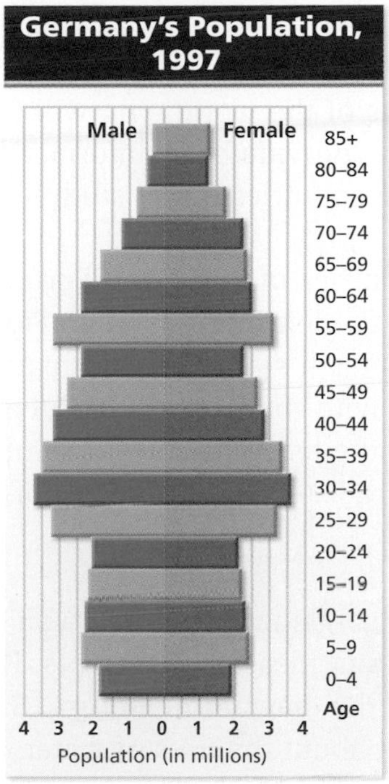

Germany's Population, 1997
Male
Female
85+
80–84
75–79
70–74
65–69
60–64
55–59
50–54
45–49
40–44
35–39
30–34
25–29
20–24
15–19
10–14
5–9
0–4
Age
4 3 2 1 0 1 2 3 4
Population (in millions)

Source: U.S. Census Bureau

Figure 15: Reading an age structure diagram

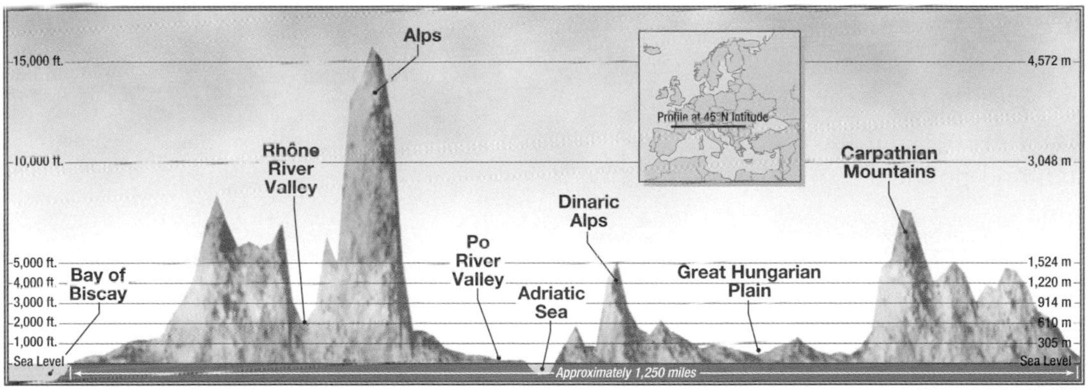

Alps
15,000 ft.
4,572 m
Profile at 45°N latitude
10,000 ft.
3,048 m
Rhône River Valley
Carpathian Mountains
Dinaric Alps
Po River Valley
5,000 ft.
4,000 ft.
3,000 ft.
2,000 ft.
1,000 ft.
Sea Level
Bay of Biscay
Adriatic Sea
Great Hungarian Plain
1,524 m
1,220 m
914 m
610 m
305 m
Sea Level
Approximately 1,250 miles

Figure 16: Reading an elevation profile

Each unit atlas includes an elevation profile. See **Figure 16**. It is a side view, or profile, of a region along a line drawn between two points.

Vertical and horizontal distances are figured differently on elevation profiles. The vertical distance (the height of a mountain, for example) is exaggerated when compared to the horizontal distance between the two points. This technique is called vertical exaggeration. If the vertical scale were not exaggerated, even tall mountains would appear as small bumps on an elevation profile.

In each unit and chapter on the various regions of the world, you will find tables that provide basic information about the countries under study.

The countries of Spain and Portugal are listed on the left in the table in **Figure 17**. You can match statistical information on the right with the name of each country listed on the left. The categories of information are listed across the top of the table.

Graphic organizers can help you understand certain ideas and concepts. For example, the diagram in **Figure 18** helps you think about the uses of water. In this diagram, one water use goes in each oval. Graphic organizers can help you focus on key facts in your study of geography.

Time lines provide highlights of important events over a period of time. The time line in **Figure 19** begins at the left with 5000 B.C., when rice was first cultivated in present-day China. The time line highlights important events that have shaped the human and political geography of China.

Spain and Portugal

Country	Population/ Growth Rate	Life Expectancy	Literacy Rate	Per Capita GDP
Portugal	9,918,040 0.1%	73, male 79, female	90% (1995)	$14,600 (1998)
Spain	39,167,744 0.1%	74, male 82, female	97% (1995)	$16,500 (1998)
United States	272,639,608 0.9%	73, male 80, female	97% (1994)	$31,500 (1998)

Sources: Central Intelligence Agency, *The World Factbook 1999; The World Almanac and Book of Facts 1999*

Figure 17: Reading a table

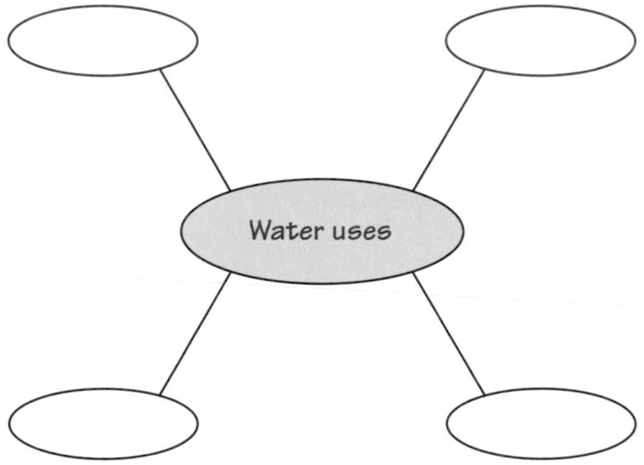
Water uses

Figure 18: Graphic organizer

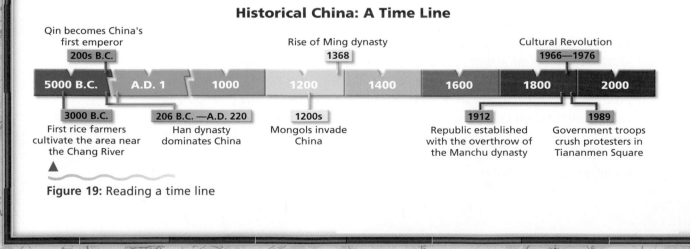

Historical China: A Time Line

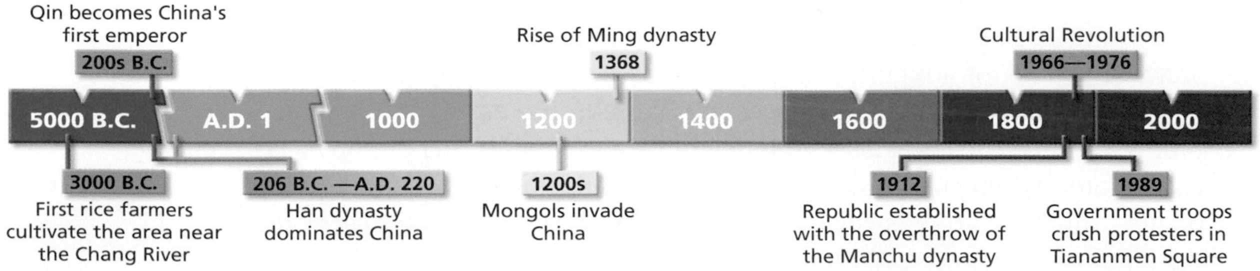
Qin becomes China's first emperor
200s B.C.
Rise of Ming dynasty
1368
Cultural Revolution
1966—1976
5000 B.C.
A.D. 1
1000
1200
1400
1600
1800
2000
3000 B.C.
First rice farmers cultivate the area near the Chang River
206 B.C. —A.D. 220
Han dynasty dominates China
1200s
Mongols invade China
1912
Republic established with the overthrow of the Manchu dynasty
1989
Government troops crush protesters in Tiananmen Square

Figure 19: Reading a time line

Corn: From Field to Consumer

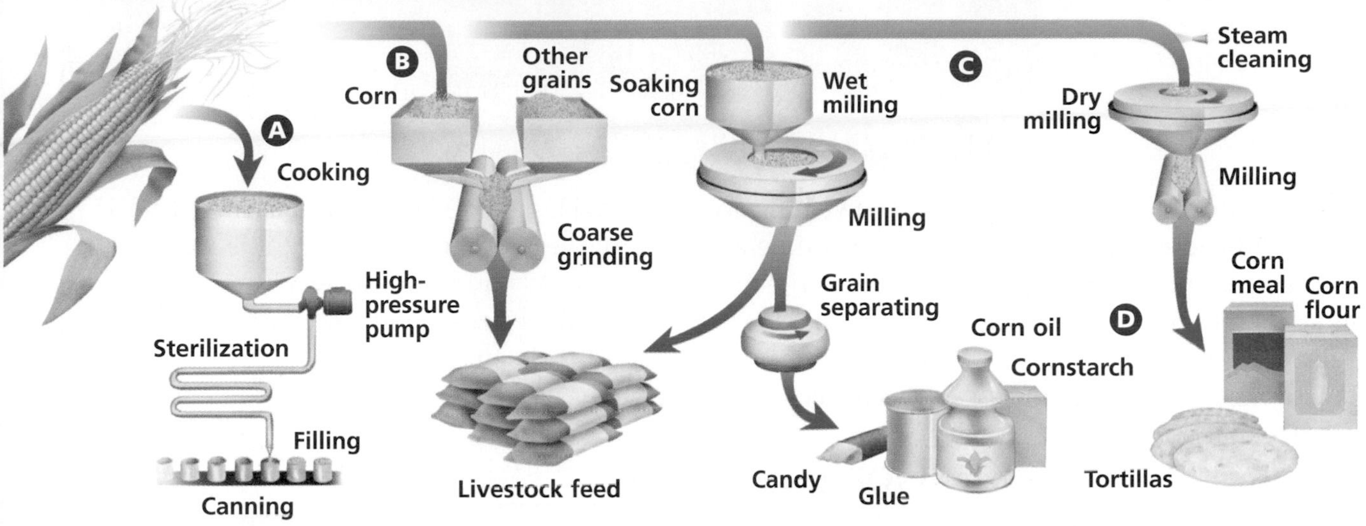

A
Cooking
Sterilization
High-pressure pump
Filling
Canning
B
Corn
Other grains
Coarse grinding
Livestock feed
Soaking corn
Wet milling
Milling
Grain separating
Candy
Glue
Corn oil
Cornstarch
C
Steam cleaning
Dry milling
Milling
Corn meal
Corn flour
D
Tortillas

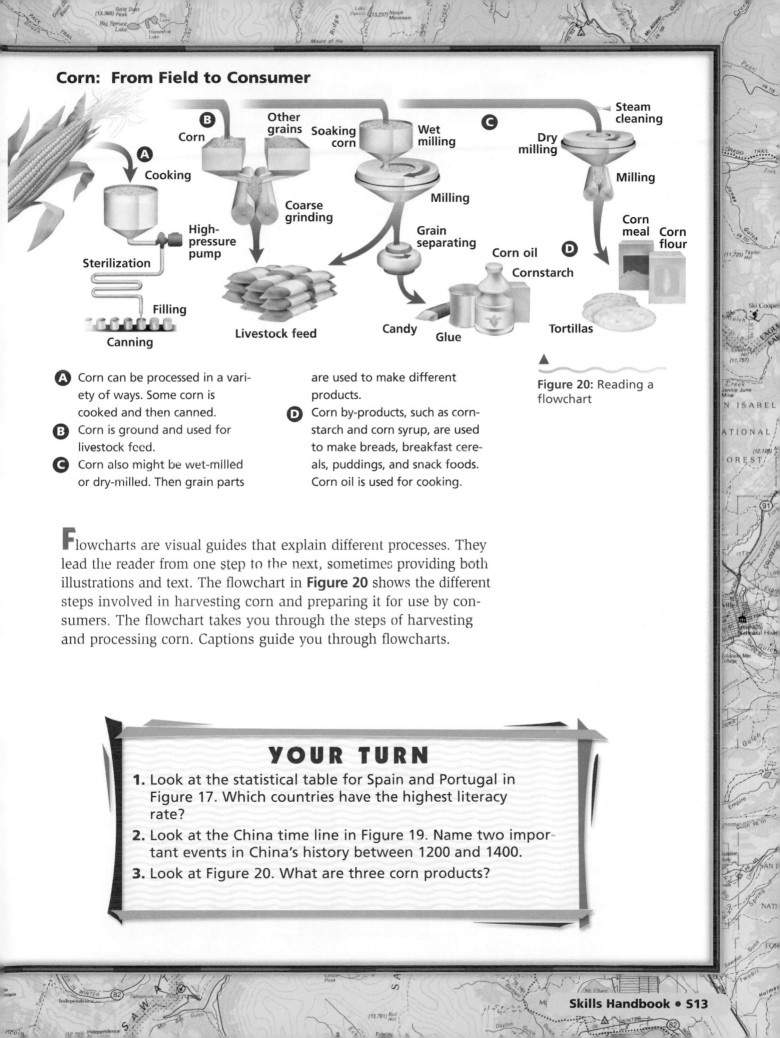

A Corn can be processed in a variety of ways. Some corn is cooked and then canned.

B Corn is ground and used for livestock feed.

C Corn also might be wet-milled or dry-milled. Then grain parts are used to make different products.

D Corn by-products, such as cornstarch and corn syrup, are used to make breads, breakfast cereals, puddings, and snack foods. Corn oil is used for cooking.

Figure 20: Reading a flowchart

Flowcharts are visual guides that explain different processes. They lead the reader from one step to the next, sometimes providing both illustrations and text. The flowchart in **Figure 20** shows the different steps involved in harvesting corn and preparing it for use by consumers. The flowchart takes you through the steps of harvesting and processing corn. Captions guide you through flowcharts.

YOUR TURN

1. Look at the statistical table for Spain and Portugal in Figure 17. Which countries have the highest literacy rate?
2. Look at the China time line in Figure 19. Name two important events in China's history between 1200 and 1400.
3. Look at Figure 20. What are three corn products?

READING A TIME-ZONE MAP

The sun is not directly overhead everywhere on Earth at the same time. Clocks are set to reflect the difference in the sun's position. Our planet rotates on its axis once every 24 hours. In other words, in one hour, it makes one twenty-fourth of a complete revolution. Since there are 360 degrees in a circle, we know that the planet turns 15 degrees of longitude each hour. (360° ÷ 24 = 15°) We also know that the planet turns in a west-to-east direction. Therefore, if a place on Earth has the sun directly overhead at this moment (noon), then a place 15 degrees to the west will have the sun directly overhead one hour from now. During that hour the planet will have rotated 15 degrees. As a result, Earth is divided into 24 time zones. Thus, time is an hour earlier for each 15 degrees you move westward on Earth. Time is an hour later for each 15 degrees you move eastward on Earth.

By international agreement, longitude is measured from the prime meridian. This meridian passes through the Royal Observatory in Greenwich, England. Time also is measured from Greenwich and is called Greenwich mean time (GMT). For each time zone east of the prime meridian, clocks must be set one hour ahead of GMT. For each time zone west of Greenwich, clocks are set back one hour from GMT. When it is noon in London, it is 1:00 P.M. in Oslo, Norway, one time zone east. However, it is 7 A.M. in New York City, five time zones west.

WORLD TIME ZONES

11 P.M.
Mid-night
1 A.M.
2 A.M.
3 A.M.
4 A.M.
5 A.M.
6 A.M.
7 A.M.
8 A.M.
9 A.M.
GREEN
8:00 A.M.
Anchorage
Vancouver
NORTH AMERICA
8:30 A.M.
Toronto
Chicago
New York
Phoenix
Los Angeles
International Date Line
Houston
Miami
Mexico City
Honolulu
Caracas
2:30 A.M.
SOUTH AMERICA
Lima
3:30 A.M.
São Paul
11:30 P.M.
10:30 P.M.
Auckland
12:45 A.M.
Buenos Aires
+11
+12
-12
-11
-10
-9
-8
-7
-6
-5
-4
-3

As you can see by looking at the map below, time zones do not follow meridians exactly. Political boundaries are often used to draw time-zone lines. In Europe and Africa, for example, time zones follow national boundaries. The mainland United States, meanwhile, is divided into four major time zones: Eastern, Central, Mountain, and Pacific. Alaska and Hawaii are in separate time zones to the west of the mainland.

Some countries have made changes in their time zones. For example, most of the United States has daylight savings time in the summer in order to have more evening hours of daylight.

The international date line is a north-south line that runs through the Pacific Ocean. It is located at 180°, although it sometimes varies from that meridian to avoid dividing countries.

At 180°, the time is 12 hours from Greenwich time. There is a time difference of 24 hours between the two sides of the 180° meridian. The 180° meridian is called the international date line because when you cross it, the date and day change. As you cross the date line from the west to the east, you gain a day. If you travel from east to west, you lose a day.

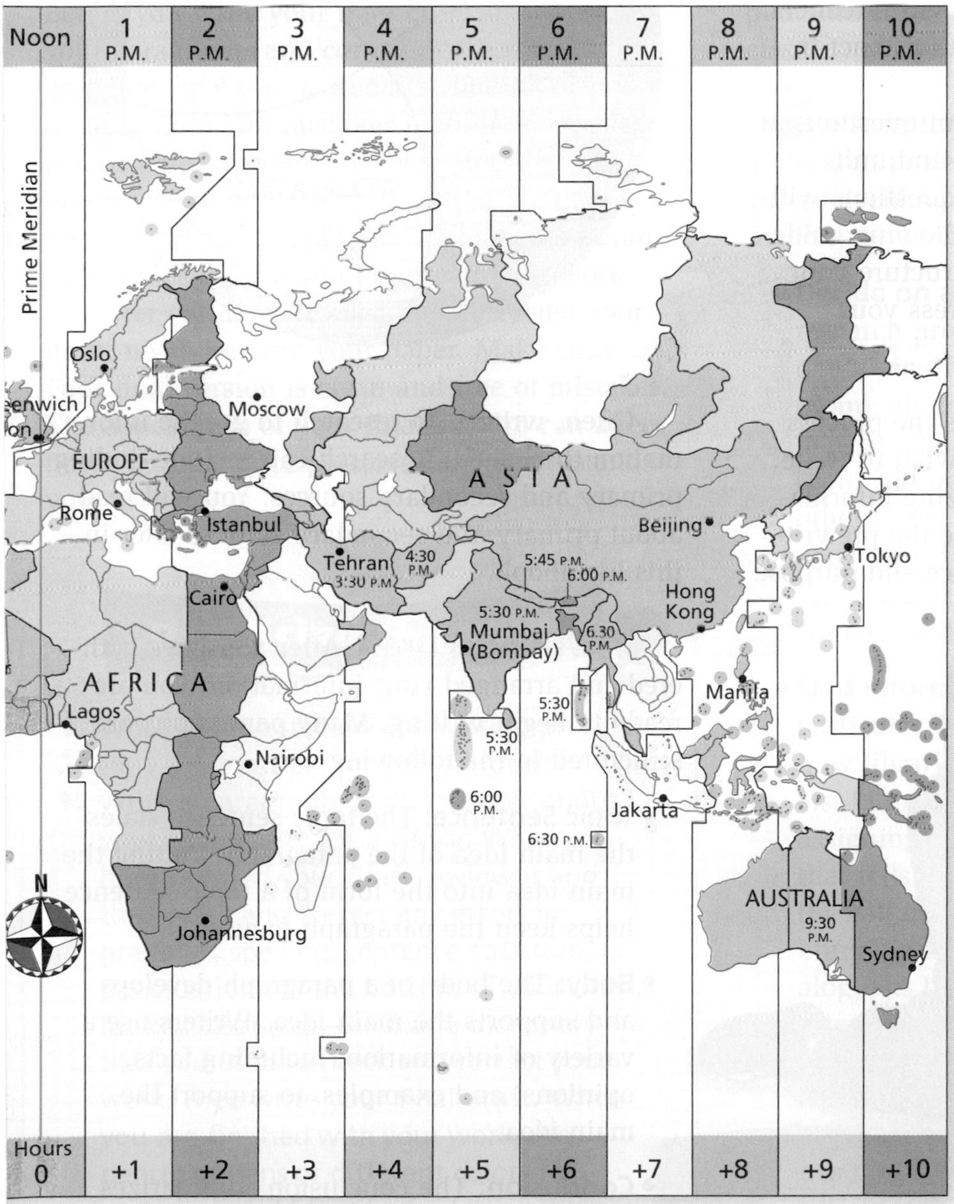

Noon
1 P.M.
2 P.M.
3 P.M.
4 P.M.
5 P.M.
6 P.M.
7 P.M.
8 P.M.
9 P.M.
10 P.M.
Prime Meridian
Oslo
Moscow
EUROPE
Rome
Istanbul
Tehran 3:30 P.M.
4:30 P.M.
5:45 P.M.
6:00 P.M.
5:30 P.M.
Mumbai (Bombay)
6:30 P.M.
5:30 P.M.
5:30 P.M.
6:00 P.M.
6:30 P.M.
ASIA
Beijing
Tokyo
Hong Kong
Manila
Jakarta
Cairo
AFRICA
Lagos
Nairobi
Johannesburg
AUSTRALIA
9:30 P.M.
Sydney
N
Hours 0
+1
+2
+3
+4
+5
+6
+7
+8
+9
+10

YOUR TURN

1. In which time zone do you live? Check your time now. What time is it in New York?
2. How many hours behind New York is Anchorage, Alaska?
3. How many time zones are there in Africa?
4. If it is 9 A.M. in the middle of Greenland, what time is it in São Paulo?

CRITICAL THINKING

The study of geography requires more than analyzing and understanding tools like graphs and maps. Throughout Holt People, Places, and Change, *you are asked to think critically about some of the information you are studying. Critical thinking is the reasoned judgment of information and ideas. The development of critical thinking skills is essential to learning more about the world around you. Helping you develop critical thinking skills is an important goal of* Holt People, Places, and Change. *The following critical thinking skills appear in the section reviews and chapter reviews of the textbook.*

Summarizing involves briefly restating information gathered from a larger body of information. Much of the writing in this textbook is summarizing. The geographical data in this textbook has been collected from many sources. Summarizing all the qualities of a region or country involves studying a large body of cultural, economic, geological, and historical information.

Finding the main idea is the ability to identify the main point in a set of information. This textbook is designed to help you focus on the main ideas in geography. The Read to Discover questions in each chapter help you identify the main ideas in each section. To find the main idea in any piece of writing, first read the title and introduction. These two elements may point to the main ideas covered in the text.

Also, write down questions about the subject that you think might be answered in the text. Having such questions in mind will focus your reading. Pay attention to any headings or subheadings, which may provide a basic outline of the major ideas. Finally, as you read, note sentences that provide additional details from the general statements that those details support. For example, a trail of facts may lead to a conclusion that expresses the main idea.

Comparing and contrasting involve examining events, points of view, situations, or styles to identify their similarities and differences. Comparing focuses on both the similarities and the differences. Contrasting focuses only on the differences. Studying similarities and differences between people and things can give you clues about the human and physical geography of a region.

Buddhist shrine, Myanmar

Stave church, Norway

Supporting a point of view involves identifying an issue, deciding what you think about it, and persuasively expressing your position. Your stand should be based on specific information. When taking a stand, state your position clearly and give reasons that support it.

Identifying points of view involves noting the factors that influence the opinions of an individual or group. A person's point of view includes beliefs and attitudes that are shaped by factors such as age, gender, race, and economic status. Identifying points of view helps us examine why people see things as they do. It also reinforces the realization that people's views may change over time or with a change in circumstances.

Identifying bias is an important critical thinking skill in the study of any subject. When a point of view is highly personal or based on unreasoned judgment, it is considered biased. Sometimes, a person's actions reflect bias. At its most extreme, bias can be expressed in violent actions against members of a particular culture or group. A less obvious form of bias is a stereotype, or a generalization about a group of people. Stereotypes tend to ignore differences within groups.

Political protest, India

Probably the hardest form of cultural bias to detect has to do with perspective, or point of view. When we use our own culture and experiences as a point of reference from which to make statements about other cultures, we are showing a form of bias called ethnocentrism.

Analyzing is the process of breaking something down into parts and examining the relationships between those parts. For example, to understand the processes behind forest loss, you might study issues involving economic development, the overuse of resources, and pollution.

Evaluating involves assessing the significance or overall importance of something. For example, you might evaluate the success of certain environmental protection laws or the effect of foreign trade on a society. You should base your evaluation on standards that others will understand and are likely to consider valid. For example, an evaluation of international relations after World War II might look at the political and economic tensions between the United States and the Soviet Union. Such an evaluation would also consider the ways those tensions affected other countries around the world.

Identifying cause and effect is part of interpreting the relationships between geographical events. A cause is any action that leads to an event; the outcome of that action is an effect. To explain geographical developments, geographers may point out multiple causes and effects. For example, geographers studying pollution in a region might note a number of causes.

Ecuador rain forest

Cleared forest, Kenya

Drought in West Texas

Dallas, Texas

Drawing inferences and drawing conclusions are two methods of critical thinking that require you to use evidence to explain events or information in a logical way. Inferences and conclusions are opinions, but these opinions are based on facts and reasonable deductions.

For example, suppose you know that people are moving in greater and greater numbers to cities in a particular country. You also know that poor weather has hurt farming in rural areas while industry has been expanding in cities. You might be able to understand from this information some of the reasons for the increased migration to cities. You could conclude that poor harvests have pushed people to leave rural areas. You might also conclude that the possibility of finding work in new industries may be pulling people to cities.

Making generalizations and making predictions are two critical thinking skills that require you to form specific ideas from a large body of information. When you are asked to generalize, you must take into account many different pieces of information. You then form a main concept that can be applied to all of the pieces of information. Many times making generalizations can help you see trends. Looking at trends can help you form a prediction. Making a prediction involves looking at trends in the past and present and making an educated guess about how these trends will affect the future.

Communications technology, rural Brazil

DECISION-MAKING AND PROBLEM-SOLVING

SKILLS

Like you, many people around the world have faced difficult problems and decisions. By using appropriate skills such as problem solving and decision making, you will be better able to choose a solution or make a decision on important issues. The following activities will help you develop and practice these skills.

Decision Making

Decision making involves choosing between two or more options. Listed below are guidelines to help you with making decisions.

1. **Identify a situation that requires a decision.** Think about your current situation. What issue are you faced with that requires you to take some sort of action?
2. **Gather information.** Think about the issue. Examine the causes of the issue or problem and consider how it affects you and others.
3. **Identify your options.** Consider the actions that you could take to address the issue. List these options so that you can compare them.
4. **Make predictions about consequences.** Predict the consequences of taking the actions listed for each of your options. Compare these possible consequences. Be sure the option you choose produces the results you want.
5. **Take action to implement a decision.** Choose a course of action from your available options, and put it into effect.

Problem Solving

Problem solving involves many of the steps of decision making. Listed below are guidelines to help you solve problems.

1. **Identify the problem.** Identify just what the problem or difficulty is that you are facing. Sometimes you face a difficult situation made up of several different problems. Each problem may require its own solution.
2. **Gather information.** Conduct research on any important issues related to the problem. Try to find the answers to questions like the following: What caused this problem? Who or what does it affect? When did it start?
3. **List and consider options.** Look at the problem and the answers to the questions you asked in Step 2. List and then think about all the possible ways in which the problem could be solved. These are your options—possible solutions to the problem.
4. **Examine advantages and disadvantages.** Consider the advantages and disadvantages of all the options that you have listed. Make sure that you consider the possible long-term effects of each possible solution. You should also determine what steps you will need to take to achieve each possible solution. Some suggestions may sound good at first but may turn out to be impractical or hard to achieve.
5. **Choose and implement a solution.** Select the best solution from your list and take the steps to achieve it.
6. **Evaluate the effectiveness of the solution.** When you have completed the steps needed to put your plan into action, evaluate its effectiveness. Is the problem solved? Were the results worth the effort required? Has the solution itself created any other problems?

Practicing the Skill

1. Chapter 24, Section 2: East Africa's History and Culture, describes the challenges of religious and ethnic conflict occurring in the region. Imagine that you are an ambassador to Rwanda. Use the decision-making guidelines to help you come up with a plan to help resolve the problems there. Be prepared to defend your decision.
2. Identify a similar problem discussed in another chapter and apply the problem-solving process to come up with a solution.

Becoming a Strategic Reader

by Dr. Judith Irvin

Everywhere you look, print is all around us. In fact, you would have a hard time stopping yourself from reading. In a normal day, you might read cereal boxes, movie posters, notes from friends, T-shirts, instructions for video games, song lyrics, catalogs, billboards, information on the Internet, magazines, the newspaper, and much, much more. Each form of print is read differently depending on your purpose for reading. You read a menu differently from poetry, and a motorcycle magazine is read differently than a letter from a friend. Good readers switch easily from one type of text to another. In fact, they probably do not even think about it, they just do it.

When you read, it is helpful to use a strategy to remember the most important ideas. You can use a strategy before you read to help connect information you already know to the new information you will encounter. Before you read, you can also predict what a text will be about by using a previewing strategy. During the reading you can use a strategy to help you focus on main ideas, and after reading you can use a strategy to help you organize what you learned so that you can remember it later. *Holt People, Places, and Change* was designed to help you more easily understand the ideas you read. Important reading strategies employed in *Holt People, Places, and Change* include:

- **A** Tools to help you **preview and predict** what the text will be about
- **B** Ways to help you **use and analyze visual information**
- **C** Ideas to help you **organize the information** you have learned

A. Previewing and Predicting

How can I figure out what the text is about before I even start reading a section?

Previewing and **predicting** are good methods to help you understand the text. If you take the time to preview and predict before you read, the text will make more sense to you during your reading.

1 Usually, your teacher will set the purpose for reading. After reading some new information, you may be asked to write a summary, take a test, or complete some other type of activity.

"After reading about Spain and Portugal, you will work with a partner to present a history of the countries to a travel group..."

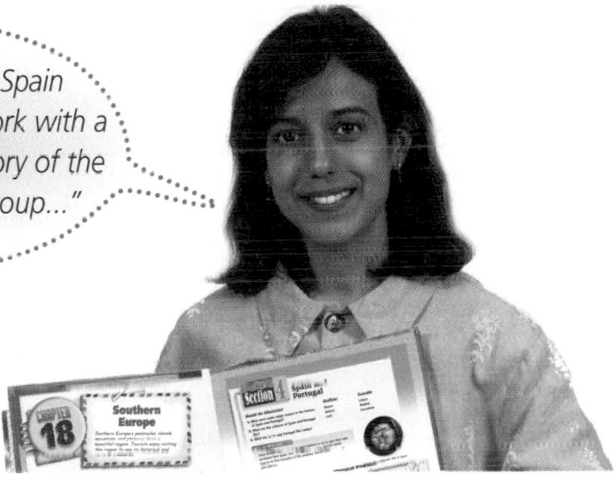

Previewing and Predicting

step 1 Identify your purpose for reading. Ask yourself what you will do with this information once you have finished reading.

step 2 Ask yourself what is the main idea of the text and what are the key vocabulary words you need to know.

step 3 Use signal words to help identify the structure of the text.

step 4 Connect the information to what you already know.

2 As you preview the text, use **graphic signals** such as headings, subheadings, and boldface type to help you determine what is important in the text. Each section of *Holt People, Places, and Change* opens by giving you important clues to help you preview the material.

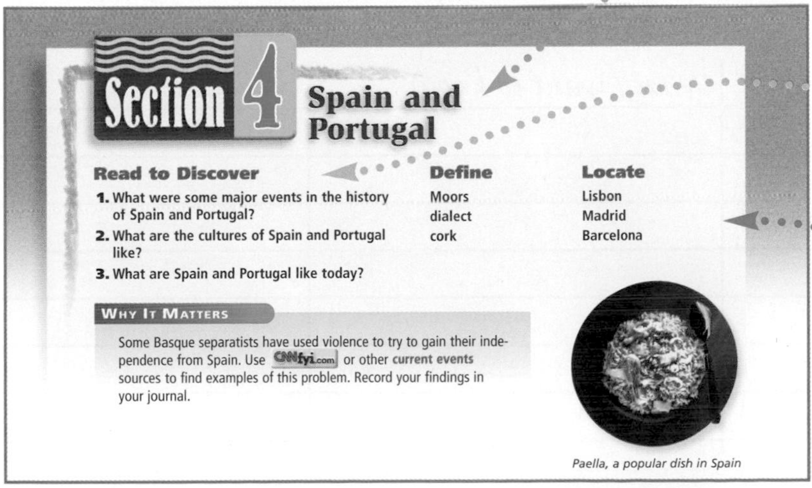

Section 4 Spain and Portugal

Read to Discover

1. What were some major events in the history of Spain and Portugal?
2. What are the cultures of Spain and Portugal like?
3. What are Spain and Portugal like today?

Define
Moors
dialect
cork

Locate
Lisbon
Madrid
Barcelona

Why It Matters

Some Basque separatists have used violence to try to gain their independence from Spain. Use CNNfyi.com or other current events sources to find examples of this problem. Record your findings in your journal.

Paella, a popular dish in Spain

Looking at the section's **main heading** and subheadings can give you an idea of what is to come.

Read to Discover questions give you clues as to the section's main ideas.

Define and **Locate** terms let you know the key vocabulary and places you will encounter in the section.

3 Other tools that can help you in previewing are **signal words**. These words prepare you to think in a certain way. For example, when you see words such as *similar to, same as,* or *different from,* you know that the text will probably compare and contrast two or more ideas. Signal words indicate how the ideas in the text relate to each other. Look at the list below for some of the most common signal words grouped by the type of text structures they include.

SIGNAL WORDS

Cause and Effect	Compare and Contrast	Description	Problem and Solution	Sequence or Chronological Order
because	different from	for instance	the question is	not long after
since	same as	for example	a solution	next
consequently	similar to	such as	one answer is	then
this led to...so	as opposed to	to illustrate		initially
if...then	instead of	in addition		before
nevertheless	although	most importantly		after
accordingly	however	another		finally
because of	compared with	furthermore		preceding
as a result of	as well as	first, second ...		following
in order to	either...or			on (date)
may be due to	but			over the years
for this reason	on the other hand			today
not only...but	unless			when

4 Learning something new requires that you connect it in some way with something you already know. This means you have to think before you read and while you read. You may want to use a chart like this one to remind yourself of the information already familiar to you and to come up with questions you want answered in your reading. The chart will also help you organize your ideas after you have finished reading.

What I know	What I want to know	What I learned

B. Use and Analyze Visual Information

How can all the pictures, maps, graphs, and time lines with the text help me be a stronger reader?

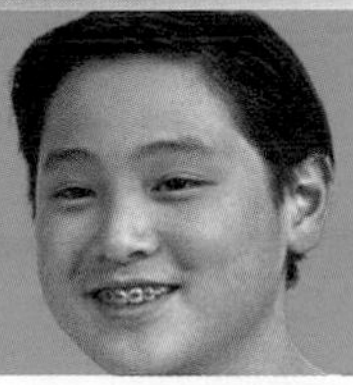

Using visual information can help you understand and remember the information presented in *Holt People, Places, and Change.* Good readers make a picture in their mind when they read. The pictures, charts, graphs, and diagrams that occur throughout *Holt People, Places, and Change* are placed strategically to increase your understanding.

1 You might ask yourself questions like these:

Why did the writer include this image with the text? What details about this image are mentioned in the text?

Analyzing Visual Information

step 1 As you preview the text, ask yourself how the visual information relates to the text.

step 2 Generate questions based on the visual information.

step 3 After reading the text, go back and review the visual information again.

step 4 Connect the information to what you already know.

2 After you have read the text, see if you can answer your own questions.

→ *Why are windmills important?*

→ *What technology do windmills use to pump water?*

→ *How might environment affect the use of windmills?*

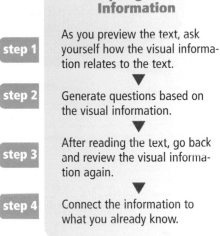

2 Maps, graphs, and charts help you organize information about a place. You might ask questions like these:

How does this map support what I have read in the text?

What does the information in this bar graph add to the text discussion?

→ *What is the purpose of this map?*

→ *What special features does the map show?*

→ *What do the colors, lines, and symbols on the map represent?*

Land Use and Resources

NORWEGIAN SEA
Greenland (DENMARK)
ATLANTIC OCEAN
NORTH SEA
BALTIC SEA
NORTHERN EURASIA
Narvik
Oslo
Stockholm
Helsinki
Copenhagen
Rostock
Hamburg
Bremen
Berlin
Warsaw
Dublin
London
Rotterdam
Brussels
RUHR
Frankfurt
Prague
Paris
Munich
Vienna
Bratislava
Budapest
Zurich
Ljubljana
Milan
Turin
Lyon
Genoa
Marseille
Bucharest
Sofia
BLACK SEA
ADRIATIC SEA
Rome
Naples
Thessaloniki
AEGEAN SEA
Athens
Oporto
Lisbon
Madrid
Barcelona
Palermo
Catania
Strait of Gibraltar
MEDITERRANEAN SEA
AFRICA
English Channel
SCALE
250
500 Miles
250
500 Kilometers
Projection: Azimuthal Equal Area

→ *What information is the writer trying to present with this graph?*

→ *Why did the writer use a bar graph to organize this information?*

Imports and Exports of Southern Europe

250
200
150
100
50
0
($ in billions)
Greece
Italy
Spain and Portugal
Imports
Exports

3 After reading the text, go back and review the visual information again.

4 Connect the information to what you already know.

C. Organize Information

Once I learn new information, how do I keep it all straight so that I will remember it?

To help you remember what you have read, you need to find a way of **organizing information**. Two good ways of doing this are by using graphic organizers and concept maps. **Graphic organizers** help you understand important relationships—such as cause and effect, compare/contrast, sequence of events, and problem/solution—within the text. **Concept maps** provide a useful tool to help you focus on the text's main ideas and organize supporting details.

Identifying Relationships

Using graphic organizers will help you recall important ideas from the section and give you a study tool you can use to prepare for a quiz or test or to help with a writing assignment. Some of the most common types of graphic organizers are shown below.

Constructing Graphic Organizers

step 1 Preview the text, looking for signal words and the main idea.

▼

step 2 Form a hypothesis as to which type of graphic organizer would work best to display the information presented.

▼

step 3 Work individually or with your classmates to create a visual representation of what you read.

Cause and Effect

Events in history cause people to react in a certain way. Cause-and-effect patterns show the relationship between results and the ideas or events that made the results occur. You may want to represent cause-and-effect relationships as one cause leading to multiple effects,

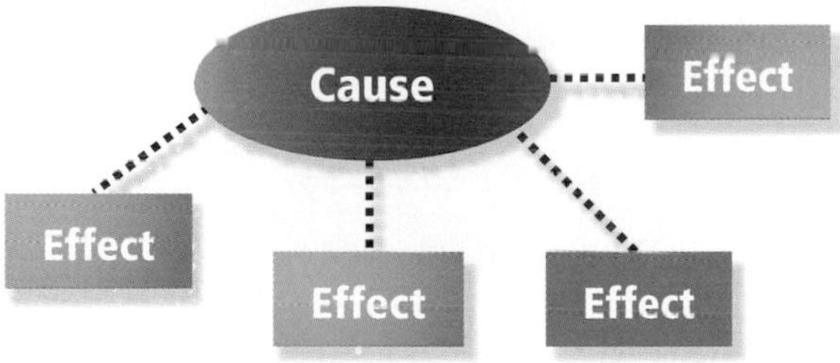
Cause
Effect
Effect
Effect
Effect

or as a chain of cause-and-effect relationships.

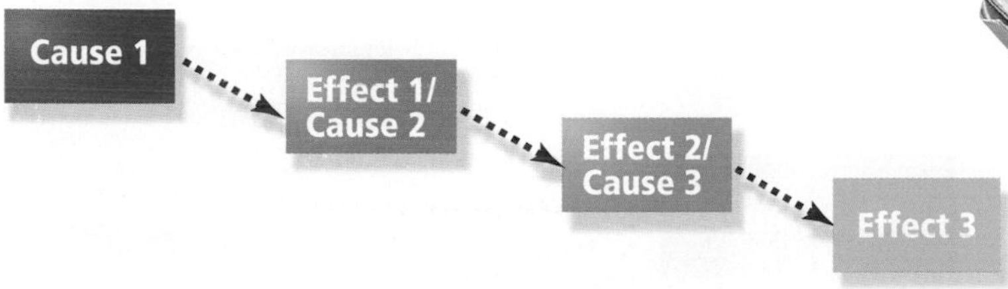
Cause 1
Effect 1/ Cause 2
Effect 2/ Cause 3
Effect 3

C. Organize Information *(continued)*

Comparing and Contrasting

Graphic organizers are often useful when you are comparing or contrasting information. Compare-and-contrast diagrams point out similarities and differences between two concepts or ideas.

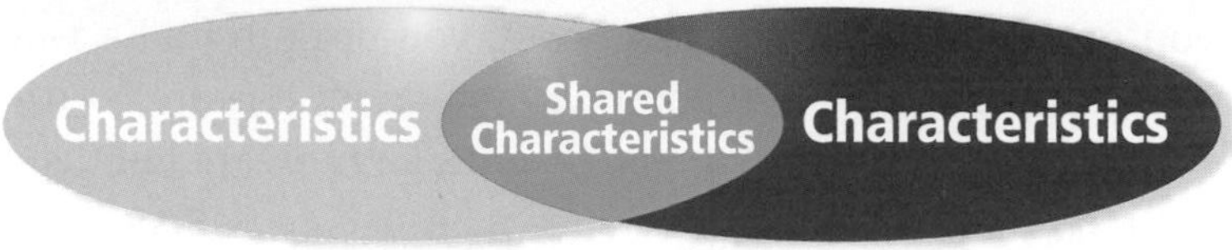
Characteristics
Shared Characteristics
Characteristics

Sequencing

Keeping track of dates and the order in which events took place is essential to understanding the history and geography of a place. Sequence or chronological-order diagrams show events or ideas in the order in which they happened.

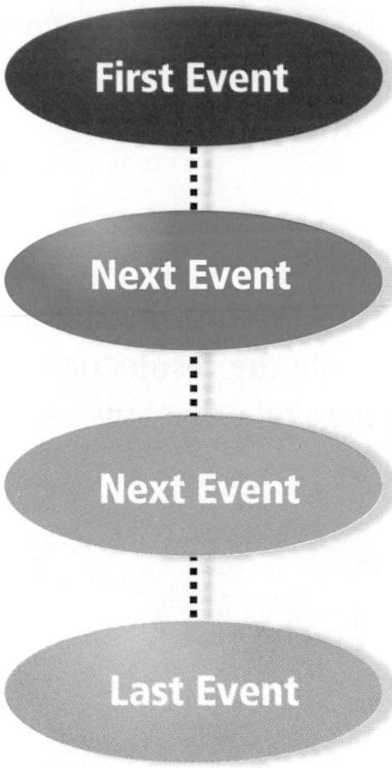
First Event
Next Event
Next Event
Last Event

Problem and Solution

Problem-solution patterns identify at least one problem, offer one or more solutions to the problem, and explain or predict outcomes of the solutions.

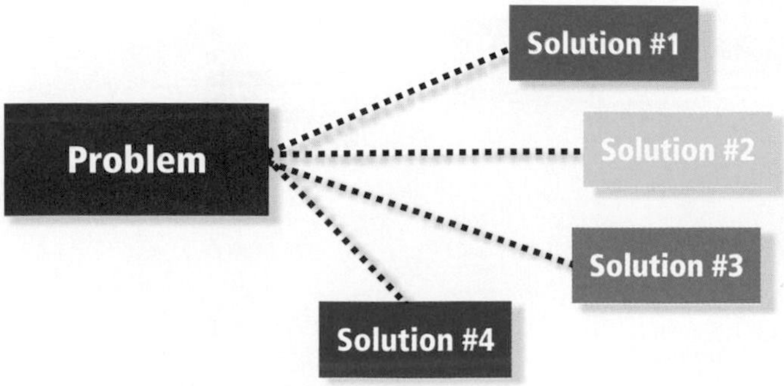
Problem
Solution #1
Solution #2
Solution #3
Solution #4

Identifying Main Ideas and Supporting Details

One special type of graphic organizer is the concept map. A concept map allows you to zero in on the most important points of the text. The map is made up of lines, boxes, circles, and/or arrows. It can be as simple or as complex as you need it to be to accurately represent the text. Here are a few examples of concept maps you might use.

Constructing Concept Maps

step 1 Preview the text, looking for what type of structure might be appropriate to display as a concept map.

step 2 Taking note of the headings, boldface type, and text structure, sketch a concept map you think could best illustrate the text.

step 3 Using boxes, lines, arrows, circles, or any shapes you like, display the ideas of the text in the concept map.

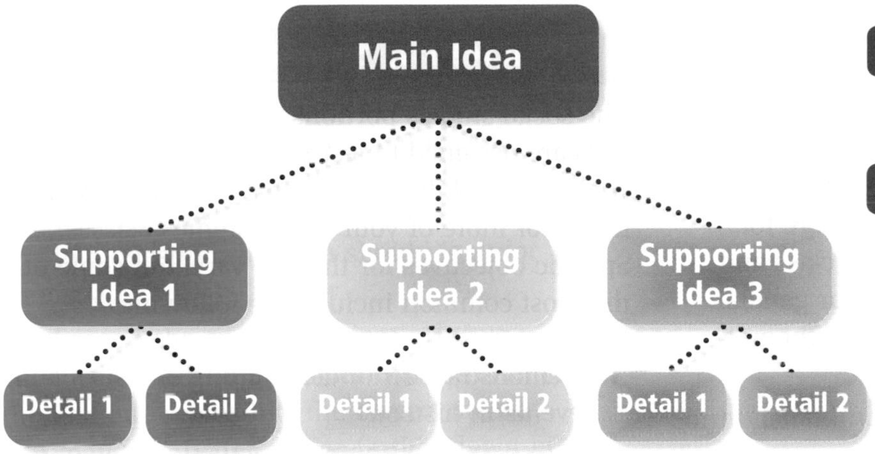
Main Idea
Supporting Idea 1
Supporting Idea 2
Supporting Idea 3
Detail 1
Detail 2
Detail 1
Detail 2
Detail 1
Detail 2

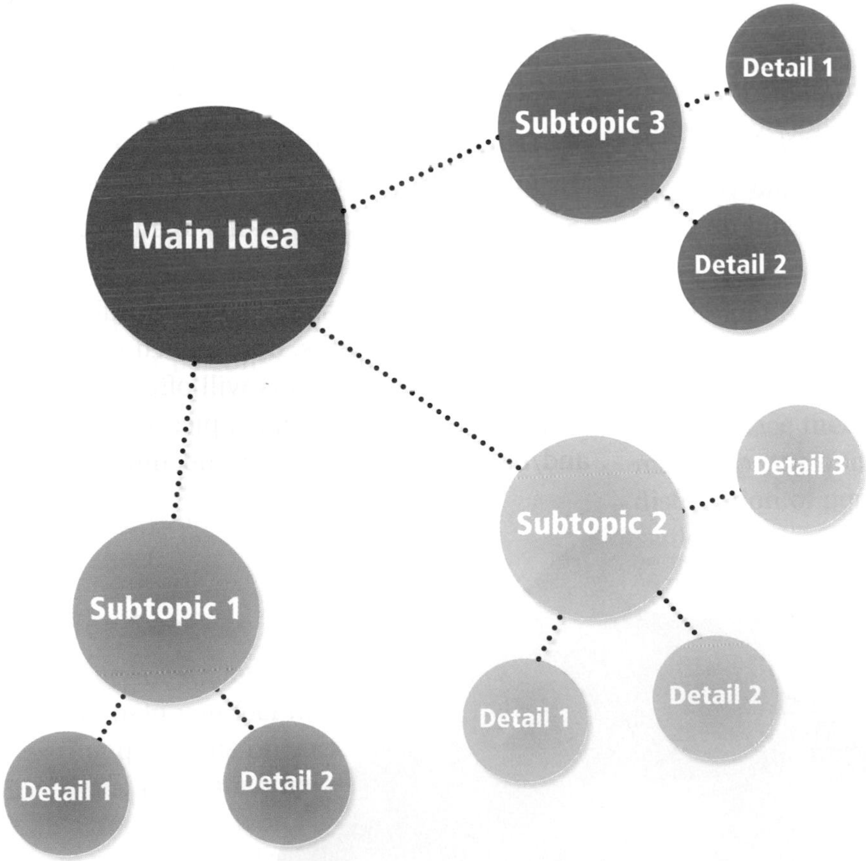
Main Idea
Subtopic 3
Detail 1
Detail 2
Subtopic 2
Detail 3
Detail 1
Detail 2
Subtopic 1
Detail 1
Detail 2

shape a region's history, culture, and geography. Questions may also ask you to understand the impact of geographic factors on major events. For example, some may ask about the effects of migration and immigration on various societies and population change. In addition, questions may test your understanding of the ways humans interact with their environment.

5. For the skills area of the tests, practice putting major events and personalities in order in your mind. Sequencing people and events by dates can become a game you play with a friend who also has to take the test. Always ask yourself "why" this event is important.
6. Follow the tips under "Ready for Reading" below when you encounter a reading passage in social studies, but remember that what you have learned about history can help you in answering reading-comprehension questions.

Ready for Reading

The main goal of the reading sections of most standardized tests is to determine your understanding of different aspects of a piece of writing. Basically, if you can grasp the main idea and the writer's purpose and then pay attention to the details and vocabulary so that you are able to draw inferences and conclusions, you will do well on the test.

Tips for Answering Multiple-Choice Questions

1. Read the passage as if you were not taking a test.
2. Look at the big picture. Ask yourself questions like, "What is the title?", "What do the illustrations or pictures tell me?", and "What is the writer's purpose?"
3. Read the questions. This will help you know what information to look for.
4. Reread the passage, underlining information related to the questions.

Types of Multiple-Choice Questions

1. **Main Idea** This is the most important point of the passage. After reading the passage, locate and underline the main idea.
2. **Significant Details** You will often be asked to recall details from the passage. Read the question and underline the details as you read, but remember that the correct answers do not always match the wording of the passage precisely.
3. **Vocabulary** You will often need to define a word within the context of the passage. Read the answer choices and plug them into the sentence to see what fits best.
4. **Conclusion and Inference** There are often important ideas in the passage that the writer does not state directly. Sometimes you must consider multiple parts of the passage to answer the question. If answers refer to only one or two sentences or details in the passage, they are probably incorrect.

5. Go back to the questions and try to answer each one in your mind before looking at the answers.
6. Read all the answer choices and eliminate the ones that are obviously incorrect.

Tips for Answering Short-Answer Questions

1. Read the passage in its entirety, paying close attention to the main events and characters. Jot down information you think is important.
2. If you cannot answer a question, skip it and come back later.
3. Words such as *compare, contrast, interpret, discuss,* and *summarize* appear often in short-answer questions. Be sure you have a complete understanding of each of these words.
4. To help support your answer, return to the passage and skim the parts you underlined.

5. Organize your thoughts on a separate sheet of paper. Write a general statement with which to begin. This will be your topic statement.
6. When writing your answer, be precise but brief. Be sure to refer to details in the passage in your answer.

Targeting Writing

On many standardized tests, you will occasionally be asked to write an essay. In order to write a concise essay, you must learn to organize your thoughts before you begin writing the actual piece. This keeps you from straying too far from the essay's topic.

Tips for Answering Composition Questions

1. Read the question carefully.
2. Decide what kind of essay you are being asked to write. Essays usually fall into one of the following types: persuasive, classificatory, compare/contrast, or "how to." To determine the type of essay, ask yourself questions like, "Am I trying to persuade my audience?", "Am I comparing or contrasting ideas?", or "Am I trying to show the reader how to do something?"
3. Pay attention to key words, such as *compare, contrast, describe, advantages, disadvantages, classify,* or *speculate.* They will give you clues as to the structure that your essay should follow.
4. Organize your thoughts on a sheet of paper. You will want to come up with a general topic sentence that expresses your main idea. Make sure this sentence addresses the question. You should then create an outline or some type of graphic organizer to help you organize the points that support your topic sentence.
5. Write your composition using complete sentences. Also, be sure to use correct grammar, spelling, punctuation, and sentence structure.
6. Be sure to proofread your essay once you have finished writing.

Gearing Up for Math

On most standardized tests you will be asked to solve a variety of mathematical problems that draw on the skills and information you have learned in class. If math problems sometimes give you difficulty, have a look at the tips below to help you work through the problems.

Tips for Solving Math Problems

1. Decide what is the goal of the question. Read or study the problem carefully and determine what information must be found.
2. Locate the factual information. Decide what information represents key facts—the ones you must have to solve the problem. You may also find facts you do not need to reach your solution. In some cases, you may determine that more information is needed to solve the problem. If so, ask yourself, "What assumptions can I make about this problem?" or "Do I need a formula to help solve this problem?"
3. Decide what strategies you might use to solve the problem, how you might use them, and what form your solution will be in. For example, will you need to create a graph or chart? Will you need to solve an equation? Will your answer be in words or numbers? By knowing what type of solution you should reach, you may be able to eliminate some of the choices.
4. Apply your strategy to solve the problem and compare your answer to the choices.
5. If the answer is still not clear, read the problem again. If you had to make calculations to reach your answer, use estimation to see if your answer makes sense.

UNIT 1

Exploring Our World

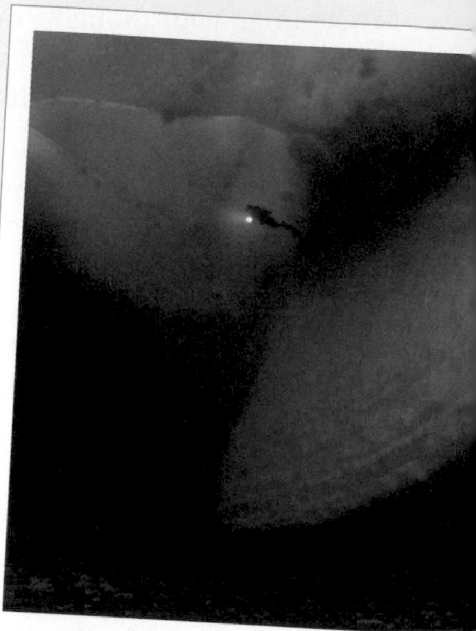

Iceberg in sea ice, Antarctica

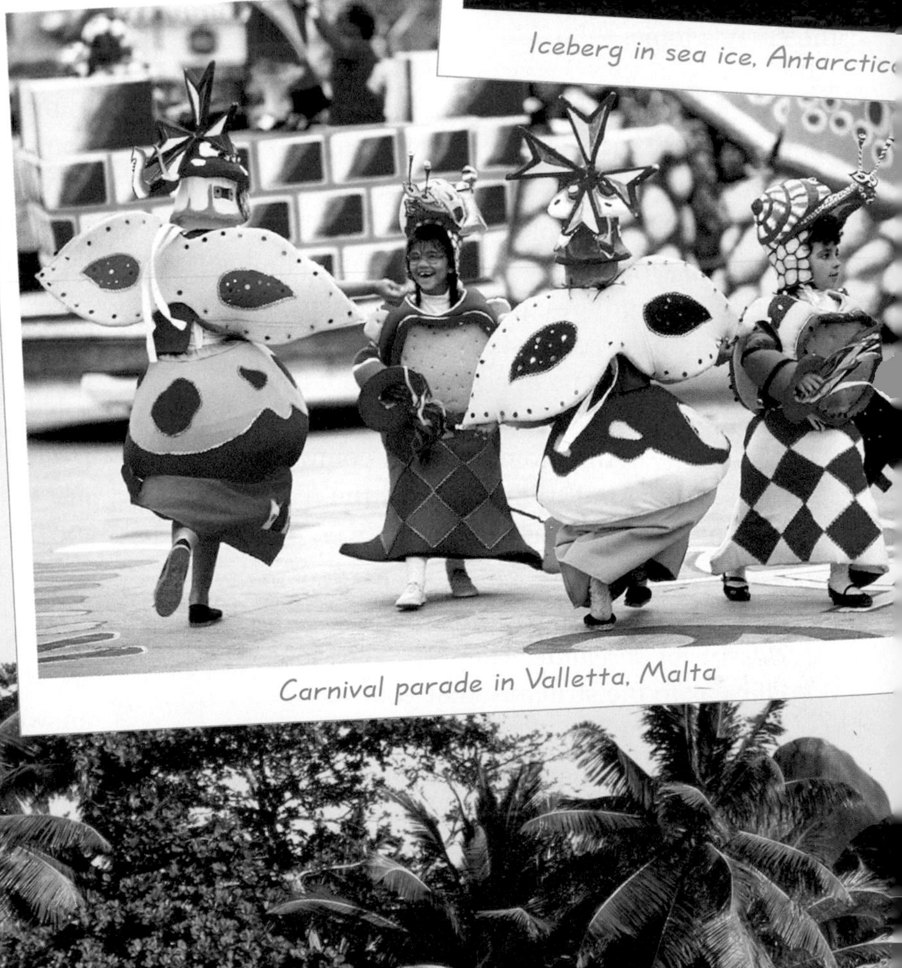

Carnival parade in Valletta, Malta

NOTES FROM THE field

A Physical Geographer in Mountain Environments

Professor Francisco Pérez studies tropical mountain environments. He is interested in the natural processes, plants, and environments of mountains. **WHAT DO YOU THINK?** *What faraway places would you like to study?*

I became attracted to mountains when I was a child. While crossing the Atlantic Ocean in a ship, I saw snow-capped Teide Peak in the Canary Islands rising from the water. It was an amazing sight.

As a physical geographer, I am interested in the unique environments of high mountain areas. This includes geological history, climate, and soils. The unusual conditions of high mountain environments have influenced plant evolution. Plants and animals that live on separate mountains sometimes end up looking similar. This happens because they react to their environments in similar ways. For example, several types of tall, weird-looking plants called giant rosettes grow in the Andes, Hawaii, East Africa, and the Canary Islands. Giant rosettes look like the top of a pineapple at the end of a tall stem.

Rosette plants, Ecuador

I have found other strange plants, such as rolling mosses. Mosses normally grow on rocks. However, if a moss plant falls to the ground, ice crystals on the soil surface lift the moss. This allows it to "roll" downhill while it continues to grow in a ball shape!

I like doing research in mountains. They are some of the least explored regions of our planet. Like most geographers, I cannot resist the attraction of strange landscapes in remote places.

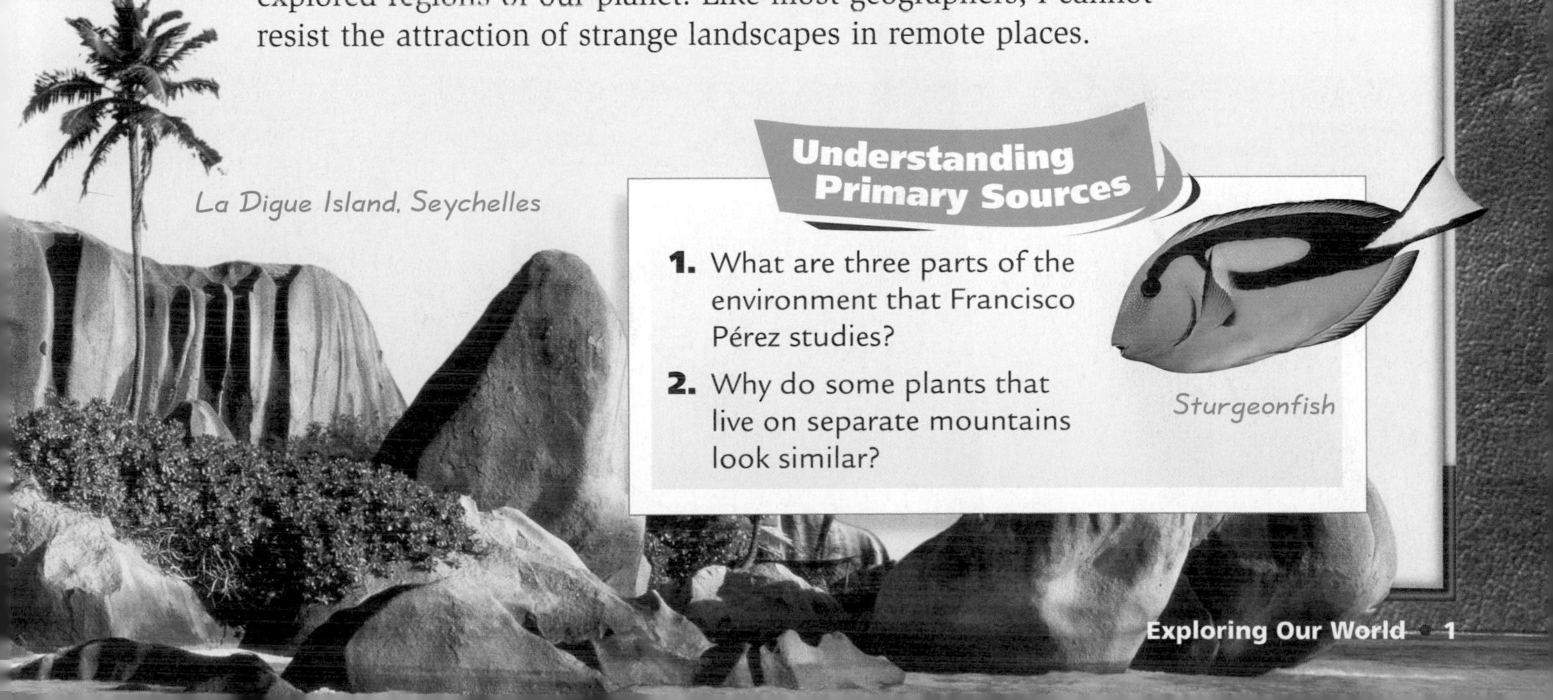
La Digue Island, Seychelles

Understanding Primary Sources

1. What are three parts of the environment that Francisco Pérez studies?
2. Why do some plants that live on separate mountains look similar?

Sturgeonfish

CHAPTER 1

A Geographer's World

Chart of the Mediterranean and Europe, 1559

Hand-held compass

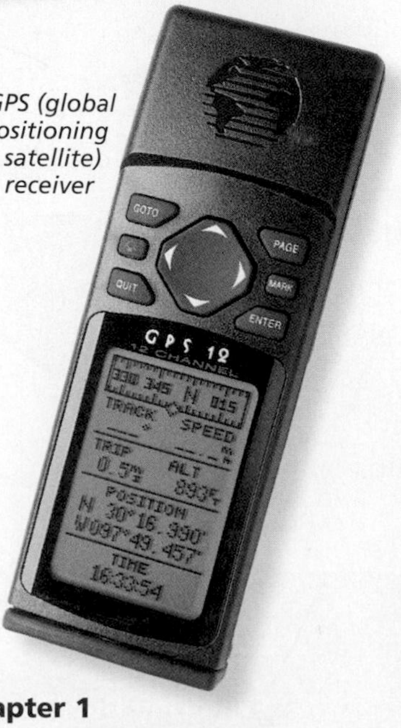
GOTO
PAGE
QUIT
MARK
ENTER
GPS 12
12 CHANNEL
TRACK
SPEED
TRIP
ALT
POSITION
TIME
GPS (global positioning satellite) receiver

Section 1 Developing a Geographic Eye

Read to Discover

1. What role does perspective play in the study of geography?
2. What are some issues or topics that geographers study?
3. At what three levels can geographers view the world?

Define

perspective
spatial perspective
geography
urban
rural

WHY IT MATTERS

What factors would you consider if you were moving to a new town or city? You would probably want to know about its geography. Use CNNfyi.com or other **current events** sources to investigate a place you might like to live. Record your findings in your journal.

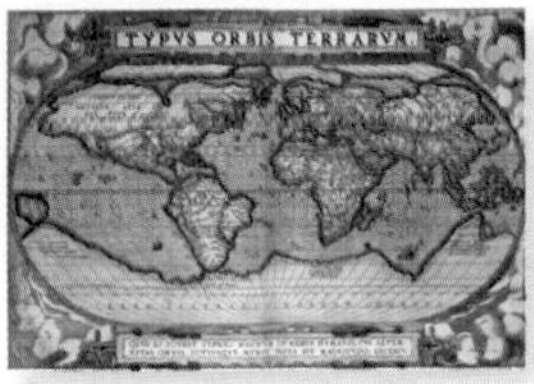
TYPVS ORBIS TERRARVM
World map, 1598

Perspectives

People look at the world in different ways. Their experiences shape the way they understand the world. This personal understanding is called **perspective**. Your perspective is your point of view. A geographer's point of view looks at where something is and why it is there. This point of view is known as **spatial perspective**. Geographers apply this perspective when they study the arrangement of towns in a state. They might also use this perspective to examine the movement of cars and trucks on busy roads.

Geographers also work to understand how things are connected. Some connections are easy to see, like highways that link cities. Other connections are harder to see. For example, a dry winter in Colorado could mean that farms as far away as northern Mexico will not have enough water.

Geography is a science. It describes the physical and cultural features of Earth. Studying geography is important. Geographically informed people can see meaning in the arrangement of things on Earth. They know how people and places are related. Above all, they can apply a spatial perspective to real life. In other words, people familiar with geography can understand the world around them.

This fish-eye view of a large city shows highway patterns.

✓ **READING CHECK:** *The World in Spatial Terms* What role does perspective play in the study of geography?

The movement of people is one issue that geographers study. For example, political and economic troubles led many Albanians to leave their country in 1991. Many packed onto freighters like this one for the trip. Geographers want to know how this movement affects the environment and other people.

Interpreting the Visual Record How do you think Albania has been affected by so many people leaving the country?

VLORA

Geographic Issues

Issues geographers study include Earth's processes and their impact on people. Geographers study the relationship between people and environment in different places. For example, geographers study tornadoes to find ways to reduce loss of life and property damage. They ask how people prepare for tornadoes. Do they prepare differently in different places? When a tornado strikes, how do people react?

Geographers also study how governments change and how those changes affect people. Czechoslovakia, for example, split into Slovakia and the Czech Republic in 1993. These types of political events affect geographic boundaries. People react differently to these changes. Some people are forced to move. Others welcome the change.

Other issues geographers study include religions, diet (or food), **urban** areas, and **rural** areas. Urban areas contain cities. Rural areas contain open land that is often used for farming.

✓ **READING CHECK:** *The Uses of Geography* What issues or topics do geographers study?

Local, Regional, and Global Geographic Studies

With any topic, geographers must decide how large an area to study. They can focus their study at a local, regional, or global level.

Local Studying your community at the local, or close-up, level will help you learn geography. You know where homes and stores are located. You know how to find parks, ball fields, and other fun places. Over time, you see your community change. New buildings are constructed. People move in and out of your neighborhood. New stores open their doors, and others go out of business.

internet connect

GO TO: go.hrw.com
KEYWORD: SJ3 CH1
FOR: Web sites about the geographer's world

Canada
United States
Grand Canyon
Mexico

The southwest is a region within the United States. One well-known place that characterizes the landscape of the southwest is the Grand Canyon. The Grand Canyon is shown in the photo at left and in the satellite image at right.

Regional Regional geographers organize the world into convenient parts for study. For example, this book separates the world into big areas like Africa and Europe. Regional studies cover larger areas than local studies. Some regional studies might look at connections like highways and rivers. Others might examine the regional customs.

Global Geographers also work to understand global issues and the connections between events. For example, many countries depend on oil from Southwest Asia. If those oil supplies are threatened, some countries might rush to secure oil from other areas. Oil all over the world could then become much more expensive.

✓ **READING CHECK:** *The World in Spatial Terms* What levels do geographers use to focus their study of an issue or topic?

go.hrw.com **Homework Practice Online**
Keyword: SJ3 HP1

Section 1 Review

Define and explain: perspective, spatial perspective, geography, urban, rural

Reading for the Main Idea

1. *The Uses of Geography* How can a spatial perspective be used to study the world?
2. *The Uses of Geography* Why is it important to study geography?

Critical Thinking

3. **Drawing Inferences and Conclusions** How do threatening weather patterns affect people, and why do geographers study these patterns?
4. **Drawing Inferences and Conclusions** Why is it important to view geography on a global level?

Organizing What You Know

5. **Finding the Main Idea** Copy the following graphic organizer. Use it to examine the issues geographers study. Write a paragraph on one of these issues.

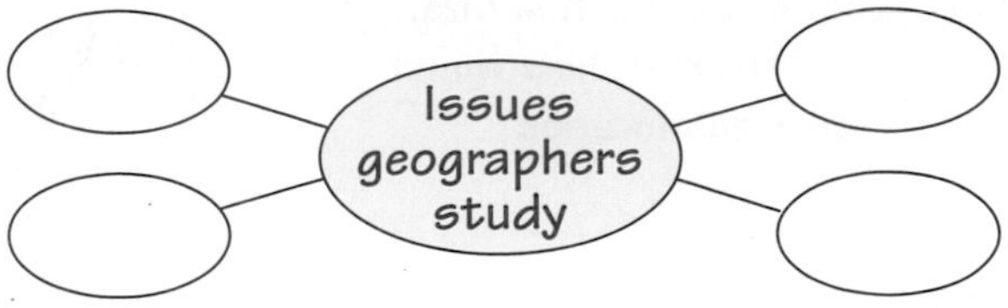
Issues geographers study

Section 2 Themes and Essential Elements

Read to Discover

1. What tools do geographers use to study the world?
2. What shapes Earth's features?
3. How do humans shape the world?
4. How does studying geography help us understand the world?

Define

absolute location
relative location
subregions
diffusion
levees

Tombs carved out of a mountain in Turkey

WHY IT MATTERS

Geographers often study the effect that new people have on a place. Use CNNfyi.com or other **current events** sources to find out how the arrival of new people has changed the United States or another country. Record your findings in your journal.

Giza
Libya
Egypt
Saudi Arabia
Sudan

The location of a place can be described in many ways.

Interpreting the Visual Record Looking at the photo of this hotel in Giza, Egypt, and at the map, how would you describe Giza's location?

Themes

The study of geography has long been organized according to five important themes, or topics of study. One theme, *location,* deals with the exact or relative spot of something on Earth. *Place* includes the physical and human features of a location. *Human-environment interaction* covers the ways people and environments affect each other. *Movement* involves how people change locations and how goods are traded, as well as the effects of these movements. *Region* organizes Earth into geographic areas with one or more shared characteristics.

✓ **READING CHECK:** ***The Uses of Geography*** What are the five themes of geography?

Six Essential Elements

Another way to look at geography is to study its essential elements, or most important parts. The six essential elements used to study geography are The World in Spatial Terms, Places and Regions, Physical Systems, Human Systems, Environment and Society, and The Uses of Geography. These six essential elements will be used throughout this textbook. They share many properties with the five themes of geography.

Location

Every place on Earth has a location. Location is defined by absolute and relative location.

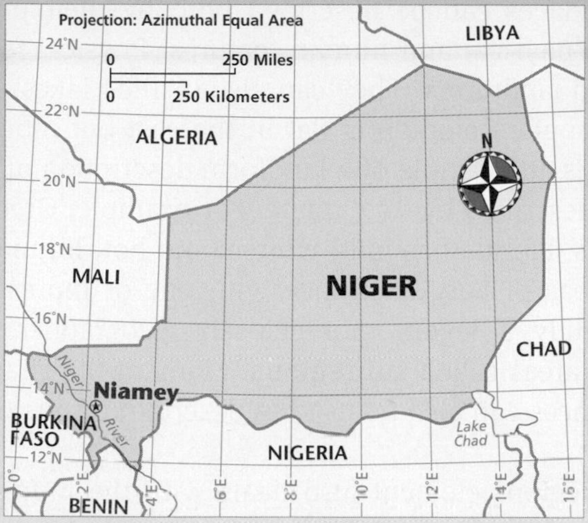

Projection: Azimuthal Equal Area
0 250 Miles
0 250 Kilometers
24°N
22°N
20°N
18°N
16°N
14°N
12°N
0°
2°E
4°E
6°E
8°E
10°E
12°E
14°E
16°E
LIBYA
ALGERIA
N
MALI
NIGER
CHAD
Niger River
Niamey
BURKINA FASO
Lake Chad
NIGERIA
BENIN

N
COAST RANGES
Sacramento R.
NEVADA
SIERRA NEVADA
YOSEMITE NATIONAL PARK
San Francisco
San Joaquin R.
PACIFIC OCEAN
COAST RANGES
CALIFORNIA
Los Angeles
0 125 250 Miles
0 125 250 Kilometers
Projection: Azimuthal Equal Area

Absolute Location: the exact spot on Earth where something is found

Example: Niamey, the capital of Niger, is located at 13°31′ north latitude and 2°07′ east longitude.

Relative Location: the position of a place in relation to other places

Example: Yosemite National Park is north of Los Angeles, California, and east of San Francisco, California.

You Be the Geographer

1. Use an atlas to find the absolute location of your city or town.
2. Write a sentence describing the relative location of your home.

The World in Spatial Terms This element focuses on geography's spatial perspective. As you learned in Section 1, geographers apply spatial perspective when they look at the location of something and why it is there. The term *location* can be used in two ways. **Absolute location** defines an exact spot on Earth. For example, the address of the Smithsonian American Art Museum is an absolute location. The address is at 8th and G Streets, N.W., in Washington, D.C. City streets often form a grid. This system tells anyone looking for an address where to go. The grid formed by latitude and longitude lines also pinpoints absolute location. Suppose you asked a pilot to take you to 52° north latitude by 175° west longitude. You would land at a location on Alaska's Aleutian Islands.

Relative location describes the position of a place in relation to another place. Measurements of direction, distance, or time can define relative location. For example, the following sentences give relative location. "The hospital is one mile north of our school." "Canada's border is about an hour's drive from Great Falls, Montana."

A geographer must be able to use maps and other geographic tools and technologies to determine spatial perspective. A geographer must

▲ Places can be described by what they do not have. This photo shows the result of a long period without rain.

also know how to organize and analyze information about people, places, and environments using geographic tools.

People travel from place to place on miles of new roadway.

Interpreting the Visual Record **What other forms of human systems are studied by geographers?**

Canada
United States
Texas
Mexico

Places and Regions Our world has a vast number of unique places and regions. Places can be described both by their physical location and by their physical and human features. Physical features include coastlines and landforms. They can also include lakes, rivers, or soil types. For example, Colorado is flat in the east but mountainous in the west. This is an example of a landform description of place. A place can also be described by its climate. For example, Greenland has long, cold winters. Florida has mild winters and hot, humid summers. Regions are areas of Earth's surface with one or more shared characteristics. To study a region more closely, geographers often divide it into smaller areas called **subregions**. Many of the characteristics that describe places can also be used to describe regions or subregions.

The Places and Regions element also deals with the human features of places and regions. Geographers want to know how people have created regions based on Earth's features and how culture and other factors affect how we see places and regions on Earth.

Physical Systems Physical systems shape Earth's features. Geographers study earthquakes, mountains, rivers, volcanoes, weather patterns, and similar topics and how these physical systems have affected Earth's characteristics. For example, geographers might study how volcanic eruptions in the Hawaiian Islands spread lava, causing landforms to change. They might note that southern California's shoreline changes yearly, as winter and summer waves move beach sand.

Geographers also study how plants and animals relate to these nonliving physical systems. For example, deserts are places with cactus and other plants, as well as rattlesnakes and other reptiles, that can

Libya
Egypt
Saudi Arabia
Aswān
Sudan

Men in rural Egypt wear a long shirt called a *galabia.* This loose-fitting garment is ideal for people living in Egypt's hot desert climate. In addition, the galabia is made from cotton, an important agricultural product of Egypt.

Interpreting the Visual Record **How does the *galabia* show how people have adapted to their environment?**

Venezuela
Colombia
Amazon River
Peru
Brazil
Bolivia

live in very dry conditions. Geographers also study how different types of plants, animals, and physical systems are distributed on Earth.

A satellite dish brings different images and ideas to people in a remote area of Brazil.

Interpreting the Visual Record How might resources have affected the use of technology here?

Human Systems People are central to geography. Our activities, movements, and settlements shape Earth's surface. Geographers study peoples' customs, history, languages, and religions. They study how people migrate, or move, and how ideas are communicated. When people move, they may go to live in other countries or move within a country. Geographers want to know how and why people move from place to place.

People move for many reasons. Some move to start a new job. Some move to attend special schools. Others might move to be closer to family. People move either when they are pushed out of a place or when they are pulled toward another place. In the Dust Bowl, for example, crop failures pushed people out of Oklahoma in the 1930s. Many were pulled to California by their belief that they would find work there. Geographers also want to know how ideas or behaviors move from one region to another. The movement of ideas occurs through communication. There are many ways to communicate. People visit with each other in person or on the phone. New technology allows people to communicate by e-mail. Ideas are also spread through films, magazines, newspapers, radio, and television. The movement of ideas or behaviors from one region to another is known as **diffusion**.

The things we produce and trade are also part of the study of human systems. Geographers study trading patterns and how countries depend on each other for certain goods. In addition, geographers look at the causes and results of conflicts between peoples. The study of governments we set up and the features of cities and other settlements we live in are also part of this study.

This woman at a railway station in Russian Siberia sells some goods that were once unavailable in her country.

Interpreting the Visual Record Which essential element is illustrated in this photo?

Environment and Society Geographers study how people and their surroundings affect each other. Their relationship can be examined in three ways. First, geographers study how humans depend on

Algeria
Mauritania
Mali
Niger
Djenne
Burkina Faso
Guinea

▲ Open-air markets like this one in Mali provide opportunities for farmers to sell their goods.

their physical environment to survive. Human life requires certain living and nonliving resources, such as freshwater and fertile soil for farming.

Geographers also study how humans change their behavior to be better suited to an environment. These changes or adaptations include the kinds of clothing, food, and shelter that people create. These changes help people live in harsh climates.

Finally, humans change the environment. For example, farmers who irrigate their fields can grow fruit in Arizona's dry climate. People in Louisiana have built **levees**, or large walls, to protect themselves when the Mississippi River floods.

The Uses of Geography Geography helps us understand the relationships among people, places, and the environment over time. Understanding how a relationship has developed can help in making plans for the future. For example, geographers can study how human use of the soil in a farming region has affected that region over time. Such knowledge can help them determine what changes have been made to the soil and whether any corrective measures need to be taken.

✓ **READING CHECK:** *The Uses of Geography* What are the six essential elements in studying geography?

go.hrw.com **Homework Practice Online**
Keyword: SJ3 HP1

Section 2 Review

Define and explain: absolute location, relative location, subregions, diffusion, levees

Reading for the Main Idea

1. *The World in Spatial Terms* How do geographers study the world?
2. *Physical Systems* What shapes Earth's features? Give examples.

Critical Thinking

3. **Finding the Main Idea** How do humans shape the world in which they live?
4. **Analyzing Information** What benefits can studying geography provide?

Organizing What You Know

5. **Summarizing** Copy the following graphic organizer. Use it to identify and describe all aspects of each of the six essential elements.

Element	Description

Section 3 The Branches of Geography

Read to Discover

1. What is included in the study of human geography?
2. What is included in the study of physical geography?
3. What types of work do geographers do?

Define

human geography
physical geography
cartography
meteorology
climatology

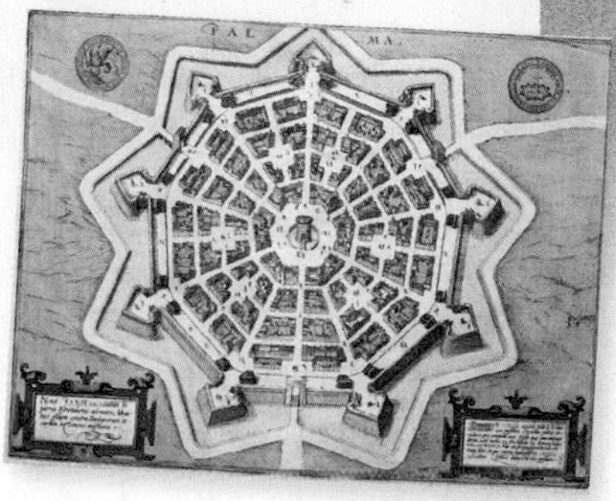

Map of an ancient fortress

WHY IT MATTERS

Nearly every year, hurricanes hit the Atlantic or Gulf coasts of the United States. Predicting weather is one of the special fields of geography. Use CNNfyi.com or other **current events** sources to find out about hurricanes. Record your findings in your journal.

Human Geography

The study of people, past or present, is the focus of **human geography**. People's location and distribution over Earth, their activities, and their differences are studied. For example, people living in different countries create different kinds of governments. Political geographers study those differences. Economic geographers study the exchange of goods and services across Earth. Cultural geography, population geography, and urban geography are some other examples of human geography. A professional geographer might specialize in any of these branches.

✓ **READING CHECK:** *Human Systems* How is human geography defined?

China
Nepal
India
Bangladesh

▲ A volunteer visits a poor area of Bangladesh. Geographers study economic conditions in regions to help them understand human geography.

Physical Geography

The study of Earth's natural landscapes and physical systems, including the atmosphere, is the focus of **physical geography**. The world is full of different landforms such as deserts, mountains, and plains. Climates affect these landscapes. Knowledge of physical systems helps geographers understand how a landscape developed and how it might change.

Connecting to Technology

A mapmaker creates a digital map.

Computer Mapping

Maps are tools that can display a wide range of information. Traditionally, maps were drawn on paper and could not be changed to suit the user. However, computers have revolutionized the art of mapmaking.

Today, mapmakers use computers to create and modify maps for different uses. They do this by using a geographic information system, or GIS. A GIS is a computer system that combines maps and satellite photographs with other kinds of spatial data—information about places on the planet. This information might include soil types, population figures, or voting patterns.

Using a GIS, mapmakers can create maps that show geographic features and relationships. For example, a map showing rainfall patterns in a particular region might be combined with data on soil types or human settlement to show areas of possible soil erosion.

The flexibility of a GIS allows people to seek answers to specific questions. Where should a new road be built to ease traffic congestion? How are changes in natural habitat affecting wildlife? These and many other questions can be answered with the help of computer mapping.

Understanding What You Read

1. How could a GIS help people change their environment?
2. What social, environmental, or economic consequences might future advances in GIS technology have?

Knowledge of physical and human geography will help you understand the world's different regions and peoples. In your study of the major world regions, you will see how physical and human geography connect to each other.

✓ **READING CHECK:** *Physical Systems* What is included in the study of physical geography?

Working as a Geographer

Geography plays a role in almost every occupation. Wherever you live and work, you should know local geography. School board members know where children live. Taxi drivers are familiar with city streets. Grocery store managers know which foods sell well in certain areas.

They also know where they can obtain these products throughout the year. Local newspaper reporters are familiar with town meetings and local politicians. Reporters also know how faraway places can affect their communities. Doctors must know if their towns have poisonous snakes or plants. City managers know whether nearby rivers might flood. Emergency workers in mountain towns check snow depth so they can give avalanche warnings. Local weather forecasters watch for powerful storms and track their routes on special maps.

Some specially trained geographers practice in the field of **cartography**. Cartography is the art and science of mapmaking. Today, most mapmakers do their work on computers. Geographers also work as weather forecasters. The field of forecasting and reporting rainfall, temperature, and other atmospheric conditions is called **meteorology**. A related field is **climatology**. These geographers, known as climatologists, track Earth's larger atmospheric systems. Climatologists want to know how these systems change over long periods of time. They also study how people might be affected by changes in climate.

▲ Experts examine snow to help forecast avalanches. They study the type of snow, weather conditions, and landforms. For example, wet snow avalanches can occur because of the formation of a particular type of ice crystal, called depth hoar, near the ground.

Governments and a variety of organizations hire geographers to study the environment. These geographers might explore such topics as pollution, endangered plants and animals, or rain forests. Some geographers who are interested in education become teachers and writers. They help people of all ages learn more about the world. Modern technology allows people all over the world to communicate instantly. Therefore, it is more important than ever to be familiar with the geographer's world.

✓ **READING CHECK:** *The Uses of Geography* What types of work do geographers perform?

go.hrw.com **Homework Practice Online**
Keyword: SJ3 HP1

Section 3 Review

Define and explain: human geography, physical geography, cartography, meteorology, climatology

Reading for the Main Idea

1. *Human Systems* What topics are included in the study of human geography?
2. *The Uses of Geography* How do people who study the weather use geography?

Critical Thinking

3. **Finding the Main Idea** Why is it important to study physical geography?
4. **Making Generalizations and Predictions** How might future discoveries in the field of geography affect societies, world economies, or the environment?

Organizing What You Know

5. **Categorizing** Copy the following graphic organizer. Use it to list geographers' professions and their job responsibilities.

Cartographer –makes maps –studies maps		

CHAPTER 1

Reviewing What You Know

Building Vocabulary

On a separate sheet of paper, write sentences to define each of the following words.

1. perspective
2. spatial perspective
3. geography
4. urban
5. rural
6. absolute location
7. relative location
8. levees
9. diffusion
10. subregions
11. human geography
12. physical geography
13. cartography
14. meteorology
15. climatology

Reviewing the Main Ideas

1. *The World in Spatial Terms* What are three ways to view geography? Give an example of when each type could be used.
2. *The World in Spatial Terms* What kind of directions would you give to indicate a place's absolute location? Its relative location?
3. *Human Systems* What is diffusion, and why is it important?
4. *Places and Regions* Why do geographers create subregions?
5. *The World in Spatial Terms* Why is cartography important? What types of jobs do geographers do?

Understanding Environment and Society

Land Use

You are on a committee that will decide whether to close a park near your school. One proposed use for the land is a building where after-school activities could be held. However, the park is the habitat of an endangered bird. Write a report describing consequences of the park closing. Then organize information from your report to create a proposal on what decision should be made.

Thinking Critically

1. **Analyzing Information** How can a geographer use spatial perspective to explain how things in our world are connected?
2. **Drawing Inferences and Conclusions** When and how do humans relate to the environment? Provide some examples of this relationship.
3. **Summarizing** How are patterns created by the movement of goods, ideas, and people?
4. **Finding the Main Idea** How are places and regions defined?
5. **Finding the Main Idea** How does studying geography help us understand the world?

Building Social Studies Skills

Map ACTIVITY

On a separate sheet of paper, match the letters on the map with their correct labels.

Africa	**Europe**
Antarctica	**North America**
Asia	**South America**
Australia	

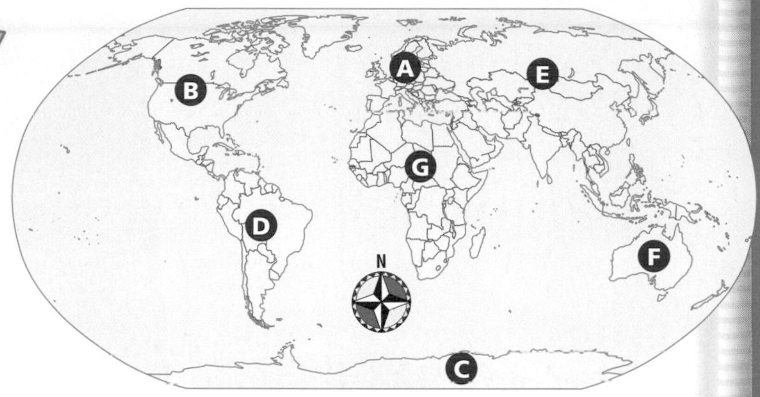

A
B
C
D
E
F
G
N

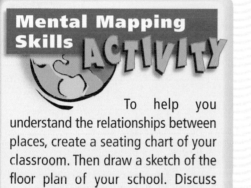

Mental Mapping Skills ACTIVITY

To help you understand the relationships between places, create a seating chart of your classroom. Then draw a sketch of the floor plan of your school. Discuss why certain areas are located in particular parts of the campus.

WRITING ACTIVITY

Write a letter persuading another student to enroll in a geography class. Include examples of professions that use geography and relate that information to the everyday life of a student. Be sure to use standard grammar, spelling, sentence structure, and punctuation.

Alternative Assessment

Portfolio ACTIVITY

Learning About Your Local Geography

Individual Project How do you define your community geographically? Is your community the area around your home or school? Write two or three sentences defining your community to share with the class.

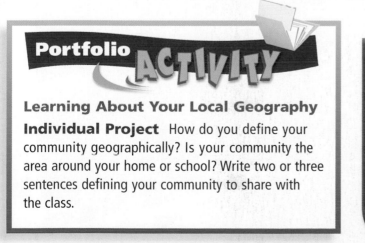

internet connect

Internet Activity: go.hrw.com
KEYWORD: SJ3 GT1

Choose a topic to explore online:

- Learn to use online maps.
- Be a virtual geographer for a day.
- Compare regions around the world.

CHAPTER 2

Planet Earth

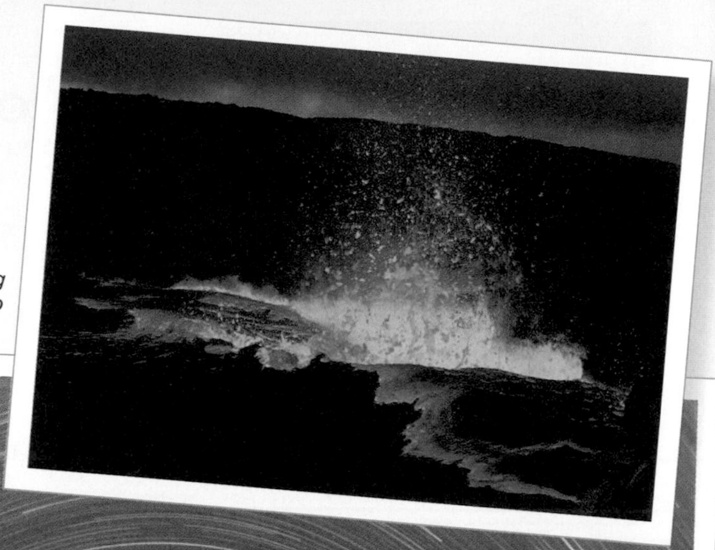

Erupting volcano

Earth as seen from space

Fossilized shell

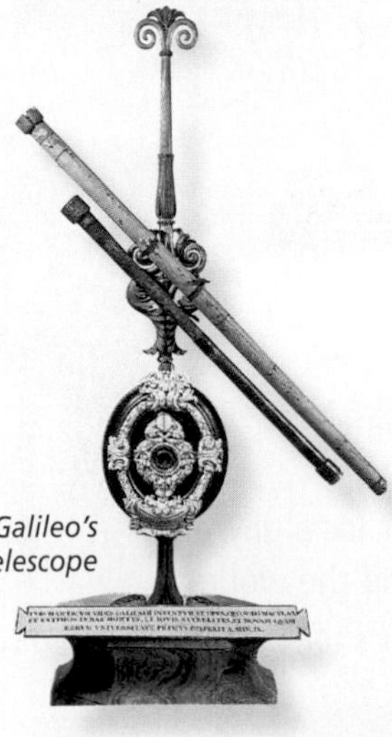

Galileo's telescope

Space observatory, Mauna Kea, Hawaii

Section 1 The Sun, Earth, and Moon

Read to Discover

1. What objects make up the solar system?
2. What causes the seasons?
3. What are the four parts of the Earth system?

Define

solar system
orbit
satellite
axis
rotation
revolution
Arctic Circle
Antarctic Circle
solstice
Tropic of Cancer
Tropic of Capricorn
equinoxes
atmosphere
ozone

Why It Matters

In 2001 scientists labeled a rocky object beyond Pluto as the new largest minor planet. Use CNNfyi.com or other **current events** sources to discover more about this huge frozen rock, called 2001 KX76. Record your findings in your journal.

Mechanical model of the solar system

The Solar System

The **solar system** consists of the Sun and the objects that move around it. The most important of those objects are the planets, their moons, and relatively small rocky bodies called asteroids. Our Sun is a star at the center of our solar system. Every object in the system travels around the Sun in an **orbit**, or path. These orbits are usually elliptical, or oval shaped.

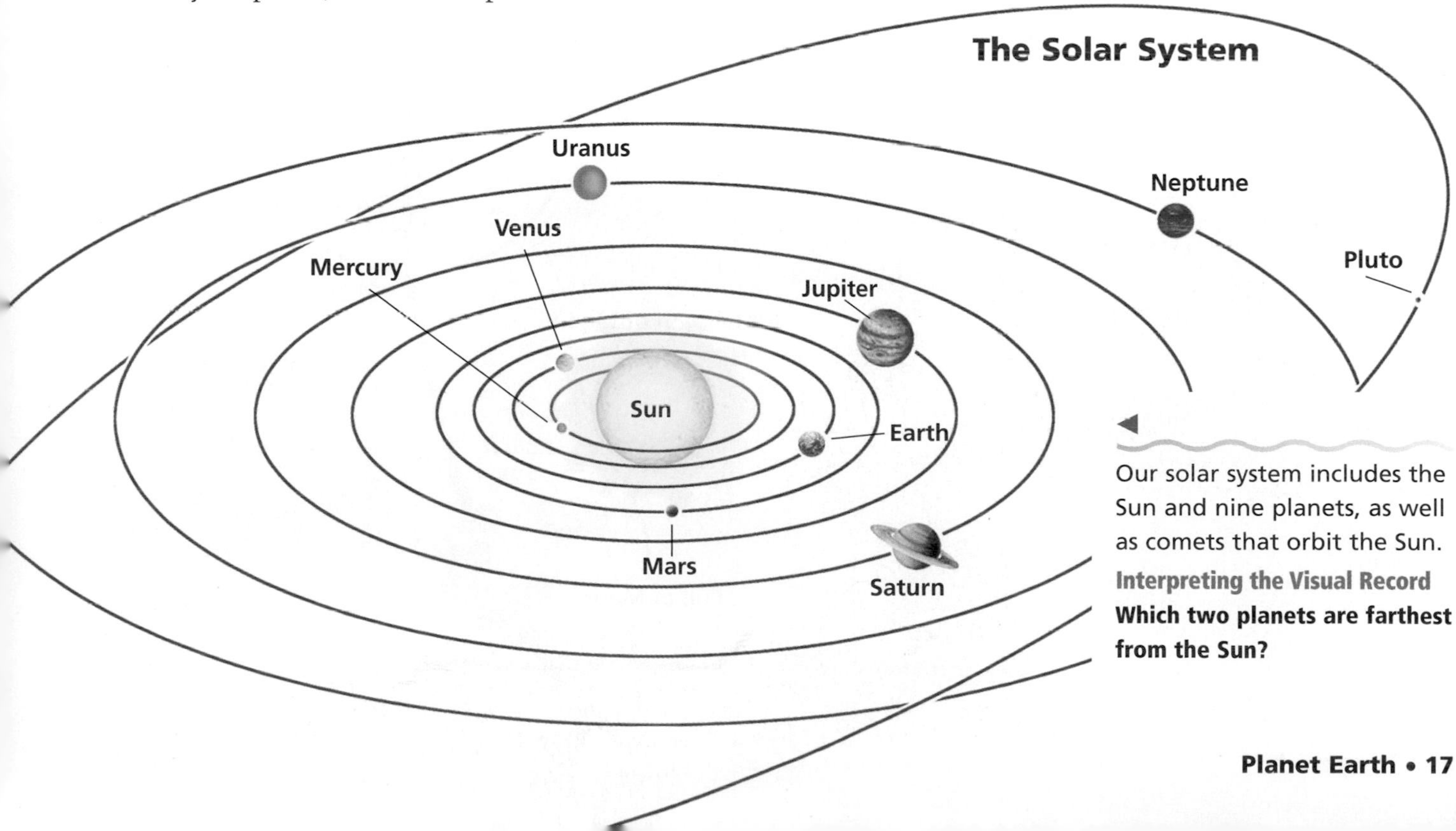
The Solar System
Uranus
Neptune
Venus
Mercury
Pluto
Jupiter
Sun
Earth
Mars
Saturn

Our solar system includes the Sun and nine planets, as well as comets that orbit the Sun.

Interpreting the Visual Record
Which two planets are farthest from the Sun?

Our Amazing Planet

Mexico's Yucatán Peninsula has a crater that stretches 200 miles (322 km) wide. Scientists believe that it is the site where a giant asteroid crashed into Earth some 65 million years ago. They think the collision caused more than half of all species, including dinosaurs, to become extinct.

The planet nearest the Sun is Mercury, followed by Venus, Earth, and Mars. Located beyond the orbit of Mars is a belt of asteroids. Beyond this asteroid belt are the planets Jupiter and Saturn. Even farther from the Sun are the planets Uranus, Neptune, and Pluto.

The Moon Some of the planets in the solar system have more than one moon. Saturn, for example, has 18. Other planets have none. A moon is a **satellite**—a body that orbits a larger body. Earth has one moon, which is about one fourth the size of Earth. Our planet is also circled by artificial satellites that transmit signals for television, telephone, and computer communications. The Moon takes about 29½ days—roughly a month—to orbit Earth.

The Moon and Sun influence physical processes on Earth. This is because any two objects in space are affected by gravitational forces pulling them together. The gravitational effects of the Sun and the Moon cause tides in the oceans here on Earth.

The Sun Compared to some other stars, our Sun is small. It is huge, however, when compared to Earth. Its diameter is about 100 times the diameter of our planet. The Sun appears larger to us than other stars. This is because it is much closer to us than other stars. The Sun is about 93 million miles (150 million km) from Earth. The next nearest star is about 25 trillion miles (40 trillion km) away.

Scientists are trying to learn if other planets in our solar system could support life. Mars seems to offer the best possibility. It is not clear, however, if life can, or ever did, exist on Mars.

✓ **READING CHECK:** *Physical Systems* What are the main objects that make up the solar system?

Effects of the Moon and Sun on Tides

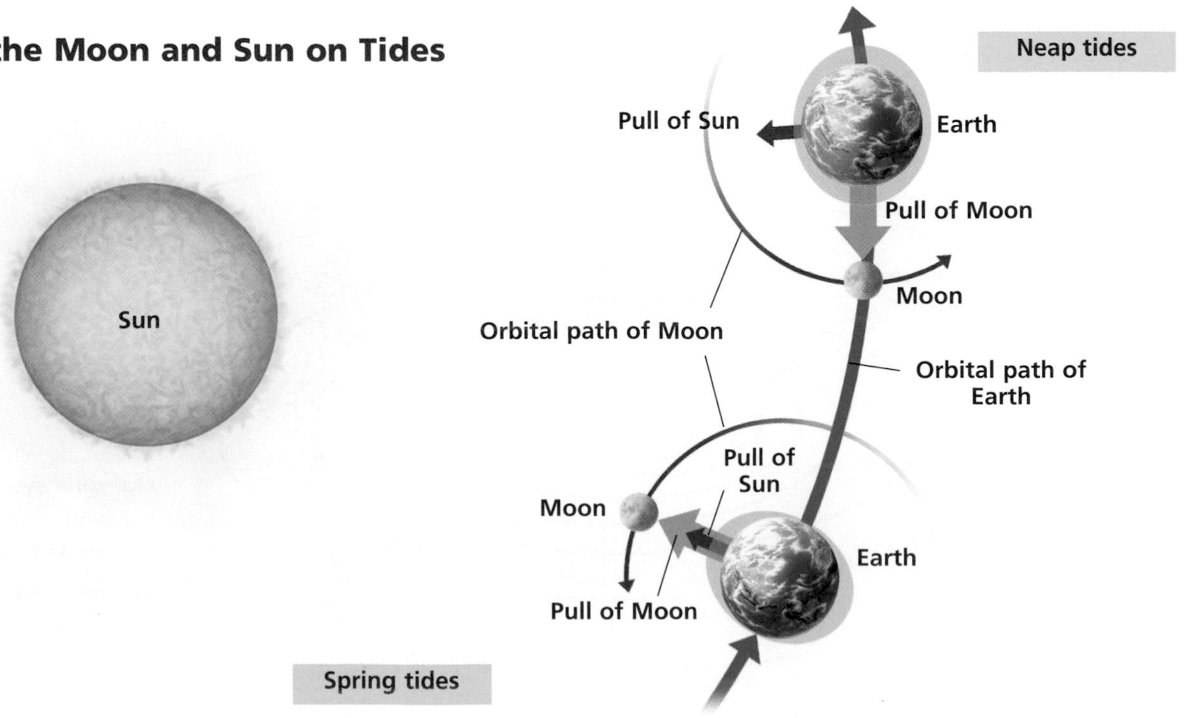
Neap tides
Pull of Sun
Earth
Pull of Moon
Moon
Sun
Orbital path of Moon
Orbital path of Earth
Pull of Sun
Moon
Earth
Pull of Moon
Spring tides

Tides are higher than normal when the gravitational pull of the Moon and the Sun combine. These tides, called spring tides, occur twice a month. Tides are lower than normal during neap tides, when the Sun and the Moon are at right angles.

Earth

Geographers are interested in how different places on Earth receive different amounts of energy from the Sun. Differences in solar energy help explain why the tropics are warm, why the Arctic region is cold, and why day is warmer than night. To understand these differences, geographers study Earth's rotation, revolution, and the tilt of its **axis**. The axis is an imaginary line that runs from the North Pole through Earth's center to the South Pole. Rotation, revolution, and tilt control the amount of solar energy reaching Earth.

▲ Photographs taken from space can tell us about Earth.

Interpreting the Visual Record Where can you see the presence of water in this view of Earth?

Rotation One complete spin of Earth on its axis is called a **rotation**. Each rotation takes 24 hours, or one day. Earth turns on its axis, but to us it appears that the Sun is moving. The Sun seems to "rise" in the east and "set" in the west. Before scientists learned that Earth revolves around the Sun, people thought that the Sun revolved around Earth. They thought Earth was at the center of the heavens.

Revolution It takes a year for Earth to orbit the Sun, or to complete one **revolution**. More precisely, it takes 365¼ days. To allow for this fraction of a day and keep the calendar accurate, every fourth year becomes a leap year. An extra day—February 29—is added to the calendar.

Tilt The amount of the Sun's energy reaching different parts of Earth varies. This is because Earth's axis is not straight up and down. It is actually tilted, or slanted, at an angle of 23.5° from vertical to the plane of Earth's orbit. Because of Earth's tilt, the angle at which the Sun's rays strike the planet is constantly changing as Earth revolves around the Sun. For this reason, the point where the vertical rays of

internet connect

GO TO: go.hrw.com
KEYWORD: SJ3 CH2
FOR: Web sites about planet Earth

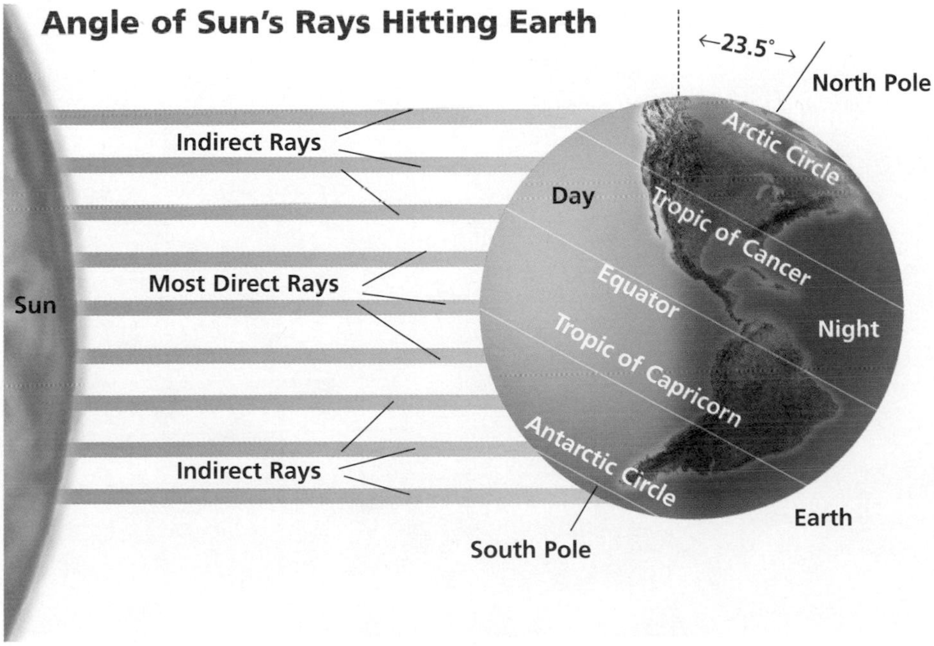
Angle of Sun's Rays Hitting Earth
23.5°
North Pole
Indirect Rays
Day
Arctic Circle
Tropic of Cancer
Most Direct Rays
Sun
Equator
Night
Tropic of Capricorn
Antarctic Circle
Indirect Rays
Earth
South Pole

◀ The tilt of Earth's axis and the position of the planet in its orbit determine where the Sun's rays will most directly strike the planet.

Interpreting the Visual Record Which areas of Earth receive only indirect rays from the Sun?

the Sun strike Earth shifts north and south of the equator. These vertical rays provide more energy than rays that strike at an angle.

✓ **READING CHECK:** *Physical Systems* How do rotation, revolution, and tilt affect solar energy reaching Earth?

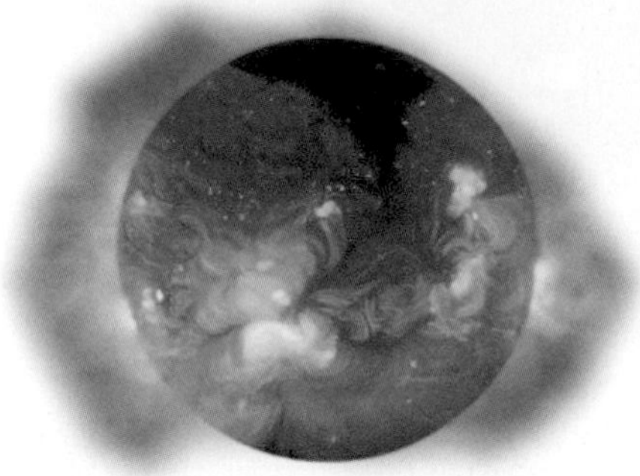

▲ The Sun's surface is always violently churning as heat flows outward from the interior.

Solar Energy and Latitude

The angle at which the Sun's rays reach Earth affects temperature. In the tropics—areas in the low latitudes near the equator—the Sun's rays are nearly vertical throughout the year. In the polar regions—the areas near the North and South Poles—the Sun's rays are always at a low angle. As a result, the poles are generally the coldest places on Earth. The **Arctic Circle** is the line of latitude located 66.5° north of the equator. It circles the North Pole. The **Antarctic Circle** is the line of latitude located 66.5° south of the equator. It circles the South Pole.

The Seasons

Each year is divided into periods of time called seasons. Each season is known for a certain type of weather, based on temperature and amount of precipitation. Winter, spring, summer, and fall are examples of seasons that are described by their average temperature. "Wet" and "dry" seasons are described by their precipitation. The seasons change as Earth orbits the Sun. As this happens, the amount of solar energy received in any given location changes.

As Earth revolves around the Sun, the tilt of the poles toward and away from the Sun causes the seasons to change.

Interpreting the Visual Record **At what point is the North Pole tilted toward the Sun?** ▼

The Seasons

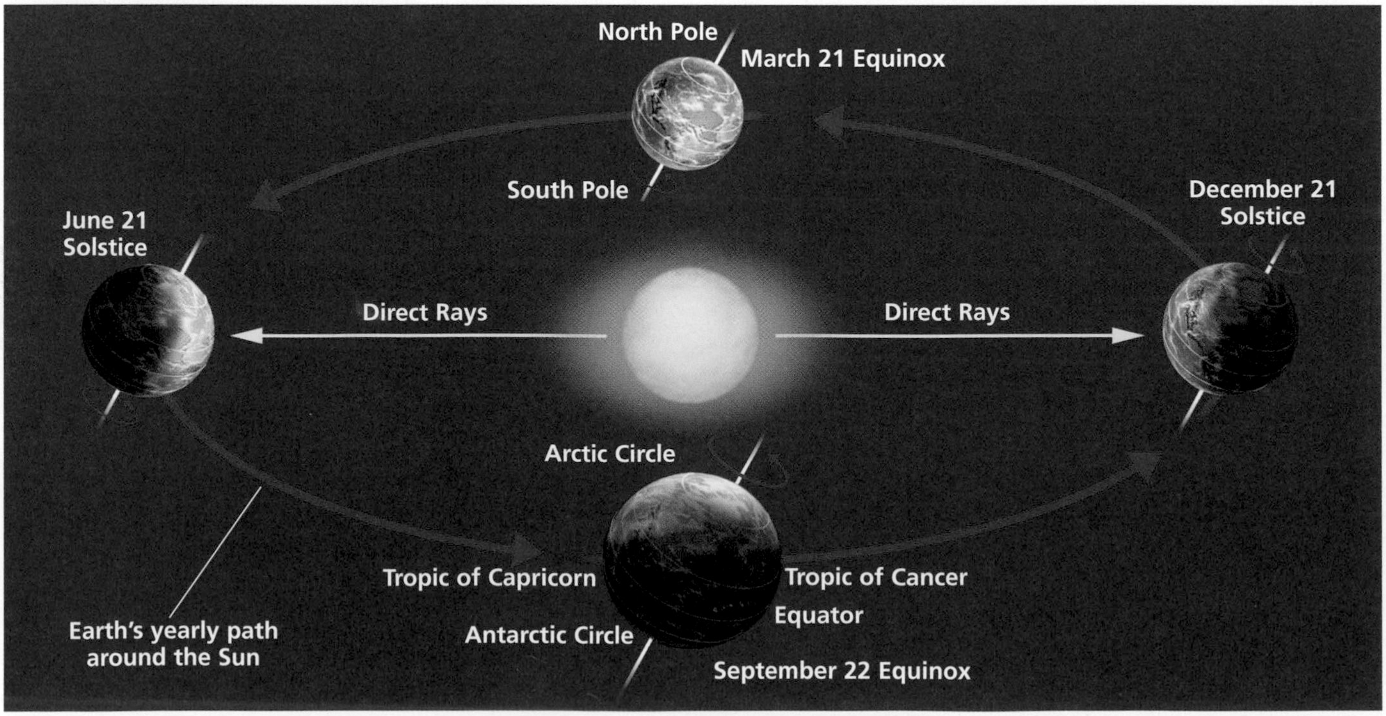
North Pole
March 21 Equinox
South Pole
June 21 Solstice
December 21 Solstice
Direct Rays
Direct Rays
Arctic Circle
Tropic of Capricorn
Tropic of Cancer
Equator
Antarctic Circle
Earth's yearly path around the Sun
September 22 Equinox

Solstice The day when the Sun's vertical rays are farthest from the equator is called a **solstice**. Solstices occur twice a year—about June 21 and about December 22. In the Northern Hemisphere the June solstice is known as the summer solstice. This is the longest day of the year and the beginning of summer. On this date the Sun's vertical rays strike Earth at the **Tropic of Cancer**. This is the line of latitude that is about 23.5° north of the equator. Six months later, about December 22, another solstice takes place. This is the winter solstice for the Northern Hemisphere. On this date the North Pole is pointed away from the Sun. The Northern Hemisphere experiences the shortest day of the year. On this date the Sun's rays strike Earth most directly at the **Tropic of Capricorn**. This line of latitude is about 23.5° south of the equator. In the Southern Hemisphere the seasons are reversed. June 21 is the winter solstice and December 22 is the summer solstice. The middle-latitude regions lie between the Tropic of Cancer and the Arctic Circle and between the Tropic of Capricorn and the Antarctic Circle.

This map shows Earth's temperatures on January 28, 1997.

Interpreting the Visual Record Which hemisphere is warmer in January?

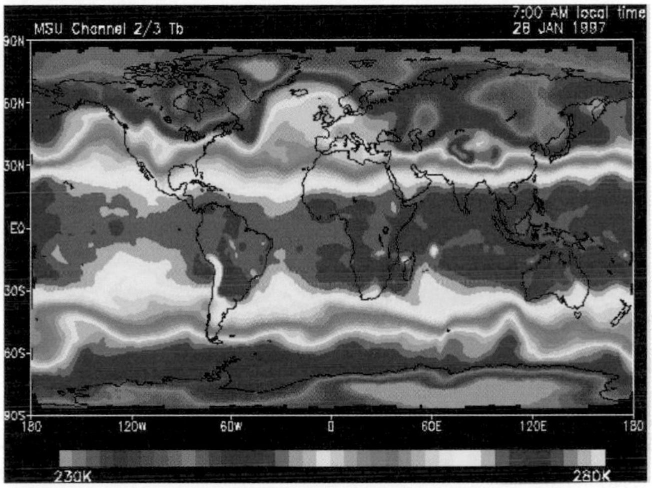
MSU Channel 2/3 Tb
7:00 AM local time
28 JAN 1997
90N
60N
30N
EQ
30S
60S
90S
180
120W
60W
0
60E
120E
180
230K
280K

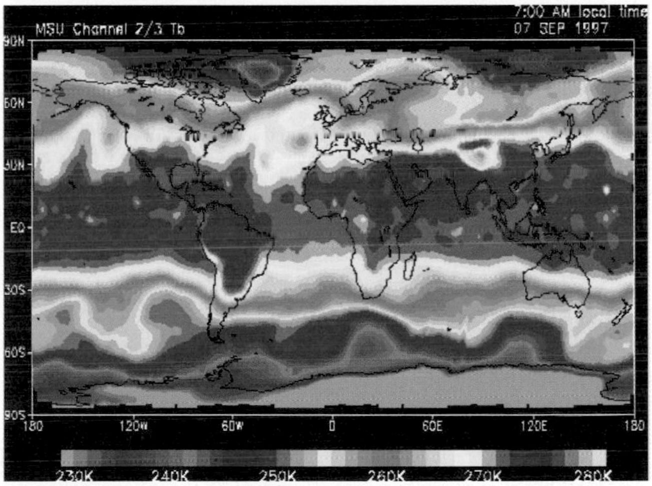
MSU Channel 2/3 Tb
7:00 AM local time
07 SEP 1997
90N
60N
30N
EQ
30S
60S
90S
180
120W
60W
0
60E
120E
180
230K
240K
250K
260K
270K
280K

This temperature map for September 7, 1997, shows summer in the Northern Hemisphere.

Equinox Twice a year, halfway between summer and winter, Earth's poles are at right angles to the Sun. The Sun's rays strike the equator directly. On these days, called **equinoxes**, every place on Earth has 12 hours of day and 12 hours of night. Equinoxes mark the beginning of spring and fall. In the Northern Hemisphere the spring equinox occurs about March 21. The fall equinox occurs there about September 22. In the Southern Hemisphere the March equinox signals the beginning of fall, and the September equinox marks the beginning of spring.

Some regions on Earth, particularly in the tropics, have seasons tied to precipitation rather than temperature. Shifting wind patterns are one cause of seasonal change. For example, in January winds from the north bring dry air to India. By June the winds have shifted, coming from the southwest and bringing moisture from the Indian Ocean. These winds bring heavy rain to India. Some places in the United States also have seasons tied to moisture. East Coast states south of Virginia have a wet season in summer. These areas also have a hurricane season, lasting roughly from June to November. Some areas of the West Coast have a dry season in summer.

The seasons affect human activities. For example, in Minnesota, people shovel snow in winter to keep the walkways clear. Students waiting for a bus must wear warm clothes. The Sun rises late and sets early. As a result, people go to work and return home in darkness.

✓ **READING CHECK:** *Physical Systems* How do the seasons relate to the Sun's energy?

The Earth System

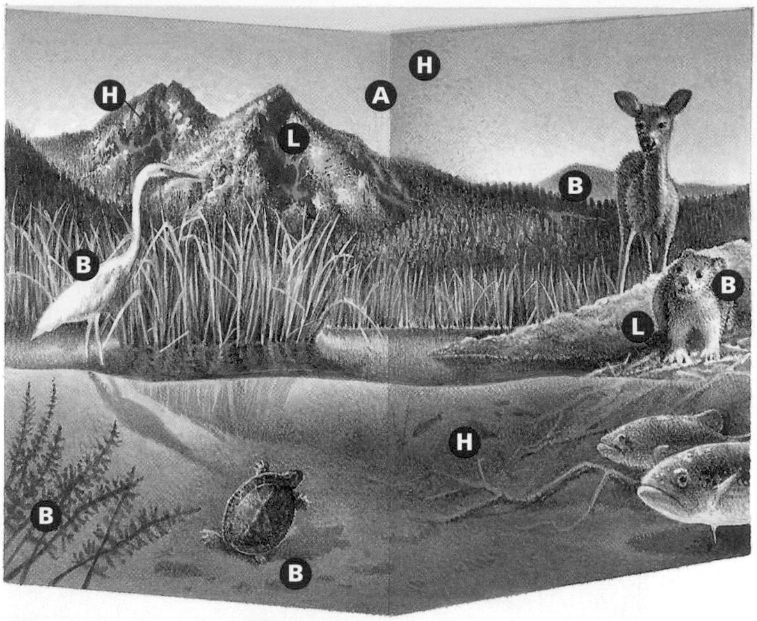
H
A
H
L
B
B
B
L
H
B
B

A Atmosphere **B** Biosphere
L Lithosphere **H** Hydrosphere

▲ The interactions of the atmosphere, lithosphere, hydrosphere, and biosphere make up the Earth system.

Interpreting the Visual Record **Which items in this image are part of the hydrosphere?**

The Earth System

Geographers need to be able to explain how and why places on Earth differ from each other. One way they do this is to study the interactions of forces and materials on the planet. Together, these forces and materials are known as the Earth system.

The Earth system has four parts: the **atmosphere**, the lithosphere, the hydrosphere, and the biosphere. The atmosphere is the layer of gases—the air—that surrounds Earth. These gases include nitrogen, oxygen, and carbon dioxide. The atmosphere also contains a form of oxygen called **ozone**. A layer of this gas helps protect Earth from harmful solar radiation. Another part of the Earth system is the lithosphere. The prefix *litho* means rock. The lithosphere is the solid, rocky outer layer of Earth, including the sea floor. The hydrosphere—*hydro* means water—consists of all of Earth's water, found in lakes, oceans, and glaciers. It also includes the moisture in the atmosphere. Finally, the biosphere—*bio* means life—is the part of the Earth system that includes all plant and animal life. It extends from high in the air to deep in the oceans.

By dividing Earth into these four spheres, geographers can better understand each part and how each affects the others. The different parts of the Earth system are constantly interacting in many ways. For example, a tree is part of the biosphere. However, to grow it needs to take in water, chemicals from the soil, and gases from the air.

✓ **READING CHECK:** *The World in Spatial Terms* What are the four parts of the Earth system?

Section 1 Review

Homework Practice Online
go.hrw.com
Keyword: SJ3 HP2

Define and explain: solar system, orbit, satellite, axis, rotation, revolution, Arctic Circle, Antarctic Circle, solstice, Tropic of Cancer, Tropic of Capricorn, equinoxes, atmosphere, ozone

Reading for the Main Idea

1. *Physical Systems* What are the major objects in the solar system?
2. *The World in Spatial Terms* What are the four parts of the Earth system?

Critical Thinking

3. **Summarizing** Which three things determine the amount of solar energy reaching places on Earth?
4. **Drawing Inferences and Conclusions** Why are the seasons reversed in the Northern and Southern Hemispheres?

Organizing What You Know

5. **Finding the Main Idea** Use this graphic organizer to explain solstice and equinox.

Solstice	⇔	Equinox

Section 2 Water on Earth

Read to Discover

1. Which processes make up the water cycle and how are they connected?
2. How is water distributed on Earth?
3. How does water affect people's lives?

Define

water vapor
water cycle
evaporation
condensation
precipitation
tributary
groundwater
continental shelf

WHY IT MATTERS

Scientists study other parts of our solar system to find out if water exists or might have existed elsewhere. Use CNNfyi.com or other **current events** sources to learn more about space agencies and their searches to detect water. Record your findings in your journal.

A limestone cavern

Characteristics of Water

Water has certain physical characteristics that influence Earth's geography. Water is the only substance on Earth that occurs naturally as a solid, a liquid, and a gas. We see water as a solid in snow and ice and as a liquid in lakes, oceans, and rivers. Water also occurs in the air as an invisible gas called **water vapor**.

Another characteristic of water is that it heats and cools slowly compared to land. Even on a very hot day, the ocean stays cool. A breeze blowing over the ocean brings cooler temperatures to shore. This keeps temperatures near the coast from getting as hot as they do farther inland. In winter the oceans cool more slowly than land. This generally keeps winters milder in coastal areas.

✓ **READING CHECK:** *Physical Systems* What are some important characteristics of water?

The Water Cycle

The circulation of water from Earth's surface to the atmosphere and back is called the **water cycle**. The total amount of water on the planet does not change. Water, however, does change its form and its location.

Water rushes through the Stewart Mountain Dam in Arizona.

Canada
United States
Stewart Mountain Dam
Mexico

The Water Cycle

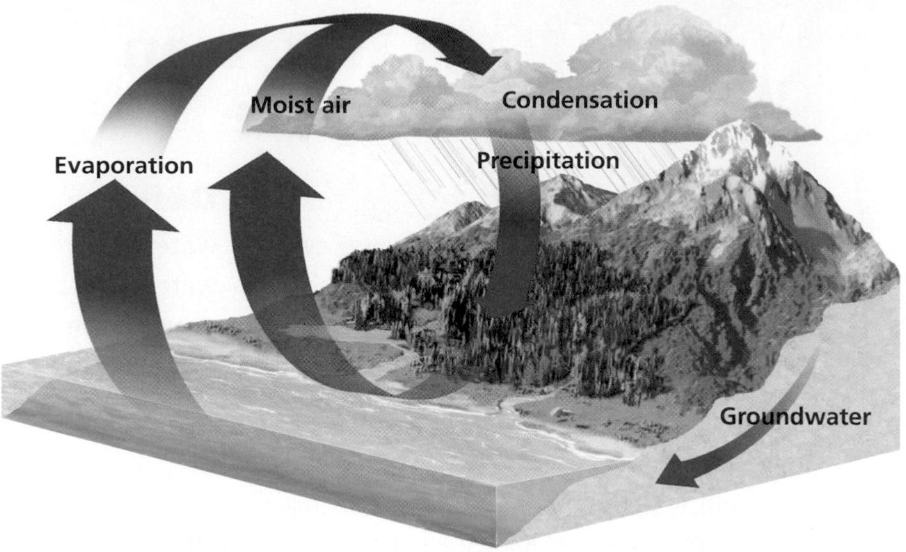

Moist air
Condensation
Evaporation
Precipitation
Groundwater

The circulation of water from one part of the hydrosphere to another depends on energy from the Sun. Water evaporates, condenses, and falls to Earth as precipitation. **Interpreting the Visual Record How would a seasonal increase in the amount of the Sun's energy received by an area change the water cycle in that area?**

The Sun's energy drives the water cycle. **Evaporation** occurs when the Sun heats water on Earth's surface. The heated water evaporates, becoming water vapor and rising into the air. Energy from the Sun also causes winds to carry the water vapor to new locations. As the water vapor rises, it cools, causing **condensation**. This is the process by which water changes from a gas into tiny liquid droplets. These droplets join together to form clouds. If the droplets become heavy enough, **precipitation** occurs—that is, the water falls back to Earth. This water can be in the form of rain, hail, sleet, or snow. The entire cycle of evaporation, condensation, and precipitation repeats itself endlessly.

✓ **READING CHECK:** *Physical Systems* What is the water cycle?

This glacier is "calving"—a mass of ice is breaking off, forming an iceberg. Most of Earth's freshwater exists as ice.

Geographic Distribution of Water

The oceans contain about 97 percent of Earth's water. About another 2 percent is found in the ice sheets of Antarctica, the Arctic, Greenland, and mountain glaciers. Approximately 1 percent is found in lakes, streams, rivers, and under the ground.

Earth's freshwater resources are not evenly distributed. There are very dry places with no signs of water. Other places have many lakes and rivers. In the United States, for example, Minnesota is dotted with more than 11,000 lakes. Dry states such as Nevada have few natural lakes. In many dry places rivers have been dammed to create artificial lakes called reservoirs.

Surface Water Water sometimes collects at high elevations, where rivers begin their flow down toward the lowlands and coasts. The first and smallest streams that form from this runoff are called headwaters. When these headwaters meet and join, they form larger streams. In turn, these streams join with other streams to form rivers. Any smaller stream or river that flows into a larger stream or river is a **tributary**. For example, the Missouri River is an important tributary of the Mississippi River, into which it flows near St. Louis, Missouri.

Lakes are usually formed when rivers flow into basins and fill them with water. Most lakes are freshwater, but some are salty. For example, the Great Salt Lake in Utah receives water from the Bear, Jordan, and Weber Rivers but has no outlet. Because the air is dry here, the rate of evaporation is very high. When the lake water evaporates, it leaves behind salts and minerals, making the lake salty.

Groundwater

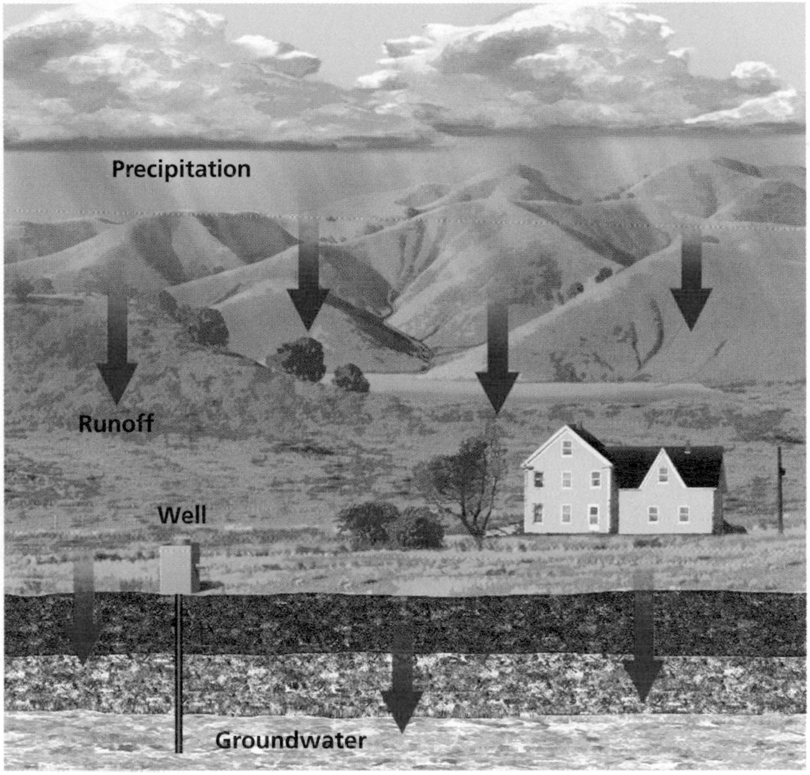
Precipitation
Runoff
Well
Groundwater

In some areas where rainfall is scarce, enough groundwater exists to support agriculture.

Interpreting the Visual Record How do people gain access to groundwater?

Groundwater Not all surface water immediately returns to the atmosphere through evaporation. Some water from rainfall, rivers, lakes, and melting snow seeps into the ground. This **groundwater** seeps down until all the spaces between soil and grains of rock are filled. In some places, groundwater bubbles out of the ground as a spring. Many towns in the United States get their water from wells—deep holes dug down to reach the groundwater. Motorized pumps allow people to draw water from very deep underground.

Oceans Most of Earth's water is found in the oceans. The Pacific, Atlantic, Indian, and Arctic Oceans connect with each other. This giant body of water covers some 71 percent of Earth's surface. These oceans also include smaller regions called seas and gulfs. The Gulf of Mexico and the Gulf of Alaska are two examples of smaller ocean areas.

Surrounding each continent is a zone of shallow ocean water. This gently sloping underwater land—called the **continental shelf**—is important to marine life. Although the oceans are huge, marine life is concentrated in these shallow areas. Deeper ocean water is home to fewer organisms. Overall, the oceans average about 12,000 feet (about 3,700 m) in depth. The deepest place is the Mariana Trench in the Pacific Ocean, at about 36,000 feet (about 11,000 m) deep.

✓ **READING CHECK:** *The World in Spatial Terms* How is water distributed on Earth?

The Continental Shelf

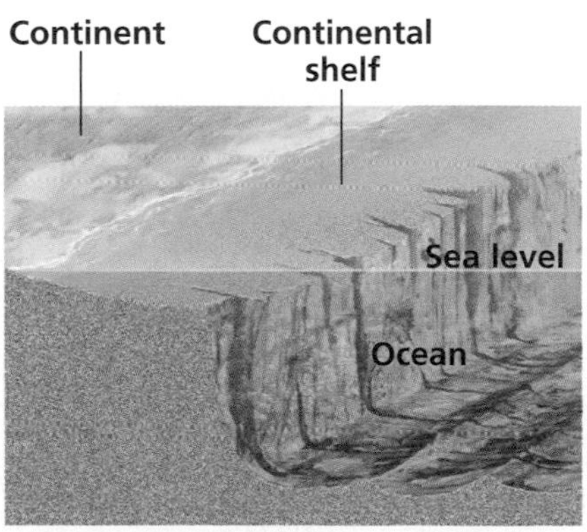
Continent
Continental shelf
Sea level
Ocean

The continental shelf slopes gently away from the continents. The ocean floor drops steeply at the edge of the shelf.

▲
This kelp forest is off the coast of southern California. The shallower parts of the oceans are home to many plants and animals.

Water Issues

Water plays an important part in our survival. As a result, water issues frequently show up in the news. Thunderstorms, particularly when accompanied by hail or tornadoes, can damage buildings and ruin crops. Droughts also can be deadly. In the mountains, heavy snowfalls sometimes cause deadly snow slides called avalanches. Heavy fog can make driving or flying dangerous. Geographers are concerned with these issues. They work on ways to better prepare for natural hazards.

Floods Water can both support and threaten life. Heavy rains can cause floods, which are the world's deadliest natural hazard. Floods kill four out of every ten people who die from natural disasters, including hurricanes, earthquakes, tornadoes, and thunderstorms.

Some floods occur in dry places when strong thunderstorms drop a large amount of rain very quickly. The water races along on the hard, dry surface instead of soaking into the ground. This water can quickly gather in low places. Creekbeds that are normally dry can suddenly surge with rushing water. People and livestock are sometimes caught in these flash floods.

Floods also happen in low-lying places next to rivers and on coastlines. Too much rain or snowmelt entering a river can cause the water to overflow the banks. Powerful storms, particularly hurricanes, can sometimes cause ocean waters to surge into coastal areas. Look at a

Canada
Davenport
United States
Mexico

Davenport, Iowa, suffered severe flooding in 1993. Many cities are located along rivers even though there is a danger of floods.
Interpreting the Visual Record Why are many cities located next to rivers?
▶

map of the United States. You will see that most major cities are located either next to a river or along a coast. For this reason, floods can be a threat to lives and property.

Flood Control Dams are a means people use to control floods. The huge Hoover Dam on the Colorado River in the United States is one example. The Aswān Dam on the Nile River in Egypt and those on the Murray River in Australia are others. Dams help protect people from floods. They also store water for use during dry periods. However, dams prevent rivers from bringing soil nutrients to areas downstream. Sometimes farming is not as productive as it was before the dams were built.

The Atatürk Dam in Turkey is 604 feet (184 m) high.

Interpreting the Visual Record How have people used dams to change their physical environment?

Clean Water The availability of clean water is another issue affecting the world's people. Not every country is able to provide clean water for drinking and bathing. Pollution also threatens the health of the world's oceans—particularly in the shallower seabeds where many fish live and reproduce.

Water Supply Finding enough water to meet basic needs is a concern in regions that are naturally dry. The water supply is the amount of water available for use in a region. It limits the number of living things that can survive in a place. People in some countries have to struggle each day to find enough water.

✓ **READING CHECK:** *Environment and Society* What are some ways in which water affects people?

Section 2 Review

go.hrw.com **Homework Practice Online**
Keyword: SJ3 HP2

Define and explain: water vapor, water cycle, evaporation, condensation, precipitation, tributary, groundwater, continental shelf

Reading for the Main Idea

1. *Physical Systems* What are the steps in the water cycle?
2. *Environment and Society* What are some major issues related to water?

Critical Thinking

3. **Analyzing Information** What are some important characteristics of water?
4. **Finding the Main Idea** Why is water supply a problem in some areas?

Organizing What You Know

5. **Sequencing** Copy the following graphic organizer. Use it to explain the water cycle.

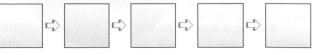

Connecting to *Technology*

Forecasting Earthquakes

Since ancient times, people have tried to forecast earthquakes. A Chinese inventor even created a device to register earthquakes as early as A.D. 132.

The theory of plate tectonics gives modern-day scientists a better understanding of how and why earthquakes occur. Earthquake scientists, known as seismologists, have many tools to help them monitor movements in Earth's crust. They try to understand when and where earthquakes will occur.

The most common of these devices is the seismograph. It measures seismic waves—vibrations produced when two tectonic plates grind against each other. Scientists believe that an increase in seismic activity may signal a coming earthquake.

A scientist with a seismograph

Other devices show shifts in Earth's crust. Tiltmeters measure the rise of tectonic plates along a fault line. Gravimeters record changes in gravitational strength caused by rising or falling land. Laser beams can detect lateral movements along a fault line. Satellites can note the movement of entire tectonic plates.

Scientists have yet to learn how to forecast earthquakes with accuracy. Nevertheless, their ongoing work may one day provide important breakthroughs in the science of earthquake forecasting.

You Be the Geographer

1. What social and economic consequences might earthquake forecasting have?
2. What technology has helped with earthquake forecasting?

Plates Moving Apart When two plates move away from each other, hot lava emerges from the gap that has been formed. The lava builds a mid-ocean ridge—a landform that is similar to an underwater mountain range. This process is currently occurring in the Atlantic Ocean where the Eurasian plate and the North American plate are moving away from each other.

Plates Sliding Tectonic plates can also slide past each other. Earthquakes occur from sudden adjustments in Earth's crust. In California the Pacific plate is sliding northwestward along the edge of the North American plate. This has created the San Andreas Fault zone. A **fault** is a fractured surface in Earth's crust where a mass of rocks is in motion.

Tectonic plates move slowly—just inches a year. If, however, we could look back 200 million years, we would see that the continents have moved a long way. From their understanding of plate tectonics, scientists proposed the theory of continental drift. This theory states that the continents were once united in a single supercontinent. They then separated and moved to the positions they are in today. Scientists call this original landmass **Pangaea** (pan-GEE-uh).

Continental Drift

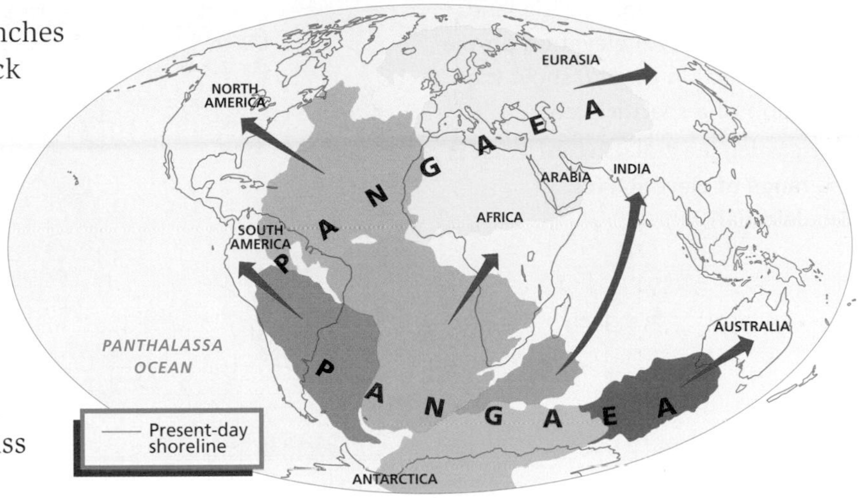

EURASIA
NORTH AMERICA
PANGAEA
ARABIA
INDIA
AFRICA
SOUTH AMERICA
AUSTRALIA
PANTHALASSA OCEAN
PANGAEA
Present-day shoreline
ANTARCTICA

About 200 million years ago it is believed there was only one continent, Pangaea, and one ocean, Panthalassa. The continental plates slowly drifted into their present-day positions.

✓ **READING CHECK:** *Physical Systems* How are primary landforms formed?

Secondary Landforms

The forces of plate tectonics build up primary landforms. At the same time, water, wind, and ice constantly break down rocks and cause rocky material to move. The landforms that result when primary landforms are broken down are called secondary landforms.

One process of breaking down and changing primary landforms into secondary landforms is called **weathering**. It is the process of breaking rocks into smaller pieces. Weathering occurs in several ways. Heat can cause rocks to crack. Water may get into cracks in rocks and freeze. This ice then expands with a force great enough to break the rock. Water can also work its way underground and slowly dissolve minerals such as limestone. This process sometimes creates caves. In

These steep peaks in Chile are part of the Andes.

Interpreting the Visual Record How do these mountains show the effects of weathering and erosion?

Elevation is the height of the land above sea level. An elevation profile is a cross-section used to show the elevation of a specific area.

Interpreting the Visual Record What is the range of elevation for Guadalcanal?

Elevation Profile: Guadalcanal

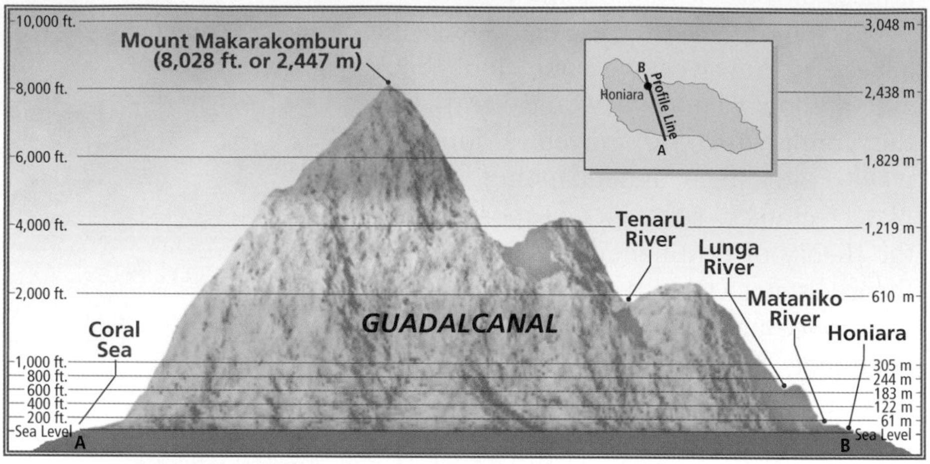
10,000 ft.
8,000 ft.
6,000 ft.
4,000 ft.
2,000 ft.
1,000 ft.
800 ft.
600 ft.
400 ft.
200 ft.
Sea Level
3,048 m
2,438 m
1,829 m
1,219 m
610 m
305 m
244 m
183 m
122 m
61 m
Sea Level
Mount Makarakomburu (8,028 ft. or 2,447 m)
Honiara
Profile Line
B
A
Tenaru River
Lunga River
Mataniko River
Honiara
Coral Sea
GUADALCANAL
A
B

some areas small plants called lichens attach to bare rock. Chemicals in the lichens gradually break down the stone. Some places in the world experience large swings in temperature. In the Arctic the ground freezes and thaws, which tends to lift stones to the surface in unusual patterns. Regardless of which weathering process is at work, rocks eventually break down into sediment. These smaller pieces of rock are called gravel, sand, silt, or clay, depending on particle size. Once weathering has taken place, water, ice, or wind can move the material and create new landforms.

✓ **READING CHECK:** *Physical Systems* What is one way in which secondary landforms are created?

Erosion

Another process of changing primary landforms into secondary landforms is **erosion**. Erosion is the movement of rocky materials to another location. Moving water is the most common force that erodes and shapes the land.

Water Flowing water carries sediment. This sediment forms different kinds of landforms depending on where it is deposited. For example, a river flowing from a mountain range onto a flat area, or plain, may deposit some of its sediment there. The sediment sometimes builds up into a fan-shaped form called an **alluvial fan**. A **floodplain** is created when rivers flood their banks and deposit sediment. A **delta** is formed when rivers carry some of their sediment all the way to the ocean. The sediment settles to the bottom where the river meets the ocean. The Nile and Mississippi Rivers have two of the world's largest deltas.

Waves in the ocean and in lakes also shape the land they touch. Waves can shape beaches into great dunes, such as on the shore of Long Island. The jagged coastline of Oregon also shows the erosive power of waves.

River water, brown with sediment, enters the ocean.

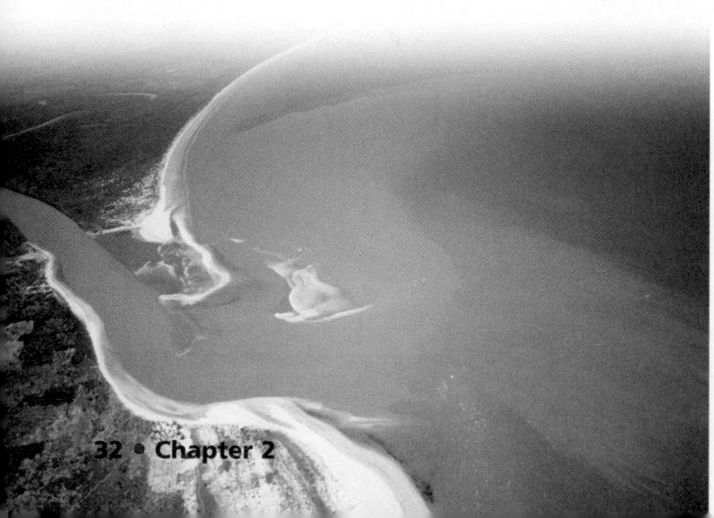

Glaciers In high mountain settings and in the coldest places on Earth are **glaciers**. These large, slow-moving rivers of ice have the power to move tons of rock.

Giant sheets of thick ice called continental glaciers cover Greenland and Antarctica. Earth has experienced several ice ages—periods of extreme cold. During the last ice age glaciers covered most of Canada and the northern United States. This ice age, which began about 2 million years ago and ended about 10,000 years ago, was broken up by warmer periods when the glaciers retreated. The Great Lakes were carved out by the movement of a continental glacier.

Wind Wind also shapes the land. Strong winds can lift soils into the air and carry them across great distances. On beaches and in deserts wind can deposit large amounts of sand to form dunes.

Blowing sand can wear down rock. The sand acts like sandpaper to polish jagged edges. An example of rocks worn down by blowing sand can be seen in Utah's Canyonlands National Park.

✓ **READING CHECK:** *Physical Systems* What forces cause erosion?

Our Amazing Planet

Waves 50 to 60 feet high, which the local people call Jaws, sometimes occur off the coast of Maui, Hawaii. They are caused by storms in the north Pacific and a high offshore ridge that focuses the waves' energy.

People and Landforms

Geographers study how people adapt their lives to different landforms. Deltas and floodplains, for example, are usually fertile places to grow food. People also change landforms. Engineers build dams to control river flooding. They drill tunnels through mountains instead of making roads over mountaintops. People have used modern technology to build structures that are better able to survive disasters like floods and earthquakes.

✓ **READING CHECK:** *Environment and Society* What are some examples of humans adjusting to and changing landforms?

Section 3 Review

go.hrw.com **Homework Practice Online** Keyword: SJ3 HP2

Define and explain: landforms, plain, plateau, isthmus, peninsula, plate tectonics, core, mantle, crust, magma, lava, continents, subduction, earthquakes, fault, Pangaea, weathering, erosion, alluvial fan, floodplain, deltas, glaciers

Reading for the Main Idea

1. *Physical Systems* How are primary landforms created?
2. *Physical Systems* What forces cause weathering and erosion?

Critical Thinking

3. **Summarizing** What is plate tectonics?
4. **Finding the Main Idea** How do people affect landforms? Give examples.

Organizing What You Know

5. **Identifying Cause and Effect** Copy the following graphic organizer. Use it to describe the movement of plates and the movement's effects.

movement		resulting landforms and changes
	⇨	
	⇨	
	⇨	

CHAPTER 2

Reviewing What You Know

Building Vocabulary

On a separate sheet of paper, write sentences to define each of the following words.

1. solar system
2. orbit
3. solstice
4. equinoxes
5. atmosphere
6. water cycle
7. evaporation
8. condensation
9. precipitation
10. landforms
11. plate tectonics
12. continents
13. earthquakes
14. weathering
15. erosion

Reviewing the Main Ideas

1. *Physical Systems* In what ways do Earth's rotation, revolution, and tilt help determine how much of the Sun's energy reaches Earth?
2. *Physical Systems* Explain how the Sun's energy drives the water cycle. Be sure to include a discussion of the three elements of the cycle.
3. *Physical Systems* How does plate tectonics relate to the continents and their landforms?
4. *Physical Systems* Describe how subduction zones are created.
5. *Physical Systems* Describe the different ways secondary landforms are created.

Understanding Environment and Society

Water Use

The availability and purity of water are important for everyone. Research the water supply in your own city or community and prepare a presentation on it. You may want to think about the following:

- Where your city or community gets its drinking water,
- Drought or water shortages that have happened in the past,
- Actions your community takes to protect the water supply.

Thinking Critically

1. **Drawing Inferences and Conclusions** How do the four parts of the Earth system help explain why places on Earth differ?
2. **Finding the Main Idea** Describe landforms that are shaped by water and wind.
3. **Drawing Inferences and Conclusions** Why do people continue to live in areas where floods are likely to occur?
4. **Identifying Cause and Effect** Describe the landforms that result (a) when two tectonic plates collide and (b) when two plates move away from each other.
5. **Summarizing** In what ways do people interact with landforms?
6. **Analyzing Information** How might mountains be primary and secondary landforms?

Building Social Studies Skills

Map ACTIVITY

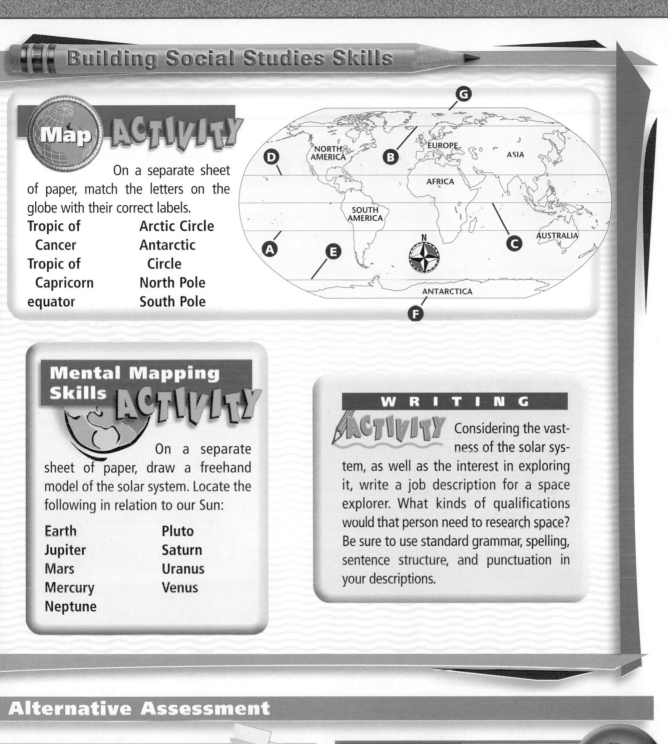

On a separate sheet of paper, match the letters on the globe with their correct labels.

Tropic of Cancer	**Arctic Circle**
Tropic of Capricorn	**Antarctic Circle**
equator	**North Pole**
	South Pole

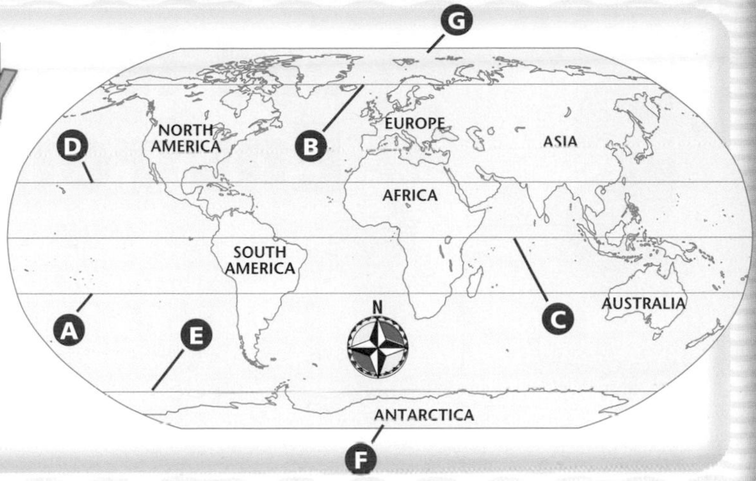

G
NORTH AMERICA
B
EUROPE
ASIA
D
AFRICA
SOUTH AMERICA
N
AUSTRALIA
A
E
C
ANTARCTICA
F

Mental Mapping Skills ACTIVITY

On a separate sheet of paper, draw a freehand model of the solar system. Locate the following in relation to our Sun:

Earth	**Pluto**
Jupiter	**Saturn**
Mars	**Uranus**
Mercury	**Venus**
Neptune	

WRITING ACTIVITY

Considering the vastness of the solar system, as well as the interest in exploring it, write a job description for a space explorer. What kinds of qualifications would that person need to research space? Be sure to use standard grammar, spelling, sentence structure, and punctuation in your descriptions.

Alternative Assessment

Portfolio ACTIVITY

Learning About Your Local Geography

Individual Project Compare the latitude and longitude of your state's capital city with that of the capitals of three countries. How might the seasons be similar or different in each city?

internet connect

Internet Activity: go.hrw.com
KEYWORD: SJ3 GT2

Choose a topic to explore online:

- Learn more about Earth's seasons.
- Discover facts about Earth's water.
- Investigate earthquakes.

CHAPTER 3

Wind, Climate, and Natural Environments

Tornado in Saskatoon, Canada

Diver, coral, and fish, Fiji Islands

Igloo at night, Alaska Range

Section 1 Winds and Ocean Currents

Read to Discover

1. How does the Sun's energy change Earth?
2. Why are wind and ocean currents important?

Define

weather
climate
greenhouse effect
air pressure
front
currents

WHY IT MATTERS

Changes in ocean temperatures create currents that affect Earth's landmasses. Use CNNfyi.com or other **current events** sources to find examples of the effects of changes in ocean temperatures, such as the La Niña weather pattern. Record your findings in your journal.

Earth from space

The Sun's Energy

All planets in our solar system receive energy from the Sun. This energy has important effects. Among the most obvious effects we see on our planet are those on **weather** and **climate**. Weather is the condition of the atmosphere at a given place and time. Climate refers to the weather conditions in an area over a long period of time. How do you think the Sun's energy affects weather and climate?

Energy Balance Although Earth keeps receiving energy from the Sun, it also loses energy. Energy that is lost goes into space. As a result, Earth—as a whole—loses as much energy as it gets. Thus, Earth's overall temperature stays about the same.

As you learned in Chapter 2, the Sun does not warm Earth evenly. The part of Earth in daylight takes in more energy than it loses. Temperatures rise. However, the rest of Earth is in darkness. That part of Earth loses more energy than it gets. Temperatures drop. In addition, when the direct rays of the Sun strike Earth at the Tropic of Cancer, it is summer in the Northern Hemisphere. Temperatures are warm. The Southern Hemisphere, on the other hand, is having winter. Temperatures are lower. The seasons reverse when the Sun's direct rays move above the Tropic of Capricorn. We can see that in any one place temperatures vary from day to day. From year to year, however, they usually stay about the same.

Stored Energy Some of the heat energy that reaches Earth is stored. One place Earth stores heat is in the air. This keeps Earth's surface warmer than if there were no air around it. The process by which

Plants—like this fossil palm found in a coal bed—store the Sun's energy. When we burn coal—the product of long-dead plants—we release the energy the plants had stored.

internet connect

GO TO: go.hrw.com
KEYWORD: SJ3 CH3
FOR: Web sites about wind, climates, and environments

The Greenhouse Effect

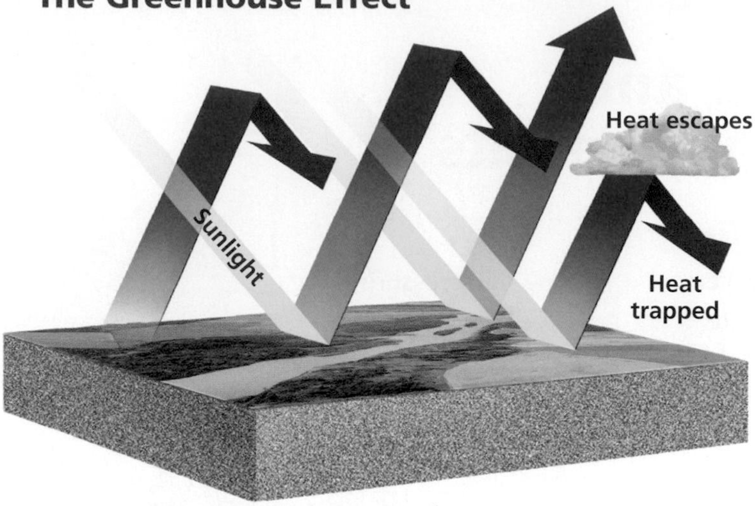
Heat escapes
Sunlight
Heat trapped

Light from the Sun passes through the atmosphere and heats Earth's surface. Most heat energy later escapes into space.

You Be the Geographer What would happen if too much heat energy remained trapped in the atmosphere?

Earth's atmosphere traps heat is called the **greenhouse effect**. In a greenhouse the Sun's energy passes through the glass and heats everything inside. The glass traps the heat, keeping the greenhouse warm.

Water and land store heat, too. As we learned in Chapter 2, water warms and cools slowly. This explains why in fall, long after temperatures have dropped, the ocean's water is only a little cooler than in summer. Land and buildings also store heat energy. For example, a brick building that has heated up all day stays warm after the Sun sets.

✓ **READING CHECK:** *Physical Systems* How does the Sun's energy affect Earth?

Wind and Currents

Air and water both store heat. When they move from place to place, they keep different parts of the world from becoming too hot or too cold. By moving air and water, winds and ocean currents move heat energy between warmer and cooler places. Different parts of the world are kept from becoming too hot or too cold.

When the wind is blowing, air is moving from one place to another. Everyone has experienced these local winds. Global winds also exist. They move air and heat energy around Earth. Ocean currents, which are caused by wind, also move heat energy.

This snow-covered waterfront town is located on Mackinac Island, Michigan.

Canada
Mackinac Island
United States
Mexico

Air Pressure To understand why there are winds, we must understand **air pressure**. Air pressure is the weight of the air. Air is a mixture of gases. At sea level, a cubic foot of air weighs about 1.25 ounces (35 grams). We do not feel this weight because air pushes on us from all sides equally. The weight of air, however, changes with the weather. Cold air weighs more than warmer air. An instrument called a barometer measures air pressure.

When air warms, it gets lighter and rises. Colder air then moves in to replace the rising air. The result is wind. Wind travels from areas of high pressure to areas of low pressure. During the day land heats up faster than water. The air over the land heats up faster as well. Along the coast lower air pressure is located over land and higher air pressure is located over water. The air above land rises, and cool air flows in to shore to take its place. At night the land cools more quickly than the water. Air pressure over the land increases, and the wind changes direction.

Earth has several major areas where air pressure stays about the same throughout the year. Along the equator is an area of low air pressure. The pressure is low because the Sun is always warming this area.

Wind shapes Earth and the life that thrives here. For example, this tree has grown in the direction blown by the area's prevailing winds.

Interpreting the Visual Record How do you think wind shapes Earth's landscape?

Reading a Weather Map

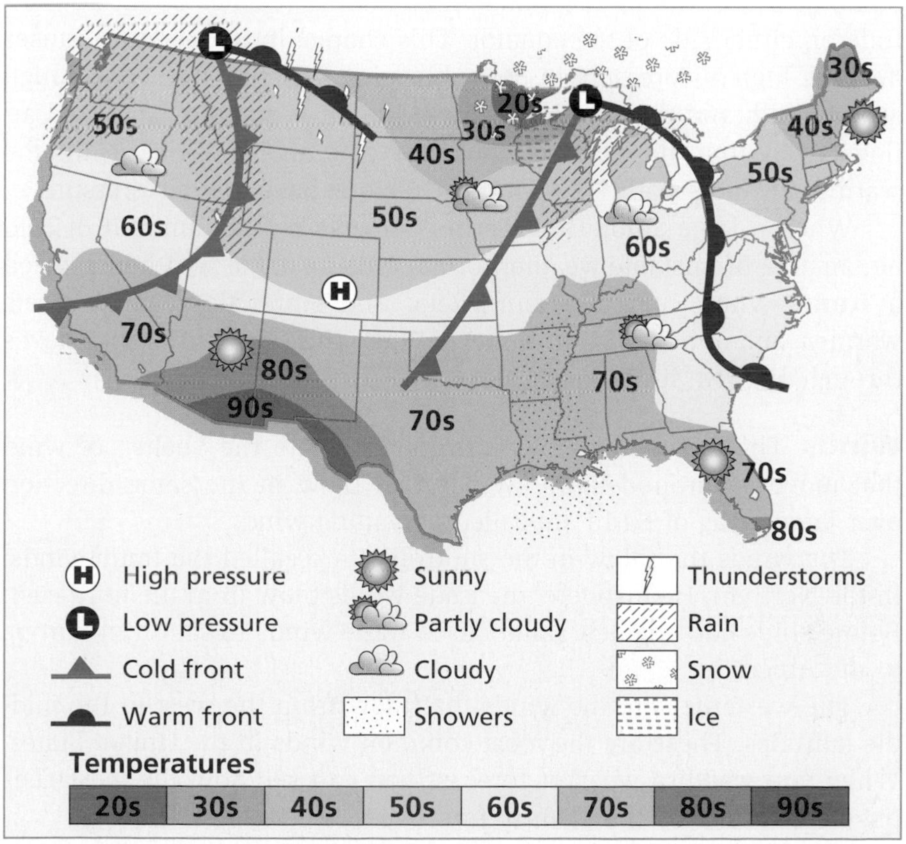
30s
20s
30s
40s
50s
50s
40s
50s
60s
60s
70s
80s
90s
70s
70s
70s
80s
High pressure
Low pressure
Cold front
Warm front
Sunny
Partly cloudy
Cloudy
Showers
Thunderstorms
Rain
Snow
Ice
Temperatures
20s
30s
40s
50s
60s
70s
80s
90s

Weather maps show atmospheric conditions as they currently exist or as they are forecast for a particular time period. Most weather maps have legends that explain what the symbols on the map mean. This map shows a cold front sweeping through the central United States. A low-pressure system is at the center of a storm bringing rain and snow to the Midwest. Notice that temperatures behind the cold front are considerably cooler than those ahead of the front.

You Be the Geographer What is the average temperature range for the southwestern states?

Pressure and Wind Systems

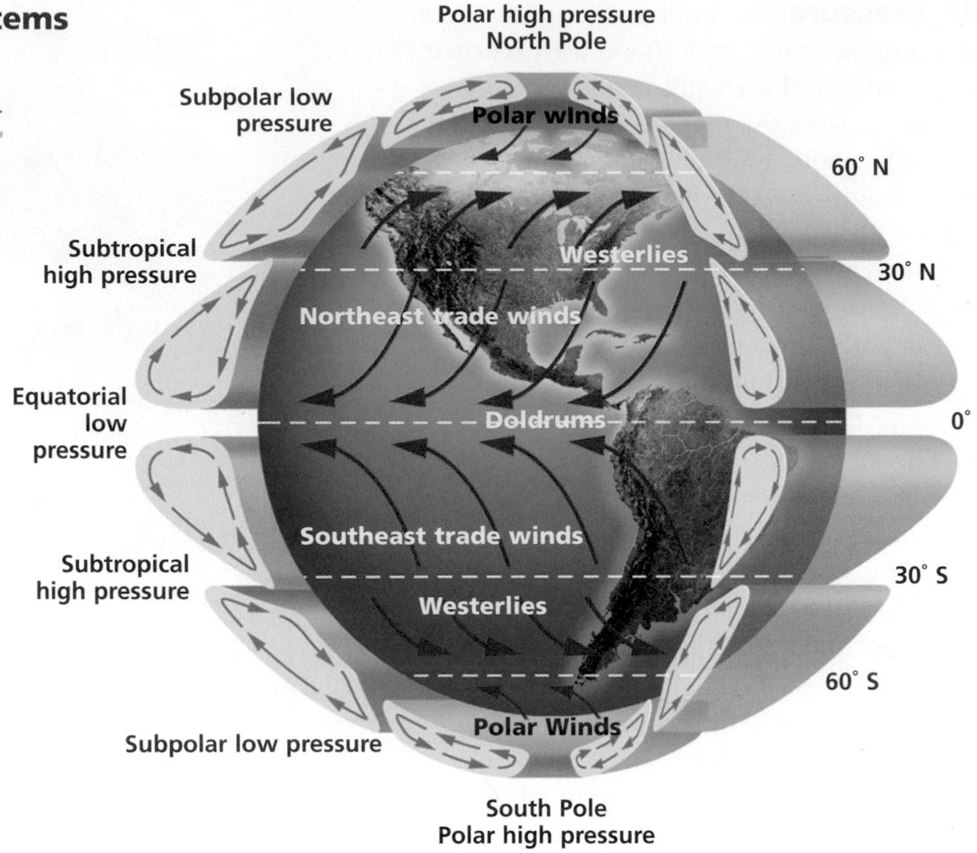
Polar high pressure
North Pole
Subpolar low pressure
Polar winds
60° N
Subtropical high pressure
Westerlies
30° N
Northeast trade winds
Equatorial low pressure
Doldrums
0°
Southeast trade winds
Subtropical high pressure
30° S
Westerlies
60° S
Subpolar low pressure
Polar Winds
South Pole
Polar high pressure

Winds between Earth's high- and low-pressure zones help regulate the globe's energy balance.

You Be the Geographer What happens when warm westerlies come into contact with cold polar winds?

This ship uses wind to travel. As more wind catches the sails, the ship moves faster.

This warm air rises along the equator and moves north and south. Some of the warm air cools and sinks once it reaches about 30° latitude on either side of the equator. This change in temperature causes areas of high air pressure in the subtropics. The pressure is also high at the North and South Poles because the air is so cold. This cold air flows away from the Poles. Because the cold air is heavier, it lifts the warmer air in its path. The subpolar regions have low air pressure.

When a large amount of warm air meets a large amount of cold air, an area of unstable weather forms. This unstable weather is called a **front**. When cold air from Arctic and Antarctic regions meets warmer air, a polar front forms. When this type of front moves through an area, it can cause storms.

Winds The major areas of air pressure create the "belts" of wind that move air around Earth. Winds that blow in the same direction over large areas of Earth are called prevailing winds.

The winds that blow in the subtropics are called the trade winds. In the Northern Hemisphere, the trade winds blow from the northeast. Before ships had engines, sailors used trade winds to sail from Europe to the Americas.

The westerlies are the winds that blow from the west in the middle latitudes. These are the most common winds in the United States. When you watch a weather forecast you can see how the westerlies push storms across the country from west to east.

Few winds blow near the equator. This area is called the doldrums. Here, warm air rises rather than blowing east or west.

Ocean Currents Winds make ocean water move in the same general directions as the air above it moves. Warm ocean water from the tropics moves in giant streams, or **currents**, to colder areas. Cold water moves in streams from the polar areas to the tropics. This moves energy between different places. Warm air and warm ocean currents raise temperatures. On the other hand, cold winds and cold ocean currents lower temperatures.

The Gulf Stream is an ocean current. It moves warm water north along the east coast of the United States. The Gulf Stream then moves across the Atlantic Ocean toward western Europe. The warm air that moves with it keeps winters mild. As a result, areas such as Ireland have warmer winters than areas in Canada that are just as far north.

Ocean currents also bring heat energy into the Arctic Ocean. In the winter, warm currents create openings in the ice. These openings give arctic whales a place to breathe. They also give people a place to catch fish. Cold water also flows out of the Arctic Ocean into warmer waters of the Pacific and Atlantic Oceans. The cold water sinks below warmer water, causing mixing. This mixing brings food to sea life.

▲ Plants and animals adapt to their particular environments on Earth.

Interpreting the Visual Record How do you think the bearded seal is able to live in Norway's cold environment?

✓ **READING CHECK:** *Physical Systems* How do winds and currents create patterns on Earth's surface?

go.hrw.com **Homework Practice Online**
Keyword: SJ3 HP3

Section 1 Review

Define and explain: weather, climate, greenhouse effect, air pressure, front, currents

Reading for the Main Idea

1. *Physical Systems* How does Earth's temperature stay balanced?
2. *Physical Systems* How does the greenhouse effect allow Earth to store the Sun's energy?

Critical Thinking

3. **Drawing Inferences and Conclusions** How would weather in western Europe be different if there were no Gulf Stream?
4. **Analyzing Information** Why were the trade winds important to early sailors?

Organizing What You Know

5. **Categorizing** Copy the following graphic organizer. Use it to show the names, locations, and directions of wind and air pressure belts.

Name	Location	Direction

CASE STUDY

HURRICANE: TRACKING A NATURAL HAZARD

Hurricanes are large circulating storms that begin in tropical oceans. Hurricanes often move over land and into populated areas. When a hurricane approaches land, it brings strong winds, heavy rains, and large ocean waves.

The map below shows the path of Hurricane Fran in 1996. Notice how Fran moved to the west and became stronger until it reached land. It began as a tropical depression and became a powerful hurricane as it passed over warm ocean waters.

Scientists who study hurricanes try to predict where these storms will travel. They want to be able to warn people in the hurricane's path. Early warnings can help people be better prepared for the deadly winds and rain. It is a difficult job because hurricanes can change course suddenly. Hurricanes are one of the most dangerous natural hazards.

One way of determining a hurricane's strength is by measuring the atmospheric pressure inside it. The lower the pressure, the stronger the storm. Hurricanes are rated on a scale of one to five. Study Table 1 to see how wind speed and air pressure are used to help determine the strength of a hurricane.

Hurricane Mitch formed in October 1998. The National Weather Service (NWS) recorded Mitch's position and strength. They learned that Mitch's pressure was one of the lowest ever recorded. The NWS estimated that Mitch's maximum sustained surface winds reached 180 miles per hour.

Table 1: Saffir-Simpson Scale

Hurricane Type	Wind Speed mph	Air Pressure mb (inches)
Category 1	74–95	more than 980 (28.94)
Category 2	96–110	965–979 (28.50–28.91)
Category 3	111–130	945–964 (27.91–28.47)
Category 4	131–155	920–944 (27.17–27.88)
Category 5	more than 155	less than 920 (27.17)

Source: Florida State University, <http://www.met.fsu.edu/explores/tropical.html>

Path of Hurricane Fran, 1996

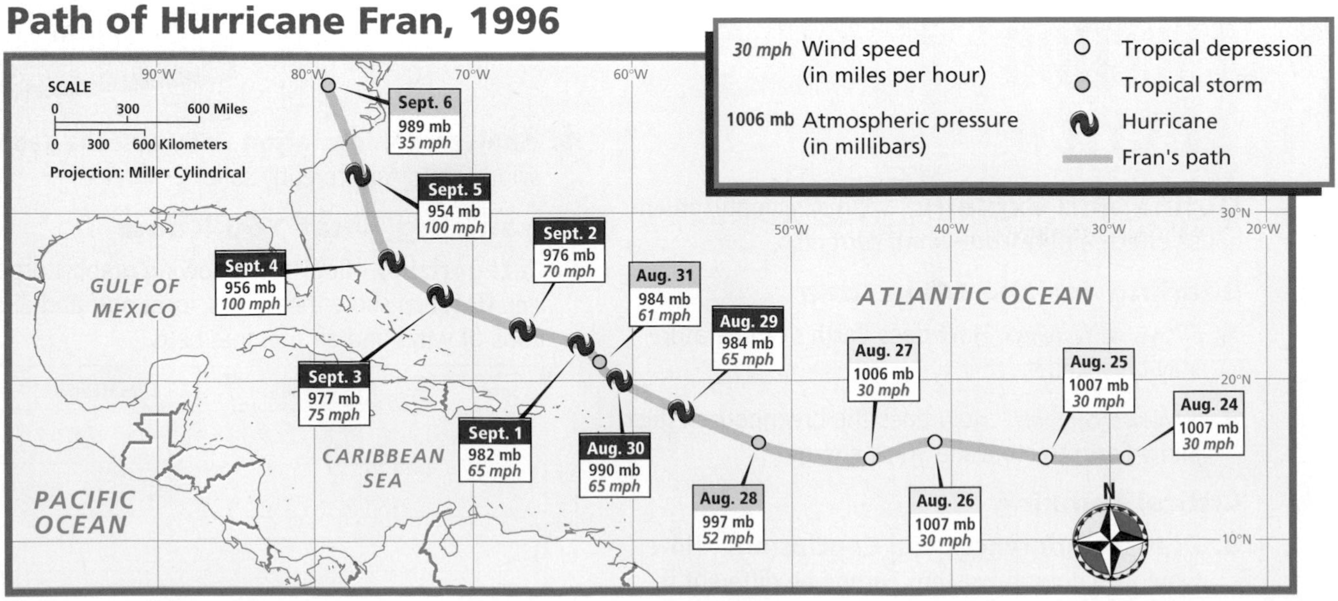
30 mph Wind speed (in miles per hour)
1006 mb Atmospheric pressure (in millibars)
Tropical depression
Tropical storm
Hurricane
Fran's path
SCALE
0 300 600 Miles
0 300 600 Kilometers
Projection: Miller Cylindrical
90°W
80°W
70°W
60°W
50°W
40°W
30°W
20°W
30°N
20°N
10°N
GULF OF MEXICO
ATLANTIC OCEAN
CARIBBEAN SEA
PACIFIC OCEAN
N
Sept. 6 989 mb 35 mph
Sept. 5 954 mb 100 mph
Sept. 4 956 mb 100 mph
Sept. 3 977 mb 75 mph
Sept. 2 976 mb 70 mph
Sept. 1 982 mb 65 mph
Aug. 31 984 mb 61 mph
Aug. 30 990 mb 65 mph
Aug. 29 984 mb 65 mph
Aug. 28 997 mb 52 mph
Aug. 27 1006 mb 30 mph
Aug. 26 1007 mb 30 mph
Aug. 25 1007 mb 30 mph
Aug. 24 1007 mb 30 mph

Table 2: Hurricane Mitch, 1998 Position and Strength

Date	Latitude (degrees)	Longitude (degrees)	Wind Speed (mph)	Pressure (millibars)	Storm Type
10/22	12 N	78 W	30	1002	Tropical depression
10/24	15 N	78 W	90	980	Category 2
10/26	16 N	81 W	130	923	Category 4
10/27	17 N	84 W	150	910	Category 5
10/31	15 N	88 W	40	1000	Tropical storm
11/01	15 N	90 W	30	1002	Tropical depression
11/03	20 N	91 W	40	997	Tropical storm
11/05	26 N	83 W	50	990	Tropical storm

Source: <http://www.met.fsu.edu/explores/tropical.html>

Hurricanes like Mitch cause very heavy rains in short periods of time. These heavy rains are particularly dangerous. The ground becomes saturated, and mud can flow almost like water. The flooding and mudslides caused by Mitch killed an estimated 10,000 people in four countries. Many people predicted that the region would not recover without help from other countries.

In the southeastern United States, many places have emergency preparedness units. The people assigned to these groups organize their communities. They provide food, shelter, and clothing for those who must evacuate their homes.

▲ This satellite image shows the intensity of Hurricane Mitch. With advanced technology, hurricane tracking is helping to save lives.

You Be the Geographer

1. Trace a map of the Caribbean. Be sure to include latitude and longitude lines.
2. Use the data about Hurricane Mitch in Table 2 to plot its path. Make a key with symbols to show Mitch's strength at each location.
3. What happened to Mitch when it reached land?

Section 2 Earth's Climate and Vegetation

Read to Discover

1. What is included in the study of weather?
2. What are the major climate types, and what types of plants live in each?

Define

rain shadow
monsoon
arid
steppe climate
hurricanes
typhoons
tundra climate
permafrost

Why It Matters

Flooding often becomes a problem during severe weather. Use CNNfyi.com or other **current events** sources to find examples of the effects of flooding on nations around the world. Record your findings in your journal.

Change
Rain
Fair
Stormy
Very Dry
BAROMETER

A barometer

Nature has many incredible sights. Lightning is one of the most spectacular occurrences. These flashes of light are produced by a discharge of atmospheric electricity.

Weather

As you have read, the condition of the atmosphere in a local area for a short period of time is called weather. Weather is a very general term. It can describe temperature, amount of sunlight, air pressure, wind, humidity, clouds, and moisture.

When warm and cool air masses come together, they form a front. Cold air lifts the warm air mass along the front. The air that is moved to higher elevations is cooled. If moisture is present in the lifted air, this cooling causes clouds to form. The moisture may fall to Earth as rain, snow, sleet, or hail. Moisture that falls in any form is called precipitation.

Another type of lifting occurs when warm, moist air is blown up against a mountain and forced to rise. The air cools as it is lifted, just as when air masses collide. Clouds form, and precipitation falls. The side of the mountain facing the wind—the windward side—often gets heavy rain. By the time the air reaches the other side of the mountain—the leeward side—it has lost most of its moisture. This can create a dry area called a **rain shadow**.

✓ **READING CHECK:** *Physical Systems* What is included in the study of weather?

Landforms and Precipitation

Windward (wet)
Leeward (dry)
Snow
Warming dry air
Rain
Cooling moist air
Rain Shadow
Ocean
Inland

As moist air from the ocean moves up the windward side of a mountain, it cools. The water vapor in the air condenses and falls in the form of rain or snow. Descending, the drier air then moves down the leeward side of the mountain. This drier air brings very little precipitation to areas in the rain shadow.

Low-Latitude Climates

If you charted the average weather in your community over a long period of time, you would be describing the climate for your area. Geographers have devised ways of describing climates based mainly on temperature, precipitation, and natural vegetation. In general, an area's climate is related to its latitude. In the low latitudes—the region close to the equator—there are two main types of climates: humid tropical and tropical savanna.

Humid Tropical Climate A humid tropical climate is warm and rainy all year. People living in this climate do not see a change from summer to winter. This is because the Sun heats the region throughout the year. The heat in the tropics causes a great deal of evaporation and almost daily rainstorms. One of the most complex vegetation systems in the world—the tropical rain forest—exists in this climate. The great rain forests of Brazil, Indonesia, and Central Africa are in the equatorial zone.

Some regions at higher latitudes have warm temperatures all year but have strong wet and dry seasons. Bangladesh and coastal India, for example, have an extreme wet season during the summer. Warm, moist air from the Indian Ocean reaches land. The air rises and cools, causing heavy rains. The rains continue until the wind changes direction in the fall. This seasonal shift of air flow and rainfall is known as a **monsoon**. A monsoon may be wet or dry. The monsoon system is particularly important in Asia.

The people of Tamil Nadu, India, adjust to the monsoon season.

Interpreting the Visual Record
What problems might people face during the wet monsoon?

SRIVIJAYALAKSHMITRASPORT
TATA
BHASKAR

Tropical Savanna Climate There is another type of tropical climate that has wet and dry seasons. However, this climate does not have the extreme shifts found in a monsoon climate. It is called a tropical savanna climate. The tropical savanna climate has a wet season soon after the warmest months. It has a dry season soon after the coolest months. Total rainfall, however, is fairly low. Vegetation in a tropical savanna climate is grass with scattered trees and shrubs.

✓ **READING CHECK:** *Physical Systems* Which climate regions are in the low latitudes?

Our Amazing Planet

In terms of loss of life, the worst natural disaster in U.S. history is still the hurricane that hit Galveston, Texas, on September 8, 1900. As many as 8,000 people died in Galveston.

Dry Climates

Temperature and precipitation are the most important parts of climate. Some regions, for example, experience strong hot and cold seasons. Other regions have wet and dry seasons. Some places are wet or dry all year long. If an area is **arid** (dry) it receives little rain. Arid regions usually have few streams and plants.

Desert Climate Most of the world's deserts lie near the tropics. The high air pressure and settling air keep these desert climate regions dry most of the time. Other deserts are located in the interiors of continents and in the rain shadows of mountains. Few plants can survive in the driest deserts, so there are many barren, rocky, or sandy areas. Dry air and clear skies permit hot daytime temperatures and rapid cooling at night.

Steppe Climate Another dry climate—the **steppe climate**—is found between desert and wet climate regions. A steppe receives more rainfall than a desert climate. However, the total amount of precipitation is still low. Grasses are the most common plants, but trees can grow along creeks and rivers. Farmers can grow crops but usually need to irrigate. Steppe climates occur in Africa, Australia, Central Asia, eastern Europe, in the Great Plains of the United States and Canada, and in South America.

✓ **READING CHECK:** *The World in Spatial Terms* What are the dry climates?

Palo Duro Canyon State Park in Texas attracts thousands of visitors each year.

Interpreting the Visual Record How can you tell that this canyon is located in a dry climate?

Canada
United States
Palo Duro State Canyon
Mexico

World Climate Regions

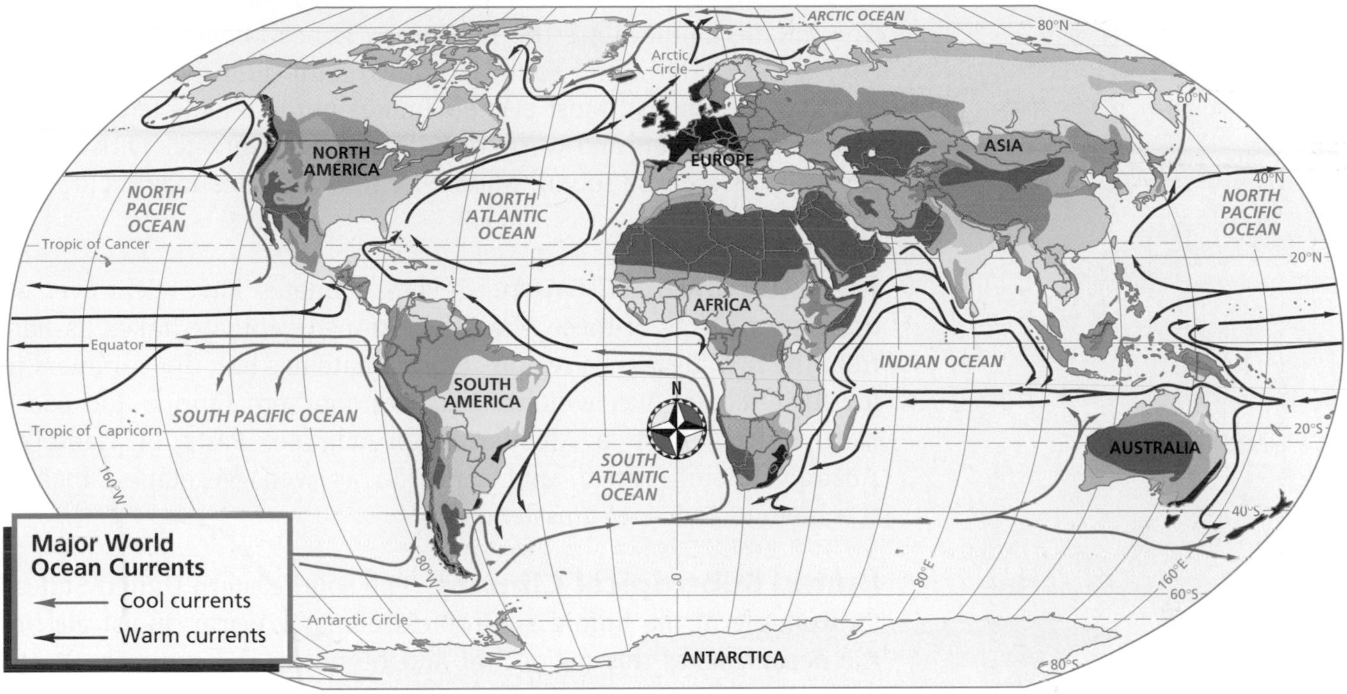
ARCTIC OCEAN
80°N
Arctic Circle
60°N
40°N
20°N
NORTH AMERICA
EUROPE
ASIA
NORTH PACIFIC OCEAN
NORTH ATLANTIC OCEAN
NORTH PACIFIC OCEAN
Tropic of Cancer
AFRICA
Equator
INDIAN OCEAN
SOUTH AMERICA
SOUTH PACIFIC OCEAN
Tropic of Capricorn
N
SOUTH ATLANTIC OCEAN
AUSTRALIA
20°S
40°S
160°W
80°W
0°
80°E
160°E
60°S
Antarctic Circle
ANTARCTICA
80°S
Major World Ocean Currents
Cool currents
Warm currents

	Climate	Geographic Distribution	Major Weather Patterns	Vegetation
Low Latitudes	HUMID TROPICAL	along the equator	warm and rainy year-round, with rain totaling anywhere from 65 to more than 450 in. (165–1,143 cm) a year	tropical rain forest
	TROPICAL SAVANNA	between the humid tropics and the deserts	warm all year; distinct rainy and dry seasons; at least 20 in. (51 cm) of rain during the summer	tropical grassland with scattered trees
Dry	DESERT	centered along 30° latitude; some middle-latitude deserts are in the interior of large continents and along their western coasts	arid; less than 10 in. (25 cm) of rain a year; sunny and hot in the tropics and sunny with wide temperature ranges during the day in middle latitudes	a few drought-resistant plants
	STEPPE	generally bordering deserts and interiors of large continents	semiarid; about 10–20 in. (25–51 cm) of precipitation a year; hot summers and cooler winters with wide temperature ranges during a day	grassland; few trees
Middle Latitudes	MEDITERRANEAN	west coasts in middle latitudes	dry, sunny, warm summers and mild, wetter winters; rain averages 15–20 in. (38–51 cm) a year	scrub woodland and grassland
	HUMID SUBTROPICAL	east coasts in the middle latitudes	hot, humid summers and mild, humid winters; rain year-round; coastal areas are in the paths of hurricanes and typhoons	mixed forest
	MARINE WEST COAST	west coasts in the upper-middle latitudes	cloudy, mild summers and cool, rainy winters; strong ocean influence; rain averages 20–60 in. (51–152 cm) a year	temperate evergreen forest
	HUMID CONTINENTAL	east coasts and interiors of upper-middle latitude continents	four distinct seasons; long, cold winters and short, warm summers; amounts of precipitation a year vary	mixed forest
High Latitudes	SUBARCTIC	higher latitudes of the interior and east coasts of continents	extremes of temperature; long, cold winters and short, warm summers; little precipitation all year	northern evergreen forest
	TUNDRA	high-latitude coasts	cold all year; very long, cold winters and very short, cool summers; little precipitation	moss, lichens, low shrubs; permafrost marshes
	ICE CAP	polar regions	freezing cold; snow and ice year-round; little precipitation	no vegetation
	HIGHLAND	high mountain regions	temperatures and amounts of precipitation vary greatly as elevation changes	forest to tundra vegetation, depending on elevation

Middle-Latitude Climates

Belgium
Germany
France
Switzerland
Italy
Côte d'Azur
Spain

The Mediterranean coast of France is part of the Riviera. The Riviera is located in a Mediterranean climate region.

Interpreting the Visual Record **What features would make this area popular with tourists?**

The middle latitudes are the two broad zones between Earth's polar circles (66.5° north and south latitudes) and the tropics (23.5° north and south latitudes). Most of the climates in the middle latitudes have cool or cold winters and warm or hot summers. Climates with wet and dry seasons are also found. Middle-latitude climates may include rain shadow deserts.

Mediterranean Climate Several climates have clear wet and dry seasons. One of these, the Mediterranean climate, takes its name from the Mediterranean region. This climate has hot, dry summers followed by cooler, wet winters. Much of southern Europe and coastal North Africa have a Mediterranean climate. Parts of California, Australia, South Africa, and Chile do as well. Vegetation includes scrub woodlands and grasslands.

Humid Subtropical Climate The southeastern United States is an example of the humid subtropical climate. Warm, moist air from the ocean makes this region hot and humid in the summer. Winters are mild, but snow falls occasionally. People in a humid subtropical climate experience **hurricanes** and **typhoons**. These are tropical storms that bring violent winds, heavy rain, and high seas. The humid subtropical climate supports areas of mixed forests where deciduous and coniferous forests blend. Deciduous trees lose their leaves during the fall each year. Coniferous trees have needle-shaped leaves that remain green year-round.

Marine West Coast Climate Some coastal areas of North America and much of western Europe have a marine west coast climate. Westerly winds carry moisture from the ocean across the land, causing winter rainfall. Evergreen forests can grow in these regions because of regular rain.

The Mediterranean has a variety of vegetation. This Mediterranean scrub forest is in Corfu, Greece.

Interpreting the Visual Record **What kinds of vegetation do you see in this scrub forest?**

Bulgaria
Macedonia
Albania
Corfu
Greece
Turkey

Humid Continental Climate Farther inland are regions with a humid continental climate. Winters in this region bring snowfall and cold temperatures, but there are some mild periods too. Summers are warm and sometimes hot. Most of the shifting weather in this climate region is the result of cold and warm air coming together along a polar front. Humid continental climates have four distinct seasons. Much of the midwestern and northeastern United States and southeastern Canada have a humid continental climate. This climate supports mixed forest vegetation.

✓ **READING CHECK:** *The World in Spatial Terms* What are the middle-latitude climates?

High-Latitude Climates

Closer to the poles we find another set of climates. They are the high-latitude climates. They have cold temperatures and little precipitation.

Subarctic Climate The subarctic climate has long, cold winters, short summers, and little rain. In the inland areas of North America, Europe, and Asia, far from the moderating influence of oceans, subarctic climates experience extreme temperatures. However, summers in these regions can be warm. In the Southern Hemisphere there is no land in the subarctic climate zone. As a result, boreal (BOHR-ee-uhl) forests are found only in the Northern Hemisphere. Trees in boreal forests are coniferous and cover vast areas in North America, Europe, and northern Asia.

Tundra Climate Farther north lies the **tundra climate**. Temperatures are cold, and rainfall is low. Usually just hardy plants, including mosses, lichens, and shrubs, survive here. Tundra summers are so short and cool that a layer of soil stays frozen all year. This frozen layer is called **permafrost**. It prevents water from draining into the soil. As a result, many ponds and marshes appear in summer.

Ice Cap Climate The polar regions of Earth have an ice cap climate. This climate

Wildlife eat the summer vegetation in the Alaskan tundra.

Interpreting the Visual Record Why is there snow on the mountain peaks during summer?

Alaska
Canada
United States

Amundsen-Scott South Pole Station
Antarctica
THE UNITED STATES OF AMERICA
WELCOMES YOU TO
AMUNDSEN-SCOTT SOUTH POLE STATION

▲ The Amundsen-Scott South Pole Station is a research center in Antarctica.

Interpreting the Visual Record **How does the design of this building show ways people have adapted to the ice cap climate?**

is cold—the monthly average temperature is below freezing. Precipitation averages less than 10 inches (25 cm) annually. Animals adapted to the cold, like walruses, penguins, and whales, are found here. No vegetation grows in this climate.

✓ **READING CHECK:** *The World in Spatial Terms* How are tundra and ice cap climates different?

Highland Climates

Mountains usually have several different climates in a small area. These climate types are known as highland climates. If you went from the base of a high mountain to the top, you might experience changes similar to going from the tropics to the Poles! The vegetation also changes with the elevation. It varies from thick forests or desert to tundra. Lower mountain elevations tend to be similar in temperature to the surrounding area. On the windward side, however, are zones of heavier rainfall or snowfall. As you go uphill, the temperatures drop. High mountains have a tundra zone and an icy summit.

✓ **READING CHECK:** *The World in Spatial Terms* What are highland climate regions?

Section 2 Review

go.hrw.com **Homework Practice Online**
Keyword: SJ3 HP3

Define and explain: rain shadow, monsoon, arid, steppe climate, hurricanes, typhoons, tundra climate, permafrost

Reading for the Main Idea

1. *Physical Systems* How is weather different from climate?

2. *The World in Spatial Terms* What are the major climate regions of the world?

Critical Thinking

3. Drawing Inferences and Conclusions Why is it important to understand weather and climate patterns?

4. Analyzing Information How does latitude influence climate?

Organizing What You Know

5. Categorizing Copy the following graphic organizer. Use it to describe Earth's climate types.

Climate	Latitudes	Characteristics

Section 3 Natural Environments

Read to Discover

1. How do environments affect life, and how do they change?
2. What substances make up the different layers of soil?

Define

extinct
ecology
photosynthesis
food chain
nutrients
plant communities
ecosystem
plant succession
humus

Why It Matters

Plants and animals depend on their environment for survival. Use CNNfyi.com or other **current events** sources to find out how conservationists work to save animals whose environments are threatened. Record your findings in your journal.

Acorns, the nut of an oak tree

Environmental Change

Geographers examine the distribution of plants and animals and the environments they occupy. They also study how people change natural environments. Changes in an environment affect the plants and animals that live in that environment. If environmental changes are extreme, some types of plants and animals may become **extinct**. This means they die out completely.

Plants use a particular environment's sunlight, water, gases, and minerals to survive.

Ecology and Plant Life The study of the connections among different forms of life is called **ecology**. One process connecting life forms is **photosynthesis**—the process by which plants convert sunlight into chemical energy. Roots take in minerals, water, and gases from the soil. Leaves take in sunlight and carbon dioxide from the air. Plant cells take in these elements and combine them to produce special chemical compounds. Plants use some of these chemicals to live and grow.

Plant growth is the basis for all the food that animals eat. Some animals, like deer, eat only plants. When deer eat plants, they store some of the plant food energy in their bodies. Other animals, like wolves, eat deer and indirectly get the plant food the deer ate. The plants, deer, and wolves together make up a **food chain**. A food chain is a series of organisms in which energy is passed along.

have deep roots that can reach water and soil nutrients far below the surface. Their spreading branches also collect large amounts of sunlight for photosynthesis.

Plants adapt to the sunlight, soil, and temperature of their region. They may also be suited to other plants found in their communities. For example, many ferns grow well in the shade found underneath trees. Some vines grow up tree trunks to reach sunlight.

Forest Succession After a Fire

A
B
C
D

A Forest fire in progress

B Early plant growth

C Middle stage

D Forest recovered

▲ Difficult conditions after a forest fire mean that the first plants to grow back must be very hardy.

You Be the Geographer In this series of photos, which plants are the first to grow back?

All of the plants and animals in an area together with the nonliving parts of their environment—like climate and soil—form what is called an **ecosystem**. The size of an ecosystem varies, depending on how it is defined. A small pond, for example, can be considered an ecosystem. The entire Earth can also be considered an ecosystem.

Ecosystems can be affected by natural events like droughts, fires, floods, severe frosts, and windstorms. Human activities can also disturb ecosystems. This happens when land is cleared for development, new kinds of plants and animals are brought into an area, or pollution is released into air and water.

Plant Succession When natural or human forces disturb a plant community, the community may be replaced by a different group of plants suited to the new conditions. The gradual process by which one group of plants replaces another is called **plant succession**.

To better understand plant succession, imagine an area just after a forest fire. The first plants to return to the area need plenty of sunshine. These plants hold the soil in place. They also provide shade for the seeds of other plants. Gradually, seeds from small trees and shrubs grow under the protection of the first plants. These new plants grow taller and begin to take more and more of the sunlight. Many of the smaller plants die. Later, taller trees in the area replace the shorter trees and shrubs that grew at first.

It is important to remember that plant communities are not permanent. The conditions they experience change over time. Some changes affect a whole region. For example, a region's climate may gradually become colder, drier, warmer, or wetter. Additional changes may occur if new plants are introduced to the community.

✓ **READING CHECK:** *Physical Systems* How do environments affect life, and how do they change?

Soils

In any discussion of plants, plant communities, or plant succession, it is important to know about the soils that support plant life. All soils are not the same. The type of soil in an area can contribute to the kinds of plants that can be grown there. It can also affect how well a plant grows. Plants need soil with minerals, water, and small air spaces if they are to survive and grow.

Soils contain decayed plant and animal matter, called **humus**. Soils rich in humus are fertile. This means they can support an abundance of plant life. Humus is formed by insects and bacteria that live in soil. They break down dead plants and animals and make the nutrients available to plant roots. Insects also make small air spaces as they move through soils. These air pockets contain moisture and gases that plant roots need for growth.

The processes that break down rocks to form soil take hundreds or even thousands of years. Over this long period of time soil tends to form layers. If you dig a deep hole, you can see these layers. Soils typically have three layers. The thickness of each layer depends on the conditions in a specific location. The top layer is called topsoil. It includes humus, insects, and plants. The layer beneath the surface soil is called the subsoil. Only the deep roots of some plants, mostly trees, reach the subsoil. Underneath this layer is broken rock that eventually breaks down into more soil. As the rock breaks down it adds minerals to the soil.

Soils can lose their fertility in several ways. Erosion by water or wind can sweep topsoil away. Nutrients can also be removed from soils by leaching. This occurs when rainfall dissolves nutrients in topsoil and washes them down into lower soil layers, out of reach of most plant roots.

✓ **READING CHECK:** *Physical Systems* What are the physical processes that produce fertile soil?

Soil Layers

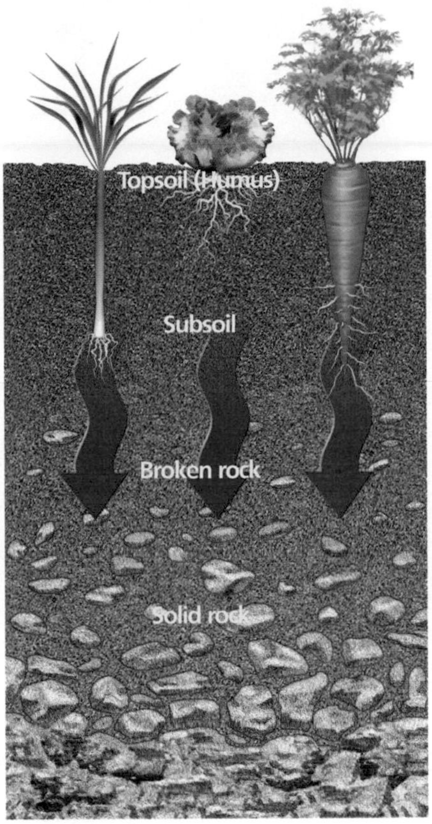
Topsoil (Humus)
Subsoil
Broken rock
Solid rock

▲ The three layers of soil are the topsoil, subsoil, and broken rock.
Interpreting the Visual Record What do you think has created the cracks in the rocky layer below the broken rock?

go.hrw.com **Homework Practice Online**
Keyword: SJ3 HP3

Section 3 Review

Define and explain: extinct, ecology, photosynthesis, food chain, nutrients, plant communities, ecosystem, plant succession, humus

Reading for the Main Idea

1. *Physical Systems* Why cannot all plants and animals live everywhere? Provide an example to illustrate your answer.
2. *Physical Systems* What makes up soil, and what produces fertile soil?

Critical Thinking

3. **Analyzing Information** What keeps tundra plant communities simple?
4. **Summarizing** How does plant succession occur?

Organizing What You Know

5. **Sequencing** Copy the following graphic organizer. Use it to describe a food chain.

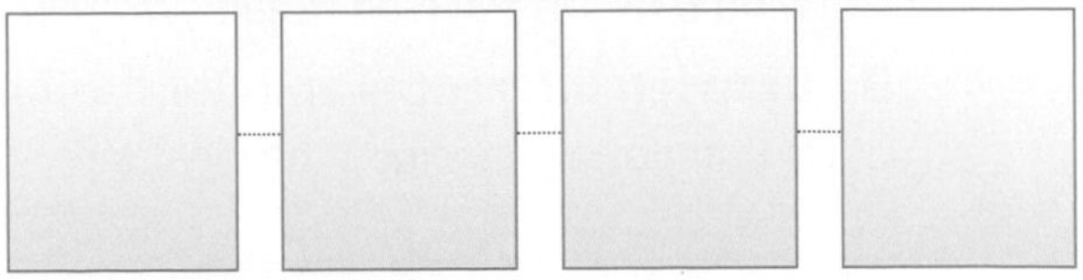

CHAPTER 3

Reviewing What You Know

Building Vocabulary

On a separate sheet of paper, write sentences to define each of the following words.

1. weather
2. climate
3. greenhouse effect
4. air pressure
5. front
6. currents
7. rain shadow
8. monsoon
9. arid
10. permafrost
11. extinct
12. ecology
13. nutrients
14. ecosystem
15. humus

Reviewing the Main Ideas

1. *The World in Spatial Terms* What are the major wind belts? Describe each.
2. *Physical Systems* How is the area around mountains affected by precipitation?
3. *The World in Spatial Terms* Into what main divisions can climate be grouped?
4. *Environment and Society* What do people do to change ecosystems?
5. *Physical Systems* What elements make up soil? How is fertile soil created?

Understanding Environment and Society

Tornadoes

Prepare an outline for a presentation on tornadoes. As you prepare your presentation from the outline, think about the following:

- How tornadoes are formed.
- How experts are able to forecast their occurrence more accurately.
- The safety precautions taken by people in tornado-prone areas.

Thinking Critically

1. **Finding the Main Idea** How does Earth store the Sun's energy?
2. **Analyzing Information** What effect do wind patterns have on ocean currents?
3. **Drawing Inferences and Conclusions** Why is it important to study the weather?
4. **Drawing Inferences and Conclusions** Why is it important to understand the concept of latitude when learning about Earth's many climates?
5. **Drawing Inferences and Conclusions** Why is it important for scientists to study soils?

Building Social Studies Skills

Map ACTIVITY

On a separate sheet of paper, match the letters on the map with their correct labels.

The following natural disasters are experienced in the United States:

- **hurricanes on the East Coast**
- **hurricanes on the Gulf Coast**
- **forest fires on the West Coast**
- **tornadoes in Texas, Oklahoma, Kansas, Nebraska, and South Dakota**

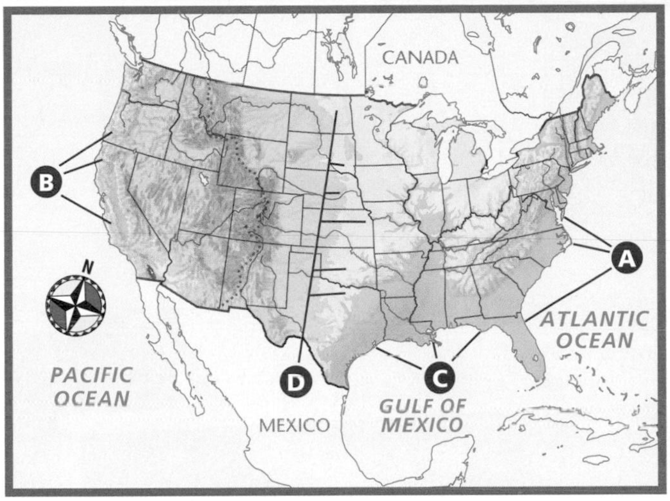

CANADA
B
A
N
ATLANTIC OCEAN
PACIFIC OCEAN
D
C
MEXICO
GULF OF MEXICO

Mental Mapping Skills ACTIVITY

Draw a freehand map of the globe. Draw lines to show the equator and low, middle, and high latitudes. Draw the continents in the appropriate areas.

WRITING ACTIVITY

After studying different climate regions, decide in which of the regions you would like to live. Write a journal entry describing what your life would be like in this particular area. Be sure to use standard grammar, spelling, sentence structure, and punctuation in your story.

Alternative Assessment

Portfolio ACTIVITY

Learning About Your Local Geography

Understanding Cause and Effect

Research your local weather patterns. Create a graph that shows how recent weather conditions have affected humans, plants, and animals in your part of the state.

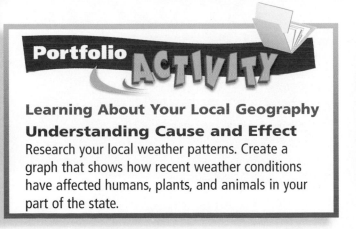

internet connect

Internet Activity: go.hrw.com
KEYWORD: SJ3 GT3

Choose a topic to explore online:

- Learn more about using weather maps.
- Follow El Niño, an ocean phenomenon that affects weather.
- Build a food web.

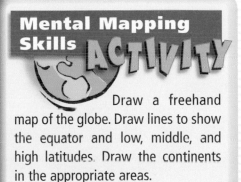

CHAPTER 4

Earth's Resources

Precious gems

Wind turbines

Valley in the Andes of Ecuador

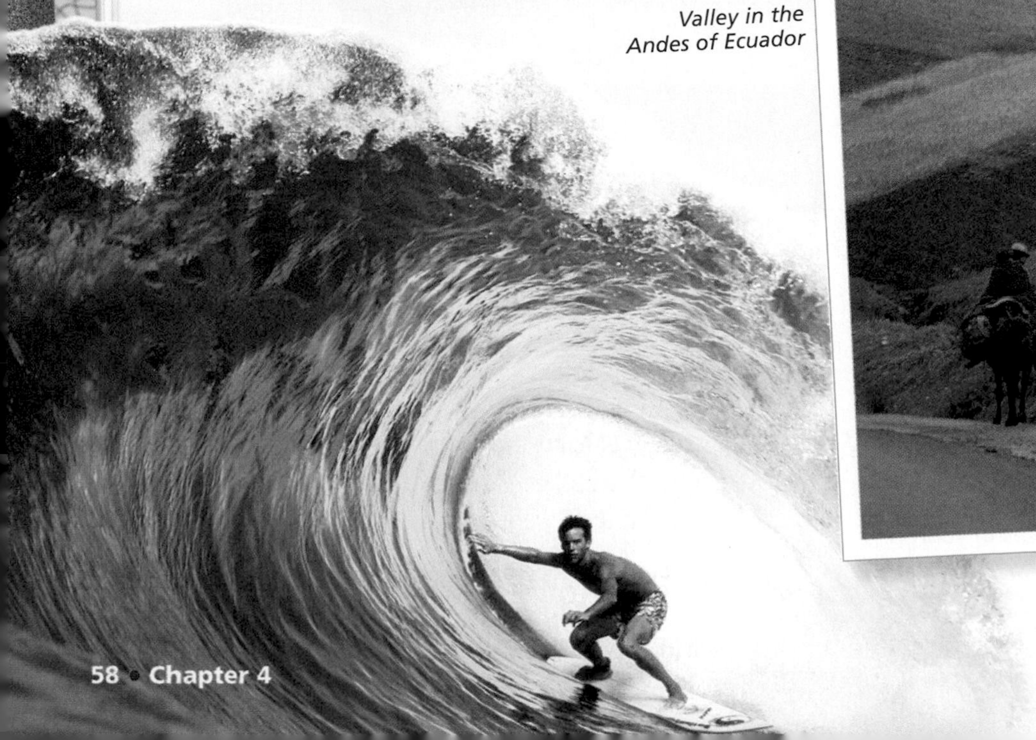

Section 1 Soil and Forests

Read to Discover

1. What physical processes produce fertile soil?
2. What processes threaten soil fertility?
3. Why are forests valuable resources, and how are they being protected?

Define

renewable resources
crop rotation
terraces
desertification
deforestation
reforestation

WHY IT MATTERS

Many people work to balance concerns about saving the rain forests with local economic needs. Use CNNfyi.com or other **current events** sources to learn more about these efforts. Record your findings in your journal.

Corn, a major food crop

Soil

Soil is one of the most important **renewable resources** on Earth. Renewable resources are those that can be replaced by Earth's natural processes.

Soil types vary depending on geographic factors. As you learned in Chapter 3, soil contains rock particles and humus. It also contains water and gases. Because soil types vary, some are better able to support plant life than others.

Soil Fertility Soil conservation—protecting the soil's ability to nourish plants—is one challenge facing farmers. Plants must take up nutrients like calcium, nitrogen, phosphorus, and potassium in order to grow. These essential nutrients may become used up if fields are always planted with the same crops. Farmers can add these nutrients to soils in the form of fertilizers, sometimes called plant food. The first fertilizers used were manures. Later, chemical fertilizers were used to increase yields.

Some farmers choose not to use chemical fertilizers. Others cannot afford to use them. They rely on other ways to keep up the soil's ability to produce. One such method is **crop rotation**. This is a system of growing different crops on the same land over a period of years.

On this farm, fields are planted with corn and alfalfa. Alfalfa is a valued crop because it replaces nutrients in the soil.

A row of poplar trees divides farmland near Aix-en-Provence, France.

Interpreting the Visual Record What effect will these trees have on erosion?

Belgium
Germany
France
Switzerland
Aix-en-Provence
Italy
Spain

Salty Soil Salt buildup is another threat to soil fertility. In dry climates farmers must irrigate their crops. They use well water or water brought by canals and ditches. Much of this water evaporates in the dry air. When the water evaporates, it leaves behind small amounts of salt. If too much salt builds up in the soil, crops cannot grow.

Erosion The problem of soil erosion is faced by farmers all over the world. Farmers have to work to keep soil from being washed away by rainfall. Soil can also be blown away by strong winds. To prevent soil loss, some farmers plant rows of trees to block the wind. Others who farm on steep hillsides build **terraces** into the slope. Terraces are horizontal ridges like stair steps. By slowing water movement the terraces stop the soil from being washed away. They also provide more space for farming.

Loss of Farmland The loss of farmland is a serious problem in many parts of the world. In some places farming has worn out the soil, and it can no longer grow crops. Livestock may then eat what few plants remain. Without plants to hold the soil in place, it may blow away. The long-term process of losing soil fertility and plant life is called **desertification**. Once this process begins, the desert can expand as people move on to better soils. They often repeat the destructive practices, damaging ever-larger areas.

Farmland is also lost when cities and suburbs expand into rural areas. Nearby farmers sell their land. The land is then used for housing or businesses, rather than for agriculture. This is happening in many poorer countries. It also happens in richer nations like the United States.

✓ **READING CHECK:** *Environment and Society* What physical processes help soil fertility, and what threatens it?

Our Amazing Planet

About 47,000 aspen trees in Utah share a root system and a set of genes. These trees are actually a single organism. These aspens cover 106 acres (43 hectares) and weigh at least 13 million pounds (5.9 million kg). Together they are probably the world's heaviest living thing.

Forests

Forests are renewable resources because new trees can be planted in a forest. If cared for properly, they will be available for future generations. Forests are important because they provide both people and wildlife with food and shelter. People depend on forests for a wide variety of products. Wood products include lumber, plywood, and shingles for building houses. Other wood-based manufactured products include cellophane, furniture, some plastics, and fibers such as rayon. Trees also supply fats, gums, medicines, nuts, oils, turpentine, waxes, and rubber. The forests are valuable not only for their products. People also use forests for recreational activities, such as camping and hiking.

▲ Villagers work on a reforestation project in Cameroon.

Deforestation The destruction or loss of forest area is called **deforestation**. It is happening in the rain forests of Africa, Asia, and Central and South America. People clear the land and use it for farming, industry, and housing. Pollution also causes deforestation.

Protecting Forests Many countries, including the United States, are trying to balance their economic needs regarding forests with conservation efforts. Since the late 1800s Congress has passed laws to protect and manage forest and wilderness areas. In addition to protecting forests, people can also plant trees in places where forests have been cut down. This replanting is called **reforestation**. In some cases the newly planted trees can be "harvested" again in a few years.

✓ **READING CHECK:** *Environment and Society* Why is preserving forests important, and how can people contribute to it?

go.hrw.com Homework Practice Online
Keyword: SJ3 HP4

Section 1 Review

Define and explain: renewable resources, crop rotation, terraces, desertification, deforestation, reforestation

Reading for the Main Idea

1. *Environment and Society* What physical processes produce fertile soil?
2. *Environment and Society* What do forests provide, and how can they be protected?

Critical Thinking

3. **Finding the Main Idea** Which two natural forces contribute to soil erosion? How can erosion be prevented?
4. **Drawing Inferences and Conclusions** Why is it important to manage forests?

Organizing What You Know

5. **Categorizing** Copy the following graphic organizer. Use it to discuss whether or not rain forests should be protected.

Reasons for . . .	Reasons against . . .

Section 2 Water and Air

Read to Discover

1. Why is water an important resource?
2. What threatens our supplies of freshwater, and how can we protect these supplies?
3. What are some problems caused by air pollution?

Define

semiarid
aqueducts
aquifers
desalinization
acid rain
global warming

A water tank

Why It Matters

Countries around the world have worked together to resolve problems regarding Earth's atmosphere. Use CNNfyi.com or other **current events** sources to learn about these efforts. Record your findings in your journal.

Water

Dry regions are found in many parts of the world, including the western United States. There are also **semiarid** regions—regions that receive a small amount of rain. Semiarid places are usually too dry for farming. However, these areas may be suitable for grazing animals.

Water Supply Many areas of high mountains receive heavy snowfall in the winter. When that snow melts, it forms rivers that flow from the mountains to neighboring regions. People in dry regions use various means to bring the water where it is needed for agricultural and other uses. They build canals, reservoirs, and **aqueducts**—artificial channels for carrying water.

Some places have water deep underground in **aquifers**. These are water-bearing layers of rock, sand, or gravel. Some are quite large. For example, the Ogallala Aquifer stretches across the Great Plains from Texas to South Dakota. People drill wells to reach the water in the aquifer.

People in dry coastal areas have access to plenty of salt water. However, they typically do not have enough freshwater. In Southwest Asia this situation is common. To create a supply of

As people make their homes in dry areas, they add to the demand for water.

Canada
United States
San Bernardino
Mexico

freshwater, people in these places have built machines that take the salt out of seawater. This process, known as **desalinization**, is expensive and takes a lot of energy. However, in some places, it is necessary.

Water Conservation In recent decades people have developed new ways to save water. Many factories now recycle water. Farmers are able to irrigate their crops more efficiently. Cities build water treatment plants to purify water that might otherwise be wasted. Some people in dry climates are using desert plants instead of grass for landscaping. This means that they do not need to water as often.

It is important for people in all climates to conserve water. Wasting water in one location could mean that less water is available for use in other places.

Canada
United States
Kansas
Mexico

Pivoting sprinklers irrigate these circular cornfields in Kansas.

Interpreting the Visual Record **Why might irrigation be necessary in these fields?**

Water Quality Industries and agriculture also affect the water supply. In many countries there are still places that cannot afford to build closed sewer systems. Some factories also operate without pollution controls because such controls would add a great deal of cost to operation.

Industrialized countries like the United States have water treatment plants and closed sewer systems. However, water can still be polluted when farmers use too much chemical fertilizer and pesticides. These chemicals can get into local streams. Waste from industries may also contain chemicals, metals, or oils that can pollute streams and rivers.

Rivers carry pollution to the oceans. The pollution can harm marine life such as fish and shellfish. Eating marine life from polluted waters can make people sick. So can drinking polluted water. Balancing industrial and agricultural needs with the need for clean water continues to be a challenge faced by many countries.

✓ **READING CHECK:** ***Environment and Society*** Why is water an important resource, and how does its availability affect people?

Air

Air is essential to life. Plants and animals need the gases in the air to live and grow.

Human activities can pollute the air and threaten the health of life on the planet. Burning fuels for heating, for transportation, and to power factories releases chemicals into the air. Particularly in large cities, these chemicals build up in the air. The chemicals create a mixture called smog.

Some cities have special problems with air pollution. Denver, Los Angeles, and Mexico City, for example, are located in bowl-shaped valleys that can trap air pollution. This pollution sometimes builds up to levels that are dangerous to people's health.

Heavy smog clouds the Los Angeles skyline.

Canada
United States
Los Angeles
Mexico

This satellite image of the Southern Hemisphere shows a thinning in the ozone layer in October 1979.

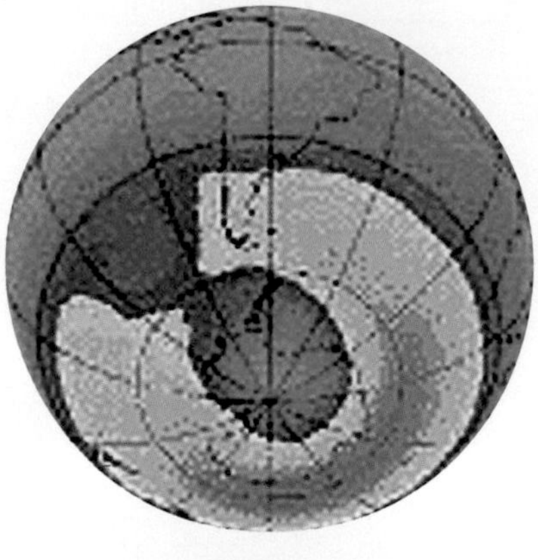

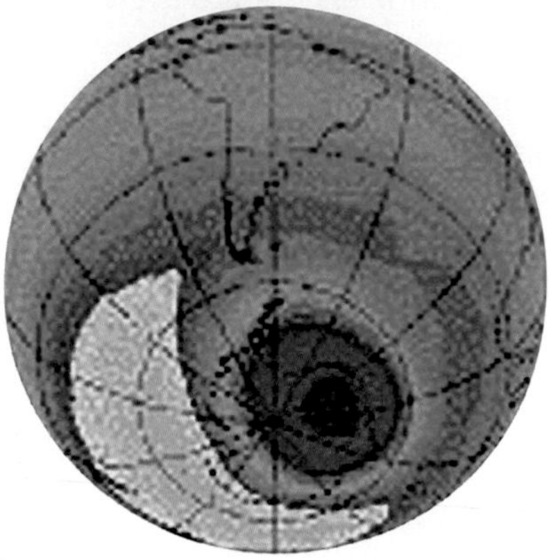

By October 1992 the thinning area, shown in purple, had grown much larger.

Acid Rain When air pollution combines with moisture in the air, it can form a mild acid. This can be similar in strength to vinegar. When it falls to the ground, this moisture is called **acid rain**. It can damage or kill trees. Acid rain can also kill fish.

Many countries have laws to limit pollution. However, pollution is an international problem. Winds can blow away air pollution, but the wind is only moving the pollution to another place. Pollution can pass from one country to another. It can even pass from one continent to another. Countries that limit their own pollution can still be affected by pollution from other countries.

Pollution and Climate Change Smog and acid rain are short-term effects of air pollution. Air pollution may also have long-term effects by changing conditions in Earth's atmosphere. Certain kinds of pollution damage the ozone in the upper atmosphere. This ozone layer protects living things by absorbing harmful ultraviolet light from the Sun. Damage to Earth's ozone layer may cause health problems in people. For example, it could lead to an increase in skin cancer.

Another concern is **global warming**—a slow increase in Earth's average temperature. The Sun constantly warms Earth's surface. The gases and water vapor in the atmosphere trap some of this heat. This helps keep Earth warm. Without the atmosphere, this heat would return to space. Evidence suggests that pollution causes the atmosphere to trap more heat. Over time this would make Earth warmer.

Scientists agree that Earth's climate has warmed during the last century. However, they disagree about exactly why. Some scientists say that temperatures have warmed because of air pollution caused by human activities, particularly the burning of fossil fuels. Others think warmer temperatures have resulted from natural causes. Scientists also disagree about what has caused the thinning of the ozone layer.

✓ **READING CHECK:** *Environment and Society* What are the different points of view about air pollution and climate change?

Section 2 Review

go.hrw.com Homework Practice Online
Keyword: SJ3 HP4

Define and explain: semiarid, aqueducts, aquifers, desalinization, acid rain, global warming

Reading for the Main Idea

1. *Environment and Society* How have people changed the environment to increase the water supply in drier areas?
2. *Environment and Society* How do people cause water pollution?
3. *Environment and Society* What kinds of human activities have polluted the air?

Critical Thinking

4. **Drawing Inferences and Conclusions** Why is desalinization rarely practiced?

Organizing What You Know

5. **Identifying Cause and Effect** Use this graphic organizer to explain air pollution.

Causes:
Air Pollution
Effects:

Section 3 Minerals

Read to Discover

1. What are minerals?
2. What are the two types of minerals?

Define

nonrenewable resources
minerals
metallic minerals
nonmetallic minerals

WHY IT MATTERS

Most minerals are dug from deep in the ground by miners. Use CNNfyi.com or other **current events** sources to learn about life as a miner. Record your findings in your journal.

Quartz crystals

Minerals

You have learned that renewable resources such as trees are always being produced. **Nonrenewable resources** are those that cannot be replaced by natural processes or are replaced very slowly.

Earth's crust is made up of substances called **minerals**. Minerals are an example of a nonrenewable resource. They provide us with many of the materials we need. More than 3,000 minerals have been identified, but fewer than 20 are common. Around 20 minerals make up most of Earth's crust. Minerals have four basic properties. First, they are inorganic. Inorganic substances are not made from living things or the remains of living things. Second, they occur naturally, rather than being manufactured like steel or brass. Third, minerals are solids in crystalline form, unlike petroleum or natural gas. Finally, minerals have a definite chemical composition or combination of elements. Although all minerals share these four properties, they can be very different from one another. Minerals are divided into two basic types: metallic and nonmetallic.

Metallic Minerals Metals, or **metallic minerals**, are shiny and can conduct heat and electricity. Metals are solids at normal room temperature. An exception is mercury, a metal that is liquid at room temperature.

Gold is one of the heaviest of all metals and is easily worked. For thousands of years people have highly valued gold. Precious metals are commonly made into jewelry and coins. Silver and platinum are other precious metals.

The Most-Common Elements in Earth's Crust

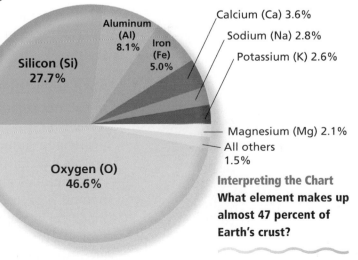

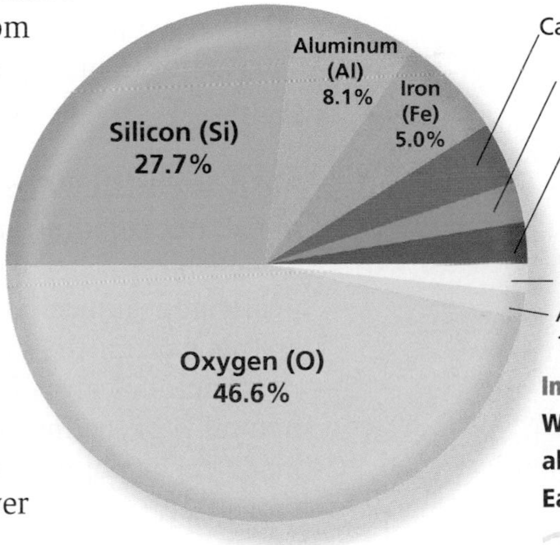
Silicon (Si) 27.7%
Aluminum (Al) 8.1%
Iron (Fe) 5.0%
Calcium (Ca) 3.6%
Sodium (Na) 2.8%
Potassium (K) 2.6%
Magnesium (Mg) 2.1%
All others 1.5%
Oxygen (O) 46.6%

Interpreting the Chart
What element makes up almost 47 percent of Earth's crust?

Connecting to Art

Art made from recycled products

Junk Art

Many Americans now make a habit of recycling. They put their cans, bottles, and newspapers by the curb for pickup or take them to recycling centers. However, some people do their recycling in a different way. They use their junk to create art.

Much recycled art is folk art. These objects have a practical purpose but are made with creativity and a sense of style. The making of folk art objects from junk is common in the world's poorer countries, where resources are scarce.

Some examples of recycled folk art include dust pans made from license plates (Mexico), jugs made from old tires (Morocco), briefcases made from flattened tin cans (Senegal), and a toy helicopter made from plastic containers and film canisters (Haiti). As scientist Stephen J. Gould has written, "In our world of material wealth, where so many broken items are thrown away rather than mended . . . we forget that most of the world fixes everything and discards nothing."

Americans do have a tradition of making recycled art, however. The Amish make quilts from old scraps of cloth. Other folk artists build whimsical figures out of bottle caps and wire. Some modern artists create sculptures from "found objects" like machine parts, bicycle wheels, and old signs. Junk art can even be fashion. One movie costume designer went to the Academy Awards ceremony wearing a dress made of credit cards!

Understanding What You Read

1. How do some societies turn junk into art?
2. Where is much recycled folk art made?

Iron is the cheapest metal. Iron can be combined with certain other minerals to make steel. Aluminum is another common metal. This lightweight metal is used in such items as soft drink cans and airplanes. We handle copper every time we pick up a penny.

Gold is a metallic mineral.

Nonmetallic Minerals Minerals that lack the characteristics of a metal are called **nonmetallic minerals**. These vary in their appearance. Quartz, a mineral often found in sand, looks glassy. Talc has a pearly appearance. Most nonmetallic minerals have a dull surface and are poor conductors of heat or electricity.

Diamonds are minerals made of pure carbon. They are the hardest naturally occurring substance. The brilliant look of diamonds has made them popular gems. Their hardness makes them valuable for industrial use. Other gemstones, like rubies, sapphires, and emeralds, are also nonmetallic minerals.

Mineral and Energy Resources in the United States

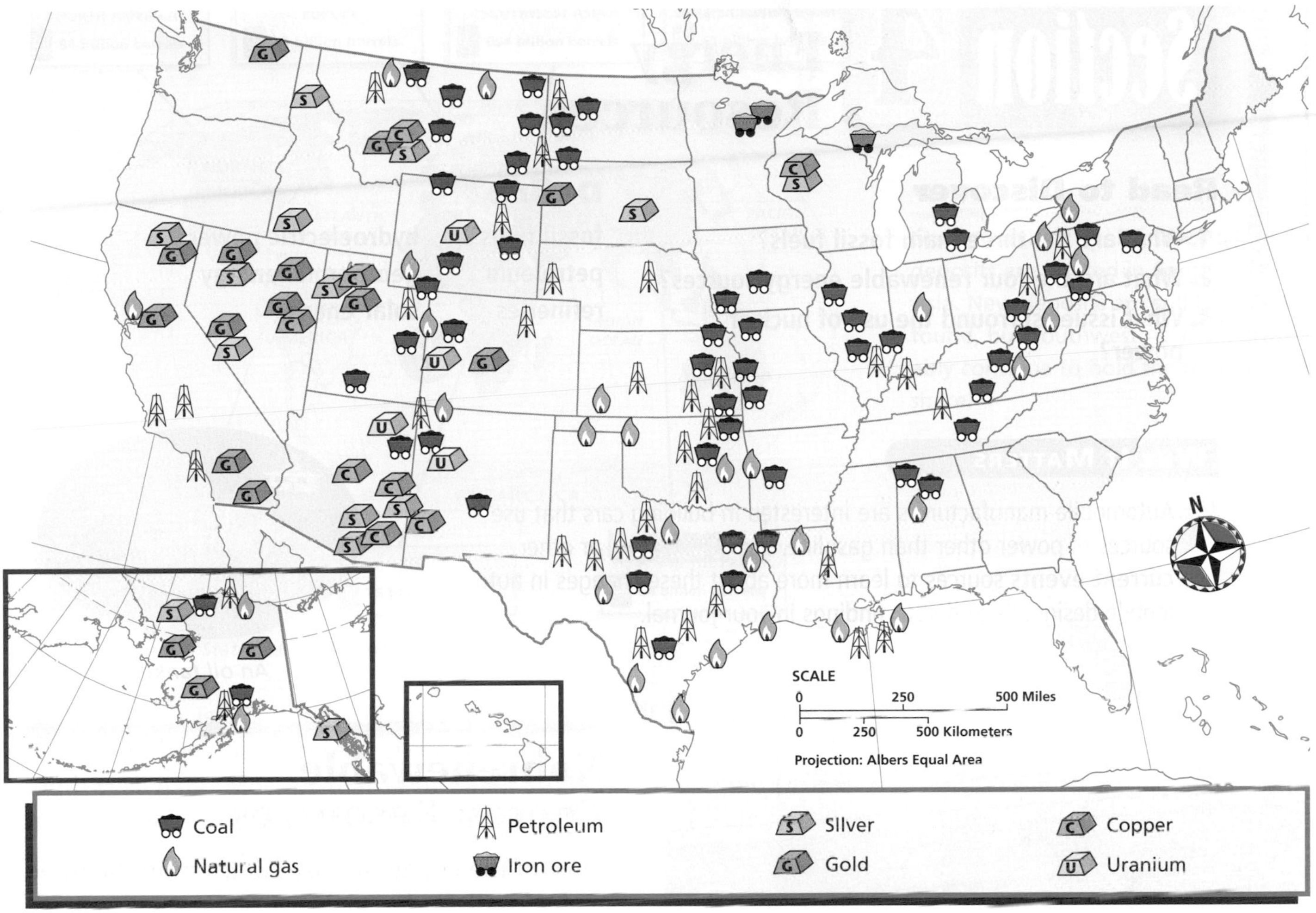
SCALE
0
250
500 Miles
0
250
500 Kilometers
Projection: Albers Equal Area
N
Coal
Natural gas
Petroleum
Iron ore
Silver
Gold
Copper
Uranium

Other mineral substances also have important uses. For example, people need salt to stay healthy. Sulfur is used in many ways, from making batteries to bleaching dried fruits. Graphite, another form of carbon, is used in making pencils.

✓ **READING CHECK:** *Physical Systems* What are the two types of minerals?

go.hrw.com **Homework Practice Online**
Keyword: SJ3 HP4

Section 3 Review

Define and explain: nonrenewable resources, minerals, metallic minerals, nonmetallic minerals

Reading for the Main Idea

1. *Physical Systems* What is a nonrenewable resource?
2. *Environment and Society* Why are minerals important? What is the difference between a metallic mineral and a nonmetallic mineral?

Critical Thinking

3. **Summarizing** How can minerals be used?
4. **Drawing Inferences and Conclusions** What makes gold such an important mineral?

Organizing What You Know

5. **Contrasting** Copy the following graphic organizer. Use it to contrast types of minerals.

Metallic minerals	Nonmetallic minerals

CHAPTER 4

Reviewing What You Know

Building Vocabulary

On a separate sheet of paper, write sentences to define each of the following words.

1. renewable resources
2. desertification
3. deforestation
4. reforestation
5. aquifers
6. acid rain
7. nonrenewable resources
8. fossil fuels
9. hydroelectric power
10. solar energy

Reviewing the Main Ideas

1. *Environment and Society* Why is fertile soil important, and how is it created?
2. *Environment and Society* What actions have people taken to increase their supply of water?
3. *Environment and Society* What are minerals, and why are they important to us?
4. *Environment and Society* For what are fossil fuels used?
5. *Environment and Society* What are the four most common renewable energy sources, and how is each used?

Understanding Environment and Society

Chernobyl

On April 26, 1986, a nuclear reactor exploded in Chernobyl. Radiation caused serious problems in Ukraine and Belarus, as well as in Eastern and Western Europe. Create an outline for a presentation based on information about the following:

- Conditions of the environment then and now.
- Preventive measures taken to prevent future accidents.

Thinking Critically

1. **Drawing Inferences and Conclusions** Why does the issue of use of rain forests cause such disagreement? What is happening to Earth's rain forests?
2. **Summarizing** What are the major causes of water and air pollution, and how does pollution affect life on this planet?
3. **Drawing Inferences and Conclusions** Why are minerals valued by society?
4. **Contrasting** How are metallic minerals different from nonmetallic minerals?
5. **Drawing Inferences and Conclusions** Why does the use of nuclear energy continue to be a debated topic?

Building Social Studies Skills

Map Activity

On a separate sheet of paper, match the letters on the map with their correct region. Then write the number of barrels of oil known to be located in each region.

- Africa
- Europe
- former Soviet Union
- South and Central America
- Southwest Asia

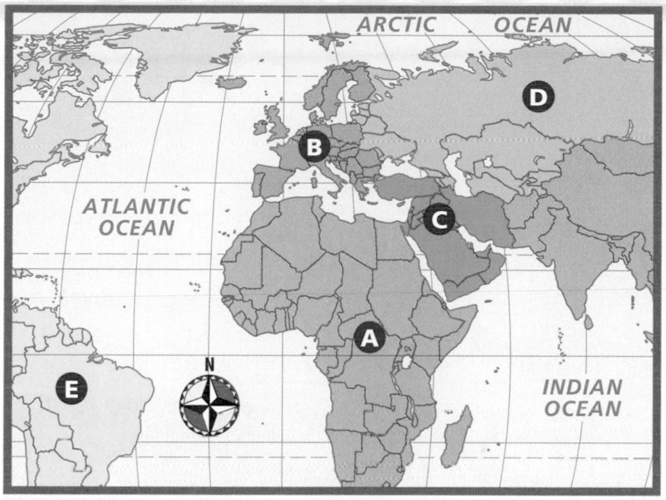

ARCTIC OCEAN
ATLANTIC OCEAN
INDIAN OCEAN
N
A
B
C
D
E

Mental Mapping Skills Activity

On a separate sheet of paper, draw a freehand map of the United States. Label areas that have copper. Compare this map with a physical map of the United States. What, if any, physical features are located in the same regions as copper deposits?

Writing Activity

Write a short paper explaining which mineral is most important to you. Justify your selection with facts you have learned. Be sure to use standard grammar, spelling, sentence structure, and punctuation.

Alternative Assessment

Portfolio Activity

Learning About Your Local Geography

Environmental Issues Study your local environment. What issues of preservation and use are important to the people of your community? How does your government handle these issues?

internet connect

Internet Activity: go.hrw.com
KEYWORD: SJ3 GT4

Choose a topic to explore Earth's resources:
- Trek through different kinds of forests.
- Investigate global warming.
- Make a recycling plan.

CHAPTER 5

The World's People

The Colosseum, Rome, Italy

1998 Olympic opening ceremony, Nagano, Japan

Easter Island, Chile

Section 1 Culture

Read to Discover

1. What is culture?
2. Why are cultural symbols important?
3. What influences how cultures develop?
4. How did agriculture affect the development of culture?

Define

culture
culture region
culture traits
ethnic groups
multicultural
race
acculturation
symbol
domestication
subsistence agriculture
commercial agriculture
civilization

WHY IT MATTERS

Throughout history, culture has both brought people together and created conflict among groups. Use CNNfyi.com or other **current events** sources to learn about cultural conflicts around the globe. Record your findings in your journal.

Flags at the South Pole

Aspects of Culture

The people of the world's approximately 200 countries speak hundreds of different languages. They may dress in different ways and eat different foods. However, all societies share certain basic institutions, including a government, an educational system, an economic system, and religious institutions. These vary from society to society and are often based on that society's **culture**. Culture is a learned system of shared beliefs and ways of doing things that guides a person's daily behavior. Most people around the world have a national culture shared with people of their own country. They may also have religious practices, beliefs, and language in common with people from other countries. Sometimes a culture dominates a particular region. This is known as a **culture region**. In a culture region, people may share certain **culture traits**, or elements of culture, such as dress, food, or religious beliefs. West Africa is an example of a culture region. Culture can also be based on a person's job or age. People can belong to more than one culture and can choose which to emphasize.

Race and Ethnic Groups Cultural groups share beliefs and practices learned from parents, grandparents, and ancestors. These groups are sometimes called **ethnic groups**. An ethnic group's shared culture may include its religion, history, language, holiday traditions, and special foods.

When people from different cultures live in the same country, the country is described as **multicultural** or multiethnic. Many countries

Thousands of Czechs and Germans settled in Texas in the mid-1800s. Dancers from central Texas perform a traditional Czech dance.

World Religions

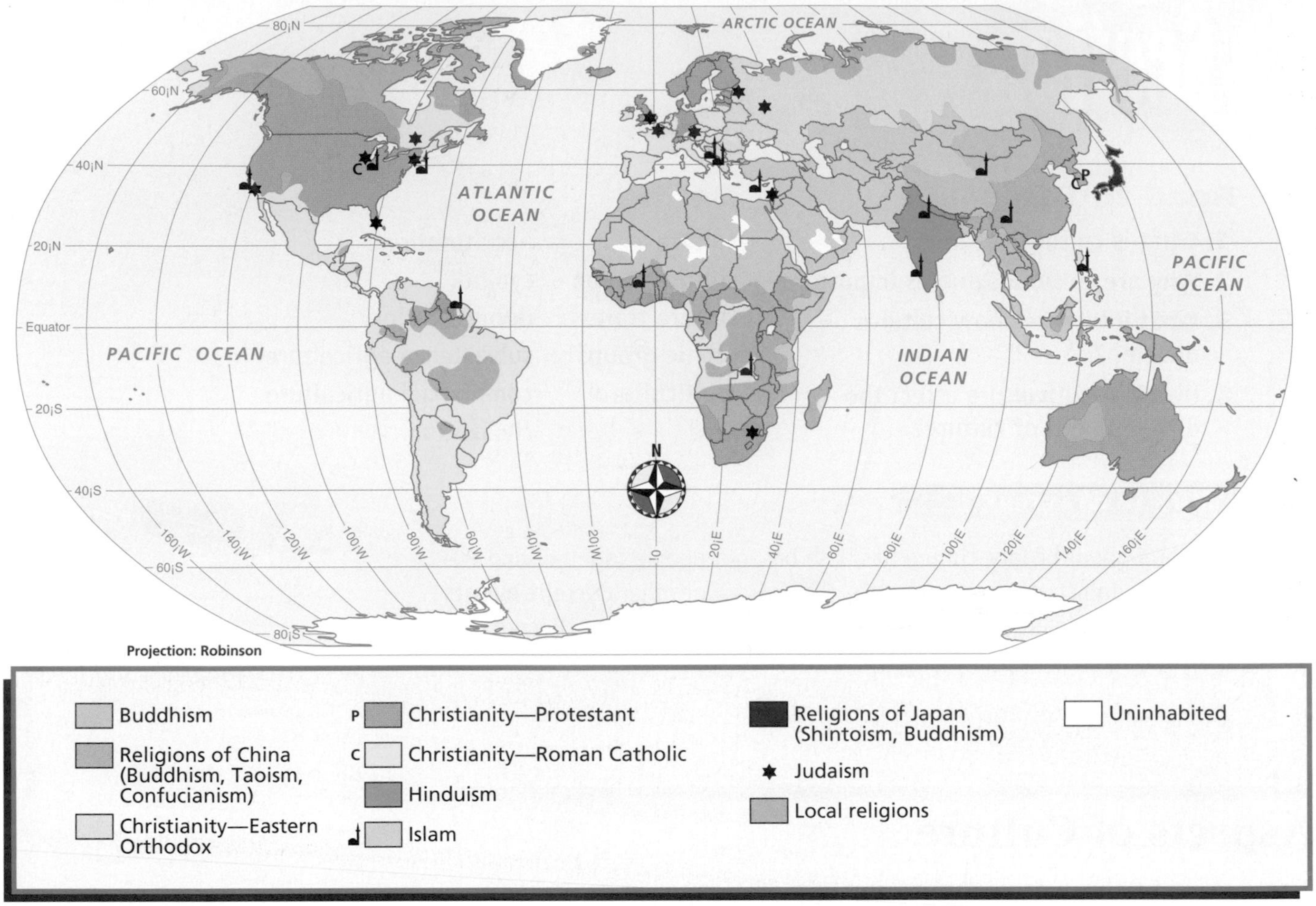
ARCTIC OCEAN
ATLANTIC OCEAN
PACIFIC OCEAN
PACIFIC OCEAN
INDIAN OCEAN
Equator
N
Projection: Robinson
Buddhism
Religions of China (Buddhism, Taoism, Confucianism)
Christianity—Eastern Orthodox
P Christianity—Protestant
C Christianity—Roman Catholic
Hinduism
Islam
Religions of Japan (Shintoism, Buddhism)
Judaism
Local religions
Uninhabited

Religion is one aspect of culture.

Canada
United States
Mexico
Miami
SUPE
FM10
MUSI

A disc jockey sits at the control board of a Miami radio station that plays Cuban music.

are multicultural. In some countries, such as Belgium, different ethnic groups have cooperated to form a united country. In other cases, such as in French-speaking Quebec, Canada, ethnic groups have frequently been in conflict. Sometimes, people from one ethnic group are spread over two or more countries. For example, Germans live in different European countries: Germany, Austria, and Czechoslovakia. The Kurds, who are a people with no country of their own, live mostly in Syria, Iran, Iraq, and Turkey.

Race is based on inherited physical or biological traits. It is sometimes confused with ethnic group. For example, the Hispanic ethnic group in the United States includes people who look quite different from each other. However, they share a common Spanish or Latin American heritage. As you know, people vary in physical appearance. Some of these differences have developed in response to climate factors like cold and sunlight. Because people have moved from region to region throughout history, these differences are not clear-cut. Each culture defines race in its own way, emphasizing particular biological and ethnic characteristics. An example can be seen in Rwanda, a country in East Africa. In this country, the Hutu and the Tutsi have carried on a bitter civil war. Although both are East African, each one considers itself different from the other. Their definition of race involves height and facial features. Around the world, people tend to identify races based on obvious physical traits. However, these definitions of race are based primarily on attitudes, not actual biological differences.

Cultural Change Cultures change over time. Humans invent new ways of doing things and spread these new ways to others. The spread of one culture's ways or beliefs to another culture is called diffusion. Diffusion may occur when people move from one place to another. The English language was once confined to England and parts of Scotland. It is now one of the world's most widely spoken languages. English originally spread because people from England founded colonies in other regions. More recently, as communication among cultures has increased, English has spread through English-language films and television programs. English has also become an international language of science and technology.

People sometimes may borrow aspects of another culture as the result of long-term contact with another society. This process is called **acculturation**. For example, people in one culture may adopt the religion of another. As a result, they might change other cultural practices to conform to the new religion. For example, farmers who become Muslim may quit raising pigs because Islam forbids eating pork.

✓ **READING CHECK:** *Human Systems* What is the definition of culture?

PRIMERICA
Travelers
YEN PING ASSOCIATION INC.
NAILS
PHỞ TỰ DO
VIETNAMESE RESTAURANT
AUTHENTIC VIETNAMESE CUISINE
Canada
United States
New York
Mexico

▲ Cultures mix in New York City's Chinatown.

Interpreting the Visual Record **Why might immigrants to a new country settle in the same neighborhood?**

internet connect

GO TO: go.hrw.com
KEYWORD: SJ3 CH5
FOR: Web sites about the world's people

Cultural Differences

A **symbol** is a sign that stands for something else. A symbol can be a word, a shape, a color, or a flag. People learn symbols from their culture. The sets of sounds of a language are symbols. These symbols have meaning for the people who speak that language. The same sound may mean something different to people who speak another language. The word *bad* means "evil" in English, "cool" to teenagers, and "bath" in German.

If you traveled to another country, you might notice immediately that people behave differently. For instance, they may speak a different language or wear different clothes. They might celebrate different holidays or salute a different flag. Symbols reflect the artistic, literary, and religious expressions of a society or culture. They also reflect that society's belief systems. Language, clothing, holidays, and flags are all symbols. Symbols help people communicate with each other and create a sense of belonging to a group.

✓ **READING CHECK:** *Human Systems* How do symbols reflect differences among societies and cultures?

Fans cheer for the U.S. Olympic soccer team.

Interpreting the Visual Record **Why do you think symbols such as flags create strong emotions?** ▼

▲ A couple prepares for a wedding ceremony in Kazakhstan.

Interpreting the Visual Record What aspects of these people's clothing indicate that they are dressed for a special event?

Development of a Culture

All people have the same basic needs for food, water, clothing, and shelter. People everywhere live in families and mark important family changes together. They usually have rituals or traditions that go with the birth of a baby, the wedding of a couple, or the death of a grandparent. All human societies need to deal with natural disasters. They must also deal with people who break the rules of behavior. However, people in different places meet these needs in unique ways. They eat different foods, build different kinds of houses, and form families in different ways. They have different rules of behavior. Two important factors that influence the way people meet basic needs are their history and environment.

History Culture is shaped by history. A region's people may have been conquered by the same outsiders. They may have adopted the same religion. They may have come from the same area and may share a common language. However, historical events may have affected some parts of a region but not others. For example, in North America French colonists brought their culture to Louisiana and Canada. However, they did not have a major influence on the Middle Atlantic region of the United States.

Cultures also shape history by influencing the way people respond to the same historical forces. Nigeria, India, and Australia were all colonized by the British. Today each nation still uses elements of the British legal system, but with important differences.

Environment The environment of a region can influence the development of culture. For example, in Egypt the Nile River is central to people's lives. The ancient Egyptians saw the fertile soils brought by the flooding of the Nile as the work of the gods. Beliefs in mountain spirits were important in many mountainous regions of the world. These areas include Tibet, Japan, and the Andes of South America.

The layout of Marrakech, Morocco, is typical of many North African cities.

Interpreting the Visual Record How are the streets and houses of Marrakech different from those in your community? ▼

Spain
Morocco
Marrakech
Algeria

Culture also determines how people use and shape their landscape. For example, city plans are cultural. Cities in Spain and its former colonies are organized around a central plaza, or square, with a church and a courthouse. On the other hand, Chinese cities are oriented to the four compass points. American cities often follow a rectangular grid plan. Many French city streets radiate out from a central core.

✓ **READING CHECK:** *Human Systems* What are some ways in which culture traits spread?

Development of Agriculture

For most of human history people ate only wild plants and animals. When the food ran out in one place, they migrated, or moved to another place. Very few people still live this way today. Thousands of years ago, humans began to help their favorite wild plant foods to grow. They probably cleared the land around their campsites and dumped seeds or fruits in piles of refuse. Plants took root and grew. People may also have dug water holes to encourage wild cattle to come and drink. People began cultivating the largest plants and breeding the tamest animals. Gradually, the wild plants and animals changed. They became dependent on people. This process is called **domestication**. A domesticated species has changed its form and behavior so much that it depends on people to survive. Domestic sheep can no longer leap from rock to rock like their wild ancestors. However, the wool of domestic sheep is more useful to humans. It can be combed and twisted into yarn.

▲ This ancient Egyptian wall painting shows domesticated cattle.

Interpreting the Visual Record Can you name other kinds of domesticated animals?

Domestication happened in many parts of the world. In Peru llamas and potatoes were domesticated. People in ancient Mexico and Central America domesticated corn, beans, squash, tomatoes, and hot peppers. None of these foods was grown in Europe, Asia, or Africa before the time of Christopher Columbus's voyages to the Americas. Meanwhile, Africans had domesticated sorghum and a kind of rice. Cattle, sheep, and goats were probably first raised in Southwest Asia. Wheat and rye were first domesticated in Central Asia. The horse was also domesticated there. These domesticated plants and animals were unknown in the Americas before the time of Columbus.

Our Amazing Planet

Thousands of years ago, domesticated dogs came with humans across the Bering Strait into North America. A breed called the Carolina dog may be descended almost unchanged from those dogs. The reddish yellow, short-haired breed also appears to be closely related to Australian dingoes.

Agriculture and Environment Agriculture changed the landscape. To make room for growing food, people cut down forests. They also built fences, dug irrigation canals, and terraced hillsides. Governments were created to direct the labor needed for these large projects. Governments also defended against outsiders and helped people resolve problems. People could now grow enough food for a whole year. Therefore, they stopped migrating and built permanent settlements.

Types of Agriculture Some farmers grow just enough food to provide for themselves and their own families. This type of farming is called **subsistence agriculture**. In the wealthier countries of the world, a small number of farmers can produce food for everyone. Each farm is large and may grow only one product. This type of farming is called **commercial agriculture**. In this system companies rather than individuals or families may own the farms.

Agriculture and Civilization Agriculture enabled farmers to produce a surplus of food—more than they could eat themselves. A few people could make things like pottery jars instead of farming. They traded or sold their products for food. With more food a family could feed more children. As a result, populations began to grow. More people became involved in trading and manufacturing. Traders and craftspeople began to live in central market towns. Some towns grew into cities, where many people lived and carried out even more specialized tasks. For example, cities often supported priests and religious officials. They were responsible for organizing and carrying out religious ceremonies. When a culture becomes highly complex, we sometimes call it a **civilization**.

✓ **READING CHECK:** *Environment and Society* In what ways did agriculture affect culture?

go.hrw.com **Homework Practice Online**
Keyword: SJ3 HP5

Section 1 Review

Define and explain: culture, culture region, culture trait, ethnic groups, multicultural, race, acculturation, symbol, domestication, subsistence agriculture, commercial agriculture, civilization

Reading for the Main Idea

1. *Human Systems* How can an individual belong to more than one cultural group?
2. *Human Systems* What institutions are basic to all societies?

Critical Thinking

3. **Drawing Inferences and Conclusions** In what ways do history and environment influence or shape a culture? What examples can you find in the text that explain this relationship?
4. **Analyzing Information** What is the relationship between the development of agriculture and culture?

Organizing What You Know

5. **Summarizing** Copy the following graphic organizer. Use it to describe culture by listing shared beliefs and practices.

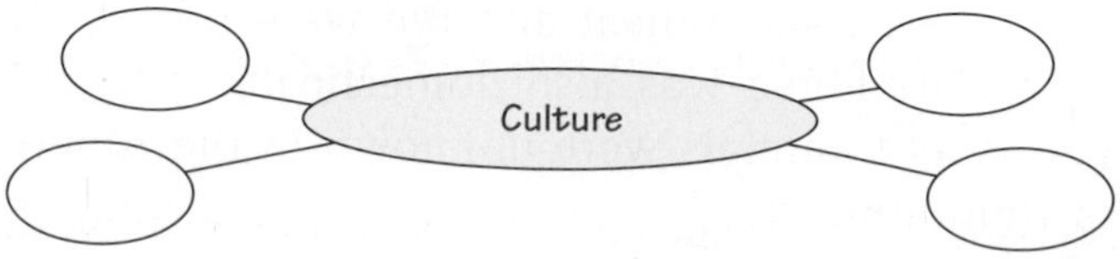
Culture

Section 2 Population, Economy, and Government

Read to Discover

1. Why does population density vary, and how has the world's population changed?
2. How do geographers describe and measure economies?
3. What are the different types of economic systems?
4. How do governments differ?

Define

primary industries
secondary industries
tertiary industries
quaternary industries
gross national product
gross domestic product
developed countries
developing countries
free enterprise
factors of production
entrepreneurs
market economy
command economy
traditional economy
democracy
unlimited government
limited government

WHY IT MATTERS

Human population has increased dramatically in the past 200 years. Use CNNfyi.com or other **current events** sources to find current projections for global or U.S. populations. Record your findings in your journal.

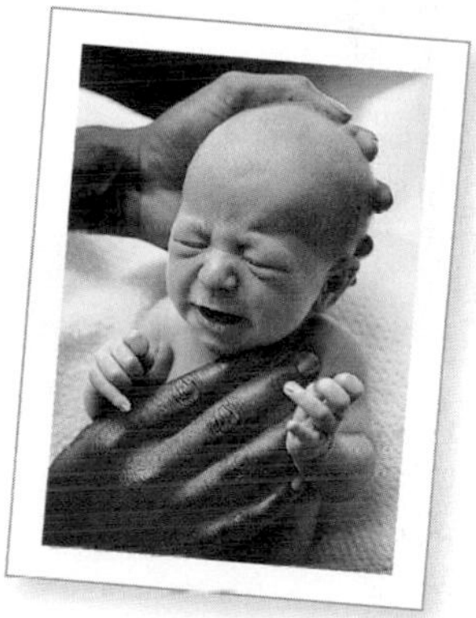

Newborn baby

Calculating Population Density

The branch of geography that studies human populations is called demography. Geographers who study it are called demographers. They look at such things as population size, density, and age trends. Some countries are very crowded. Others are only thinly populated. Demographers measure population density by dividing a country's population by its area. The area is stated in either square miles or square kilometers. For example, the United States has 74 people for every square mile (29/sq km). Australia has just 6 people per square mile (2.3/sq km). Japan has 869 people per square mile (336/sq km), and Argentina has 35 people per square mile (14/sq km).

These densities include all of the land in a country. However, people may not be able to live on some land. Rugged mountains, deserts, frozen lands, and other similar places usually have very few people. Instead, people tend to live in areas where the land can be farmed. Major cities tend to be located in these same regions of dense population.

✓ **READING CHECK:** *Human Systems* What is population density?

Shoppers crowd a street in Tokyo, Japan.

China
Russia
North Korea
South Korea
Tokyo
Japan

Differences in Population Density

Looking at this book's maps of world population densities allows us to make generalizations. Much of eastern and southern Asia is very densely populated. There are dense populations in Western Europe and in eastern areas of North America. There are also places with very low population densities. Canada, Australia, and Siberia have large areas where few people live. The same is true for the Sahara Desert. Parts of Asia, South America, and Africa also have low population densities.

Heavily populated areas attract large numbers of people for different reasons. Some places have been densely populated for thousands of years. Examples include the Nile River valley in Egypt and the Huang River valley in China. These places have fertile soil, a steady source of water, and a good growing climate. These factors allow people to farm successfully. People are also drawn to cities. The movement of people from farms to cities is called urbanization. In many countries people move to cities when they cannot find work in rural areas. In recent years this movement has helped create huge cities. Mexico City, Mexico; São Paulo, Brazil; and Lagos, Nigeria, are among these giant cities. Some European cities experienced similar rapid growth when they industrialized in the 1800s. During that period people left farms to come to the cities to work in factories.

✓ **READING CHECK:** *Human Systems* Why does population density vary?

World Population Growth

Population in billions
12
11
10
9
8
7
6
5
4
3
2
1
0
A.D. 1
100
200
300
400
500
600
700
800
900
1000
1100
1200
1300
1400
1500
1600
1700
1800
1900
2000
2100

Source: U.S. Census

Interpreting the Chart **Approximately when did world population growth begin to increase significantly?**

▲

Population Growth

Researchers estimate that about 10,000 years ago the world's entire human population was less than 10 million. The annual number of births was roughly the same as the annual number of deaths.

After people made the shift from hunting and gathering to farming, more food was available. People began to live longer and have more children. The world's population grew. About 2,000 years ago, the world had some 200 million people. By A.D. 1650 the world's population had grown to about 500 million. By 1850 there were some 1 billion people. Better health care and food supplies helped more babies survive into adulthood and have children. By 1930 there were 2 billion people on Earth. Just 45 years later that number had doubled to 4 billion. In 1999 Earth's population reached 6 billion. By the year 2025 the world's population could grow to about 9 billion.

Births add to a country's population. Deaths subtract from it. The number of births per 1,000 people in a year is called the birthrate. Similarly, the death rate is the annual number of deaths per 1,000 people. The birthrate minus the death rate equals the rate of natural increase. This number is expressed as a percentage. A country's population changes when people enter or leave the country.

✓ **READING CHECK:** *Human Systems* What is the rate of natural increase?

Economic Activity

All of the activities that people do to earn a living are part of a system called the economy. This includes people going to work, making things, selling things, buying things, and trading services. Economics is the study of the production, distribution, and use of goods and services.

Types of Economic Activities Geographers divide economic activities into primary, secondary, tertiary, and quaternary industries. **Primary industries** are activities that directly involve natural resources or raw materials. These industries include farming, mining, and cutting trees.

The products of primary industries often have to go through several stages before people can use them. **Secondary industries** change the raw materials created by primary activities into finished products. For example, the sawmill that turns a tree into lumber is a secondary industry.

Tertiary industries handle goods that are ready to be sold to consumers. The stores that sell products are included in this group. The trucks and trains that move products to stores are part of this group. Banks, insurance companies, and government agencies are also considered tertiary industries.

The fourth part of the economy is known as **quaternary industries**. People in these industries have specialized skills. They work mostly with information instead of goods. Researchers, managers, and administrators fall into this category.

A

B

C

D

A **Primary industry:** A dairy farmer feeds his cows.
B **Secondary industry:** Cheese is prepared in a factory.
C **Tertiary industry:** A grocer is selling cheese to a consumer.
D **Quaternary industry:** A technician inspects dairy products in a lab.

Economic Indicators A common means of measuring a country's economy is the **gross national product** (GNP). The GNP is the value of all goods and services that a country produces in one year. It includes goods and services made by factories owned by that country's citizens but located in foreign countries. Most geographers use **gross domestic product** (GDP) instead of GNP. GDP includes only those goods and services produced within a country. GDP divided by the country's population is called per capita GDP. This figure shows individual purchasing power and is useful for comparing levels of economic development.

✓ **READING CHECK:** *Human Systems* What are primary, secondary, tertiary, and quaternary industries?

CHAPTER 5 Reviewing What You Know

Building Vocabulary

On a separate sheet of paper, write sentences to define each of the following words.

1. culture
2. ethnic groups
3. multicultural
4. acculturation
5. symbol
6. domestication
7. subsistence agriculture
8. civilization
9. limited government
10. entrepreneurs
11. command economy
12. market economy
13. factors of production
14. free enterprise
15. carrying capacity

Reviewing the Main Ideas

1. *Human Systems* What is culture, and why should people study it?
2. *Environment and Society* What is the difference between subsistence and commercial agriculture?
3. *Human Systems* What are some of the different ways countries organize governments?
4. *Human Systems* Why are telecommunications devices useful as economic indicators?
5. *Environment and Society* How do population growth rates affect resources?

Understanding Environment and Society

Domestication

Do you know how, when, and why people first domesticated dogs, cats, pigs, and hawks? What about oranges? Pick a domesticated plant or animal to research. As you prepare your presentation consider the following:

- Where the crop or animal was first domesticated.
- Differences between it and its wild ancestors.
- Humans spreading it to new areas.

Thinking Critically

1. **Drawing Inferences and Conclusions** Why are ethnic groups sometimes confused with races?
2. **Making Generalizations and Predictions** Over the past 2,000 years, how many times has world population doubled? By when is it projected to double again? What might be the effect of this increase?
3. **Finding the Main Idea** What are the four basic divisions of industry? Give examples.
4. **Summarizing** What are the three economic systems, and what are the benefits of the U.S. free-enterprise system?
5. **Making Generalizations and Predictions** Do you think Earth has a carrying capacity for its human population? Why or why not?
6. **Summarizing** Explain unlimited and limited government. Give examples of each.

Building Social Studies Skills

Map Activity

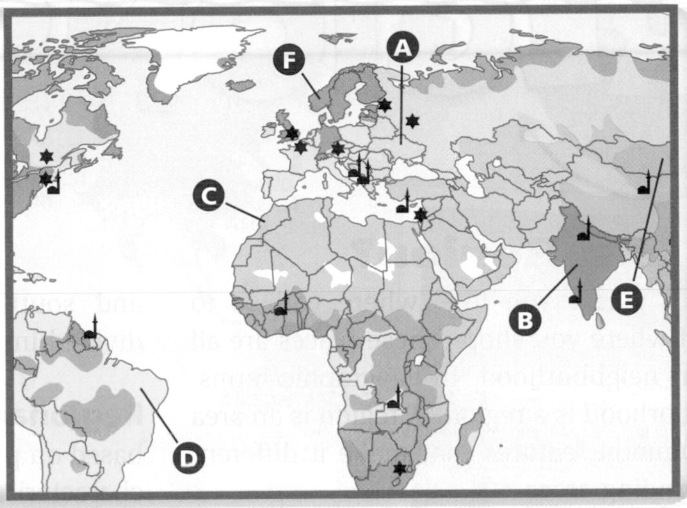

A
B
C
D
E
F

On a separate sheet of paper, match the letters on the map with their correct labels.

- Buddhism
- Christianity—Eastern Orthodox
- Christianity—Protestant
- Christianity—Roman Catholic
- Hinduism
- Islam

Mental Mapping Skills Activity

Draw a map of the world and label Japan, Australia, the United Kingdom, and Argentina. Based on your knowledge of climates, population density, and resources, which of these countries probably depend on imported food? Which ones probably export food? Express this information on your map.

Writing Activity

Study the economy of your local community. Has the local economy grown or declined since 1985? Why? Predict how your local area could change economically during the next 10 years. Be sure to use standard grammar, spelling, sentence structure, and punctuation.

Alternative Assessment

Portfolio Activity

Learning About Your Local Geography

Factors of Production Recall the discussion of the factors of production. Create a model showing how these factors influence the economy of your community.

internet connect

go.hrw.com

Internet Activity: go.hrw.com
KEYWORD: SJ3 GT5

Choose a topic to explore online:

- Visit famous buildings and monuments around the world.
- Compare facts about life in different countries.
- Examine world population growth.

UNIT 2

Chapter 6
3,700,000 B.C–A.D. 476
The Ancient World

Gold funeral mask of Pharaoh Tutankhamen

Greek vase showing potters at work

Ancient Chinese art

2,500,000 B.C. | 500,000 B.C. | 8000 B.C. | 4000 B.C. | 1 B.C. | A.D. 500

2,500,000 B.C.
Science and Technology
The first stone tools appear.

c. 400,000 B.C.–100,000 B.C.
Global Events
The first *Homo sapiens* appear.

c. 8000 B.C.
Science and Technology
Agricultural societies develop in Mesopotamia.

c. 3200 B.C.
Politics
Upper and Lower Egypt are united.

c. 2500 B.C.
Global Events
The Harappan civilization appears in the Indus River valley.

c. Late 1000s B.C.
Politics
The Zhou dynasty begins in China.

c. 800s B.C.–700s B.C.
Politics
Sparta and Athens develop into powerful city-states.

A.D. 476
Global Events
The Western Roman Empire falls.

The Acropolis, Athens

Chapter 7
A.D. 432–1800
The World in Transition

Viking carving of a lion's head

Crusaders at the gates of Jerusalem

800
Politics
Charlemagne is crowned Emperor of the Romans by Pope Leo III.

800–900s
Politics
The Vikings invade Western Europe.

1096
Global Events
The first Crusade begins.

1271
Global Events
Marco Polo begins his trip to China.

1347–1351
Global Events
The Black Death sweeps through Europe.

c. 1450
Science and Technology
Johannes Gutenberg invents the movable type printing press.

1492
Global Events
Christopher Columbus makes his first voyage to America.

1517
Daily Life
Martin Luther posts his 95 theses.

1632
Science and Technology
Galileo proves that Earth revolves around the Sun.

1762
Politics
Catherine the Great becomes Empress of Russia.

1000 | 1200 | 1400 | 1600 | 1800

Catherine the Great, empress of Russia

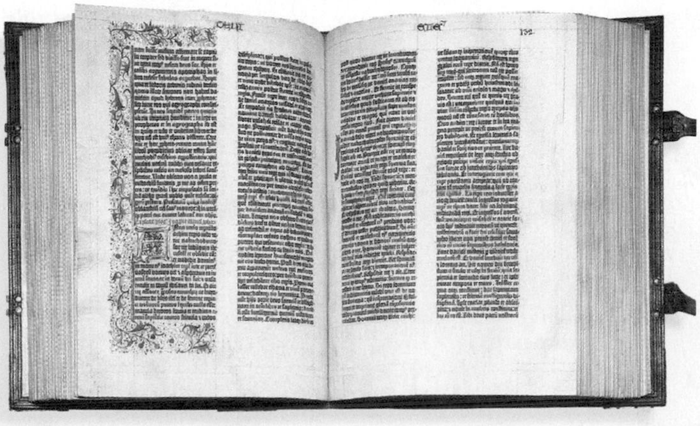

A Gutenberg Bible

Galileo Galilei

UNIT 2

Chapters 8 & 9
1550–Present
The Modern World

M
W
R

Plate celebrating the coronation of William III and Mary II

Women marching on Versailles during the French Revolution

1550 | **1650** | **1700** | **1750** | **1800**

1558
Politics
Elizabeth I becomes queen of England.

1594-95
The Arts
William Shakespeare writes *Romeo and Juliet*.

1687
Science and Technology
Isaac Newton publishes his most famous work, *Principia*.

1688
Politics
The Glorious Revolution occurs in England.

1737
Science and Technology
Samuel F. B. Morse invents the telegraph.

1763
Global Events
The Seven Years' War ends.

1769
Science and Technology
James Watt builds the first steam engine.

1776
Politics
The American colonies declare independence from Great Britain.

1789
Politics
The United States Constitution is ratified.

1789
Politics
The French Revolution begins.

Re-creation of Shakespeare's Globe Theatre

William Shakespeare

Early steam locomotive

Glider flown by the Wright brothers

Russian President Boris Yeltsin (center)

1850
1900
1950
2000

1815
Global Events
Napoléon is defeated at Waterloo.

1865
Daily Life
Slavery is abolished in the United States at the end of the Civil War

1903
Science and Technology
The Wright brothers build the first working airplane.

1917
Global Events
The United States enters World War I.

1917
Politics
The Russian Revolution is fought.

1929
Daily Life
The Great Depression begins.

1945
Global Events
World War II ends.

1957
Science and Technology
The first artificial satellite in space, *Sputnik,* is launched.

1989
Global Events
The Soviet Union collapses.

2001
Global Events
Terrorists attack the World Trade Center in New York and the Pentagon in Washington, D.C.

World War I

September 11 interfaith memorial

Emergence of Agriculture

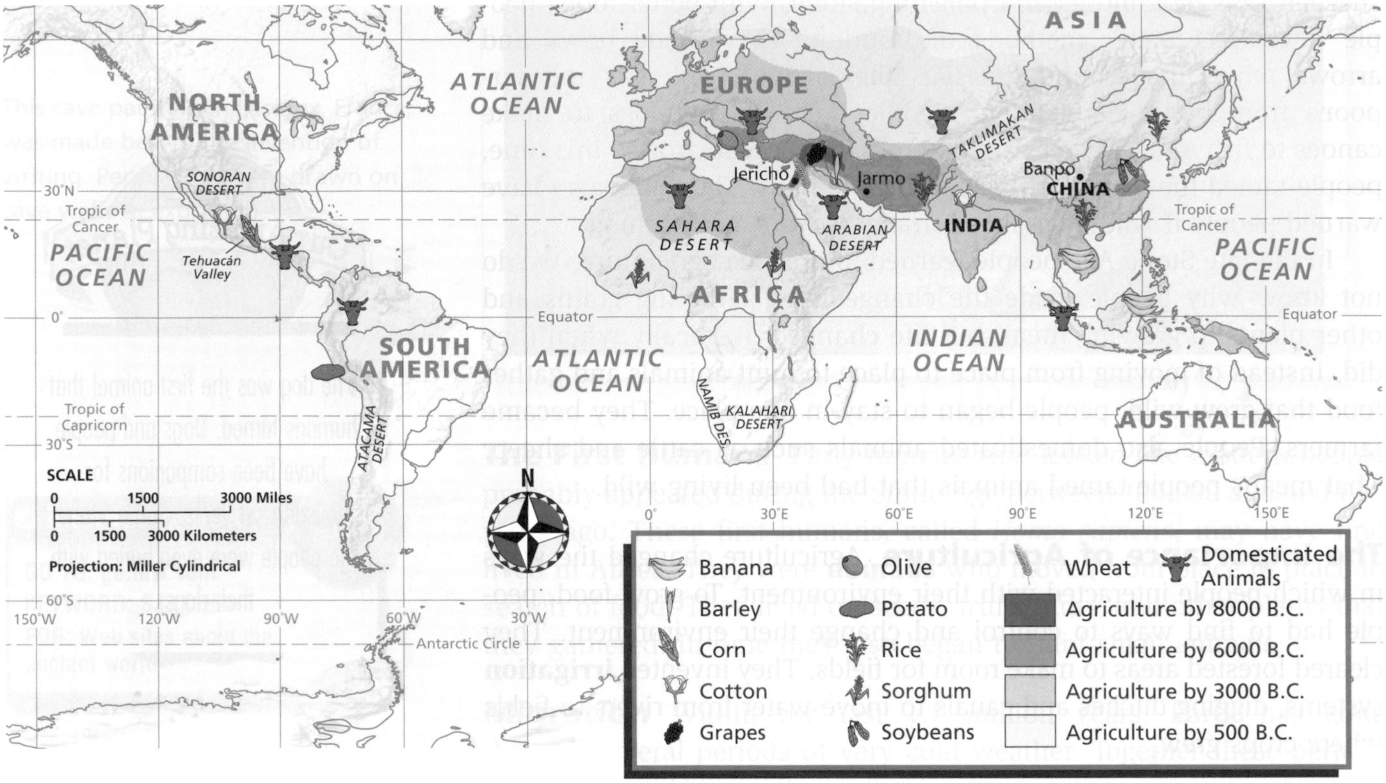

NORTH AMERICA
SONORAN DESERT
Tehuacán Valley
PACIFIC OCEAN
ATLANTIC OCEAN
SOUTH AMERICA
ATACAMA DESERT
EUROPE
Jericho
Jarmo
SAHARA DESERT
ARABIAN DESERT
AFRICA
NAMIB DES.
KALAHARI DESERT
ASIA
TAKLIMAKAN DESERT
Banpo
CHINA
INDIA
INDIAN OCEAN
AUSTRALIA
Tropic of Cancer
Tropic of Capricorn
Equator
Antarctic Circle
SCALE
0 1500 3000 Miles
0 1500 3000 Kilometers
Projection: Miller Cylindrical
N
Banana
Barley
Corn
Cotton
Grapes
Olive
Potato
Rice
Sorghum
Soybeans
Wheat
Domesticated Animals
Agriculture by 8000 B.C.
Agriculture by 6000 B.C.
Agriculture by 3000 B.C.
Agriculture by 500 B.C.

The practice of agriculture spread over a period of thousands of years.

Interpreting the Map Where was agriculture first developed?

Because of the ways it changed people's lives, the development of agriculture was enormously important. In fact, learning how to grow food prepared the way for a new chapter in the story of human life—the story of civilization.

✓ **READING CHECK:** *Summarizing* How did agriculture change the ways in which people lived?

People made stone and ivory tools during the Stone Age.

The Beginnings of Civilization

Historians describe civilization as having four basic characteristics. First, a civilization is made up of people who live in an organized society, not simply as a loosely connected group. Second, people are able to produce more food than they need to survive. Third, they live in towns or cities with some form of government. And fourth, they practice **division of labor**. This means that each person performs a specific job.

Agriculture and Civilization How did the development of agriculture affect the growth of civilization? Before agriculture, people spent almost all of their time simply finding food. When people were able to grow their own food, they could produce more than they needed to survive. This meant that some people did not have to grow food at all. They had time to develop other skills, such as making pottery, cloth, and other goods. These people could trade the goods they produced and the services they offered for food or other needs.

Trade Once people began to trade, they had to deal with each other in more complex ways than before. Disagreements arose, creating a need for laws. Governments and priesthoods developed to fill that need. Governments made laws and saw that they were obeyed. Religion taught people what they should and should not do.

When people traded, they traveled to places where their goods were wanted and where they could get the things they wanted and needed. Some places where people exchanged goods grew into cities. In these cities, people traded not only goods but also ideas. Over time people built palaces, temples, and other public buildings in their cities.

The Development of Writing Trade, like business today, required people to keep records. Written languages may have developed from this need. The invention of written language began about 3,000 B.C. Farmers also needed a method to keep track of seasonal cycles. They had to know when it was time to plant new crops and when they could expect rain. Over time, they developed calendars.

Once they had writing and calendars, people began to keep written records of events. **History**, which is the written record of human civilization, had begun.

✓ READING CHECK: *Identifying Cause and Effect* How did trade lead to the development of writing?

Development of Writing: One Theory

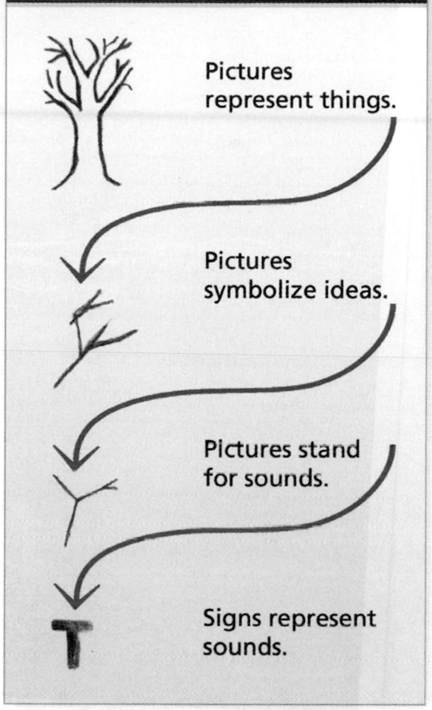

Pictures represent things.
Pictures symbolize ideas.
Pictures stand for sounds.
Signs represent sounds.

▲ The invention of the alphabet may have begun from pictures. This flowchart shows the possible development of the letter T.

River Valley Civilizations

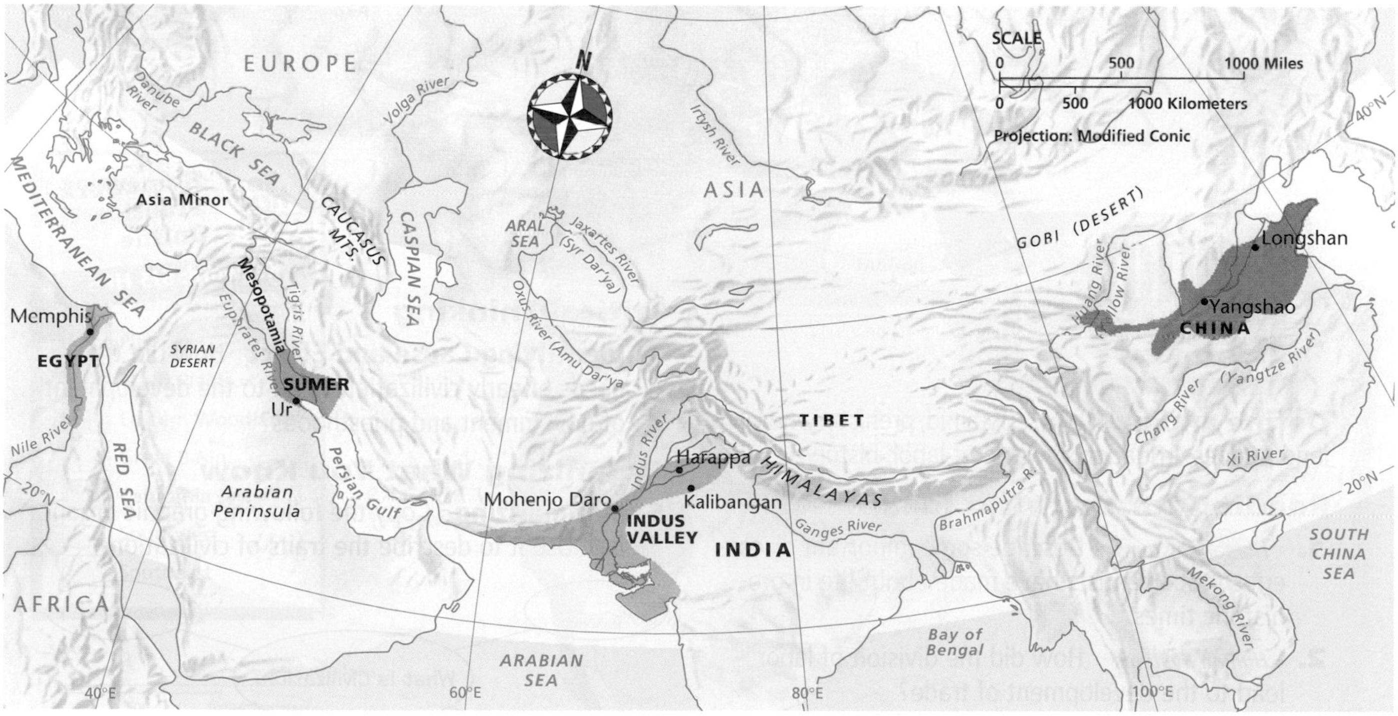

EUROPE
Danube River
BLACK SEA
Volga River
N
Irtysh River
SCALE
0 500 1000 Miles
0 500 1000 Kilometers
Projection: Modified Conic
40°N
MEDITERRANEAN SEA
Asia Minor
CAUCASUS MTS.
CASPIAN SEA
ASIA
ARAL SEA
Jaxartes River (Syr Darya)
GOBI (DESERT)
Longshan
Huang River
Yellow River
Memphis
Mesopotamia
Tigris River
Euphrates River
Oxus River (Amu Darya)
Yangshao
CHINA
EGYPT
SYRIAN DESERT
SUMER
Ur
Chang River
(Yangtze River)
TIBET
Nile River
RED SEA
Persian Gulf
Indus River
Harappa
HIMALAYAS
Xi River
20°N
Arabian Peninsula
Mohenjo Daro
Kalibangan
Brahmaputra R.
INDUS VALLEY
Ganges River
INDIA
SOUTH CHINA SEA
AFRICA
Mekong River
Bay of Bengal
ARABIAN SEA
40°E
60°E
80°E
100°E

Section 3 The Greek and Roman Worlds

Read to Discover

1. How did ancient Greek civilization develop?
2. What events led to the birth and decline of the Roman Empire?
3. How did Christianity begin?

Define

city-states
direct democracy
republic
aqueduct

Locate

Aegean Sea
Greece
Crete
Athens
Italy
Rome
Adriatic Sea
Mediterranean Sea
Alps
Jerusalem

WHY IT MATTERS

Both the Greek and Roman governments were based on the idea that people can govern themselves. Use CNNfyi.com or other **current events** sources to find out about how citizens of the United States and other countries take part in government.

Greek coins, c. 500s B.C.

Aegean Civilization, c. 1450 B.C.-700 B.C.

BLACK SEA
Bosporus
THRACE
MACEDONIA
SEA OF MARMARA
Mt. Olympus
40°N
Dardanelles (Hellespont)
Troy
THESSALY
Asia Minor
AEGEAN SEA
IONIA
GREECE
MYCENAEANS
ATTICA
Mycenae
Athens
Tiryns
Peloponnesus
Pylos
Delos
IONIAN SEA
N
Kos
Thera
Rhodes
36°N
MINOANS
Knossos
Crete
SCALE
0 75 150 Miles
0 75 150 Kilometers
Projection: Lambert Conformal Conic
MEDITERRANEAN SEA
28°E

The Early Greeks

By 2000 B.C. civilizations were developing in the Nile River valley and the Fertile Crescent. At the same time another civilization was forming near the Balkan peninsula and the Aegean Sea. The people who settled this area later became known as the Greeks. From the Greeks came many of the ideas that formed the foundation for modern western civilization.

Geography and Greek Civilization

Geography has much to do with the way the early Greeks lived. Greece is a rugged country that is made up of many peninsulas and islands separated by narrow waters. The land is covered with high mountains. They separated groups of people who lived in the valleys. These landforms contributed to the development of separate communities rather than one large and united kingdom. Because it was difficult to travel through the mountains, some Greeks preferred to travel by sea. Many became fighters, sailors, and traders.

Connecting to Art

The Toreador fresco

Frescoes Today, on the island of Crete, visitors can see the ruins of the palace of King Minos. When the palace was first built around 1500 B.C., the walls were covered with beautiful, colorful paintings called frescoes. The paintings were damaged over the years, but some of them have been carefully restored so that people can tell how they first looked. Many of the paintings show scenes from nature. Some are of birds, fish, dolphins, and other animals.

The largest of these paintings is called the *Toreador Fresco*. A toreador is a bullfighter. It shows ancient Minoan athletes jumping over a bull. The bull jumper at the right is a woman.

Understanding What You Read

1. Why did the paintings have to be restored?
2. What do the paintings tell us about life on the island of Crete in ancient times?

The Minoans About 100 years ago on the island of Crete, scientists found the remains of the earliest Greek civilization. By 2000 B.C., the Minoan people had developed a great civilization. From the evidence scientists found, we know that the Minoans built cities and grand palaces that even had running water. We also know that they developed a system of writing and that Minoan artists carved beautiful statues from gold, ivory, and stone. Because Crete's soil was very poor, farming was not very productive. Many people became sailors and fishers. By 1400 B.C., the Minoan civilization began to decline. It was conquered by a group that lived on the Greek mainland, the Mycenaeans (my-suh-NEE-unhz).

The Mycenaeans The Mycenaeans controlled the Greek mainland from about 1600 B.C. to about 1200 B.C. They were a warlike people who lived in tribes. Each tribe had its own chief. The Mycenaean tribes built fort-like cities surrounded by stone walls. They carried out raids on other peoples throughout the eastern Mediterranean. Once they conquered the Minoans, they adopted many aspects of their civilization. For example, they used the Minoan system of writing. By 1200 B.C. earthquakes and wars had destroyed most of the Mycenaean cities. A later Greek poet named Homer wrote a long poem called the *Iliad*, which pulls together about 400 years of historical events, legends, and folk tales. It tells the story of the Trojan War. The Mycenaeans were the Greeks Homer wrote about in that story.

✓ **READING CHECK:** *Analyzing* How did the geography of the land affect the way the Minoans lived?

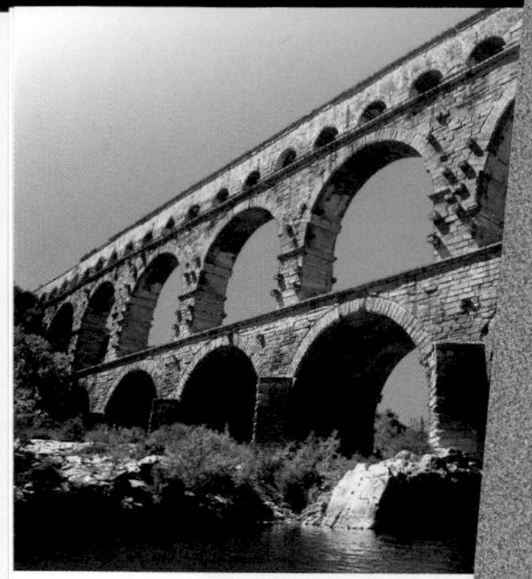

Aqueducts were stone ca
carried water from moun
the city.

This modern stain
shows Jesus surrou
According to the
Matthew, Jesus sa
should change to
like children.

Interpreting the V
do you think Jesu

CHAPTER 6 Reviewing What You Know

Building Vocabulary

On a separate sheet of paper, write sentences to define each of the following words.

1. hominid
2. prehistory
3. nomads
4. land bridges
5. irrigation
6. civilization
7. division of labor
8. history
9. migrated
10. hieroglyphics
11. quipu
12. city-states
13. direct democracy
14. republic
15. aqueduct

Reviewing the Main Ideas

1. *Human Systems* What are the four characteristics of civilization?
2. *Environment and Society* How did the development of agriculture lead to the growth of villages and towns?
3. *Environment and Society* What are some of the resources early people in the Americas depended on for survival?
4. *Environment and Society* Why did the city-states in ancient Greece develop differently from each other?
5. *Human Systems* What were some of the ancient Romans' achievements?

Understanding History and Society

The Road to Civilization

People of the early civilizations lived very differently from the first humans. Make a flow chart that shows the development of civilization from nomadic hunters and gatherers to city dwellers. As you prepare your presentation about human development, consider the following:

- How people made better tools.
- How agriculture changed society.
- How trade affected the way people lived.

Thinking Critically

1. **Drawing Conclusions** Why is the ability to make and use tools an important step in human development?
2. **Drawing Inferences** Why are the developments of a calendar, a system of counting, and a system of writing so important to a civilization?
3. **Predicting** How do you think civilization might change in the future?
4. **Comparing and Contrasting** How were the cultures of the ancient Greeks and the ancient Romans similar? How were they different?
5. **Identifying Cause and Effect** Give at least two reasons why civilizations decline.

Building Social Studies Skills

Map ACTIVITY

On a separate sheet of paper, match the letters on the map with their correct labels.

Macedonia **Asia Minor**
Ionian Sea **Athens**
Aegean Sea **Crete**
Knossos

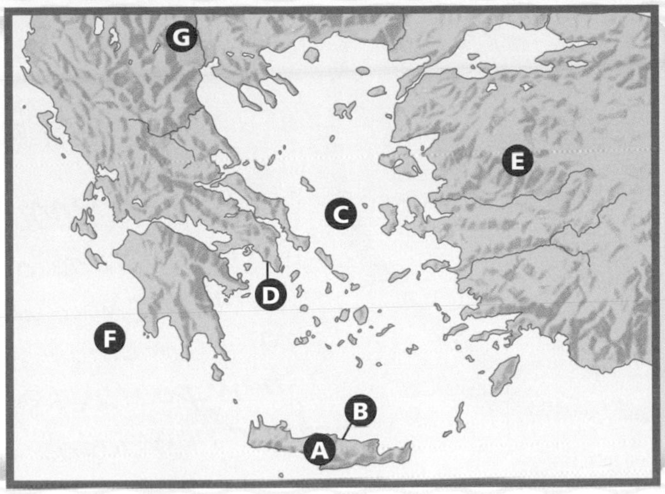
G
E
C
D
F
B
A

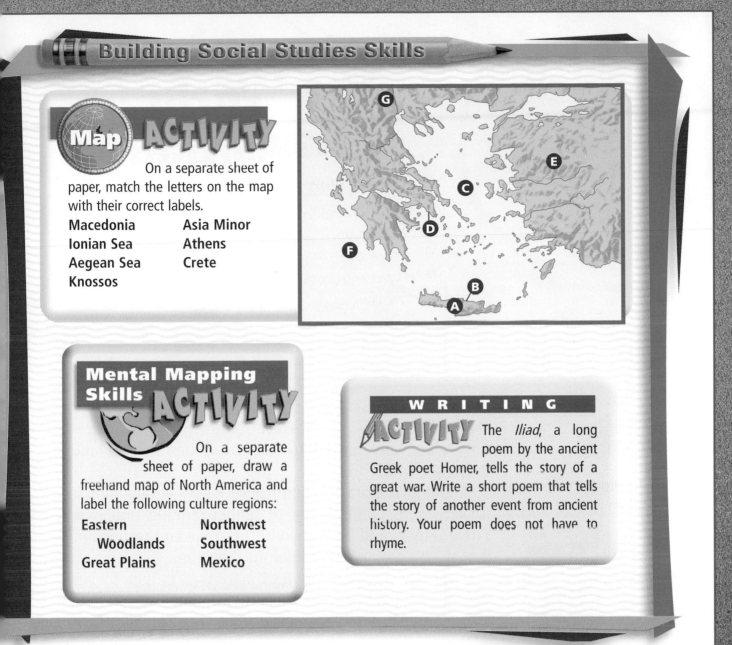

Mental Mapping Skills ACTIVITY

On a separate sheet of paper, draw a freehand map of North America and label the following culture regions:

Eastern Woodlands **Northwest**
Great Plains **Southwest**
Mexico

WRITING ACTIVITY

The *Iliad*, a long poem by the ancient Greek poet Homer, tells the story of a great war. Write a short poem that tells the story of another event from ancient history. Your poem does not have to rhyme.

Alternative Assessment

Portfolio ACTIVITY

Learning About Your Local History

Early Settlers Research how your town or city was founded. On poster board, create a display that shows who the first people were to settle in your town.

internet connect

Internet Activity: go.hrw.com
KEYWORD: SJ3 GT6

Choose a topic to explore about the ancient world:
- List different divisions of labor in early civilizations.
- Report on Minoan civilization.
- Create a newspaper article about ancient Athens.

CHAPTER 7

The World in Transition

The next 2000 years in human history were a time of great change. In this chapter you will read about the growth of new empires, the development of new political systems, and the search for new ideas.

During the Middle Ages about 1,000 years ago, society was separated into distinct classes. Certain young women of the time who were born into noble families had to undergo training on how to behave.

Young girls from the families of lesser nobles often went to live in the households of higher-ranking noblewomen. There they would be trained in the skills and responsibilities that were expected of women in their rank.

Generally a young noblewoman was taught to sew, to weave, to cook, to play musical instruments, and to sing. She also learned the social conduct that was proper for women of the nobility. In some cases girls and young women were also instructed in the skills of household supervision.

Young noblewoman from the Middle Ages

Knight with female admirers

Papal palace in Avignon, France

Section 1 The Middle Ages

Read to Discover

1. What were the Middle Ages?
2. What was society like during the Middle Ages?
3. How did the Middle Ages come to an end?

Define

feudalism
nobles
fief
vassals
knight
chivalry
manors
serfs
clergy
cathedrals
Crusades
middle class
vernacular

Locate

France
England
Normandy
Norway
Denmark
Sweden
Jerusalem
Spain

Why It Matters

The desire to control Jerusalem, which led to the Crusades, is still a cause of conflict. Use CNNfyi.com or other **current events** sources to learn what is happening in Jerusalem today. Record your findings in your journal.

A medieval knight

The Rise of the Middle Ages

In the year A.D. 476, the last of the western Roman emperors was defeated by invading Germanic tribes. These invaders from the north brought new ideas and traditions that gradually developed into new ways of life for people in Europe. Historians see the years between the last of the Roman emperors and the beginnings of the modern world in about 1500 as a period of change. Because it falls between the ancient and modern worlds, this time in history is called the Middle Ages or the medieval period. *Medieval* comes from the Latin for "middle age."

The time from the 400s to around 1000 is known as the Early Middle Ages. As this period began, the Roman system of laws and government had broken down. Western Europe was in a state of disorder. It was divided into many kingdoms ruled by kings who had little authority. For example, Britain was largely controlled by two Germanic tribes, the Angles and the Saxons. These groups had established several independent kingdoms.

Nobles in the Middle Ages built their own castles for protection.

Between 1347 and 1351 the Black Death killed about one third of Europe's entire population.

The Growth of Cities As Europe's economy got stronger, cities grew. Centers for trade and industry, cities attracted merchants and craftsmen as well as peasants, who hoped to find opportunities for better lives and more freedom. Both the manorial system and the feudal system began to fall apart.

During the Middle Ages, cities were crowded and dirty. When disease struck, it spread rapidly. In 1347 a deadly disease called the Black Death swept through Europe. Even this disastrous plague, however, had some positive effects. With the decrease in population came a shortage of labor. This meant that people could begin to demand higher wages for their work.

Education and Literature Most people could not read or write. As cities grew and trade increased, so did the demand and need for education. Between the late 1000s and the late 1200s, four important universities developed in England, France, and Italy. By the end of the 1400s, many more universities had opened throughout Europe.

A lecturer teaches at a university during the Middle Ages. Medieval universities taught religion, the liberal arts, medicine, and law.

Most people during the Middle Ages did not speak, read, or write Latin, the language of the Church. They spoke **vernacular** languages—everyday speech that varied from place to place. Writers such as Dante Alighieri in Italy and Geoffrey Chaucer in England began writing literature in vernacular languages. Dante is best known for *The Divine Comedy.* Chaucer's most famous work is *The Canterbury Tales*.

The End of the Middle Ages The decline of feudalism and the manorial system, the growth of stronger central governments, the growth of cities, and a renewed interest in education and trade brought an end to the Middle Ages. In addition, stronger kings challenged the power of the Catholic church. By the end of the 1400s, a new age had begun.

✓ **READING CHECK:** *Finding the Main Idea* Why did kings become more powerful after the Crusades?

Section 1 Review

go.hrw.com Homework Practice Online
Keyword: SJ3 HP7

Define and explain: feudalism, nobles, fief, vassals, knight, chivalry, manors, serfs, clergy, cathedrals, Crusades, middle class, vernacular

Reading for the Main Idea

1. *Human Systems* Why is the time between the A.D. 400s and about 1500 called the Middle Ages?
2. *Human Systems* What was life like in the Middle Ages?
3. *Human Systems* What led to the end of the Middle Ages?

Critical Thinking

4. **Evaluating** Why is Magna Carta considered one of the most important documents in European history?

Organizing What You Know

5. **Analyzing** Copy the following graphic organizer. Use the right-hand column to describe briefly each person's responsibility.

Person	Responsibility
noble	
vassal	

Section 2 The Renaissance and Reformation

Read to Discover

1. What were the main interests of Renaissance scholars?
2. How did people's lives change during the Renaissance?
3. What changes took place during the Reformation and Counter-Reformation?

Define

Renaissance
humanists
Reformation
Protestants
Counter-Reformation

Locate

Rome
Florence

WHY IT MATTERS

Works of Renaissance art have remained popular for hundreds of years. Use CNNfyi.com or other **current events** sources to learn about Renaissance paintings displayed in museums around the world today. Record your findings in your journal.

Leonardo da Vinci's sketch of a flying machine

New Interests and New Ideas

The Crusades and trade in distant lands caused great changes in Europe. During their travels, traders and Crusaders discovered scholars who had studied and preserved Greek and Roman learning. While trading in Southwest Asia and Africa, people learned about achievements in science and medicine. Such discoveries encouraged more curiosity. During the 1300s, this new creative spirit developed and sparked a movement known as the **Renaissance** (re-nuh-SAHNS). This term comes from the French word for "rebirth." The Renaissance brought fresh interest in exploring the achievements of the ancient world, its ideas, and its art.

Beginning of the Renaissance The Renaissance started in Italy. Italian cities such as Florence and Venice had become rich through industry and trade. Among the population was a powerful middle class. Many members of this class were wealthy and well-educated. They had many interests beside their work. Many studied ancient history, the arts, and education. They used their fortunes to support painters, sculptors, and architects, and to encourage learning. Scholars revived the learning of ancient Greece and Rome. Enthusiasm for art and literature increased. Over time the ideas of the Renaissance spread from Italy into other parts of Europe.

▲ The powerful Medici family ruled Florence for most of the Renaissance. Banker Cosimo de' Medici, seen here, was a great supporter of the arts.

The Humanities As a result of increased interest in ancient Greece and Rome, scholars encouraged the study of subjects that had been taught in ancient Greek and Roman schools. These subjects, including history, poetry, and grammar, are called the humanities.

The Counter-Reformation In response to the rise of Protestantism, the Catholic Church attempted to reform itself. This movement is called the **Counter-Reformation**. Church leaders began to focus more on spiritual matters and on making Church teachings easier for people to understand. They also attempted to stop the spread of Protestantism. Since about 1478, Spanish leaders had put on trial and severely punished people who questioned Catholic teachings. Leaders of what was called the Spanish Inquisition saw their fierce methods as a way to protect the Catholic Church from its enemies. During the Counter-Reformation, the pope brought the Spanish Inquisition to Rome.

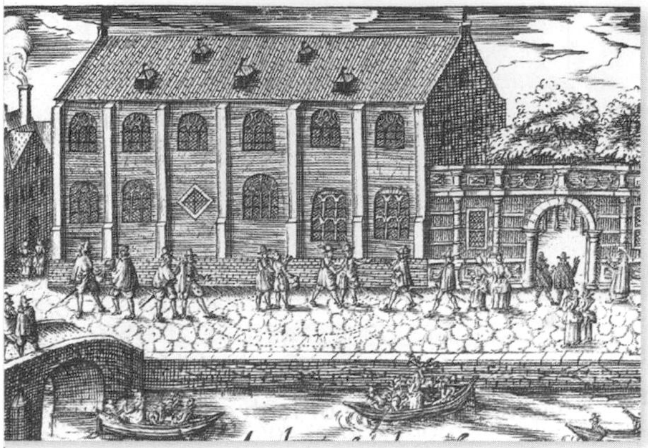

Many schools, including the Dutch University of Leiden shown here, were established during the Reformation.

Interpreting the Visual Record What goal of the Renaissance humanists was shared by both Catholics and Protestants?

Results of Religious Struggle Terrible religious wars broke out in France, Germany, the Netherlands, and Switzerland after the Reformation. By the time these wars ended, important social and political changes had occurred in Europe. Many different churches arose in Europe.

A stronger interest in education arose. Catholics saw education as a tool to strengthen people's belief in the teachings of the Church. Protestants believed that people could find their own way to Christian faith by studying the Bible. Although both Catholics and Protestants placed importance on literacy, the ability to read, education did not make people more tolerant. Both Catholic and Protestant leaders opposed views that differed from their own.

As Protestantism became more popular, the Catholic Church lost some of its power. It was no longer the only church in Europe. As a result, it lost some of the tremendous political power it had held there. As the power of the Church and the pope decreased, the power of monarchs and national governments increased.

✓ **READING CHECK:** *Identifying Cause and Effect* How did the religious conflicts of the 1500s change life in Europe?

go.hrw.com **Homework Practice Online** Keyword: SJ3 HP7

Section 2 Review

Define and explain: Renaissance, humanists, Reformation, Protestants, Counter-Reformation

Reading for the Main Idea

1. *Human Systems* What brought about the Renaissance?
2. *Human Systems* What were some important changes in daily life during the Renaissance?
3. *Human Systems* After the Reformation and Counter-Reformation, how was life in Europe different?

Critical Thinking

4. **Drawing Inferences** Why did national governments gain strength as the power of the Catholic Church declined?

Organizing What You Know

5. **Categorizing** Copy and complete the following graphic organizer with the achievements of some key people of the Renaissance and the Reformation.

Person	Achievement

Section 3 Exploration and Conquest

Read to Discover

1. What was the Scientific Revolution?
2. What started the Age of Exploration?
3. How was the English monarchy different from others in Europe?
4. What was the relationship between England and its American colonies?

Define

Scientific Revolution
Age of Exploration
colony
mercantilism
absolute authority
limited monarchy
Parliament
Puritan
constitution
Restoration

Locate

India
China
Spain
Portugal
Mexico
Bahamas
France
Russia
Austria
England

Why It Matters

Countries often try to increase their power through conquest. Use CNNfyi.com or other **current events** sources to find examples of conquest going on today. Record your findings in your journal.

Galileo's telescope

The Scientific Revolution

You have read that Renaissance humanists encouraged learning, curiosity, and discovery. The spirit of the Renaissance paved the way for a development during the 1500s and 1600s known as the **Scientific Revolution**. During this period, Europeans began looking at the world in a different way. Using new instruments such as the microscope and the telescope, they made more accurate observations than were possible before. They set up scientific experiments and used mathematics to learn about the natural world.

This scientific approach produced new knowledge in the fields of astronomy, physics, and biology. For example, in 1609 Galileo Galilei built a telescope and observed the sky. He eventually proved that an earlier scientist, Copernicus, had been correct in saying that the planets circle the sun. Earlier, people had believed that the planets moved around the Earth. In 1687 Sir Isaac Newton explained the law of gravity. In the 1620s William Harvey discovered the circulation of blood.

Other discoveries and advances such as better ships, improved maps, compasses and other sailing equipment allowed explorers to venture farther over the seas than before. These discoveries paved the way for the Age of Exploration.

✓ **READING CHECK:** *Identifying Cause and Effect* What brought about the Scientific Revolution?

The model pictured below is of an English explorer's ship. Although they appear tiny and fragile by today's standards, ships like this carried European explorers to new lands around the world.

This map shows the routes taken by Portuguese, Spanish, French, English, and Dutch explorers. They sailed both east and west to discover new lands.

Interpreting the Map Find Magellan's course on the map. Describe the route he found from the Atlantic Ocean to the Pacific Ocean.

The Dutch artist Jan Vermeer, who painted during the 1600s, often showed his subjects in the midst of work activities. Vermeer's *The Astronomer* shows research and work connected to mapmaking.

European Explorations, 1492–1535

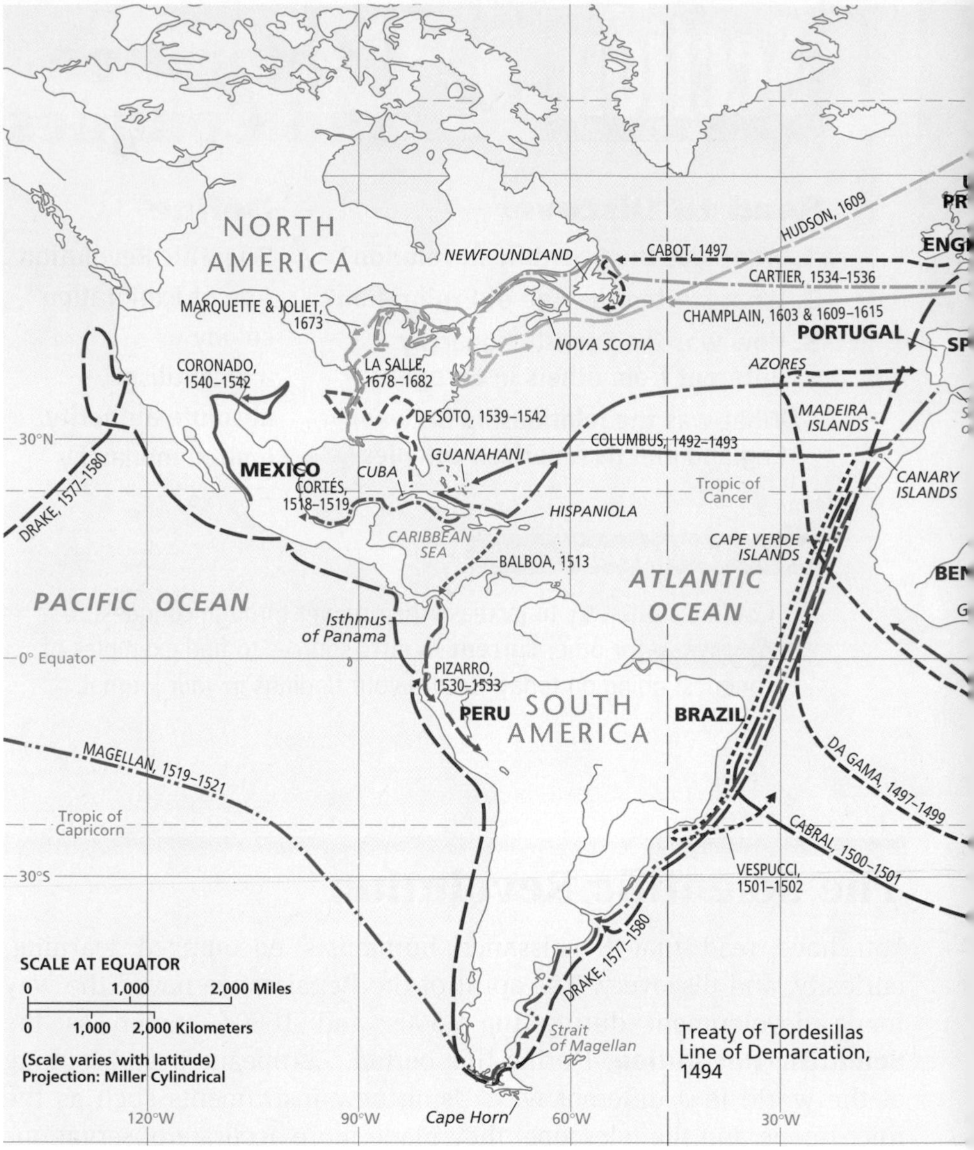
NORTH AMERICA
SOUTH AMERICA
PACIFIC OCEAN
ATLANTIC OCEAN
NEWFOUNDLAND
CABOT, 1497
HUDSON, 1609
CARTIER, 1534–1536
CHAMPLAIN, 1603 & 1609–1615
PORTUGAL
AZORES
NOVA SCOTIA
MARQUETTE & JOLIET, 1673
CORONADO, 1540–1542
LA SALLE, 1678–1682
DE SOTO, 1539–1542
MADEIRA ISLANDS
COLUMBUS, 1492–1493
GUANAHANI
CANARY ISLANDS
MEXICO
CORTÉS, 1518–1519
CUBA
Tropic of Cancer
HISPANIOLA
CARIBBEAN SEA
CAPE VERDE ISLANDS
BALBOA, 1513
DRAKE, 1577–1580
Isthmus of Panama
30°N
0° Equator
30°S
Tropic of Capricorn
PIZARRO, 1530–1533
PERU
BRAZIL
MAGELLAN, 1519–1521
DA GAMA, 1497–1499
CABRAL, 1500–1501
VESPUCCI, 1501–1502
SCALE AT EQUATOR
0 1,000 2,000 Miles
0 1,000 2,000 Kilometers
(Scale varies with latitude)
Projection: Miller Cylindrical
Strait of Magellan
Treaty of Tordesillas Line of Demarcation, 1494
Cape Horn
120°W
90°W
60°W
30°W

The Age of Exploration

Europeans were eager to find new and shorter sea routes so that they could trade with India and China for spices, silks, and jewels. The combination of curiosity, technology, and the demand for new and highly valued products launched a period known as the **Age of Exploration**.

A member of the Portuguese royal family named Prince Henry encouraged Portugal to become a leader in exploration. He wanted to find a route to the rich spice trade of India. Portuguese explorers did eventually succeed in finding a way. They reached India by sailing around Africa.

Hoping to find another route to India, Spain sponsored the voyage of the Italian navigator Christopher Columbus. He hoped to find a direct route to India by sailing westward across the Atlantic Ocean. In

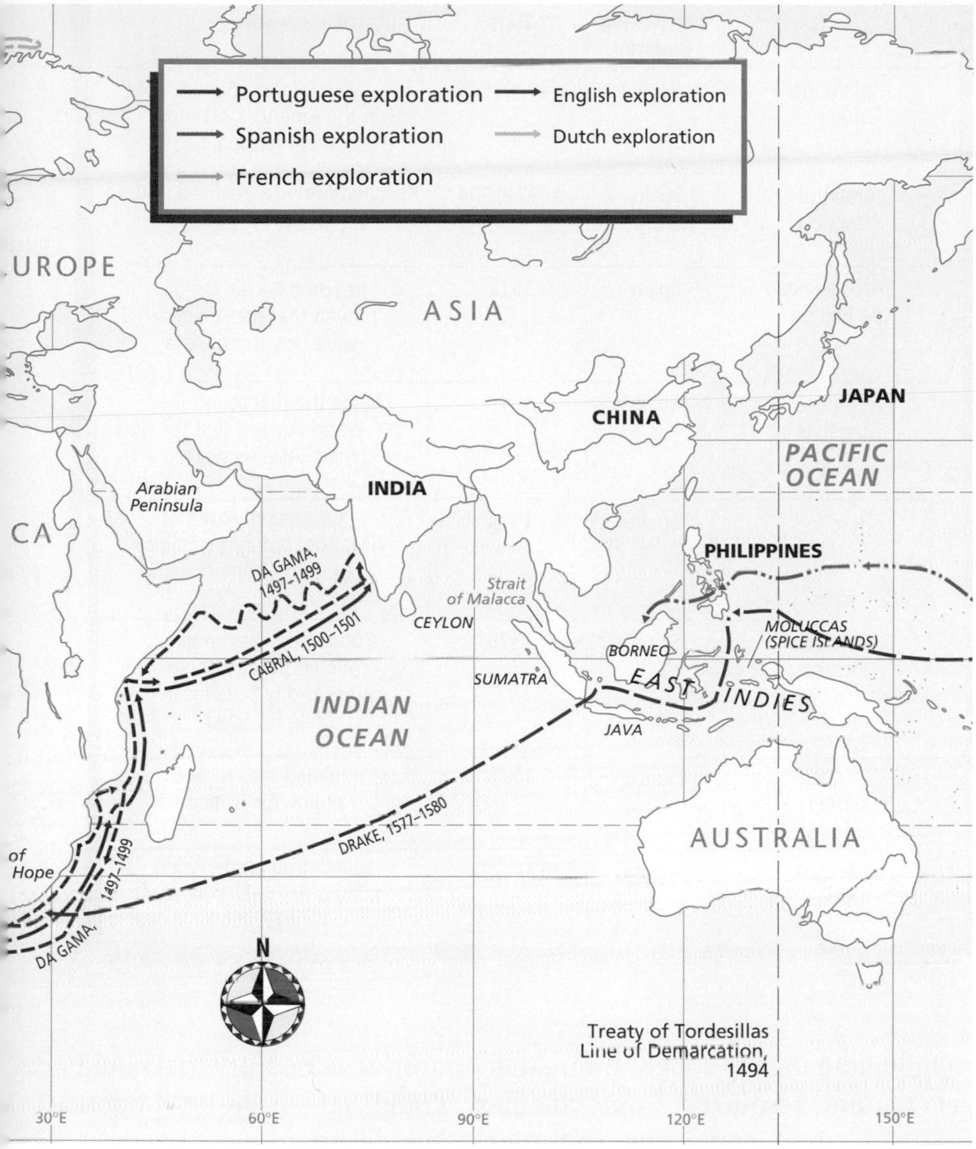
Portuguese exploration
Spanish exploration
French exploration
English exploration
Dutch exploration
UROPE
ASIA
CHINA
JAPAN
PACIFIC OCEAN
INDIA
Arabian Peninsula
PHILIPPINES
DA GAMA, 1497–1499
Strait of Malacca
CEYLON
CABRAL, 1500–1501
MOLUCCAS (SPICE ISLANDS)
BORNEO
SUMATRA
EAST INDIES
INDIAN OCEAN
JAVA
DRAKE, 1577–1580
AUSTRALIA
of Hope
1497–1499
DA GAMA,
N
Treaty of Tordesillas Line of Demarcation, 1494
30°E
60°E
90°E
120°E
150°E

Sailors of the 1500s had many new tools such as this astrolabe to hold a course and measure their progress. A sailor would sight a star along the bar of the astrolabe. By lining the bar with markings on the disk, he could figure out the latitude of the ship's position.

1492 Columbus reached an island in what is now called the Bahamas. Because he had no idea that the Americas lay between Europe and Asia, Columbus believed he had reached the east coast of India.

Later Spanish explorers who knew of the Americas were motivated more by the promise of conquest and riches than by curiosity and the opening of trade routes. The chart on the following page provides an overview of the major explorers from the late 1400s through the 1500s, their voyages, and their accomplishments.

Conquest and Colonization Over time the Spanish, French, English, Dutch, and others established American colonies. A **colony** is a territory controlled by people from a foreign land. As they expanded overseas, Europeans developed an economic theory called **mercantilism**. This theory said that a government should do everything it could to increase its wealth. One way it could do so was by

European Explorers

Name	Sponsoring Country	Date	Accomplishment
Christopher Columbus	Spain	1492–1504	Discovered islands in the Americas, claimed them for Spain
Amerigo Vespucci	Spain, Portugal	1497–1504	Reached America, realized it was not part of Asia
Vasco Núñez de Balboa	Spain	1513	Reached Pacific Ocean, proved that the Americas were not part of Asia
Ferdinand Magellan	Spain	1519	Made the first round-the-world voyage, first to reach Asia by water
Hernán Cortés	Spain	1519	Conquered Aztec civilization, brought smallpox to Central America
Francisco Pizarro	Spain	1530	Conquered Inca empire, claimed the land from present-day Ecuador to Chile for Spain
Jacques Cartier	France	1535	Claimed the Quebec region for France
Sir Francis Drake	England	1577–1580	Sailed around the World, claimed the California coast for England

Interpreting the Chart Which explorer do you think made the most important discovery? Give reasons for your answer.

European explorers sailed in search of goods like gold and cinnamon. In addition, some found new foods, like tomatoes, to bring back to Europe.

selling more than it bought from other countries. A country that could get natural resources from colonies would not have to import resources from competing countries. The desire to win overseas sources of materials helped fuel the race for colonies. The Age of Exploration changed both Europe and the lands it colonized. Colonized lands did benefit from these changes. However, in general, Europe gained the most. During this time, goods, plants, animals, and even diseases were exchanged between Europe and the Americas.

The Slave Trade A tragic result of exploration and colonization was the spread of slavery. During the 1500s Europeans began to use enslaved Africans to work in their colonies overseas. In exchange for slaves, European merchants shipped cotton goods, weapons, and liquor to Africa. These slaves were sent across the Atlantic to the Americas, where they were traded for goods such as sugar and cotton. These goods were then sent to Europe in exchange for manufactured products to be sold in the Americas. Conditions aboard the slave ships were horrific, and slaves were treated brutally. Many died crossing the Atlantic.

✓ **READING CHECK:** *Identifying Cause and Effect* What were two results of European exploration?

Monarchies in Europe

Wealth flowed into European nations from their colonies. At the same time the Church's power over rulers and governments lost strength. The power of monarchs increased. In France, Russia, and Central Europe, monarchs ruled with **absolute authority**, meaning they alone had the power to make all the decisions about governing their nation. This situation would not change much until the 1700s.

France was ruled by a royal family called the Bourbons. Its most powerful member was Louis XIV, who ruled France from 1643 to 1715. Like many European monarchs, Louis believed that he had been chosen by God to rule. He had absolute control of the government and made all important decisions himself. Under Louis, France became a very powerful nation. In Russia, the Romanov dynasty came to power in the early 1600s. The most powerful of the Romanov czars was Peter the Great, who took the throne in 1682. He wanted to make Russia more like countries in Western Europe. Like Louis XIV, Peter the Great was an absolute monarch who strengthened his country. In Central Europe, two great families competed for power. The Habsburgs ruled the Austrian Empire, while the Hohenzollerns controlled Prussia to the north.

England's situation was different. When King John signed Magna Carta during the Middle Ages, he set a change in motion for England's government. England became a **limited monarchy**. This meant that the powers of the king were limited by law. By the 1500s, **Parliament**, an assembly made up of nobles, clergy, and common people, had gained the power to pass laws and make sure they were upheld.

English Civil War English monarchs such as Henry VIII and Elizabeth I had to work with or around Parliament to achieve their political goals. Later English monarchs fought with Parliament for power. Some even went to war over this issue. The struggle between king and Parliament reached its peak in the mid-1600s. Armies of Parliament supporters under Oliver Cromwell defeated King Charles I, ended the monarchy, and proclaimed England a commonwealth, a nation in which the people held most of the authority.

A special court tried Charles I for crimes against the people. Oliver Cromwell, a **Puritan**, took control of England. Puritans were a group of Protestants who thought that the Church of England was too much like the Catholic Church. The Puritans were a powerful group in Parliament at the time, and Cromwell was their leader.

Empress Maria Theresa of Austria was a member of the Habsburg family.

Oliver Cromwell led the Puritan forces that overthrew the English monarchy. He ruled England from 1653 to 1658.

The death warrant of Charles I was signed and sealed by members of Parliament. Parliament chose to behead King Charles I in public.

Interpreting the Visual Record
Why might Parliament have decided to have Charles I beheaded where everyone could see?

Cromwell's Commonwealth Cromwell controlled England for about five years. He used harsh methods to create a government that represented the people. Twice he tried to establish a **constitution**, a document that outlined the country's basic laws, but his policies were unpopular. Discontent became widespread. In 1660, two years after Cromwell died, Parliament invited the son of Charles I to rule England. Thus the English monarchy was restored under Charles II. This period of English history was called the **Restoration**.

Last Change in Government Cheering crowds greeted Charles II when he reached London. One observer recalled that great celebrations were held in the streets, which were decorated with flowers and tapestries. People hoped that the Restoration would bring peace and progress to England.

Although England had a king again, the Civil War and Cromwell's commonwealth had made lasting changes in the government. Parliament strictly limited the king's power.

Charles II, shown here as a boy, became king following the fall of Cromwell's commonwealth in 1660.

The Glorious Revolution When Charles II died, his brother became King James II. James's belief in absolute rule angered Parliament. They demanded that he give up the throne and invited his daughter, Mary, and her Dutch husband, William of Orange, to replace him. This transfer of power, which was accomplished without bloodshed, was called the Glorious Revolution. The day before William and Mary took the throne in 1689, they had to agree to a document called the Declaration of Rights. It stated that Parliament would choose who ruled the country. It also said that the ruler could not make laws, impose taxes, or maintain an army without Parliament's approval. By 1700 Parliament had replaced the monarchy as the major source of political power in England.

✓ **READING CHECK:** *Drawing Inferences* How did the English Civil War and events that followed affect the English government?

English Colonial Expansion

During the 1600s, English explorers began claiming and conquering lands overseas. In 1607 the British established Jamestown in what is now the state of Virginia. Jamestown was the first permanent English settlement in North America. In 1620, settlers founded Plymouth in what is now Massachusetts.

The settlers at Jamestown settled close by the James River.

Interpreting the Visual Record

Why do you think the colonists built their settlement in the manner shown here?

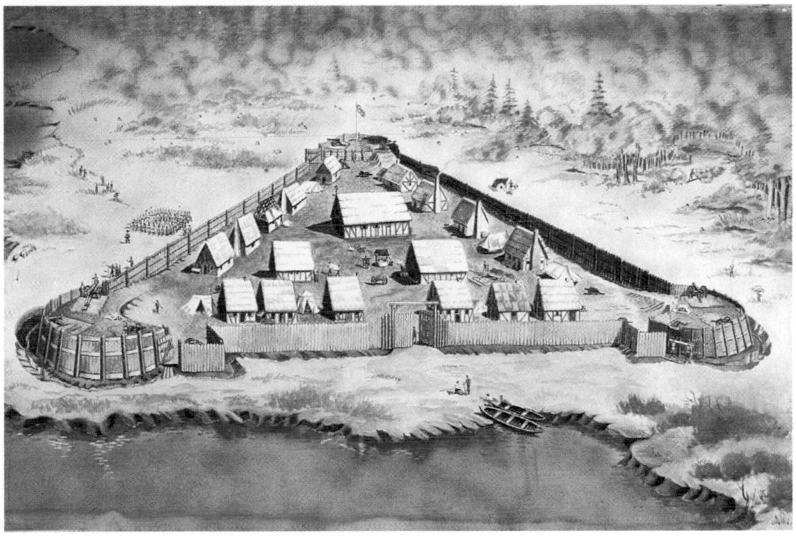

Colonial Williamsburg Foundation

Mercantilism and the British Colonies The British government, with its policy of mercantilism, thought that the colonies should exist only for the benefit of England. Parliament passed laws that required colonists to sell certain products only to Britain, even if another country would pay a higher price. Other trade laws imposed taxes on sugar and other goods that the colonies bought from non-British colonies.

Resistance in the Colonies The American colonists saw these trade laws as a threat to their liberties. They found many ways to break the laws. For example, they avoided paying taxes whenever and however they could. Parliament, however, continued to impose new taxes. With each new tax, colonial resistance increased. Relations between England and the colonies grew steadily worse. The stage was set for revolution.

✓ **READING CHECK:** *Finding the Main Idea* How did England regard the American colonies?

Section 3 Review

Define and explain: Scientific Revolution, Age of Exploration, colony, mercantilism, absolute authority, limited monarchy, Parliament, Puritan, constitution, Restoration

Reading for the Main Idea

1. *Human Systems* How did the Scientific Revolution aid European exploration?
2. *Places and Regions* What prompted Europeans to explore and colonize land overseas?
3. *Human Systems* How was England different from other monarchies in Europe?

Critical Thinking

4. **Drawing Inferences** How did England's treatment of the American colonies set the stage for revolution?

Organizing What You Know

5. **Summarizing** Copy the following graphic organizer. Use it to show how the slave trade worked between Europe, Africa, and the Americas. Alongside each arrow, list the items that were traded along that route.

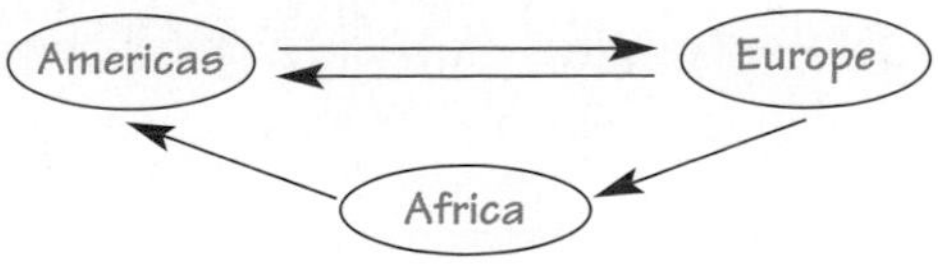
Americas
Europe
Africa

CHAPTER 7

Reviewing What You Know

Building Vocabulary

On a separate sheet of paper, write a sentence to define each of the following words:

1. feudalism
2. vassals
3. chivalry
4. manors
5. serfs
6. clergy
7. vernacular
8. Renaissance
9. humanists
10. Reformation
11. Protestants
12. Scientific Revolution
13. colony
14. mercantilism
15. constitution

Reviewing the Main Ideas

1. *Human Systems* What did vassals receive in exchange for serving kings and nobles?
2. *Human Systems* What was humanism?
3. *Human Systems* What were the results of the Reformation and Counter-Reformation?
4. *Environment and Society* How did the Scientific Revolution pave the way for European exploration?
5. *Human Systems* What was mercantilism?

Understanding History and Society

The Feudal System

Throughout Europe in the Middle Ages, the feudal system was the most important political structure. Create a chart to explain the relationships among kings, lords, vassals, and knights. Consider the following:

- Who granted lands and who received the grants.
- What a king or lord expected from his vassals.

Thinking Critically

1. **Evaluating** Why was Magna Carta one of the most important documents in European history?
2. **Identifying Cause and Effect** Why did the growth of cities and trade during the High Middle Ages increase the need for education?
3. **Contrasting** How did political power in Europe change after the Counter-Reformation?
4. **Supporting a Point of View** How did mercantilism both help and harm Great Britain as a colonial power?
5. **Identifying Cause and Effect** How did the English Civil War change politics in Great Britain?

Building Social Studies Skills

Map Activity

On a separate sheet of paper, match the letters on the map with their correct labels.

Spain
Portugal
North America
Mexico
South America
Europe

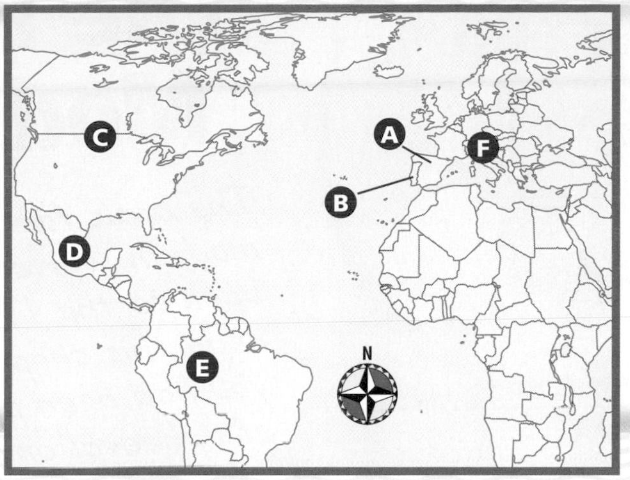

A
B
C
D
E
F
N

Mental Mapping Skills Activity

On a separate sheet of paper, draw a freehand map like the one in the Map Activity. On your map, sketch and label each of the following explorers' routes:

Columbus
Magellan
Drake

Writing Activity

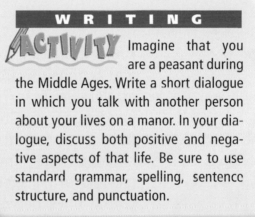

Imagine that you are a peasant during the Middle Ages. Write a short dialogue in which you talk with another person about your lives on a manor. In your dialogue, discuss both positive and negative aspects of that life. Be sure to use standard grammar, spelling, sentence structure, and punctuation.

Alternative Assessment

Portfolio Activity

Learning About Your Local History

Local Artists and Writers The Renaissance produced many great artists and writers. Conduct research on the Internet or in your local library to find out about artists and writers in your state or region. Write a brief report on one of these artists or writers. Keep a list of sources you used to get your information.

internet connect

Internet Activity: go.hrw.com
KEYWORD: SJ3 GT7

Choose a topic to explore about the world in transition:

- Write a report on daily life in the Middle Ages.
- Create a biography of a Renaissance artist or writer.
- Learn more about an explorer described in this chapter.

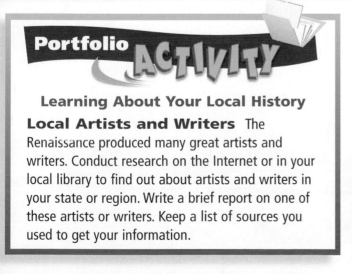

CHAPTER 8

The Birth of the Modern World

The basis for the democratic and modern world we live in today dates back to the 1700s and 1800s. When you read this chapter, you might just wish you had been part of this stirring time of upheaval and great accomplishment.

Drummer boy from the American Revolution

From the mid-1760s through the mid-1770s, British policies and actions toward the 13 colonies in North America became intolerable. Many colonists called Patriots believed that independence from Great Britain was necessary to guarantee their freedom and right to a government of, for, and by the people.

When the American Revolution started in April 1775, patriots of all ages joined the fight for independence. Many young boys between the ages of 14 and 16 enlisted in the American army. Other boys, some as young as six, served as drummers for the troops, like the one pictured on this page. Their job was to signal commands, which sometimes put them in the midst of battle.

The American navy had its share of young sailors as well. Small boys served as deckhands or "powder monkeys." They carried ammunition to the gunners during battle.

Revolutionary War cannon

Colonial Williamsburg Foundation

Harbor at Charleston, South Carolina

Section 1 The Enlightenment

Read to Discover

1. What was the Enlightenment?
2. What ideas about government did Enlightenment thinkers suggest?
3. How did the Enlightenment lead to changes in society?

Define

Enlightenment
reason
secularism
individualism
popular sovereignty
social contract

WHY IT MATTERS

Our American government and way of life are largely based on the ideas of the Enlightenment. Use CNNfyi.com or other **current events** sources to find out how these ideas continue to cause changes today all around the world. Record your findings in your journal.

Monticello, home of American Enlightenment thinker, Thomas Jefferson

The Birth of a New Age

You have read about how greatly European society changed during the Middle Ages, the Renaissance, the Reformation, and the Scientific Revolution. You have also learned how advances in science and technology paved the way for exploration and expansion overseas. As time went on, many changes in the world continued to take place, especially in people's thinking about their relationship with their nation's government.

From the mid 1600s through the 1700s, most European countries were ruled by monarchs. These rulers increasingly wanted absolute control over their governments and their subjects. Many, although not all, literary people, scientists, and philosophers, or thinkers, in these countries saw the need for change. They believed it was necessary to combat the political and social injustices people suffered every day. These critics claimed that the monarchs and nobility took too much from the common people and gave back too little. They wanted a new social order that was fairer for all people. These ideas were published in books, pamphlets, plays, and newspapers. Historians call this era of new ideas the **Enlightenment**.

✓ **READING CHECK:** *Identifying Cause and Effect* What about the political and social order of European nations caused many people to want change?

▲ John Locke (1632-1704) was an important English philosopher. He is considered the founder of the Enlightenment in England.

Mary Wollstonecraft was a British writer of the Enlightenment. She argued that women should have the same rights as men, including the right to an equal education.

Enlightenment Thinking

The Enlightenment is also called the Age of Reason. At this time, scientists began to use **reason**, or logical thinking, to discover the laws of nature. They believed that the laws of nature governed the universe and all its creatures. Some also thought there was a natural law that governed society and human behavior. They tried to use their powers of reasoning to discover this natural law. By following natural law, they hoped to solve society's problems and improve people's lives.

While religion was important to some thinkers, other thinkers played down its importance. Playing down the importance of religion became known as **secularism**. The ideas of secularism and **individualism**—a belief in the political and economic independence of individuals—would later influence some ideas about the separation of church and state in government. These ideas led to more rights for all people, individual freedoms, and government by the people.

The Enlightenment in England The English philosopher John Locke believed that natural law gave individuals the right to govern themselves. Locke wrote that freedom was people's natural state. He thought individuals possessed natural rights to life, liberty, and property. Locke also claimed people should have equality under the law.

Much of Locke's writing focused on government. Locke argued that government should be based on an agreement between the people and their leaders. According to Locke, people give their rulers the power to rule. If the ruler does not work for the public good, the people have the right to change the government. Locke's writings greatly influenced other thinkers of the Enlightenment. They also influenced the Americans who shaped and wrote the Declaration of Independence and the Constitution.

internet connect

GO TO: go.hrw.com
KEYWORD: SJ3 CH8
FOR: Web sites about the birth of the modern world

The Enlightenment in France In France, the thinkers of the Enlightenment believed that science and reason could work together to improve people's lives. They spoke out strongly for individual rights, such as freedom of speech and freedom of worship.

ENCYCLOPÉDIE,
OU
DICTIONNAIRE RAISONNÉ
DES SCIENCES,
DES ARTS ET DES MÉTIERS,
TOME PREMIER.
A PARIS,
M. DCC. LI.
AVEC APPROBATION ET PRIVILEGE DU ROY.

The Encyclopedia, published by Enlightenment philosophers, became the most famous publication of the period.

Voltaire The French writer Voltaire was a leading voice of the Enlightenment. As a young man, Voltaire became a famous poet and playwright. He used his wit to criticize the French monarchy, the nobility, and the religious controls of the church. His criticisms got him into trouble. He eventually went to England after being imprisoned twice.

In England, Voltaire was delighted by the freedom of speech he found. In defense of this freedom, he wrote, "I may disapprove of what you say, but I will defend to the death your right to say it."

Voltaire also studied the writings of John Locke. When Voltaire returned to France, he published many essays and tales. These writings explored Enlightenment ideas, such as justice, good government, and human rights.

Our Amazing Planet

In 1717, when Voltaire was 23, he spent eleven months in prison for making fun of the government. During that time, he wrote his first play. Its success made him the greatest playwright in France.

Rousseau Jean-Jacques Rousseau (roo-SOH) was another French thinker of the Enlightenment. He believed that people could only preserve their freedom if they chose their own government, and that good government must be controlled by the people. This belief is called **popular sovereignty**.

Rousseau's most famous book, *The Social Contract*, published in 1762, expressed his views. "Man was born free, and everywhere he is in chains," Rousseau wrote. He meant that people in society lose the freedom they have in nature. Like Locke, Rousseau believed that government should be based on an agreement made by the people. He called this agreement the **social contract**.

Jean-Jacques Rousseau

The Encyclopedia *The Encyclopedia* was the most famous publication of the Enlightenment. It brought together the writings of Voltaire, Rousseau, and other philosophers. The articles in *The Encyclopedia* covered science, religion, government, and the arts. Many articles criticized the French government and the Catholic church. Some philosophers went to jail for writing these articles. Nevertheless, the *Encyclopedia* helped spread Enlightenment ideas.

✓ **READING CHECK:** *Summarizing* What did the thinkers of the Enlightenment believe?

In France, writers and artists gathered each week at meetings like the one shown in this painting. Their purpose was to discuss the new ideas of the Enlightenment.

Interpreting the Visual Record

How might the group pictured here encourage the free sharing of ideas?

We the People
of the United States, in Order to form a more perfect Union, esta
insure domestic Tranquility, provide for the common defence, promote the general Welfare, and secure the Blessings of Liberty
and our Posterity, do ordain and establish this Constitution for the United States of America.
Article I
Article II

▲ The philosopher Baron de Montesquieu (MOHN-tes-kyoo) thought governments should be divided into three branches. His ideas helped the writers of the U.S. Constitution form our government.

The Enlightenment and Society

When the philosophers began to publish their ideas, there was little freedom of expression in Europe. Most countries were ruled by absolute monarchs. Few people dared to criticize the court or the nobility. Most nations had official religions, and there was little toleration of other faiths.

As time passed, Enlightenment ideas about freedom, equality, and government became more influential. Eventually, they inspired the American and French revolutions. In that way, the Enlightenment led to more freedom for individuals and to government by the people.

Section 1 Review

go.hrw.com Homework Practice Online
Keyword: SJ3 HP8

Define and explain Enlightenment, reason, secularism, individualism, popular sovereignty, social contract

Reading for the Main Idea

1. *Human Systems* Why was the Enlightenment also called the Age of Reason?
2. *Human Systems* What important ideas about government came from Enlightenment thinkers?

Critical Thinking

3. **Drawing Conclusions** Why might the French nobility and the church dislike *The Encyclopedia*?
4. **Analyzing** In what ways did John Locke and other philosophers of the Enlightenment help pave the way for democracy in the United States?

Organizing What You Know

5. **Categorizing** Copy the following graphic organizer. Use details from the chapter to fill it in. Then write a title for the chart.

Writer	Country	Important Ideas
Locke		
Voltaire		
Rousseau		

Section 2 The Age of Revolution

Read to Discover

1. What started the American Revolution and what were its results?
2. How did the French Revolution change France?
3. How did Europe change during and after the Napoléonic Era?

Define

Patriots
Loyalists
alliance
oppression
Reign of Terror
balance of power
reactionaries

WHY IT MATTERS

The revolutions of the 1700s in the United States and France gave many new rights and freedoms to ordinary citizens. Use CNNfyi.com or other **current events** sources to find examples of recent revolutions that have occurred in countries around the world.

No
Stamp Act

Colonial Williamsburg Foundation

American teapot with anti-Stamp Act slogan

The American Revolution

Enlightenment philosophers' ideas about freedom, equality, and government were not confined to Europe in the 1700s. By the 1750s, the British had established 13 colonies along the Atlantic Coast in North America. These British colonists had developed a new way of life and a new relationship with their home country. The colonists held their own elections and made their own laws. However, the colonists were still British subjects, and they had no representation in the British Parliament.

The Growing Conflict While the British had colonies along the Atlantic Coast in North America, the French colonies—New France—lay to the north and west. As British colonists pushed westward into French-controlled territory, tensions mounted.

France and Great Britain had long been enemies in Europe. In 1754, their conflict spilled over into North America, sparking the French and Indian War. In Europe this war was called the Seven Years' War. It began in 1756 and ended in 1763. As the victor in this war, the British gained control of most of North America.

To help pay for the war, the British taxed goods that their colonists in North America needed. Many colonists thought these new taxes were unfair, since they had no representatives in Parliament to express their views. Americans resisted the new taxes by refusing to buy British goods.

AMERICA
HONI SOIT QVI MAL Y PENSE
DIEU ET MON DROIT
V SHILLINGS

▲ The Stamp Act required Americans to purchase stamps like this one and to place them on many types of public documents.

IN CONGRESS. JULY 4. 1776.

The unanimous Declaration of the thirteen united States of America.

The Declaration of Independence declared the American colonies free from British control. It was adopted on July 4, 1776—now celebrated as Independence Day.

As their unhappiness increased, the colonies united against the British. In 1774, 12 colonies sent representatives to the First Continental Congress. The Congress pledged to stop trade with Britain until the colonies had representation in Parliament.

Some American colonists believed the best way to guarantee their rights was to break away from British rule. Colonists called **Patriots** wanted independence. They made up one third of the population. Another third, the **Loyalists**, wanted to remain loyal to Great Britain. The rest of the colonists were undecided.

The Declaration of Independence In 1776 the Continental Congress adopted the Declaration of Independence. Thomas Jefferson was the Declaration's main author. The Declaration clearly showed the influence of Enlightenment thinkers, especially Locke and Rousseau. The Declaration stated that that "all men are created equal" and have the right to "life, liberty, and the pursuit of happiness." The ideal of individual liberty was only applied in a limited way. Women and slaves were not included. Nevertheless, the Declaration was still a great step forward toward equality and justice.

Locke's and Rousseau's ideas about popular sovereignty were clearly seen in the Declaration. It stated that all powers of government come from the people. It said that no government can exist without the consent of its citizens and that government is created to protect individual rights. In addition, it stated that if a government fails to protect these rights, the people may change it and set up a new government.

The first battle of the American Revolution was fought in Lexington, Massachusetts, on April 19, 1775.

War and Peace By the time the Declaration of Independence was written, the colonies were already at war with Great Britain. At first, the British seemed unbeatable. Then in late 1777, France formed an **alliance** with the Americans. An alliance is an agreement formed to help both sides. By helping the Americans, France hoped to weaken the British Empire.

In 1781 the American forces—commanded by George Washington—and their French allies defeated the main British army in Virginia. The Americans had won the Revolutionary War. The final peace terms were settled in the Treaty of Paris in 1783. The British recognized the independence of the United States. All land east of the Mississippi now belonged to the new country.

✓ **READING CHECK:** *Finding the Main Idea* How did the ideas of the Enlightenment influence the American Revolution?

Effects of American Independence

In 1777 the Americans adopted a plan of government called the Articles of Confederation. The Articles set up a central government, but it was purposely weak. Many Americans did not trust that a central government would always protect the individual rights and liberties they had fought for in the Revolution. Thus Congress could not levy taxes or coin money. It could not regulate trade. Within 10 years, however, it became clear that a weak central government was not helping the country to work as a whole.

In May 1787 delegates from all the states met at a convention in Philadelphia to revise the Articles. The delegates soon realized that making changes in the Articles would not be enough. They decided instead to write a new constitution.

After choosing George Washington to preside over the convention, the delegates went to work. They wanted a strong central government. They also wanted some powers kept for the states. As a result, the new Constitution they wrote set up a federal system of government. This is a system of government in which power is divided between a central government and individual states. The central government was given several important powers. It could declare war, raise armies, and make treaties. It could coin money and regulate trade with foreign countries. The states and the people kept all other powers. The Constitution was approved in 1789. The federal government had three branches. Each branch acted as a check on the power of the others. The executive branch enforced the laws. The legislative branch made the laws. The judicial branch interpreted the laws.

The American Revolution and the writing of the U.S. Constitution were major events in world history. Enlightenment ideas were finally put into practice. The success of the American democracy also encouraged people around the world. They realized they could fight for political freedoms, too.

Of course, American democracy in 1789 was not perfect. Women had few rights, and slaves had no rights at all. Still, the world now had a democratic country that inspired the loyalty of most of its citizens.

READING CHECK: *Comparing and Contrasting* How was the new Constitution different from the old Articles of Confederation?

The United States in 1783

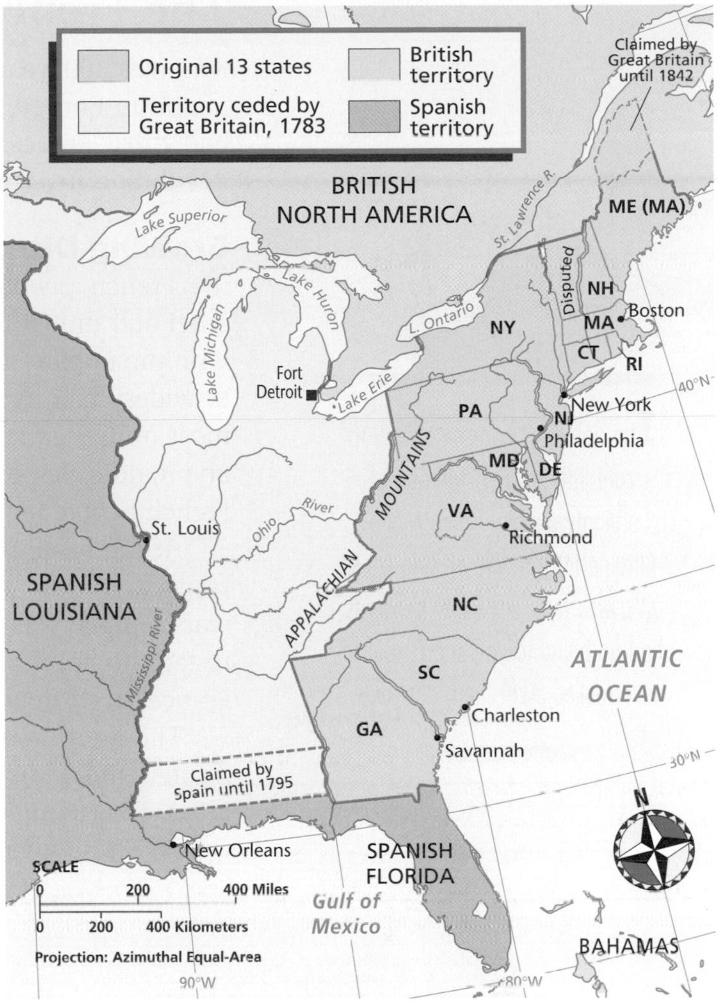

Original 13 states
Territory ceded by Great Britain, 1783
British territory
Spanish territory
Claimed by Great Britain until 1842
BRITISH NORTH AMERICA
Lake Superior
Lake Michigan
Lake Huron
L. Ontario
Lake Erie
St. Lawrence R.
Fort Detroit
ME (MA)
Disputed
NH
MA
Boston
CT
RI
NY
PA
NJ
New York
Philadelphia
MD
DE
VA
Richmond
NC
SC
GA
Charleston
Savannah
APPALACHIAN MOUNTAINS
Ohio River
St. Louis
Mississippi River
SPANISH LOUISIANA
Claimed by Spain until 1795
New Orleans
SPANISH FLORIDA
Gulf of Mexico
ATLANTIC OCEAN
BAHAMAS
N
40°N
30°N
90°W
80°W
SCALE
0 200 400 Miles
0 200 400 Kilometers
Projection: Azimuthal Equal-Area

The Treaty of Paris doubled the size of the United States.

Interpreting the Map **What nation controlled the region to the south of the United States? To the north? To the west?**

George Washington (1732–1799) led the American troops to victory in the Revolution and was elected the first president of the United States.

The French Revolution

For over 100 years France had been the largest and most powerful nation in Europe. For all of this time, a monarch with absolute power had ruled France. Yet within months of the beginning of the French Revolution in 1789, the king lost all power.

Our Amazing Planet

The nobles of France seemed to care little for the suffering of ordinary people. When Marie-Antoinette, the wife of King Louis XVI, was told that many peasants had no bread to eat, she is said to have replied, "Let them eat cake."

Growing Discontent As the United States won its independence, the French people struggled against **oppression**. Oppression is the cruel and unjust use of power against others. By the 1770s discontent with the nobility was widespread. Food shortages and rising prices led to widespread hunger. To make matter worse, the nobles, who owned most of the land, raised rents. Taxes were also raised on the peasants and middle classes while the nobles and the clergy paid no taxes. Some French people took to the streets, rioting against high prices and taxes.

At the same time, the French monarchy was losing authority and respect. Due to the king's expensive habits and spending on foreign wars, France was in deep debt. To pay the debts, King Louis XVI tried to tax the nobles and the clergy. When they refused to pay the taxes, France faced financial collapse.

The French peasants and middle classes had different complaints against the king. They did, however, share certain Enlightenment ideas. For example, they spoke of liberty and equality as their natural rights. These ideas united them against the king and nobles.

The Outbreak of Revolution
In 1789 a group representing the majority of the people declared itself to be the National Assembly. It was determined to change the existing government. This action marked the beginning of the French Revolution.

When Louis XVI moved troops into Paris and Versailles, there was fear that the soldiers would drive out the National Assembly by force. In Paris, the people took action. Angry city dwellers destroyed the Bastille prison, which they called a symbol of royal oppression. The violence spread as peasants attacked manor houses and monasteries throughout France.

◄ On July 14, 1789, a crowd destroyed the Bastille, freeing its prisoners. Bastille Day marked the spread of the Revolution and is celebrated in France every July 14.

The National Assembly quickly took away the privileges of the clergy and nobles. Feudalism was ended and peasants were freed from their old duties. The National Assembly also adopted the *Declaration of the Rights of Man and Citizen*. This document stated that men are born equal and remain equal under the law. It guaranteed basic rights and also defined the principles of the French Revolution—liberty, equality, and fraternity.

The End of the Monarchy In 1791 the National Assembly completed a constitution for France. This constitution allowed for the king to be the head of the government, but limited his authority. The constitution divided the government into three branches—executive, legislative, and judicial. Louis XVI pretended to agree to this new government. In secret, he tried to overthrow it. When he and his family tried to escape France in 1791, they were arrested and sent back to Paris.

BILITÉ DE
LARÉPUB
LIQUE.
LIBERTÉ,
EGALITÉ,
FRATERNI
TÉ OU LA
MORT

This poster summarizes the main goals of the French Revolution: liberty, equality, and fraternity. Fraternity means "brotherhood."

The French Republic In 1792 a new group of people, the National Convention, gathered and declared France a republic. The National Convention also put Louis XVI on trial as an enemy of the state. Urged on by a lawyer named Maximilien Robespierre, the members found the king guilty. In 1793, the king was sent to the guillotine, a machine that dropped a huge blade to cut off a person's head.

Robespierre was the leader of a political group known as the Jacobins. Many of the Jacobins wanted to bring about sweeping reforms that would benefit all classes of French society. As the French Revolution went on, the Jacobins gained more and more power. By the time Louis XVI was executed, Robespierre was probably the most powerful man in France. He and his allies controlled the actions of the National Convention.

The frequent use of the guillotine shocked people in France, Europe, and the United States. As a result, the French Revolution lost many supporters.

A group called the Jacobins controlled the National Convention. Robespierre was a powerful leader of the Jacobins.

Under Robespierre, the National Convention looked for other enemies. Anyone who had supported the king or criticized the revolution was a suspect. Thousands of people—nobles and peasants alike—died at the guillotine. This period, called the **Reign of Terror**, ended in 1794 when Robespierre himself was put to death. Despite the terror, the revolutionaries did achieve some goals. They replaced the monarchy with a republic. They also gave peasants and workers new political rights. They opened new schools and supported the idea of universal elementary education. They established wage and price controls in an effort to stop inflation. They abolished slavery in France's colonies. They encouraged religious tolerance.

Between 1795 and 1799, a government called the Directory tried to govern France. A new two-house legislature was created to make laws. This legislature also elected five officials called directors to run the government. The people selected to be directors, however, could not agree on many issues. They were corrupt and quarreled about many issues. They quickly became unpopular with the French people. In addition, by 1799 enemy armies were again threatening France. Food shortages were causing panic in the cities. Many French people concluded their country needed one strong leader to restore law and order.

✓ **READING CHECK:** *Summarizing* Why did many French peasants and poor workers support the Revolution?

Napoléon had a way of getting the public's attention. He was very popular with the French people.

The Napoléonic Era

In 1799 a young general named Napoléon Bonaparte overthrew the Directory and took control of the French government. Most people in France accepted Napoléon. In turn he supported the changes brought about by the Revolution. In 1804 France was declared an empire, and Napoléon was crowned emperor.

Napoléon as Emperor In France Napoléon used his unlimited power to restore order. He organized French law into one system—the Napoléonic Code. He set up the Bank of France to run the country's finances. Influenced by the Enlightenment, he built schools and universities.

A brilliant general, Napoléon won many land battles in Europe. By 1809 he ruled the Netherlands and Spain. He forced Austria and Prussia to be France's allies. He abolished the Holy Roman Empire. He also unified the northern Italian states into the Kingdom of Italy, under his control. Within five years of becoming emperor, Napoléon had reorganized and dominated Europe. Because of the important role that he played, the wars that France fought from 1796 until 1815 are called the Napoléonic Wars.

Napoléon also made changes in the lands he controlled. He put the Napoléonic Code into effect in the countries he conquered and abolished feudalism and serfdom. He also introduced new military techniques throughout Europe. Without intending to, the French increased feelings of loyalty and patriotism among the people Napoléon had conquered. In some places this increased opposition to French rule. Over time, the armies of Napoléon's enemies grew stronger.

In 1812 Napoléon invaded Russia with more than 500,000 soldiers. The invasion was a disaster. The cold Russian winter, hunger, and disease claimed the lives of most of the French soldiers. Napoléon finally ordered his soldiers to retreat.

BONAPARTE

This painting captures the glory of Napoléon as a military leader.

Napoléon's Defeat The monarchs of Europe took advantage of Napoléon's weakened state. Prussia, Austria, and Great Britain joined together to invade France. These allies captured Paris in 1814. Napoléon gave up the throne and went into exile on the island of Elba, near Italy. Louis XVIII, the brother of the executed king, was made the new king of France.

The following year Napoléon made a short-lived attempt to retake his empire. This period is known as the Hundred Days. Between March and June of 1815, Napoléon regained control of France. The king fled into exile. Soon, however, Napoléon's enemies sent armies against him. The other European nations defeated him at Waterloo in Belgium. Napoléon was sent to St. Helena, a small island in the South Atlantic. He lived there under guard and died in 1821. In 1840 the British allowed the French to bring Napoléon's remains back to Paris, where they lie to this day.

Governments of France, 1774–1814

1774	Louis XVI becomes king.
1789	Third Estate, as the National Assembly, assumes power.
1791	Legislative Assembly, with Louis XVI as constitutional monarch, begins rule.
1799	Napoléon establishes himself as First Consul.
1804	Napoléon is crowned emperor.
1814	Napoléon is defeated and the monarchy is restored.

After being ruled as a republic and then an empire, France became a monarchy once again in 1814.

Europe After Napoléon During the years of Napoléon's rule, France had become bigger and stronger than the other countries in Europe. After Napoléon's defeat, delegates from all over Europe met at the Congress of Vienna. Their goal was to bring back the **balance of power** in Europe. Having a balance of power is a way to keep peace by making sure no one nation or group of nations becomes too powerful.

Napoléon had not always upheld the ideals of the French Revolution, but he did extend their influence throughout Europe. This led other governments to fear that rebellions against monarchy might spread. Having defeated Napoléon, the major European powers wanted to restore order, keep the peace, and suppress the ideas of the revolution.

Many delegates to the Congress of Vienna were **reactionaries**. Reactionaries not only oppose change. They would like to actually undo certain changes. In this case they wanted to return to an earlier political system. These delegates were not comfortable with the ideals of the French Revolution, such as liberty and equality. They worried that these ideals would overturn the monarchies in their own countries.

One of the most influential leaders at the Congress of Vienna was Prince Metternich of Austria. To protect his absolute power in Austria, Metternich suppressed ideas such as freedom of speech and of the press. He encouraged other leaders to censor newspapers and to spy on individuals they suspected of revolutionary activity.

The Congress of Vienna redrew the map of Europe. Lands that Napoléon had conquered were taken away from France. In the end, France's boundaries were returned to where they had been in 1790. Small countries around France were combined into bigger, stronger ones. This was done to prevent France from ever again threatening the peace of Europe. France also had to pay other countries for the damages it had caused. Ruling families were returned to their thrones in Spain, Portugal, and parts of Italy. Switzerland alone kept its constitutional government but had to promise to remain neutral in European wars.

The Congress of Vienna also led to an alliance between Great Britain, Russia, Prussia, and Austria. The governments of these countries agreed to work together to keep order in Europe. For 30 years the alliance successfully prevented new revolutions in Europe.

Many of Europe's royal families came to Vienna during the winter of 1814–15. They attended balls while diplomats and rulers discussed the situation of Europe after Napoléon.

✓ **READING CHECK:** *Drawing Conclusions* Why did the other countries of Europe want to defeat Napoléon?

Section 2 Review

go.hrw.com Homework Practice Online
Keyword: SJ3 HP8

Define and explain Patriots, Loyalists, alliance, oppression, Reign of Terror, balance of power, reactionaries

Reading for the Main Idea

1. *Human Systems* Why did the 13 American colonies rebel against Great Britain?
2. *Human Systems* What were the causes and effects of the French Revolution?
3. *Human Systems* How did Napoléon change France and the rest of Europe?

Critical Thinking

4. **Supporting a Point of View** Many people argue that the United States was not really created until 1789. Why do you think this is so? Explain your answer.

Organizing What You Know

5. **Identifying Time Order** Copy the following time line. Use it to list some important events of both the American Revolution and the French Revolution.

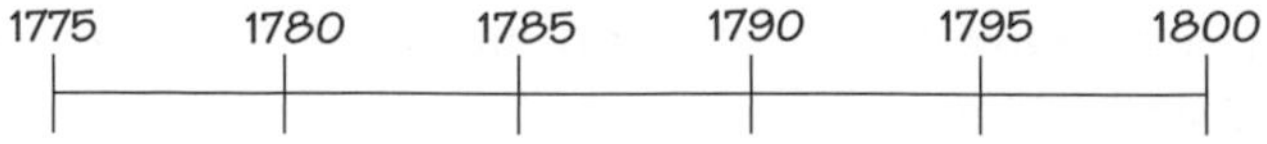
1775
1780
1785
1790
1795
1800

Section 3 The Industrial Revolution

Read to Discover

1. How did the Industrial Revolution begin?
2. What developments in transportation and communications helped spread industrial development?
3. What features of business affected life in the Industrial Age?

Define

Industrial Revolution
factors of production
capital
factories
capitalism
mass production

An early steam locomotive

WHY IT MATTERS

The high standards of living that most Americans enjoy today were made possible by the Industrial Revolution. Use CNNfyi.com or other **current events** sources to find out more about industry and industrialized nations.

The Origins of the Industrial Revolution

In the early 1700s inventors began putting the ideas of the Scientific Revolution to work by creating many new machines. Advances in industry, business, transportation, and communications changed people's lives around the world in almost every way. This period, which lasted through the 1700s and 1800s, was called the **Industrial Revolution**.

New Needs in Agriculture The first stages of the Industrial Revolution took place in agricultural communities in Great Britain. Ways of dividing, managing, and using the land had changed greatly since the Middle Ages. People had begun to think about land in new ways. Wealthy farmers began to buy more land to increase the size of their farms. Small farmers, unable to compete with these large operations, sometimes lost their land. At the same time, Europe's population continued to grow, which meant that the demand for food grew as well. Farmers recognized the need to improve farming methods and increase production.

One such farmer was Jethro Tull. He invented a new farm machine, called a seed drill, for planting seeds in straight rows. More inventors soon followed with other new farm machines. The machinery made farms more productive, and farmers were able to grow more food with fewer workers. As a result, many farm workers lost their jobs. Many of these people moved to cities to look for other kinds of work.

▲ This painting shows the original McCormick reaper, used to cut grain. It was invented by Cyrus H. McCormick in 1831.

Factors of Production The Industrial Revolution began in Great Britain because the country had the right **factors of production**. These are items necessary for industry to grow. They include land, natural resources, workers, and **capital**. Capital refers to the money and tools needed to make a product.

Great Britain had rich deposits of coal and iron ore. It also had many rivers to provide water power for **factories** and transportation. Money was available, since many British people had grown wealthy during the 1700s. They were willing to invest their money in new businesses. The British government allowed people to start businesses and protected their property. Labor was available since many ex-farm workers needed jobs.

Our Amazing Planet

One early water-powered machine in an English mill was said to spin more than 300 million yards of silk thread every day!

✓ **READING CHECK:** *Summarizing* What factors of production helped Great Britain to develop early industries?

The Growth of Industry

As mentioned earlier, agricultural needs led to new machines and methods for farming. People in other industries began to wonder how machines could help them as well. For example, before the early 1700s, British people had spun thread and woven their own cloth at home on simple spinning wheels and looms. It was a slow process, and the demand for cloth was always greater than the supply.

This painting shows one artist's view of a factory. By 1800, textiles made in English factories were shipped all over the world.

The Textile Industry To speed up cloth making in the early 1700s, English inventors built new types of spinning machines and looms. In 1769 Richard Arkwright invented a water-powered spinning machine. He eventually set up his spinning machines in mills and hired workers to run them. Workers earned a fixed rate of pay for a set number of hours of work. Arkwright brought his workers and machinery together in a large building called a factory. Arkwright's arrangement with his workers was the beginning of the factory system.

In 1785 Edmund Cartwright built a water-powered loom. It could weave cloth much faster than could a hand loom. In fact, one worker with a powered loom could produce as much cloth as several people with traditional ones. Each new invention that improved the spinning and weaving process led to more inventions and improvements.

The factory system soon spread to other industries. Machines were invented to make shoes, clothing, furniture, and other goods. Machines were also used for printing, papermaking, lumber and food processing, and for making other machines. More and more British people went to work in factories and mills.

▲ New industries needed much steel for machinery. The Bessemer converter, invented in the 1850s, was a cheaper, better way to make steel.

The Steam Engine Early machines in factories were driven by water power. This system, however, had drawbacks. It meant that a factory had to be located on a stream or river, preferably next to a waterfall or dam. In many cases these streams and rivers were far from raw materials and overland transportation routes. The water flow in rivers can change from season to season, and sometimes rivers run dry. People recognized that a lighter, movable, and more dependable power source was needed. Many inventors thought using steam power to run machines was the answer.

Steam engines boil water and use the steam to do work. Early steam engines were not efficient though. In 1769 James Watt, a Scottish inventor, built a modern steam engine that did work well. With Watt's invention, steam power largely replaced water power. This meant that factories could be built anywhere.

The factory system changed the lives of workers. In the past, workers had taken years to learn their trades. In a factory, however, a worker could learn to run a machine in just a day or two. Factory owners hired unskilled workers—often young men, women, and children—and paid them as little as possible. As a result, the older skilled workers were often out of work.

✓ **READING CHECK:** *Cause and Effect* How was the textile industry created in Great Britain?

The Spread of the Industrial Revolution

Great Britain quickly became the world's leading industrial power. British laws encouraged people to use capital to set up factories. Great Britain's stable government was good for industry too.

The rest of Europe did not develop industry as quickly. For one thing, the French Revolution and Napoléon's wars had disrupted Europe's economies. That made it difficult to put the factors of production to work. Many countries also lacked the resources needed to industrialize.

These steamboats from the 1850s carried people and goods on the Mississippi River.

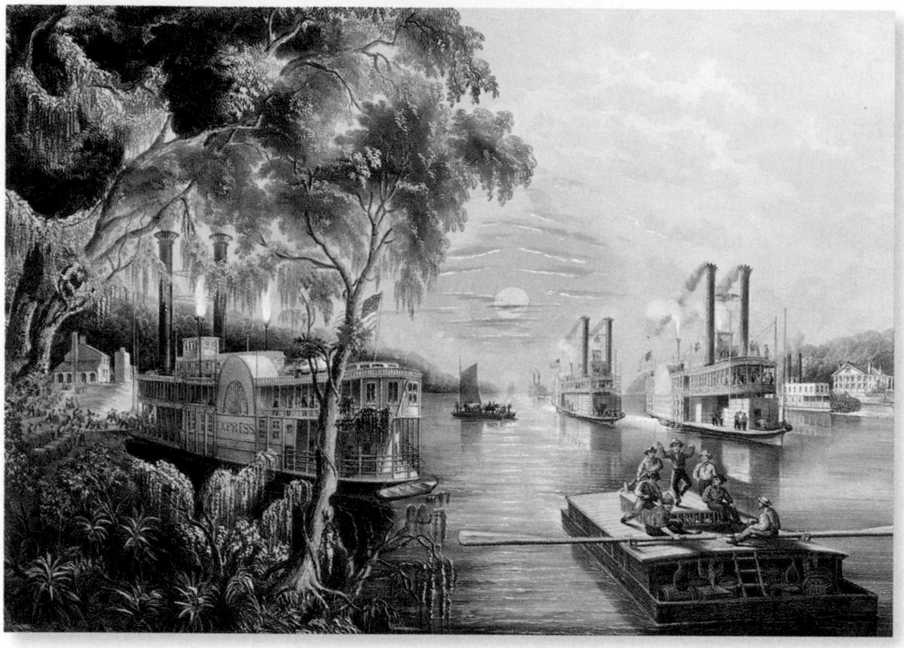

The Industrial Revolution did spread quickly to the United States though. The United States had a stable government, rich natural resources, and a growing labor force. Americans were quick to adapt British inventions and methods to their own industries.

Transportation Since the Middle Ages, horse-drawn wagons had been the main form of transportation in Europe. Factory owners needed better transportation to get raw materials and send goods to market. To move goods faster, stone-topped roads were built in Europe and the United States. Canals were dug to link rivers. The steam engine was also put to work in transportation. In 1808 American inventor Robert Fulton built the first steamboat. Within a few decades, steamships were crossing the Atlantic.

Steam also powered the first railroads. An English engineer, George Stephenson, perfected a steam locomotive that ran on rails. By the 1830s, railways were being built across Great Britain, mainland Europe, and the United States.

Communication Even before 1800, scientists had known that electricity and magnetism were related. American inventor Samuel F. B. Morse put this knowledge to practical use. Morse sent an electrical current through a wire. The current made a machine at the other end click. Morse also invented a code of clicking dots and dashes to send messages this way.

Morse's inventions—the telegraph and the Morse code—brought about a major change in communications. Telegraph wires soon stretched across continents and under oceans. Suddenly information and ideas could travel at the speed of electricity.

The telegraph revolutionized communications in the 1850s. This device is a telegraph receiver.

Life in the Industrial Age

The 1800s are sometimes called the Industrial Age. This was an age of new inventions. It was a time when businesses found new ways to produce and distribute goods. The owners of factories in the Industrial Age often became very wealthy. Low factory wages, however, meant many workers faced poverty.

The Rise of Capitalism In the late 1800s European and American individuals owned and operated factories. This economic system is called **capitalism**. In a capitalist system, individuals or companies, not the government, control the factors of production.

The early capitalists wanted to make as much profit as possible from their factories. They divided each manufacturing process into a series of steps. Each worker performed just one of the steps, over and over again. This division of labor meant workers could produce more goods in less time.

Factory owners used machines to make the parts for their products. These parts were identical and interchangeable. To speed up production, the parts were carried to the workers in the factory. Each worker added one part, and the product moved on to the next worker. This method of production is called an assembly line.

In the early 1900s, Henry Ford used an assembly line to build cars.

Interpreting the Visual Record **How do you think the assembly line might have made work easier for these people?**

Mass Production The division of labor, interchangeable parts, and the assembly line made mass production possible. **Mass production** is a system of producing large numbers of identical items. Mass production lowered the cost of clothing, furniture, and other goods. It allowed more people to buy manufactured products and to enjoy a higher standard of living.

✓ **READING CHECK:** *Finding the Main Idea* What is capitalism and how did it affect the Industrial Revolution?

go.hrw.com **Homework Practice Online**

Keyword: SJ3 HP8

Section 3 Review

Define and explain Industrial Revolution, factors of production, capital, factories, capitalism, mass production

Reading for the Main Idea

1. *Environmental and Society* Where did the Industrial Revolution begin and why?
2. *Human Systems* What advances in transportation and communications helped to spread the Industrial Revolution?
3. *Human Systems* How did capitalism and mass production affect people's standard of living in the late 1800s?

Critical Thinking

4. **Drawing Conclusions** Why do you think the steam engine was such an important invention of the Industrial Revolution?

Organizing What You Know

5. **Categorizing** Copy the following graphic organizer. Use it to describe some important inventions of the Industrial Revolution.

Invention	Inventor	Importance
seed drill		
spinning machine		
water-powered loom		
steam engine		
steam locomotive		
telegraph		

Section 4 Expansion and Reform

Read to Discover

1. How did life in Europe and America change after 1850?
2. What led to reforms in the later 1800s?
3. How did nationalism change the map of Europe in the mid-1800s?

Define

working class
literacy
emigrate
suburbs
reform
suffragettes
nationalism

Why It Matters

By the later 1800s, new ideas and technology began to improve city life. Use CNNfyi.com or other **current events** sources to find out about solutions to today's urban problems.

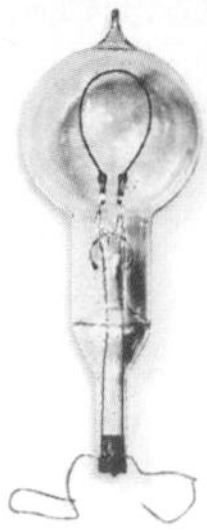

Thomas Edison's electric light bulb

The Rise of the Middle Class

The Industrial Revolution changed how people in Europe and America worked and lived. Industries and cities grew, and new inventions made life easier.

During the later 1800s many people became better educated. Some became wealthy. This group included bankers, doctors, lawyers, professors, engineers, factory owners, and merchants. Also in this group were the managers who helped keep industries running. Together these people and their families were known as the middle class. Membership in the middle class was based upon economic standing rather than upon birth.

Doctors were one of the groups who made up the middle class of the late 1800s. Medical advances made during this period made their jobs safer and more efficient.

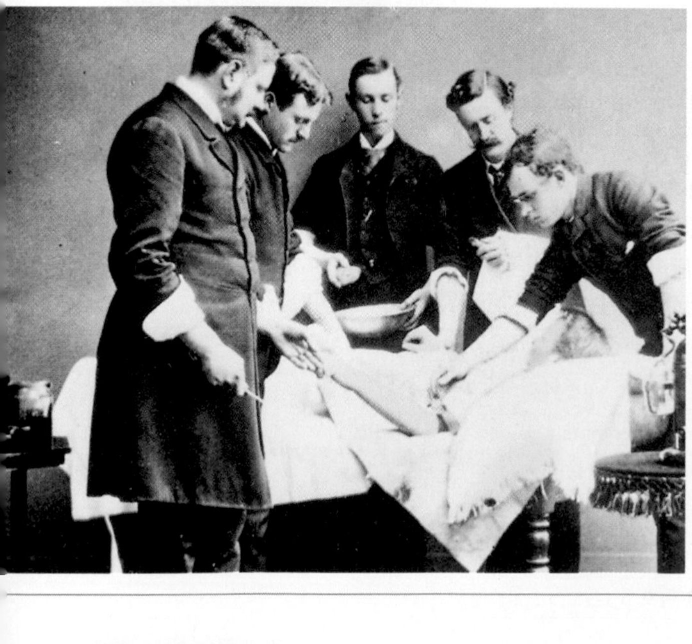

The ideas of the middle class influenced many areas of life in Western Europe and in the United States. Over time, the middle class's wealth, social position, lifestyle, and political power grew. Government leaders began turning to some middle-class individuals for advice, particularly about business and industry.

Many middle-class families had enough money that women did not need to work outside the home. They cleaned, cooked, and took care of the children, often with hired help. In the mid-1800s, however, many middle-class women started to express a desire for roles outside the home.

For some women, doing something outside the home meant independence. It was also a way to earn a living. During the late 1800s more jobs opened up to women. They became nurses, secretaries, telephone operators, and teachers.

✓ **READING CHECK:** *Finding the Main Idea* What role did the middle class play in the society of the late 1800s?

▲ After 1870, more and more women went to high school. For the first time they began to study the same subjects as men did.

The Growth of Society

The middle class was not the only group of people to enjoy the benefits of the Industrial Age. By the 1870s life was improving in some ways for both the middle class and the **working class,** people who worked in factories and mines.

Technology and Communication In the 1870s a tremendous new power source was developed. That power source was electricity. This led to a new wave of inventions in Western Europe and the United States. The electric generator produced the power needed to run all kinds of machines and engines. Thomas Edison's electric light bulb created a new way of lighting rooms, streets, and cities. Alexander Graham Bell's telephone made it possible to transmit the human voice over long distance.

In the late 1800s the first successful gasoline-driven automobile was built. In 1908 American inventor Henry Ford produced the Model T. This was the first automobile to become popular with American buyers.

◀ Scientists of the 1800s used microscopes like this one to study cells.

Other Advances Advances in science and medicine also transformed people's lives. Scientists discovered more about the connection between food and health. This new knowledge, plus new information about diseases, made it possible for people to live healthier, longer lives.

Scientists of this time also made great advances in the fields of chemistry and physics. For example, they formed new theories about the structure of the atom and organized all known elements into the periodic table. It was also at this time that X-rays were discovered and first used in medicine. Scientists like Max Planck and Albert Einstein developed new ideas that changed the study of physics. Their ideas were the basis for the work of many later experiments.

Several new fields of study, together called the social sciences, gained popularity during this period. Scholars saw these fields as a way to study people as members of society. The social sciences include such fields as economics, politics, anthropology, and psychology. The study of history also changed. Historians searched for evidence of the past in documents, diaries, letters, and other written sources. As a result, new views of history began to emerge from their research.

Public Education After 1870, governments in Europe and the United States required all children to attend school. The spread of education had many benefits. As **literacy**—the ability to read—became widespread, more books and magazines were published. Newspapers that carried stories from all over the world also became very popular. By reading them, citizens became more informed about their governments.

The World

As greater numbers of people learned to read, newspapers competed for their attention. They published eye-catching stories and cartoons.

Arts and Entertainment City dwellers of the late 1800s found themselves with more time and money for entertainment. Theaters opened to meet a demand for concerts, plays, and vaudeville shows. Art collections were made available to the public by displaying them in museums. Free public libraries opened in many cities. Sports became more organized, and cities began to sponsor teams with official rules and national competitions. Many cities began to construct public parks. These parks allowed people who lived in the cities to enjoy outdoor activities. By the end of the 1800s many of these parks had begun to include playgrounds for children.

A Growing Population One of the greatest changes of the later 1800s was the rapid growth of cities in the United States. Faced with crowded, dirty cities and seeking new opportunities, many Europeans chose to emigrate to the United States. To **emigrate** means to leave one country to live in another. The United States was not the only destination for these emigrants. Many also chose to seek new lives in South America, Africa, Australia, and New Zealand.

Between 1870 and 1900 more than 10 million people left Europe for the United States. These newcomers hoped to find economic opportunities. Some sought political and religious freedom as well.

This is a painting of a croquet game in a public park. It reflects the increased participation in free-time activities during the late 1800s.

Interpreting the Visual Record **What does this painting suggest about sports in the later 1800s?**

CONNECTING TO *Art*

A New Art Period

Works of art not only show the values of an artist but also the values of the society in which the artist lives. The American and French Revolutions, for example, changed society deeply. Many artists were inspired to paint stirring scenes from history and nature. These artists were called *romantics*. Their scenes showed life to be more exciting and satisfying than it normally is.

By the mid-1800s, however, many artists had rejected romanticism. These artists instead wanted to portray life as it really was. A style called *realism* developed. The realists painted ordinary living conditions and familiar settings. They tried to re-create what they saw around them, accurately and honestly.

Honore Daumier was a French realist. He painted *The Washerwoman* during the Industrial Revolution in France, a time when many city workers were struggling to survive. The subject in the painting is one of these workers.

Understanding What You Read

1. How was realism different from romanticism?
2. What types of subjects and scenes might a realist paint?

City Improvements Faced with rapidly growing populations and changes in society, many cities needed civic improvements. Local governments began to provide water and sewer service to city dwellers. Many streets were also paved. In 1829 London organized a police force. Many other cities soon had police forces, too.

Cities around the world grew rapidly in the 1800s. By the early 1900s, more people lived in cities than in the country. Many cities—including New York, London, Paris, and Berlin—had populations of more than 1 million.

Cities also created public transportation systems. Horse-drawn streetcars and buses were used mainly within cities. Trains, however, could take people far outside a city. As a result, some people began to move outside cities to areas called **suburbs**. These people usually took trains into cities each morning and returned to their homes in the suburbs at night.

✓ **READING CHECK:** *Summarizing* What were some advances of the later 1800s?

Our Amazing Planet

Between 1865 and 1900 most American cities doubled or tripled in size. Much of this growth was due to immigration. Many immigrants to the United States moved to New York City. By 1900 the city's population was nearly five times larger than it had been in 1850.

Political and Social Reform

In addition to great advances in technology, communications, science, and medicine, the mid-1800s and early 1900s saw many political and social reforms. To **reform** something is to remove its faults. Around the world, citizens worked to improve their governments and societies.

Emmeline Pankhurst (1858–1928) led many demonstrations and marches on behalf of the women's suffrage movement in Great Britain.

Great Britain In Great Britain reformers passed laws that allowed male factory workers in cities to vote. Laws were also passed to improve conditions in factories, and slavery was abolished. New laws were passed to provide health insurance, unemployment insurance, and money for the elderly.

Beginning in the late 1800s, many women in Great Britain became **suffragettes**. These women campaigned for their right to vote. They were led by outspoken women like Emmeline Pankhurst. British women gained this right in 1928.

France A revolution in France in 1848 forced the king from the throne. A new government called the Second Republic was established. It guaranteed free speech and gave the vote to all men. In 1875, a new French constitution established the Third Republic. This constitution lasted for nearly 70 years.

RÉPUBLIQUE FRANÇAISE.
Combat du peuple parisien dans les journées des 22, 23 et 24 Février 1848.

In 1848, French citizens overthrew the king and set up the Second Republic.

United States The issue of slavery divided the United States in the mid-1800s. In late 1860 and early 1861 several southern states broke from the Union to form the Confederate States of America. The Civil War followed and raged until 1865 when the Confederacy surrendered. Congress then amended the Constitution to abolish slavery and grant citizenship to former slaves. The vote was given to all men, regardless of race or color.

Many reforms were the results of efforts by women such as Elizabeth Cady Stanton and Lucretia Mott. As early as 1848 they had campaigned for the abolition of slavery, equality for women, and the right to vote. In the 1890s and early 1900s, the movement for women's right to vote grew stronger. The Nineteenth Amendment to the Constitution, ratified in 1920, finally gave women this right.

✔ **READING CHECK:** *Comparing and Contrasting* How were reforms in Great Britain, France, and the United States in the mid-1800s and early 1900s similar?

Nationalism in Europe

Nationalism is the love of one's country more than the love of one's native region or state. In the 1800s, nationalism led to the unification of Italy and of Germany. It was also a driving force for change in Russia.

In the early 1800s the Congress of Vienna had divided Italy into several states, some of which were ruled by Austria. In the 1850s and 1860s, a nationalist named Giuseppe Garibaldi led a movement to unify these states. He and his army defeated the Austrians and their French allies and drove them out of Italy. Largely because of his efforts, most of present-day Italy had been unified by 1861. In that year Victor Emmanuel II was made the king of Italy.

Germany in the mid-1800s was a patchwork of 39 independent states. The largest was Prussia, ruled by William I. In 1862 he appointed Otto von Bismarck one of his advisers. Both men wanted to make Germany into a powerful unified country. Bismarck convinced the other German states to join in this effort and to declare war first on Austria, Prussia's chief rival, and then on France. After the war, the German states were joined together into the German Empire. William I became the first kaiser, or emperor.

▲ Otto von Bismarck (1815–1898) was known for his strong will and determination.

In the 1800s Russia had more territory and people than any other country in Europe. Its economy, however, was not as developed as those of other countries. People from Russia's many ethnic groups felt very little unity with each other. In the 1850s Czar Alexander II tried to introduce major reforms. He freed all the serfs in Russia and introduced political changes. Later czars, however, tried to undo these reforms. Censorship and discrimination against minorities became widespread. This repression created an explosive situation in Russia. In 1905, a group of revolutionaries tried to overthrow the czar but failed.

✓ **READING CHECK:** *Drawing Inferences* How did nationalism help reshape nations?

Section 4 Review

go.hrw.com **Homework Practice Online** Keyword: SJ3 HP8

Define and explain working class, literacy, emigrate, suburbs, reform, suffragettes, nationalism

Reading for the Main Idea

1. *Human Systems* What allowed people's lives to improve during the last half of the 1800s?
2. *Human Systems* How did reforms of the later 1800s and early 1900s affect people's lives?
3. *Human Systems* How did nationalism lead to the unification of Italy and Germany in the mid-1800s?

Critical Thinking

4. **Analyzing** What effect did immigration of the later 1800s have on the United States?

Organizing What You Know

5. **Categorizing** Copy the following chart. List the home country of each leader. Then give details about his accomplishments.

Leader	Country	Accomplishments
Giuseppe Garibaldi		
Otto von Bismarck		
Czar Alexander II		

CHAPTER 8 Reviewing What You Know

Building Vocabulary

On a separate sheet of paper, write sentences to define each of the following.

1. Enlightenment
2. reason
3. individualism
4. popular sovereignty
5. Patriots
6. alliance
7. oppression
8. factors of production
9. capital
10. capitalism
11. mass production
12. literacy
13. emigrate
14. reform
15. nationalism

Reviewing the Main Ideas

1. *Human Systems* What did Enlightenment thinkers hope to discover?
2. *Human Systems* What led to the defeat of the British in the American Revolution?
3. *Environment and Society* What conditions in Great Britain gave rise to the Industrial Revolution?
4. *Environment and Society* How did education change greatly in Europe and the United States during the later 1800s and what were the benefits?
5. *Human Systems* What were the effects of nationalism on European nations in the late 1800s?

Understanding History and Society

Plans for Reform

Imagine you are the mayor of a large European city in the mid-1800s. Using a chart, make a presentation that lists and describes the reforms and changes you think should be made in your city. Consider the following:

- Health and safety issues.
- Communication and transportation needs.
- Education needs.

Thinking Critically

1. **Analyzing** How did Enlightenment ideas influence American democracy?
2. **Drawing Conclusions** Why did revolutions break out in America and France in the late 1700s?
3. **Analyzing** How did Napoléon Bonaparte change France and the rest of Europe in the early 1800s?
4. **Supporting a Point of View** Which three advances in the later 1800s do you think changed people's lives the most? Explain your answer.
5. **Evaluating** Why was the middle class so important to the Industrial Revolution?

Building Social Studies Skills

Map Activity

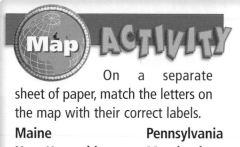

On a separate sheet of paper, match the letters on the map with their correct labels.

Maine	**Pennsylvania**
New Hampshire	**Maryland**
Massachusetts	**Virginia**
Connecticut	**North Carolina**
New York	**Georgia**

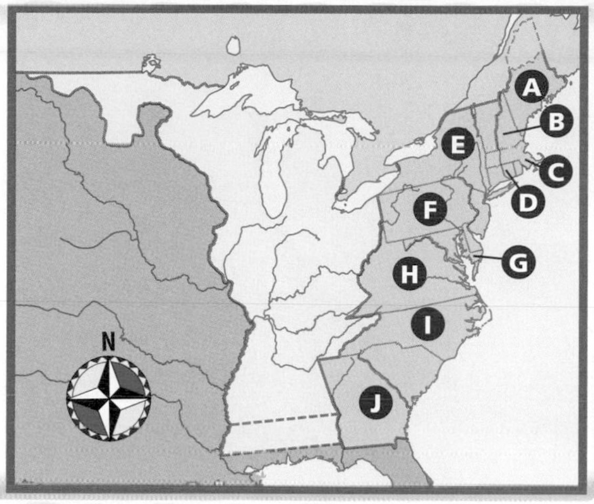

A
B
C
D
E
F
G
H
I
J
N

Mental Mapping Skills Activity

On a separate sheet of paper, draw a freehand map of Europe in the late 1800s. Make a key for your map and label the following:

Great Britain	**Italy**
France	**Russia**
Germany	**Austria**

Writing Activity

Imagine you are a news reporter in France in 1789, just as the French Revolution is breaking out. Write a news story about why the French people are in revolt and what they hope to achieve. Be sure to use standard grammar, spelling, sentence structure, and punctuation.

Alternative Assessment

Portfolio Activity

Learning About Your Local History

Industries in Your Town Research one or two of the main industries of your town, region, or state. Create a chart to explain when, where, why, and how the industry or industries were developed.

internet connect

Internet Activity: go.hrw.com
KEYWORD: SJ3 GT8

Choose a topic to explore about the birth of the modern world:

- Explore the ideas of the Enlightenment.
- Investigate the causes of the French Revolution.
- Understand capitalism.

CHAPTER 9

The Modern World

The 1900s were filled with change. Great wars, economic depressions, horrible injustices, and tremendous technological advances have all taken place. You will find out how it all happened in this chapter.

One of the events that affected the world in the 1900s was the Great Depression. In the early 1930s millions of workers throughout the world could not find jobs and people had no money to buy goods.

During the Great Depression, young people faced special problems. In some cases, parents expected children to work when the parents themselves could not. Children were often a burden in poor families. For many youngsters, running away seems the only solution. At one point, almost 250,000 teenaged "hoboes" were roaming the United States. Many of these young people searched for any kind of work or odd job that they could find.

Poster from the Great Depression

YEARS OF DUST
RESETTLEMENT ADMINISTRATION
Rescues Victims
Restores Land to Proper Use

Migrant child

TEXAS 1939
122654
FARM
DRIVE SAFELY

Depression-era farmhouse

Section 1 World War I

Read to Discover

1. What were the causes of World War I?
2. How did science and technology make this war different from earlier wars?
3. How was the world changed because of World War I?

Define

militarism
U-boats
armistice

Locate

England
France
Germany
Russia
Austria-Hungary
Ottoman Empire
Serbia
Sarajevo

WHY IT MATTERS

World War I started in the Balkans—a region that is still the scene of much conflict. Use CNNfyi.com or other **current events** sources to learn what is happening in this region today. Record your findings in your journal.

BOOTE

German poster from World War I

Beginning of World War I

By the early 1900s, countries across Europe were competing for power. They built up strong armies to protect themselves and their interests. Powerful nations feared each other. Tensions were high. The stage was set for war.

The spirit of nationalism was still strong in Europe in the early 1900s. Nationalism is a fierce pride in one's country. Many European countries wanted more power and more land. They built strong armies and threatened to use force to get what they wanted. The use of strong armies and the threat of force to gain power is called **militarism**.

Europe's leaders did not trust one another. To protect their nations against strong enemies, they formed alliances. An alliance is an agreement between countries. If a country is attacked, its allies—the members of the alliance—help it fight.

By 1907 Europe was divided into two opposing sides. Germany, Austria-Hungary, and Italy had formed one alliance. England, France, and Russia had formed another.

The attention of both alliances was soon drawn to the Balkans, a region in southeastern Europe. In 1878 Serbia, part of this region, had become an independent country. Serbian nationalists now wanted control of Bosnia and Herzogovina, which belonged to Austria-Hungary.

On June 28, 1914, a Serbian nationalist shot and killed the heir to the Austro-Hungarian throne, Archduke Francis Ferdinand. As a result, Austria-Hungary declared war on Serbia. Russia supported Serbia; Germany supported Austria-Hungary. With Russia and its allies on one side and Germany and its allies on the other, conflict quickly spread.

▲ This drawing of the killing of Archduke Francis Ferdinand in Sarajevo was published in French newspapers.

internet connect

GO TO: go.hrw.com
KEYWORD: SJ3 CH9
FOR: Web sites about the modern world

In August 1914 Germany declared war on Russia. Russia was allied with France, so Germany declared war on France, too. England declared war on Germany. Japan also declared war on Germany. England, France, Russia, and Japan became known as the Allied Powers. The alliance of Germany, Austria-Hungary, the Ottoman Empire, and Bulgaria was called the Central Powers. Later in the war, Italy left the Central Powers and joined the Allied Powers. Eventually, the Allied Powers included 32 countries.

✓ **READING CHECK:** *Identifying Cause and Effect* How did militarism and alliances help set the stage for war in Europe?

A New Kind of War

New weapons played a major role in World War I. Germany introduced submarines, which were called **U-boats**. This name is short for "underwater boats." Germany also introduced poison gas, which was later used by both sides and caused great loss of life. Other new weapons included large, long-range cannons and the machine gun. Machine guns could kill hundreds of people in a few minutes.

World War I was also the first war to use the airplane. At first airplanes were used mainly to observe enemy troops. Later, machine guns were placed on airplanes, so they could fire on troops and shoot at each other in the sky. England also introduced the tank during the war. This huge, heavy vehicle could not be easily stopped. With machine guns mounted on them, tanks could kill large numbers of soldiers.

The Allied Powers and the Central Powers divided Europe into two opposing sides.

Europe at the Beginning of World War I

10°W
0°
60°N
50°N
40°N
NORWAY
SWEDEN
FINLAND
Petrograd
RUSSIA
ATLANTIC OCEAN
NORTH SEA
DENMARK
BALTIC SEA
GREAT BRITAIN
NETHERLANDS
London
GERMAN EMPIRE
Berlin
Vistula River
Dnieper R.
English Channel
BELGIUM
Rhine R.
LUXEMBOURG
Paris
ALSACE-LORRAINE
Danube R.
Vienna
FRANCE
SWITZERLAND
AUSTRIA-HUNGARY
Bay of Biscay
ROMANIA
BLACK SEA
BOSNIA AND HERZEGOVINA
Sarajevo
SERBIA
Danube R.
BULGARIA
ADRIATIC SEA
ITALY
PORTUGAL
SPAIN
Corsica (FRENCH)
Sardinia (ITALIAN)
Rome
MONTENEGRO
ALBANIA
Balkan Peninsula
OTTOMAN EMPIRE
Tigris R.
Allied Powers
Neutral Countries
Central Powers
National capital
SCALE
0 200 400 Miles
0 200 400 Kilometers
Projection: Azimuthal Equal-Area
N

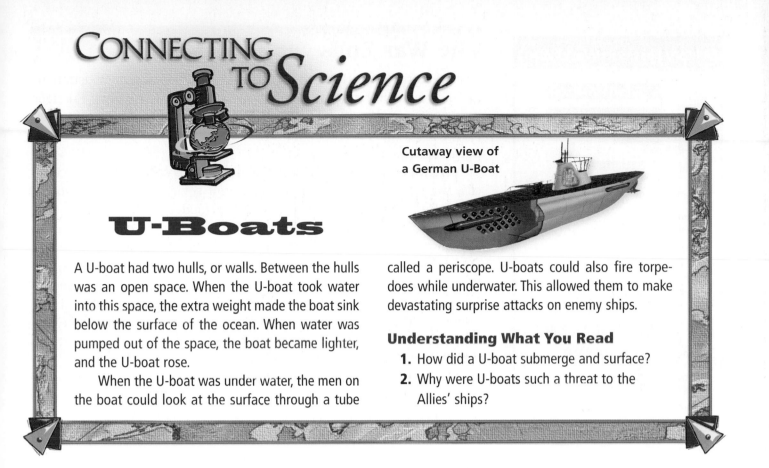

CONNECTING TO *Science*

U-Boats

Cutaway view of a German U-Boat

A U-boat had two hulls, or walls. Between the hulls was an open space. When the U-boat took water into this space, the extra weight made the boat sink below the surface of the ocean. When water was pumped out of the space, the boat became lighter, and the U-boat rose.

When the U-boat was under water, the men on the boat could look at the surface through a tube called a periscope. U-boats could also fire torpedoes while underwater. This allowed them to make devastating surprise attacks on enemy ships.

Understanding What You Read

1. How did a U-boat submerge and surface?
2. Why were U-boats such a threat to the Allies' ships?

The Early Years of the War Early in the war, Germany attacked France. The German army almost reached Paris, the French capital. However, Russia attacked Germany and Austria-Hungary, forcing Germany's attention east. At sea, England used its powerful navy to stop supplies from reaching Germany by ship. Germany used its deadly U-boats to sink ships carrying supplies to Great Britain.

At first, both sides thought they would win a quick victory. They were wrong. Armies dug in for a long and costly fight. World War I would go on for four years.

The United States and World War I At first, the United States stayed out of World War I. In 1917, however, Germany tried to persuade Mexico to join the Central Powers. The Germans promised to help Mexico retake Arizona, New Mexico, and Texas from the United States after the war. This angered many Americans.

At the same time, German U-boats were attacking American ships carrying supplies to the Allies. Many ships were sunk and many Americans died.

The United States had another motivation for joining the war. The major Allied countries had moved toward democracy, but the Central Powers had not. President Woodrow Wilson told Congress that "the world must be made safe for democracy." On April 6, 1917, the United States declared war on Germany.

American soldiers march through Paris during World War I.

✓ **READING CHECK:** *Summarizing* Why did the United States enter World War I?

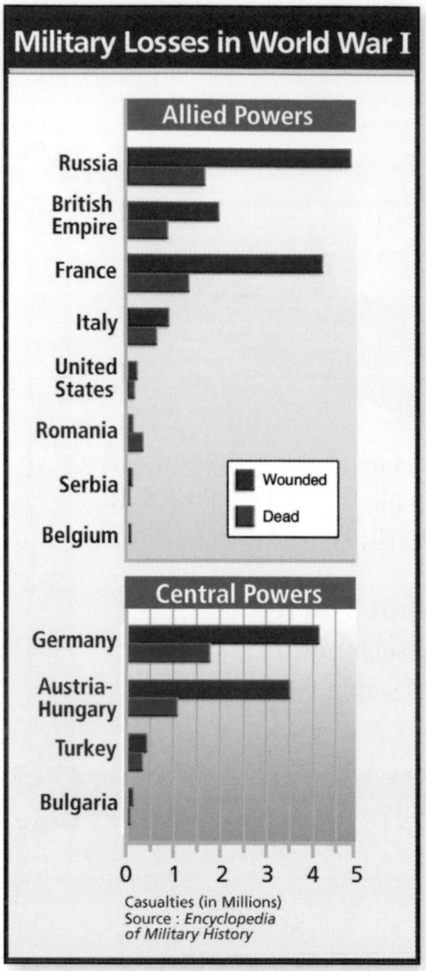
Military Losses in World War I
Allied Powers
Russia
British Empire
France
Italy
United States
Romania
Serbia
Belgium
Wounded
Dead
Central Powers
Germany
Austria-Hungary
Turkey
Bulgaria
0 1 2 3 4 5
Casualties (in Millions)
Source : *Encyclopedia of Military History*

Interpreting the Graph Which of the Allied Powers had the highest number of total casualties? Which of the Central Powers had the highest casualties?

The War Ends

During World War I, Russian citizens held protests and demonstrations because they did not have enough food and because so many Russians were dying in the war. The Russian army joined the people in their protests. In March 1917 the czar, or king, was overthrown and put in prison.

A new government was set up. Political groups called soviets, or councils, were also formed. The most powerful soviet leader was Vladimir Lenin. He offered the Russian people peace, food, and land. Lenin's ideas were part of an economic and political system known as communism. On November 7, 1917, Lenin's followers took control of Russia.

Lenin's government signed a peace treaty with the Central Powers, and Russia withdrew from the war. In 1918 Lenin's followers established a communist party. Some Russians wanted the czar to return, and Civil War broke out. The Communists won. In 1922 they renamed their country the Union of Soviet Socialist Republics, or the Soviet Union.

With Russia out of the war, the tide began to turn in favor of Germany. The German army advanced on Paris. However, when the United States entered the war, the German army was pushed back to its own border. Germany's allies began to surrender. At last, Germany itself surrendered. An **armistice** was signed. An armistice is an agreement to stop fighting.

The fighting stopped on November 11, 1918. More than 8.5 million soldiers had been killed, and 21 million more wounded. Millions who did not fight died from starvation, disease, and bombs.

Making Peace In January 1919 the Allied nations met near Paris to decide what would happen now that the war was over. This meeting came to be known as the Paris Peace Conference.

President Wilson wanted fair peace terms to end the war. He felt that harsh terms might lead to future wars. His ideas were called the Fourteen Points. These ideas called for no secret treaties, freedom of the seas for everyone, and the establishment of an association of nations to promote peace and international cooperation. That association, the League of Nations, was formed later but the United States never joined.

▲ Allied Leaders at the Paris Peace Conference. President Woodrow Wilson is at the far right.

Other Allied leaders wanted to punish Germany. They felt that Germany had started the war and should pay for it. They believed that the way to prevent future wars was to make sure that Germany could never become powerful again.

The agreement these leaders finally reached became known as the Treaty of Versailles. Germany was forced to admit it had started the war and to pay money to the Allies. Germany also lost territory. The treaty stated that Germany could not make tanks, military planes, large weapons, or submarines. The United States never agreed to the Treaty of Versailles. It eventually signed a separate peace treaty with Germany.

A New Europe World War I changed the map of Europe. France and Belgium gained territory that had belonged to Germany. Austria, and Hungary became separate countries. Poland and Czechoslovakia gained their independence. Bosnia and Herzegovina, Croatia, Montenegro, Serbia, and Slovenia were united as Yugoslavia. Finland, Estonia, Latvia, and Lithuania, all of which had been part of Russia, also became independent nations. Bulgaria and the Ottoman Empire likewise lost territory.

✓ **READING CHECK:** *Comparing and Contrasting* How did the peace terms Woodrow Wilson wanted compare to those in the Treaty of Versailles?

A New World

After World War I, the world was very different. New ideas, new art, new music, and new kinds of books reflected the feeling that the world no longer made sense. Some writers called the people who had been through the war "the lost generation." Composers wrote music that sounded different from the music people were used to hearing. Many people thought it didn't sound pretty. Artists like Pablo Picasso and Salvador Dali created paintings that looked more like scenes from dreams than from the real world. People were tired of war. They wanted to have fun, and not worry so much about what might happen tomorrow. Jazz music, which gave musicians more freedom, became popular. Women wanted more freedom. They began to wear their hair and their skirts short. In the United States, women demanded and won the right to vote.

✓ **READING CHECK:** *Drawing Inferences* Why were there so many new ideas and new kinds of art after World War I?

Women vote in the United States, c. 1920.

go.hrw.com Homework Practice Online
Keyword: SJ3 HP9

Section 1 Review

Define and explain: militarism, U-boats, armistice

Reading for the Main Idea

1. *Human Systems* What was Europe like just before World War I?
2. *Human Systems* What role did science and technology play in the war?
3. *Human Systems* How did World War I change the world?

Critical Thinking

4. **Drawing Inferences and Conclusions** How might World War I have been different if there had not been alliances in Europe?

Organizing What You Know

5. **Categorizing** Copy the following chart. Use it to list the members of each alliance.

Allied Powers	Central Powers

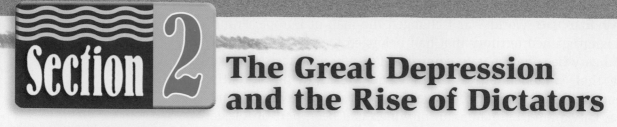

Section 2 The Great Depression and the Rise of Dictators

Read to Discover

1. What led to the Great Depression?
2. What is a dictatorship?
3. How did the Great Depression help dictators come to power in Europe?

Define

stock market
bankrupt
Great Depression
New Deal
dictator
fascism
communism
police state
collective farms

WHY IT MATTERS

Some countries in today's world are ruled by dictators. Use CNNfyi.com or other **current events** sources to find examples of dictators and learn how they came to power. Record your findings in your journal.

Dorothea Lange's photograph Migrant Mother

THE BANK OF UNITED STATES
THE BANK OF UNITED STATES

During the stock market crash, people rushed to get money out of banks.

The Great Depression

During the 1920s industrialized countries such as the United States and Great Britain experienced great economic growth. However, less than 10 years later, many of these countries struggled with high rates of unemployment and poverty.

Causes of the Depression During World War I, much farmland in Europe was destroyed. Farmers all over the world planted more crops to sell food to European countries. Many American farmers borrowed money to buy farm machinery and more land. When the war ended, there was less demand for food in Europe. Prices went down. Farmers could not pay back the money they had borrowed. Many lost their land.

During the 1920s, the **stock market** did very well. The stock market is an organization through which shares of stock in companies are bought and sold. People who buy stock are buying shares in a company. If people sell their stock when the price per share has risen above the original price, they make a profit.

In the 1920s, stock prices rose very high and many people invested their money in the stock market. People thought stock prices would stay high, so they borrowed money to buy more stocks. Unfortunately, stock prices fell. Low stock prices made people rush to sell their shares before they lost any more money. So many people all selling stock at once drove prices down even more quickly. Finally the stock market crashed, or hit bottom, on October 29, 1929.

People who had borrowed to buy stocks suddenly had to pay back the money. They rushed to the banks to take money out. But the banks did not have enough money to give everyone their savings all at once. In a very short time, banks, factories, farms, and people went **bankrupt**. This meant they had no more money.

This is a breadline in New York City, during the Great Depression. People who could not find jobs stood in these lines to receive free food from the government.

This was the beginning of the **Great Depression**. All over the world, prices and wages fell, banks closed, business slowed or stopped, and people could not find jobs. Many people were poor. Many did not even have enough money to buy food. Some people sold apples on street corners to make a little money.

Governments around the world tried to lessen the effects of the Great Depression. Some limited the number of imports they allowed into their countries. They thought this would encourage citizens to buy products made by businesses in their own countries. This plan did not work. In fact, the loss of foreign markets for their products drove many countries even further into debt.

The New Deal In 1932 Franklin D. Roosevelt became president of the United States. He created a program to help end the Great Depression. This program was called the **New Deal**. The federal government gave money to each state to help people. The government also created jobs. It hired people to construct buildings and roads and work on other projects.

Laws were passed to regulate banks and stock exchanges better. In 1938, Congress passed the Fair Labor Standards Act. It established the lowest amount of money a worker could be paid to keep a healthy standard of living. Many people today refer to it as the minimum wage law. Congress also guaranteed workers the right to form unions so they could demand better pay and better working conditions. The Social Security Act, passed in 1935, created benefits for people who were unemployed or elderly.

Under the New Deal, the United States became deeply involved in the well-being of its citizens. For the first time, the government created large-scale social programs to better the lives of American citizens. The New Deal did not, however, completely end the Great Depression in the United States. Government programs helped the economy grow somewhat, but they were not enough to solve the economic crisis completely. The Great Depression would not end in the United States until World War II.

Our Amazing Planet

The Great Depression affected the entire world. By 1932, more than 30 million people throughout the world could not find jobs.

✓ **READING CHECK:** *Identifying Cause and Effect* How did the Great Depression start?

The Rise of Dictators in Europe

As the Great Depression continued in Europe, life got harder. Many people became unhappy with their governments, which were not able to help them. In some countries, people were willing to give up democracy to have strong leaders who promised them more money and better lives. It was easy for dictators to take control of these governments. A **dictator** is an absolute, or total, ruler. A government ruled by a dictator is called a dictatorship. Powerful dictators seized control of Italy and Germany.

When he became dictator of Italy, Benito Mussolini took the title *il Duce* (il DOO-chay), Italian for "the leader."

Italy Becomes a Dictatorship Benito Mussolini told the Italians that he had the answers to their problems. Mussolini called his ideas **fascism** and started the Fascist Party. Fascism was a political movement that put the needs of the nation above the needs of the individual. The nation's leader was supposed to represent the will of the nation. The leader had total control over the people and the economy.

Fascist nations became strong through militarism. Their leaders feared communism for a good reason. **Communism** promised a society in which property would be shared by everyone. Mussolini promised that he would not let communists take over Italy. He also promised he would bring Italy out of the Great Depression and return Italy to the glory of the Roman Empire.

In 1924, the Fascist Party won Italy's national election. Mussolini took control of the government and became a dictator. He turned Italy into a police state. A **police state** is a country in which the government has total control over people and uses secret police to find and punish people who rebel or protest.

Hitler was a very powerful speaker. He often twisted the truth in his speeches. He claimed that the bigger a lie was, the more likely people would be to believe it.

Germany After World War I many Germans felt that their government had betrayed them by signing the Treaty of Versailles. Many also blamed the German government for the unemployment and inflation brought by the Great Depression. Several groups attempted to overthrow and replace the old government. Eventually a new party called the Nazi Party gained power. It too was a fascist party. Adolf Hitler was its leader.

Hitler promised to break the treaty of Versailles. He said he would restore Germany's economy, rebuild Germany's military power, and take back territory that Germany had lost after the war. Hitler told the Germans that they were superior to other people. Many Germans eagerly listened to Hitler's message. They thought he would restore Germany to its former power.

The Nazis quickly gained power in Germany. In 1933 Hitler took control of the German government. He made himself dictator and used the title *der Führer* (FYOOR-ur), which is German for "the leader." He turned Germany into a police state. Newspapers and political parties that opposed the Nazis were outlawed. Groups of people that Hitler claimed were inferior, especially Jews, lost their civil liberties.

Hitler began to secretly rebuild Germany's army and navy. He was going to make Germany a mighty nation again. He called his rule the Third Reich. *Reich* is the German word for *empire*. In 1936 Hitler formed a partnership with Mussolini called the Rome-Berlin Axis.

The Soviet Union Russia had suffered terribly during World War I. Lenin's Communist government had promised an ideal society in which people would share things and live well. However, most Russians remained poor.

After Lenin died, Joseph Stalin gained control of the Communist Party. Stalin's government took land from farmers and forced farmers to work on large **collective farms** owned and controlled by the central government. Stalin also tried to industrialize the Soviet Union. However, for ordinary Russians food and manufactured goods remained scarce.

Religious worship was forbidden. Artists were even told what kind of pictures to make. Secret police spied on people. If people did not obey Stalin's policies they were arrested and put in jail or killed. Scholars think that by 1939 more than 5 million people had been arrested, deported, sent to forced labor camps, or killed.

For many years, many Soviet people thought Joseph Stalin was a great hero. Later, people became more aware of his responsibility for the deaths of millions of Russians for "crimes against the state."

✓ **READING CHECK:** *Analyzing* How did Hitler use the Treaty of Versailles to help him gain power in Germany?

go.hrw.com **Homework Practice Online**
Keyword: SJ3 HP9

Section Review 2

Define and explain: stock market, bankrupt, Great Depression, New Deal, dictator, fascism, communism, police state, collective farms

Reading for the Main Idea

1. *Human Systems* What happened during the Great Depression?
2. *Human Systems* What is life like in a dictatorship?
3. *Human Systems* How did European dictators take advantage of the Great Depression to gain power?

Critical Thinking

4. **Making Inferences and Conclusions** How were Woodrow Wilson's concerns about the Treaty of Versailles proven correct by the rise of Adolf Hitler?

Organizing What You Know

5. **Identifying Cause and Effect** Copy the following graphic organizer. Fill it in to summarize what happened in the Great Depression.

Cause	Effect
Europe needs food during the war.	
The war ends and crop prices fall.	
Stock prices rise very high.	
People rush to sell their stocks.	
People rush to take money out of the banks.	

Section 3 Nationalism in Latin America

Read to Discover

1. What were European colonies in Latin America like, and how did they win their independence?
2. Why did dictatorships replace some democracies in Latin America?
3. How have relations between the United States and Latin American countries changed over time?

Define

revolutionaries
economic nationalism

Locate

Haiti
Cuba
Mexico
Central America
Panama Canal

WHY IT MATTERS

The United States is still very involved in Latin American affairs. Use CNNfyi.com or other **current events** sources to find examples of U.S. involvement in Latin America. Record your findings in your journal.

Red and green coffee beans still on the branch

The Changing Face of Latin America

Life in Latin America changed greatly in the 1500s after conquerors claimed the land for European countries. The Portuguese controlled Brazil. The much larger Spanish territory stretched from what is now Kansas all the way to the southern tip of South America.

Spanish colonists created a new civilization in the Americas. They forced many Indian people there to work their large farms and mine for silver and gold. Rich supplies of precious metals as well as agricultural products were shipped to Europe. Most of the workers had no land rights and received none of the wealth that resulted from their labor.

For more than three hundred years, Spain ruled its colonies strictly. Very little changed until the early 1800s. By that time, wars in Europe had weakened Spain. The people of the United States and France had overthrown their old governments. Colonial leaders throughout Latin America were inspired to break away from Spanish rule.

▲ Explorer Hernán Cortés conquered the mighty Aztec civilization and claimed Mexico for Spain. Cortés is pictured here capturing the Aztec ruler Moctezuma II.

Interpreting the Visual Record

According to this picture, what advantages did the Spanish have over the Aztec?

Moves for Independence

Over time, colonists in Latin America no longer thought of themselves as Europeans. Each colony had developed its own way of life, and wanted to control its own government. Colonists did not want to pay taxes to a country that was taking rich resources without giving much back. Nationalist movements began to gather strength.

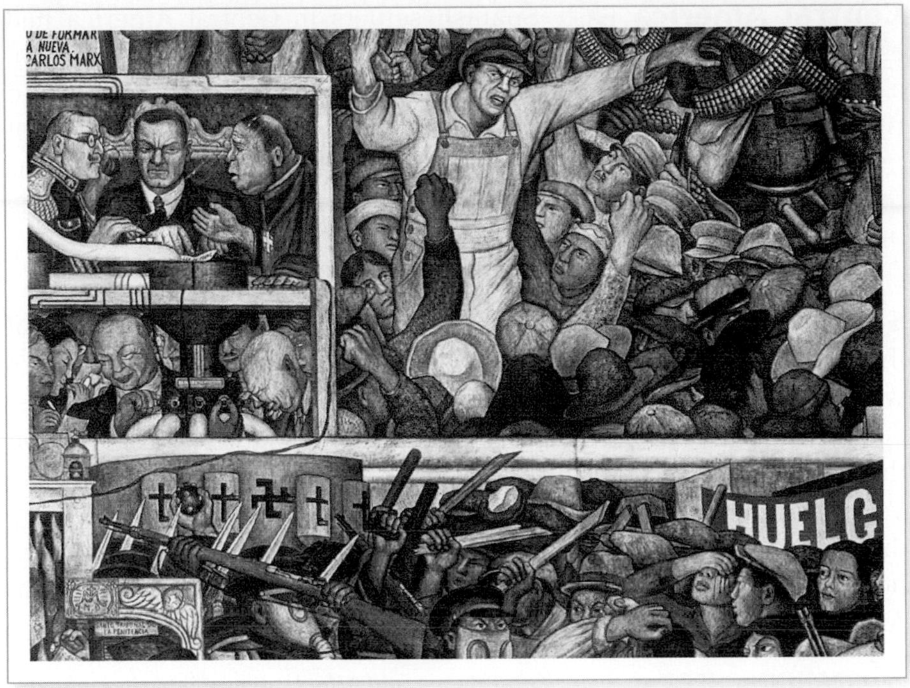
A NUEVA
CARLOS MARX
HUELG

Mexican artist Diego Rivera painted pictures that showed the historical, social, and economic problems of his country. Other Latin American countries faced many of the same problems as Mexico.

Hispaniola Columbus had claimed the Caribbean island of Hispaniola for Spain in the 1400s. France had later taken over the western end of the island. The French Revolution in Europe inspired the slaves. Led by Toussaint L'Ouverture, they rebelled in 1791 and eventually gained their freedom. In 1804 L'Ouverture took control of the newly independent country of Haiti. The former Spanish colony on Hispaniola broke away from Haiti in the mid-1800s and became known as the Dominican Republic.

Mexico In 1810 the Mexican people revolted against Spanish rule. After a struggle that lasted until 1821, Mexico finally won its independence. American and European investments helped Mexico grow economically, but most Mexicans remained poor.

Although Mexico was independent, political unrest continued over the next 100 years. During the 1820s and early 1830s, many Americans moved from the United States to a part of northern Mexico now known as Texas. Eventually, the Texans broke away from Mexico. In 1845 Texas became part of the United States. This event helped trigger a war between Mexico and the United States.

Unrest in Mexico increased in the early 1900s. The government was under the dictatorship of Porfirio Díaz. Once again, the rich people became richer and controlled much of the country's land. Most people, however remained poor and had no land of their own. In 1910, they began to revolt. The Mexican Revolution continued for many years and involved various leaders and groups.

Land reform was one of the main goals of the revolution. Over time, large farms were broken up and given to villages. At the same time, the Mexican government became more involved in the national economy than it had been before the revolution. Many foreign-owned businesses were forced out of Mexico.

Pancho Villa (VEE-yah) was a Mexican revolutionary and leader.

Central America Early Spanish settlers in Central America had established colonies with towns and large farm estates. As in Mexico, a few rich people owned the land, and most workers had no land rights. Although these colonies won independence from Spain, not much changed after Spanish officials left. Foreign countries such as the United States and Great Britain built railroads and developed big businesses. Most local people continued to be poor.

Simón Bolívar (1783-1830) was called "the Liberator."

South America The demand for self-rule spread to other parts of the Americas. One of the most famous Latin American **revolutionaries** was Simón Bolívar. Called "the Liberator," Bolívar led a revolt against Spain that lasted 10 years. In 1821 Bolívar became president of a nation that eventually included the present-day countries of Colombia, Venezuela, Ecuador, and Panama. A few years later the Spanish were driven out of Peru. In 1825 the new country of Bolivia was named in honor of Bolívar. By the early 1830s, almost all the colonies in Latin America ruled themselves.

✓ READING CHECK: *Identifying Cause and Effect* How did feelings of nationalism affect Latin America in the 1800s?

Challenges

The new nations of Latin America were now free to govern themselves. However, they still faced the challenge of improving people's lives. Revolutions changed the governments in these new countries, but they usually replaced one group of powerful families with another one. Life for most poor farmers, plantation workers, and city people hardly changed.

This painting depicts Theodore Roosevelt leading the Rough Riders into battle during the Spanish-American War.

The United States and Latin America During the late 1800s and early 1900s, the United States was a powerful political and economic force in Latin America. In 1898 the United States went to war with Spain to help Cuba win its independence. Many Americans felt that the Spanish were too harsh in their treatment of the Cubans. At the end of the war, Cuba and Puerto Rico came under U.S. control, as did the Philippines in the Pacific Ocean. Cuba became fully independent in 1902. In 1903 the United States helped Panama revolt against Colombia. Panama became an independent nation. The next year Panama allowed the United States to begin construction on the Panama Canal. The canal opened in 1914, connecting the Atlantic Ocean with the Pacific Ocean. The United States controlled the canal and the territory around it.

In 1904 President Theodore Roosevelt announced that if the independence of any country in the Western Hemisphere were in danger, the United States would act to help. He also said that the United States would make sure that Latin American countries repaid loans. This policy angered many Latin Americans.They thought the plan was just an excuse for the United States to interfere in Latin American affairs. They did not think the United States had the right to take on this power.

✓ **READING CHECK:** *Evaluating* How did many Latin Americans feel about the relationship between the United States and Latin America?

The Rise of Dictators

Before World War I, Latin America was mainly a farming region. After the war, the region's economy started to grow and change. Oil became a major export. Mining grew rapidly. There was rapid growth of electric and hydroelectric power generation. The energy allowed many Latin American countries to begin to industrialize. A stronger economy led to changes in other areas of Latin American life. Cities grew. There were more jobs and opportunities for education. To supply labor for growing industries, some countries encouraged Europeans to immigrate.

Then the Great Depression struck. It affected Latin American nations in the same ways as other nations. Prices fell for many of Latin America's exports. Some countries could not pay their debts. People lost their jobs and could not find new jobs. More and more people became unhappy with their governments.

As in Europe, economic problems led to political problems. Some constitutional governments were overthrown, and dictators took over. In many Latin American countries, the military influenced or controlled the new governments.

In the past the United States had often stepped in to influence events in Latin America. This had led to tension between many Latin American countries and the United States. During the 1930s, President Franklin D. Roosevelt tried to improve relations between the United States and Latin America. He began a program he called the Good Neighbor Policy. The United States would cooperate with Latin American countries but would not interfere with their governments.

✓ **READING CHECK:** *Drawing Inferences* Why did President Roosevelt think the Good Neighbor Policy would improve relations between the United States and Latin America?

Our Amazing Planet

The Panama Canal is about 51 miles long. Before it was built, a ship sailing from New York City to San Francisco had to travel about 15,000 miles around South America. After the canal was built, the same trip was about 6,000 miles.

Like most of Latin America, Mexico City improved its economy in the 1920s.

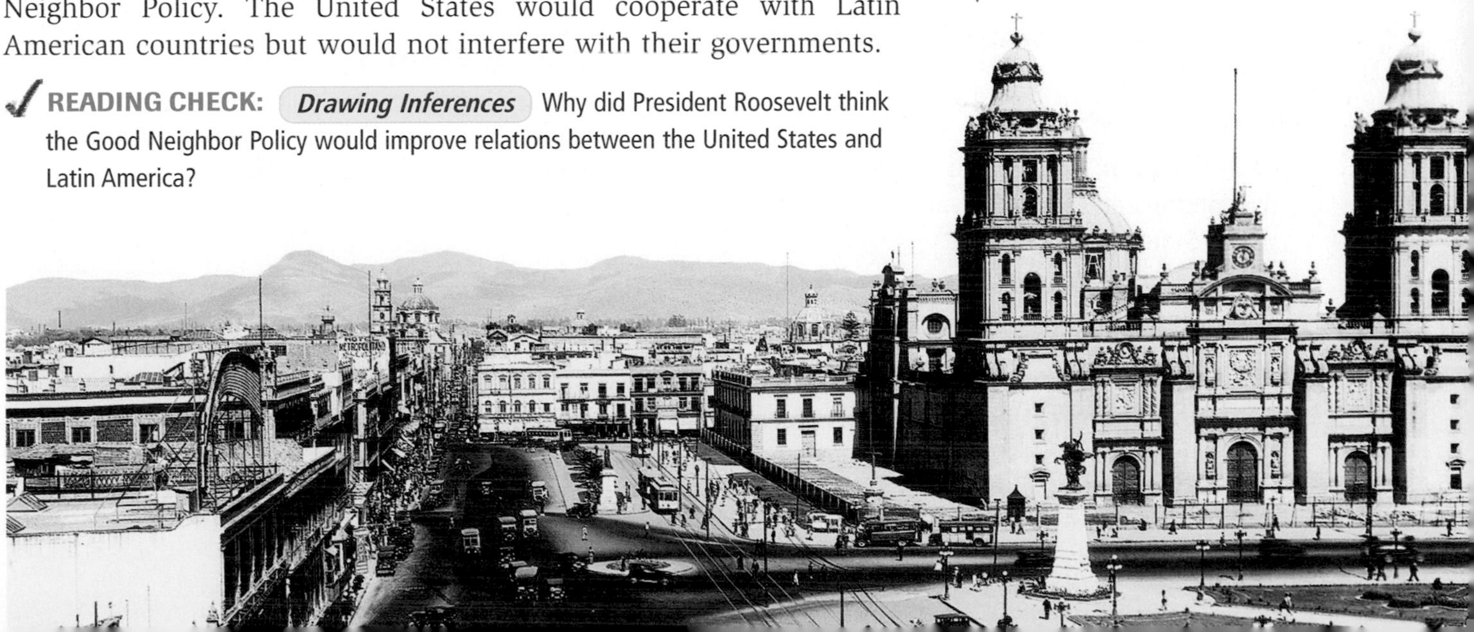

Economic Independence

During the 1930s, many Latin American leaders wanted economic independence from the United States and Europe. Because of the global depression, international markets for Latin American goods were weak. Imported goods, however, were costly. Thus Latin American countries had no choice but to develop their own industries to make goods. This gave rise to **economic nationalism**. This means putting the economic interests of one's own country above the interests of other countries. Before this time other countries, such as the United States and Great Britain, had basically controlled the Latin American economy.

Mexican president Lázaro Cárdenas (center) nationalized Mexico's oil industry. Cárdenas, who came from a poor family, promised the Mexican people economic reform.

One example of economic nationalism can be seen in Mexico in 1938. Mexican workers wanted better pay from American- and British-owned oil companies, but the oil companies would not increase their wages. Mexican president Lázaro Cárdenas nationalized the oil industry. That means that the government seized ownership and control of all the oil companies in Mexico.

The Mexican president's actions angered Great Britain, but the Mexican and British governments eventually worked out an agreement. The Mexican people were happy that Mexico was gaining more control of its own economy. Today many Mexicans think of March 13, 1938—the day the oil companies were nationalized—as the beginning of Mexico's economic independence.

✓ **READING CHECK:** *Analyzing* Why did economic nationalism become important to the leaders of Latin America?

go.hrw.com Homework Practice Online
Keyword: SJ3 HP9

Section 3 Review

Define and explain: revolutionaries, economic nationalism

Reading for the Main Idea

1. *Human Systems* How would you describe the relationship between Latin America and the United States?
2. *Human Systems* How was Latin America changed by economic nationalism?

Critical Thinking

3. **Comparing/Contrasting** How was President Theodore Roosevelt's 1904 policy toward Latin America different from President Franklin D. Roosevelt's Good Neighbor Policy?

Organizing What You Know

4. **Summarizing** Copy the following graphic organizer. Fill it in, listing the movements, ideas, and policies that affected Latin America in each period.

1791-1831	1898-1918	1919-1933	1934-1938

Section 4 World War II

Read to Discover

1. What were the causes of World War II?
2. What was the Holocaust?
3. How did World War II end?

Define

aggression
anti-Semitism
genocide
Holocaust

Locate

Japan
Italy
Germany
Hawaii
Ethiopia
Poland
Sicily
Pearl Harbor
Normandy

WHY IT MATTERS

Acts of aggression still happen. Use CNNfyi.com or other **current events** sources to find examples of aggression in today's world. Record your findings in your journal.

National Iwo Jima Memorial Monument

Threats to World Peace

During the 1930s, Japan, Italy, and Germany committed acts of aggression against other countries. **Aggression** is warlike action, such as an invasion or an attack. At first, little was done to stop them. Eventually, their actions led to a full-scale war that involved much of the world.

In 1931, Japanese forces took control of Manchuria, a part of China. The League of Nations protested, but took no military action to stop Japan. Continuing its aggressive actions, Japan succeeded in controlling about one fourth of China by 1939. At about the same time, Italy invaded Ethiopia, a country in East Africa. Many countries protested, but they did not want to go to war again. Like Japan, Italy saw that the rest of the world would not try hard to stop its aggression.

Pablo Picasso painted *Guernica* after the Spanish town of the same name was bombed.

Interpreting the Visual Record **What human feelings about war does Picasso express?**

Women cry as they give the Nazi salute to German troops in Sudentenland.

Interpreting the Visual Record Why do you think these women are showing strong feelings?

Modewaren

Spanish Civil War In 1936, civil war broke out in Spain. On one side were fascists led by General Francisco Franco. Both Italy and Germany sent troops and supplies to help Franco's forces. On the other side were Loyalists, people loyal to the elected Spanish government. The Soviet Union sent aid to the Loyalists. Volunteers from France, Great Britain, and the United States also fought on their side, but their help was not enough. In 1939, the fascists defeated the Loyalists. Franco set up a dictatorship. He ended free elections and most civil rights. By the end of the 1930s, it was clear that fascism was growing in Europe.

Hitler's Aggressions In the late 1930s many Germans lived in Austria, Czechoslovakia, and Poland. Hitler wanted to unite these countries to bring all Germans together. In 1938 German soldiers marched into Austria, and Hitler declared Austria to be part of the Third Reich. Great Britain and France protested but did not attack Germany. Later that year Hitler took over the Sudentenland, a region of western Czechoslovakia. Other European countries were worried, but they still did not want a war. Hitler soon conquered the rest of Czechoslovakia.

Eventually Britain and France realized they could not ignore Hitler. They asked the Soviet Union to be their ally in a war against Germany. However, Soviet leader Joseph Stalin had made a secret plan with Hitler. They decided that their countries would never attack each other. This deal was called the German-Soviet nonaggression pact.

In September 1939 Hitler invaded Poland. Two days later, Great Britain and France declared war on Germany. World War II had begun. On one side were Germany, Italy, and Japan. They called themselves the Axis Powers, or the Axis. Great Britain, France, and other countries that fought against the Axis called themselves the Allies.

✓ **READING CHECK:** ***Drawing Inferences*** How might British and French leaders have prevented World War II?

Joseph Stalin (second from right) made an agreement that the Soviet Union and Germany would not attack each other.

Carrying whatever belongings they can, people in northern France try to escape from attacks.

War

At the beginning of the war, the Germans won many victories. Poland fell in one month. In 1940 Germany conquered Denmark, Norway, the Netherlands, Belgium, and Luxembourg. In June 1940 Germany invaded and quickly defeated France. In less than one year, Hitler had gained control of almost all of western Europe. Next he sent German planes to bomb Great Britain. The British fought back with their own air force. This struggle became known as the Battle of Britain.

In June 1941, Hitler turned on his ally and invaded the Soviet Union. As winter set in, however, the Germans found themselves vulnerable to Soviet attacks. Without enough supplies, Hitler's troops were defeated by a combination of the freezing Russian winter and the Soviet Red Army. For the first time in the war, German soldiers were forced to retreat.

The United States Many people in the United States did not want their country to go to war. The United States sent supplies, food, and weapons to the British but did not actually enter the war until 1941. In that year Japan was taking control of Southeast Asia and the Pacific. Seeing the United States as a possible enemy, Japanese military leaders attempted to destroy the U.S. naval fleet in the Pacific. On December 7, 1941, Japan launched a surprise air attack on the naval base at Pearl Harbor, Hawaii. The attack sank or damaged U.S. battleships and killed more than 2,300 American soldiers. The next day President Franklin D. Roosevelt announced that the United States was at war with Japan. Great Britain also declared war on Japan. Three days later, Germany and Italy—both allies of Japan—declared war on the United States. In response, Congress declared war on both countries.

✓ **READING CHECK:** *Evaluating* How were Hitler's invasion of the Soviet Union and Japan's attack on Pearl Harbor turning points in the war?

Our Amazing Planet

After France was forced to sign a peace agreement with Germany and Italy in 1940, some French groups escaped to North Africa or to Great Britain and formed the Free French army. Others remained in France and formed an "underground" movement to resist the Germans secretly.

EXTRA
Los Angeles Times
Night Pictorial
RACE RESULTS
IT'S WAR!
Hostilities Declared by Japanese; 350 Reported Killed In Hawaii Raid
U.S. Battleships Hit; 7 Die in Honolulu
Air Bombs Rained on Pacific Bases
Air Guards, Attention!

Newspapers around the country ran headlines similar to this one after the Japanese attack on Pearl Harbor.

Interpreting the Visual Record **How do you think Americans felt when they saw headlines like this one?**

The Holocaust

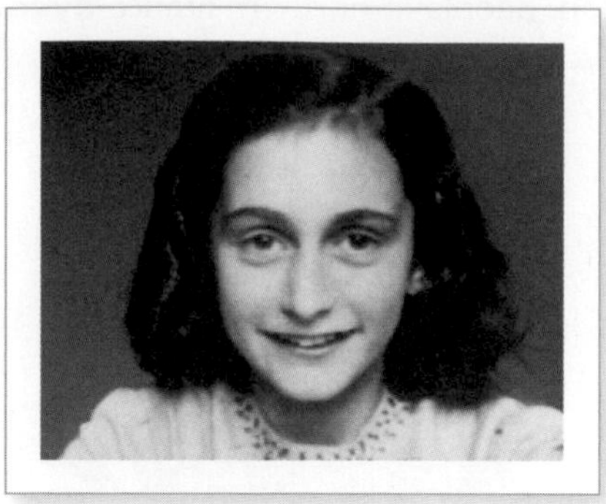

▲ Anne Frank (1930-1945) was a Jewish teenager. During the Holocaust her family hid in an attic for two years to escape the Nazis. Anne kept a diary in which she wrote her thoughts and feelings.

Hitler believed that Germans were a superior people, and planned to destroy or enslave people whom he believed were inferior. Hitler hated many peoples, but he particularly hated the Jews. Hatred of Jews is called **anti-Semitism**. The Nazis rounded up Europe's Jews and imprisoned them in concentration camps.

Death Camps In 1941, Hitler ordered the destruction of Europe's entire Jewish population. The Nazis built death camps in Poland to carry out this plan. People who could work were forced into slave labor. Those who could not work were sent to gas chambers where they were killed. Some Jews were shot in large groups. Thousands of other people died from conditions in the camps. The dead were buried in mass graves or burned in large ovens.

By the time the Nazi government fell, its leaders and followers had murdered an estimated 6 million European Jews. The Nazi **genocide**, the planned killing of a race of people, is called the **Holocaust**. Millions of non-Jews were also killed.

Resisting the Nazis Some Jews tried to fight back. Others hid. Most, however, were unable to escape. Many Europeans ignored what was happening to the Jews, but some tried to save people from the Holocaust. The Danes helped about 7,000 Jews escape to Sweden. In Poland and Czechoslovakia, the German businessman Oskar Schindler saved many Jews by employing them in his factories.

✓ **READING CHECK:** *Summarizing* What were Nazi concentration camps like?

Peace Memorial Park marks the spot where the first atomic bomb was dropped August 6, 1945, in Hiroshima, Japan. ▼

The End of the War

In 1942 the Germans tried to capture the Soviet city of Stalingrad. The battle lasted six months, but the Soviet defenders held out. The Germans were never able to take the city. This was a major blow to the Germans, who never fully recovered from this defeat. At the same time, American and British forces defeated the Germans in Africa. The war began to turn in favor of the Allies. That same year in the Pacific Japan lost several important battles. Led by the United States, Allied forces—including troops from Australia and New Zealand—began a campaign to regain some of the Pacific islands Japan had taken. Slowly, the Allies pushed the Japanese forces back across the Pacific Ocean.

In the summer of 1943 the Allies captured the island of Sicily in Italy. Italians forced Mussolini to resign, and Italy's new leader dissolved the Fascist Party. In September, Italy agreed to stop fighting the Allies.

Victory in Europe On June 6, 1944, Allied forces landed on the beaches of Normandy in northern France. This was the D-Day invasion. The invasion was a success. In August, Allied troops entered Paris. By September they were at Germany's western border. With the

Soviets attacking Germany from the east, the Nazis' defenses fell apart. On April 30 Hitler killed himself, and within a week, Germany surrendered.

Victory over Japan Fighting continued in the Pacific. The Allies bombed Japan, but the Japanese would not surrender. Finally President Harry Truman decided to use the atomic bomb against Japan. On August 6, 1945, the most powerful weapon the world had ever seen was dropped on the city of Hiroshima. The bomb reduced the city to ashes and destroyed the surrounding area. About 130,000 people were killed and many more were injured. Countless more people died later. On August 9 another atomic bomb was dropped on the Japanese city of Nagasaki. Five days later Japan surrendered.

A New Age World War II resulted in more destruction than any other war in history. More than 50 million people were killed, and millions more were wounded. Unlike in most earlier wars, many of the people killed were civilians. Civilians are people who are not in the military. Millions were killed in the Holocaust. Thousands were killed by bombs dropped on cities in Europe and Japan. Thousands more died in prison camps in Japan and the Soviet Union. In time, people began to question how such cruel acts against human life and human rights were allowed to happen and how they could be prevented in the future.

The American use of the atomic bomb began the atomic age. With it came many questions and fears. How would this new weapon be used? What effect would it have on future wars? After World War II, world leaders would struggle with these questions.

Losses of the Major Wartime Powers in World War II, 1939 - 1945

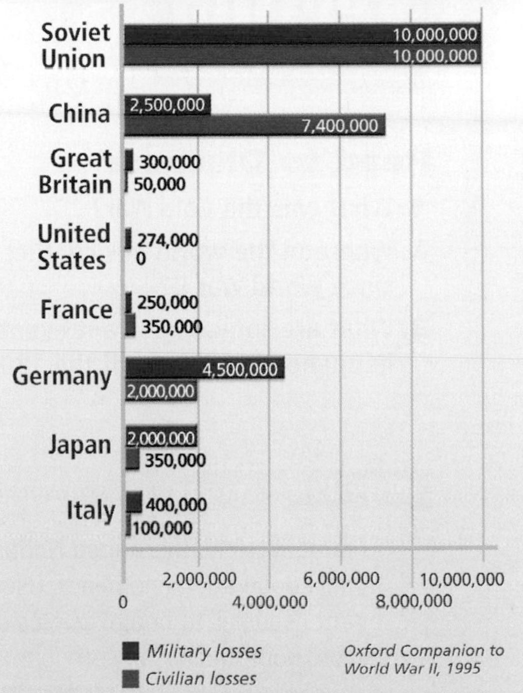
Soviet Union
10,000,000
10,000,000
China
2,500,000
7,400,000
Great Britain
300,000
50,000
United States
274,000
0
France
250,000
350,000
Germany
4,500,000
2,000,000
Japan
2,000,000
350,000
Italy
400,000
100,000
0
2,000,000
4,000,000
6,000,000
8,000,000
10,000,000
Military losses
Civilian losses
Oxford Companion to World War II, 1995

Interpreting the Graph **What three countries had the highest civilian losses? What do you think caused these losses?**

✓ **READING CHECK:** *Analyzing* How was World War II unlike any war that came before it?

go.hrw.com **Homework Practice Online** **Keyword: SJ3 HP9**

Section 4 Review

Define and explain: aggression, anti-Semitism, genocide, Holocaust

Reading for the Main Idea

1. *Human Systems* What events led to World War II?
2. *Human Systems* What happened during the Holocaust?
3. *Human Systems* What were the results of World War II?

Critical Thinking

4. **Cause and Effect** How did the rise of fascism in Europe lead to World War II?

Organizing What You Know

5. **Drawing Inferences and Conclusions** Copy the following graphic organizer. Fill it in, telling why each event was important in the war.

Event	Why Important?
Hitler invades Poland.	
Hitler gains control of western Europe.	
Germany invades the Soviet Union.	
Japan attacks Pearl Harbor.	
The Allies invade Europe on D-Day.	
The United States drops the atomic bomb on Japan.	

Section 5 The World Since 1945

Read to Discover

1. What was the Cold War?
2. Where in the world has conflict arisen since World War II?
3. What are some important events that happened at the end of the 1900s?

Define

bloc
arms race
partition
globalization

Locate

Israel
China
Korea
Vietnam
Cuba

WHY IT MATTERS

Created in 1945, the United Nations continues to promote international cooperation and peace. Use CNNfyi.com or other **current events** sources to find examples of UN action to stop violence. Record your findings in your journal.

compact discs

The Cold War

Although the Soviet Union and the United States were allies in World War II, the alliance fell apart after the war. The former allies clashed over ideas about freedom, government, and economics. Because this struggle did not turn into a shooting or "hot" war, it is known as the Cold War.

A Struggle of Ideas The struggle that started the Cold War was between two ideas—communism and capitalism. Communism is an economic system in which a central authority controls the government and the economy. Capitalism is a system in which businesses are privately owned. During the Cold War, the Soviet government functioned as a dictatorship which controlled the economy. However, the United States and other democratic nations practiced some form of capitalism.

In June 1948 the Soviets set up a blockade along the East German border to prevent supplies from getting into West Berlin. The people of West Berlin faced starvation. The United States and Great Britain organized an airlift to supply West Berlin. Food and supplies were flown in daily to the people.

Europe Divided After World War II Joseph Stalin, leader of the Soviet Union, brought most countries in Eastern Europe under communist control. The Soviet Union and those communist-controlled countries were known as the Eastern bloc. A **bloc** is a group of nations united under a common idea or for a common purpose. The United States and the democracies in Western Europe were known as the Western bloc. While Western countries experienced periods of great economic growth, industries in most communist countries did not develop. People in these countries suffered from shortages of goods, food, and money.

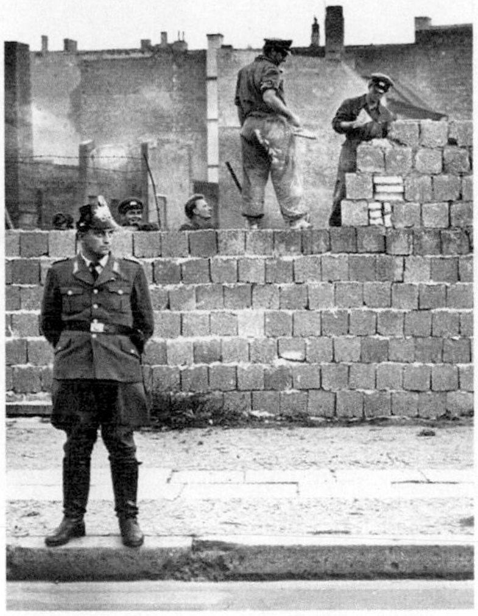

▲ The Berlin Wall did not stop people from trying to reach West Berlin. More than 130 people died trying to escape over the heavily guarded wall.

Interpreting the Visual Record Why do you think people risked death to escape communism?

Two Germanies After World War II the Allies divided Germany into four zones to keep it from becoming powerful again. Britain, France, the United States, and the Soviet Union each controlled a zone. Germany could no longer have an army, and the Nazi Party was outlawed. By 1948, the Western Allies were ready to unite their zones, but the Soviets did not want Germany united as a democratic nation. The next year the American, British, and French zones became the Federal Republic of Germany, or West Germany. The Soviets established the German Democratic Republic, or East Germany. The city of Berlin, although part of East Germany, was divided into East and West Berlin, with West Berlin under Allied control. The Berlin Wall, which became a famous symbol of the Cold War, separated the two parts of the city.

The Soviet Union After Stalin Joseph Stalin, who had led the Soviet Union through World War II, died in 1953. The next Soviet leader was Nikita Khrushchev. He criticized Stalin's policies and reduced the government's control over the economy.

During the 1950s and 1960s some Eastern bloc nations tried to break free of communism. In East Germany, Czechoslovakia, and Hungary, for example, people rebelled against Soviet control, but the Soviets crushed these revolts.

20°W
10°W
0°
SCALE
0
300
600 Miles
0
300
600 Kilometers
Projection: Azimuthal Equal-Area
NATO nations
Warsaw Pact nations
Other Communist nations
Neutral nations
Iron Curtain
The United States and Canada are the North American members of NATO.
FINLAND
NORWAY
SWEDEN
BALTIC SEA
SOVIET UNION
NORTHERN IRELAND
NORTH SEA
UNITED KINGDOM
DENMARK
IRELAND
NETHERLANDS
POLAND
50°N
GERMAN DEM. REP.
ATLANTIC OCEAN
N
BELGIUM
UKRAINE
CZECHOSLOVAKIA
FED. REP. OF GERMANY
LUXEMBOURG
FRANCE
CRIMEA
AUSTRIA
HUNGARY
ROMANIA
SWITZ.
LIECH.
BLACK SEA
YUGOSLAVIA
BULGARIA
ANDORRA
SAN MARINO
ITALY
40°N
MONACO
PORTUGAL
SPAIN
ALBANIA
TURKEY
AEGEAN SEA
GREECE
10°W
MEDITERRANEAN SEA
20°E
30°E

In this picture U.S. President Harry Truman signs the North Atlantic Pact, which created NATO. Shown above is the NATO emblem.

Interpreting the Visual Record How would you explain the NATO emblem?

The United Nations World leaders did not want the Cold War to turn "hot." Although the League of Nations had failed to prevent World War II, people still wanted an international organization that could settle problems peacefully. In April, 1945, the United Nations (UN) was created. Its purpose was to solve economic and social problems as well as to promote international cooperation and maintain peace. Representatives of 50 countries formed the original United Nations. Today there are nearly 200 member nations. The six official languages of the United Nations are Arabic, Chinese, English, French, Russian, and Spanish. The headquarters of the United Nations are in New York City. It also has offices in Geneva, Switzerland, and Vienna, Austria.

New Alliances Fearing war but hoping to preserve peace, nations around the world formed new alliances. In 1949, 12 Western nations, including the United States, created the North Atlantic Treaty Organization (NATO). In 1954 the Southeast Asia Treaty Organization (SEATO) was created in an attempt to halt the spread of communism in Southeast Asia. Many Eastern bloc countries, including the Soviet Union, signed the Warsaw Pact in 1955. The Warsaw Pact countries had more total troops than the NATO members. This difference in the number of troops encouraged the Western powers to rely on nuclear weapons to establish a balance of power.

Mikhail Gorbachev, with his wife, Raisa. In 1990, Gorbachev won the Nobel Peace Prize for his reform work in the Soviet Union.

The End of the Cold War Throughout the Cold War, the Soviet Union and the United States had been a waging an **arms race**. The countries competed to create more advanced weapons and to have more nuclear missiles than each other. The arms race was expensive and took its toll on the already shaky Soviet economy.

In 1985, Mikhail Gorbachev became head of the Soviet Union. He reduced government control of the economy and increased individual liberties, such as freedom of speech and the press. He also improved relations with the United States. These reforms in the Soviet Union encouraged democratic movements in Eastern bloc countries. In 1989, Poland and Czechoslovakia threw off communist rule. In November, the Berlin Wall came down. In October 1990, East and West Germany became one democratic nation. Soviet republics also began to seek freedom and independence. By the end of 1991, the Soviet Union no longer existed. The Cold War was over. The arms race could stop.

In October 1990 young people in Berlin wave German flags to celebrate the reunification of Germany.

The breakup of the Soviet Union created several independent countries. Russia was the largest of these new nations. Its new leader was Boris Yeltsin. Under Yeltsin, Russia moved toward democracy. Yeltsin also improved Russia's relations with the West. In 2000, Vladimir Putin became leader of Russia. Under Putin, relations with the United States improved further.

Some tension arose, however, between Russia and the former Soviet republics. For example, Russia and the Ukraine clashed over military issues in the 1990s.

✓ **READING CHECK:** *Evaluating* How did the end of the Soviet Union affect the world?

Israel's Knesset, or parliament, meets here. The Knesset is the supreme power in Israel.

Other World Conflicts

Since the end of World War II, many conflicts have shaken the world. Some have been resolved, while others continue to threaten world peace. The lessons of two world wars and the threat of mass destruction that would result from a nuclear war has kept these conflicts contained. World War III has not occurred, and the hope of people everywhere is that it never will.

Southwest Asia After World War I Britain said it would help create a Jewish homeland in Palestine, a region of Southwest Asia. Many Arab nations, however, wanted an Arab state in Palestine. In 1947 the UN voted to **partition**, or divide, Palestine, creating both a Jewish state and an Arab state. While the Arabs rejected this plan, Jewish leaders in Palestine accepted it. In May 1948, Israel was established as a Jewish state.

The establishment of Israel enraged many Palestinian Arabs and Arab nations. Attacked by neighboring Arab countries, Israel fought back. By early 1949 a cease-fire was reached. Israel survived, but Palestinian Arabs had no homeland. In 1967, tensions between Israel and its Arab neighbors exploded into war again. In what became known as the Six-Day War, Israel captured territory from Egypt, Syria, and Jordan. After the Six-Day War, the Palestine Liberation Organization (PLO), led by Yasir Arafat, launched many attacks on Israel.

Russia
China
North Korea
Demilitarized Zone
South Korea

At the end of the Korean War, the two sides set up a neutral area, called the demilitarized zone, or DMZ. It is a buffer zone, and no military forces from either side may enter the area.

The many attempts to bring peace to the Middle East have failed. The Israelis and the Arabs do not trust each other. Both sides make demands that the other side will not meet. When one side commits acts of violence, the other side strikes back. The failure to achieve peace in the Middle East continues to be one of the most disturbing issues facing the world.

Korea At the end of World War II the Soviet Union controlled northern Korea. U.S. troops controlled southern Korea. A Communist government took power, and in 1950, North Korea invaded South Korea. The United Nations sent troops to stop the invasion. The Korean War lasted until 1953, when a cease-fire was signed. Korea remains divided.

Cuba In 1959 Fidel Castro established a Communist government in Cuba. In 1961 President John F. Kennedy approved an invasion of Cuba by anti-Castro forces. The invasion failed, and Castro turned to the Soviet Union for support. The Soviet Union, which by this time possessed nuclear weapons, sent nuclear missiles to Cuba. Kennedy demanded that the missiles be withdrawn, but Khruschev refused. NATO and Warsaw Pact military forces prepared for combat. For several days the Cuban missile crisis held the world on the brink of nuclear war. Finally, the Soviet Union agreed to remove its missiles, and the United States promised it would not invade Cuba.

Vietnam Vietnam had been a colony of France for more than 60 years. In 1945 Ho Chi Minh, a Communist leader, declared Vietnam independent. In 1954 Vietnam became divided. North Vietnam was communist. South Vietnam was not. In the late 1950s, when North Vietnam invaded South Vietnam, the United States sent troops to South Vietnam to fight the communists. Many Americans were unhappy that the country had become involved in this war, and American troops pulled out of Vietnam in 1973. South Vietnam surrendered in 1975. Nearly 1.7 million Vietnamese and about 58,000 Americans lost their lives in the Vietnam War. In 1976 Vietnam was united under a Communist government.

Northern Ireland When the Republic of Ireland gained independence from Great Britain in 1922, the territory of Northern Ireland remained part of Britain. The Protestant majority in Northern Ireland controlled both the government and the economy. This caused resentment among Northern Irish Catholics. During the late 1960s Catholic protests began to turn violent. The British have tried to resolve the conflict both through political means and military force. While the situation has improved, a permanent peaceful solution has not yet been found.

The Breakup of Yugoslavia Yugoslavia was created after World War I by uniting several formerly independent countries. These included Bosnia, Croatia, Slovenia, and Serbia. After the fall of communism in Eastern Europe, Eastern Orthodox Serbs tried to dominate parts of Yugoslavia where people were mainly Roman Catholic or Muslim. Fighting broke out between Serbia and Croatia, which was mainly Roman Catholic. Yugoslavia was once again divided into several countries in the early 1990s, but this did not end the violence. In 1992 Bosnian Serbs began a campaign of terror and murder intended to drive the Muslims out of Bosnia. Finally, NATO bombed Serbian targets in 1995, and the fighting stopped. Several Serb leaders were tried as war criminals.

The War on Terrorism On September 11, 2001, terrorists attacked the World Trade Center in New York City and the Pentagon in Washington, D.C. Following these attacks, the United States asked for support of nations around the world. Many nations, including Russia, China, Cuba, Pakistan, and Saudi Arabia, supported the United States in what President George W. Bush called a "war on terrorism." That show of support indicated that nations of the world might be beginning to leave behind some of the struggles of the last century.

✓ **READING CHECK:** *Evaluating* What has prevented conflicts in different parts of the world from becoming world wars?

▲ After the Vietnam War more than a million people fled Vietnam by boat.
Interpreting the Visual Record **What kinds of conditions might make people willing to leave their homes?**

Croatia
Bosnia and Herzegovina
Mostar
Yugoslavia

◄ Mostar, the unofficial capital of Bosnia and Herzegovina, was bombed heavily in the 1990s.

CHAPTER 9

Reviewing What You Know

Building Vocabulary

On a separate sheet of paper, write sentences to define each of the following words.

1. militarism
2. armistice
3. stock market
4. bankrupt
5. dictator
6. fascism
7. police state
8. revolutionaries
9. economic nationalism
10. aggression
11. anti-Semitism
12. genocide
13. bloc
14. arms race
15. globalization

Reviewing the Main Ideas

1. *Human Systems* What ideas, actions, and incidents were major causes of World War I?
2. *Human Systems* How did dictators come to power in Europe during the 1930s?
3. *Human Systems* How did nationalism change Latin America?
4. *Human Systems* What single event finally caused the United States to enter World War II?
5. *Human Systems* How did the Cold War shape the second half of the 1900s?

Understanding History and Society

The Changing World Map

The world map has changed a great deal during the 1900s. Create a presentation that shows some of these changes. Your presentation should include a chart that describes the changes and shows where and when they happened. As you prepare your chart, consider the changes that occurred:

- After World War I.
- After World War II.
- After the Cold War.

Thinking Critically

1. **Drawing Conclusions** How did the Treaty of Versailles help set the stage for World War II?
2. **Evaluating** How did President Roosevelt's program, the New Deal, help workers?
3. **Comparing and Contrasting** How has U.S. policy in Latin America changed over the years? Why did it change?
4. **Analyzing** What role did aggression, and the response of world leaders to aggression, play in World War II?
5. **Evaluating** What prevented conflicts from becoming major world wars in the late 1900s?

Building Social Studies Skills

Map ACTIVITY

On a separate sheet of paper, match the letters on the map with their correct labels.

Austria	Italy
France	Poland
Germany	Russia
Great Britain	

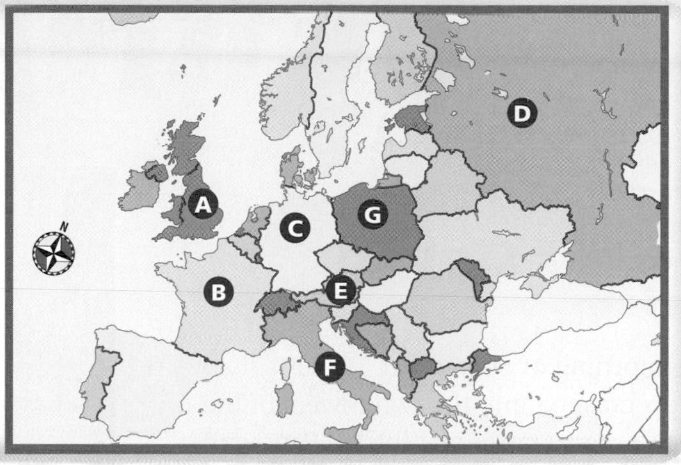

A
B
C
D
E
F
G
N

Mental Mapping Skills ACTIVITY

On a separate sheet of paper, draw a freehand map of Western Europe. Label Germany, Italy, France, and Great Britain. Shade the countries that sided with the Allies in World War II one color. Shade the countries that were Axis Powers a different color. Make a key for your map.

WRITING ACTIVITY

Imagine that you are making a film about a family in the United States during the Great Depression. Write a summary of the film you would like to make. List characters who will appear in the film, events that will occur, problems that will arise, and how the characters will solve them. Be sure to use standard grammar, spelling, sentence structure, and punctuation.

Alternative Assessment

Portfolio ACTIVITY

Learning About Your Local History

Historical People and Places

Research how your town is connected to an event from the 1900s. This link might be a person, place, building, or statue. Write a report on this person, place, or object and explain its historical importance. Include photographs or drawings in your report.

internet connect

Internet Activity: go.hrw.com
KEYWORD: SJ3 GT9

Choose a topic about the modern world.

- Learn about the effects of the Treaty of Versailles.
- Write a report about Anne Frank.
- Create a poster about the causes and effects of global warming.

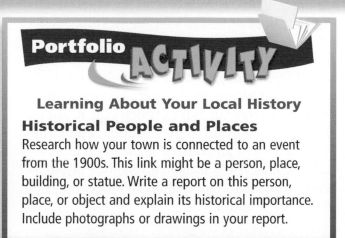

FOCUS ON GOVERNMENT

Combating Global Terrorism

Early in the morning of September 11, 2001, two passenger jets crashed into the two towers of the World Trade Center. Another jet hit the Pentagon outside of Washington, D.C., and a fourth crashed in southern Pennsylvania. All of these planes were piloted by terrorists, people who use violence to achieve political goals. An investigation by the U.S. government led officials to conclude that al Qaeda, a terrorist organization led by Osama bin Laden, was responsible for these attacks. At the time of the attacks, bin Laden was living in Afghanistan, a landlocked country in Southwest Asia.

President George W. Bush addressed a joint session of Congress on September 20. During the session he pledged to use the full might of the nation in a war on international terrorism

The War on Terror The terrorist attacks of September 11, 2001, were not the first on American soil or American interests. Terrorists tried to destroy the World Trade Center in New York in 1993. American citizens and embassies abroad have also been targeted. U.S. allies have also been victims of terrorists. For years, the U.S. government and its allies went to great lengths to combat terrorism. The terrible attacks of September 11, however, demanded the strongest possible retaliation.

Calling the attacks an act of war, President George W. Bush declared war on terrorism. "Either you are with us or you are with the terrorists," President Bush told the world.

The New York City sky filled with smoke after the attack.

Forming an International Coalition The United States wanted to combat terrorists on a global scale. To do that, President Bush formed an international coalition. Great Britain was an early partner in the coalition, and Prime Minister Tony Blair enlisted the support of many nations. A new era in global relations began as China, Russia, and more than 50 other countries joined the coalition.

Southwest Asia: Political

BLACK SEA
GEORGIA
Tbilisi
ARMENIA
Yerevan
Ankara
TURKEY
CYPRUS
Nicosia
LEBANON
Beirut
ISRAEL
Jerusalem
Tigris
Baku
CASPIAN SEA
Ural River
KAZAKHSTAN
Astana
ARAL SEA
SYRIA
Damascus
Euphrates River
Amman
JORDAN
IRAQ
Baghdad
AZERBAIJAN
TURKMENISTAN
Ashgabat
UZBEKISTAN
KYRGYZSTAN
Tashkent
Tehran
TAJIKISTAN
Dushanbe
Basra
Kuwait City
KUWAIT
IRAN
Kabul
AFGHANISTAN
Islamabad
Indus River
Manama
BAHRAIN
QATAR
Doha
PERSIAN GULF
SAUDI ARABIA
Riyadh
UNITED ARAB EMIRATES
Abu Dhabi
Masqat (Muscat)
Karachi
PAKISTAN
New Delhi
INDIA
OMAN
YEMEN
Sanaa

▲ Afghanistan is a landlocked country. It shares borders with Pakistan, Iran, Turkmenistan, Uzbekistan, and Tajikistan.

▲ Much of Afghanistan is covered by rugged mountainous terrain. This landscape provided hiding places for al Qaeda terrorist camps and cells.

Some countries supplied military support for the fight against terrorists in Afghanistan. Others, including Pakistan and Uzbekistan, allowed coalition forces to use their air bases near Afghanistan. The coalition included many Muslim and Arab nations.

Coalition forces achieved victory quickly in Afghanistan. By the end of 2001, the Taliban, Afghanistan's ruling government, was forced from power and many al Qaeda terrorists were captured or killed. Despite this success, the war on terrorism is not over. Terrorist cells are still active in other countries. President Bush warned that new battles will have to be fought to eliminate them.

A New Government for Afghanistan

After the fall of the Taliban, representatives from all over Afghanistan formed a new government. Their country faced difficult problems. Years of war had left the country in ruins. As part of the war on terrorism, coalition forces provided food and medical care and also promised to rebuild Afghanistan.

Homeland Security While fighting terrorism in Afghanistan, the U. S. government also acted to block future terrorist attacks at home. The nation's borders and coastline are patrolled more carefully. New procedures make air travel more secure.

President Bush also created the Office of Homeland Security. Its job is to coordinate different security and intelligence agencies. As a result, officials can better identify people with links to terrorists.

Understanding What You Read

1. How are the United States and other nations fighting global terrorism?
2. In what ways are Americans defending their homeland against terror?

GeoSKILLS

Building Skills for Life: Using Visual Evidence

We learn about the past from many different sources. One important source of information is visual evidence. Paintings, statues, drawings, and photographs are all examples of visual evidence. Pictures and paintings provide many clues about life in the past. Sometimes they show the clothing people wore, the houses they lived in, or the games they played. Often they document, or prove, that certain events were an important part of a culture.

As with all historical sources, you need to study visual evidence carefully. Often, artists and photographers only show what they want you to see. To use visual evidence effectively, follow these steps:

1. **Identify the visual evidence.** Study a picture or painting carefully. Pay attention to details. Ask yourself who the subjects of the picture are and what they might be doing. Look at the painting on this page. How would you describe the people you see? What are they doing?

Pieter Brueghel the Elder painted this scene in the 1500s.

2. **Evaluate the visual evidence.** Remember, a picture or photo does not always show the whole story. The artist or photographer might have left out details on purpose. Thinking about the artist's purpose will help you decide whether visual evidence is reliable. What purpose do you think Brueghel had for painting his picture? Do you think it is a reliable record of how some people lived?

3. **Learn from the visual evidence.** After studying a picture carefully, use the details that you note to draw conclusions. Your conclusions should help you understand how some people lived at a particular time and place in the past. What conclusions can you draw from the details in Brueghel's painting?

PRACTICING THE SKILL

1. Study an old family album or library book that contains photographs taken long ago in your city or state. What do the pictures tell you about life in the time in which they were taken?
2. Study a picture in a newspaper or magazine without reading the caption. What story does the photo tell about our culture? Why do you think the photographer has chosen to document this event in this way?
3. What visual evidence would best capture our way of life today? Choose five pictures. Explain why each one might help people of the future understand American life today.

HANDS ON GEOGRAPHY

Paintings, drawings, statues, sculpture, and photographs are all types of visual evidence. Historians study the details in visual evidence to draw conclusions about the past.

Look at the two examples of visual evidence below. The first is a sculpture. It shows a battle that took place in ancient Greece about 2,500 years ago. The second is a painting from 1862 of a British railway station. What details do you notice in each example? What information do they help you to know?

This relief shows the Battle of Marathon that took place in 490 B.C.

Artist William Frith painted this scene in 1862.

Lab Report

1. Look at the sculpture of the Battle of Marathon. What conclusions can you draw about warfare in ancient Greece?
2. Look at the painting. What do you think the artist's purpose was for painting this scene?

UNIT 3

United States and Canada

CHAPTER 10 & 11
The United States

CHAPTER 12
Canada

Canadian Rocky Mountains

CN Tower and SkyDome, Toronto, Canada

An Englishman in Texas

Jon Hall grew up in the London suburbs. He studied Greek and Latin as a student in Texas. Here he contrasts what he sees as the British and Texan attitudes toward personal space and sports. **WHAT DO YOU THINK?** *How do you think people in your community feel about these topics?*

As an Englishman, the absence in Texas of fences and walls and clearly marked boundaries made me rather nervous at first. In London, with thousands of people in a small space, everyone is uptight about fencing off *their* little bit of land. In Texas, front yards and parks and parking lots sprawl casually without boundaries. And Texans really are more open and friendly than others. On the street, in a store, in a restaurant, greeting strangers is just the thing to do.

Brits and Texans support sports differently. In Britain, the spectators tend to be males between 15 and 45 years old—definitely not a family atmosphere. But at Texas football games, you'll see grandparents with their grandkids and guys and gals on dates. At the high school level too, there is much wider participation: the band, cheerleaders, parents, fans. I played soccer for my high school and most Saturdays we'd have a crowd of about seven.

Street scene in Austin, Texas

American teenagers

Understanding Primary Sources

1. Why does Jon Hall think the people of London are more concerned about boundaries than Texans?
2. According to Jon Hall, what gives Texas football games a "family atmosphere?"

American buffalo

The United States and Canada

Elevation Profile

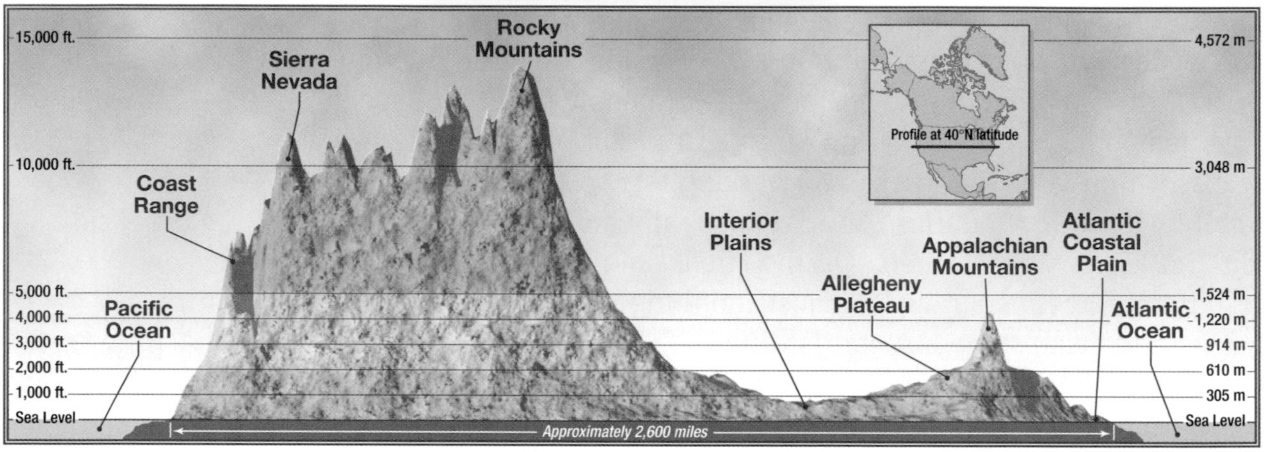
15,000 ft.
10,000 ft.
5,000 ft.
4,000 ft.
3,000 ft.
2,000 ft.
1,000 ft.
Sea Level
4,572 m
3,048 m
1,524 m
1,220 m
914 m
610 m
305 m
Sea Level
Rocky Mountains
Sierra Nevada
Coast Range
Pacific Ocean
Interior Plains
Allegheny Plateau
Appalachian Mountains
Atlantic Coastal Plain
Atlantic Ocean
Profile at 40°N latitude
Approximately 2,600 miles

GEOSTATS:

Highest point in North America: Mount McKinley, Alaska–20,320 ft. (6,194 m)

Lowest point in North America: Death Valley, California–282 ft. below sea level (86 m below sea level)

Largest lake in North America: Lake Superior–31,800 sq. mi. (82,362 sq km)

World's highest tides: Bay of Fundy, Nova Scotia, Canada–as high as 70 ft. (21 m)

The United States and Canada: Comparing Sizes

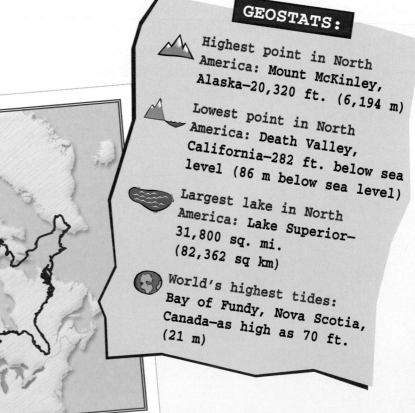

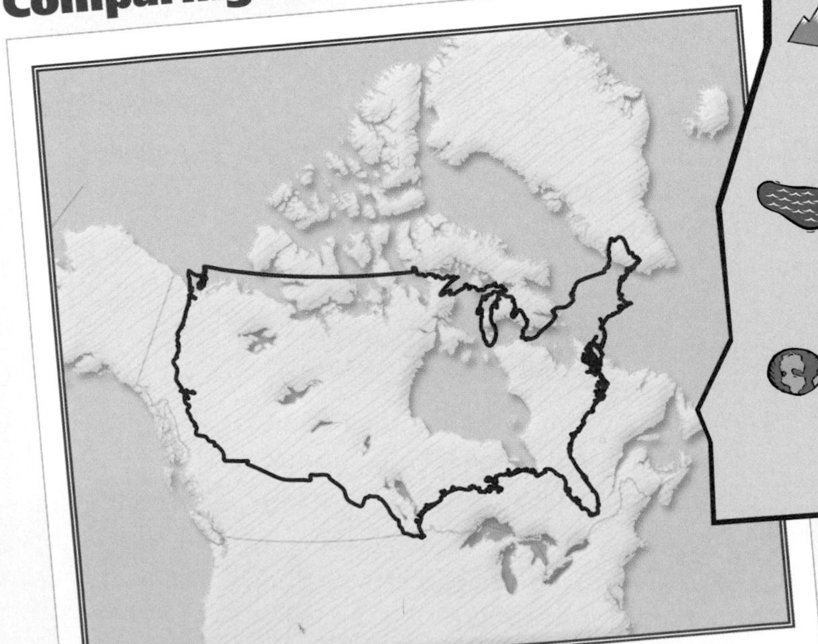

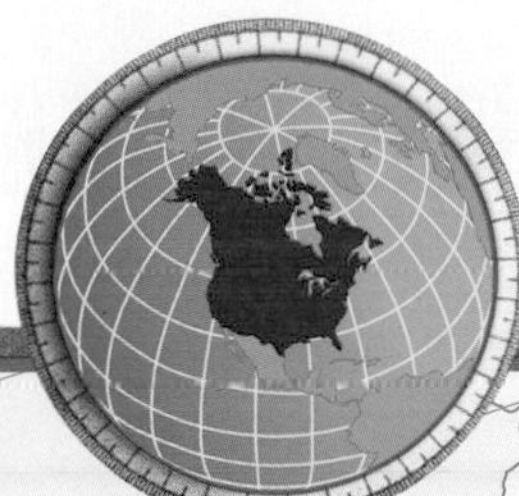

United States and Canada: Physical

UNIT 3 ATLAS

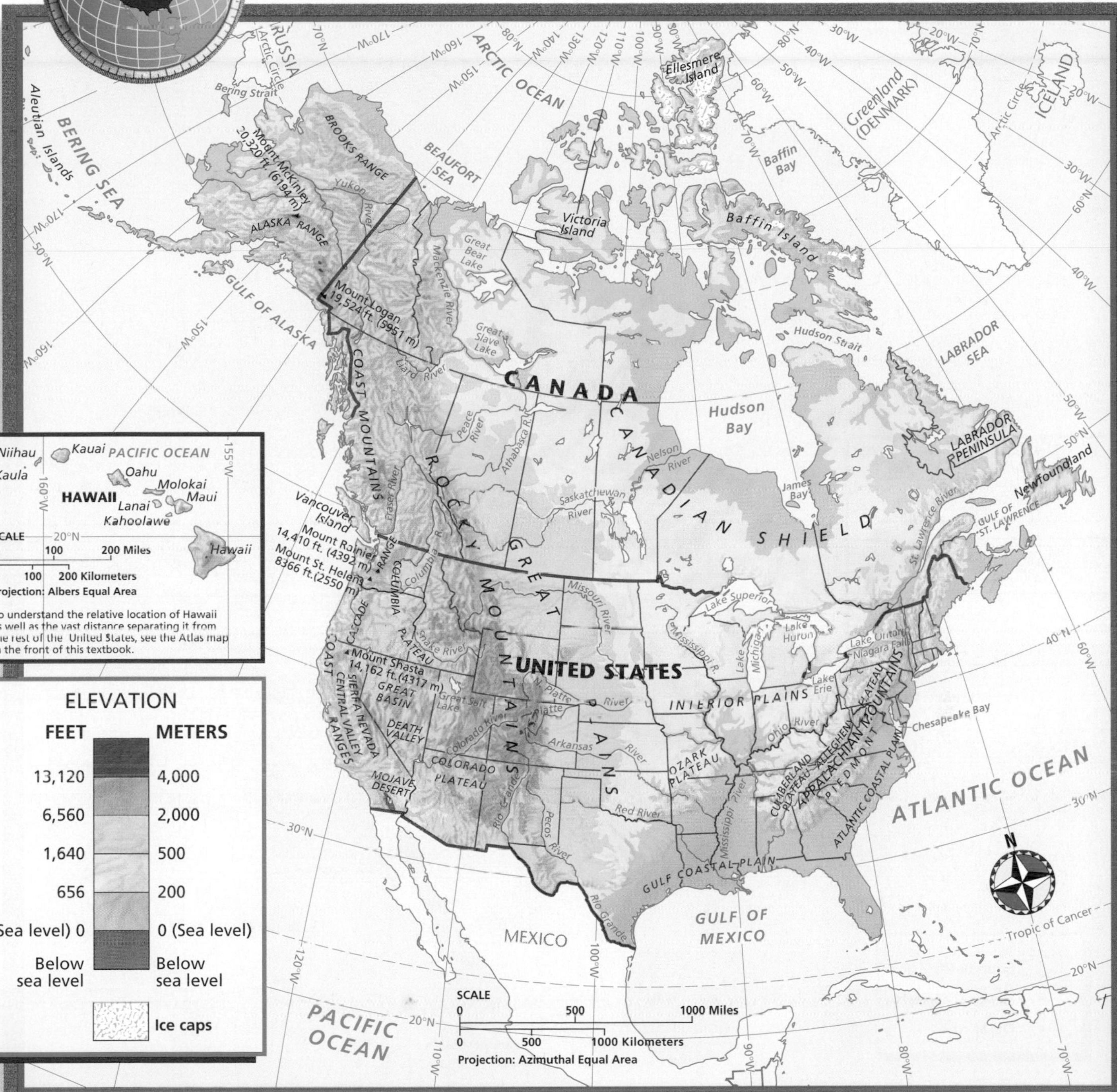

RUSSIA
Arctic Circle
Bering Strait
Aleutian Islands
BERING SEA
ARCTIC OCEAN
BROOKS RANGE
Mount McKinley 20,320 ft. (6194 m)
ALASKA RANGE
Yukon River
BEAUFORT SEA
GULF OF ALASKA
Mount Logan 19,524 ft. (5951 m)
Ellesmere Island
Greenland (DENMARK)
ICELAND
Baffin Bay
Victoria Island
Baffin Island
Great Bear Lake
Mackenzie River
Great Slave Lake
Hudson Strait
LABRADOR SEA
Liard River
CANADA
COAST MOUNTAINS
Peace River
Athabasca R.
CANADIAN SHIELD
Hudson Bay
LABRADOR PENINSULA
Newfoundland
Nelson River
James Bay
Saskatchewan River
GULF OF ST. LAWRENCE
St. Lawrence River
ROCKY MOUNTAINS
GREAT PLAINS
Vancouver Island
Fraser River
Mount Rainier 14,410 ft. (4392 m)
Mount St. Helens 8366 ft. (2550 m)
CASCADE RANGE
COLUMBIA PLATEAU
Columbia R.
Missouri River
Lake Superior
Mississippi R.
Lake Michigan
Lake Huron
Lake Ontario
Niagara Falls
Lake Erie
Snake River
Mount Shasta 14,162 ft. (4317 m)
UNITED STATES
COAST RANGES
SIERRA NEVADA
CENTRAL VALLEY
GREAT BASIN
Great Salt Lake
N. Platte River
Platte
INTERIOR PLAINS
DEATH VALLEY
Colorado River
Arkansas River
Ohio River
OZARK PLATEAU
ALLEGHENY PLATEAU
APPALACHIAN MOUNTAINS
CUMBERLAND PLATEAU
PIEDMONT
Chesapeake Bay
ATLANTIC COASTAL PLAIN
MOJAVE DESERT
COLORADO PLATEAU
Rio Grande
Pecos River
Red River
Mississippi River
ATLANTIC OCEAN
GULF COASTAL PLAIN
N
GULF OF MEXICO
MEXICO
Tropic of Cancer
PACIFIC OCEAN
SCALE
0 500 1000 Miles
0 500 1000 Kilometers
Projection: Azimuthal Equal Area
Niihau
Kauai
PACIFIC OCEAN
Kaula
Oahu
Molokai
HAWAII
Lanai
Maui
Kahoolawe
Hawaii
SCALE
0 100 200 Miles
0 100 200 Kilometers
Projection: Albers Equal Area
To understand the relative location of Hawaii as well as the vast distance separating it from the rest of the United States, see the Atlas map in the front of this textbook.
ELEVATION
FEET
METERS
13,120
4,000
6,560
2,000
1,640
500
656
200
(Sea level) 0
0 (Sea level)
Below sea level
Below sea level
Ice caps

1. *Places and Regions* Where is the highest point in North America? Which southwestern desert includes an area below sea level?
2. *Places and Regions* Which two large lakes are entirely within Canada?
3. *Places and Regions* What are four tributaries of the Mississippi River?

Critical Thinking

4. **Drawing Inferences and Conclusions** Compare this map to the **population map** of the region. What is one physical feature that many of the largest cities have in common? What is the connection between the cities' locations and these physical features?

United States and Canada: Political

ARCTIC OCEAN
BERING SEA
Bering Strait
Arctic Circle
RUSSIA
BEAUFORT SEA
GULF OF ALASKA
ALASKA (U.S.)
Ellesmere Island
Greenland (DENMARK)
ICELAND
Baffin Bay
Victoria Island
Baffin Island
YUKON TERRITORY
NORTHWEST TERRITORIES
NUNAVUT
Iqaluit
Hudson Strait
LABRADOR SEA
CANADA
Hudson Bay
James Bay
NEWFOUNDLAND
LABRADOR
Newfoundland
BRITISH COLUMBIA
ALBERTA
Edmonton
Calgary
SASKATCHEWAN
MANITOBA
ONTARIO
QUEBEC
Winnipeg
Vancouver Island
Vancouver
Seattle
GULF OF ST. LAWRENCE
PRINCE EDWARD ISLAND
NEW BRUNSWICK
NOVA SCOTIA
Quebec
Montreal
Ottawa
Toronto
Niihau
Kauai
PACIFIC OCEAN
Kaula
Oahu
Molokai
HAWAII
Lanai
Maui
Kahoolawe
Hawaii
SCALE
0 100 200 Miles
0 100 200 Kilometers
Projection: Albers Equal Area
To understand the relative location of Hawaii as well as the vast distance separating it from the rest of the United States, see the Atlas map in the front of this textbook.
WASH.
MONT.
N. DAK.
MINN.
OREG.
IDAHO
S. DAK.
WIS.
MICH.
UNITED STATES
WYO.
NEBR.
IOWA
Chicago
Detroit
ILL.
IND.
OHIO
PA.
N.Y.
VT.
N.H.
MAINE
Boston
MASS.
CT.
R.I.
New York
N.J.
Philadelphia
Washington, D.C.
DEL.
MD.
Chesapeake Bay
San Francisco
NEV.
UTAH
Denver
COLO.
CALIF.
KANS.
MO.
W. VA.
VA.
KY.
Los Angeles
San Diego
ARIZ.
N. MEX.
OKLA.
ARK.
TENN.
N.C.
S.C.
Atlanta
GA.
Phoenix
Dallas
TEXAS
ALA.
MISS.
LA.
FLA.
San Antonio
Houston
Miami
PACIFIC OCEAN
ATLANTIC OCEAN
GULF OF MEXICO
MEXICO
Tropic of Cancer
N
Boundaries
National capitals
Other cities
SCALE
0 500 1000 Miles
0 500 1000 Kilometers
Projection: Azimuthal Equal Area

1. *Places and Regions* Compare this map to the **physical map** of the region. What physical feature forms part of the border between the United States and Mexico?

Critical Thinking

2. **Comparing** Compare this map to the **climate** and **population maps**. Which U.S. border—the Canadian or Mexican—has a denser population? Why?
3. **Comparing** Which Canadian province or territory appears to be the largest? the second largest? Why is it hard to compare their sizes?

United States and Canada: Climate

UNIT 3 ATLAS

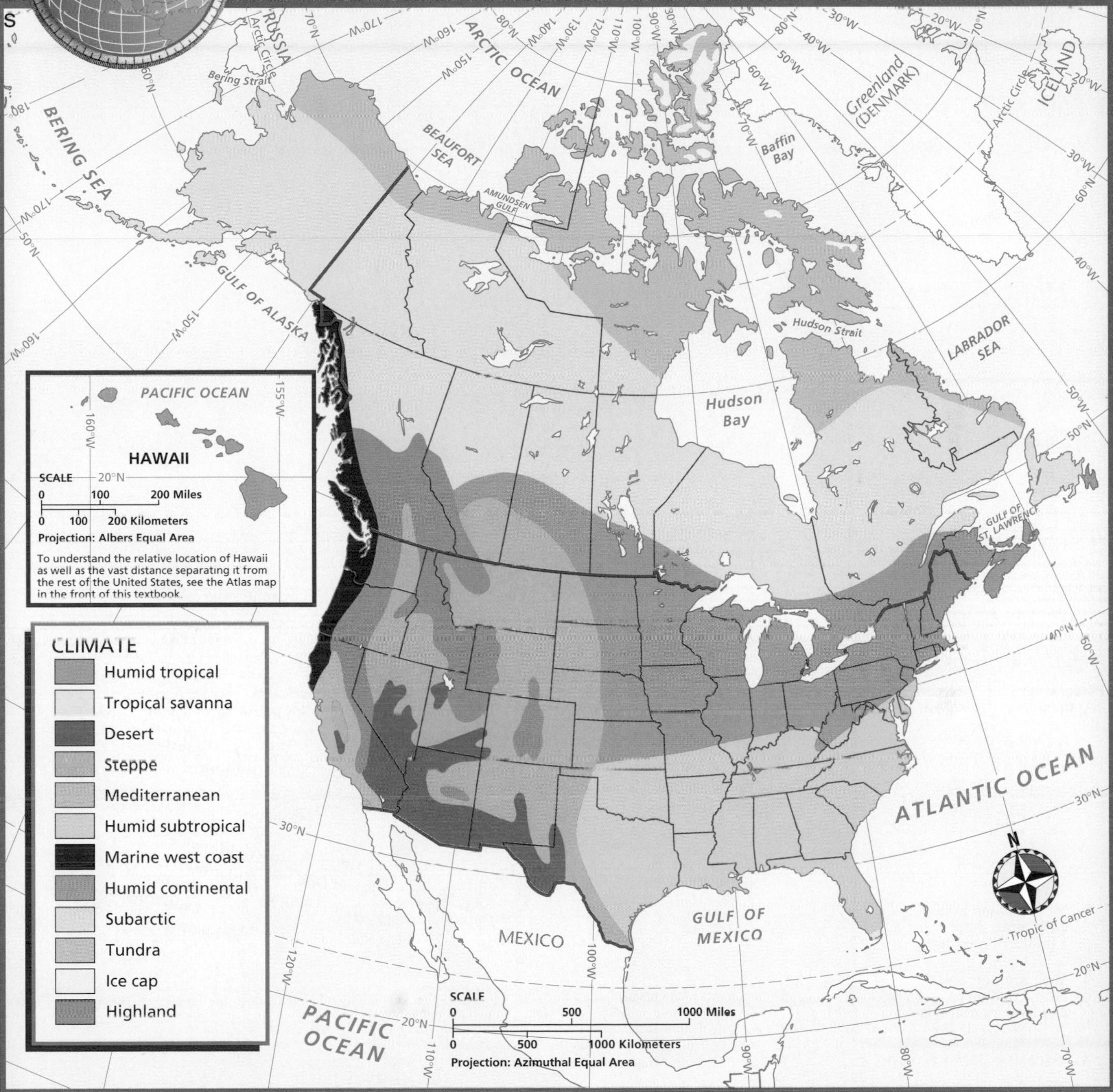

ARCTIC OCEAN
BEAUFORT SEA
AMUNDSEN GULF
BERING SEA
Bering Strait
RUSSIA
Arctic Circle
Greenland (DENMARK)
ICELAND
Baffin Bay
Hudson Strait
LABRADOR SEA
Hudson Bay
GULF OF ST. LAWRENCE
GULF OF ALASKA
ATLANTIC OCEAN
GULF OF MEXICO
MEXICO
PACIFIC OCEAN
Tropic of Cancer
PACIFIC OCEAN
HAWAII
SCALE
0 100 200 Miles
0 100 200 Kilometers
Projection: Albers Equal Area
To understand the relative location of Hawaii as well as the vast distance separating it from the rest of the United States, see the Atlas map in the front of this textbook.
CLIMATE
Humid tropical
Tropical savanna
Desert
Steppe
Mediterranean
Humid subtropical
Marine west coast
Humid continental
Subarctic
Tundra
Ice cap
Highland
SCALE
0 500 1000 Miles
0 500 1000 Kilometers
Projection: Azimuthal Equal Area
N

1. *Places and Regions* Which U.S. state has the greatest diversity of climates? What are three states that have only one climate type?

2. *Places and Regions* Compare this map to the **physical** and **population maps** of the region. Which climate region contains the most big cities? Which climate regions do not have big cities?

Critical Thinking

3. **Comparing** Compare this map to the **physical map**. What may have limited settlement of the U.S. Great Plains?

United States and Canada: Population

UNIT 3 ATLAS

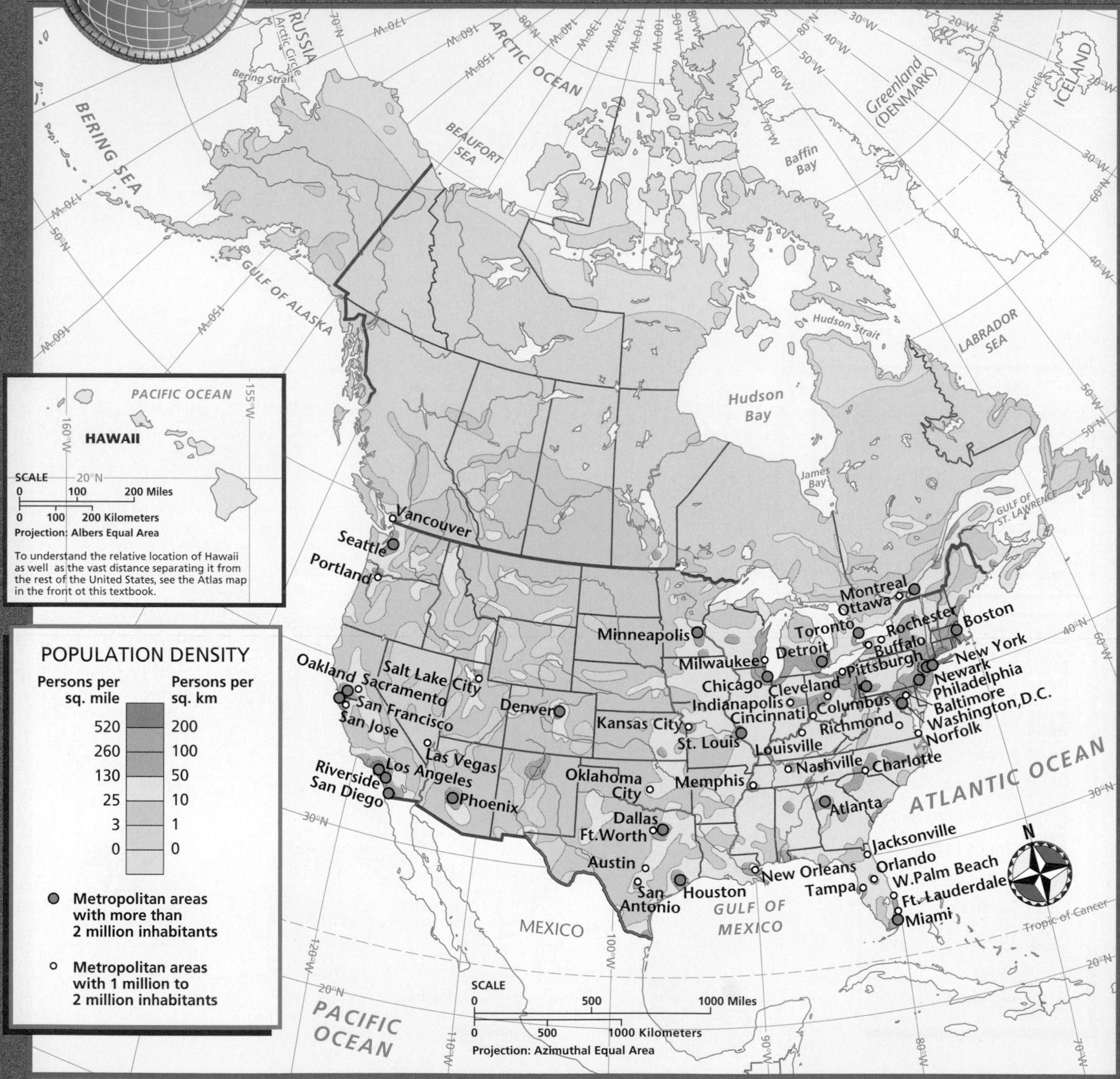

PACIFIC OCEAN
HAWAII
SCALE
0 100 200 Miles
0 100 200 Kilometers
Projection: Albers Equal Area
To understand the relative location of Hawaii as well as the vast distance separating it from the rest of the United States, see the Atlas map in the front ot this textbook.
POPULATION DENSITY
Persons per sq. mile
Persons per sq. km
520 200
260 100
130 50
25 10
3 1
0 0
Metropolitan areas with more than 2 million inhabitants
Metropolitan areas with 1 million to 2 million inhabitants
RUSSIA
BERING SEA
Bering Strait
ARCTIC OCEAN
BEAUFORT SEA
GULF OF ALASKA
Baffin Bay
Greenland (DENMARK)
ICELAND
Hudson Strait
LABRADOR SEA
Hudson Bay
James Bay
GULF OF ST. LAWRENCE
ATLANTIC OCEAN
GULF OF MEXICO
MEXICO
PACIFIC OCEAN
Tropic of Cancer
Vancouver
Seattle
Portland
Oakland
Sacramento
San Francisco
San Jose
Salt Lake City
Las Vegas
Los Angeles
Riverside
San Diego
Phoenix
Denver
Minneapolis
Milwaukee
Chicago
Indianapolis
Cincinnati
Kansas City
St. Louis
Louisville
Nashville
Memphis
Oklahoma City
Dallas
Ft. Worth
Austin
San Antonio
Houston
New Orleans
Atlanta
Charlotte
Jacksonville
Orlando
Tampa
W. Palm Beach
Ft. Lauderdale
Miami
Detroit
Toronto
Cleveland
Columbus
Pittsburgh
Buffalo
Rochester
Montreal
Ottawa
Boston
New York
Newark
Philadelphia
Baltimore
Washington, D.C.
Richmond
Norfolk
SCALE
0 500 1000 Miles
0 500 1000 Kilometers
Projection: Azimuthal Equal Area
N

1. *Places and Regions* Which country appears to have a larger population?
2. *Places and Regions* What are Canada's two largest cities?
3. *Places and Regions* Based on the map, which area of the United States do you think was settled first? Why?

Critical Thinking

4. **Analyzing Information** Use the map on this page to create a chart, graph, database, or model of population centers in the United States and Canada.

United States and Canada: Land Use and Resources

UNIT 3 ATLAS

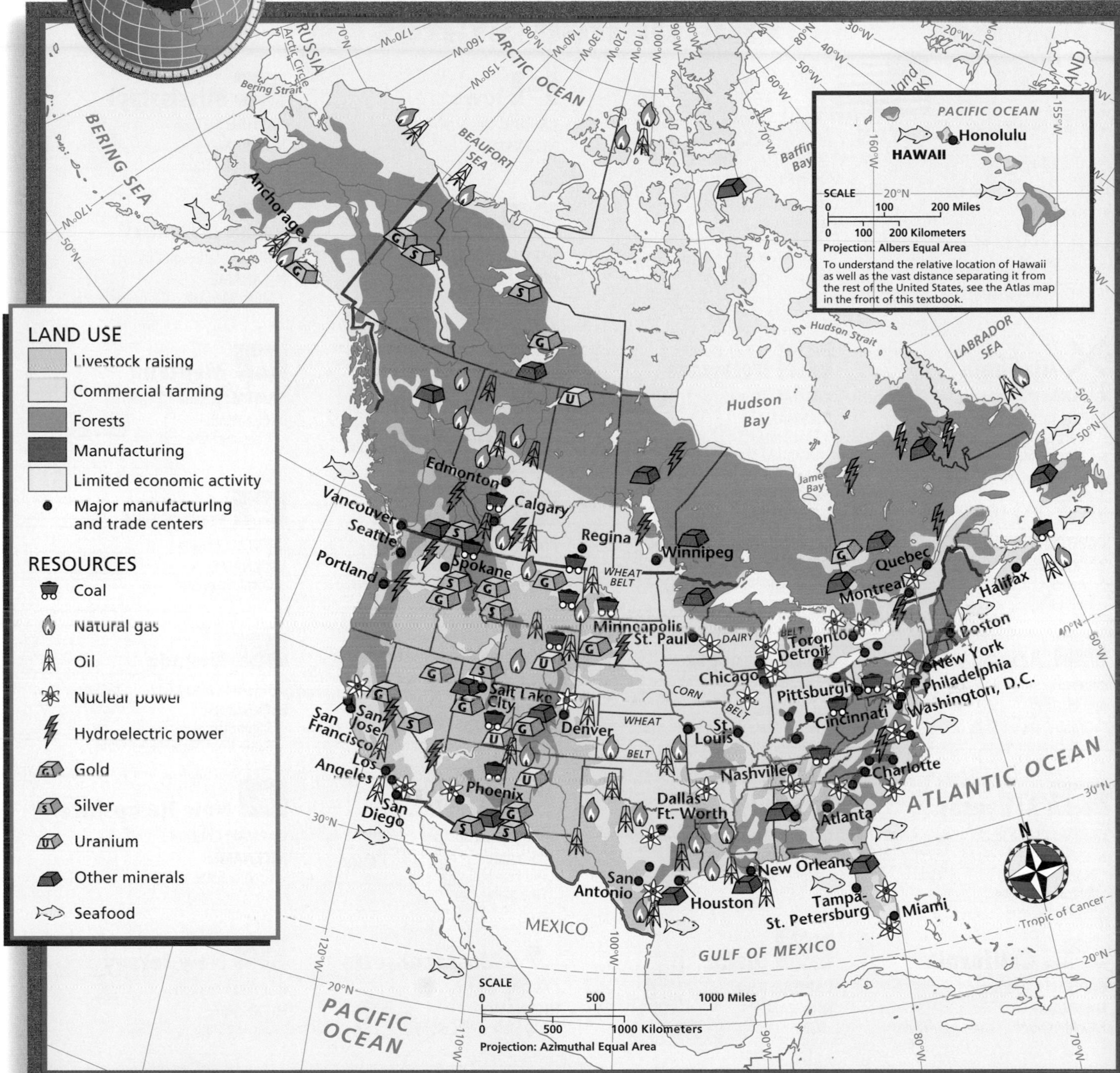

LAND USE
Livestock raising
Commercial farming
Forests
Manufacturing
Limited economic activity
Major manufacturing and trade centers
RESOURCES
Coal
Natural gas
Oil
Nuclear power
Hydroelectric power
Gold
Silver
Uranium
Other minerals
Seafood
PACIFIC OCEAN
Honolulu
HAWAII
SCALE
0
100
200 Miles
0
100
200 Kilometers
Projection: Albers Equal Area
To understand the relative location of Hawaii as well as the vast distance separating it from the rest of the United States, see the Atlas map in the front of this textbook.
RUSSIA
Arctic Circle
Bering Strait
BERING SEA
ARCTIC OCEAN
BEAUFORT SEA
Baffin Bay
Hudson Strait
LABRADOR SEA
Hudson Bay
James Bay
Anchorage
Edmonton
Calgary
Vancouver
Seattle
Portland
Spokane
Regina
Winnipeg
Quebec
Montreal
Halifax
Boston
Toronto
Detroit
New York
Philadelphia
Washington, D.C.
Minneapolis
St. Paul
Chicago
Pittsburgh
Cincinnati
St. Louis
Salt Lake City
Denver
San Francisco
San Jose
Los Angeles
San Diego
Phoenix
Nashville
Charlotte
Atlanta
Dallas
Ft. Worth
San Antonio
Houston
New Orleans
Tampa-St. Petersburg
Miami
WHEAT BELT
DAIRY BELT
CORN BELT
WHEAT BELT
ATLANTIC OCEAN
GULF OF MEXICO
MEXICO
PACIFIC OCEAN
Tropic of Cancer
N
SCALE
0
500
1000 Miles
0
500
1000 Kilometers
Projection: Azimuthal Equal Area

1. Places and Regions Look at the **physical map**. In which area of North America are gold, silver, and uranium found?

2. Places and Regions Which two states on the Gulf of Mexico produce large amounts of oil and natural gas?

3. Environment and Society Which type of land use is most common throughout Canada?

Critical Thinking

4. **Analyzing Information** Create a chart, graph, database, or model of economic activities in the United States and Canada.

Fast Facts

The United States

UNITED STATES

CAPITAL: Washington, D.C.

AREA: 3,717,792 sq. mi. (9,629,091 sq km)

POPULATION: 281,421,906

MONEY: U.S. dollar (US$)

LANGUAGES: English, Spanish (spoken by a large minority)

Alabama
CAPITAL: Montgomery
NICKNAME: Heart of Dixie, Camellia State

Alaska
CAPITAL: Juneau
NICKNAME: The Last Frontier (unofficial)

Arizona
CAPITAL: Phoenix
NICKNAME: Grand Canyon State

Arkansas
CAPITAL: Little Rock
NICKNAME: Natural State, Razorback State

California
CAPITAL: Sacramento
NICKNAME: Golden State

Colorado
CAPITAL: Denver
NICKNAME: Centennial State

Connecticut
CAPITAL: Hartford
NICKNAME: Constitution State, Nutmeg State

Delaware
CAPITAL: Dover
NICKNAME: First State, Diamond State

Florida
CAPITAL: Tallahassee
NICKNAME: Sunshine State

Georgia
CAPITAL: Atlanta
NICKNAME: Peach State, Empire State of the South

Hawaii
CAPITAL: Honolulu
NICKNAME: Aloha State

Idaho
CAPITAL: Boise
NICKNAME: Gem State

Illinois
CAPITAL: Springfield
NICKNAME: Prairie State

Indiana
CAPITAL: Indianapolis
NICKNAME: Hoosier State

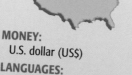

Iowa
CAPITAL: Des Moines
NICKNAME: Hawkeye State

Kansas
CAPITAL: Topeka
NICKNAME: Sunflower State

Kentucky
CAPITAL: Frankfort
NICKNAME: Bluegrass State

Louisiana
CAPITAL: Baton Rouge
NICKNAME: Pelican State

Maine
CAPITAL: Augusta
NICKNAME: Pine Tree State

Maryland
CAPITAL: Annapolis
NICKNAME: Old Line State, Free State

Massachusetts
CAPITAL: Boston
NICKNAME: Bay State, Old Colony

Michigan
CAPITAL: Lansing
NICKNAME: Great Lakes State, Wolverine State

Minnesota
CAPITAL: St. Paul
NICKNAME: Gopher State, North Star State

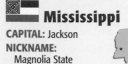

Mississippi
CAPITAL: Jackson
NICKNAME: Magnolia State

Missouri
CAPITAL: Jefferson City
NICKNAME: Show Me State

Montana
CAPITAL: Helena
NICKNAME: Treasure State

Nebraska
CAPITAL: Lincoln
NICKNAME: Cornhusker State

Nevada
CAPITAL: Carson City
NICKNAME: Sagebrush State, Battle Born State, Silver State

New Hampshire
CAPITAL: Concord
NICKNAME: Granite State

New Jersey
CAPITAL: Trenton
NICKNAME: Garden State

New Mexico
CAPITAL: Santa Fe
NICKNAME: Land of Enchantment

New York
CAPITAL: Albany
NICKNAME: Empire State

Countries, states, provinces, and territories not drawn to scale.

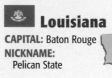

North Carolina
CAPITAL: Raleigh
NICKNAME: Tar Heel State, Old North State

Pennsylvania
CAPITAL: Harrisburg
NICKNAME: Keystone State

Texas
CAPITAL: Austin
NICKNAME: Lone Star State

North Dakota
CAPITAL: Bismarck
NICKNAME: Peace Garden State

Rhode Island
CAPITAL: Providence
NICKNAME: Little Rhody, Ocean State

Utah
CAPITAL: Salt Lake City
NICKNAME: Beehive State

West Virginia
CAPITAL: Charleston
NICKNAME: Mountain State

Ohio
CAPITAL: Columbus
NICKNAME: Buckeye State

South Carolina
CAPITAL: Columbia
NICKNAME: Palmetto State

Vermont
CAPITAL: Montpelier
NICKNAME: Green Mountain State

Wisconsin
CAPITAL: Madison
NICKNAME: Badger State

Oklahoma
CAPITAL: Oklahoma City
NICKNAME: Sooner State

South Dakota
CAPITAL: Pierre
NICKNAME: Coyote State, Mount Rushmore State

Virginia
CAPITAL: Richmond
NICKNAME: Old Dominion

Wyoming
CAPITAL: Cheyenne
NICKNAME: Equality State, Cowboy State

Oregon
CAPITAL: Salem
NICKNAME: Beaver State

Tennessee
CAPITAL: Nashville
NICKNAME: Volunteer State

Washington
CAPITAL: Olympia
NICKNAME: Evergreen State

Canada

CANADA
CAPITAL: Ottawa
AREA: 3,890,695 sq. mi. (9,976,140 sq km)
POPULATION: 31,592,805
MONEY: Canadian dollar (Can$)
LANGUAGES: English (official), French (official)

Nova Scotia
CAPITAL: Halifax

Saskatchewan
CAPITAL: Regina

Nunavut
CAPITAL: Iqaluit

Yukon Territory
CAPITAL: Whitehorse

Alberta
CAPITAL: Edmonton

New Brunswick
CAPITAL: Fredericton

Ontario
CAPITAL: Toronto

British Columbia
CAPITAL: Victoria

Newfoundland
CAPITAL: St. John's

Prince Edward Island
CAPITAL: Charlottetown

Manitoba
CAPITAL: Winnipeg

Northwest Territories
CAPITAL: Yellowknife

Quebec
CAPITAL: Quebec

internet connect
COUNTRY STATISTICS
GO TO: go.hrw.com
KEYWORD: SJ3 FactsU3
FOR: more facts about the United States and Canada

Sources: Central Intelligence Agency, *The World Factbook 2001; The World Almanac and Book of Facts 2001*

CHAPTER 10

The Geography and History of the United States

Many different groups have settled in the United States. Here you will read about one of the first of these groups, the Pilgrims.

In November 1620 a small ship sailing from England was blown off course into a harbor near what is now Provincetown, Massachusetts. It was the *Mayflower*, which had been bound for Virginia. The weary voyagers "fell upon their knees and blessed the God of Heaven, who had brought them over the vast and furious ocean," wrote William Bradford, a leader of the group.

The voyagers had indeed been over a "furious ocean." For more than two months, the *Mayflower* had been blown about by violent storms. The passengers were sick and weak, and they had landed far north of their destination at the wrong time of year. The "howling wilderness" terrified many of them, and the weather was cold and getting colder. While their shipmates huddled on board, some of the passengers searched for a place to settle. By mid-December they had found a site—Plymouth, named after the English port from which they had sailed.

Puritan couple dressed for church

Pilgrims landing at Plymouth Rock

Early American colonial settlement

Detail, Courtesy of the Pilgrim Society, Plymouth, Massachusetts

Section 1 Physical Geography

Read to Discover

1. What are the major physical features of the United States?
2. What climate regions are found in the United States?
3. What natural resources does the United States have?

Define

contiguous
Continental Divide
basins

Locate

Coastal Plain
Appalachian Mountains
Interior Plains
Rocky Mountains
Great Lakes
Mississippi River
Great Plains
Columbia River
Great Basin
Colorado Plateau
Sierra Nevada
Cascade Range
Aleutian Islands

Why It Matters

Some of the U.S. states are at risk for earthquakes. Use CNNfyi.com or other **current events** sources to find out about earthquakes in the United States. Record your findings in your journal.

Bald eagle

The United States: Physical-Political

PACIFIC OCEAN
CANADA
UNITED STATES
ROCKY MOUNTAINS
GREAT PLAINS
INTERIOR PLAINS
GREAT BASIN
COLORADO PLATEAU
SIERRA NEVADA
CENTRAL VALLEY
CASCADE RANGE
APPALACHIAN MOUNTAINS
PIEDMONT
ATLANTIC COASTAL PLAIN
GULF COASTAL PLAIN
ATLANTIC OCEAN
GULF OF MEXICO
MEXICO
Straits of Florida
Tropic of Cancer
Florida Keys
Lake Superior
Lake Michigan
Lake Huron
Lake Erie
Lake Ontario
Great Salt Lake
Columbia River
Missouri River
Mississippi R.
Mississippi River
Ohio River
Seattle
Portland
San Francisco
Los Angeles
San Diego
Las Vegas
Phoenix
Denver
Dallas
Austin
San Antonio
Houston
New Orleans
Chicago
Detroit
Atlanta
Miami
Baltimore
Washington, D.C.
Philadelphia
New York
Boston
WA OR CA NV ID MT WY UT AZ CO NM ND SD NE KS OK TX MN IA MO AR LA WI IL MI IN OH KY TN MS AL GA FL SC NC VA WV PA NY VT NH ME MA CT RI NJ DE MD
ARCTIC OCEAN
Arctic Circle
BROOKS RANGE
AK
Mount McKinley 20,320 ft. (6194 m)
ALASKA RANGE
Aleutian Islands
PACIFIC OCEAN
0 500 Miles
0 500 Kilometers
Niihau
Kauai
Kaula
Oahu
Molokai
Maui
Lanai
Kahoolawe
HI
Hawaii
SCALE
0 100 200 Miles
0 100 200 Kilometers
Projection: Albers Equal Area
To understand the relative location of Hawaii, as well as the vast distance separating it from the rest of the United States, see the Atlas map.
ELEVATION
FEET METERS
13,120 4,000
6,560 2,000
1,640 500
656 200
(Sea level) 0 0 (Sea level)
Below sea level Below sea level
Continental Divide
National capital
Other cities
SCALE
0 250 500 Miles
0 250 500 Kilometers
Projection: Azimuthal Equal Area
N
50°N
30°N
20°N
100°W
80°W

internet connect

GO TO: go.hrw.com
KEYWORD: SJ3 CH10
FOR: Web sites about the United States

Physical Features

The 48 **contiguous** American states and the District of Columbia lie between the Atlantic and Pacific Oceans. Contiguous states are those that border each other. Two states are not contiguous: Alaska, to the northwest of Canada, and Hawaii, in the Pacific Ocean. The United States also has territories in the Pacific Ocean and the Caribbean Sea. We will now look at the physical features of the 50 states. You can use the map on the next page to follow along.

The East The eastern United States rises from the Coastal Plain to the Appalachian Mountains. The Coastal Plain is a low region that lies close to sea level. It rises gradually inland. The Coastal Plain stretches from New York to Mexico along the Atlantic and Gulf of Mexico coasts.

The Appalachians include mountain ranges and river valleys from Maine to Alabama. The mountains are very old. Erosion has lowered and smoothed the peaks for more than 300 million years. The highest mountain in the Appalachians rises to just 6,684 feet (2,037 m).

At the foot of the Appalachians, between the mountains and the Coastal Plain, is the Piedmont. The Piedmont is a region of rolling plains. It begins in New Jersey and extends as far south as Alabama.

The Interior Plains Vast plains make up most of the United States west of the Appalachians. This region is called the Interior Plains. The Interior Plains stretch westward to the Rocky Mountains.

After the last ice age, glaciers shrank. They left rolling hills, lakes, and major river systems in the northern Interior Plains. The Great Lakes were created by these retreating ice sheets. From west to east, the Great Lakes are Lake Superior, Lake Michigan, Lake Huron, Lake Erie, and Lake Ontario.

The Mississippi River and its tributaries drain the Interior Plains. Along the way, they deposit rich soils that produce fertile farmlands. A tributary is a stream or river that flows into a larger stream or river. Tributaries of the Mississippi include the Missouri and Ohio Rivers.

The Great Smoky Mountains of Tennessee are a range of the Appalachian Mountains.

Interpreting the Visual Record
What clues from this photograph might tell you that these mountains are very old?

▼

Canada
United States
Mexico

Physical Regions of the United States and Canada

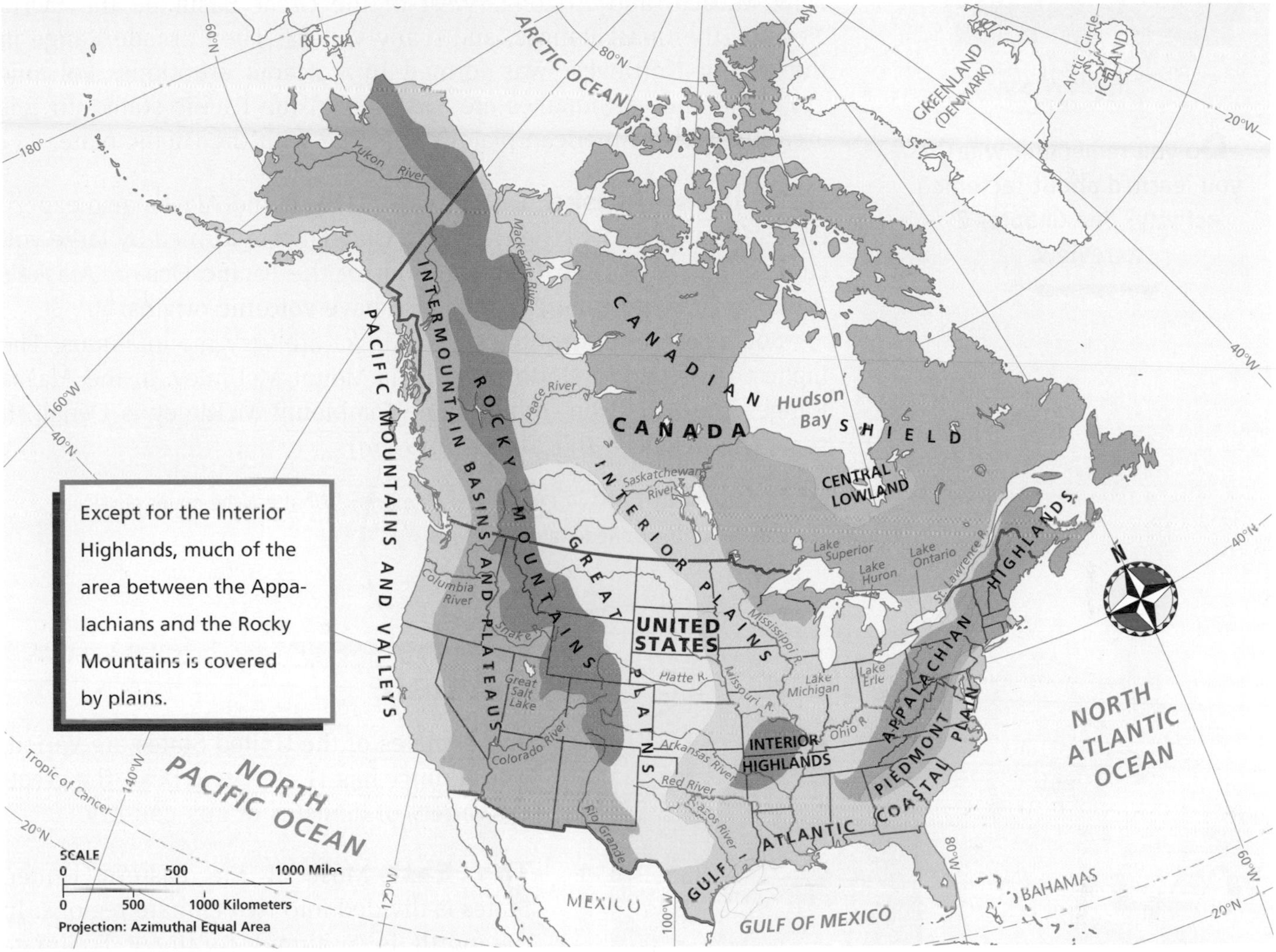
Except for the Interior Highlands, much of the area between the Appalachians and the Rocky Mountains is covered by plains.
RUSSIA
ARCTIC OCEAN
GREENLAND (DENMARK)
ICELAND
Arctic Circle
Yukon River
Mackenzie River
Peace River
Saskatchewan River
Columbia River
Snake R.
Great Salt Lake
Colorado River
Rio Grande
Platte R.
Missouri R.
Mississippi R.
Arkansas River
Red River
Brazos River
Ohio R.
St. Lawrence R.
Lake Superior
Lake Huron
Lake Michigan
Lake Erie
Lake Ontario
Hudson Bay
CANADIAN SHIELD
CANADA
CENTRAL LOWLAND
INTERIOR PLAINS
GREAT PLAINS
ROCKY MOUNTAINS
INTERMOUNTAIN BASINS AND PLATEAUS
PACIFIC MOUNTAINS AND VALLEYS
UNITED STATES
INTERIOR HIGHLANDS
APPALACHIAN HIGHLANDS
PIEDMONT
ATLANTIC COASTAL PLAIN
GULF
NORTH PACIFIC OCEAN
NORTH ATLANTIC OCEAN
GULF OF MEXICO
MEXICO
BAHAMAS
Tropic of Cancer
80°N
60°N
40°N
20°N
180°
160°W
140°W
120°W
100°W
80°W
60°W
40°W
20°W
N
SCALE
0 500 1000 Miles
0 500 1000 Kilometers
Projection: Azimuthal Equal Area

In some places on its way to the Gulf of Mexico, the great Mississippi River is 1.5 miles (2.4 km) wide!

The flattest part of the Interior Plains is the Great Plains region. It lies closest to the Rocky Mountains. The region has a higher elevation than the rest of the Interior Plains. The Great Plains extend from Mexico in the south into Canada in the north.

The West As we continue westward, we reach the Rocky Mountains. The Rockies include a series of mountain ranges separated by high plains and valleys. They extend from Mexico to the cold Arctic. Many Rocky Mountain peaks reach more than 14,000 feet (4,267 m).

Running along the crest of the Rockies is the **Continental Divide**. It divides the flow of North America's rivers. Rivers east of the divide, such as the Missouri, flow eastward. Rivers west of the divide, such as the Columbia, flow westward.

West of the Rockies is a region of plateaus and **basins**. A basin is a region surrounded by higher land, such as mountains. The Great Basin in Nevada and Utah, for example, is surrounded by high mountains. Southeast of the Great Basin is

The Rio Grande cuts through Big Bend National Park along the Texas-Mexico border.

Interpreting the Visual Record What landforms are found in this area?

Canada
United States
Big Bend
Mexico

BUILD on WHAT You Know

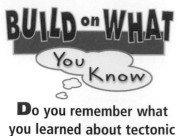

Do you remember what you learned about tectonic activity? See Chapter 2 to review.

the Colorado Plateau. The Colorado Plateau lies in Utah, Colorado, New Mexico, and Arizona. West of the Great Basin lie the Sierra Nevada, the Coast Ranges, and many valleys. The Cascade Range in the Pacific Northwest was formed by volcanic eruptions. Volcanic eruptions and earthquakes are a danger in the Pacific states. In this area, the North American plate is colliding with the Pacific plate.

Hawaii and Alaska Farther west, Hawaii and Alaska also experience tectonic activity. The Hawaiian Islands were formed by large volcanoes that have risen from the floor of the Pacific Ocean. Alaska's Aleutian (uh-LOO-shuhn) Islands also have volcanic origins.

Southeastern and south-central Alaska are very mountainous. The highest mountain in North America is Mount McKinley, in the Alaska Range. The American Indian name for Mount McKinley is Denali. It soars to a height of 20,320 feet (6,194 m).

✓ **READING CHECK:** *Places and Regions* What are the major physical features of the United States?

A Winter storm in Massachusetts
B Spring meadow in California
C Summer in Florida
D Fall in Colorado

Climate

The climates of the United States are varied. The country has 11 climate types—the greatest variety of climates of any country.

The East Most of the eastern United States is divided into two climate regions. In the north is a humid continental climate with snowy winters and warm, humid summers. Southerners experience the milder winters and warm, humid summers of a humid subtropical climate. Coastal areas often experience tropical storms. Southern Florida, with a tropical savanna climate, is warm all year.

The Interior Plains Humid continental, humid subtropical, and steppe climates meet in the interior states. People there sometimes experience violent weather, such as hail and tornadoes. The steppe climate of the Great Plains supports wide grasslands. Summers are hot, and droughts can be a problem. Blinding snowstorms called blizzards sometimes occur during winters, which can be very cold.

The West Climates in the West are mostly dry. Steppe and varied highland climates dominate much of the Rocky Mountain region. Temperatures and the amount of rain and snow vary.

Much of the Southwest has a desert climate. The West Coast has two climate types. The forested north has a wet and mild marine west coast climate. A drier Mediterranean climate is found in the south.

Except in the southeast, most of Alaska has very cold subarctic and tundra climates. Hawaii is the only state within the tropics. Northeasterly trade winds bring rain to eastern sides of the islands. Hawaii's western slopes have a drier tropical savanna climate.

✓ **READING CHECK:** *The World in Spatial Terms* What climate regions are found in the United States?

Our Amazing Planet

Redwoods, the tallest trees in the world, grow in California and Oregon. They can grow well over 300 feet (90 m) high with trunks 20 feet (6 m) in diameter. Some redwood trees are more than 1,500 years old!

Natural Resources

The United States has many resources. Some of the most productive farmlands in the world are found in the Interior Plains. Ranches and farms produce beef, wheat, corn, and soybeans. California, Florida, Texas, and other areas grow fruit, vegetables, and cotton.

Alaska, California, Texas, and other states supply oil and natural gas. Coal and other minerals are found in Appalachian and western states. Gold and silver mines also operate in some western states.

Forests, especially in the Northwest and the Southeast, are important sources of lumber. The Atlantic Ocean, Gulf of Mexico, and Pacific Ocean are rich sources of fish and other seafood. The natural beauty of the country is also a valuable resource for tourism. All these resources help support industry and other economic activities.

✓ **READING CHECK:** *Places and Regions* What natural resources does the United States have?

go.hrw.com Homework Practice Online
Keyword: SJ3 HP10

Section 1 Review

Define and explain: contiguous, Continental Divide, basins

Working with Sketch Maps On a map of the United States that you draw or that your teacher provides, label the following: Coastal Plain, Appalachian Mountains, Interior Plains, Rocky Mountains, Great Lakes, Mississippi River, Great Plains, Columbia River, Great Basin, Colorado Plateau, Sierra Nevada, Cascade Range, and Aleutian Islands.

Reading for the Main Idea

1. *Places and Regions* What are the two major mountain regions in the United States? What major landform region lies betweeen them?
2. *Places and Regions* What resources are found in the country? Why are they important for the economy?
3. *Places and Regions* What parts of the United States have particularly rich farmlands?

Critical Thinking

4. **Drawing Inferences and Conclusions** The Rockies are higher than the Appalachians. How is this fact a clue to the relative age of the two mountain systems?

Organizing What You Know

5. **Categorizing** Copy the following graphic organizer. Use it to categorize the major physical features and climates of the East, Interior Plains, and West.

	Physical Features	Climates
East		
Interior Plains		
West (including Alaska, and Hawaii)		

Section 2 The History of the United States

Read to Discover

1. How did early colonists from Europe change North America?
2. How did the United States change during the late 1700s and early 1800s?
3. How has the United States changed in the last 50 years?

Define

plantations
frontier
ratified
pioneers
abolitionist
seceded
Emancipation Proclamation

Why It Matters

The idea that people have right to decide their own government is still at work today. Use CNNfyi.com or other **current events** sources to find out about how people in the United States take part in the government. Record your findings in your journal.

An American quilt from the 1800s

▲ Plains Indians hunted buffalo for food and used the skins to make clothing and cover their teepees.

Colonizing North America

You know that the history of the United States is connected to the history of Europe and many other countries in the world. You have already learned some early U.S. history. However, there is much more to know about how our land became the great country it is today. Our history has been made by people from many different cultures. It is filled with earth-shattering events and ordinary, everyday happenings. It is a story of great discoveries, courageous journeys, sweeping political movements, and constant change.

The Indians of North America The first people who shaped the land we live on were various American Indian peoples. They had lived in what is now the United States for thousands of years before Europeans arrived. From the Atlantic coast to the Pacific coast, American Indians developed ways of life that were strongly influenced by their environments. For examples, the Iroquois hunted in the Woodlands of the Northeast. The Natchez raised crops in the rich soil of the Southeast. The Lakota Sioux and other Plains people were both buffalo hunters and farmers. In the Southwest, the Navajo and Apache mostly hunted and herded animals while the Hopi and the Zuni (ZOO-nee) mostly farmed. The Tlingit (TLING-kut) of Alaska fished.

The New Colonists In the 1490s and 1500s Europeans from Spain, France, the Netherlands, and other countries began to travel to the Americas. During the 1600s the English also began claiming lands and establishing colonies. In 1607 they established Jamestown in what is now Virginia. It was the first permanent English settlement in America. In 1620, settlers founded Plymouth in what is now Massachusetts. Sometimes the settlers made friends with the Indians living there. More often Indians and settlers fought.

Overland travel was difficult in the early colonies. For a long time water transportation was the colonists' main link to the outside world. In fact nearly all early colonial settlements were ports located on natural harbors or navigable rivers. New settlers migrated by sea to the growing coastal towns and inland trading posts on rivers.

▲ Enslaved Africans were brought to colonial Jamestown in Dutch ships like the one shown in this painting.

Enslaved Africans In the early 1600s thousands of enslaved Africans were brought to North America. Most were brought to the southern colonies to work on **plantations**. A plantation is a large farm that grows mainly one crop to sell. Plantations were common in the southern colonies because of the area's rich soils and mild climates. Most colonial plantations produced large crops of cotton or tobacco.

A much larger group of enslaved Africans were brought to the islands of the West Indies in the Caribbean Sea and to South America They were forced to work on large sugarcane plantations. Thousands of Africans died during the passage across the Atlantic.

The Metropolitan Museum of Art

◀ This painting shows a southern plantation as a small community.

Interpreting the Visual Record How do you think products from this plantation were sent to markets?

▲ This painting shows a scene of the Boston Massacre, March 5, 1770. British troops in Boston opened fire on an angry crowd, killing several.

Interpreting the Visual Record How do you think the people of Boston reacted to the Boston Massacre?

Life in the Colonies By the mid-1700s many British citizens had settled in 13 colonies along the Atlantic coast. Some came in search of wealth. Others came seeking religious freedom. Settlers had also come from Scotland, Ireland, Germany, France, Sweden, and other countries. They contributed greatly to the growth of the colonies. Many individuals owned and worked small farms, but the climate and soils in the southern colonies were ideal for a large-scale agricultural economy. The colonies in the north—the New England and Middle colonies—became centers for trade, shipbuilding, and fishing. Cities such as Boston and New York became major seaports.

Farming, trading, and fishing were only a few ways the colonists earned a living. There were also craftsworkers, such as carpenters and blacksmiths, who produced a variety of goods. As colonial economies grew, colonists did not need to import as many goods from England.

Most of the people who came to America settled along the coast. As these areas became more crowded people began to move to the **frontier**. The frontier referred to land to the west of the colonies that was not already settled by the Europeans. These unsettled lands, however, were not empty. They were Indian lands.

The British were not alone in taking over Indian lands. The French and Spanish also claimed lands that had long been home to American Indians. The French had established a fur-trading business with some Indians, and many Indian tribes remained allies of the French for many years.

The 13 Colonies

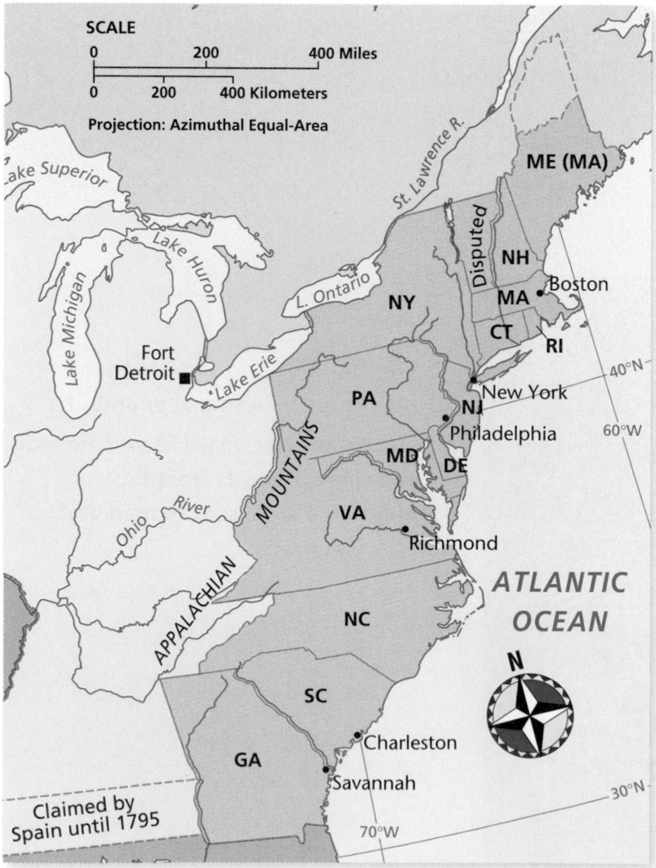

SCALE
0
200
400 Miles
0
200
400 Kilometers
Projection: Azimuthal Equal-Area
Lake Superior
St. Lawrence R.
ME (MA)
Lake Huron
Lake Michigan
L. Ontario
Disputed
NH
NY
MA
Boston
CT
RI
Fort Detroit
Lake Erie
40°N
PA
New York
NJ
Philadelphia
60°W
MD
DE
MOUNTAINS
Ohio River
VA
Richmond
ATLANTIC OCEAN
APPALACHIAN
NC
N
SC
Charleston
GA
Savannah
30°N
Claimed by Spain until 1795
70°W

Trouble Brewing At the same time, British colonists were moving onto lands claimed by the French. The British and French had already been fighting wars in Europe for years. In 1754 the conflict spilled over to North America in what was called the French and Indian War. The British colonists fought not only the French but also their Indian allies.

By 1763 Great Britain had won the war. However, it had been a very expensive war. To raise money, the British Parliament began to impose new restrictions on the colonists and establish new taxes. The colonists said that Parliament had no right to tax them without the consent of their own colonial assemblies. They called this "taxation without representation." Some refused to buy British goods.

A worried Parliament sent British soldiers to Boston to control the protests. Each new British act only made the colonies work more closely together. Slowly the 13 colonies were becoming united.

✓ **READING CHECK:** *Summarizing* What was colonial life like during the 1600s and early 1700s?

American Independence

In April 1775, British troops near Boston tried to capture gunpowder and weapons stored by the colonists. Fighting broke out near the towns of Lexington and Concord. The American Revolution had begun.

The Declaration of Independence was signed on July 4, 1776, but the American Revolution dragged on for five years. Eventually, however, George Washington was able to defeat British general Cornwallis and get him to surrender in 1781. This battle, the Battle of Yorktown, was the last major battle of the Revolution.

▲ The signing of the U.S. Constitution took place in Philadelphia on September 17, 1787.

In 1787 the Americans wrote a new Constitution that set up the federal system of government with three main branches—executive, legislative, and judicial. Each had distinct powers and acted as a check on the others so that no one branch had all the power. This is the system of government we have today. The Constitution was **ratified**, or approved, by the states in 1788 and took effect in 1789.

Westward Expansion

In the 1790s and 1800s many Americans and immigrants migrated west of the Appalachians in search of more and better farmland. These new settlers were called **pioneers**. They were people who were leading the way into new areas. The boundaries of the United States shifted as settlement spread westward. By the 1820s, pioneers had crossed the Mississippi River and settled as far south as Texas. By the mid-1800s the country stretched from the Atlantic to the Pacific coast.

Albert Bierstadt, *Emigrants Crossing the Plains,* 1867, oil on canvas, AO1.IT: The National Cowboy Hall of Fame and Western Heritage Center, Oklahoma City, OK

◀ This painting by American artist Albert Bierstadt (1830–1902) shows a group of pioneers heading west across the Great Plains.

Interpreting the Visual Record What does Bierstadt's painting suggest about American ideas of the West during the 1800s?

Territorial Expansion of the United States

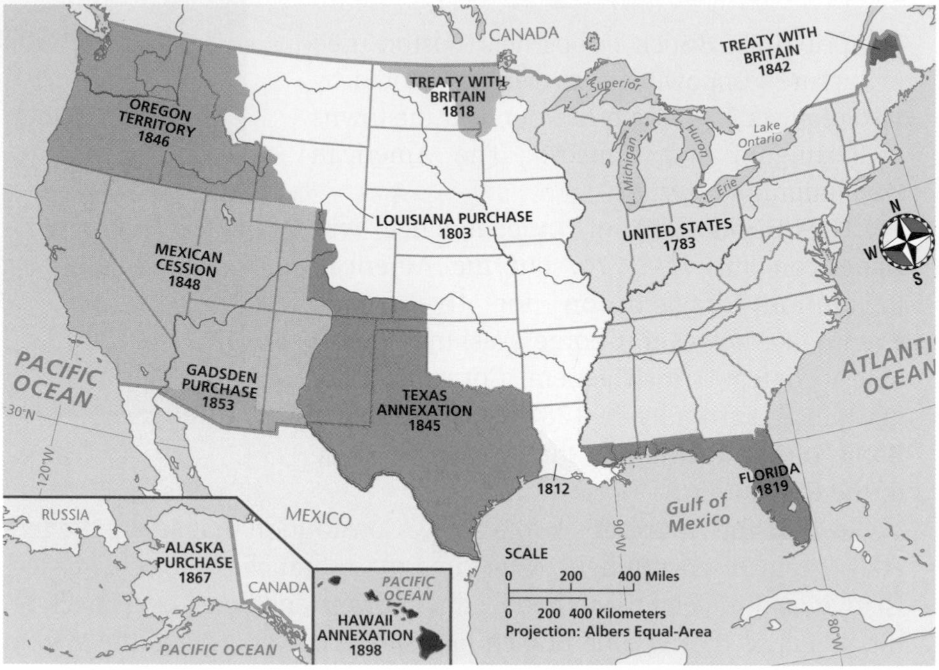
CANADA
TREATY WITH BRITAIN 1842
TREATY WITH BRITAIN 1818
OREGON TERRITORY 1846
L. Superior
L. Michigan
L. Huron
Lake Ontario
L. Erie
LOUISIANA PURCHASE 1803
UNITED STATES 1783
MEXICAN CESSION 1848
N
W
S
PACIFIC OCEAN
GADSDEN PURCHASE 1853
TEXAS ANNEXATION 1845
ATLANTIC OCEAN
30°N
120°W
1812
FLORIDA 1819
Gulf of Mexico
RUSSIA
MEXICO
ALASKA PURCHASE 1867
CANADA
PACIFIC OCEAN
PACIFIC OCEAN
HAWAII ANNEXATION 1898
SCALE
0 200 400 Miles
0 200 400 Kilometers
Projection: Albers Equal-Area
90°W
80°W

Within 100 years of independence, the borders of the United States had expanded to the Pacific Ocean. New land was added through annexation, purchase, treaty, and war.

Interpreting the Map How did the United States gain most of its territory after 1783? Which was the largest single addition?

Most of the people in mining camps were young, unmarried men. The camps were rather wild, with a lot of crime and fighting.

Interpreting the Visual Record What parts of this scene suggest that the town has grown rapidly?

The government sold land cheaply or gave it away to encourage people to settle new areas. Many people arrived on the Pacific coast after gold was discovered in California in 1848. However, few people settled in the deserts and mountains of the western United States or in the Great Plains. They called this area the Great American Desert. Most people believed it was too dry to support farming.

As pioneers moved westward they began to have bitter conflicts with American Indians. Many of the Indians did not own land as individuals. Instead, they considered land a shared resource. As settlers occupied and divided up land, they pushed American Indians farther west and onto reservations. Many died from warfare or from diseases carried by settlers.

✓ **READING CHECK:** ***Summarizing*** What problem developed between the settlers and the American Indians as the United States expanded?

The Granger Collection, N

The Civil War

By 1830 the northeastern United States was industrializing. Industries and railroads spread. In the South, however, the economy was based on export crops like tobacco and cotton. As you have read, farmers grew those crops on plantations with the labor of enslaved Africans. The North, with its factories and large cities, had less use for slave labor. Economic differences between the North and South, and the South's insistence on maintaining slavery, eventually led to war.

President Abraham Lincoln

The Slavery Issue The Missouri Compromise of 1820 let Missouri enter the Union as a slave state and divided the rest of U.S. territory into slave and free areas. Many people, however, wanted to abolish slavery altogether. As new states entered the Union, bitter arguments raged over whether each state would allow slavery. As the election of 1860 approached, the issue of slavery threatened to rip apart the country.

In 1860 Abraham Lincoln was elected president. He was an **abolitionist**, someone who wanted to end slavery. In response, South Carolina **seceded** from, or left, the United States. Other southern states soon followed. These states formed the Confederate States of America.

Lincoln argued that states had no right under the Constitution to secede. He said that the government must put down the rebellion. The long, bloody Civil War began in 1861. It caused much suffering, as families were divided and property was destroyed. The war finally ended in 1865 when the Confederacy surrendered. Bitter feelings about the war, however, lasted into the next century.

During the war, Lincoln issued the **Emancipation Proclamation**. This document freed slaves in the states that were in rebellion. When the war ended, Congress passed three amendments ending slavery and guaranteeing the former slaves rights. However, the laws were often ignored. Life did not get much better for many former slaves.

Our Amazing Planet

More than 600,000 Americans died in the Civil War. This was more than in any other war the United States has fought before or since.

During the Civil War soldiers on each side were often ordered to attack well-defended positions. This led to many casualties.

Interpreting the Visual Record **Whose point of view do you think the artist is trying to portray? Why?**

The development of steamships during the second half of the 1800s allowed a great increase in immigration to the United States and Canada. In this image from the late 1800s, immigrants in search of new opportunities come ashore at Ellis Island, New York.

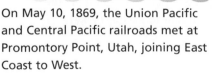

Elizabeth Cady Stanton (1815–1902) campaigned for women's rights. Her efforts helped start the women's suffrage movement, to get women the right to vote.

Growth and Expansion After the War Most of the Civil War had been fought in the South. It took a long time for the South to recover and rebuild. In the meantime, the rest of the country changed rapidly during the later 1800s. More railroads and industry expanded, settlers pushed west, and more and more people were immigrating, or moving, to the United States.

The first transcontinental railroad was completed in 1869. It linked the eastern United States with California. This railroad made it much easier to move goods and people across the country. Railroads also allowed major cities to develop far from navigable waterways.

With new agricultural machinery, farms could produce more food using fewer people than ever before. Irrigation and better plows allowed farmers to grow crops in the Great American Desert. As a result, people's views of the region changed and they began to settle the area.

The development of industry attracted more people to the country's growing cities. Some came from rural areas. However, many were immigrants, mostly from Europe. Many European immigrants settled in the industrial cities of the Northeast. Millions of immigrants poured into the United States during the later 1800s and early 1900s, making the nation the most diverse in the world. By 1920 more Americans lived in cities than rural areas.

✓ **READING CHECK:** *Finding the Main Idea* Why did many Americans and immigrants move westward during the 1800s?

On May 10, 1869, the Union Pacific and Central Pacific railroads met at Promontory Point, Utah, joining East Coast to West.

The 1900s and Beyond

In the 1900s the United States experienced major social, economic, and technological changes. The country fought in World War I in 1917–18 and suffered through the Great Depression in the 1930s. U.S. forces also fought in World War II from 1941 to 1945. Since the mid-1900s the United States has been one of the richest and most powerful countries in the world.

After World War II the United States and the Soviet Union became rivals in the Cold War. Both countries built huge military forces and developed nuclear weapons. The two countries never formally went to war against each other. However, they supported different sides in small wars around the world. Since the collapse of the Soviet Union in 1991, the United States and Russia have had better relations.

The 1950s and 1960s saw the rise of the Civil Rights Movement. Presidents John F. Kennedy and Lyndon B. Johnson introduced reforms which ended many forms of segregation and discrimination. Hispanics, Native Americans, and women also fought for and won gains in the fight for equal treatment and equal opportunity.

The last decade has seen rapid advances in computer technology. The development of the microchip shrank the size and cost of computers and made them accessible to many Americans. The Internet, a global network of computers, helps link people around the world. Other communication tools such as cellular phones and fax machines have made communication easier as well. All of this technology has sparked an information revolution that has changed our lives forever. More than ever, the future of the United States holds promise for all Americans.

Dr. Martin Luther King, Jr., was a key leader of the Civil Rights Movement. He delivered his famous "I Have a Dream" speech at the Lincoln Memorial in Washington, D.C., in August 1963.

✓ **READING CHECK:** *Finding the Main Idea* How have computer technology and the Internet changed Americans' lives?

go.hrw.com **Homework Practice Online** Keyword: SJ3 HP10

Section 2 Review

Define and explain: plantations, frontier, ratified, pioneers, abolitionist, seceded, Emancipation Proclamation

Reading for the Main Idea

1. *Environment and Society* How did North America change after the early colonists arrived?
2. *Human Systems* What major events changed in the United States between the late 1700s and the mid-1800s?
3. *Human Systems* How has the United States changed since the mid-1900s?

Critical Thinking

4. **Drawing Conclusions** During which period in U.S. history do you think our country changed the most? Why?

Organizing What You Know

5. **Identifying Time Order** Copy the time line below into your notebook. Use it to list some important dates, periods, and events that occurred during the 1800s.

1800 ——————————————————— 1900

Connecting to *History*

An ATTACK on America

On the morning of September 11, 2001, the United States experienced one of the greatest tragedies in its history. Terrorists—individuals who use violence to achieve political goals—hijacked four commercial airliners flying out of airports in Boston, Massachusetts; Newark, New Jersey; and Washington, D.C. The terrorists crashed two of the planes into the twin towers of New York City's World Trade Center, causing the buildings to collapse. The third plane hit the Pentagon—the headquarters for the U.S. Department of Defense—and the fourth crashed in rural Pennsylvania. Thousands of people were killed or injured in the attacks.

Smoke rises from the site of the World Trade Center towers.

Immediately after September 11, the federal government launched a massive investigation to find out who was responsible for the brutal attacks. Investigators soon named Osama bin Laden and his Afghanistan-based terrorist network, al Qaeda, as the chief suspects in the attacks. U.S. leaders demanded that the ruling government of Afghanistan, the Taliban, turn bin Laden over to U.S. authorities, but Taliban leaders refused. The United States then began building an international coalition to help in its effort to fight terrorism. Countries pledging their support included Great Britain, Russia, Pakistan, and Saudi Arabia.

President George W. Bush, addressing Congress

U.S. leaders also put in place increased security measures to better protect Americans from terrorist threats. On September 20, 2001, President George W. Bush announced the appointment of Governor Tom Ridge of Pennsylvania to the new cabinet-level position of homeland security director. Key goals of the new position included improving airport security and protecting vital systems such as transportation, water sources, and power networks from attack. President Bush also signed antiterrorism legislation to give law-enforcement agencies greater freedom in performing their duties. Other new domestic-security measures focused on the development of response plans in the event of biological and chemical terrorism. The necessity of these measures was clear after Americans were exposed to anthrax-causing compounds that had been sent through the mail. Anthrax is a potentially deadly disease caused by a spore-forming bacterium. The federal government has set aside billions of dollars to prevent and respond to such biological or chemical threats.

Multifaith memorial service for the victims

While establishing security measures to protect Americans at home, the U.S. government also took decisive steps to limit terrorist threats abroad. With international support, the United States mobilized military forces for an air and ground war against the Taliban and al Qaeda. Despite the loss of several American lives in combat, the Taliban government was forced from power by mid-November, and hundreds of al Qaeda and Taliban soldiers were captured. However, small groups of al Qaeda and Taliban supporters remained hidden in Afghanistan and Pakistan and continued to attack U.S. and allied forces in the region. President Bush acknowledged that the war on terrorism would be a long one: "Afghanistan is just the beginning of the war against terror. . . . Across the world and across the years, we will fight these evil ones, and we will win."

FIRE DEPARTMENT
CITY OF
NEW YORK

Firefighters played a key role in the search and recovery efforts at the attack sites.

Understanding What You Read

1. What is terrorism?
2. Why is international support needed to fight terrorism?

U.S. aircraft carrier departing as part of a battlegroup launched in response to the September 11 attacks

CHAPTER 10

Reviewing What You Know

Building Vocabulary

On a separate sheet of paper, write sentences to define each of the following words.

1. contiguous
2. Continental Divide
3. basins
4. plantations
5. frontier
6. ratified
7. pioneers
8. abolitionist
9. seceded
10. Emancipation Proclamation

Reviewing the Main Ideas

1. *Places and Regions* What are the two major mountain regions of the United States?
2. *Places and Regions* Where are the dry climate regions located in the United States?
3. *Environment and Society* How did North America change in the 1600s and 1700s when European colonists arrived?
4. *Human Systems* How did people's lives change in the United States between 1830 and 1900?
5. *Environment and Society* What changes occurred in the United States after World War II?

Understanding History and Society

The Transcontinental Railroad

The completion of the first transcontinental railroad linked the West Coast of the United States with the East Coast. Prepare a presentation about the building of this railroad, considering the following:

- When and where the building of the railroad lines began, and when and where it was completed.
- Problems railroad workers faced.
- The effect the Transcontinental Railroad had on American life.

Thinking Critically

1. **Contrasting** How is the physical geography of the Appalachians different from that of the Rocky Mountains? Why is this true?
2. **Drawing Inferences and Conclusions** Why do you think the Mississippi River is important to agriculture in the South?
3. **Contrasting** How do you think the pioneers' and American Indians' viewpoints about the land and its use differed?
4. **Finding the Main Idea** Why did it take the South a long time to recover and rebuild after the Civil War?
5. **Finding the Main Idea** Why is the Internet such an important technological advance in the United States?

Building Social Studies Skills

Map ACTIVITY

On a separate sheet of paper, match the letters on the map with their correct labels.

Atlantic Ocean	Great Lakes
Pacific Ocean	New York City
Alaska	Los Angeles
Hawaii	Miami
Gulf of Mexico	Chicago

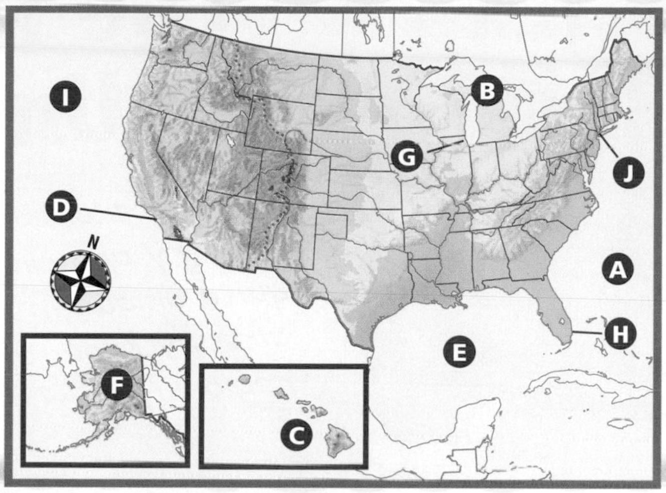

I
B
G
J
D
N
A
H
E
F
C

Mental Mapping Skills ACTIVITY

On a separate sheet of paper, draw a freehand outline map of the United States. Label the following territories that were purchased in the 1800s:

Louisiana Purchase	Mexican Cession
Texas Annexation	Gadsden Purchase
Oregon Territory	

WRITING ACTIVITY

You might be familiar with the song "America the Beautiful." It reminds the listener of the physical beauty of the United States—"from sea to shining sea." Write a short poem, song, or rap describing the physical geography of the eastern, interior, or western United States.

Alternative Assessment

Portfolio ACTIVITY

Learning About Your Local History

Historical Buildings Research the buildings in your town to find out which are the oldest or which have historical significance. Take a photograph or make a drawing of one building. Write a paragraph to explain the part the building played in your town's history.

internet connect

go.hrw.com

Internet Activity: go.hrw.com
KEYWORD: SJ3 GT10

Choose a topic to explore about the United States:

- Experience life in the early colonies.
- Search letters and journal entries written by soldiers in the Civil War.
- Explore the advance of civil rights in the United States.

CHAPTER 11

The Regions of the United States

The different regions that make up our country are similar in some ways and quite unique in others. What do you already know about the different regions?

In this chapter you'll learn about the land, climate, and economy of the different regions in the United States. In the rest of the book, you will meet people from all over the world. Each of them has cultural traditions—beliefs and behaviors—that are different from yours. However, each has many things in common.

To learn about American culture, we are going to start by meeting an American: you. What beliefs do you have? What do you like to eat? What language do you speak at home? What kind of music do you like? Which holidays do you celebrate? These things and others reflect something about our American culture as well as our diversity.

Section 1 The Northeast

Read to Discover

1. What are some features of the Northeast?
2. What kinds of landforms and climates are found in New England and the Middle Atlantic states?
3. How do physical features affect the economies of New England and the Middle Atlantic states?

Define

megalopolis
moraine
second-growth forests
estuary

Locate

White Mountains
Green Mountains
Longfellow Mountains
Berkshire Hills
Cape Cod
Nantucket
Martha's Vineyard
Chesapeake Bay
Susquehanna River
Washington, D.C.
Philadelphia
Baltimore

Why It Matters

Millions of tourists visit the Northeast every year. Use CNNfyi.com or other **current events** sources to learn about a place you might like to visit there. Record your findings in your journal.

The Statue of Liberty in New York City

Northeastern United States: Physical-Political

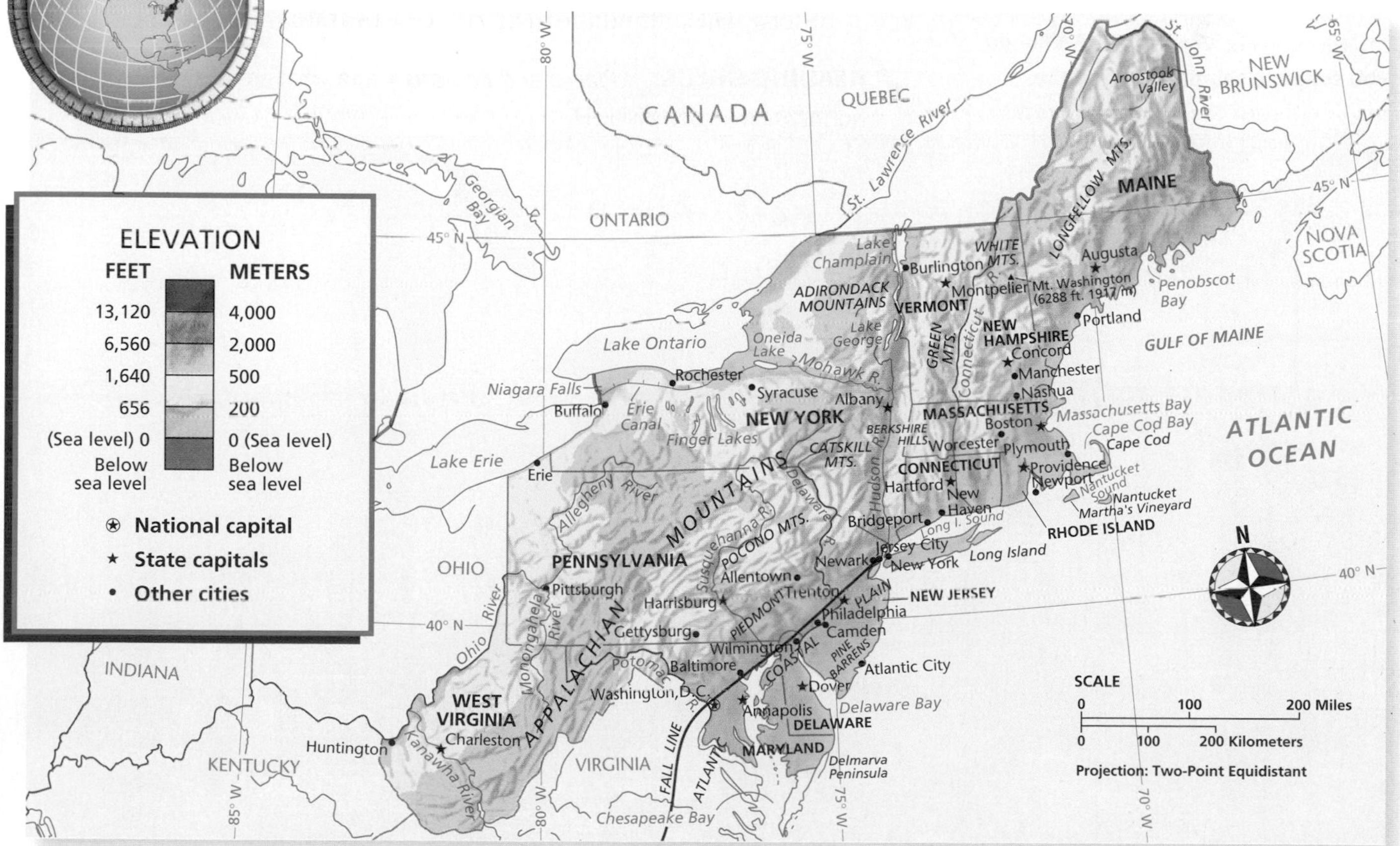

ELEVATION
FEET
METERS
13,120
4,000
6,560
2,000
1,640
500
656
200
(Sea level) 0
0 (Sea level)
Below sea level
Below sea level
National capital
State capitals
Other cities
CANADA
QUEBEC
ONTARIO
NEW BRUNSWICK
NOVA SCOTIA
St. Lawrence River
St. John River
Aroostook Valley
Georgian Bay
LONGFELLOW MTS.
MAINE
Augusta
Portland
Penobscot Bay
GULF OF MAINE
Lake Champlain
Burlington
WHITE MTS.
Montpelier
Mt. Washington (6288 ft. 1917 m)
VERMONT
GREEN MTS.
ADIRONDACK MOUNTAINS
Lake Ontario
Oneida Lake
Lake George
Mohawk R.
NEW HAMPSHIRE
Concord
Manchester
Nashua
Connecticut R.
Rochester
Syracuse
Albany
Niagara Falls
Buffalo
Erie Canal
Finger Lakes
NEW YORK
BERKSHIRE HILLS
MASSACHUSETTS
Boston
Massachusetts Bay
Cape Cod Bay
Cape Cod
ATLANTIC OCEAN
Worcester
Plymouth
CATSKILL MTS.
Hudson R.
CONNECTICUT
Hartford
Providence
Newport
Nantucket Sound
Nantucket
Martha's Vineyard
RHODE ISLAND
New Haven
Bridgeport
Long I. Sound
Long Island
Lake Erie
Erie
Allegheny River
MOUNTAINS
Delaware R.
POCONO MTS.
Susquehanna R.
PENNSYLVANIA
Allentown
Newark
Jersey City
New York
OHIO
Pittsburgh
Harrisburg
Trenton
PIEDMONT
PLAIN
NEW JERSEY
Philadelphia
Camden
Gettysburg
Ohio River
Monongahela River
INDIANA
Wilmington
Baltimore
COASTAL
PINE BARRENS
Atlantic City
Potomac R.
APPALACHIAN
WEST VIRGINIA
Charleston
Washington, D.C.
Dover
Annapolis
Delaware Bay
DELAWARE
FALL LINE
ATLANTIC
MARYLAND
Delmarva Peninsula
Huntington
Kanawha River
KENTUCKY
VIRGINIA
Chesapeake Bay
SCALE
0
100
200 Miles
0
100
200 Kilometers
Projection: Two-Point Equidistant
N
45° N
40° N
85° W
80° W
75° W
70° W
65° W

The Northeast

New England States	Middle Atlantic States
Connecticut	Delaware
Maine	Maryland
Massachusetts	New Jersey
New Hampshire	New York
Rhode Island	Pennsylvania
Vermont	West Virginia

A View of the Northeast

Although the Northeast is the smallest region in the United States, it is the most heavily populated. It has the country's greatest concentration of cities, factories, banks, universities, and transportation centers. The region is home to New York City, the country's largest city, and Washington, D.C., its capital.

The states of the Northeast are grouped into two subregions. The New England states are located in the northeastern portion of the country. The Middle Atlantic states stretch from the Appalachians to the Atlantic coast. There are six states in each subregion.

Megalopolis Overlapping the two subregions of the Northeast is a huge densely populated urban area. This area is called a **megalopolis**. A megalopolis is a string of cities that have grown together. This urban area stretches along the Atlantic coast from Boston to Washington, D.C. Major cities that are part of the megalopolis include New York City, Philadelphia, and Baltimore. At least 40 million people live in this area.

Except for Washington, D.C., all of these cities were founded during the colonial era. They grew because they were important seaports. Today they are major industrial and financial centers as well. These cities are connected by roads, railroads, and airline routes. Many of the world's largest companies have home offices in these cities. Washington, D.C. is the country's capital and the center of government offices. D.C. stands for District of Columbia.

✓ **READING CHECK:** *Places and Regions* Into what areas is the Northeastern region divided?

internet connect

GO TO: go.hrw.com
KEYWORD: SJ3 CH11
FOR: Web sites about regions of the United States

New York City is an important seaport.

Interpreting the Visual Record **Why do you suppose shipping helped the major cities of the Northeast grow?**

Canada
New York
United States
Mexico

New England

The New England states are famous for their scenic beauty and varied landforms. The subregion has also been the site of many important events in American history. The Pilgrims landed here in 1620 and were soon followed by other colonists. In the late 1700s, New England was the center of the American Revolution.

Canada
Vermont
United States
Mexico

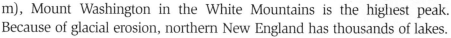

▲ Small towns and beautiful scenery can be found throughout Vermont and the rest of New England.

Landforms The Appalachian Mountains cross much of northern New England. The Appalachian system is actually made up of many small ranges. In New England, these include New Hampshire's White Mountains, Vermont's Green Mountains, and Maine's Longfellow Mountains. At 6,288 feet (1,917 m), Mount Washington in the White Mountains is the highest peak. Because of glacial erosion, northern New England has thousands of lakes.

Southern New England mainly is a hilly region. As glaciers pushed to the Atlantic coast, they left rock material in the form of hundreds of hills. The Berkshires of western Massachusetts are the highest hilly region. The only plains in New England are along the Atlantic coast and in the Connecticut River valley.

New England's coastline varies greatly from north to south. In the north, the scenic coast of Maine is made of granite. Granite is a hard, speckled rock. Maine's coast is rugged and rocky with many narrow inlets, bays, peninsulas, and islands.

Glaciers are responsible for the features of the southern New England coast. Cape Cod and the islands of Nantucket and Martha's Vineyard are glacial **moraine** materials. A moraine is a ridge of rocks, gravel, and sand piled up by the huge ice sheets.

BUILD on WHAT
You Know

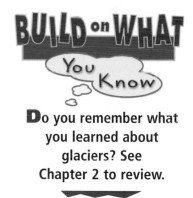

Do you remember what you learned about glaciers? See Chapter 2 to review.

Climate New England has a humid continental climate. Each autumn the region's brightly colored leaves attract tourists. Winter sports fans like its snowy winters. In the summer, fog is common along the coast. Very rarely during the summer, a hurricane may strike the coast of southern New England. More common are winter storms from the North Atlantic called northeasters. These storms bring cold, snowy weather with strong winds and high ocean waves.

Economy Dairy farming is the region's most important agricultural activity. Other important crops are cranberries and potatoes. However, a short growing season and rocky terrain limit farming in New England. As a result, most farms in this region are small. Some are now used as second homes or retirement retreats.

Cool, shallow waters off the coast are good fishing areas. Cod and shellfish are the most valuable seafood. The U.S. government has set rules to prevent overfishing in some areas.

Shipbuilding was a major industry in colonial New England. Builders used wood from the region's forests. Nearly all of New England's forests today are **second-growth forests**. These are the trees that cover an area after the original forest has been cut.

New England was the country's first industrial area. Textile mills and shoe factories were built along rivers and swift streams. The water was a handy power source for factories. Today, many banks, investment houses, and insurance companies are based in the region. In addition, the area has many respected colleges and universities. These schools include Harvard, Yale, the Massachusetts Institute of Technology, and many others.

✓ **READING CHECK:** *Places and Regions* Why was New England better suited for industrial growth than for agriculture?

Canada
United States
Pennsylvania
Mexico

▲ These Pennsylvania miners are waiting to enter one of the many coal mines in the Middle Atlantic states.

Middle Atlantic States

About one fifth of the U.S. population lives in the Middle Atlantic states subregion. It is one of the world's most industrialized and urbanized areas.

Landforms Three landform regions cross the Middle Atlantic states. They are the Coastal Plain, the Piedmont, and the Appalachian Mountains. The Coastal Plain stretches across all of the Middle Atlantic states except West Virginia. This flat plain does not rise much above sea level. Long Island and Chesapeake Bay are both part of the Coastal Plain.

Chesapeake Bay is fed by the Susquehanna River. It is the largest **estuary** on the Atlantic coast. An estuary is a body of water where salty seawater and freshwater mix. As Ice Age glaciers melted along this coast, the sea level rose. The rising sea filled low river valleys and formed the bay.

Inland from the Coastal Plain is the Piedmont. This region slopes down from the Appalachians to the Coastal Plain. Where these regions meet, rivers plunge over rapids and waterfalls. These rivers supplied waterpower for the early towns and cities.

The northern part of the Appalachian Mountains crosses the Middle Atlantic states. Several major rivers cut through the Appalachians here on their way to the Atlantic Ocean. These include the Potomac, Susquehanna, Delaware, and Hudson rivers.

Climates The Middle Atlantic states have two major climate types. The north has a humid continental climate, while the south has a humid subtropical climate. Summers in both climate regions can be very hot and humid. Winds passing over the warm Gulf Stream and the Gulf of Mexico bring hot humid air inland.

During winter, arctic air from the north sometimes enters the region. Winters are colder away from the coast, particularly in the north. Snowfall can be heavy in some areas, especially in the Appalachians and upstate New York. Like the New England coast, the Middle Atlantic coast may experience hurricanes and northeasters.

Economy Soils are better for farming in the Middle Atlantic states than in New England. However, the region's expanding cities have taken over most of the available farmland.

Major coal-mining areas are found in the Appalachians, particularly in West Virginia and Pennsylvania. Coal is used in steelmaking. The steel industry helped make Pittsburgh, in western Pennsylvania, the largest industrial city in the Appalachians.

Today nearly every kind of manufacturing and service industry can be found in the Middle Atlantic states. Major seaports allow farmers and companies to ship their products to markets around the world. In addition, tourists visit natural and historical sites. These include Niagara Falls between New York and Canada and Gettysburg, a major Civil War battleground in Pennsylvania.

▲ Developments like Camden Yards baseball stadium and a new harbor have strengthened the economy of Baltimore, Maryland.

✓ **READING CHECK:** *Physical Systems* How are the climates of the Middle Atlantic states similar to those of New England?

Section 1 Review

go.hrw.com Homework Practice Online
Keyword: SJ3 HP11

Define and explain: megalopolis, moraine, second-growth forest, estuary

Working with Sketch Maps On a map of the United States that you draw or that your teacher provides, label the following: White Mountains;Green Mountains; Longfellow Mountains; Berkshire Hills; Cape Cod; Nantucket; Martha's Vineyard; Chesapeake Bay; Susquehanna River; Washington, D.C.; Philadelphia; Baltimore.

Reading for the Main Idea

1. *Human Systems* What are some characteristics of the Northeast?

2. *Human Systems* What types of landforms and climates are found in New England and in the Middle Atlantic states?

3. *Human Systems* How do landforms and climate affect the economies of New England and the Middle Atlantic states?

Critical Thinking

4. Drawing Conclusions What kinds of environmental challenges might threaten the cities of the megalopolis? Why do you think this?

Organizing What You Know

5. Categorizing Categorizing Copy the following graphic organizer. Use it to categorize the major landforms and climates of the Northeast.

	Landforms	Climates
New England		
Middle Atlantic states		

Millions of tourists visit the South every year.

Interpreting the Visual Record **How does the region's climate help attract visitors?**

Climate

Most people who live in the South, particularly along the Coastal Plain, are used to a humid subtropical climate. Winters are mild, and summers are long, hot, and humid. Not all of the South, however, has a subtropical climate. In higher areas such as the Appalachians and Ozarks, temperatures are cooler. Because it is so large, Texas experiences several different climates. These include humid, subtropical, desert, and highland climates.

Most of the South receives between 40 and 60 inches (100 and 150 cm) of rainfall per year. Thunderstorms, which often create dangerous lightning and tornadoes, bring much of this rain to the region. Some areas of the Appalachians may experience occasional winter snowstorms. During late summer and early fall, hurricanes may strike coastal areas.

✓ **READING CHECK:** *Places and Regions* What types of storms are common in the South?

Economy

Historically, the South was mainly rural and agricultural. In recent decades, however, the region has attracted many new industries. As the economy has grown, so have many cities. Houston is now the fourth-largest city in the country. Dallas-Fort Worth, Atlanta, Miami, and New Orleans have also grown to be major cities and commercial centers.

Agriculture Although agriculture is no longer the South's major economic activity, many small towns and farming areas stretch across the region. The region has long been a major producer of cotton, tobacco, and citrus fruit. In recent years, some farmers have decided to **diversify**. This means that farmers are producing a variety of crops instead of just one.

Resources The coastal waters of the Gulf of Mexico and the Atlantic are rich in ocean life. Though all the southern coastal states have fishing industries, Louisiana and Texas are the leaders. The shallow waters around the Mississippi Delta produce great quantities of oysters, shrimp, and other seafood. The major mineral and energy resources of the region include coal, sulfur, salt, phosphates, oil, and natural gas. Oil is found in Texas and Louisiana. These two states also lead the country in the production of sulfur. Florida has the country's largest phosphate-mining industry. Phosphates are used to make fertilizer. Much of it is exported to Japan and other Asian nations.

Industry Today many textile factories operate in the Piedmont areas of Georgia, the Carolinas, and Virginia. The Texas Gulf Coast and the lower Mississippi River area have huge oil refineries. Houston, New Orleans, and other major seaports ship the oil. Some cities such as Austin, Texas, also have computer, software, and publishing companies.

Canada
United States
Mexico

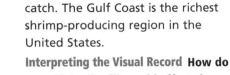

A Louisiana shrimper clears the day's catch. The Gulf Coast is the richest shrimp-producing region in the United States.

Interpreting the Visual Record How do you think oil spills could affect the local economy here?

Warm weather and beautiful beaches draw many vacationers to resorts in the South. People vacation in eastern Virginia, Florida, and the coastal islands of the Carolinas and Texas. Tourist attractions in cities like New Orleans, San Antonio, and Nashville also attract many visitors.

Many cities in the South have important links with countries in Central and South America. Miami is an important travel connection with Caribbean countries, Mexico, and South America. Atlanta, Houston, and Dallas also are major transportation centers.

✓ **READING CHECK:** *Places and Regions* How does geography affect the economic resources of the South?

Our Amazing Planet

Florida produces about 75 percent of the oranges and grapefruits grown in the United States.

go.hrw.com Homework Practice Online
Keyword: SJ3 HP11

Section Review 2

Define and explain: barrier islands, wetlands, sediment, diversify

Working with Sketch Maps On the map that you created in Section 1, label the 12 states of the South. Then label the following: Everglades, Okefenokee Swamp, Mississippi Delta, Blue Ridge Mountains, Great Smoky Mountains, Cumberland Plateau, Ozark Plateau, Interior Plains, Atlanta, Houston, New Orleans, Miami, Dallas.

Reading for the Main Idea

1. *Places and Regions* What areas of the South are wetlands?
2. *Places and Regions* Which southern state has many climates? What are these climates?
3. *Places and Regions* How has the economy of the South changed in recent years?

Critical Thinking

4. **Supporting a Point of View** Use what you learned in this section, and what you know to support this statement: Industry should continue to grow in the South.

Organizing What You Know

5. **Summarizing** Copy the following graphic organizer. Use it to describe the resources and industries that contribute to the economy of the South.

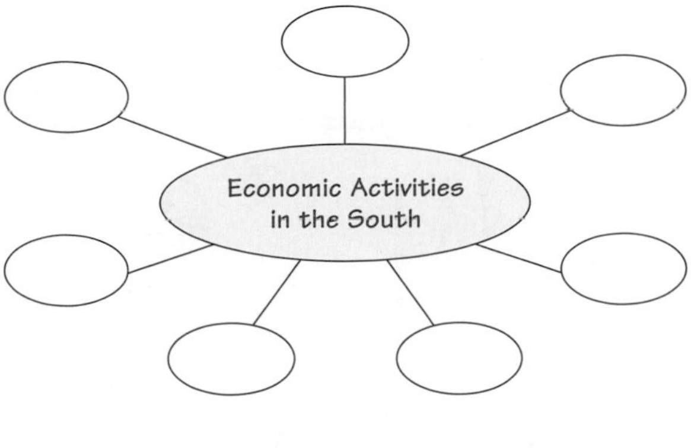
Economic Activities in the South

Section 3 The Midwest

Read to Discover

1. What types of landforms and climates are found in the Midwest?
2. What are some agricultural products grown in the region?
3. What are the main industries of the Midwest?

Define

droughts
Corn Belt
Dairy Belt

Locate

Chicago
Detroit

Why It Matters

Managing pollution is a challenge for the U.S. government. Use CNNfyi.com or other **current events** sources to find out pollution problems and clean-up efforts in the Midwest. Record your findings in your journal.

Gateway Arch, St. Louis, Missouri

Midwestern United States: Physical-Political

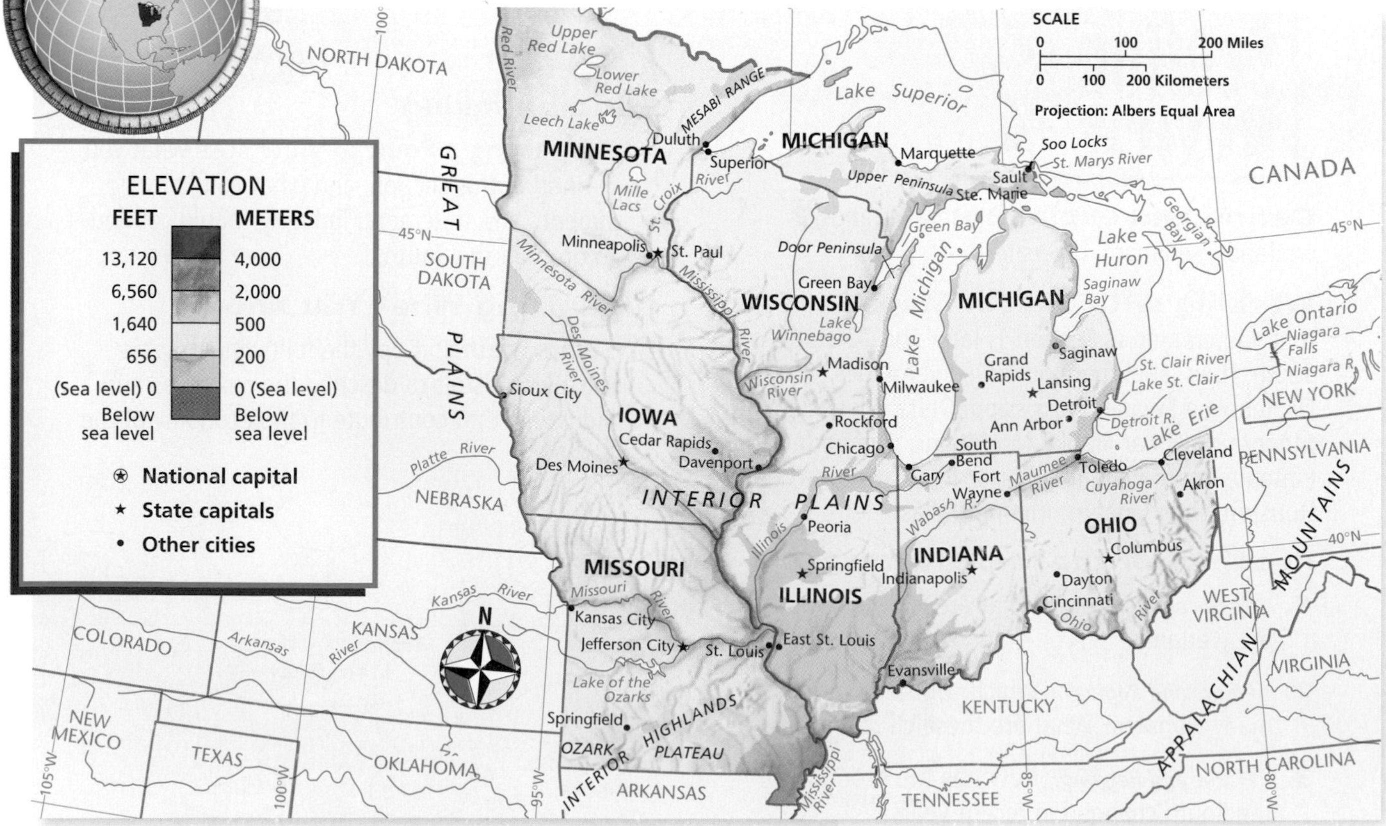

SCALE
0 100 200 Miles
0 100 200 Kilometers
Projection: Albers Equal Area
ELEVATION
FEET METERS
13,120 4,000
6,560 2,000
1,640 500
656 200
(Sea level) 0 0 (Sea level)
Below sea level Below sea level
National capital
State capitals
Other cities
NORTH DAKOTA
SOUTH DAKOTA
NEBRASKA
KANSAS
COLORADO
NEW MEXICO
TEXAS
OKLAHOMA
ARKANSAS
MINNESOTA
IOWA
MISSOURI
WISCONSIN
ILLINOIS
INDIANA
MICHIGAN
OHIO
KENTUCKY
TENNESSEE
WEST VIRGINIA
VIRGINIA
NORTH CAROLINA
PENNSYLVANIA
NEW YORK
CANADA
GREAT PLAINS
INTERIOR PLAINS
OZARK PLATEAU
INTERIOR HIGHLANDS
APPALACHIAN MOUNTAINS
MESABI RANGE
Upper Peninsula
Door Peninsula
Lake Superior
Lake Michigan
Lake Huron
Lake Erie
Lake Ontario
Lake St. Clair
Georgian Bay
Saginaw Bay
Green Bay
Upper Red Lake
Lower Red Lake
Leech Lake
Mille Lacs
Lake Winnebago
Lake of the Ozarks
Soo Locks
St. Marys River
St. Clair River
Detroit R.
Niagara Falls
Niagara R.
Red River
St. Croix River
Minnesota River
Mississippi River
Des Moines River
Wisconsin River
Illinois River
Chicago River
Wabash R.
Maumee River
Cuyahoga River
Ohio River
Platte River
Kansas River
Arkansas River
Missouri River
Duluth
Superior
Marquette
Sault Ste. Marie
Minneapolis
St. Paul
Green Bay
Madison
Milwaukee
Grand Rapids
Lansing
Saginaw
Detroit
Ann Arbor
Sioux City
Cedar Rapids
Davenport
Des Moines
Rockford
Chicago
Gary
South Bend
Fort Wayne
Toledo
Cleveland
Akron
Peoria
Springfield
Indianapolis
Columbus
Dayton
Cincinnati
Kansas City
Jefferson City
St. Louis
East St. Louis
Evansville
Springfield
45°N
40°N
100°
95°W
85°W
80°W
105°W
100°W
N

Landforms and Climate

The Midwest includes eight states: Ohio, Michigan, Indiana, Illinois, Wisconsin, Minnesota, Iowa, and Missouri. All but Iowa and Missouri have shorelines on the Great Lakes, the largest freshwater lake system in the world.

Most of the Midwest lies within the Interior Plains, a region of flat plains and low hills. The most rugged areas are in the Ozark Plateau, which stretches into southern Missouri. During the Ice Age the northern part of the region was eroded by glaciers. These glaciers created the Great Lakes. They also left behind thin soils and many thousands of smaller lakes.

The entire Midwest has a humid continental climate with four distinct seasons. The whole region experiences cold arctic air and snow in winter. The region is subject to thunderstorms, tornadoes, and occasional summer **droughts**. Droughts are periods when little rain falls and crops are damaged.

Our Amazing Planet

The northern part of the Midwest has thousands of lakes. Minnesota alone has more than 10,000 lakes.

✓ **READING CHECK:** *Places and Regions* In which landform and climate regions are the Midwest located?

Economy

Agriculture Good soils and flat land have helped make the Midwest one of the world's great farming regions. Farmers produce corn, dairy products, and soybeans and raise cattle. The core of the Midwest's corn-growing region is the **Corn Belt**. It stretches from central Ohio to central Nebraska. Much of the corn is used to feed livestock, such as beef cattle and hogs.

States in the **Dairy Belt** are major producers of milk, cheese, and other dairy products. Most of the Dairy Belt is pasture. Located north of the Corn Belt, the area includes Wisconsin and most of Minnesota and Michigan.

Corn: From Field to Consumer

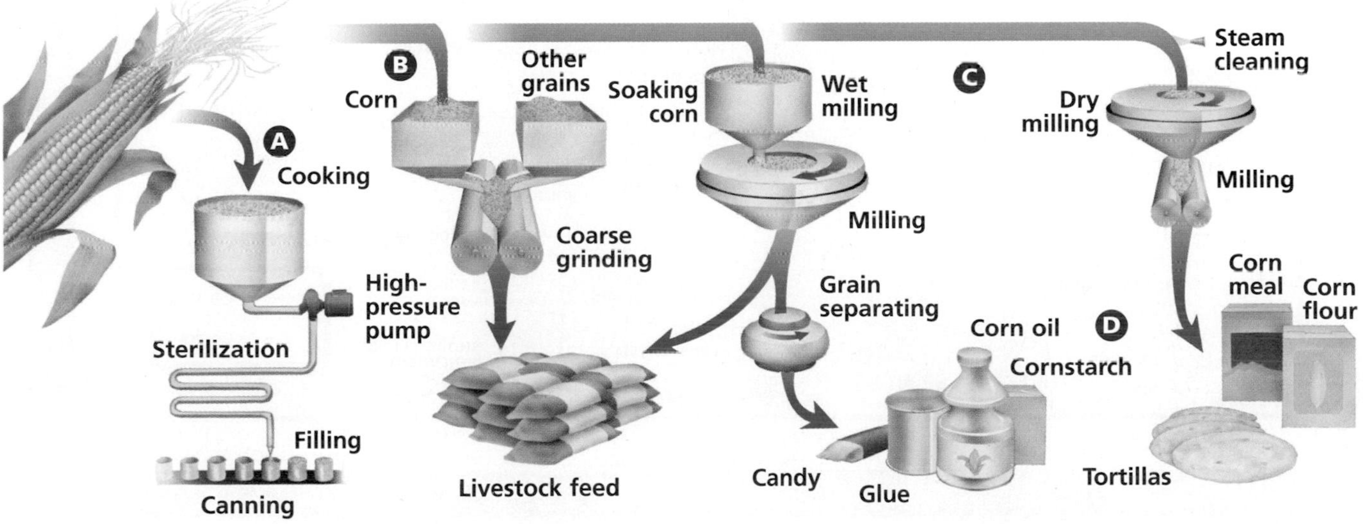

A
Cooking
Sterilization
High-pressure pump
Filling
Canning
B
Corn
Other grains
Coarse grinding
Livestock feed
Soaking corn
Wet milling
Milling
Grain separating
C
Steam cleaning
Dry milling
Milling
Corn oil
D
Cornstarch
Candy
Glue
Corn meal
Corn flour
Tortillas

Ⓐ Corn can be processed in a variety of ways. Some corn is cooked and then canned.
Ⓑ Corn is ground and used for livestock feed.
Ⓒ Corn also might be wet-milled or dry-milled. Then grain parts are used to make different products.
Ⓓ Corn by-products, such as cornstarch and corn syrup, are used to make breads, breakfast cereals, and snack foods.

CONNECTING TO *Technology*

The Great Lakes and St. Lawrence Seaway

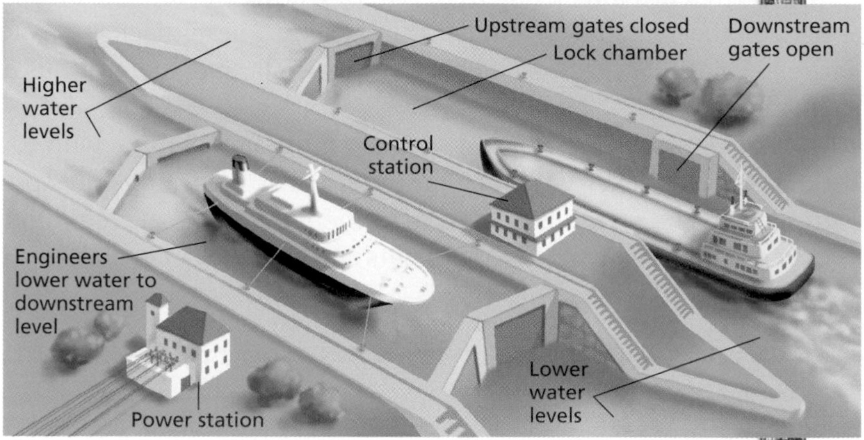

Upstream gates closed
Downstream gates open
Lock chamber
Higher water levels
Control station
Engineers lower water to downstream level
Power station
Lower water levels

Moving through a canal lock

The St. Lawrence Seaway permits ships to go between the Great Lakes and the Atlantic Ocean. This waterway's canals and locks allow ships to move from one water level to another. The difference in water levels is significant. For example, Lake Erie is about 570 feet (174 m) above sea level. Farther to the east, Montreal is about 100 feet (30 m) above sea level. Ships moving from one water level to another enter a lock. The water level inside the lock is raised or lowered. It is changed to match the water level in the waterway ahead of the ship. From there, the ship can move on to the next lock.

Understanding What You Read

1. What U.S. cities are located along the shores of the Great Lakes? Why might they have been established here?
2. Which of the Great Lakes lies at the highest elevation? Which lies at the lowest elevation?

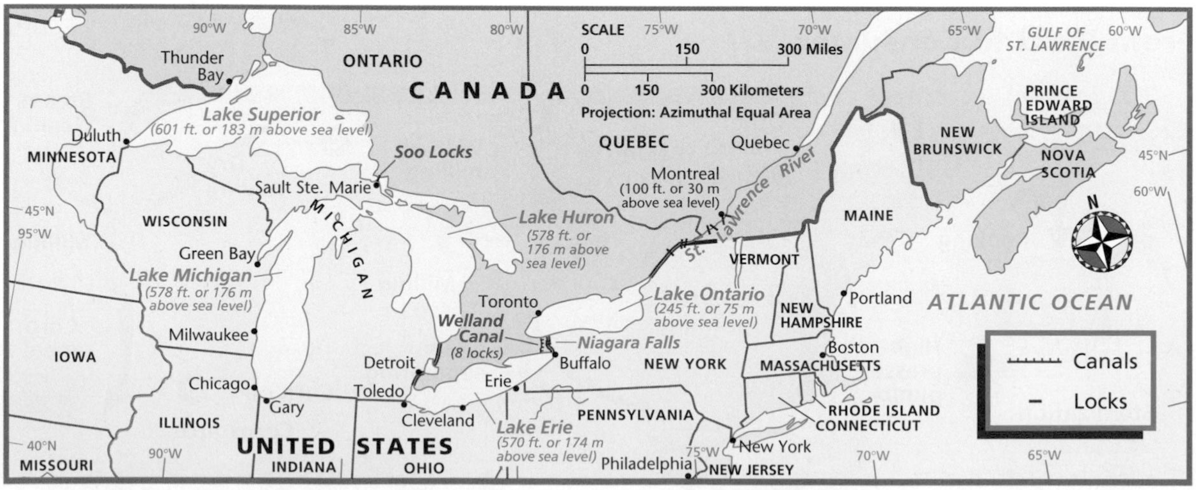

SCALE
0 150 300 Miles
0 150 300 Kilometers
Projection: Azimuthal Equal Area
CANADA
ONTARIO
QUEBEC
Thunder Bay
Lake Superior
(601 ft. or 183 m above sea level)
Duluth
MINNESOTA
Soo Locks
Sault Ste. Marie
WISCONSIN
MICHIGAN
Green Bay
Lake Michigan
(578 ft. or 176 m above sea level)
Milwaukee
IOWA
Chicago
Gary
ILLINOIS
MISSOURI
INDIANA
OHIO
UNITED STATES
Lake Huron
(578 ft. or 176 m above sea level)
Toronto
Welland Canal
(8 locks)
Niagara Falls
Detroit
Toledo
Cleveland
Erie
Buffalo
Lake Erie
(570 ft. or 174 m above sea level)
Lake Ontario
(245 ft. or 75 m above sea level)
NEW YORK
PENNSYLVANIA
Philadelphia
NEW JERSEY
New York
Montreal
(100 ft. or 30 m above sea level)
Quebec
St. Lawrence River
VERMONT
NEW HAMPSHIRE
MAINE
Portland
Boston
MASSACHUSETTS
RHODE ISLAND
CONNECTICUT
NEW BRUNSWICK
NOVA SCOTIA
PRINCE EDWARD ISLAND
GULF OF ST. LAWRENCE
ATLANTIC OCEAN
Canals
Locks
N
90°W
85°W
80°W
75°W
70°W
65°W
60°W
45°N
40°N
95°W

Many of the Midwest's products are shipped to markets by water. One route is along the Mississippi River to the Gulf of Mexico. The other is through the Great Lakes.

Industry Chicago, Illinois, is one of the busiest shipping ports on the Great Lakes and has one of the world's busiest airports. Chicago is linked to the rest of the region by highways and railroads. In the late 1800s, its industries attracted many immigrants. They worked in steel mills, meat-packing plants, and other businesses. Today, Chicago is the third-largest city in the United States.

Other Midwest cities such as Cleveland, Detroit, and Milwaukee were also founded on important transportation routes, either on the Great Lakes or on major rivers. The locations of these cities gave industries access to nearby farm products, coal, and iron ore. Those resources have supported thriving industries such as food processing, iron, steel, machinery, and automobile manufacturing. Detroit, Michigan, has been the nation's leading automobile producer since the early 1900s.

On the upper Mississippi River, Minneapolis and St. Paul are major distribution centers for agricultural and industrial products from the upper Midwest. On the western bank of the Mississippi River is St. Louis. About two hundred years ago, it became the center for pioneers heading west and the nation's leading riverboat port.

The Midwest's traditional industries declined in the late 1900s. In addition, industrial pollution threatened the Great Lakes and surrounding areas. In response, companies have modernized their plants and factories. The region has also attracted new industries. Many produce high-technology products. The Midwest is again a prosperous region. Stricter pollution laws have made many rivers and the Great Lakes much cleaner.

Canada
Chicago
United States
Mexico

The Sears Tower (at left) in downtown Chicago is one of the world's tallest buildings.

✓ **READING CHECK:** *Places and Regions* What are the major economic activities of the Midwest?

go.hrw.com **Homework Practice Online**
Keyword: SJ3 HP11

Section 3 Review

Define and explain: droughts, Corn Belt, Dairy Belt

Working with Sketch Maps On the map that you created in Section 2, label the eight states of the Midwest. Then label Chicago, Detroit, and St. Louis.

Reading for the Main Idea

1. *Places and Regions* Which Midwestern states are in the Corn Belt? Which are in the Dairy Belt?
2. *Places and Regions* Why are Chicago and Detroit important Midwestern cities?
3. *Human Systems* How do farm and industrial products from the Midwest get to markets elsewhere?

Critical Thinking

4. **Drawing Inferences and Conclusions** How might the physical geography of the Midwest be different if the Ice Age had not occurred?

Organizing What You Know

5. **Cause and Effect** Copy the following graphic organizer. Use it to show how location on important transportation routes helped the economy of Midwest cities to grow.

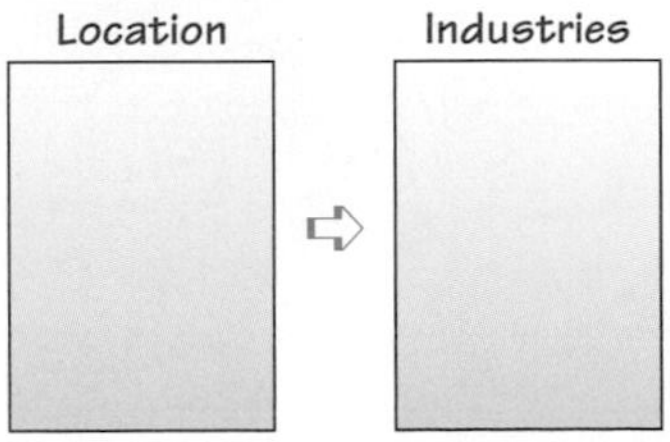

Location
Industries

Section 4 The Interior West

Read to Discover

1. What are the major landform regions of the Interior West?
2. What are the characteristics of the Interior West's climates?
3. What economic activities are important in the Interior West?

Define

badlands
chinooks
Wheat Belt
center-pivot irrigation
strip mining
national parks

Locate

Phoenix
Las Vegas
Denver

Hopi Kachina

Why It Matters

Parts of the Interior West have experienced droughts. Use CNNfyi.com or other **current events** sources to find out about droughts in this region. Record your findings in your journal.

Interior West: Physical-Political

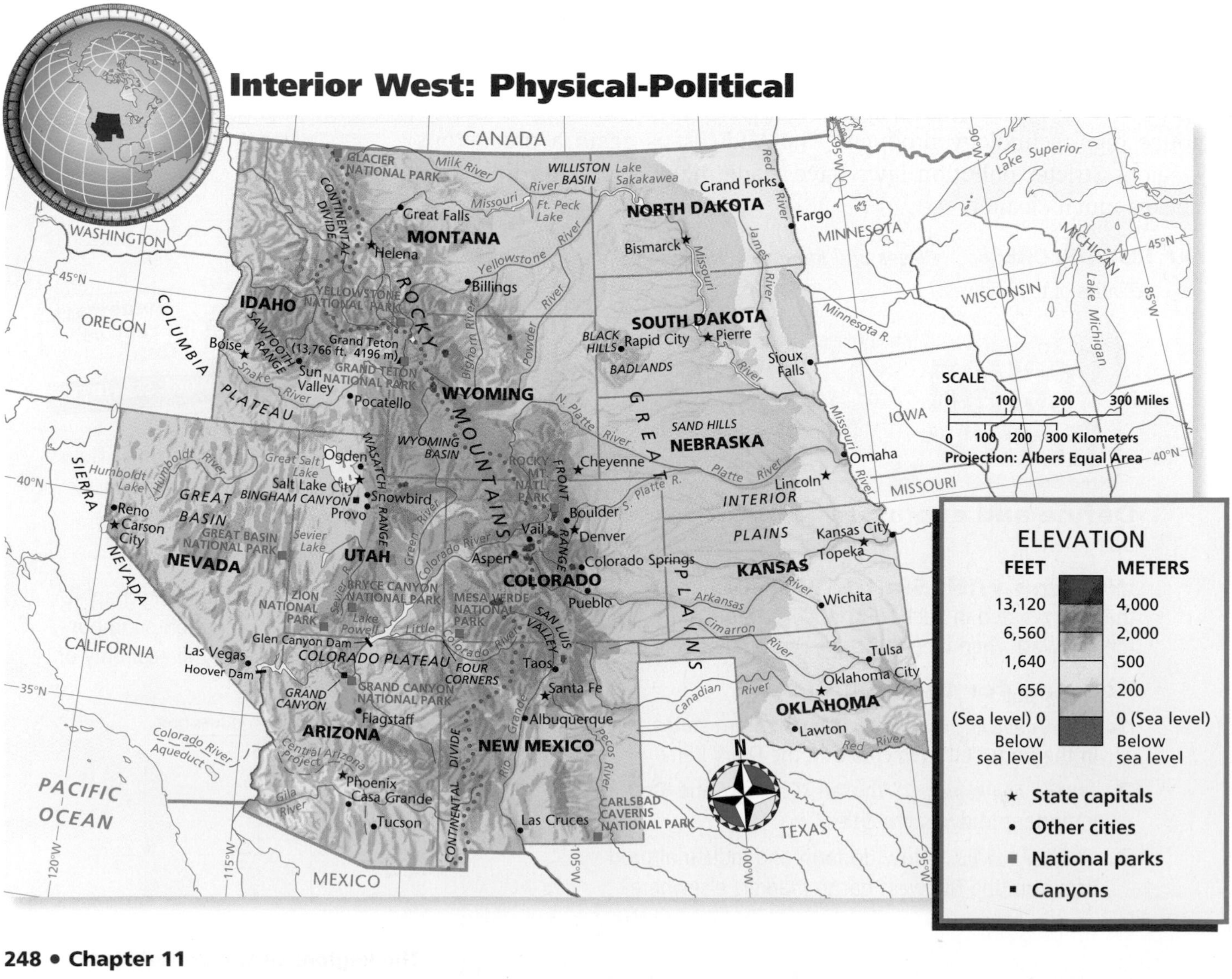

CANADA
GLACIER NATIONAL PARK
CONTINENTAL DIVIDE
Milk River
Missouri River
WILLISTON BASIN
Lake Sakakawea
Ft. Peck Lake
Great Falls
MONTANA
Helena
NORTH DAKOTA
Grand Forks
Fargo
Bismarck
Red River
James River
WASHINGTON
Yellowstone River
Billings
MINNESOTA
Lake Superior
MICHIGAN
WISCONSIN
Lake Michigan
Minnesota R.
IDAHO
YELLOWSTONE NATIONAL PARK
ROCKY MOUNTAINS
OREGON
COLUMBIA PLATEAU
SAWTOOTH RANGE
Boise
Snake River
Grand Teton (13,766 ft. 4196 m)
Sun Valley
GRAND TETON NATIONAL PARK
Pocatello
Bighorn River
Powder River
SOUTH DAKOTA
BLACK HILLS
Rapid City
Pierre
BADLANDS
Sioux Falls
WYOMING
N. Platte River
GREAT PLAINS
SAND HILLS
NEBRASKA
IOWA
Omaha
Missouri River
Lincoln
MISSOURI
SIERRA NEVADA
Humboldt Lake
Humboldt River
Great Salt Lake
Ogden
Salt Lake City
WASATCH RANGE
WYOMING BASIN
ROCKY MT. NAT'L PARK
FRONT RANGE
Cheyenne
Platte River
S. Platte R.
INTERIOR PLAINS
GREAT BASIN
BINGHAM CANYON
Snowbird
Provo
Reno
Carson City
GREAT BASIN NATIONAL PARK
Sevier Lake
NEVADA
UTAH
Green River
Colorado River
Boulder
Vail
Denver
Aspen
Colorado Springs
COLORADO
Pueblo
KANSAS
Kansas City
Topeka
Arkansas River
Wichita
ZION NATIONAL PARK
BRYCE CANYON NATIONAL PARK
MESA VERDE NATIONAL PARK
SAN LUIS VALLEY
Lake Powell
Cimarron River
Glen Canyon Dam
CALIFORNIA
Las Vegas
Hoover Dam
COLORADO PLATEAU
FOUR CORNERS
Taos
Tulsa
Oklahoma City
GRAND CANYON
GRAND CANYON NATIONAL PARK
Santa Fe
Canadian River
OKLAHOMA
Flagstaff
Albuquerque
Lawton
ARIZONA
NEW MEXICO
Red River
Colorado River Aqueduct
Central Arizona Project
Rio Grande
Pecos River
PACIFIC OCEAN
Phoenix
Casa Grande
Tucson
Gila River
CARLSBAD CAVERNS NATIONAL PARK
Las Cruces
TEXAS
MEXICO
N
45°N
40°N
35°N
120°W
115°W
105°W
100°W
95°W
90°W
85°W
SCALE
0 100 200 300 Miles
0 100 200 300 Kilometers
Projection: Albers Equal Area
ELEVATION
FEET METERS
13,120 4,000
6,560 2,000
1,640 500
656 200
(Sea level) 0 0 (Sea level)
Below sea level Below sea level
★ State capitals
• Other cities
■ National parks
▪ Canyons

Landforms

The Interior West includes the states of North Dakota, South Dakota, Nebraska, Kansas, Oklahoma, Montana, Wyoming, Colorado, Idaho, Utah, Nevada, New Mexico, and Arizona. These states occupy three landform regions: the Great Plains, the Rocky Mountains, and the Intermountain West.

The Great Plains were formed over millions of years by the depositing of sediment from mountains. Rivers carried this sediment onto the plains, slowly increasing their elevation. The plains are known for their flat, sweeping horizons. A few areas, however, feature more varied landforms. The Sand Hills of Nebraska are ancient, grass-covered sand dunes. In the Dakotas, rugged areas of soft rock called **badlands** are found. Badlands are areas that have been eroded by wind and water into small gullies. They have little vegetation or soil.

West of the Great Plains are the Rocky Mountains. They stretch from the Arctic through Idaho, Montana, Wyoming, Utah, Colorado, and New Mexico. The Rockies are actually a series of mountain ranges, passes, and valleys.

Two other major landforms, the Great Basin and the Colorado Plateau, are located west of the Rockies. They are both part of the Intermountain West region. The rivers of the Great Basin do not reach the sea. Instead they flow into low basins and dry up. There they leave behind dry lake beds or salt flats. The Colorado Plateau is known for its deep canyons. The largest of these is the Grand Canyon.

✓ **READING CHECK:** *Places and Regions* What kinds of landforms are found in the Interior West?

Canada
Wyoming
United States
Mexico

▲ Storms like this one are common on the Great Plains of Wyoming.

Canada
United States
Rocky Moutains
Mexico

◀ The Rocky Mountains create beautiful views in much of Colorado. The highest mountain peaks reach elevations where trees cannot grow.

Canada
United States
Arizona
Mexico

These cacti are native to the desert climate of Arizona. The short plant is a teddy bear cholla (CHOY-yuh). The tall cactus is a saguaro (suh-WAHR-uh).

Climate

Most of the Great Plains region has a steppe climate. They are semiarid and become drier toward the west. Temperatures can vary greatly. Winter temperatures in some areas can drop to -40°F (-40°C), while summer temperatures might rise above 110°F (43°C). Droughts are a major climate hazard in this region. During drought periods, dust storms may cover huge areas. In addition, strong, dry winds blow from the Rocky Mountains onto the Great Plains. These winds are called **chinooks**.

The highland climates of the Rocky Mountain region vary, depending on elevation. Semiarid grasslands usually are found at the foot of the mountains. Most of the slopes, on the other hand, are forested. The forests capture the winter snowfall and form the source for the rivers that flow across the Great Plains. Climates in the Great Basin and the Colorado Plateau also vary. Arizona, New Mexico, and Nevada have mostly desert climates. Utah and southern Idaho have mainly steppe climates. Some parts of this region lie in the rain shadow created by the Rocky Mountains. These areas receive almost no rain at all. This is particularly true in low-lying areas of the Great Basin.

Because the region's climate is so varied, many types of vegetation grow in the Interior West. The Great Plains were once covered with grasses, shrubs, and sagebrush. Most of the native vegetation, however, has been cut to allow farming and ranching. The drier desert areas of the Southwest have less vegetation. Bushes and cacti are the most common plants in the region.

✓ **READING CHECK:** *Places and Regions* Why do the Rockies have several different types of climate?

BUILD on WHAT You Know

Do you remember what you learned about the steppe climate? See Chapter 3 to review.

Canada
United States
Grand Canyon
Mexico

The Colorado River flows through Marble Canyon in Arizona.

Interpreting the Visual How do you think this canyon was formed?

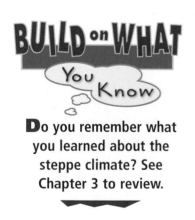

Economy

Ranching became important in the Interior West in the 1800s. Great herds of cattle and flocks of sheep roamed the Great Plains. Today, both ranching and wheat farming are common. The greatest wheat-growing area is known as the **Wheat Belt**. It stretches across the Dakotas, Montana, Nebraska, Kansas, Oklahoma, Colorado, and Texas.

Wheat from the Great Plains is shipped to other countries.

Irrigation Because this region receives relatively little rainfall, farmers depend on irrigation to water their crops. Much of the farmland in the Interior West must be irrigated. One method of irrigation uses long sprinkler systems mounted on wheels. The wheels rotate slowly. In this way, the sprinkler irrigates the area within a circle. This is called **center-pivot irrigation**.

Historically most of the water used to irrigate fields in the Interior West was drawn from underground aquifers. Overuse of this water, however, has drained much of the water from these aquifers. As a result, some farmers have begun to seek new sources for water. They want to preserve some of the region's valuable groundwater.

Canada
Wyoming
United States
Mexico

Workers have dug this pit to mine coal near Sheridan, Wyoming. Wyoming has the largest coal deposits in the Interior West.

Our Amazing Planet

Yellowstone is the country's oldest national park, dating back to 1872. Yellowstone National Park has about 200 geysers—including the famous Old Faithful—and 10,000 hot springs.

Mining and Industry Mining is a key economic activity in the Rocky Mountains. Early prospectors struck large veins of gold and silver there. Today Arizona, New Mexico, and Utah are leading copper-producing states. Nevada is a leading gold-mining state. Lead and many other ores are also found in the Interior West.

However, mining can cause problems. For example, coal miners in parts of the Great Plains strip away soil and rock. This process is called **strip mining**. This kind of mining leads to soil erosion and other problems. Today, laws require miners to restore damaged areas.

One of the Interior West's greatest resources is its natural beauty. The U.S. government has set aside large scenic areas known as **national parks**. Among these are Yellowstone, Grand Teton, Rocky Mountain, and Glacier National Parks. Tourists are also drawn to other areas of the Rocky Mountains. Ski resorts like Aspen and Vail in Colorado and Taos in New Mexico attract many people to the region. Another popular attraction is Mount Rushmore. In the early 1900s, sculptors carved the faces of four presidents into one of the Black Hills of South Dakota. Las Vegas, Nevada, is likewise one of the country's most popular tourist destinations.

Interior West cities like Phoenix, Arizona, and Denver, Colorado, are growing rapidly. The population of Phoenix, for example, has nearly doubled since 1980. Many retirement communities have sprung up in the desert. After World War II, the federal government built dams, military bases, and major highways in the area. The widespread use of air conditioning has made the Phoenix area even more attractive.

✓ **READING CHECK:** *Places and Regions* What makes agriculture possible in the climate of the Great Plains?

go.hrw.com **Homework Practice Online**
Keyword: SJ3 HP11

Section 4 Review

Define and explain: badlands, chinooks, Wheat Belt, center-pivot irrigation, strip mining, national parks

Working with Sketch Maps On the map that you created for Section 3, label the 13 Interior West states. Then label Phoenix and Las Vegas.

Reading for the Main Idea

1. *Places and Regions* What landform regions and climates are found in the Interior West?
2. *Human Systems* How does geography contribute to the economy of the Interior West?

Critical Thinking

3. **Drawing Inferences** Why has the U.S. government created national parks in this region?
4. **Drawing Inferences and Conclusions** Would cities such as Phoenix be experiencing such rapid growth if air conditioning had not been invented? Why?

Organizing What You Know

5. **Identifying Cause and Effect** Copy the following graphic organizer. Use it to describe landforms of the Interior West and what created them.

Landform	Description	Formation
Badlands		
Great Basin		
Grand Canyon		

Section 5 The Pacific States

Read to Discover

1. What types of landforms do the different Pacific states share?
2. How do the climates of the Pacific states differ?
3. How do the Pacific states contribute to the economy of the United States?

Define

caldera

Locate

Coast Ranges
Sierra Nevada
Death Valley
Willamette Valley
Cascades
Los Angeles
Seattle

Why It Matters

Several computer and software companies are located in the Pacific states. Use CNNfyi.com or other **current events** sources to find out what changes have taken place in these industries. Record your findings in your journal.

Computer microchip

Pacific States: Physical-Political

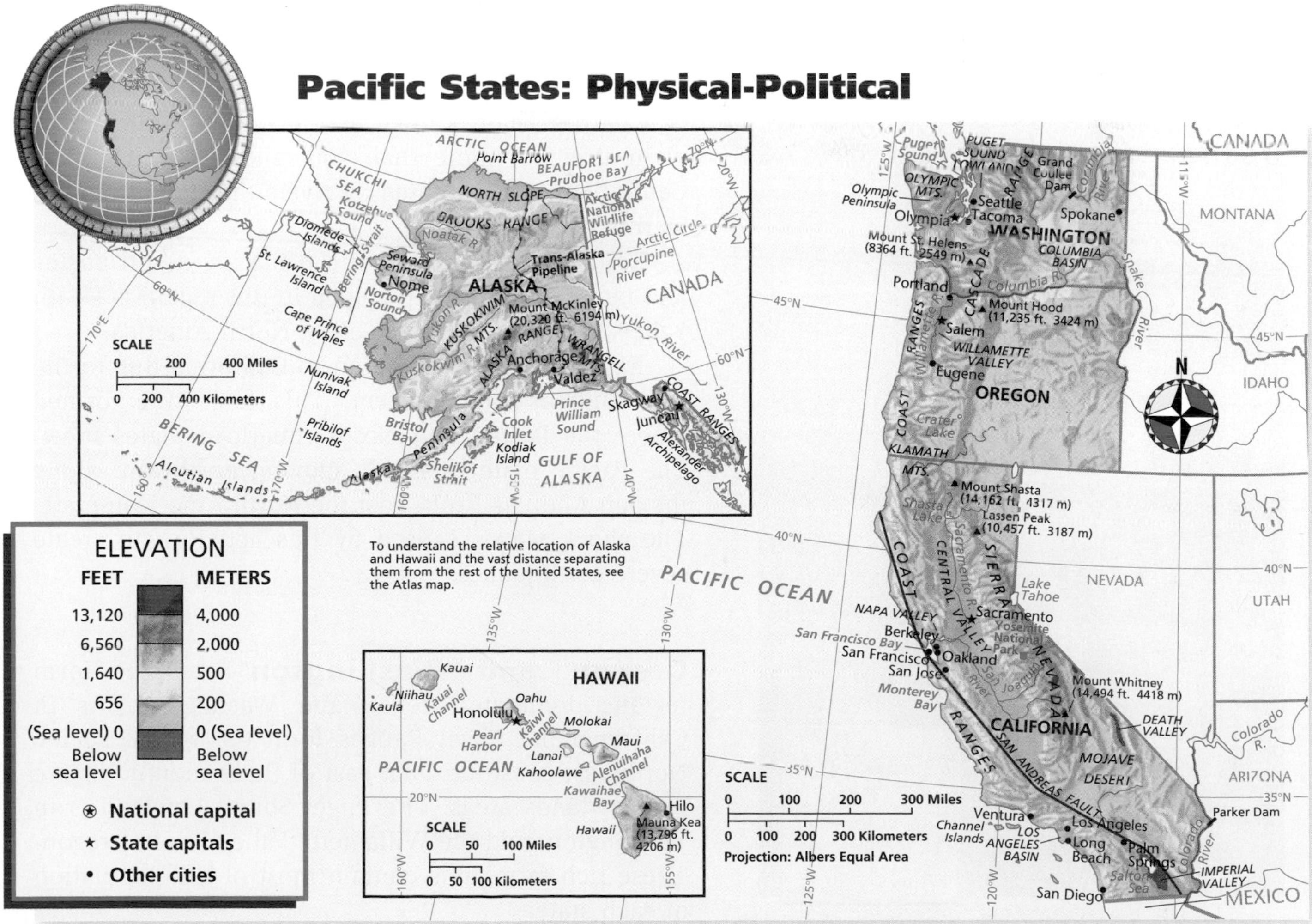
ARCTIC OCEAN
Point Barrow
BEAUFORT SEA
Prudhoe Bay
CHUKCHI SEA
Kotzebue Sound
NORTH SLOPE
BROOKS RANGE
Arctic National Wildlife Refuge
Noatak R.
Arctic Circle
Diomede Islands
Bering Strait
Seward Peninsula
Trans-Alaska Pipeline
Porcupine River
St. Lawrence Island
Nome
Norton Sound
ALASKA
CANADA
Cape Prince of Wales
KUSKOKWIM MTS.
Mount McKinley (20,320 ft. 6194 m)
ALASKA RANGE
Yukon River
Yukon R.
Kuskokwim R.
Anchorage
WRANGELL MTS.
Valdez
SCALE
0 200 400 Miles
0 200 400 Kilometers
Nunivak Island
Prince William Sound
Skagway
COAST RANGES
Juneau
Alexander Archipelago
Pribilof Islands
Bristol Bay
Cook Inlet
Kodiak Island
Alaska Peninsula
Shelikof Strait
GULF OF ALASKA
BERING SEA
Aleutian Islands
ELEVATION
FEET
METERS
13,120
4,000
6,560
2,000
1,640
500
656
200
(Sea level) 0
0 (Sea level)
Below sea level
Below sea level
National capital
State capitals
Other cities
To understand the relative location of Alaska and Hawaii and the vast distance separating them from the rest of the United States, see the Atlas map.
PACIFIC OCEAN
HAWAII
Kauai
Niihau
Kaula
Kauai Channel
Oahu
Honolulu
Pearl Harbor
Kaiwi Channel
Molokai
Lanai
Maui
Kahoolawe
Alenuihaha Channel
Kawaihae Bay
Hilo
Mauna Kea (13,796 ft. 4206 m)
Hawaii
PACIFIC OCEAN
SCALE
0 50 100 Miles
0 50 100 Kilometers
Puget Sound
PUGET SOUND LOWLAND
Grand Coulee Dam
Columbia River
Olympic Peninsula
OLYMPIC MTS.
Seattle
Olympia
Tacoma
Spokane
CASCADE RANGE
WASHINGTON
COLUMBIA BASIN
Mount St. Helens (8364 ft. 2549 m)
Snake River
Portland
Columbia R.
Mount Hood (11,235 ft. 3424 m)
Salem
WILLAMETTE VALLEY
Willamette R.
Eugene
COAST RANGES
OREGON
Crater Lake
KLAMATH MTS.
MONTANA
IDAHO
CANADA
N
Mount Shasta (14,162 ft. 4317 m)
Lassen Peak (10,457 ft. 3187 m)
Shasta Lake
CENTRAL VALLEY
Sacramento R.
SIERRA NEVADA
Lake Tahoe
NEVADA
UTAH
NAPA VALLEY
Sacramento
Yosemite National Park
Berkeley
San Francisco Bay
San Francisco
Oakland
San Jose
Monterey Bay
San Joaquin River
Mount Whitney (14,494 ft. 4418 m)
COAST RANGES
CALIFORNIA
DEATH VALLEY
Colorado R.
SAN ANDREAS FAULT
MOJAVE DESERT
ARIZONA
SCALE
0 100 200 300 Miles
0 100 200 300 Kilometers
Projection: Albers Equal Area
Ventura
Channel Islands
LOS ANGELES BASIN
Los Angeles
Long Beach
Palm Springs
Parker Dam
Colorado River
Salton Sea
IMPERIAL VALLEY
San Diego
MEXICO

BUILD on WHAT You Know

Do you remember what you learned about plate tectonics? See Chapter 2 to review.

A View of the Pacific States

If you looked at a map, you might wonder why California, Oregon, Washington, Alaska, and Hawaii are grouped together as a region. Alaska and Hawaii are separated from each other and from the 48 contiguous states. Contiguous states are those that border each other. Yet these states share a physical environment characterized by mountains, volcanoes, and earthquakes. They share cultural, political, and economic similarities as well. In addition, each of the states is working to protect fragile wilderness areas, fertile agricultural lands, and valuable natural resources. In many cases, these features are what first attracted people to the region.

Landforms

California California can be divided into four major landform areas. They are the Coast Ranges, the Sierra Nevada, the Central Valley, and the desert basins and ranges. The Coast Ranges form a rugged coastline along the Pacific.

The Sierra Nevada range lies east of the Coast Ranges. It is one of the longest and highest mountain ranges in the United States. Mount Whitney, the highest peak in the 48 contiguous states, rises above the Sierra Nevada.

Canada
Los Angeles
United States
Mexico

The San Andreas Fault caused a severe earthquake in Los Angles in 1994. Scientists warn that future severe earthquakes threaten California.

Between the Sierra Nevada and the Coast Ranges is a narrow plain known as the Central Valley. This plain stretches more than 400 miles (644 km). The Central Valley is irrigated by rivers that flow from the Sierra Nevada.

To the east of the Sierra Nevada are desert basins and mountain ranges. Included in this region is Death Valley, the lowest point in all of North America.

Earthquakes are common in California due to the San Andreas Fault system. This fault was formed where the Pacific and North American plates meet. The Pacific plate is slowly moving northward along the San Andreas Fault, past the North American plate. The shock waves caused by this activity can create severe earthquakes.

Oregon and Washington Four landform regions dominate Oregon and Washington. As in California the Coast Ranges form the scenic Pacific Northwest coastline. Just east of these mountains are two lowlands areas. The Puget Sound Lowland is in Washington, and the Willamette Valley lies in Oregon. These rich farmlands contain most of the population of each state.

Canada
Crater Lake
United States
Mexico

Crater Lake is what remains of a volcanic mountain that erupted more than 6,000 years ago.

The Cascades are a volcanic mountain range stretching across both states into northern California. The range includes Oregon's Crater Lake, the deepest lake in the United States. Crater Lake fills a huge **caldera**. A caldera is a large depression formed after a major eruption and collapse of a volcanic mountain.

East of the Cascades is a region of dry basins and mountains. Much of this area is known as the Columbia Basin. It is drained by the Columbia River.

Alaska and Hawaii Alaska occupies a huge peninsula that juts out from the northwestern part of North America. The volcanic Aleutian Islands form an arc to the southwest. The mountain ranges of Alaska are some of the most rugged in the world. The state has more than 3 million lakes. Ice fields and glaciers cover 4 percent of the state.

The Hawaiian Islands are a chain of eight major islands and more than 100 smaller islands. Although the islands are volcanic in origin, only one has active volcanoes. This is Hawaii, the largest of the islands. The Hawaiian Islands have scenic coasts with coral reefs that erode into fine, white beach sand.

✓ **READING CHECK:**
Identifying Cause and Effect
What causes severe earthquakes in California?

Sunlight reflects off the rugged cliffs of Kalau Valley on the Hawaiian island of Kauai.

Interpreting the Visual Why do you suppose few roads have been built in some parts of Kauai?

Alaska
Canada
United States

Only animals that can survive cold harsh climates, like the polar bear, live in northern Alaska.

Climate

The climates of the Pacific states vary. Seven different climates can be found within this region. They range from tropical to tundra climates.

California The northern coast of California has a marine west coast climate. Along the southern coast and in central California, the climate is Mediterranean. Temperatures are warm all year, even in winter. Summers are dry with hot winds. The basins of eastern California experience desert and steppe climates. Summer temperatures in Death Valley often reach 120° F (49° C).

Oregon and Washington The Cascades divide Oregon and Washington into two climate regions. To the west, the climate is marine west coast. Temperatures are mild year-round, with cloudy, rainy winters and warm, sunny summers. To the east of the Cascades are drier desert and steppe climates.

Alaska and Hawaii A marine west coast climate is found along the southeast coast of Alaska. Most of the state, especially the interior, has a subarctic climate. Summers are short, while winters are long and severe. Most precipitation is in the form of snow. The northern area of Alaska along the Arctic Ocean has a tundra climate.

Hawaii has little daily or seasonal temperature change. During Honolulu's coldest month, the temperature averages 72° F (22° C). It averages 81° F (27° C) during the warmest month. The climate of the eastern slopes of the islands is humid tropical with heavy rainfall.

✓ **READING CHECK:** *Supporting a Point of View* Which climate of the Pacific states would you prefer? Why?

Our Amazing Planet

Part of the island of Kauai in Hawaii is considered the wettest place in the world.

Alaska
Canada
United States

The Trans-Alaska Pipeline snakes across mountain ranges and tundra.

Economy

Each of the Pacific states contributes to the economy of the United States. California is the leading agricultural producer and leading industrial state. Crops include cotton, nuts, vegetables, and fruit. Aerospace, construction, entertainment, computers, software, and tourism are important industries in the state.

Forests and fish are two of the most important resources in Oregon and Washington. Seattle, Washington, is home to many important industries, including a major computer software company.

Alaska's economy is largely based on oil, forests, and fish. Hawaii's natural beauty, mild climate, and fertile soils are its most important resources. Hawaii's volcanic soils and climate are ideal for growing sugarcane, pineapples, and coffee. Millions of tourists visit the islands each year. Both states lack diverse agriculture and industry. As a result most goods must be imported from other states.

✓ **READING CHECK:** *Drawing Conclusions* What can you conclude about how Hawaii contributes to the U.S. economy as a result of having a mild climate and fertile soils?

Canada
United States
Mexico

The cutting down of many trees in Olympic National Forest of Washington has left irregular patterns in the forest.

Interpreting the Visual Record
Why do you think the lumber industry has been the focus of environmental debates?

Section Review 5

go.hrw.com **Homework Practice Online**
Keyword: SJ3 HP11

Define and explain: caldera

Working with Sketch Maps On the map that you created for Section 4, label the five Pacific states. Then label the following places: Coast Ranges, Sierra Nevada, Death Valley, Willamette Valley, Cascades, Los Angeles, Seattle.

Reading for the Main Idea

1. *Places and Regions* What are five physical features of the Pacific states?
2. *Places and Regions* What are the seven climates of the Pacific states?
3. *Human Systems* What resources, agricultural products, and industries are important to the economy of the Pacific states?

Critical Thinking

4. **Analyzing** How might severe hurricane damage affect Hawaii's economy?

Organizing What You Know

5. **Categorizing** Copy the following graphic organizer. Use it to categorize the different landform areas in each of the Pacific states.

State	Landform Areas
California	
Oregon	
Washington	
Alaska	
Hawaii	

CHAPTER 11

Reviewing What You Know

Building Vocabulary

On a separate sheet of paper, write sentences to define each of the following words.

1. megalopolis
2. moraine
3. estuary
4. barrier islands
5. wetlands
6. sediment
7. diversify
8. droughts
9. Corn Belt
10. Dairy Belt
11. badlands
12. chinooks
13. Wheat Belt
14. strip mining
15. caldera

Reviewing the Main Ideas

1. *Places and Regions* What has helped the megalopolis in the Northeast become a major industrial and financial center?
2. *Places and Regions* Why are many coastal areas of the South covered by wetlands?
3. *Places and Regions* What factors have helped to make the Midwest a great farming region?
4. *Places and Regions* What mining problems has the Interior West faced and how are they being corrected?
5. *Places and Regions* Why are California, Oregon, Washington, Alaska, and Hawaii grouped together as a region?

Understanding History and Society

Resource Use

Coal is an important natural resource in parts of the United States. The coal mining industry has created many jobs. As you prepare an oral report about this industry, consider the following:

- In which states coal mining is important.
- How coal is mined.
- How coal mining affects the environment.

Thinking Critically

1. **Evaluating** Are regions defined solely on the basis of location? Explain your answer.
2. **Analyzing** What natural forces have contributed to shaping the landforms in the regions of the United States?
3. **Drawing Conclusions** Why is tourism important to many regions?
4. **Supporting a Point of View** In which region or state in particular would you most like to live in the future? Explain your answer.
5. **Making Generalizations and Predictions** Why have most regions developed high-technology industries? What do you think will happen in the future to these industries?

Building Social Studies Skills

Map ACTIVITY

On a separate sheet of paper, match the letters on the map with their correct labels.

Aleutian Islands	**Detroit**
Arctic Ocean	**Hawaii**
Cape Cod	**New Orleans**
Chesapeake Bay	**Phoenix**
Crater Lake	**Seattle**

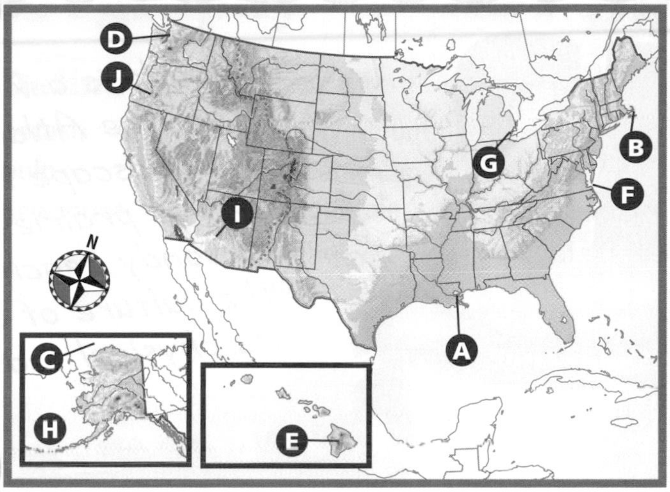
D
J
B
G
F
I
N
A
C
H
E

Mental Mapping Skills ACTIVITY

On a separate sheet of paper, draw a freehand map of the United States. Make a key for your map and label the following:

Everglades	**Ozark Plateau**
Grand Canyon	**San Andreas Fault**
Mississippi Delta	**Lake Erie**
White Mountains	**Sierra Nevada**

WRITING ACTIVITY

Each region of the United States welcomes tourists. Pleasant climates, natural sites, and historic sites attract visitors. Write a short travel ad for a magazine describing the attractions of one region. Be sure to use standard grammar, spelling, sentence structure, and punctuation.

Alternative Assessment

Portfolio ACTIVITY

Learning About Your Local Geography

Research Project Research the climate of your state. Find out the typical weather conditions for the area in which you live. Create a chart that shows the average temperature, rainfall, and other precipitation for each season.

internet connect

Internet Activity: go.hrw.com
KEYWORD: SJ3 GT11

Choose a topic to explore about the regions of the United States:

- Examine growth and development along the Great Lakes and St. Lawrence River.
- Create a brochure on Hawaii's environment.
- Create a newspaper article on the Gulf Coast of Texas.

GEORGE DAWE & SON LTD
127979
098022
ATLANTIC CRUISER
MISS MORGAN
Greenland
Canada
Avalon Peninsula
United States

The harbor at Avalon Peninsula is home to many fishing boats. **Interpreting the Visual Record Why do you think most people in the Maritime Provinces live in coastal cities?**

The Eastern Provinces

New Brunswick, Nova Scotia, and Prince Edward Island are often called the Maritime Provinces. **Maritime** means "on or near the sea." Each of these provinces is located near the ocean. Prince Edward Island is a small island, and Nova Scotia occupies a peninsula. New Brunswick has coasts on the Gulf of St. Lawrence and on the Bay of Fundy. Newfoundland is usually not considered one of the Maritime Provinces. It includes the island of Newfoundland and a large region of the mainland called Labrador.

A short growing season and poor soils make farming difficult in the eastern provinces. Most of the region's economy is related to forestry and fishing.

Many people in the eastern provinces are descendants of families that emigrated from the British Isles. In addition, many French-speaking families have moved from Quebec to New Brunswick. Most of the region's people live in coastal cities. The cities have industrial plants and serve as fishing and shipping ports. Halifax, Nova Scotia, is the region's largest city.

✓ **READING CHECK:** *Places and Regions* Why are most of the eastern provinces called the Maritime Provinces?

Our Amazing Planet

Canada's Bay of Fundy has some of the highest tides in the world—up to 70 feet (21 m). The tide brings water from the North Atlantic into the narrow bay. The bore, or leading wave of the incoming water, can roar like a big truck as the tide rushes in.

The Heartland

Inland from the eastern provinces are Quebec and Ontario. More than half of all Canadians live in these heartland provinces. In fact, the chain of cities that extends from Windsor, Ontario, to the city of Quebec is the country's most urbanized region.

Connecting to Literature

Anne of Green Gables

by Lucy Maud Montgomery

Canada's smallest province, Prince Edward Island, was the birthplace (in 1874) of one of the country's best-loved writers. Lucy Maud Montgomery based her Anne of Green Gables *series on the island she loved. She created characters and situations that lived in the minds of readers. Since its publication in 1908,* Anne of Green Gables *put the tiny island on the map, inspiring tours and festivals. It has even drawn tourists from as far away as Japan. They come to capture the spirit of the brave orphan. In this passage, young Anne is being driven to Green Gables by her new guardian, Matthew. He is kind but hardly imaginative!*

Anne says, "When I don't like the name of a place or a person I always imagine a new one and always think of them so. There was a girl at the asylum [orphanage] whose name was Hepzibah Jenkins, but I always imagined her as Rosalia DeVere." . . .

They had driven over the crest of a hill. Below them was a pond. . . . A bridge spanned it midway and from there to its lower end, where an amber-hued belt of sand hills shut it in from the dark-blue gulf beyond, the water was a glory of many shifting hues. . . .

"That's Barry's pond," said Matthew.

"Oh, I don't like that name, either. I shall call it—let me see—the Lake of Shining Waters. Yes, that is the right name for it. I know because of the thrill. When I hit on a name that suits exactly it gives me a thrill. Do things ever give you a thrill?"

Matthew ruminated.[1] "Well now, yes. It always kind of gives me a thrill to see them ugly white grubs[2] that spade up in the cucumber beds. I hate the look of them."

"Oh, I don't think that can be exactly the same kind of thrill. Do you think it can? There doesn't seem to be much connection between grubs and lakes of shining waters, does there? But why do other people call it Barry's pond?"

"I reckon because Mr. Barry lives up there in that house."

Analyzing Primary Sources

1. Why is *Anne of Green Gables* popular outside of Prince Edward Island?
2. How does imagination affect a person's view of the world?

Definitions [1]ruminate: to think over in the mind slowly [2]grubs: wormlike insect larvae

Day draws to a close in Toronto, Ontario. The city is located at the site of a trading post from the 1600s. Today Toronto is one of North America's major cities.

Quebec The city of Quebec is the capital of the province. The city's older section has narrow streets, stone walls, and French-style architecture. Montreal is Canada's second-largest city and one of the largest French-speaking cities in the world. About 3.3 million people live in the Montreal metropolitan area. It is the financial and industrial center of the province. Winters in Montreal are very cold. People in the city center use underground passages and overhead tunnels to move between buildings.

Ontario Ontario is Canada's leading manufacturing province. It is also Canada's most populous province. About 4.7 million people live in the metropolitan area of Toronto, Ontario's capital. Toronto is a major center for industry, finance, education, and culture. Toronto's residents have come from many different regions, including China, Europe, and India. Between Toronto and Montreal lies Ottawa, Canada's capital. In Ottawa many people speak both English and French. It has grand government buildings, parks, and several universities.

✓ **READING CHECK:** *Places and Regions* What are the major cities of Canada's heartland?

The Western Provinces

Farther to the west are the major farming regions of Manitoba, Saskatchewan, and Alberta. These three provinces are called the Prairie Provinces. Along the Pacific coast is British Columbia.

Canada's Prairie Provinces are home to productive farms like this one near Brandon, Manitoba.

Interpreting the Visual Record What can you tell about the physical geography of this region of Canada?

The Prairie Provinces More people live in Quebec than in all of the Prairie Provinces combined. The southern grasslands of these provinces are part of a rich wheat belt. Farms here produce far more wheat than Canadians need. The extra wheat is exported. Oil and natural gas production also are important in Alberta. Rocky Mountain resorts in western Alberta attract many tourists. The major cities of the Prairie Provinces are Edmonton, Calgary, and Winnipeg.

British Columbia British Columbia is Canada's westernmost province. This mountainous province has rich natural resources, including forests, salmon, and important minerals. Almost 4 million people live in British Columbia. Nearly half of them are in the coastal city of Vancouver. Vancouver is a multicultural city with large Chinese and Indian populations. It also is a major trade center.

✓ **READING CHECK:** *Environment and Society* How does geography affect the location of economic activities in the Prairie Provinces?

Our Amazing Planet

In the St. Elias Mountains in the Yukon Territory is the world's largest nonpolar ice field. The field covers an area of 15,822 square miles (40,570 sq km) and stretches into Alaska.

The Inuit have long hunted beluga whales for meat, blubber, and skin.

The Canadian North

Canada's vast northern lands include the Yukon Territory, the Northwest Territories, and Nunavut (NOO-nah-vuht). Nunavut is a new territory created for the **Inuit** (Eskimos) who live there. *Nunavut* means "Our Land" in the Inuit language. Nunavut is part of Canada, but the people have their own local government. The three territories cover more than one third of Canada but are home to only about 100,000 people. Boreal forests, tundra, and frozen Arctic ocean waters separate isolated towns and villages.

✓ **READING CHECK:** Who lives in Nunavut?

go.hrw.com **Homework Practice Online**
Keyword: SJ3 HP12

Section 3 Review

Define and explain: regionalism, maritime, Inuit

Working with Sketch Maps On the map that you created in Section 2, locate and label the major cities of Canada's provinces and territories. Where are most of these major cities located? What may have led to their growth?

Reading for the Main Idea

1. *Places and Regions* How does regionalism affect Canada's culture?
2. *The World in Spatial Terms* Into which provincial groups is Canada divided?

Critical Thinking

3. **Drawing Inferences and Conclusions** What makes the heartland a good area in which to settle?
4. **Finding the Main Idea** Why was Nunavut created?

Organizing What You Know

5. **Categorizing** Use the following graphic organizer to identify Canada's regions and provinces.

Region	Provinces

CHAPTER 12

Reviewing What You Know

Building Vocabulary

On a separate sheet of paper, write sentences to define each of the following words.

1. potash
2. pulp
3. newsprint
4. provinces
5. dominion
6. Métis
7. regionalism
8. maritime
9. Inuit

Reviewing the Main Ideas

1. *Places and Regions* How is the physical geography of Canada similar to that of the United States?
2. *Places and Regions* What types of natural resources can be found in Canada? Where is Canada's major wheat-farming area?
3. *Human Systems* What groups of people have made Canada their home?
4. *Human Systems* How do the people of Quebec show their regionalism?
5. *Places and Regions* What is Ottawa's relative location? Why is the city important?

Understanding Environment and Society

Resource Use

The Canadian economy depends on industries such as fishing, lumber, mining, and fossil fuels. As you create a presentation for your class, you may want to think about:

- Actions the Canadian government might take to conserve Canada's resources.
- What might happen if nothing is done to conserve Canada's resources.

Thinking Critically

1. **Comparing** How is Canada's government similar to that of the United States?
2. **Finding the Main Idea** How has immigration changed Canada?
3. **Drawing Inferences and Conclusions** How have past events shaped current conflicts in Canada?
4. **Drawing Inferences and Conclusions** If fishing and lumber are the primary industries of the Maritime Provinces, what are some likely secondary industries? List three industries.
5. **Summarizing** What geographic factors are responsible for economic activities in the Canadian Provinces?

Building Social Studies Skills

Map Activity

On a separate sheet of paper, match the letters on the map with their correct labels.

Great Slave Lake
Great Bear Lake
Newfoundland
Prince Edward Island
Manitoba
Alberta
Toronto
Calgary
Vancouver
Nunavut

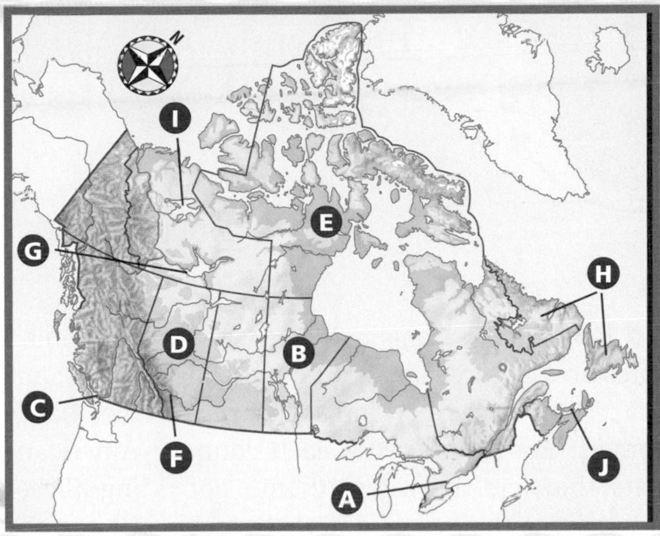

N
I
E
G
H
D
B
C
F
J
A

Mental Mapping Skills Activity

On a separate sheet of paper, draw a map of Canada and label the following:

British Columbia
Great Lakes
Hudson Bay
Ontario
Ottawa
Quebec
Saskatchewan
Yukon Territory

Writing Activity

Write three paragraphs explaining where in Canada you might like to live and why. Name a province and describe the geographic, climatic, political, and cultural features that make it attractive to you. Be sure to use standard grammar, sentence structure, spelling, and punctuation.

Alternative Assessment

Portfolio Activity

Learning About Your Local Geography

Individual Project Canada's cold climate helped make winter sports popular there. What sports are popular in your region? How do they compare with Canada's sports? Create a thematic map of your region that shows the location of different sporting activities.

internet connect

go.hrw.com

Internet Activity: go.hrw.com
KEYWORD: SJ3 GT12

Choose a topic to explore about Canada:

- Take a trip to the Yukon Territory.
- Learn about Canada's First Nations.
- Meet the people of Quebec.

FOCUS ON

ECONOMY

NAFTA

Borders and Barriers Canada, Mexico, and the United States are the three largest countries in North America. They have very large and productive economies. Borders separate each country and create barriers between them. For example, one barrier is the use of different types of currency in each country. In Canada, people use Canadian dollars. In Mexico, they use Mexican pesos. In the United States, people use U.S. dollars. You cannot buy a cheeseburger in Canada with Mexican pesos because of this barrier. Another barrier is the different laws that each country has. This creates a barrier to law enforcement.

The NAFTA agreement was signed by the leaders of Mexico, the United States, and Canada in 1992 and took effect on January 1, 1994. NAFTA created the largest free trade area in the world.

Some barriers between Canada, the United States, and Mexico are being removed. For example, barriers to trade are changing. The North American Free Trade Agreement (NAFTA) is causing these changes. With NAFTA, Canada, the United States, and Mexico have agreed to follow some common rules about trading. These new rules make it easier to trade across borders.

Beginnings of NAFTA NAFTA began on January 1, 1994. The purpose of NAFTA is to improve nearly all aspects of trade between the three countries. It promotes free trade by lowering or removing taxes on goods traded between Canada, the United States, and Mexico. For example, NAFTA eliminates tariffs between them. A tariff is a kind of tax. Tariffs are paid on goods that are exported to other countries. For example, when apples are exported from the United States to Japan, Japan collects a tariff.

Because of NAFTA, many agricultural and industrial products are not taxed when they are imported from the other member countries. Therefore, these goods can be easily traded from one country to another. NAFTA also eases barriers for corporations. For example, a company might be based in the United States. That company is now able to set up factories in Mexico without the problem of special taxes or tariffs.

NAFTA Trade Flows

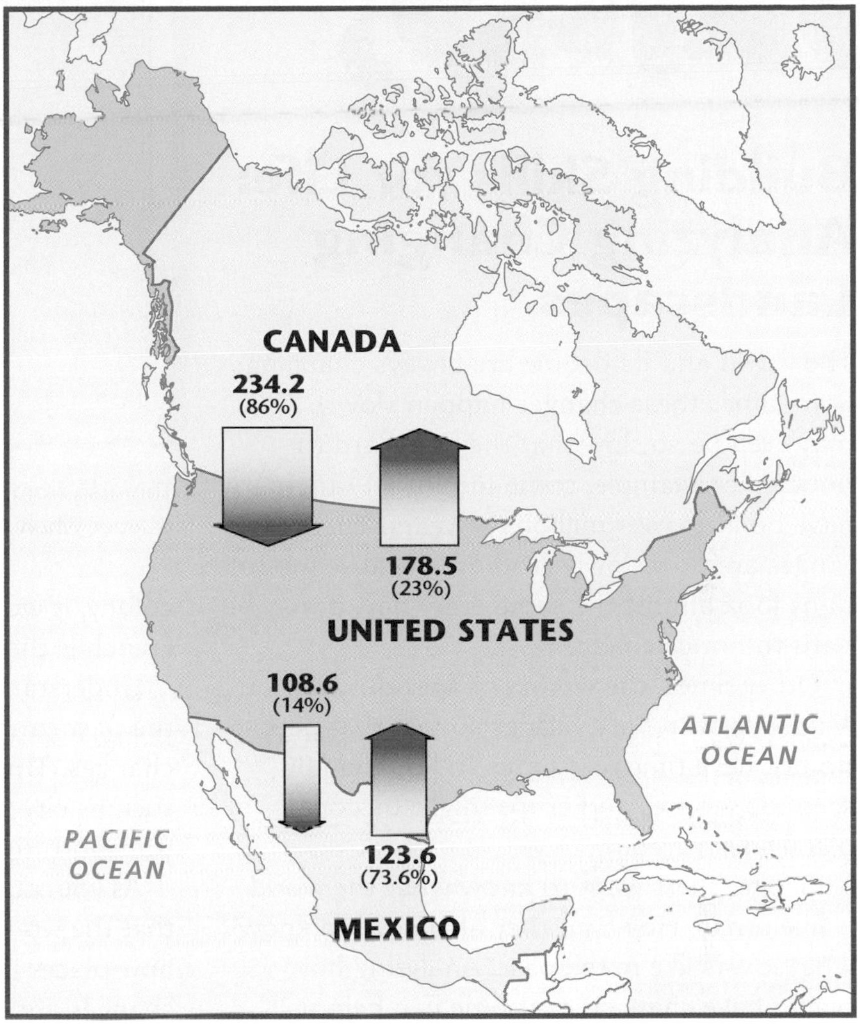

CANADA
234.2
(86%)
178.5
(23%)
UNITED STATES
108.6
(14%)
123.6
(73.6%)
MEXICO
PACIFIC OCEAN
ATLANTIC OCEAN

This map shows trade among the United States and its NAFTA partners in billions of U.S. dollars. Numbers in parentheses show the percentage of each country's total exports. Trade among all three countries has greatly increased since NAFTA began in 1994.

Removing Barriers Some people in both the United States and Canada have criticized the NAFTA agreement. They believe NAFTA has caused many Americans and Canadians to lose their jobs. Some corporations have closed factories in the United States and Canada. These corporations then opened new factories in Mexico. People are also worried that NAFTA might harm the environment. Under NAFTA, fewer environmental laws and regulations must be followed. This may cause environmental problems such as increased pollution or pesticide use.

Other people support NAFTA. They point out that trade among Canada, the United States, and Mexico has increased since NAFTA began. There are now more jobs in all three countries. For example, the United States exports more agricultural products to Mexico now. NAFTA also helps all three countries by increasing their total production of goods. For example, T-shirts are made from cotton. With NAFTA, cotton grown in Mexico, the United States, or Canada is cheaper than cotton from other countries. This helps cotton growers in all NAFTA countries.

The borders between Canada, the United States, and Mexico are slowly becoming less important. NAFTA is removing trade barriers between these countries and increasing their economic connections.

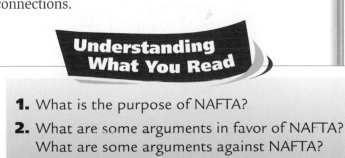

Understanding What You Read

1. What is the purpose of NAFTA?
2. What are some arguments in favor of NAFTA? What are some arguments against NAFTA?

GeoSKILLS

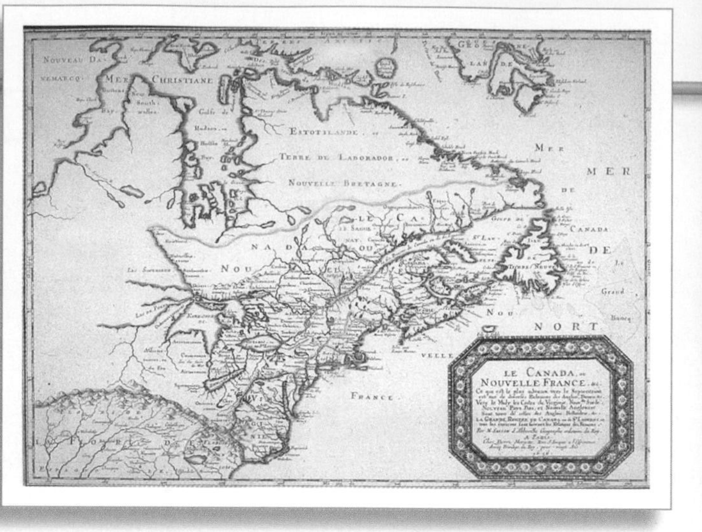
MER CHRISTIANE
ESTOTILANDE
TERRE DE LABORADOR
NOUVELLE BRETAGNE
MER
MER
DE
CANADA
NORT
FRANCE
LE CANADA, ou
NOUVELLE FRANCE

This map from the mid-1600s shows Quebec when it was a French colony.

Building Skills for Life: Analyzing Changing Landscapes

The world and its people are always changing. Sometimes these changes happen slowly. They may even be so slow that they are hard to notice. For example, some mountain ranges have built up over millions of years. These ranges are now slowly eroding. Because mountains look almost the same every day, it may be hard to notice changes.

Other times, the world changes quickly. Mudslides can bury villages so fast that people do not have time to escape. In less than 30 seconds, houses and crops might be completely destroyed.

Geographers want to know what the world is like today. However, they also need to know what it was like in the past. Analyzing how places have changed over time can help us better understand the world. For example, suppose you took a trip to Quebec. You would notice that most people there speak French. If you knew that Quebec used to be a French colony, it would help you understand why French is the main language today.

Understanding how places have changed in the past can also help us predict future changes. This is an important goal for people such as city planners, government officials, and transportation engineers.

As you study geography, try to remember that the world is always changing. Think about how places have changed and why these changes are important. Ask yourself how places might change in the future. Be aware that maps, photographs, newspapers, and other tools of geography can become outdated. After all, the world does not wait for geography!

PRACTICING THE SKILL

1. Find an area in your community that you think is changing quickly. Observe the changes. Are new businesses, houses, or roads being built? Are the changes big or small?
2. Talk to a parent, grandparent, or neighbor. Ask how your community, town, or city has changed during the last 20 to 30 years. What are some of the major changes? Does this person remember some old places that are no longer there?
3. Look for an old book, magazine, or map. Try to find one that is at least 30 years old. How is it different from a current book, magazine, or map?

HANDS ON GEOGRAPHY

You can analyze changing landscapes by comparing old photographs of a place to new ones. Important changes might be easy to see. For example, new buildings and new roads often stand out on the more recent photographs.

Look at the two photographs below. They show a small section of Las Vegas, Nevada. The photograph on the left was taken in 1963. The photograph on the right was taken 35 years later in 1998. Now compare the two photographs. What do you notice?

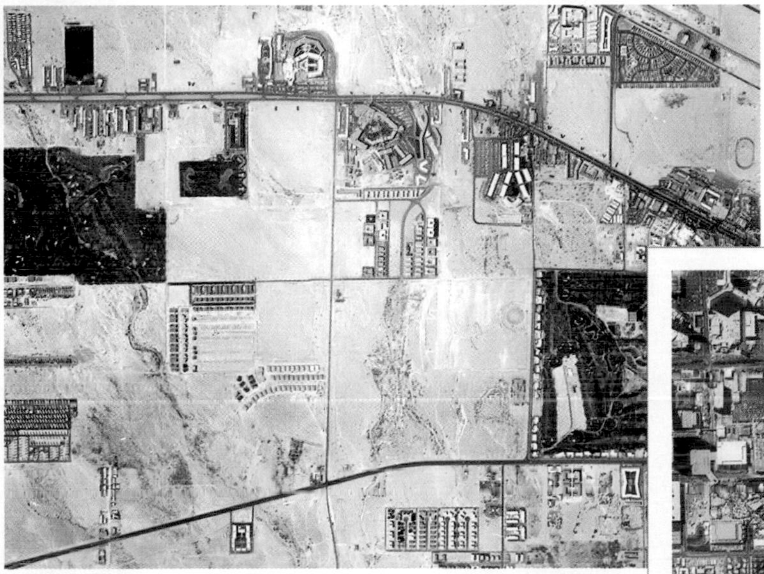

Las Vegas, 1963

Las Vegas, 1998

Lab Report

1. How do you know these two photographs show the same place? What evidence do you see?
2. How did this section of Las Vegas change between 1963 and 1998? Do you think these are big changes or small ones?
3. Find a street map of Las Vegas and try to figure out exactly what part of the city the photographs show. Then compare the map with the 1998 photograph. What information does the map give about this section of the city?

UNIT 4

Middle and South America

CHAPTER 13
Mexico

CHAPTER 14
Central America and the Caribbean Islands

CHAPTER 15
Caribbean South America

CHAPTER 16
Atlantic South America

CHAPTER 17
Pacific South America

Congress Building, Brasília, Brazil

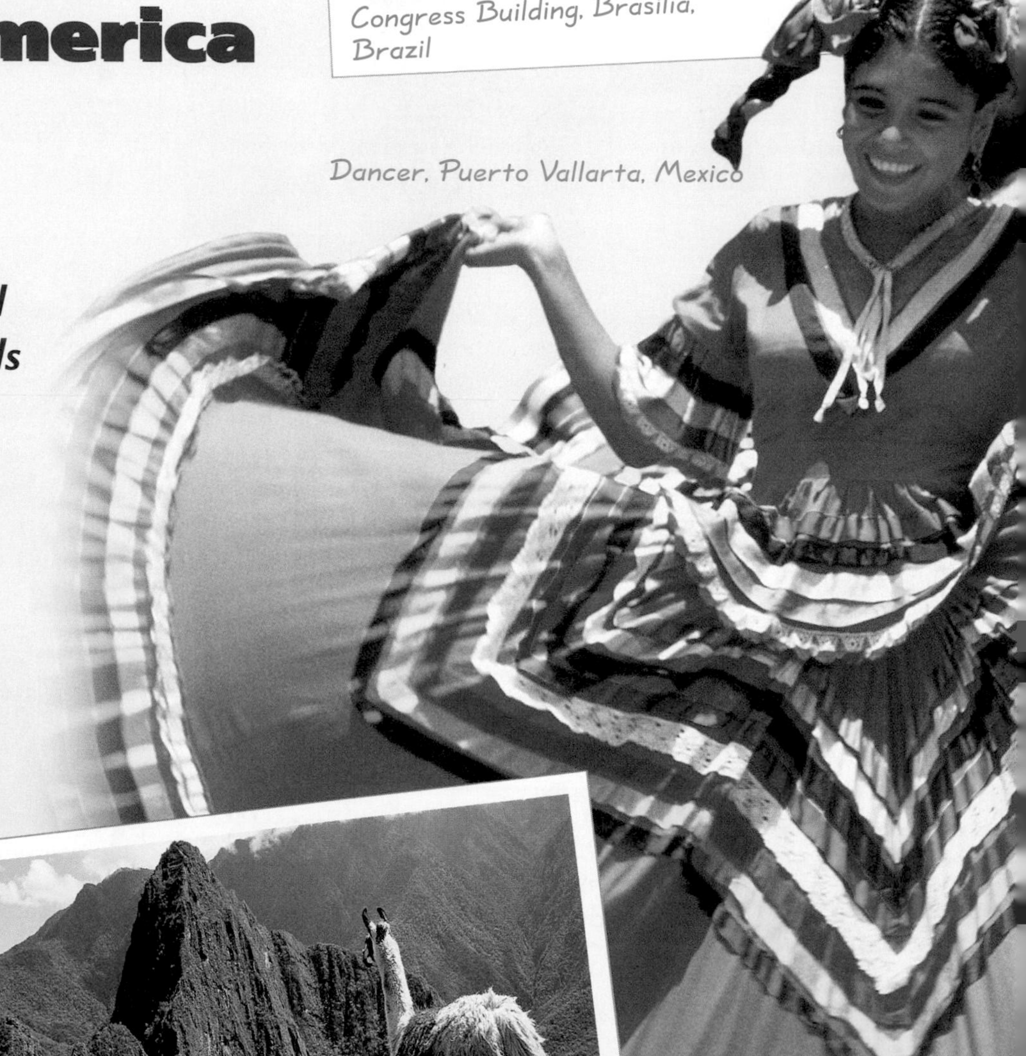
Dancer, Puerto Vallarta, Mexico

Machu Picchu, Peru, and llama

Notes from the Field

A Conservationist in Costa Rica

Sandy Wiseman works for a conservation organization in Canada. He often organizes trips to rain forests. Here Dr. Wiseman tells about a morning hike through a Costa Rican forest. **WHAT DO YOU THINK?** *Which of the animals he mentions would you like to see for yourself?*

Birds of many kinds were already active in the canopy. From high in the treetops, parrots and parakeets were squawking and feeding, not just themselves but dozens of other creatures with the fruit they dropped to the forest floor.

A tiny clear-winged butterfly floated in jerks along the path and came to rest on a leaf over the trail. Its transparent wings made it almost invisible. Later I spotted a small anteater. Only after it heard me reach for my camera did it stand up with nose held high to taste the air. The anteater spread wide its hooked forepaws as if to invite a hug, in a defensive pose. Within a minute it resumed its foraging, shuffling, and sniffing into the forest.

I now thought better of hurrying through the woods. I would sit for a while and take in my surroundings. With patient observation and quiet thought,the richness of the rain forest rekindles [renews] marvel and wonder.

Clear-winged butterfly, Costa Rica

Understanding Primary Sources

1. How do the parrots and parakeets feed other animals?
2. How does Sandy Wiseman react to seeing the creatures in the rain forest?

Blue poison dart frog

Middle and South America

Elevation Profile

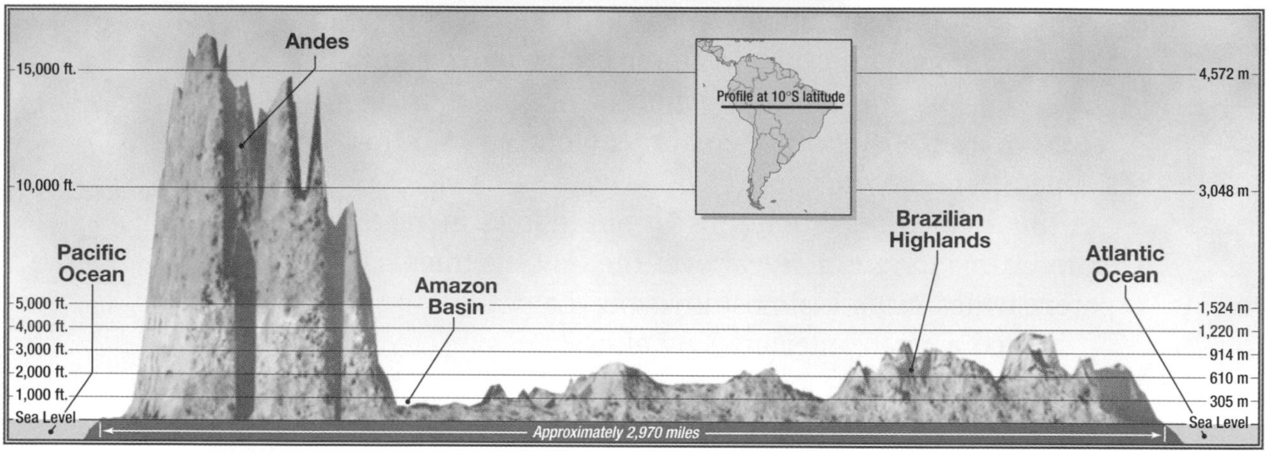
Andes
15,000 ft.
4,572 m
Profile at 10°S latitude
10,000 ft.
3,048 m
Pacific Ocean
Amazon Basin
Brazilian Highlands
Atlantic Ocean
5,000 ft.
4,000 ft.
3,000 ft.
2,000 ft.
1,000 ft.
Sea Level
1,524 m
1,220 m
914 m
610 m
305 m
Sea Level
Approximately 2,970 miles

The United States and Middle and South America: Comparing Sizes

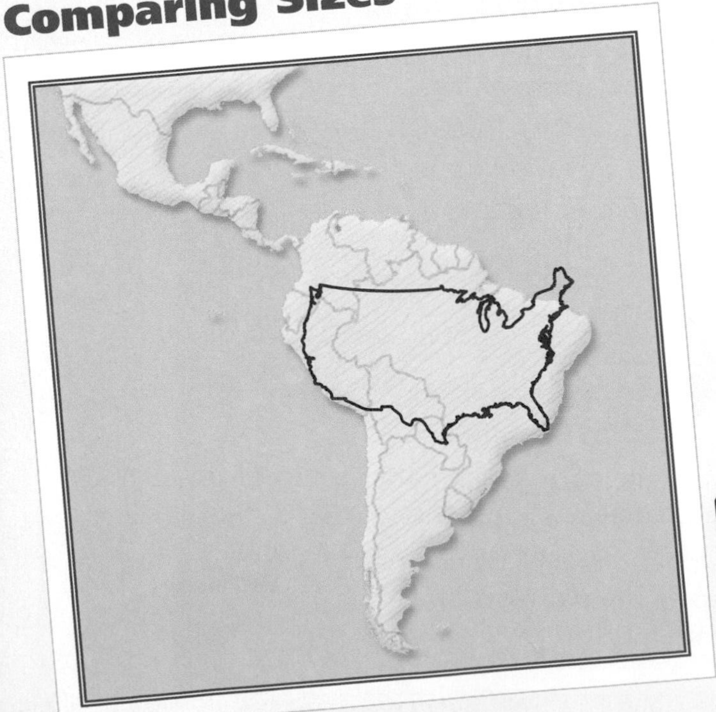

GEOSTATS:

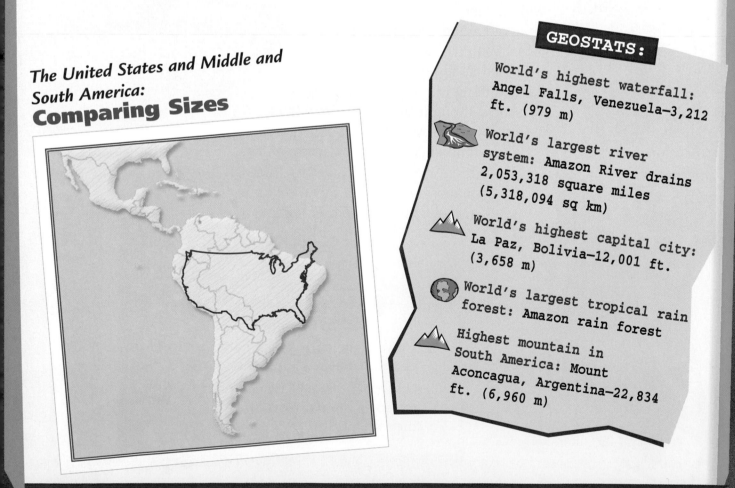

World's highest waterfall: Angel Falls, Venezuela–3,212 ft. (979 m)

World's largest river system: Amazon River drains 2,053,318 square miles (5,318,094 sq km)

World's highest capital city: La Paz, Bolivia–12,001 ft. (3,658 m)

World's largest tropical rain forest: Amazon rain forest

Highest mountain in South America: Mount Aconcagua, Argentina–22,834 ft. (6,960 m)

Middle and South America: Physical

UNITED STATES
Bermuda (U.K.)
GULF OF MEXICO
ATLANTIC OCEAN
Tropic of Cancer
BAHAMAS
GREATER ANTILLES
CUBA
JAMAICA
Hispaniola
LESSER ANTILLES
YUCATÁN PENINSULA
MEXICO
BELIZE
GUATEMALA
HONDURAS
EL SALVADOR
NICARAGUA
Lake Nicaragua
COSTA RICA
PANAMA
Panama Canal
ISTHMUS OF PANAMA
CARIBBEAN SEA
BAJA CALIFORNIA
SIERRA MADRE OCCIDENTAL
SIERRA MADRE ORIENTAL
Rio Grande
Rio Bravo
VENEZUELA
Lake Maracaibo
LLANOS
Orinoco River
Angel Falls
GUYANA
SURINAME
FRENCH GUIANA (FRANCE)
GUIANA HIGHLANDS
COLOMBIA
Cauca R.
Magdalena R.
ECUADOR
Galápagos Islands (ECUADOR)
Equator
Rio Negro
AMAZON BASIN
Amazon River
PERU
BRAZIL
São Francisco R.
BRAZILIAN HIGHLANDS
BRAZILIAN PLATEAU
PACIFIC OCEAN
Lake Titicaca
BOLIVIA
Lake Poopó
Paraguay River
Paraná R.
ATACAMA DESERT
Gran Chaco
PARAGUAY
Iguaçu Falls
Tropic of Capricorn
CHILE
Paraná River
Uruguay R.
URUGUAY
Mount Aconcagua 22,834 ft. (6960 m)
PAMPAS
ANDES
ARGENTINA
Río de la Plata
ATLANTIC OCEAN
PATAGONIA
Falkland Islands (U.K.)
TIERRA DEL FUEGO
CAPE HORN
SCALE
0 500 1000 Miles
0 500 1000 Kilometers
Projection: Azimuthal Equal Area
ELEVATION
FEET METERS
13,120 4,000
6,560 2,000
1,640 500
656 200
(Sea level) 0 0 (Sea level)
Below sea level Below sea level
N
30°N
20°N
10°N
10°S
20°S
30°S
40°S
50°S
100°W
90°W
80°W
70°W
60°W
50°W
40°W
30°W
20°W
110°W
120°W
130°W
140°W

1. Places and Regions Which country has two highland regions and a large plateau?
2. Places and Regions Which country has two large peninsulas that extend into different oceans?
3. Places and Regions Which island groups separate the Caribbean Sea from the Gulf of Mexico and the Atlantic Ocean?

Critical Thinking

4. **Drawing Inferences and Conclusions** Find central Mexico on the map. Why do you think east-west travel might be difficult in this area? What physical feature do you think would make travel easier in northern Brazil?

Guatemala

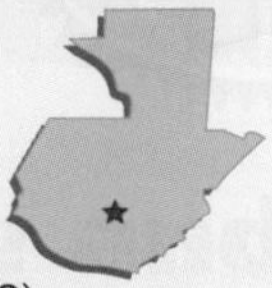

CAPITAL: Guatemala City
AREA: 42,042 sq. mi. (108,890 sq km)
POPULATION: 12,974,361
MONEY: quetzal (GTQ)
LANGUAGES: Spanish, Quiche, Cakchiquel, Kekchi
CHILDREN BORN/WOMAN: 4.6

Guyana

CAPITAL: Georgetown
AREA: 83,000 sq. mi. (214,970 sq km)
POPULATION: 697,181
MONEY: Guyanese dollar (GYD)
LANGUAGES: English, ethnic dialects
CHILDREN BORN/WOMAN: 2.1

Haiti

CAPITAL: Port-au-Prince
AREA: 10,714 sq. mi. (27,750 sq km)
POPULATION: 6,964,549
MONEY: gourde (HTG)
LANGUAGES: French (official), Creole
CHILDREN BORN/WOMAN: 4.4

Honduras

CAPITAL: Tegucigalpa
AREA: 43,278 sq. mi. (112,090 sq km)
POPULATION: 6,406,052
MONEY: lempira (HNL)
LANGUAGES: Spanish, ethnic languages
CHILDREN BORN/WOMAN: 4.2

Jamaica

CAPITAL: Kingston
AREA: 4,243 sq. mi. (10,990 sq km)
POPULATION: 2,665,636
MONEY: Jamaican dollar (JMD)
LANGUAGES: English, Creole
CHILDREN BORN/WOMAN: 2.1

Mexico

CAPITAL: Mexico City
AREA: 761,602 sq. mi. (1,972,550 sq km)
POPULATION: 101,879,171
MONEY: Mexican peso (MXN)
LANGUAGES: Spanish, Mayan, Nahuatl, ethnic languages
CHILDREN BORN/WOMAN: 2.6

Nicaragua

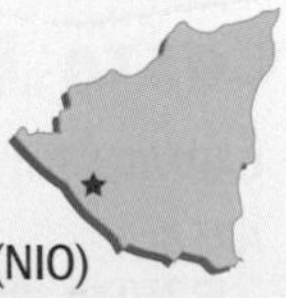

CAPITAL: Managua
AREA: 49,998 sq. mi. (129,494 sq km)
POPULATION: 4,918,393
MONEY: gold cordoba (NIO)
LANGUAGES: Spanish (official), English, ethnic languages
CHILDREN BORN/WOMAN: 3.2

Panama

CAPITAL: Panama City
AREA: 30,193 sq. mi. (78,200 sq km)
POPULATION: 2,845,647
MONEY: balboa (PAB)
LANGUAGES: Spanish (official), English
CHILDREN BORN/WOMAN: 2.3

Paraguay

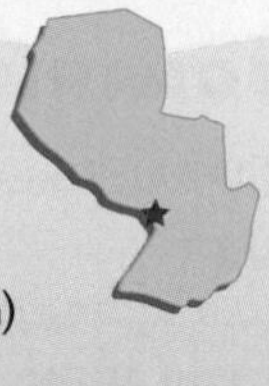

CAPITAL: Asunción
AREA: 157,046 sq. mi. (406,750 sq km)
POPULATION: 5,734,139
MONEY: guarani (PYG)
LANGUAGES: Spanish (official), Guarani
CHILDREN BORN/WOMAN: 4.1

Peru

CAPITAL: Lima
AREA: 496,223 sq. mi. (1,285,220 sq km)
POPULATION: 27,483,864
MONEY: nuevo sol (PEN)
LANGUAGES: Spanish (official), Quechua (official), Aymara
CHILDREN BORN/WOMAN: 3.0

Countries not drawn to scale.

UNIT 4 ATLAS

PUERTO RICO (U.S. Commonwealth)

CAPITAL: San Juan
AREA: 3,515 sq. mi. (9,104 sq km)
POPULATION: 3,937,316
MONEY: U.S. dollar (USD)
LANGUAGES: Spanish, English
CHILDREN BORN/WOMAN: 1.9

SAINT KITTS AND NEVIS

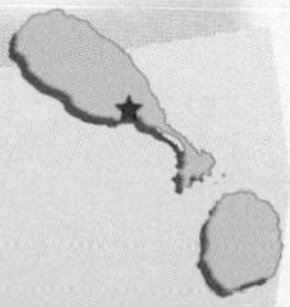

CAPITAL: Basseterre
AREA: 101 sq. mi. (261 sq km)
POPULATION: 38,756
MONEY: East Caribbean dollar (XCD)
LANGUAGES: English
CHILDREN BORN/WOMAN: 2.4

SAINT LUCIA

CAPITAL: Castries
AREA: 239 sq. mi. (620 sq km)
POPULATION: 158,178
MONEY: East Caribbean dollar (XCD)
LANGUAGES: English (official), French patois
CHILDREN BORN/WOMAN: 2.4

SAINT VINCENT AND THE GRENADINES

CAPITAL: Kingstown
AREA: 150 sq. mi. (389 sq km)
POPULATION: 115,942
MONEY: East Caribbean dollar (XCD)
LANGUAGES: English, French patois
CHILDREN BORN/WOMAN: 2.1

SURINAME

CAPITAL: Paramaribo
AREA: 63,039 sq. mi. (163,270 sq km)
POPULATION: 433,998
MONEY: Surinamese guilder (SRG)
LANGUAGES: Dutch (official), English, Sranang Tongo
CHILDREN BORN/WOMAN: 2.5

TRINIDAD AND TOBAGO

CAPITAL: Port-of-Spain
AREA: 1,980 sq. mi. (5,128 sq km)
POPULATION: 1,169,682
MONEY: Trinidad and Tobago dollar (TTD)
LANGUAGES: English, Hindi, French, Spanish
CHILDREN BORN/WOMAN: 1.8

URUGUAY

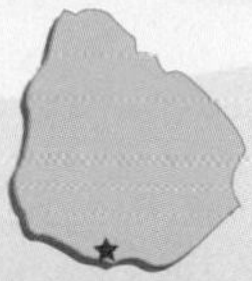

CAPITAL: Montevideo
AREA: 68,039 sq. mi. (176,220 sq km)
POPULATION: 3,360,105
MONEY: Uruguayan peso (UYU)
LANGUAGES: Spanish, Portunol
CHILDREN BORN/WOMAN: 2.4

VENEZUELA

CAPITAL: Caracas
AREA: 352,143 sq. mi. (912,050 sq km)
POPULATION: 23,916,810
MONEY: bolivar (VEB)
LANGUAGES: Spanish (official), many ethnic languages
CHILDREN BORN/WOMAN: 2.5

internet connect

COUNTRY STATISTICS
GO TO: go.hrw.com
KEYWORD: SJ3 FactsU4
FOR: more facts about Middle and South America

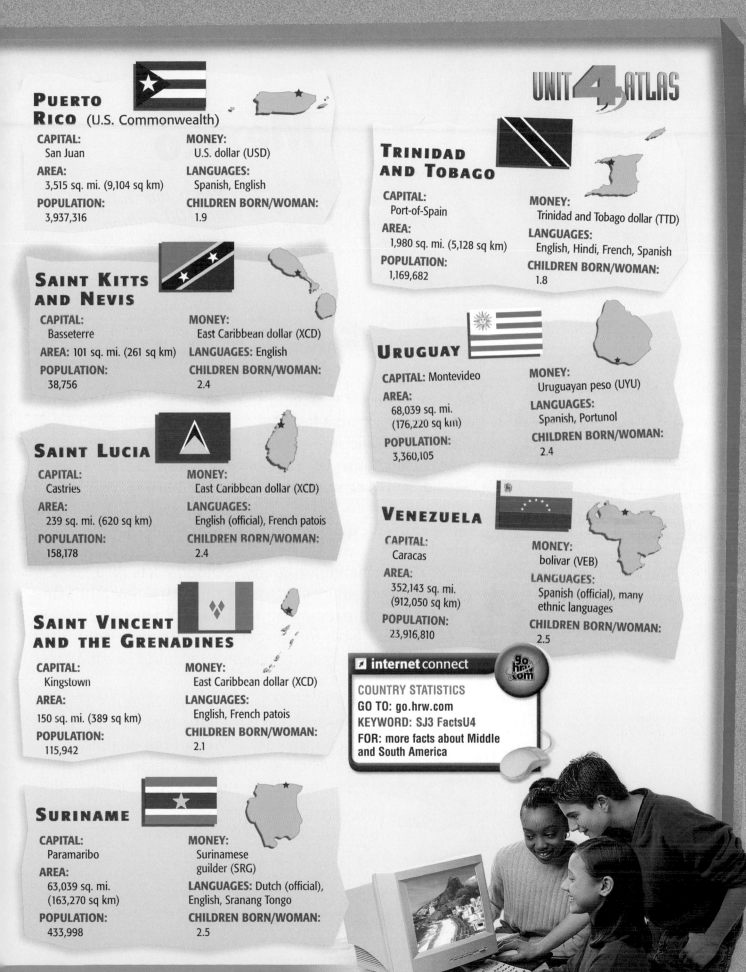

CHAPTER 13

Mexico

Now we will study Mexico, our neighbor to the south. More than 100 million people live in Mexico. Below you will meet Ellie, a Mexican student.

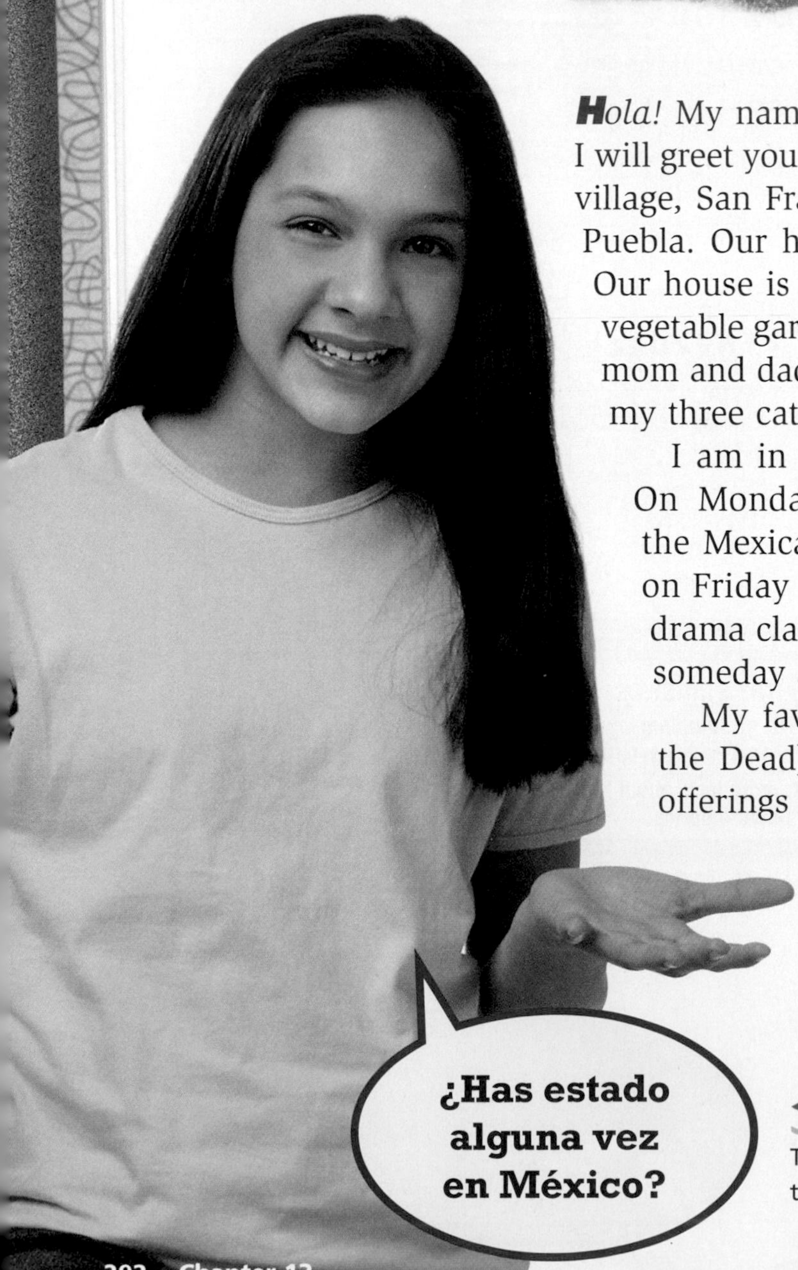
¿Has estado alguna vez en México?

Hola! My name is Ellie, and I am 14. If you are my friend, I will greet you with a fast kiss on the cheek. I live in a small village, San Francisco Acatepec, on the edge of the city of Puebla. Our house is made of adobe and has a big yard. Our house is surrounded by a big adobe wall. We have a vegetable garden, flowers, and a lot of trees. I live with my mom and dad, my older brother (he's in the ninth grade), my three cats, and two dogs.

I am in the eighth grade. School starts at 8:00 A.M. On Monday mornings, we salute the flag and sing the Mexican national anthem. School ends at 2:15 but on Friday I have to stay till 4:45 to take an additional drama class. I love drama since I want to be an actress someday and a marine biologist.

My favorite holiday is Dia de los Muertos (Day of the Dead). On that day, we make bread and put out offerings to honor the dead. We put out clothes, sugar cane, chocolate, sugar candy skulls, flowers, bread, pictures, incense, and candles.

Translation: Have you ever been to Mexico?

Section 1 Physical Geography

Read to Discover

1. What are the main physical features of Mexico?
2. What climate types, plants, and animals are found in Mexico?
3. What are Mexico's main natural resources?

Define

sinkholes

Locate

Gulf of Mexico
Baja California
Gulf of California
Río Bravo (Rio Grande)
Mexican Plateau
Sierra Madre Oriental
Sierra Madre Occidental
Mount Orizaba
Yucatán Peninsula

Scarlet macaw

WHY IT MATTERS

The Río Bravo (Rio Grande) marks the border between the United States and Mexico. Use CNNfyi.com or other **current events** sources to find information on this major river. Record your findings in your journal.

Mexico: Physical-Political

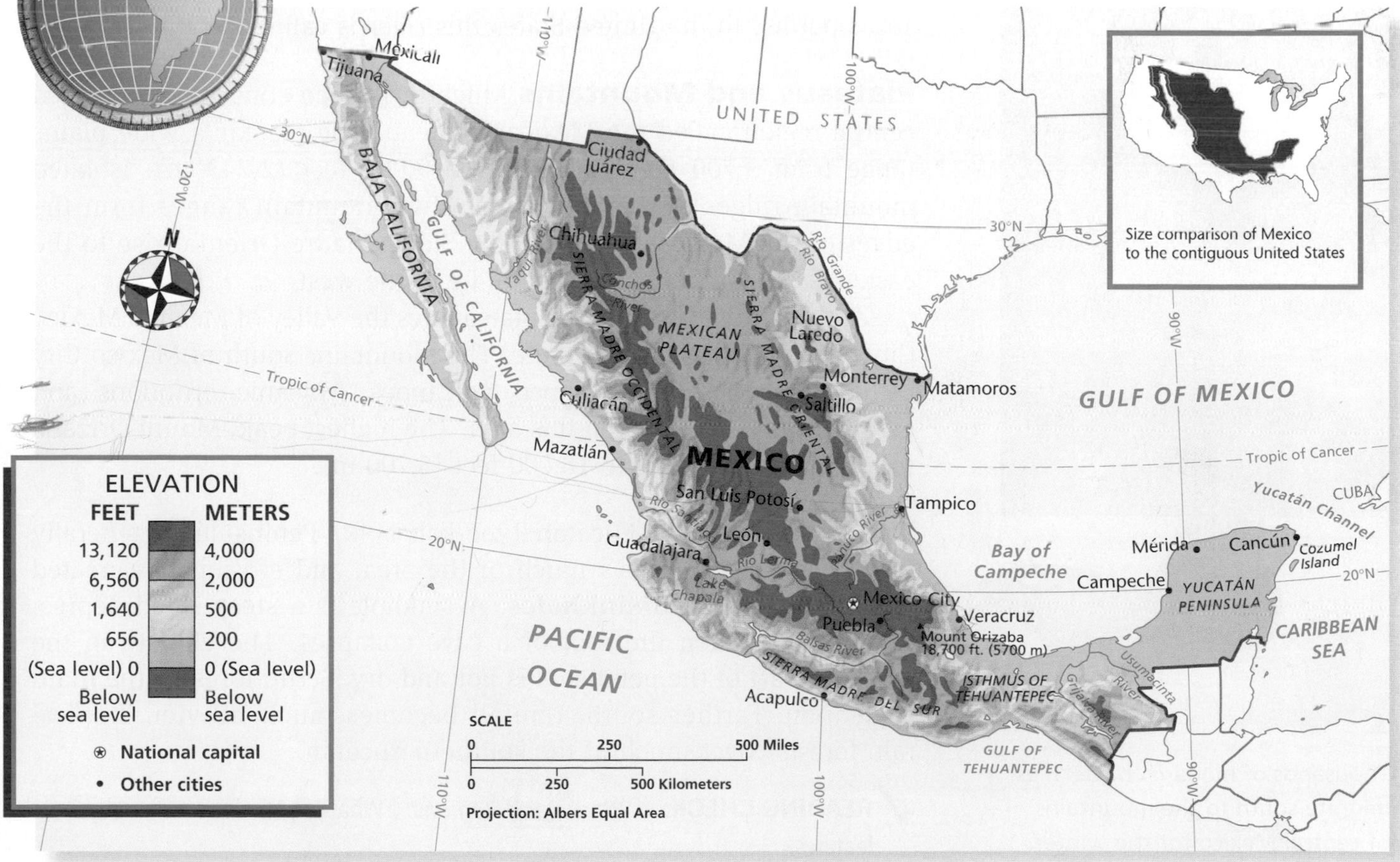

UNITED STATES
Mexicali
Tijuana
Ciudad Juárez
Chihuahua
BAJA CALIFORNIA
GULF OF CALIFORNIA
SIERRA MADRE OCCIDENTAL
MEXICAN PLATEAU
SIERRA MADRE ORIENTAL
Rio Grande
Río Bravo
Nuevo Laredo
Monterrey
Matamoros
Saltillo
Culiacán
Mazatlán
MEXICO
San Luis Potosí
Tampico
León
Guadalajara
Lake Chapala
Mexico City
Puebla
Veracruz
Mount Orizaba 18,700 ft. (5700 m)
Balsas River
SIERRA MADRE DEL SUR
Acapulco
ISTHMUS OF TEHUANTEPEC
GULF OF TEHUANTEPEC
Bay of Campeche
Campeche
Mérida
Cancún
Cozumel Island
YUCATÁN PENINSULA
Yucatán Channel
CUBA
CARIBBEAN SEA
GULF OF MEXICO
PACIFIC OCEAN
Tropic of Cancer
30°N
20°N
120°W
110°W
100°W
90°W
N
Size comparison of Mexico to the contiguous United States
ELEVATION
FEET
METERS
13,120
4,000
6,560
2,000
1,640
500
656
200
(Sea level) 0
0 (Sea level)
Below sea level
Below sea level
National capital
Other cities
SCALE
0
250
500 Miles
0
250
500 Kilometers
Projection: Albers Equal Area

United States
Mexico
Mt. Orizaba
Guatemala

Volcanic Mount Orizaba rises southeast of Mexico City.

Interpreting the Visual Record What kinds of climates do you think people living in this area might experience?

internet connect

GO TO: go.hrw.com
KEYWORD: SJ3 CH13
FOR: Web sites about Mexico

Physical Features

Mexico is a large country. It has a long coast on the Pacific Ocean. It has a shorter one on the Gulf of Mexico. In far southern Mexico, the two bodies of water are just 137 miles (220 km) apart. This part of Mexico is called the Isthmus of Tehuantepec (tay-WAHN-tah-pek). The Caribbean Sea washes the country's sunny southeastern beaches. Beautiful Caribbean and Pacific coastal areas attract many tourists.

Baja (BAH-hah) California is a long, narrow peninsula. It extends south from Mexico's northwestern border with the United States. The peninsula separates the Gulf of California from the Pacific Ocean. One of Mexico's few major rivers, the Río Bravo, forms the Mexico-Texas border. In the United States this river is called the Rio Grande.

Plateaus and Mountains Much of Mexico consists of a rugged central region called the Mexican Plateau. The plateau's wide plains range from 3,700 feet (1,128 m) to 9,000 feet (2,743 m). Isolated mountain ridges rise much higher. Two mountain ranges form the edges of the Mexican Plateau. The Sierra Madre Oriental rise to the east. The Sierra Madre Occidental lie in the west.

At the southern end of the plateau lies the Valley of Mexico. Mexico City, the capital, is located there. The mountains south of Mexico City include towering, snowcapped volcanoes. Volcanic eruptions and earthquakes are a threat in this area. The highest peak, Mount Orizaba (oh-ree-SAH-buh), rises to 18,700 feet (5,700 m).

The Yucatán The Yucatán (yoo-kah-TAHN) Peninsula is generally flat. Limestone underlies much of the area, and erosion has created numerous caves and **sinkholes**. A sinkhole is a steep-sided depression formed when the roof of a cave collapses. The climate in the northern part of the peninsula is hot and dry. Scrub forest is the main vegetation. Farther south, rainfall becomes much heavier. Tropical rain forests cover much of the southern Yucatán.

Thousands of monarch butterflies migrate south to the mountains of central Mexico for the winter.

✓ **READING CHECK:** *Places and Regions* What are Mexico's major physical features?

The States of Mexico

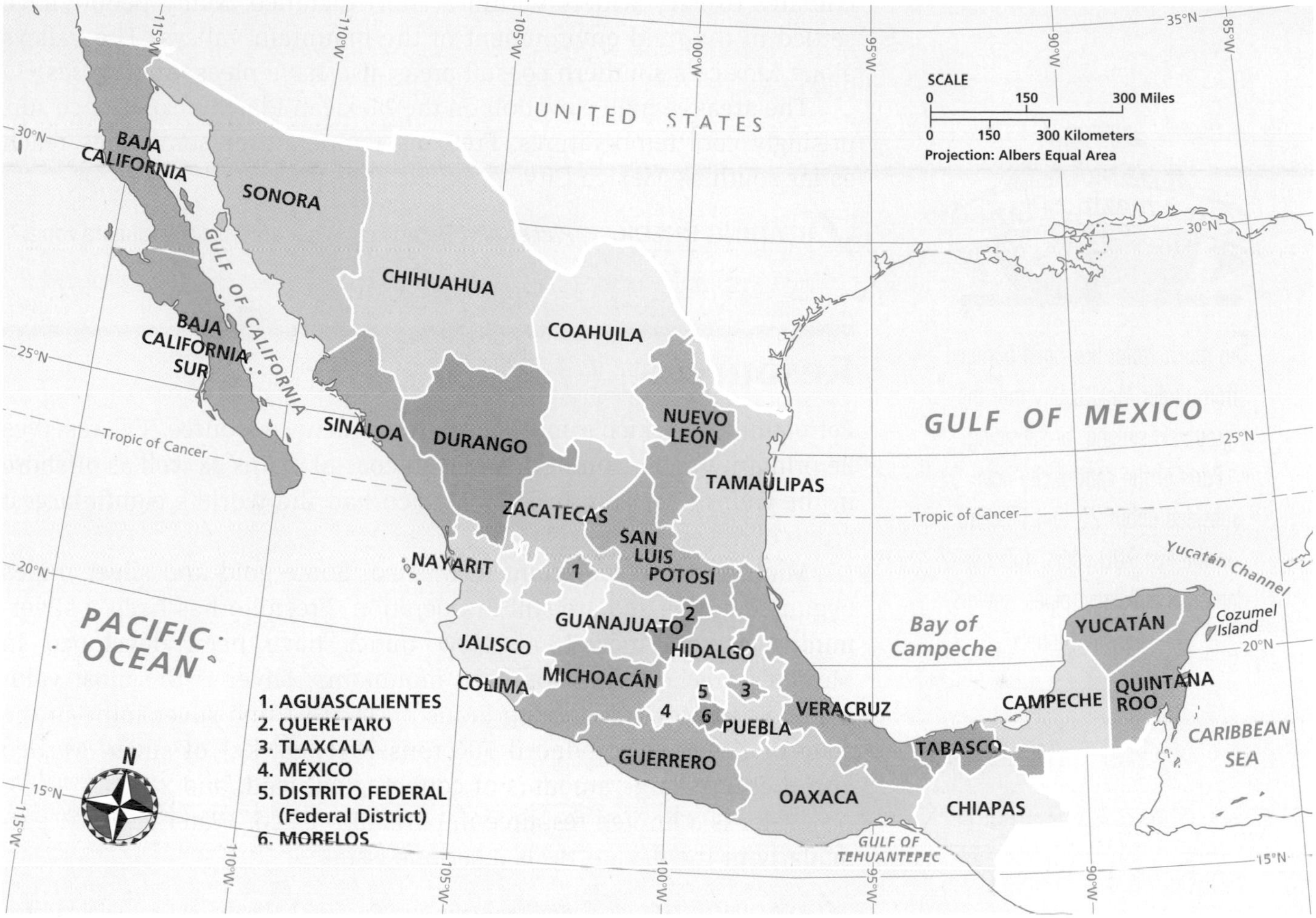

UNITED STATES
SCALE
0 150 300 Miles
0 150 300 Kilometers
Projection: Albers Equal Area
BAJA CALIFORNIA
SONORA
GULF OF CALIFORNIA
CHIHUAHUA
COAHUILA
BAJA CALIFORNIA SUR
SINALOA
DURANGO
NUEVO LEÓN
TAMAULIPAS
GULF OF MEXICO
Tropic of Cancer
ZACATECAS
SAN LUIS POTOSÍ
NAYARIT
Yucatán Channel
PACIFIC OCEAN
GUANAJUATO
JALISCO
HIDALGO
Bay of Campeche
YUCATÁN
Cozumel Island
COLIMA
MICHOACÁN
QUINTANA ROO
CAMPECHE
VERACRUZ
PUEBLA
TABASCO
CARIBBEAN SEA
GUERRERO
OAXACA
CHIAPAS
GULF OF TEHUANTEPEC
1. AGUASCALIENTES
2. QUERÉTARO
3. TLAXCALA
4. MÉXICO
5. DISTRITO FEDERAL (Federal District)
6. MORELOS
N
35°N
30°N
25°N
20°N
15°N
115°W
110°W
105°W
100°W
95°W
90°W
85°W

Climate, Vegetation, and Wildlife

Mexico's climate varies by region. Its mountains, deserts, and forests also support a variety of plants and animals.

A Tropical Area Mexico extends from the middle latitudes into the tropics. It has desert, steppe, savanna, and humid tropical climates. Most of northern Mexico is dry. There, Baja California's Sonoran Desert meets the Chihuahuan (chee-WAH-wahn) Desert of the plateau. Desert scrub vegetation and dry grasslands are common. Cougars, coyotes, and deer can be found in some areas of the north.

The forested plains along Mexico's southeastern coast are hot and humid much of the year. Summer is the rainy season. Forests cover about 20 percent of Mexico's land area. Tropical rain forests provide a home for anteaters, jaguars, monkeys, parrots, and other animals.

Many varieties of cactus thrive in the Sonoran Desert.

Interpreting the Visual Record Why do you think large trees are not found in the Sonoran Desert?

Nogales
United States
Mexico
Guatemala

Climate Variations In some areas changes in elevation cause climates to vary widely within a short distance. Many people have settled in the mild environment of the mountain valleys. The valleys along Mexico's southern coastal areas also have pleasant climates.

The areas of high elevation on the Mexican Plateau experience surprisingly cool temperatures. Freezing temperatures sometimes reach as far south as Mexico City.

✓ **READING CHECK:** *Places and Regions* What are Mexico's climate zones?

Our Amazing Planet

So much water has been pumped from under Mexico City that the ground is sinking, or subsiding. Parts of the central city have subsided about 25 feet (7.6 m) in the last 100 years. This has damaged buildings, pipes, sewers, and subway tunnels.

Resources

Petroleum is Mexico's most important energy resource. Oil reserves lie primarily under southern and Gulf coastal plains as well as offshore in the Gulf of Mexico. In 1997 Mexico had the world's eighth-largest crude oil reserves.

Mining is also important in Mexico. Some gold and silver mines begun centuries ago are still in operation. Fresnillo has been a silver-mining center since 1569. New mines have been developed in Mexico's northern and southern mountains. Silver is the most valuable part of Mexico's mining industry. In 1997 one silver mine in the state of Zacatecas produced 706 tons (641,037 kg) of silver. Mexico also produces large amounts of copper, gold, lead, and zinc.

Water is a limited resource in parts of Mexico. Water scarcity, particularly in the dry north, is a serious issue.

✓ **READING CHECK:** *Environment and Society* What problems might water scarcity cause for Mexican citizens?

go.hrw.com **Homework Practice Online**
Keyword: SJ3 HP13

Section 1 Review

Define and explain: sinkholes

Working with Sketch Maps On a map of Mexico that you draw or that your teacher provides, label the following: Gulf of Mexico, Baja California, Gulf of California, Río Bravo (Rio Grande), Mexican Plateau, Sierra Madre Oriental, Sierra Madre Occidental, Mount Orizaba, and Yucatán Peninsula. In a caption, describe the Yucatán.

Reading for the Main Idea

1. *Places and Regions* What are Mexico's major physical features?
2. *Places and Regions* What are the major climate zones of Mexico?

Critical Thinking

3. **Drawing Inferences and Conclusions** Based on physical features and climate, which areas of Mexico provide the best conditions for people to live?
4. **Drawing Inferences and Conclusions** How do you think Mexico's geography affects movement and communication between different parts of the country?

Organizing What You Know

5. **Summarizing** Copy the following graphic organizer. Use it to describe Mexico's physical geography.

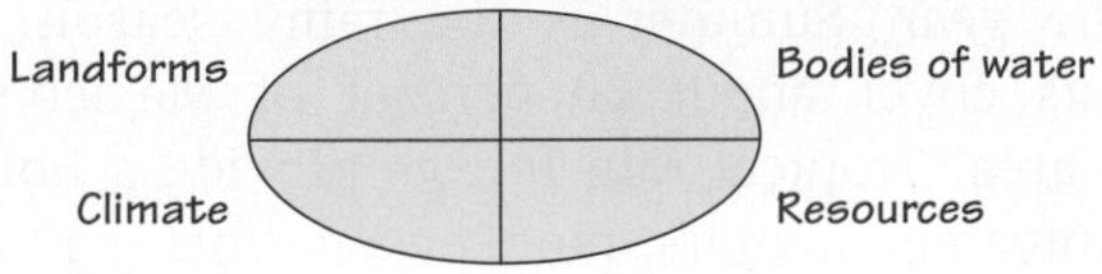

Landforms
Bodies of water
Climate
Resources

Section 2 History and Culture

Read to Discover

1. What early cultures developed in Mexico?
2. What was Mexico like under Spanish rule and after independence?
3. What are some important features of Mexican culture?

Define

chinampas
conquistadores
epidemic
empire
mestizos
mulattoes
missions
ejidos
haciendas

Why It Matters

There are many aspects of Spanish influence still found in present-day Mexico. Use CNNfyi.com or other **current events** sources to find information about Mexican history. Record your findings in your journal.

An Aztec serpent pendant

Early Cultures

Mesoamerica (*meso* means "in the middle") is the cultural area including Mexico and much of Central America. Many scientists think the first people to live in Mesoamerica arrived from the north about 12,000 years ago. By about 5,000 years ago, people in Mesoamerica were growing beans, peppers, and squash. They also domesticated an early form of corn. It eventually developed into the corn that we see today.

By about 1500 B.C. many people throughout the region were living in small farming villages. Along the humid southern coast of the Gulf of Mexico lived the Olmec people. The Olmec built temples, pyramids, and huge statues. They traded carved jade and obsidian, a volcanic stone, throughout eastern Mexico.

By about A.D. 200, other complex cultures were developing in what is now Mexico. Many of these civilizations had large city centers. Those centers had apartments, great avenues, open plazas, and pyramid-shaped temples. Some temple areas throughout Mesoamerica had stone ball courts. Players on those courts competed in a game somewhat like basketball. However, this ball game was not simply a sport. It had deep religious importance. Players who lost might be sacrificed to the gods.

Maya ruins include stone carvings and pyramid-type structures. Figures such as this Chac Mool are thought to represent the rain god.

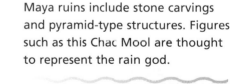

This copy of an original Aztec tax record shows items that were to be collected as tribute.

Interpreting the Visual Record What items besides tunics and headgear can you identify?

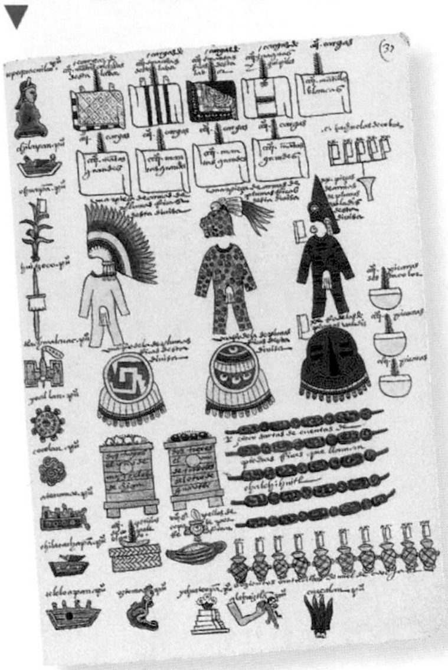

The Maya

Maya civilization developed in the tropical rain forest of southeastern Mexico, Guatemala, Belize, and Honduras. Maya city-states were at their peak between about A.D. 250 and 800. The Maya made accurate astronomical calculations and had a detailed calendar. Modern scholars can now read some Maya writing. This has helped us understand their civilization.

The Maya grew crops on terraced hillsides and on raised fields in swampy areas. They dug canals, piling the rich bottom mud onto the fields alongside the canals. This practice enriched the soil. Using this productive method of farming, the Maya supported an extremely dense population.

Sometime after A.D. 800, Maya civilization collapsed. The cities were abandoned. This decline may have been caused by famine, disease, warfare, or some combination of factors. However, the Maya did not die out. Millions of people of Maya descent still live in Mexico and Central America today.

The Aztec

A people called the Aztec began moving into central Mexico from the north about A.D. 1200. They later established their capital on an island in a lake in the Valley of Mexico. Known as Tenochtitlán (tay-nawch-teet-LAHN), this capital grew into a splendid city. Its population in 1519 is estimated to have been at least 200,000. It was one of the largest cities in the world at that time. The Aztec conquered other Indian peoples around them. They forced these peoples to pay taxes and provide captives for sacrifice to Aztec gods.

The Aztec practiced a version of raised-field agriculture in the swampy lakes of central Mexico. The Aztec called these raised fields ***chinampas*** (chuh-NAM-puhs). There they grew the corn, beans, and peppers that most people ate. Only rich people in this society ate meat. On special occasions common people sometimes ate dog meat. The upper classes also drank chocolate.

✓ **READING CHECK:** What were the main features of Mexico's early civilizations?

The Maya ruins of Tulum, an ancient Maya ceremonial and religious center, lie on the Caribbean coast.

Interpreting the Visual Record Why do you think the Maya built a large wall around this city?

United States
Mexico
Tulum National Park
Guatemala

CONNECTING TO *History*

TENOCHTITLÁN

Tenochtitlán—now Mexico City—was founded by the Aztec in the early 1300s. According to their legends, they saw an eagle sitting atop a cactus on a swampy island in Lake Texcoco. The eagle held a snake in its mouth. A prophecy had instructed them to build a city where they saw such an eagle.

Within 200 years this village had become an imperial capital and the largest city in the Americas. It was a city of pyramids, palaces, markets, and gardens. Canals and streets ran through the city. Stone causeways connected the island to the mainland.

Bernal Díaz, a Spanish soldier, described his first view of the Aztec capital in 1519.

"When we saw so many cities and villages built in the water and other great towns on dry land and that straight and level Causeway going towards [Tenochtitlán], we were amazed and said that it was like the enchantments they tell of in the legend of Amadis, on account of the great towers and temples and buildings rising from the water, and all built of masonry. And some of our soldiers asked whether the things that we saw were not a dream."

The Spaniards went on to conquer the Aztec and destroy Tenochtitlán. On the ruins they built Mexico City. They also drained Lake Texcoco to allow the city to expand.

Understanding What You Read

1. Where and when was Tenochtitlán first built?
2. What was the Spaniards' reaction to Tenochtitlán?

A sketch map of the Aztec capital of Tenochtitlán

Colonial Mexico and Independence

Spanish Conquest Hernán Cortés, a Spanish soldier, arrived in Mexico in 1519 with about 600 men. These **conquistadores** (kahn-kees-tuh-DAWR-ez), or conquerors, had both muskets and horses. These were unknown in the Americas at that time. However, the most important factor in the conquest was disease. The native people of the Americas had no resistance to European diseases. The first **epidemic**, or widespread outbreak, of smallpox struck central Mexico in 1520. The death toll from disease greatly weakened the power of the Aztec. In 1521 Cortés completed his conquest of the Aztec and the other American Indian peoples of southern Mexico. They named the territory New Spain.

Colonial Mexico During this period, Spain ruled an **empire**. An empire is a system in which a central power controls a number of

BUILD on WHAT You Know

Do you remember what you learned about population density? See Chapter 5 to review.

Our Amazing Planet

Mexico City was 250 miles (400 km) away from the center of the 1985 earthquake on Mexico's Pacific coast. However, the city suffered heavy damage and thousands of deaths. The city sits on a former lake bed. The loose soil under the city made the damage worse.

Mexico's Culture Regions

Mexico's 31 states and one federal district can be grouped into six culture regions. These regions are highly diverse in their resources, climate, population, and other features.

Greater Mexico City Greater Mexico City is Mexico's most developed and crowded region. This area includes Mexico City and about 50 smaller cities. More than 20 million people live there. It is one of the most heavily populated urban areas in the world.

Mexico City is also one of the world's most polluted cities. Thousands of factories and millions of automobiles release exhaust and other pollutants into the air. Surrounding mountains trap the resulting **smog**—a mixture of smoke, chemicals, and fog. Smog can cause health problems like eye irritation and breathing difficulties.

Wealth and poverty exist side by side in Mexico City. The city has very poor slums. It also has busy highways, modern office buildings, high-rise apartments, museums, universities, and old colonial cathedrals.

Central Interior Mexico's central interior region lies north of the capital. It extends toward both coasts. Many cities here began as mining or ranching centers during the colonial period. Small towns with a central square and a colonial-style church are common.

The region has many fertile valleys and small family farms. In recent years the central interior has attracted new industries from overcrowded Mexico City. As a result, cities like Guadalajara are growing rapidly.

Oil Coast The forested coastal plains between Tampico and Campeche (kahm-PAY-chay) were once lightly settled. However, the population has grown as oil production in this region has increased. In addition, large forest areas are being cleared for farming and ranching.

United States
Mexico
Mexico City
Guatemala

Smog covers Mexico City. The city continues to work toward solutions to challenges facing it as one of the world's largest cities.

Interpreting the Visual Record What two words do you think the word *smog* comes from?

Southern Mexico Many people in southern Mexico speak Indian languages. They live in the country's poorest region. It has few cities and little industry. Subsistence farming is common. Poverty and corrupt local governments have led to unrest. In the 1990s people in the state of Chiapas staged an antigovernment uprising.

Northern Mexico Northern Mexico has become one of the country's most prosperous and modern areas. NAFTA has helped the region's economy grow. Monterrey and Tijuana are important cities here. Factories called ***maquiladoras*** (mah-kee-lah-DORH-ahs) are located along the northern border and are often foreign-owned.

American music, television, and other forms of entertainment are popular near the border. Many Mexicans cross the border to shop, work, or live in the United States. In recent decades, the U.S. government has increased its efforts to stop illegal immigration across the border.

The Yucatán Most of the Yucatán Peninsula is sparsely populated. Mérida is this region's major city. As in other parts of Mexico, some farmers in the region practice **slash-and-burn agriculture**, in which an area of forest is burned to clear it for planting. The ashes enrich the soil. After a few years of planting crops, the soil is exhausted. The farmer then moves on to a new area of forest. Farmers can return to previously farmed areas years later.

Maya ruins and sunny beaches have made tourism a major industry in this area. The popular resort of Cancún and the island of Cozumel are located here.

Celebrations, such as Danza de Los Viejitos—Dance of the Old Men—are popular throughout Mexico.

✓ READING CHECK: *Human Systems* What are the six culture regions of Mexico?

go.hrw.com Homework Practice Online
Keyword: SJ3 HP13

Section 3 Review

Define and explain: inflation, cash crops, smog, *maquiladoras*, slash-and-burn agriculture

Working with Sketch Maps On the map you created in Section 2, label Tijuana, Ciudad Juárez, Acapulco, Mazatlán, Cancún, Mexico City, Guadalajara, Tampico, Campeche, and Monterrey. Which city is the national capital? Which cities are located at or near sea level? Which are located at higher elevations?

Reading for the Main Idea

1. *Human Systems* What are three economic problems faced by Mexico in recent decades?
2. *Human Systems* What are Mexico's six culture regions? Describe a feature of each.

Critical Thinking

3. Analyzing Information How have changes in the price of oil affected Mexico?
4. Drawing Inferences and Conclusions Why would farmers in Mexico grow only cash crops?

Organizing What You Know

5. Categorizing Copy the following graphic organizer. Use it to list key facts about the population and economy of each culture region in Mexico.

	Population	Economy
Greater Mexico City		
Central interior		
Oil coast		
Southern Mexico		
Northern Mexico		
Yucatán		

Section 2 Central America

Read to Discover

1. What was Central America's early history like?
2. How is the region's history reflected in its people today?
3. What are the countries of Central America like today?

Define

cacao
dictators
cardamom
civil war
ecotourism

Locate

Guatemala City
Lake Nicaragua
San José
Panama City
Panama Canal

WHY IT MATTERS

Civil wars caused great damage and disruption in Central America during the 1980s and early 1990s. Use CNNfyi.com or other **current events** sources to find out about conditions in Central American countries today. Record your findings in your journal.

Ancient jaguar pendant from Panama

Mexico
Belize
Xunantunich
Guatemala
Honduras

Maya ruins can be found here in Belize and in other parts of Central America and Mexico.

History

More than 35 million people live in the countries of Central America. These countries have a shared history.

Early History The early peoples of Central America developed different cultures and societies. The Maya, for example, built large cities with pyramids and temples. People of Maya descent still live in Guatemala and parts of Mexico. Many of their ancient customs and traditions still influence modern life.

In the early 1500s European countries began establishing colonies in the region. Most of Central America came under the control of Spain. In the 1600s the British established the colony of British Honduras, which is now Belize. The British also occupied the Caribbean coast of Nicaragua.

European colonists established large plantations. They grew crops like tobacco and sugarcane. They forced the Central American Indians to work on the plantations. Some Indians were sent to work in gold mines elsewhere in the Americas. In addition, many Africans were brought to the region as slaves.

Independence Costa Rica, El Salvador, Guatemala, Honduras, and Nicaragua declared independence from Spain in 1821. They formed the United Provinces of Central America, but separated from each other in 1838–1839. Panama, once part of Colombia, became independent in 1903. The British left Nicaragua in the late 1800s. British Honduras gained independence as Belize in 1981.

✓ READING CHECK: *Human Systems* What role did Europeans play in the region's history?

Our Amazing Planet

Lake Nicaragua was probably once part of an ocean bay. It is a freshwater lake, but it also has some oceanic animal life. This animal life includes the Lake Nicaragua shark. It grows to a length of about 8 to 10 feet (2.4 to 3 m).

Culture

Central America's colonial history is reflected in its culture today. In what ways do you think this is true?

People, Languages, and Religion The region's largest ethnic group is mestizo. Mestizos are people of mixed European and Indian ancestry. People of African ancestry make up a significant minority. Various Indian peoples also live in the region.

Spanish is the official language in most countries. However, many people speak Indian languages. In the former British colony of Belize, English is the official language.

Many Central Americans practice religions brought to the region by Europeans. Most are Roman Catholics. Spanish missionaries converted many Indians to Catholicism. However, Indian religions have influenced Catholicism in the region. Protestant Christians are a large minority in some countries, particularly Belize.

Guatemalans celebrate the Christian holiday *Semana Santa*, or Holy Week. The street is covered with colored sand and flowers.

Interpreting the Visual Record How important do Christian holidays appear to be in the region?

Mexico
Belize
Guatemala
Antigua Guatemala
Honduras

Caribbean Islands

Country	Population/ Growth Rate	Life Expectancy	Literacy Rate	Per Capita GDP
Antigua and Barbuda	66,970 0.7%	69, male 73, female	89%	$8,200
Bahamas	297,852 .93%	67, male 74, female	98%	$15,000
Barbados	275,330 0.5%	71, male 76, female	97%	$14,500
Cuba	11,184,023 0.4%	74, male 79, female	96%	$1,700
Dominica	70,786 -.98%	71, male 77, female	94%	$4,000
Dominican Republic	8,581,447 1.6%	71, male 76, female	82%	$5,700
Grenada	89,227 -0.06%	63, male 66, female	98%	$4,400
Haiti	6,964,549 1.4%	47, male 51, female	45%	$1,800
Jamaica	2,665,636 0.5%	74, male 78, female	85%	$3,700
St. Kitts and Nevis	38,756 -0.11%	68, male 74, female	97%	$7,000
St. Lucia	158,178 1.23%	69, male 76, female	67%	$4,500
St. Vincent and the Grenadines	115,942 0.4%	71, male 74, female	96%	$2,800
Trinidad and Tobago	1,169,682 -0.51%	66, male 71, female	98%	$9,500
United States	281,421,906 0.9%	74, male 80, female	97%	$36,200

Sources: Central Intelligence Agency, *The World Factbook 2001;* U.S. Census Bureau

Interpreting the Chart Why might life expectancy be greater in some Caribbean island countries than in others?

Culture

Today, nearly every Caribbean island shows the signs of past colonialism and slavery. These signs can be seen in the region's culture.

People, Languages, and Religion

Most islanders are of African or European descent or are a mixture of the two. Much smaller numbers of Asians also live there. Chinese and other Asians came to work on the plantations after slavery ended in the region.

English, French, and mixtures of European and African languages are spoken on many islands. For example, Haitians speak French and Creole. Creole is a Haitian dialect of French. Spanish is spoken in Cuba, the Dominican Republic, Puerto Rico, and some small islands. Dutch is the main language on several territories of the Netherlands.

Another sign of the region's past are the religions practiced there. Protestant Christians are most numerous on islands that were British territories. Former French and Spanish territories have large numbers of Roman Catholics. On all the islands, some people practice a combination of Catholicism and traditional African religions. One of these religions is **Santería**. Santería began in Cuba and spread to nearby islands and parts of the United States. It has roots in West African religions and traditions.

Food, Festivals, and Music Caribbean cooking today relies on fresh fruits, vegetables, and fish or meat. Milk or preserved foods like cheese or pickled fish are seldom used. Cooking has been influenced by foods brought from Africa, Asia, and elsewhere. For example, the samosa—a spicy, deep-fried pastry—has its origins in India. Other popular foods include mangoes, rice, yams, and okra.

People on each Caribbean island celebrate a variety of holidays. One of the biggest and most widespread is Carnival. Carnival is a time of feasts and parties before the Christian season of Lent. It is celebrated with big parades and beautiful costumes.

The islands' musical styles are popular far beyond the Caribbean. Trinidad and Tobago is the home of steel-drum and **calypso** music. Jamaica is famous as the birthplace of **reggae** music. **Merengue** is the national music and dance of the Dominican Republic.

Caribbean musical styles have many fans in the United States. However, the United States has influenced Caribbean culture as well. For example, baseball has become a popular sport in the region. It is particularly popular in the Dominican Republic and Cuba. A number of successful professional baseball players in the United States come from Caribbean countries.

✓ **READING CHECK:** *Human Systems* How do the cultures of the Caribbean islands reflect historical events?

The Caribbean Islands Today

Now we will look at the largest island countries. We also will examine the island territory of Puerto Rico.

Cuba Cuba is the largest and the most populous country in the Caribbean. It is about the size of Tennessee but has more than twice the population. It is located just 90 miles (145 km) south of Florida. Havana, the capital, is the country's largest and most important city.

Cuba has had a Communist government since Fidel Castro seized power in 1959. Cuba has supported Communist **guerrilla** movements trying to overthrow other governments. A guerrilla takes part in irregular warfare, such as raids.

Many Cubans who oppose Castro have become **refugees** in the United States. A refugee is someone who flees to another country, usually for economic or political reasons. Many Cuban refugees and their families have become U.S. citizens. Most live in Florida.

The U.S. government has banned trade with Cuba. It also has restricted travel by U.S. citizens to the island since the 1960s. For years Cuba received economic aid and energy supplies from the Soviet Union. The collapse of the Soviet Union in the early 1990s has hurt Cuba's economy.

Today, private businesses remain limited in Cuba. Most farmland is organized into **cooperatives** and government-owned sugarcane

Puerto Rico
Port of Spain
Trinidad
Venezuela

A girl joins the Carnival celebration in Trinidad and Tobago.

Interpreting the Visual Record What does the elaborate costume imply about the popularity of Carnival?

A worker cuts sugarcane in central Cuba. Sugarcane is Cuba's most important cash crop.

Cuba
Jamaica

plantations. A cooperative is an organization owned by its members and operated for their mutual benefit.

Sugarcane remains Cuba's most important crop and export. Tourism has also become an important part of the economy. There has been debate in the United States over ending the ban on trade and travel to Cuba.

Haiti Haiti occupies the mountainous western third of the island of Hispaniola. It is the poorest country in the Americas. It is also one of the most densely populated. Its people have suffered under many corrupt governments during the last two centuries. Many Haitian refugees have come to the United States to escape poverty and political violence.

Port-au-Prince (pohr-toh-PRINS) is the national capital and center of industry. Coffee and sugarcane are two of the country's most important crops. Most Haitians farm small plots. Many grow **plantains**. Plantains are a type of banana used in cooking.

Dominican Republic The Dominican Republic occupies the eastern part of Hispaniola. It is a former Spanish colony. The capital is Santo Domingo. Santo Domingo was the first permanent European settlement in the Western Hemisphere.

Other Island Countries

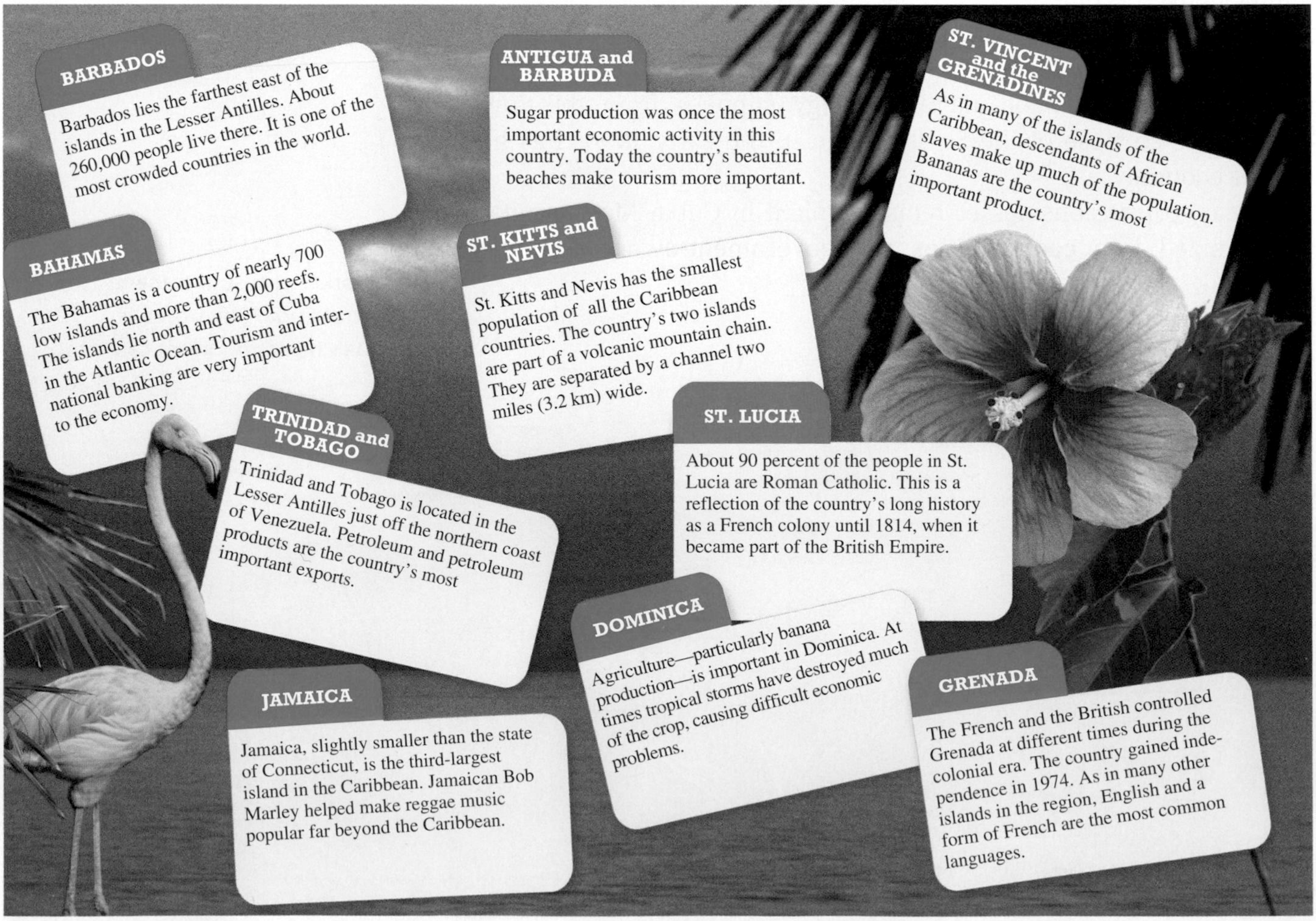
BARBADOS
Barbados lies the farthest east of the islands in the Lesser Antilles. About 260,000 people live there. It is one of the most crowded countries in the world.
ANTIGUA and BARBUDA
Sugar production was once the most important economic activity in this country. Today the country's beautiful beaches make tourism more important.
ST. VINCENT and the GRENADINES
As in many of the islands of the Caribbean, descendants of African slaves make up much of the population. Bananas are the country's most important product.
BAHAMAS
The Bahamas is a country of nearly 700 low islands and more than 2,000 reefs. The islands lie north and east of Cuba in the Atlantic Ocean. Tourism and international banking are very important to the economy.
ST. KITTS and NEVIS
St. Kitts and Nevis has the smallest population of all the Caribbean countries. The country's two islands are part of a volcanic mountain chain. They are separated by a channel two miles (3.2 km) wide.
TRINIDAD and TOBAGO
Trinidad and Tobago is located in the Lesser Antilles just off the northern coast of Venezuela. Petroleum and petroleum products are the country's most important exports.
ST. LUCIA
About 90 percent of the people in St. Lucia are Roman Catholic. This is a reflection of the country's long history as a French colony until 1814, when it became part of the British Empire.
DOMINICA
Agriculture—particularly banana production—is important in Dominica. At times tropical storms have destroyed much of the crop, causing difficult economic problems.
JAMAICA
Jamaica, slightly smaller than the state of Connecticut, is the third-largest island in the Caribbean. Jamaican Bob Marley helped make reggae music popular far beyond the Caribbean.
GRENADA
The French and the British controlled Grenada at different times during the colonial era. The country gained independence in 1974. As in many other islands in the region, English and a form of French are the most common languages.

The Dominican Republic is not a rich country. However, its economy, education, health care, and housing are more developed than Haiti's. Agriculture and tourism are important parts of the Dominican Republic's economy.

Puerto Rico Puerto Rico is the easternmost of the Greater Antilles. Once a Spanish colony, today it is a U.S. **commonwealth**. A commonwealth is a self-governing territory associated with another country. Puerto Ricans are U.S. citizens. However, they have no voting representation in the U.S. Congress.

Unemployment is higher and wages are lower in Puerto Rico than in the United States. Still, American aid and investment have helped make the economy of Puerto Rico more developed than those of other Caribbean islands. Puerto Ricans continue to debate whether their island should remain a commonwealth. Some want it to become an American state or an independent country.

Cuba
Ocho Rios
Jamaica

▲ Ocho Rios, Jamaica, and other beautiful Caribbean resorts and beaches attract many tourists.

Interpreting the Visual Record **Why do you think cruise ships like the one in the photo are a popular way to travel in the Caribbean?**

Other Islands Jamaica, in the Greater Antilles, is the largest of the remaining Caribbean countries. The smallest country is St. Kitts and Nevis in the Lesser Antilles. The smallest U.S. state, Rhode Island, is nearly 12 times larger! For more about other Caribbean countries and the Bahamas, see the Other Island Countries illustration.

A number of Caribbean and nearby islands are territories of other countries. These territories include the U.S. and British Virgin Islands. The Netherlands and France also have Caribbean territories. Bermuda, an Atlantic island northwest of the Caribbean, is a British territory.

✓ **READING CHECK:** *Human Systems* How are Puerto Rican citizens' political rights different from those of other U.S. citizens?

go.hrw.com Homework Practice Online
Keyword: SJ3 HP14

Section 3 Review

Define and explain: Santería, calypso, reggae, merengue, guerrilla, refugees, cooperatives, plantains, commonwealth

Working with Sketch Maps On the map you created in Section 2, label the Caribbean countries, Havana, Port-au-Prince, and Santo Domingo.

Reading for the Main Idea

1. *Human Systems* When did European powers establish colonies in the Caribbean islands?
2. *Human Systems* What ethnic groups make up the region's population today?
3. *Human Systems* Why have Cubans and Haitians come to the United States as refugees?

Critical Thinking

4. **Comparing/Contrasting** What do the histories of Caribbean countries have in common with the history of the United States? How are they different?

Organizing What You Know

5. **Sequencing** Copy the following graphic organizer. Use it to show important events and periods in the history of the Caribbean islands since 1492.

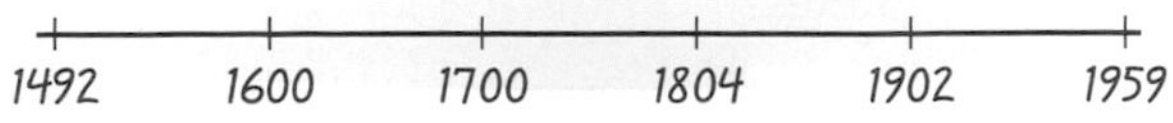

1492
1600
1700
1804
1902
1959

Section 2 Colombia

Read to Discover

1. What are the main periods of Colombia's history?
2. What is Colombia like today?

Define

El Dorado
cassava

Locate

Colombia
Bogotá
Cauca River
Magdalena River

WHY IT MATTERS

Colombia remains a country troubled by violence and conflict. Use CNNfyi.com or other **current events** sources to learn more about problems in Colombia. Record your findings in your journal.

Pre-Columbian gold armor

Early History

Advanced cultures have lived in Colombia for centuries. Some giant mounds of earth, stone statues, and tombs found in Colombia are more than 1,500 years old.

The Chibcha In western Colombia, the Chibcha people had a well-developed civilization. The Chibcha practiced pottery making, weaving, and metalworking. Their gold objects were among the finest in ancient America.

The Chibcha had an interesting custom. New rulers were covered with gold dust and then taken to a lake to wash the gold off. Gold and emerald objects were thrown into the water as the new ruler washed. This custom inspired the legend of **El Dorado** (el duh-RAH-doh), or "the Golden One." The old legend of El Dorado describes a marvelous, rich land.

Spanish Conquest Spanish explorers arrived on the Caribbean coast of South America about 1500. They were helping to expand Spain's new empire. The Spanish conquered the Chibcha and seized much of their treasure. Spaniards and their descendants set up large estates. Powerful Spanish landlords forced South American Indians and enslaved Africans to work the land.

Giant stone figures near the headwaters of the Magdalena River are part of the San Agustín culture.

Interpreting the Visual Record How might the location of these figures in a remote area have helped to preserve them?

Venezuela
Colombia
Magdalena River
Brazil
Peru

Independence In the late 1700s people in Central and South America began struggling for independence from Spain. After independence was achieved, the republic of Gran Colombia was created. It included Colombia, Ecuador, Panama, and Venezuela. In 1830 the republic dissolved, and New Granada, now Colombia, was created. Present-day Panama was once part of New Granada.

After independence, debate raged in Colombia. People argued over how much power the central government and the Roman Catholic Church should have. Part of the problem had to do with the country's rugged geography. The different regions of Colombia had little contact with each other. They developed separate economies and identities. Uniting these different groups into one country was hard. Outbreaks of violence throughout the 1800s and 1900s killed thousands of people.

✓ **READING CHECK:** *Environment and Society* What geographic factors influenced Colombia's ability to control its territory?

Colombia

Country	Population/ Growth Rate	Life Expectancy	Literacy Rate	Per Capita GDP
Colombia	40,349,388 1.6%	67, male 75, female	91%	$6,200
United States	281,421,906 0.9%	74, male 80, female	97%	$36,200

Sources: Central Intelligence Agency, *The World Factbook 2001;* U.S. Census Bureau

Interpreting the Chart How much larger is the U.S. population than that of Colombia?

Colombia Today

Colombia is Caribbean South America's most populous country. The national capital is Bogotá, a city located high in the eastern Andes. Most Colombians live in the fertile valleys and basins among the mountain ranges because those areas are moderate in climate and good for farming. Rivers, such as the Cauca and Magdalena, flow down from the Andes to the Caribbean. They help connect settlements between the mountains and the coast. Cattle ranches are common in the Llanos. Few people live in the tropical rain forest regions in the south.

The guard tower of an old Spanish fort stands in contrast with the modern buildings of Cartagena, Colombia.

Interpreting the Visual Record Why might the Spanish have chosen this location for a fort?

Cartagena
Venezuela
Colombia
Brazil
Peru

Connecting to Science

Fighting Malaria

Botanical print of a gray cinchona

Malaria is a disease usually transmitted by mosquitoes. It is common in the tropics. For centuries malaria was also widespread in Europe, but Europeans had no remedy. Native peoples in the South American rain forest did have a treatment, though. They used the powdered bark of the cinchona tree, which contains the drug quinine. The history of quinine and the struggle to obtain it is a story of great adventure.

The Spanish first discovered cinchona in the 1500s, when they conquered Peru. Shipments of the bark were soon arriving in Europe, where quinine was produced. Later, some countries tried to control the supply of bark. However, the Dutch smuggled cinchona seeds out of South America. They set up their own plantations in the East Indies. Before long, the Netherlands controlled most of the world's supply of quinine.

During World War II, the Axis Powers seized the Netherlands. As a result, the Allies lost their source of quinine. A crisis was prevented when some quinine was smuggled out of Germany and sold on the black market. Since then, scientists have developed synthetic drugs for the treatment of malaria. However, quinine remains an important drug. It is used to treat heart disease and is a key ingredient in tonic water.

Understanding What You Read

1. How did native peoples' use of the cinchona tree change the world?
2. How did political decisions during World War II affect the use of quinine?

BUILD on WHAT You Know

Do you remember what you learned about renewable and nonrenewable resources? See Chapter 4 to review.

Economy Colombia's economy relies on several valuable resources. Rich soil produces world-famous Colombian coffee. Only Brazil produces more coffee. Other major export crops include bananas, corn, rice, and sugarcane. **Cassava** (kuh-SAH-vuh), a tropical plant with starchy roots, is an important food crop. Colombian farms also produce flowers that are exported around the world. In fact, only the Netherlands exports more cut flowers than Colombia.

In recent years oil has become Colombia's leading export. Oil is found mainly in eastern Colombia. Other natural resources include iron ore, gold, coal, and tin. Most of the world's emeralds also come from Colombia.

Even with these rich resources, many Colombians have low incomes. Colombia faces the same types of problems as other countries in Central and South America. For example, urban poverty and rapid population growth remain a challenge in Colombia.

Venezuela
Colombia
Neiva
Peru
Brazil

Folk dancers get ready to perform in Neiva, Colombia.

Interpreting the Visual Record What aspects of culture can you see in this photograph?

Cultural Life The physical geography of Colombia has isolated its regions from one another. This is one reason why the people of Colombia are often known by the area in which they live. African traditions have influenced the songs and dances of the Caribbean coast. Traditional music can be heard in some remote areas. In addition to music, many Colombians enjoy soccer. They also play a Chibcha sport called *tejo*, a type of ringtoss game. Roman Catholicism is the country's main religion.

Conflict is a serious problem in Colombia today. Border conflicts with Venezuela have gone on for many years. Many different groups have waged war with each other and with Colombia's government. These groups have controlled large areas of the country. Many farmers have been forced off of their land, and the economy has been damaged. Because of this instability, the future of Colombia is uncertain.

✓ **READING CHECK:** *Human Systems* How have historical events affected life in Colombia today?

Section 2 Review

go.hrw.com **Homework Practice Online**
Keyword: SJ3 HP15

Define and explain: El Dorado, cassava

Working with Sketch Maps On the map you created in Section 1, label Colombia, Bogotá, and the Cauca and Magdalena Rivers.

Reading for the Main Idea

1. *Human Systems* Why did Spanish explorers come to Colombia?
2. *Human Systems* What are some characteristics of Colombia's culture?

Critical Thinking

3. **Finding the Main Idea** How have Colombia's varied landscapes affected its history?
4. **Summarizing** How have conflicts in Colombia affected its economy?

Organizing What You Know

5. **Sequencing** Copy the following graphic organizer. Use it to describe Colombia's historical periods.

Early history	Spanish period	Independence	Colombia today

Section 3 Venezuela

Read to Discover

1. How did the Spanish contribute to Venezuela's history?
2. What are some characteristics of Venezuela's culture?

Define

indigo
caudillos
llaneros
pardos

Locate

Venezuela
Caracas
Lake Maracaibo

WHY IT MATTERS

Changing oil prices can have a dramatic effect on the Venezuelan economy. Use CNNfyi.com or other **current events** sources to find information about current oil prices. Record your findings in your journal.

Empanadas

History of Venezuela

There were many small tribes of South American Indians living in Venezuela before the Spanish arrived. Most were led by chiefs and survived by a combination of hunting and farming.

Indigo was an important crop in Venezuela during colonial times.

Indigo

Spanish Conquest Christopher Columbus landed on the Venezuelan coast in 1498. By the early 1500s the Spanish were exploring the area further. They forced South American Indians to dive for pearls and pan for gold. There was little gold, however. The settlers had to turn to agriculture. They grew **indigo** (IN-di-goh) and other crops. Indigo is a plant used to make a deep blue dye. South American Indians were forced to work the fields. When many of them died, plantation owners brought in enslaved Africans to take their place. Some slaves were able to escape. They settled in remote areas and governed themselves.

Margarita Island in Venezuela was the site of a Spanish fort in the 1500s.

Margarita Island
Venezuela
Colombia
Brazil
Peru

Independence Partly because the colony was so poor, some people in Venezuela revolted against Spain. Simón Bolívar led the fight against the Spanish armies. Bolívar is considered a hero in many South American countries because he led wars of independence throughout the region. The struggle for independence finally ended in 1830, when Venezuela became an independent country.

Throughout the 1800s Venezuelans suffered from dictatorships and civil wars. The country's military leaders were called **caudillos** (kow-THEE-yohs). After oil was discovered, some caudillos kept the country's oil money for themselves. In 1958 the last dictator was forced out of power.

Our Amazing Planet

Venezuela is home to the anaconda—the longest snake in the world. Adult anacondas are more than 15 feet (4.6 m) long.

Oil Wealth By the 1970s Venezuela was earning huge sums of money from oil. This wealth allowed part of the population to buy luxuries. However, about 80 percent of the population still lived in poverty. Many of these people moved to the cities to find work. Some settled on the outskirts in shacks that had no running water, sewers, or electricity.

Venezuela's wealth drew many immigrants from Europe and from other South American countries. However, in the 1980s oil prices dropped sharply. Because Venezuela relied on oil for most of its income, the country suffered when prices decreased.

✓ **READING CHECK:** *Human Systems* How did the Spanish contribute to Venezuela's history?

Venezuela Today

Most Venezuelans live along the Caribbean coast and in the valleys of the nearby mountains. About 85 percent live in cities and towns. Caracas (kuh-RAHK-uhs), the capital, is the center of Venezuelan culture. It is a large city with a modern subway system, busy expressways, and tall office buildings. However, slums circle the city. Poverty in rural areas is also widespread. Still, Venezuela is one of South America's wealthiest countries. It is developing rapidly.

Venezuela

Country	Population/ Growth Rate	Life Expectancy	Literacy Rate	Per Capita GDP
Venezuela	23,916,810 1.6%	70, male 77, female	91%	$6,200
United States	281,421,906 0.9%	74, male 80, female	97%	$36,200

Sources: Central Intelligence Agency, *The World Factbook 2001;* U.S. Census Bureau

Interpreting the Chart What is the average life expectancy for someone from Venezuela?

Economy Venezuela's economy is based on oil production. Lake Maracaibo (mah-rah-KY-boh) is a bay of the Caribbean Sea. The rocks under the lake are particularly rich in oil. However, the country is trying to reduce its dependence on oil income.

The Guiana Highlands in the southeast are rich in other minerals, such as iron ore for making steel. Dams on tributaries of the Orinoco River produce hydroelectricity.

Llaneros herd cattle on the large ranches of the Llanos.

Interpreting the Visual Record How do these *llaneros* look similar to cowboys in the United States?

Agriculture Northern Venezuela has small family farms and large commercial farms. ***Llaneros*** (lah-NE-rohs)—cowboys of the Venezuelan Llanos—herd cattle on the many ranches in this region. Few people live in the Guiana Highlands. Some small communities of South American Indians practice traditional slash-and-burn agriculture there.

Cultural Life More than two thirds of Venezuela's population are ***pardos***. They are people of mixed African, European, and South American Indian ancestry. Native groups make up only about 2 percent of the population. They speak more than 25 different languages. Spanish is the official language. Most of the people are Roman Catholics. Some Venezuelan Indians follow the religious practices of their ancestors.

The *joropo,* a lively foot-stomping couples' dance, is Venezuela's national dance. *Toros coleados* is a local sport. In this rodeo event, the contestant pulls a bull down by grabbing its tail. Baseball and soccer are also popular in Venezuela.

✓ **READING CHECK:** *Human Systems* What are some aspects of Venezuela's culture?

go.hrw.com Homework Practice Online
Keyword: SJ3 HP15

Section 3 Review

Define and explain: indigo, caudillos, *llaneros, pardos*

Working with Sketch Maps On the map you created in Section 2, label Venezuela, Caracas, and Lake Maracaibo. How does elevation affect the climate of Caracas?

Reading for the Main Idea

1. *Environment and Society* Why did Spanish settlers in Venezuela have to turn to agriculture?
2. *Human Systems* Who led Venezuela's revolt against Spain?

Critical Thinking

3. **Drawing Inferences and Conclusions** Why might Venezuela try to reduce its dependence on oil exports?
4. **Comparing** Compare the population densities of the Caribbean coast and the Guiana Highlands.

Organizing What You Know

5. **Analyzing Information** Copy the following graphic organizer. Use it to explain how oil is related to the history, urban poverty, and economy of Venezuela.

Oil	History	
	Urban poverty	
	Economy	

Section 4 The Guianas

Read to Discover

1. Which countries influenced the early history of the Guianas?
2. How are Guyana, Suriname, and French Guiana similar today?

Define

indentured servants
pidgin languages

Locate

Guyana
Suriname
French Guiana
Georgetown
Paramaribo
Devil's Island
Kourou
Cayenne

WHY IT MATTERS

French Guiana is the site of a modern space center. Use CNNfyi.com or other **current events** sources to find space-related sites that talk about the European Space Agency. Record your findings in your journal.

Decorated Djuka canoe paddle

Early History of the Guianas

Dense tropical rain forests cover much of the region east of Venezuela. Rugged highlands lie to the south. The physical environment of this region kept it somewhat isolated from the rest of South America. Thus, the three countries known as the Guianas (gee-AH-nuhz) have a history quite different from the rest of the continent.

European Settlement Spain was the first European country to claim the Guianas. The Spanish eventually lost the region to settlers from Great Britain, France, and the Netherlands. Sometimes a war fought in Europe determined which country held this corner of South America. The Europeans established coffee, tobacco, and cotton plantations. They brought Africans to work as slaves on these plantations. Sugarcane later became the main crop.

Asian Workers European countries made slavery illegal in the mid-1800s. Colonists in the Guianas needed a new source of labor for their plantations. They brought **indentured servants** from India, China, and Southeast Asia. Indentured servants agree to work for a certain period of time, often in exchange for travel expenses. As these people worked together, they developed **pidgin languages**. Pidgin languages are simple so that people who speak different languages can understand each other.

✓ **READING CHECK:** *Human Systems* What countries influenced the early history of the Guianas?

This Hindu temple is located in Cayenne, French Guiana.

Interpreting the Visual Record
Which architectural features resemble other buildings you have seen? Which features are different?

Guyana
Suriname
Cayenne
French Guiana
Brazil

The Guianas

Country	Population/ Growth Rate	Life Expectancy	Literacy Rate	Per Capita GDP
French Guiana	177,562 / 2.7%	73, male 80, female	83%	$6,000
Guyana	697,181 / .07%	61, male 66, female	98%	$4,800
Suriname	433,998 / 0.6%	69, male 74, female	93%	$3,400
United States	281,421,906 / 0.9%	74, male 80, female	97%	$36,200

Sources: Central Intelligence Agency, *The World Factbook 2001;* U.S. Census Bureau

Interpreting the Chart Why might the populations of Guyana and Suriname be growing slowly?

The Guianas Today

The area formerly known as British Guiana gained its independence in 1966 and became Guyana. In 1975 Dutch Guiana broke away from the Netherlands to become Suriname. French Guiana remains a part of France.

Guyana *Guyana* (gy-AH-nuh) is a South American Indian word that means "land of waters." Nearly all of Guyana's agricultural lands are located along the narrow coastal plains. Guyana's most important agricultural products are rice and sugar. The country's major mineral resource is bauxite.

Guyana has a diverse population. About half of its people are of South Asian descent. Most of these people farm small plots of land or run small businesses. About one third of the population is descended from African slaves. These people control most of the large businesses and hold most of the government positions. More than one third of the country's population lives in Georgetown, the capital.

Suriname The resources and economy of Suriname (soohr-uh-NAH-muh) are similar to those of Guyana. Many farms in Suriname are found in coastal areas. Aluminum is a major export. Interior forests also supply lumber for export to other countries.

Like Guyana, Suriname has a diverse population. There are South Asians, Africans, Chinese, Indonesians, and people of mixed heritage. Muslim, Hindu, Roman Catholic, and Protestant houses of worship line the streets of the national capital, Paramaribo (pah-rah-MAH-ree-boh). Nearly half of the country's people live there.

Our Amazing Planet

The goliath bird-eating spider of northeastern South America is the largest spider in the world. The record holder had a leg span more than 11 inches (28 cm) across. That is as big as a dinner plate!

Bigi Poika
Guyana
French Guiana
Suriname
Brazil

A woman cooks cassava cakes in Bigi Poika, Suriname.

Guyana
Cayenne
Suriname
French Guiana
Brazil

Carnival is a time for celebration in Cayenne, French Guiana.

French Guiana French Guiana (gee-A-nuh) has a status in France similar to that of a state in the United States. It sends representatives to the French Parliament in Paris. France used to send some of its criminals to Devil's Island. This island was a prison colony just off French Guiana's coast. Prisoners there suffered terribly from overwork. Devil's Island was closed in the early 1950s.

Today, forestry and shrimp fishing are the most important economic activities. Agriculture is limited to the coastal areas. The people of French Guiana depend heavily on imports for their food and energy. France developed the town of Kourou (koo-ROO) into a space center. The European Space Agency launches satellites from this town.

More than 160,000 people live in French Guiana, mostly in coastal areas. About two thirds of the people are descended from Africans. Other groups include Europeans, Asians, and South American Indians. The national capital is Cayenne (keye-EN).

✓ **READING CHECK:** *Human Systems* How is French Guiana different from Guyana and Suriname?

go.hrw.com **Homework Practice Online**
Keyword: SJ3 HP15

Section 4 Review

Define and explain: indentured servants, pidgin languages

Working with Sketch Maps On the map you created in Section 3, label Guyana, Suriname, French Guiana, Georgetown, Paramaribo, Devil's Island, Kourou, and Cayenne.

Reading for the Main Idea

1. *Environment and Society* What crops did early settlers raise in the Guianas?
2. *Human Systems* Why did colonists in the Guianas bring indentured servants from Asia?

Critical Thinking

3. **Drawing Inferences and Conclusions** Why might the people of French Guiana prefer to remain a part of France?
4. **Drawing Inferences and Conclusions** Why do you think few people live in the interior of the Guianas?

Organizing What You Know

5. **Categorizing** Copy the following graphic organizer. Use it to describe the Guianas. Fill in the ovals with features of Guyana, Suriname, and French Guiana. In the center, list features they have in common.

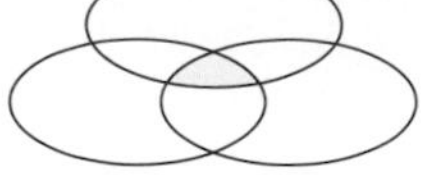

CHAPTER 15

Reviewing What You Know

Building Vocabulary

On a separate sheet of paper, write sentences to define each of the following

1. cordillera
2. *tepuís*
3. Llanos
4. El Dorado
5. cassava
6. indigo
7. caudillos
8. *llaneros*
9. *pardos*
10. indentured servants
11. pidgin languages

Reviewing the Main Ideas

1. *Places and Regions* What are the five common elevation zones in the Andes region?
2. *Places and Regions* What are three resources found in Caribbean South America?
3. *Environment and Society* How did geography affect political upheavals throughout the history of Colombia?
4. *Human Systems* Why did Venezuela revolt against Spanish colonial rule?
5. *Human Systems* How does the political status of French Guiana differ from that of Guyana and Suriname?

Understanding Environment and Society

Resource Use

Venezuela and Colombia both depend on income from oil exports. Create a presentation in which you use a map, graph, chart, model, or database showing the problems this could cause. You may want to think about the following:

- Why it is risky for a country to rely heavily on a single industry.
- How a country might diversify its export products.

Thinking Critically

1. **Finding the Main Idea** Why is the Orinoco River important to Caribbean South America?
2. **Finding the Main Idea** How might rapid population growth contribute to poverty in the region?
3. **Analyzing Information** Why is Roman Catholicism the main religion in Caribbean South America?
4. **Drawing Inferences and Conclusions** Why do you think most Venezuelans live along the Caribbean coast and in the valleys of the nearby mountains?
5. **Drawing Inferences and Conclusions** How are pidgin languages in the Guianas an example of cultural cooperation?

Building Social Studies Skills

Map Activity

On a separate sheet of paper, match the letters on the map with their correct labels.

Andes
Guiana Highlands
Orinoco River
Magdalena River
Lake Maracaibo
Devil's Island
Llanos

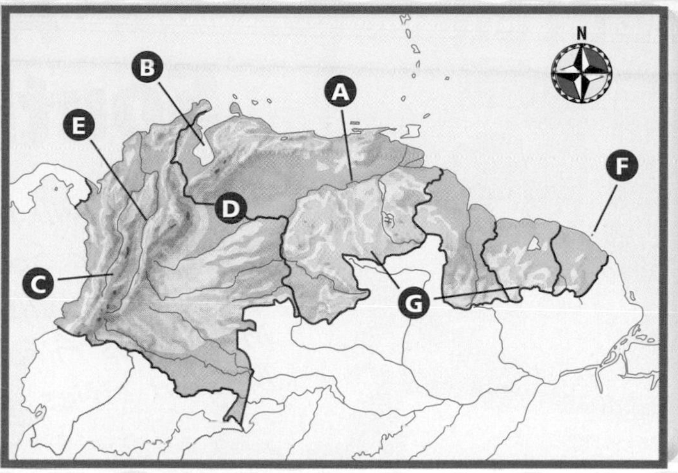

N
A
B
C
D
E
F
G

Mental Mapping Skills Activity

On a separate sheet of paper, draw a freehand map of Caribbean South America. Make a key for your map and label:

Atlantic Ocean
Caribbean Sea
Colombia
French Guiana
Guyana
Pacific Ocean
Suriname
Venezuela

Writing Activity

Imagine that you are a teacher living in Caracas, Venezuela. Use the chapter map to write a quiz, with answers, for students in your geography class on the geography, economy, and people of Venezuela. Be sure to use standard grammar, sentence structure, spelling, and punctuation.

Alternative Assessment

Portfolio Activity

Learning About Your Local Geography

Research Project Many South American Indians build homes using local resources. Draw illustrations of some of the oldest buildings in your community. Describe the materials used.

internet connect

Internet Activity: go.hrw.com
KEYWORD: SJ3 GT15

Choose a topic to explore about Caribbean South America:

- Trek through the Guiana Highlands.
- Search for the treasures of El Dorado.
- Ride with the *llaneros* of Venezuela.

CHAPTER 16

Atlantic South America

Now we will look at the four countries of Atlantic South America. Below, Mercedes tells us about growing up in Buenos Aires, one of the region's biggest cities.

¡Hola!
Me llamo Mercedes.
Soy de Argentina.

Hi! I am 13, and I live in Buenos Aires, the capital of Argentina. I live in an apartment with my mom, father, two brothers, and a sister.

I wake up at 6:30 A.M. to get ready for school. For breakfast I have a cup of tea and bread with butter and *dulce de leche* (a caramel spread). It is delicious!

In school I take 12 different classes in one year. They include math, Spanish, art, geography, biology, and language (English). School ends at 1:30 P.M. every day, and then I go home to eat lunch. My mother makes us a large meal that includes meat, pasta or potatoes, soup, and salad. At 2:00 P.M., I go back to school for English.

My favorite holiday is Christmas. My whole family goes to my grandparents' house. We barbecue *lechón* (pork) for dinner and have different types of salads. We eat *turrón*, a honey and almond bar, and a special sweet bread with fruit. At midnight everyone opens their presents.

Translation: Hi! My name is Mercedes. I am from Argentina.

Section 1 Physical Geography

Read to Discover

1. What landforms and rivers are found in Atlantic South America?
2. What are the region's climates, vegetation, and wildlife like?
3. What are some of the region's important resources?

Define

Pampas
estuary
soil exhaustion

Locate

Amazon River
Brazilian Highlands
Brazilian Plateau
Gran Chaco
Patagonia
Tierra del Fuego
Andes
Paraná River
Paraguay River
Río de la Plata

WHY IT MATTERS

Itaipu Dam, on the Paraná River between Brazil and Paraguay, is an important source of hydroelectric power. Use CNNfyi.com or other **current events** sources to find out more about dam projects and their consequences. Record your findings in your journal.

Amazon rain forest monkey

Atlantic South America: Physical-Political

SOUTH AMERICA
AMAZON BASIN
Solimões River (Amazon R.)
Amazon River
Manaus
Belém
Equator
BRAZIL
São Francisco River
PACIFIC OCEAN
ATLANTIC OCEAN
MATO GROSSO PLATEAU
Brasília
BRAZILIAN HIGHLANDS
Salvador
BRAZILIAN PLATEAU
Paraguay R.
Pilcomayo River
A N D E S
PARAGUAY
Asunción
Rio de Janeiro
São Paulo
Tropic of Capricorn
GRAN CHACO
Paraná River
Iguaçu R.
Uruguay River
Mount Aconcagua 22,834 ft. (6969 m)
Córdoba
Rosario
URUGUAY
PAMPAS
Buenos Aires
Montevideo
Río de la Plata
ARGENTINA
PATAGONIA
TIERRA DEL FUEGO
CAPE HORN
N
SCALE
0 500 1000 Miles
0 500 1000 Kilometers
Projection: Modified Chamberlin Trimetric
ELEVATION
FEET METERS
13,120 4,000
6,560 2,000
1,640 500
656 200
(Sea level) 0 0 (Sea level)
Below sea level Below sea level
National capitals
Other cities
Size comparison of Atlantic South America to the contiguous United States
90°W 80°W 70°W 60°W 50°W 40°W 30°W 20°W 100°W
10°S 20°S 30°S 40°S 50°S

Resources

One of the region's greatest resources is the Amazon rain forest. The rain forest provides food, wood, natural rubber, medicinal plants, and many other products. However, large areas of the rain forest are being cleared for mining, ranching, and farming.

Commercial agriculture is found throughout the region. In some areas, however, planting the same crop every year has caused **soil exhaustion**. Soil exhaustion means that the soil has lost nutrients needed by plants. Overgrazing is also a problem in some places.

The region's mineral wealth includes gold, silver, copper, and iron. There are oil deposits in the region, particularly in Brazil and Patagonia. Some of the region's large rivers provide hydroelectric power. One of the world's largest hydroelectric dams is the Itaipu Dam on the Paraná River. The dam lies between Brazil and Paraguay.

✓ **READING CHECK:** *Environment and Society* How have humans modified the region's environment?

◄ People are clearing large areas of the Amazon rain forest by burning and by cutting.

Interpreting the Visual Record **Why do you think someone would choose to clear rain forest areas by burning rather than by cutting?**

go.hrw.com **Homework Practice Online**
Keyword: SJ3 HP16

Section 1 Review

Define and explain: Pampas, estuary, soil exhaustion

Working with Sketch Maps On an outline map of the region that you draw or that your teacher provides, label the following: Amazon River, Brazilian Highlands, Brazilian Plateau, Gran Chaco, Patagonia, Tierra del Fuego, Andes, Paraná River, Paraguay River, and Río de la Plata.

Reading for the Main Idea

1. *Places and Regions* What major landforms lie between the Amazon River basin and Patagonia?
2. *Places and Regions* What sets the Amazon River apart from all of the world's other rivers?
3. *Places and Regions* Why is the Patagonia desert dry?

Critical Thinking

4. **Drawing Inferences and Conclusions** How do you think soil exhaustion in Brazil could lead to more deforestation?

Organizing What You Know

5. **Categorizing** Copy the following graphic organizer. Use it to describe Atlantic South America.

Climates	Vegetation and wildlife	Resources

Section 2 Brazil

Read to Discover

1. What is the history of Brazil?
2. What are important characteristics of Brazil's people and culture?
3. What are Brazil's four major regions like today?

Define

favelas

Locate

Rio de Janeiro
São Paulo
Manaus
Belém
Salvador
São Francisco River
Mato Grosso Plateau
Brasília

WHY IT MATTERS

The Amazon rain forest is a tremendous resource for Brazil. Use CNNfyi.com or other **current events** sources to find out more about the Amazon region. Record your findings in your journal.

Brazil nuts

History

Most Brazilians are descended from three groups of immigrants. The first group included peoples who probably migrated to the Americas from northern Asia long ago. The second was made up of Portuguese and other Europeans who came after 1500. Africans brought as slaves made up the third group.

First Inhabitants Brazil's first human inhabitants arrived in the region thousands of years ago. They spread throughout the tropical rain forests and savannas.

These peoples developed a way of life based on hunting, fishing, and small-scale farming. They grew crops such as sweet potatoes, beans, and cassava. The root of the cassava plant is ground up and used as an ingredient in many foods in Brazil today. It also is used to make tapioca. Tapioca is a common food in grocery stores in the United States and other countries.

Europeans and Africans After 1500, Portuguese settlers began to move into Brazil. Favorable climates and soil helped make Brazil a large sugar-growing colony. Colonists brought slaves from Africa to work alongside Brazilian Indians on large sugar plantations. Sugar plantations eventually replaced forests along the Atlantic coast.

As elsewhere in the region, Brazilian Indians fought back against early European colonists. However, the Indians could not overcome powerful European forces.

CHAPTER 16

Reviewing What You Know

Building Vocabulary

On a separate sheet of paper, write sentences to define each of the following words.

1. Pampas
2. estuary
3. soil exhaustion
4. favelas
5. *encomienda*
6. gauchos
7. Mercosur
8. landlocked

Reviewing the Main Ideas

1. *Human Systems* Which country in Atlantic South America was a Portuguese colony? What colonial power controlled the other countries before they became independent?
2. *Places and Regions* What major river systems drain much of northern and central Atlantic South America? What economic roles do they play?
3. *Places and Regions* Which is the richest region in Brazil? Which is the poorest?
4. *Places and Regions* What and where is the Río de la Plata?
5. *Places and Regions* What is the most important agricultural area in Argentina?

Understanding Environment and Society

Resource Use

Paraguay and Uruguay both harness energy through hydroelectric dams. Create a presentation on the use of dams for hydroelectric power. Consider the following:

- Government decisions to expand the use of hydroelectric power.
- Benefits of hydroelectric power.
- How hydroelectric power is harnessed.

Thinking Critically

1. How are European influences reflected in the religions, languages, and other cultural characteristics of the countries of Atlantic South America?
2. Why are large areas of Brazil's tropical rain forest being cleared?
3. How do the climates of northern Brazil and southern Argentina differ?
4. How might Mercosur help the economies of the region's countries?
5. How are the ethnic populations of Uruguay and Paraguay different?

Building Social Studies Skills

Map ACTIVITY

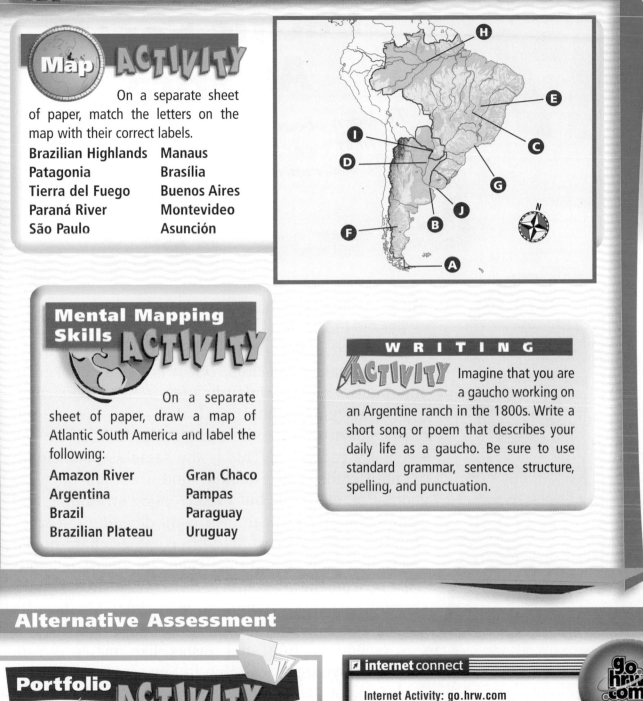

On a separate sheet of paper, match the letters on the map with their correct labels.

Brazilian Highlands
Patagonia
Tierra del Fuego
Paraná River
São Paulo
Manaus
Brasília
Buenos Aires
Montevideo
Asunción

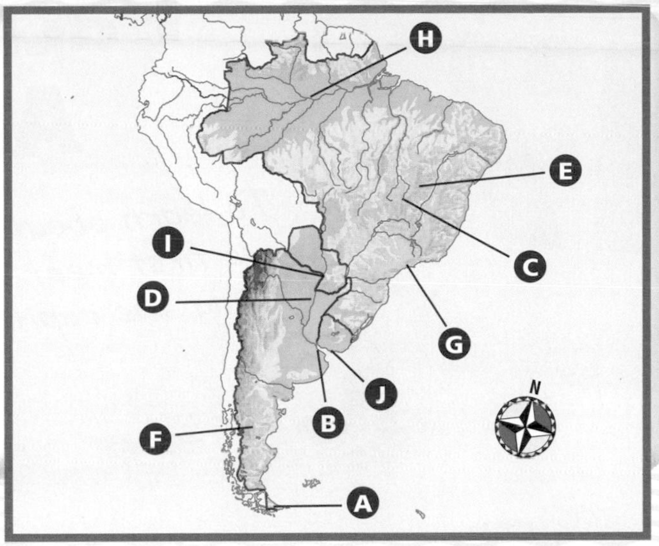

H
E
C
I
D
G
J
B
F
A
N

Mental Mapping Skills ACTIVITY

On a separate sheet of paper, draw a map of Atlantic South America and label the following:

Amazon River
Argentina
Brazil
Brazilian Plateau
Gran Chaco
Pampas
Paraguay
Uruguay

WRITING ACTIVITY

Imagine that you are a gaucho working on an Argentine ranch in the 1800s. Write a short song or poem that describes your daily life as a gaucho. Be sure to use standard grammar, sentence structure, spelling, and punctuation.

Alternative Assessment

Portfolio ACTIVITY

Learning About Your Local Geography

Research Project Ranching is a major economic activity in Atlantic South America. Interview a member of a business organization. Then create a business profile of your community. Identify the role of entrepreneurs in your profile.

internet connect

Internet Activity: go.hrw.com
KEYWORD: SJ3 GT16

Choose a topic to explore about Atlantic South America:

- Journey along the Amazon River.
- Compare Uruguayans and Paraguayans.
- Celebrate the Brazilian Carnival.

CHAPTER 17

Pacific South America

To learn about Pacific South America, we first meet Mariana. She lives in Lima, the capital of Peru.

As tumpa ta runasimita rimani.

Hi! My name is Mariana Gonzales. I am 13 years old. I live in Lima, Peru, with my parents and my twin brother, Alejo. We speak Spanish. There is a Peruvian language called Quechua, but it is mostly spoken in the Andes. I understand only a few words of Quechua. I go to a French school, so I also speak French and some English. I am in the third grade of what we call secondary education. This is the same as your eighth or ninth grade. I love biology and art. I am not very good at other sports, but I really enjoy swimming and badminton. My favorite dish is *ají de gallina*, a spicy chicken dish. We eat it with potatoes, hard-boiled eggs, black olives, and rice. There are lots of delicious exotic fruits in my country. Have you heard of cherimoya, papaya, *cocona*, or *maracuyá*? My favorite dessert is *lucuma* ice cream. It's made from a yellowish fruit and tastes like maple syrup. My favorite place to go in Lima is the Museo de Oro, or "gold museum". The incredible jewelry and other objects there really bring my country's ancient history to life.

Translation: I speak a little Quechua.

Section 1 Physical Geography

Read to Discover

1. What are the major physical features of the region?
2. What climates and vegetation exist in this region?
3. What are the region's major resources?

Define

strait
selvas
Peru Current
El Niño

Locate

Andes
Strait of Magellan
Tierra del Fuego
Cape Horn
Amazon River
Iquitos
Altiplano
Lake Titicaca
Lake Poopó
Atacama Desert

WHY IT MATTERS

The Atacama Desert offers a large variety of natural features including mountains, geysers, and the "Valley of the Moon." Use CNNfyi.com or other **current events** sources to discover other natural wonders of this area. Record your findings in your journal.

Peruvian hummingbird

Pacific South America: Physical-Political

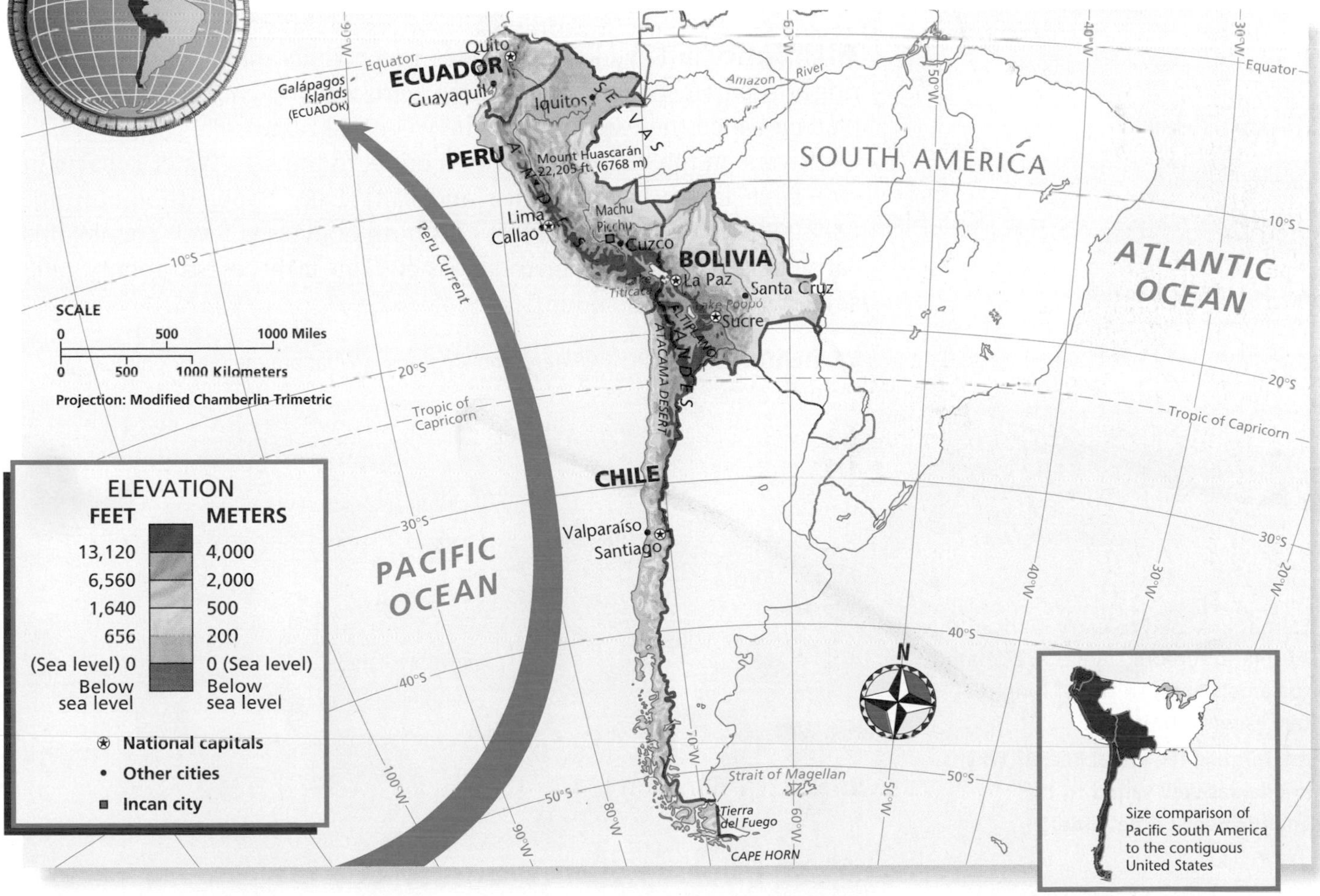

Quito
ECUADOR
Guayaquil
Galápagos Islands (ECUADOR)
Equator
Iquitos
SELVAS
PERU
Mount Huascarán 22,205 ft. (6768 m)
ANDES
Lima
Callao
Machu Picchu
Cuzco
BOLIVIA
La Paz
Santa Cruz
Titicaca
Lake Poopó
Sucre
ALTIPLANO
ATACAMA DESERT
Peru Current
Amazon River
SOUTH AMERICA
ATLANTIC OCEAN
Tropic of Capricorn
CHILE
Valparaíso
Santiago
PACIFIC OCEAN
Strait of Magellan
Tierra del Fuego
CAPE HORN
N
SCALE
0 500 1000 Miles
0 500 1000 Kilometers
Projection: Modified Chamberlin Trimetric
ELEVATION
FEET METERS
13,120 4,000
6,560 2,000
1,640 500
656 200
(Sea level) 0 0 (Sea level)
Below sea level Below sea level
National capitals
Other cities
Incan city
Size comparison of Pacific South America to the contiguous United States

internet connect

GO TO: go.hrw.com
KEYWORD: SJ3 CH17
FOR: Web sites about Pacific South America

Physical Features

Shaped like a shoestring, Chile (CHEE-lay) stretches about 2,650 miles (4,264 km) from north to south. However, at its broadest point Chile is just 221 miles (356 km) wide. As its name indicates, Ecuador (E-kwuh-dawr) lies on the equator. Peru (puh-ROO) forms a long curve along the Pacific Ocean. Bolivia (buh-LIV-ee-uh) is landlocked.

Mountains The snowcapped Andes run through all four of the region's countries. Some ridges and volcanic peaks rise more than 20,000 feet (6,096 m) above sea level. Because two tectonic plates meet at the region's edge, earthquakes and volcanoes are constant threats. Sometimes these earthquakes disturb Andean glaciers, sending ice and mud rushing down the mountain slopes.

In Chile's rugged south, the peaks are covered by an ice cap. This ice cap is about 220 miles (354 km) long. Mountains extend to the continent's southern tip. There, the Strait of Magellan links the Atlantic and Pacific Oceans. A **strait** is a narrow passageway that connects two large bodies of water. The large island south of the strait is Tierra del Fuego, or "land of fire." It is divided between Chile and Argentina. At the southernmost tip of the continent, storms swirl around Chile's Cape Horn. Many other islands lie along Chile's southern coast.

Tributaries of the Amazon River begin high in the Andes. In fact, ships can travel upriver about 2,300 miles (3,700 km) on the Amazon. This allows ships to sail from the Atlantic Ocean to Iquitos, Peru.

BUILD on WHAT You Know

Do you remember what you learned about earthquakes? See Chapter 2 to review.

Altiplano In Ecuador, the Andes range splits into two ridges. The ridges separate further in southern Peru and Bolivia. A broad, high plateau called the Altiplano lies between the ridges.

Rivers on the Altiplano have no outlet to the sea. Water collects in two large lakes, Lake Titicaca and salty Lake Poopó (poh-oh-POH). Lake Titicaca lies at 12,500 feet (3,810 m) above sea level. Large ships carry freight and passengers across it. The lake covers about 3,200 square miles (8,288 sq km).

✓ **READING CHECK:** *Places and Regions* What are the major physical features of the region?

Llamas are used to carry loads in the Altiplano region. Llamas are related to camels and can travel long distances without water.

Interpreting the Visual Record Why are llamas well suited to the environment of the Andes?

Colombia
Napo River
Ecuador
Brazil
Peru

Canoes are an important form of transportation along the Napo River in eastern Ecuador.

Interpreting the Visual Record **What type of vegetation does this region have?**

Climate and Vegetation

Climate and vegetation vary widely in Pacific South America. Some areas, such as Chile's central valley, have a mild Mediterranean climate. Other areas have dry, wet, or cold weather conditions.

Grasslands and Forests Mountain environments change with elevation. The Altiplano region between the mountain ridges is a grassland with few trees. Eastern Ecuador, eastern Peru, and northern Bolivia are part of the Amazon River basin. These areas have a humid tropical climate. South Americans call the thick tropical rain forests in this region ***selvas***. In Bolivia the rain forest changes to grasslands in the southeast. Far to the south, southern Chile is covered with dense temperate rain forests. Cool, rainy weather is typical of this area of rain forests.

Deserts Northern Chile contains the Atacama Desert. This desert is about 600 miles (965 km) long. Rain is extremely rare, but fog and low clouds are common. They form when the cold **Peru Current** chills warmer air above the ocean's surface. Cloud cover keeps air near the ground from being warmed by the Sun. The area receives almost no sunshine for about six months of the year. Yet it seldom rains. As a result, coastal Chile is one of the cloudiest—and driest—places on Earth.

In Peru, rivers cut through the dry coastal region. They bring snowmelt down from the Andes. About 50 rivers cross Peru. The rivers have made settlement possible in these dry areas.

Our Amazing Planet

The Atacama Desert is one of the driest places on Earth. Some spots in the desert have not received any rain for more than 400 years. Average rainfall is less than 0.004 inches (0.01 cm) per year.

A Bolivian miner uses a jackhammer to mine for tin.

El Niño About every two to seven years, an ocean and weather pattern affects the dry Pacific coast. This weather pattern is called **El Niño**. Cool ocean water near the coast warms. As a result, fish leave what is normally a rich fishing area. Areas along the coast often suffer flooding from heavy rains. El Niño is caused by the buildup of warm water in the Pacific Ocean. Ocean and weather events around the world can be affected. Some scientists think that greenhouse gases made a long El Niño during the 1990s even worse.

✓ **READING CHECK:** *Physical Systems* How does El Niño affect Earth?

Resources

The countries of Pacific South America have many important natural resources. The coastal waters of the Pacific Ocean are rich in fish. Forests in southern Chile and east of the Andes in Peru and Ecuador provide lumber. In addition, the region has oil, natural gas, silver, gold, and other valuable mineral resources. Bolivia has large deposits of tin. It also has resources such as copper, lead, and zinc. Chile has large copper deposits. In fact, Chile is the world's leading producer and exporter of copper.

✓ **READING CHECK:** *Environment and Society* How has Chile's copper supply affected its economy?

Section 1 Review

go.hrw.com Homework Practice Online Keyword: SJ3 HP17

Define strait, *selvas,* Peru Current, El Niño

Working with Sketch Maps On a map of South America that you draw or that your teacher provides, label the following: Andes, Strait of Magellan, Tierra del Fuego, Cape Horn, Amazon River, Iquitos, Altiplano, Lake Titicaca, Lake Poopó, and Atacama Desert. Where is Lake Titicaca, and what is it like?

Reading for the Main Idea

1. *Places and Regions* What is the main landform region of Pacific South America?
2. *Physical Systems* What is El Niño? What effect does El Niño have on coastal flooding in Peru?

Critical Thinking

3. **Finding the Main Idea** What would you encounter on a journey from Iquitos, Peru, to Tierra del Fuego?
4. **Making Generalizations and Predictions** What problem would people living on the dry coast of Chile experience, and how could they solve it?

Organizing What You Know

5. **Categorizing** Copy the following graphic organizer. Use it to describe the landforms, climate, vegetation, and sources of water of Pacific South America.

	Western	Central	Eastern
Landforms			
Climate			
Vegetation			
Water sources			

Section 2 History and Culture

Read to Discover

1. What were some achievements of the region's early cultures?
2. What was the Inca Empire like?
3. What role did Spain play in the region's history?
4. What governmental problems have the region's people faced?

Define

quinoa
quipus
viceroy
creoles
coup

Locate

Cuzco
Machu Picchu

An ancient gold ornament from Peru

WHY IT MATTERS

Hiram Bingham of Yale University discovered the ruins of the "lost city" of Machu Picchu in 1911. Use CNNfyi.com or other **current events** sources to learn more about famous historical sites in Pacific South America. Record your findings in your journal.

Early Cultures

Thousands of years ago, agriculture became the basis of the region's economy. To raise crops in the steep Andes, early farmers cut terraces into the mountainsides. Peoples of the region developed crops that would be important for centuries to come. They domesticated **quinoa** (KEEN-wah), a native Andean plant that yields nutritious seeds. They also grew many varieties of potatoes. Domesticated animals included the llama (LAH-muh) and alpaca (al-PA-kuh). Both have thick wool and are related to camels. Early inhabitants raised and ate guinea pigs, which are related to mice. The people wove many fabrics from cotton and wool. These fabrics had complicated, beautiful patterns.

Peru's first advanced civilization reached its height in about 900 B.C. The main town was located in an Andean valley. This town contained large stone structures decorated with carved jaguars and other designs. Later, people in coastal areas used sophisticated irrigation systems to store water and control flooding. They also built pyramids about 100 feet (30 m) high. Huge stone carvings remain near the Bolivian shores of Lake Titicaca. They were carved by the people of the Tiahuanaco (TEE-uh-wuh-NAH-koh) culture. Another people scratched outlines of animals and other shapes into the surface of the Peruvian desert. These designs are hundreds of feet long.

✓ **READING CHECK:** *Human Systems* What were some achievements of the region's early cultures?

This Peruvian woman is separating seeds from the quinoa plant.

Peru
Brazil
Machu Picchu
Bolivia
Chile

The ruins of Machu Picchu, an Inca city, were discovered in 1911.
Interpreting the Visual Record **Why might the Inca have chosen this site for a settlement?**

The Inca

By the early 1500s, one people ruled most of the Andes region. This group, the Inca, conquered the other cultures around them. They controlled an area reaching from what is now southern Colombia to central Chile. The Inca Empire stretched from the Pacific Coast inland to the *selvas* of the Amazon rain forest. Perhaps as many as 12 million people from dozens of different ethnic groups were included. The Inca called their empire Tawantinsuyu (tah-WAHN-tin-SOO-yoo), which means "land of the four quarters." Four highways that began in the Inca capital, Cuzco (KOO-skoh), divided the kingdom into four sections.

The Inca Empire The Inca adopted many of the skills of the people they ruled. They built structures out of large stone blocks fitted tightly together without cement. Buildings in the Andean city of Machu Picchu have survived earthquakes and the passing of centuries. Inca metalworkers created gold and silver objects, some decorated with emeralds. Artists made a garden of gold plants with silver stems. They even made gold ears for the corn plants.

Perhaps the Inca's greatest achievement was the organization of their empire. Huge irrigation projects turned deserts into rich farmland that produced food for the large population. A network of thousands of miles of stone-paved roads connected the empire. Along the highways were rest houses, temples, and storerooms. The Inca used storerooms to keep supplies of food. For example, they stored potatoes that had been freeze-dried in the cold mountain air.

To cross the steep Andean valleys, the Inca built suspension bridges of rope. The Inca had no wheeled vehicles or horses. Instead, teams of runners carried messages throughout the land. An important message could be moved up to 150 miles (241 km) in one day.

The runners did not carry letters, however, because the Inca did not have a written language. Instead, they used **quipus** (KEE-pooz). Quipus were complicated systems of knots tied on strings of various colors. Numerical information about important events, populations, animals, and grain supplies was recorded on quipus. Inca officials were trained to read the knots' meaning.

Quipus were used by the Inca to keep records.
Interpreting the Visual Record
How might quipus have made it easier for the Inca to control their empire?

Civil War Although it was rich and efficient, the Inca Empire did not last long. When the Inca emperor died in 1525, a struggle began. Two of his sons fought over who would take his place. About seven years later, his son Atahualpa (ah-tah-WAHL-pah) won the civil war.

✓ **READING CHECK:** *Human Systems* What was the Inca's greatest achievement?

CONNECTING TO *Technology*

Inca Roads

The road system was one of the greatest achievements of Inca civilization. The roads crossed high mountains, tropical rain forests, and deserts.

The main road, Capac-nan, or "royal road," connected the capitals of Cuzco and Quito. These cities were more than 1,500 miles (2,414 km) apart. This road crossed jungles, swamps, and mountains. It was straight for most of its length. Inca roads were built from precisely cut stones. One Spanish observer described how the builders worked.

"The Indians who worked these stones used no mortar; they had no steel for cutting and working the stones, and no machines for transporting them; yet so skilled was their work that the joints between the stones were barely noticeable."

Another longer highway paralleled the coast and joined Capac-nan, creating a highly efficient network. Along these roads were rest houses. The Inca also built suspension bridges to span deep ravines. They built floating bridges to cross wide rivers.

When the Spanish conquered the region in the 1530s, they destroyed the road system. Today, only fragments of the Inca roads still exist.

Inca roads had stairways to cross steep peaks.

Understanding What You Read

1. How might the road system have allowed the Inca to control their territory?
2. What were the main features of the Inca road system?

Spain in Pacific South America

While on his way to Cuzco to be crowned, Atahualpa met Spanish explorer Francisco Pizarro. Pizarro's small group of men and horses had recently landed on the continent's shore. Pizarro wanted Inca gold and silver.

Conquest and Revolt Pizarro captured Atahualpa, who ordered his people to fill a room with gold and silver. These riches were supposed to be a ransom for his freedom. However, Pizarro ordered the Inca emperor killed. The Spaniards continued to conquer Inca lands.

Colombia
Ecuador
Brazil
Peru
Cuzco
Bolivia
Chile

▲ The stonework of an Inca temple in Cuzco now forms the foundation of this Catholic church.

Interpreting the Visual Record **What does this photo suggest about how the Spanish viewed the religious practices of the Inca?**

By 1535 the Inca Empire no longer existed. The last Inca rulers fled into the mountains. A tiny independent state in the foothills of the eastern Andes survived several decades more.

The new Spanish rulers often dealt harshly with the South American Indians. Many Indians had to work in gold and silver mines and on the Spaniards' plantations. Inca temples were replaced by Spanish-style Roman Catholic churches. A **viceroy**, or governor, appointed by the king of Spain enforced Spanish laws and customs.

From time to time, the people rebelled against their Spanish rulers. In 1780 and 1781 an Indian named Tupac Amarú II (too-PAHK ahm-AHR-oo) led a revolt. This revolt spread, but was put down quickly.

Independence By the early 1800s, the desire for independence had grown in South America. The people of Pacific South America began to break away from Spain. **Creoles**, American-born descendants of Europeans, were the main leaders of the revolts. Chile became an independent country in 1818. Ecuador achieved independence in 1822, and Peru became independent two years later. Bolivia became independent in 1825. In the 1880s Bolivia lost a war with Chile. As a result, Bolivia lost its strip of seacoast and became landlocked.

✓ **READING CHECK:** *Human Systems* What was Spain's role in the region's history?

Simón Bolívar was a soldier and political leader in the early 1800s. He fought against the Spanish and helped win independence for several South American countries. ▼

Government

Since gaining their independence, the countries of Pacific South America have had periods during which their governments were unstable. Often military leaders have taken control and limited citizens' rights. However, in recent decades the region's countries have moved toward more democratic forms of government. These governments now face the challenge of widespread poverty.

Ecuador is a democracy. Ecuador's government is working to improve housing, medical care, and literacy. Bolivia has suffered from a series of violent revolutions and military governments. It is now also a democracy. Bolivia has had one of the most stable elected governments in the region in recent years.

Peru's recent history has been particularly troubled. A terrorist group called the Sendero Luminoso, or "shining path," was active in the 1980s. The group carried out deadly guerrilla attacks. With the arrest of the group's leader in 1992, hopes for calm returned. Peru has an elected president and congress.

Young Peruvians hold a political campaign rally.

Chile has also recently ended a long violent period. In 1970, Chileans elected a president who had been influenced by communist ideas. A few years later he was overthrown and killed during a military **coup** (KOO). A coup is a sudden overthrow of a government by a small group of people. In the years after the coup, the military rulers tried to crush their political enemies. The military government was harsh and often violent. Thousands of people were imprisoned or killed. In the late 1980s the power of the rulers began to weaken. After more than 15 years of military rule, Chileans rejected the military dictatorship. A new, democratic government was created. Chileans now enjoy many new freedoms.

✓ **READING CHECK:** *Human Systems* How has unlimited government been a problem for some of the nations in the region?

Section 2 Review

go.hrw.com **Homework Practice Online** Keyword: SJ3 HP17

Define and explain: quinoa, quipus, viceroy, creoles, coup

Working with Sketch Maps On the map you created in Section 1, label Cuzco and Machu Picchu. Then shade in the area ruled by the Inca. What may have limited Inca expansion eastward?

Reading for the Main Idea

1. *Human Systems* How did the Inca communicate across great distances?
2. *Environment and Society* What attracted the Spanish conquerors to Pacific South America?

Critical Thinking

3. **Analyzing Information** What governmental problems have many of the region's nations experienced?
4. **Drawing Inferences and Conclusions** Why do you think many leaders of the independence movement were creoles rather than Spaniards?

Organizing What You Know

5. **Sequencing** Copy the following graphic organizer. Use it to show important events in the history of Pacific South America.

GeoSKILLS

▲ Many people from Japan migrated to the area around São Paulo, Brazil in the 1900s.

Building Skills for Life: Understanding Migration Patterns

People have always moved to different places. This movement is called migration. Understanding migration patterns is very important in geography. These patterns help explain why certain places are the way they are today. In South America, for example, there are people whose ancestors came from Africa, Asia, Europe, and North America. All of these people migrated to South America sometime in the past.

Why do people migrate? There are many different reasons. Sometimes, people do not want to move, but they are forced to. This is called forced migration. Other times, people migrate because they are looking for a better life. This is an example of voluntary migration.

Geographers who study migration patterns often use the words *push* and *pull*. They identify situations that push people out of places. For example, wars often push people away. They also identify situations that pull people to new places. A better job might pull someone to a new place. Usually, people migrate for a combination of reasons. They might be pushed from a place because there is not enough farmland. They might also be pulled to a new place by good farmland.

Geographers are also interested in barriers to migration. Barriers make it harder for people to migrate. There are cultural barriers, economic barriers, physical barriers, and political barriers. For example, deserts, mountains, and oceans can make it harder for people to migrate. Unfamiliar languages and ways of life can also block migration.

Migration changes people and places. Both the places that people leave and the places where they arrive are changed. Can you think of some ways that migration has changed the world?

PRACTICING THE SKILL

1. List some factors that can push people out of a place or pull them to a new place.
2. Research the migration of your ancestors or a friend's ancestors. Where did they come from? When did they migrate? Why?
3. Imagine you had to migrate to a new place. Where would you go? Why would you pick this place? Do you think you would be scared, excited, or both?

HANDS ON GEOGRAPHY

The following passage was written by a woman from Argentina who migrated to the United States. Read the passage and then answer the Lab Report questions.

"My nephew and I came from a faraway country called Argentina. When I mention this country to others, they say, "Oh, Argentina! It is so beautiful!" However, as beautiful as Argentina is, life there is very difficult now.

In Argentina, there are three social classes: rich, middle class, and poor. The middle class, of which I am a member, is the largest. We are the workers and the businesspeople. Because of bad economic decisions and corrupt government, the middle class has almost disappeared. Factories have closed, and people have no work. The big companies move to other countries. The small businesses depend on the big companies and often have to close. Argentina has a very high rate of unemployment. Many people are hungry.

My husband and I had some friends who worked in Argentina. They advised us to sell everything we owned and move to Houston. They told us that life was better there and they had relatives who would help us find a house to rent. They told us a lawyer would help us put our papers in order so we could work. I had a small sewing shop with some sewing machines, which I sold so I could travel."

Poverty and unemployment are problems in some parts of Argentina.
Interpreting the Visual Record What evidence can you see of poor living conditions?

Lab Report

1. What pushed the author out of Argentina?
2. Why did she choose Houston as her destination?
3. According to the author, what do other people think Argentina is like? does she agree?

UNIT 5

Geirangerfjord, Norway

Europe

CHAPTER 18
Southern Europe

CHAPTER 19
West-Central Europe

CHAPTER 20
Northern Europe

CHAPTER 21
Eastern Europe

Regatta on the Grand Canal, Venice, Italy

A Professor in the Czech Republic

Meredith Walker teaches English at Clemson University. She also teaches English As a Second Language courses. Here she describes a visit to Prague, the capital of the Czech Republic. **WHAT DO YOU THINK?** ***Does Prague sound like a city you would like to see?***

The castle in Prague sits on a hill high above the Vltava River. This river divides the city. A castle has stood on that hillside for 1,000 years. Rising from the inner courtyard of the castle is a huge medieval building, St. Vitus' Cathedral. Together, the castle and cathedral look almost magical, especially at night when spotlights shine on them. The castle is the most important symbol of the city. A great Czech writer, Franz Kafka, believed that the castle influenced everything and everyone in the city.

Another important landmark in Prague is Charles Bridge, one of eight bridges that cross the Vltava River. The bridge is part of the route that kings once traveled on their way to the castle to be crowned. Today, large crowds of tourists walk there. Many stop to photograph some of the 22 statues that line the bridge. No cars are allowed on the bridge today.

The first time I walked across the bridge, heading up toward the castle, it was at night. Fireworks were lighting the sky all around me. It was a colorful welcome.

Street scene in Prague, Czech Republic

Portuguese girls in native costume

Understanding Primary Sources

1. How does the city's physical geography help make the castle a symbol of Prague?
2. How did the fireworks display affect Meredith Walker's feelings about Prague?

Whooper swan

Europe

Elevation Profile

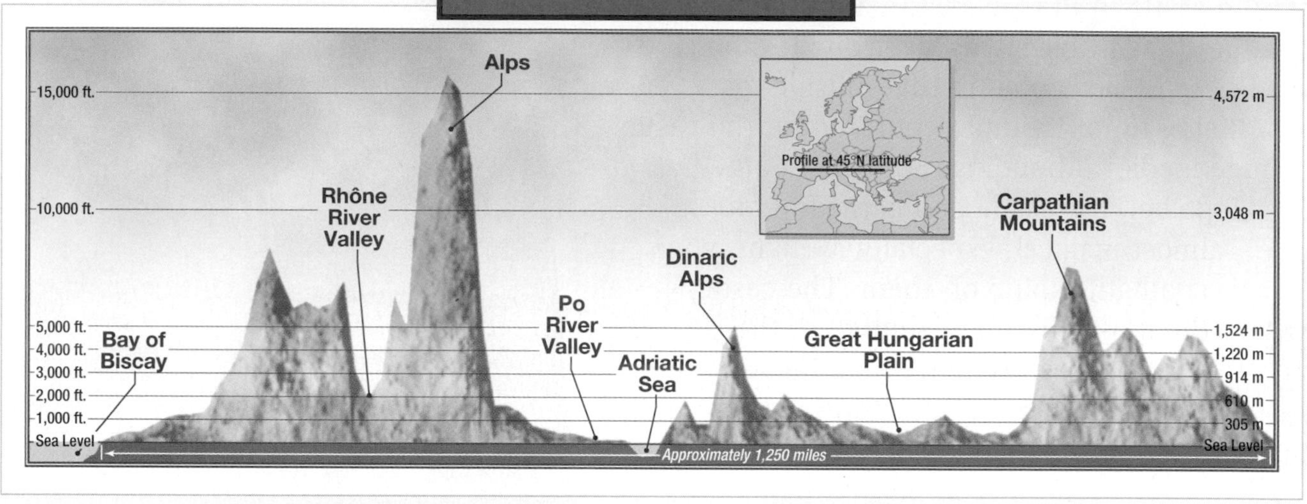
Alps
Rhône River Valley
Po River Valley
Adriatic Sea
Dinaric Alps
Great Hungarian Plain
Carpathian Mountains
Bay of Biscay
Profile at 45°N latitude
15,000 ft.
10,000 ft.
5,000 ft.
4,000 ft.
3,000 ft.
2,000 ft.
1,000 ft.
Sea Level
4,572 m
3,048 m
1,524 m
1,220 m
914 m
610 m
305 m
Sea Level
Approximately 1,250 miles

GEOSTATS:

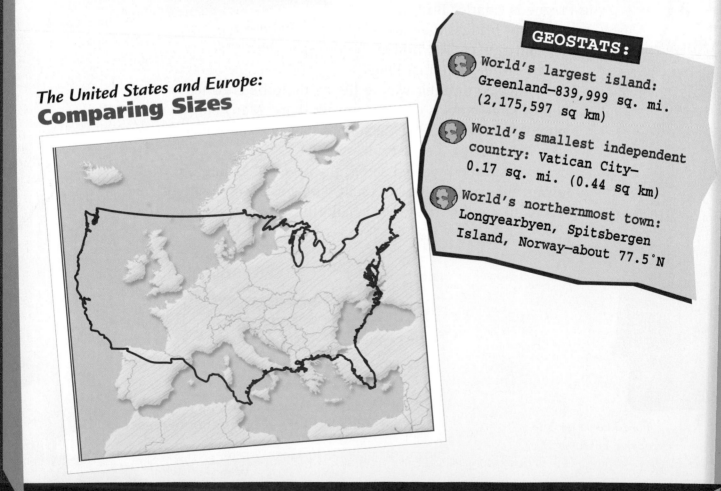

- World's largest island: Greenland–839,999 sq. mi. (2,175,597 sq km)
- World's smallest independent country: Vatican City–0.17 sq. mi. (0.44 sq km)
- World's northernmost town: Longyearbyen, Spitsbergen Island, Norway–about 77.5°N

The United States and Europe: Comparing Sizes

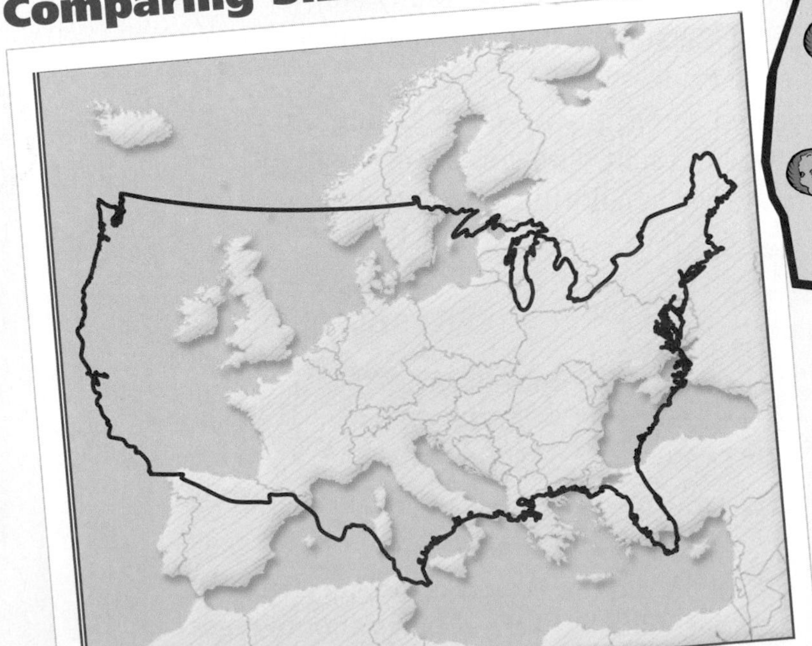

Europe: Physical

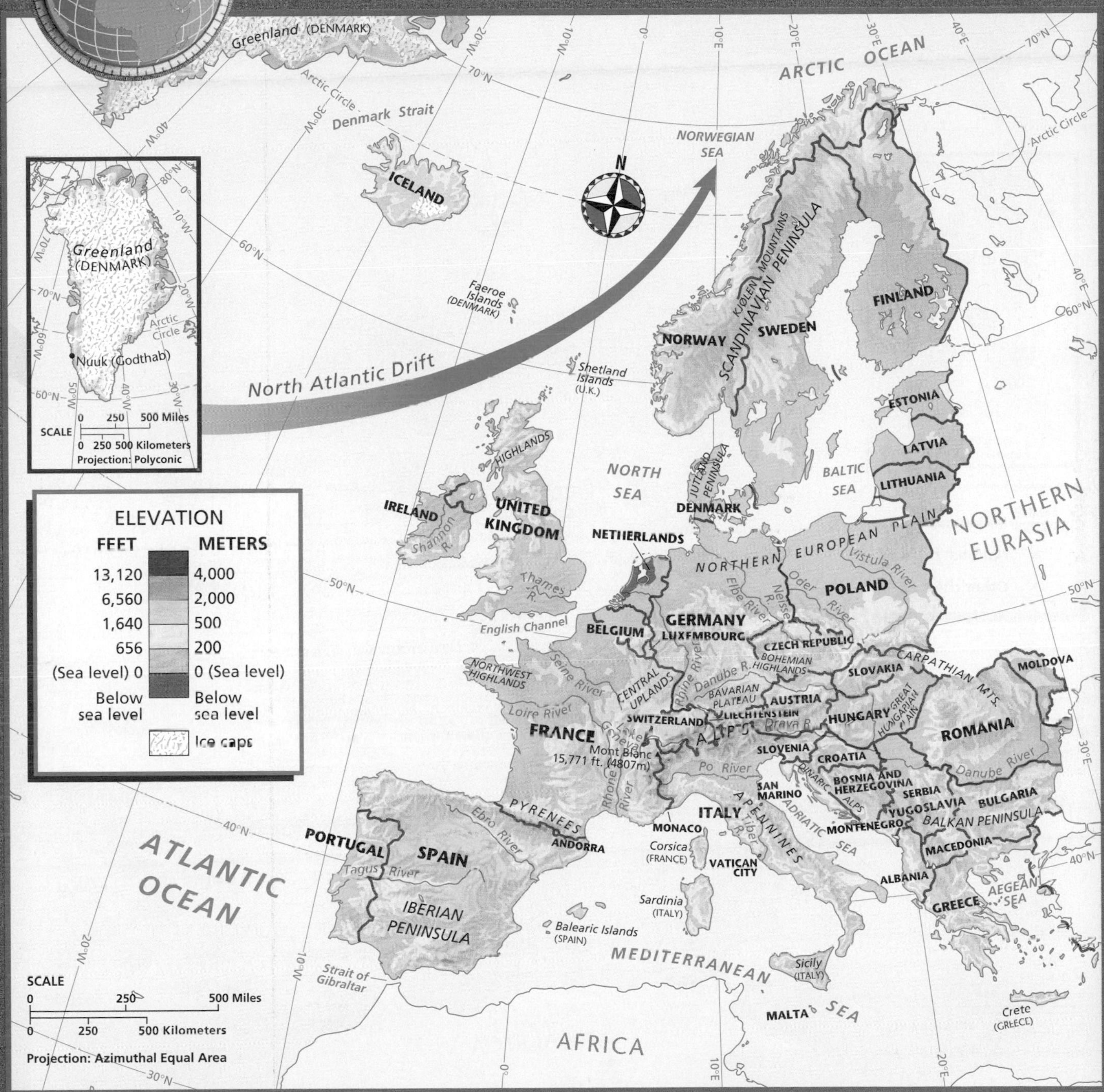
Greenland (DENMARK)
Arctic Circle
Denmark Strait
ARCTIC OCEAN
NORWEGIAN SEA
ICELAND
Faeroe Islands (DENMARK)
Shetland Islands (U.K.)
North Atlantic Drift
KJOLEN MOUNTAINS
SCANDINAVIAN PENINSULA
NORWAY
SWEDEN
FINLAND
ESTONIA
LATVIA
LITHUANIA
BALTIC SEA
NORTH SEA
JUTLAND PENINSULA
DENMARK
HIGHLANDS
IRELAND
Shannon R.
UNITED KINGDOM
Thames R.
NETHERLANDS
NORTHERN EUROPEAN PLAIN
NORTHERN EURASIA
Vistula River
Oder River
Neisse R.
Elbe River
POLAND
GERMANY
BELGIUM
LUXEMBOURG
English Channel
CZECH REPUBLIC
BOHEMIAN HIGHLANDS
SLOVAKIA
CARPATHIAN MTS.
MOLDOVA
NORTHWEST HIGHLANDS
Seine River
CENTRAL UPLANDS
Rhine River
Danube R.
BAVARIAN PLATEAU
AUSTRIA
LIECHTENSTEIN
HUNGARY
GREAT HUNGARIAN PLAIN
ROMANIA
Loire River
FRANCE
SWITZERLAND
Lake Geneva
Mont Blanc 15,771 ft. (4807m)
ALPS
Drava R.
SLOVENIA
CROATIA
Po River
Rhone River
DINARIC ALPS
BOSNIA AND HERZEGOVINA
SERBIA
YUGOSLAVIA
Danube River
BULGARIA
SAN MARINO
MONTENEGRO
BALKAN PENINSULA
PYRENEES
ANDORRA
MONACO
ITALY
APENNINES
ADRIATIC SEA
MACEDONIA
Tiber R.
PORTUGAL
SPAIN
Ebro River
Tagus River
Corsica (FRANCE)
VATICAN CITY
ALBANIA
ATLANTIC OCEAN
IBERIAN PENINSULA
Sardinia (ITALY)
GREECE
AEGEAN SEA
Balearic Islands (SPAIN)
MEDITERRANEAN SEA
Strait of Gibraltar
Sicily (ITALY)
MALTA
Crete (GREECE)
AFRICA
SCALE
0 250 500 Miles
0 250 500 Kilometers
Projection: Azimuthal Equal Area
Greenland (DENMARK)
Arctic Circle
Nuuk (Godthab)
0 250 500 Miles
SCALE
0 250 500 Kilometers
Projection: Polyconic
ELEVATION
FEET METERS
13,120 4,000
6,560 2,000
1,640 500
656 200
(Sea level) 0 0 (Sea level)
Below sea level Below sea level
Ice caps

1. *Places and Regions* What are two mountain ranges that occupy peninsulas?
2. *Places and Regions* What are the two major plains of Europe? Which is larger?

Critical Thinking

3. **Analyzing Information** In the days before air travel, which physical feature would have made it difficult to travel between Italy and the countries to its north?
4. **Analyzing Information** Which physical feature would have made travel between Greece, Italy, and Spain fairly easy?

Europe: Political

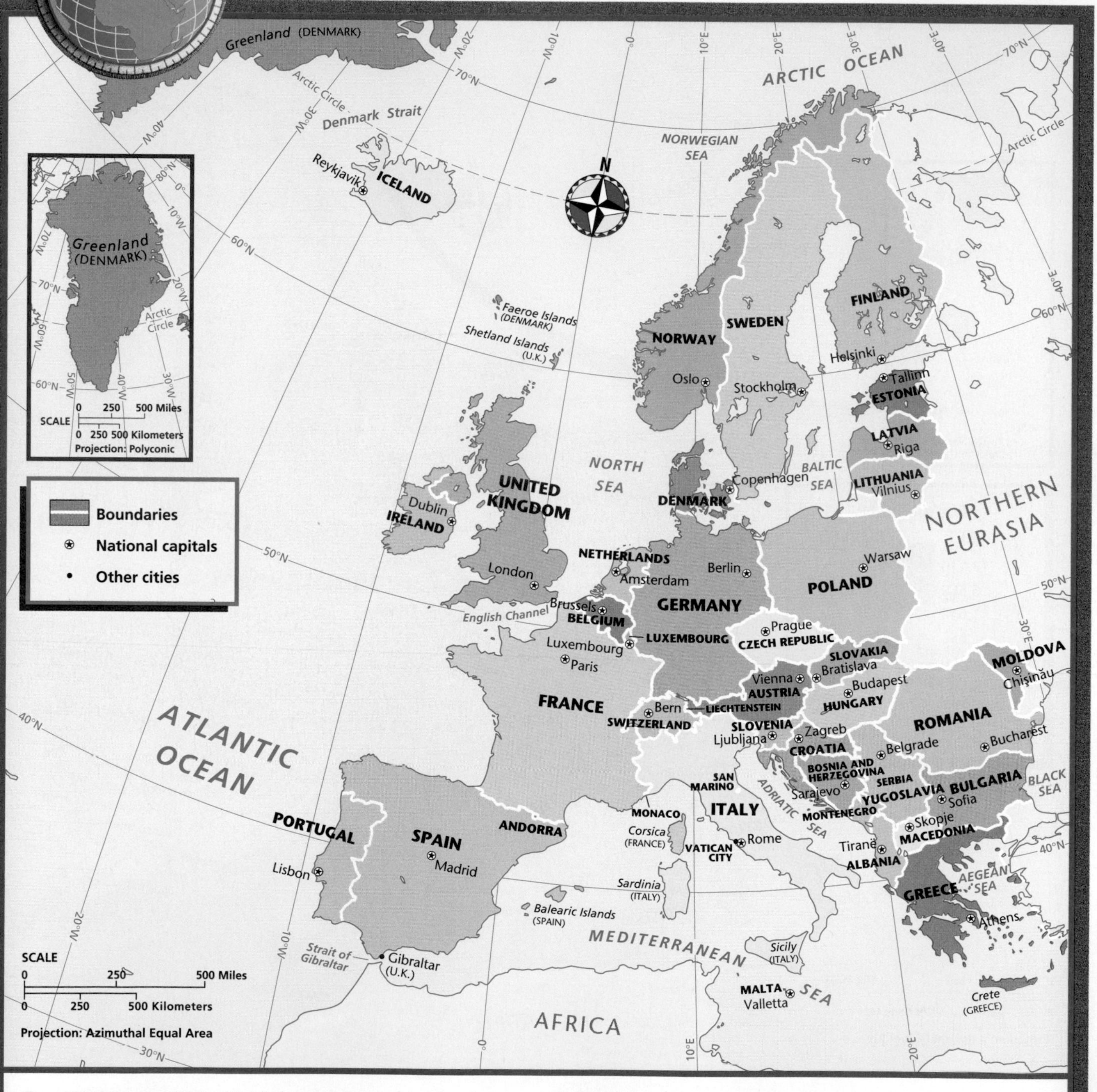
Greenland (DENMARK)
Arctic Circle
Denmark Strait
ARCTIC OCEAN
NORWEGIAN SEA
Reykjavik
ICELAND
N
Greenland (DENMARK)
Arctic Circle
0 250 500 Miles
SCALE
0 250 500 Kilometers
Projection: Polyconic
Faeroe Islands (DENMARK)
Shetland Islands (U.K.)
NORWAY
SWEDEN
FINLAND
Oslo
Stockholm
Helsinki
Tallinn
ESTONIA
LATVIA
Riga
LITHUANIA
Vilnius
Copenhagen
BALTIC SEA
NORTH SEA
DENMARK
UNITED KINGDOM
Dublin
IRELAND
Boundaries
National capitals
Other cities
NORTHERN EURASIA
NETHERLANDS
Amsterdam
Berlin
Warsaw
POLAND
London
GERMANY
Brussels
BELGIUM
English Channel
LUXEMBOURG
Luxembourg
Paris
Prague
CZECH REPUBLIC
SLOVAKIA
Bratislava
MOLDOVA
Chişinău
Vienna
AUSTRIA
Budapest
HUNGARY
FRANCE
Bern
LIECHTENSTEIN
SWITZERLAND
SLOVENIA
Ljubljana
Zagreb
CROATIA
ROMANIA
Bucharest
Belgrade
BOSNIA AND HERZEGOVINA
SERBIA
Sarajevo
YUGOSLAVIA
BULGARIA
Sofia
BLACK SEA
ATLANTIC OCEAN
SAN MARINO
MONACO
ITALY
ADRIATIC SEA
MONTENEGRO
Skopje
MACEDONIA
PORTUGAL
SPAIN
ANDORRA
Madrid
Corsica (FRANCE)
VATICAN CITY
Rome
Tiranë
ALBANIA
Lisbon
Sardinia (ITALY)
AEGEAN SEA
GREECE
Athens
Balearic Islands (SPAIN)
MEDITERRANEAN SEA
Sicily (ITALY)
Strait of Gibraltar
Gibraltar (U.K.)
MALTA
Valletta
Crete (GREECE)
AFRICA
SCALE
0 250 500 Miles
0 250 500 Kilometers
Projection: Azimuthal Equal Area

1. *Places and Regions* Which countries border both the Atlantic and the Mediterranean?

2. *Places and Regions* Compare this map to the **physical map** of the region. Which physical feature helps form the boundary between Spain and France?

Critical Thinking

3. **Comparing** Which countries have the shortest coastlines on the Adriatic Sea?

4. **Drawing Inferences and Conclusions** The United Kingdom has not been invaded successfully since A.D. 1066. Why?

Europe: Climate

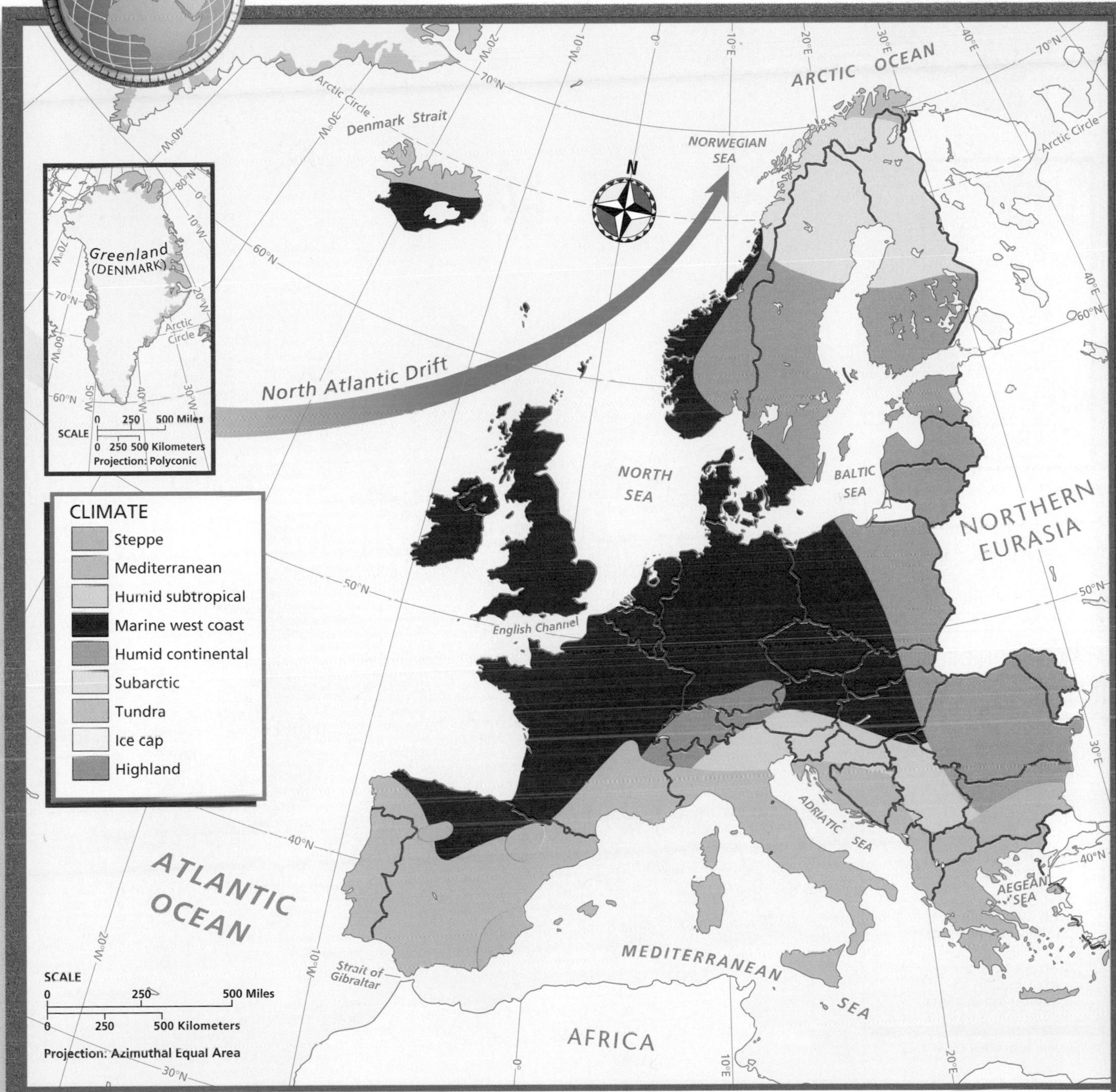

ARCTIC OCEAN
Arctic Circle
Denmark Strait
NORWEGIAN SEA
North Atlantic Drift
NORTH SEA
BALTIC SEA
NORTHERN EURASIA
English Channel
ADRIATIC SEA
AEGEAN SEA
ATLANTIC OCEAN
MEDITERRANEAN SEA
Strait of Gibraltar
AFRICA
Greenland (DENMARK)
SCALE
0 250 500 Miles
0 250 500 Kilometers
Projection: Polyconic
CLIMATE
Steppe
Mediterranean
Humid subtropical
Marine west coast
Humid continental
Subarctic
Tundra
Ice cap
Highland
SCALE
0 250 500 Miles
0 250 500 Kilometers
Projection: Azimuthal Equal Area

1. *Physical Systems* Which climate type takes its name from a sea in the region?
2. *Places and Regions* Which two independent countries have climate types that are not found in any other European country? Which climate types do these two countries have?

Critical Thinking

3. **Comparing** Compare this map to the **physical** and **population maps**. Which physical feature in central Europe has a highland climate and relatively few people? This physical feature is in which countries?

Europe: Population

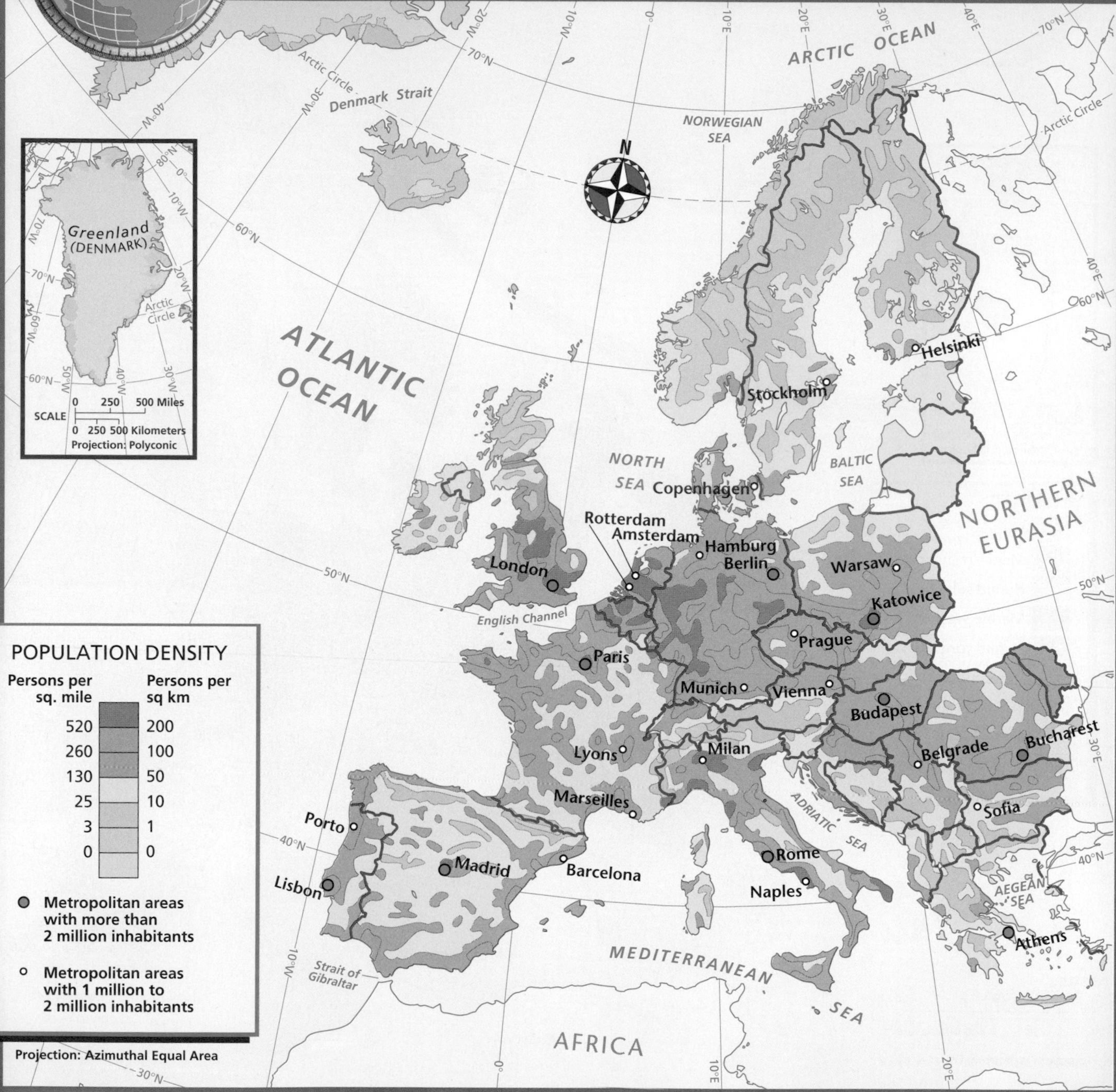
ARCTIC OCEAN
NORWEGIAN SEA
Denmark Strait
Arctic Circle
ATLANTIC OCEAN
NORTH SEA
BALTIC SEA
NORTHERN EURASIA
English Channel
ADRIATIC SEA
AEGEAN SEA
MEDITERRANEAN SEA
Strait of Gibraltar
AFRICA
Greenland (DENMARK)
SCALE
0 250 500 Miles
0 250 500 Kilometers
Projection: Polyconic
Helsinki
Stockholm
Copenhagen
Rotterdam
Amsterdam
Hamburg
Berlin
Warsaw
London
Katowice
Prague
Paris
Munich
Vienna
Budapest
Lyons
Milan
Belgrade
Bucharest
Marseilles
Sofia
Porto
Madrid
Barcelona
Rome
Lisbon
Naples
Athens
POPULATION DENSITY
Persons per sq. mile
Persons per sq km
520 200
260 100
130 50
25 10
3 1
0 0
Metropolitan areas with more than 2 million inhabitants
Metropolitan areas with 1 million to 2 million inhabitants
Projection: Azimuthal Equal Area

1. *Places and Regions* Examine the **climate map**. Why are northern Norway, Sweden, and Finland so thinly populated?
2. *Places and Regions* Compare this map to the **political map**. Which countries have between 25 and 130 persons per square mile in all areas?

Critical Thinking

3. **Analyzing Information** Use the map to create a chart, graph, database, or model of population centers in Europe.

Europe: Land Use and Resources

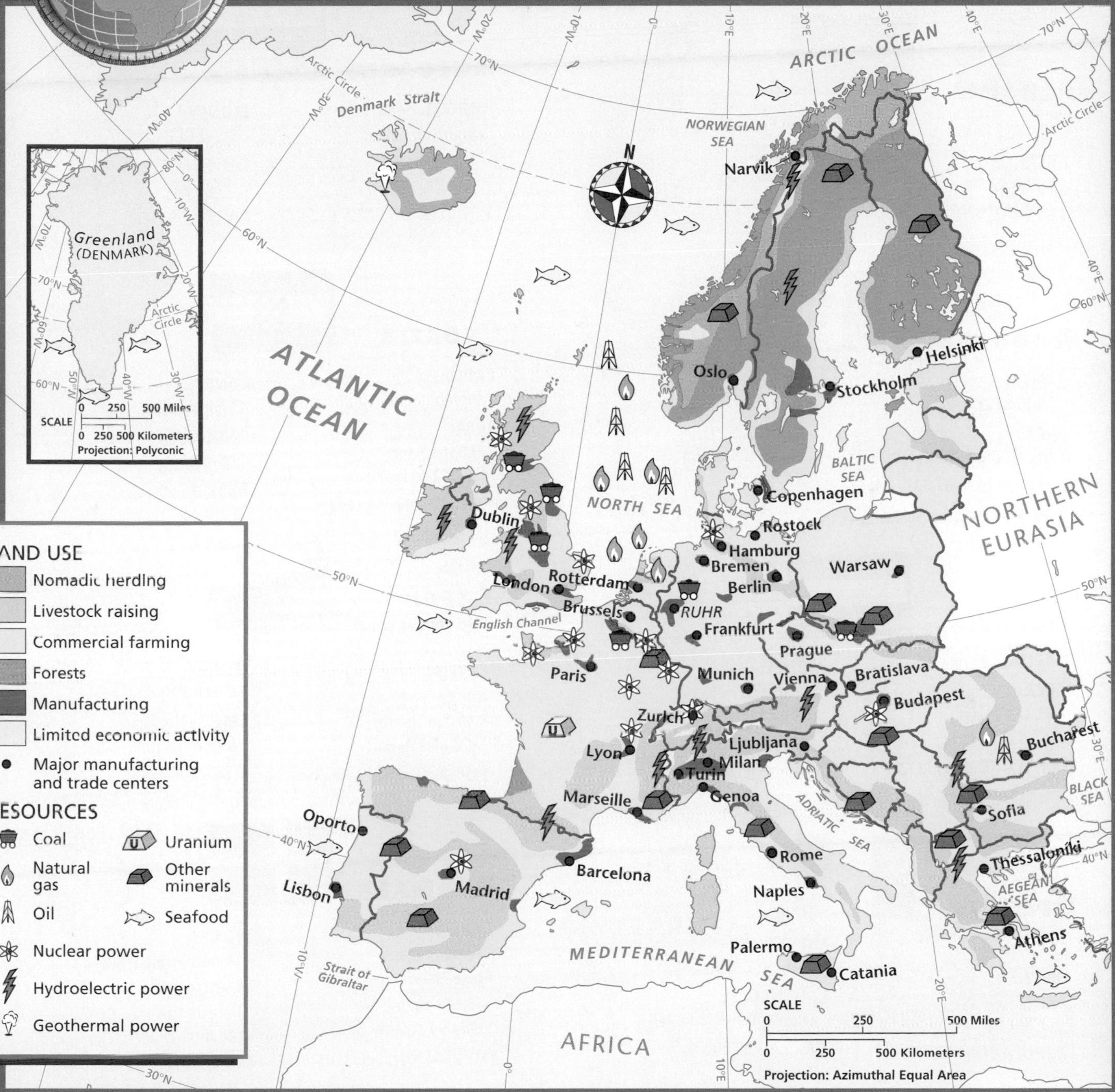
ARCTIC OCEAN
NORWEGIAN SEA
Denmark Strait
Arctic Circle
ATLANTIC OCEAN
NORTH SEA
BALTIC SEA
English Channel
NORTHERN EURASIA
ADRIATIC SEA
BLACK SEA
AEGEAN SEA
MEDITERRANEAN SEA
Strait of Gibraltar
AFRICA
RUHR
Narvik
Oslo
Stockholm
Helsinki
Copenhagen
Rostock
Hamburg
Bremen
Berlin
Warsaw
Dublin
London
Rotterdam
Brussels
Frankfurt
Prague
Paris
Munich
Vienna
Bratislava
Budapest
Zurich
Lyon
Ljubljana
Milan
Turin
Genoa
Marseille
Bucharest
Sofia
Thessaloníki
Athens
Oporto
Lisbon
Madrid
Barcelona
Rome
Naples
Palermo
Catania
Greenland (DENMARK)
SCALE
0 250 500 Miles
0 250 500 Kilometers
Projection: Polyconic
Projection: Azimuthal Equal Area
LAND USE
Nomadic herding
Livestock raising
Commercial farming
Forests
Manufacturing
Limited economic activity
Major manufacturing and trade centers
RESOURCES
Coal
Uranium
Natural gas
Other minerals
Oil
Seafood
Nuclear power
Hydroelectric power
Geothermal power

1. Places and Regions What is the only country in the region that uses geothermal power?
2. Places and Regions Which country in the region mines uranium?
3. Places and Regions In which body of water is oil and gas production concentrated?

Critical Thinking

4. **Analyzing Information** Use the map on this page to create a chart, graph, database, or model of economic activities in Europe.

Fast Facts

Europe

ALBANIA

CAPITAL: Tiranë

AREA: 11,100 sq. mi. (28,748 sq km)

POPULATION: 3,510,484

MONEY: lek (ALL)

LANGUAGES: Albanian, Greek

CARS: data not available

ANDORRA

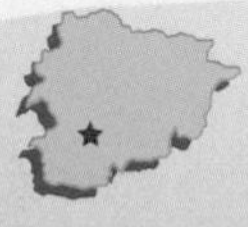

CAPITAL: Andorra la Vella

AREA: 181 sq. mi. (468 sq km)

POPULATION: 67,627

MONEY: euro (€), 1-01-2002

LANGUAGES: Catalan (official), French Castilian

CARS: 35,358

AUSTRIA

CAPITAL: Vienna

AREA: 32,378 sq. mi. (83,858 sq km)

POPULATION: 8,150,835

MONEY: euro (€), 1-01-2002

LANGUAGES: German

CARS: 3,780,000

BELGIUM

CAPITAL: Brussels

AREA: 11,780 sq. mi. (30,510 sq km)

POPULATION: 10,258,762

MONEY: euro (€), 1-01-2002

LANGUAGES: Dutch, French, German

CARS: 4,420,000

BOSNIA AND HERZEGOVINA

CAPITAL: Sarajevo

AREA: 19,741 sq. mi. (51,129 sq km)

POPULATION: 3,922,205

MONEY: marka (BAM)

LANGUAGES: Croatian, Serbian, Bosnian

CARS: data not available

BULGARIA

CAPITAL: Sofia

AREA: 42,822 sq. mi. (110,910 sq km)

POPULATION: 7,707,495

MONEY: lev (BGL)

LANGUAGES: Bulgarian

CARS: 1,650,000

CROATIA

CAPITAL: Zagreb

AREA: 21,831 sq. mi. (56,542 sq km)

POPULATION: 4,334,142

MONEY: Croatian kuna (HRK)

LANGUAGES: Croatian

CARS: 698,000

CZECH REPUBLIC

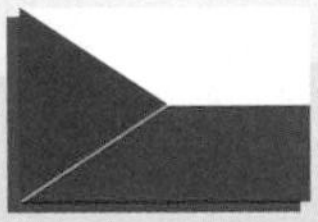

CAPITAL: Prague

AREA: 30,450 sq. mi. (78,866 sq km)

POPULATION: 10,264,212

MONEY: Czech koruna (CZK)

LANGUAGES: Czech

CARS: 4,410,000

DENMARK

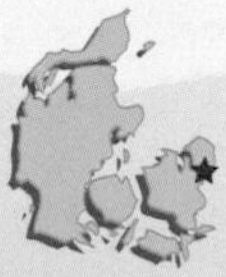

CAPITAL: Copenhagen

AREA: 16,639 sq. mi. (43,094 sq km)

POPULATION: 5,352,815

MONEY: Danish krone (DKK)

LANGUAGES: Danish, Faroese, Greenlandic (an Inuit dialect), German

CARS: 1,790,000

ESTONIA

CAPITAL: Tallinn

AREA: 17,462 sq. mi. (45,226 sq km)

POPULATION: 1,423,316

MONEY: Estonian kroon (EEK)

LANGUAGES: Estonian (official), Russian, Ukrainian, English, Finnish

CARS: 338,000

Countries not drawn to scale.

FINLAND

CAPITAL: Helsinki
AREA: 130,127 sq. mi. (337,030 sq km)
POPULATION: 5,175,783
MONEY: euro (€), 1-01-2002
LANGUAGES: Finnish, Swedish
CARS: 1,940,000

FRANCE

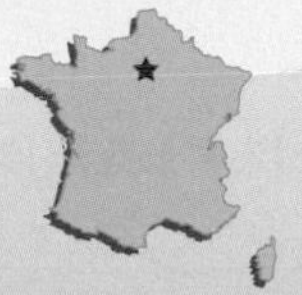

CAPITAL: Paris
AREA: 211,208 sq. mi. (547,030 sq km)
POPULATION: 59,551,227
MONEY: euro (€), 1-01-2002
LANGUAGES: French
CARS: 25,500,000

GERMANY

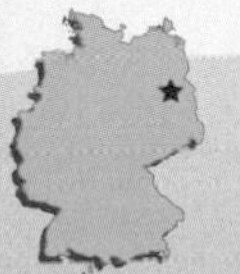

CAPITAL: Berlin
AREA: 137,846 sq. mi. (357,021 sq km)
POPULATION: 83,029,536
MONEY: euro (€), deutsche mark (DM)
LANGUAGES: German
CARS: 41,330,000

GREECE

CAPITAL: Athens
AREA: 50,942 sq. mi. (131,940 sq km)
POPULATION: 10,623,835
MONEY: euro (€), 1-01-2002
LANGUAGES: Greek (official), English, French
CARS: 2,340,000

HUNGARY

CAPITAL: Budapest
AREA: 35,919 sq. mi. (93,030 sq km)
POPULATION: 10,106,017
MONEY: forint (HUF)
LANGUAGES: Hungarian
CARS: 2,280,000

ICELAND

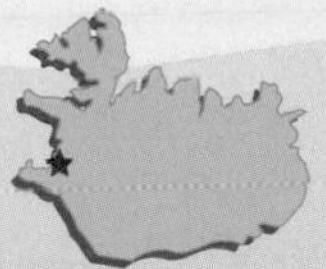

CAPITAL: Reykjavik
AREA: 39,768 sq. mi. (103,000 sq km)
POPULATION: 277,906
MONEY: Icelandic krona (ISK)
LANGUAGES: Icelandic
CARS: 132,468

IRELAND

CAPITAL: Dublin
AREA: 27,135 sq. mi. (70,280 sq km)
POPULATION: 3,840,838
MONEY: euro (€), 1-01-2002
LANGUAGES: English, Irish (Gaelic)
CARS: 1,060,000

ITALY

CAPITAL: Rome
AREA: 116,305 sq. mi. (301,230 sq km)
POPULATION: 57,679,825
MONEY: euro (€), 1-01-2002
LANGUAGES: Italian, German, French, Slovene
CARS: 31,000,000

LATVIA

CAPITAL: Riga
AREA: 24,938 sq. mi. (64,589 sq km)
POPULATION: 2,385,231
MONEY: Latvian lat (LVL)
LANGUAGES: Lettish (official), Lithuanian, Russian
CARS: 252,000

LIECHTENSTEIN

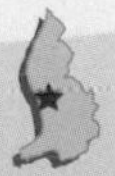

CAPITAL: Vaduz
AREA: 62 sq. mi. (160 sq km)
POPULATION: 32,528
MONEY: Swiss franc (CHF)
LANGUAGES: German
CARS: data not available

Sources: Central Intelligence Agency, *The World Factbook 2001; The World Almanac and Book of Facts 2001;* population figures are 2001 estimates.

Lithuania

CAPITAL: Vilnius
AREA: 25,174 sq. mi. (65,200 sq km)
POPULATION: 3,610,535
MONEY: litas (LTL)
LANGUAGES: Lithuanian (official), Polish, Russian
CARS: 653,000

Luxembourg

CAPITAL: Luxembourg
AREA: 998 sq. mi. (2,586 sq km)
POPULATION: 429,080
MONEY: euro (€), Luxembourg franc (LuxF)
LANGUAGES: Luxembourgish, German, French
CARS: 231,666

Macedonia

CAPITAL: Skopje
AREA: 9,781 sq. mi. (25,333 sq km)
POPULATION: 2,046,209
MONEY: Macedonian denar (MKD)
LANGUAGES: Macedonian, Albanian, Turkish, Serbo-Croatian
CARS: 263,000

Malta

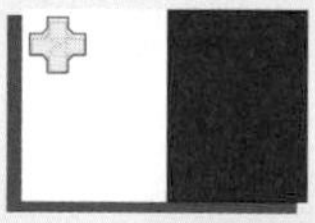

CAPITAL: Valletta
AREA: 122 sq. mi. (316 sq km)
POPULATION: 394,583
MONEY: Maltese lira (MTL)
LANGUAGES: Maltese (official), English (official)
CARS: 122,100

Moldova

CAPITAL: Chișinău
AREA: 13,067 sq. mi. (33,843 sq km)
POPULATION: 4,431,570
MONEY: Moldovan leu (MDL)
LANGUAGES: Moldovan (official), Russian, Gagauz
CARS: 169,000

Monaco

CAPITAL: Monaco
AREA: 0.75 sq. mi. (1.95 sq km)
POPULATION: 31,842
MONEY: euro (€), 1-01-2002
LANGUAGES: French (official), English, Italian, Monegasque
CARS: 17,000

Netherlands

CAPITAL: Amsterdam
AREA: 16,033 sq. mi. (41,526 sq km)
POPULATION: 15,981,472
MONEY: euro (€), 1-01-2002
LANGUAGES: Dutch
CARS: 5,810,000

Norway

CAPITAL: Oslo
AREA: 125,181 sq. mi. (324,220 sq km)
POPULATION: 4,503,440
MONEY: Norwegian krone (NOK)
LANGUAGES: Norwegian
CARS: 1,760,000

Poland

CAPITAL: Warsaw
AREA: 120,728 sq. mi. (312,685 sq km)
POPULATION: 38,633,912
MONEY: zloty (PLN)
LANGUAGES: Polish
CARS: 7,520,000

Portugal

CAPITAL: Lisbon
AREA: 35,672 sq. mi. (92,391 sq km)
POPULATION: 10,066,253
MONEY: euro (€), 1-01-2002
LANGUAGES: Portuguese
CARS: 2,950,000

Countries not drawn to scale.

Romania

CAPITAL: Bucharest
AREA: 91,699 sq. mi. (237,500 sq km)
POPULATION: 22,364,022
MONEY: leu (ROL)
LANGUAGES: Romanian, Hungarian, German
CARS: 2,390,000

San Marino

CAPITAL: San Marino
AREA: 23.6 sq. mi. (61.2 sq km)
POPULATION: 27,336
MONEY: euro (€), 1-01-2002
LANGUAGES: Italian
CARS: 24,825

Slovakia

CAPITAL: Bratislava
AREA: 18,859 sq. mi. (48,845 sq km)
POPULATION: 5,414,937
MONEY: Slovak koruna (SKK)
LANGUAGES: Slovak (official), Hungarian
CARS: 994,000

Slovenia

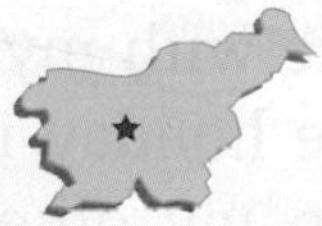

CAPITAL: Ljubljana
AREA: 7,820 sq. mi. (20,253 sq km)
POPULATION: 1,930,132
MONEY: tolar (SIT)
LANGUAGES: Slovenian, Serbo-Croatian
CARS: 657,000

Spain

CAPITAL: Madrid
AREA: 194,896 sq. mi. (504,782 sq km)
POPULATION: 40,037,995
MONEY: euro (€), peseta (Pta)
LANGUAGES: Castilian Spanish, Catalan, Galician
CARS: 15,300,000

Sweden

CAPITAL: Stockholm
AREA: 173,731 sq. mi. (449,964 sq km)
POPULATION: 8,875,053
MONEY: Swedish krona (SEK)
LANGUAGES: Swedish
CARS: 3,700,000

Switzerland

CAPITAL: Bern
AREA: 15,942 sq. mi. (41,290 sq km)
POPULATION: 7,283,274
MONEY: Swiss franc (CHF)
LANGUAGES: German, French, Italian
CARS: 3,320,000

United Kingdom

CAPITAL: London
AREA: 94,525 sq. mi. (244,820 sq km)
POPULATION: 59,647,790
MONEY: British pound (GBP)
LANGUAGES: English, Welsh, Scottish form of Gaelic
CARS: 25,590,000

Vatican City

CAPITAL: Vatican City
AREA: 0.17 sq. mi. (0.44 sq km)
POPULATION: 890
MONEY: euro (€), 1-01-2002
LANGUAGES: Italian, Latin
CARS: data not available

Yugoslavia

CAPITAL: Belgrade
AREA: 39,517 sq. mi. (102,350 sq km)
POPULATION: 10,677,290
MONEY: New Yugoslav dinar (YUM)
LANGUAGES: Serbian, Albanian
CARS: 1,000,000

internet connect
COUNTRY STATISTICS
GO TO: go.hrw.com
KEYWORD: SJ3 FactsU5
FOR: more facts about Europe

Sources: Central Intelligence Agency, *The World Factbook 2001; The World Almanac and Book of Facts 2001;* population figures are 2001 estimates.

Section 3 Italy

Read to Discover

1. What was the early history of Italy like?
2. How has Italy added to world culture?
3. What is Italy like today?

Define

pope
Renaissance
coalition governments

Locate

Rome
Genoa
Naples
Milan
Turin
Florence

WHY IT MATTERS

Leonardo da Vinci and Galileo are just two famous Italians who have made significant contributions to science and art. Use CNNfyi.com or other **current events** sources to find examples of recent Italian scientists and artists. Record your findings in your journal.

Artifact from a warrior's armor, 400s B.C.

Switzerland
Austria
France
Italy
Rome

▲ The Appian Way was a road from Rome to Brindisi. It was started in 312 B.C. by the emperor Claudius.

Interpreting the Visual Record How do you think this road has withstood more than 2,000 years of use?

History

About 750 B.C. a tribe known as the Latins established the city of Rome on the Tiber River. Over time, these Romans conquered the rest of Italy. They then began to expand their rule to lands outside Italy.

Roman Empire At its height about A.D. 100, the Roman Empire stretched westward to what is now Spain and Portugal and northward to England and Germany. The Balkans, Turkey, parts of Southwest Asia, and coastal North Africa were all part of the empire. Roman laws, roads, engineering, and the Latin language could be found throughout this huge area. The Roman army kept order, and people could travel safely throughout the empire. Trade prospered. The Romans made advances in engineering, including roads and aqueducts—canals that transported water. They also learned how to build domes and arches. Romans also produced great works of art and literature.

About A.D. 200, however, the Roman Empire began to weaken. The western part, with its capital in Rome, fell in A.D. 476. The eastern part, the Byzantine Empire, lasted until 1453.

Roman influences in the world can still be seen today. Latin developed into the modern languages of French, Italian, Portuguese, Romanian, and Spanish. Many English words have Latin origins as well. Roman laws and political ideas have influenced the governments and legal systems of many modern countries.

Switzerland
Austria
France
Italy
Rome

The Colosseum is a giant amphitheater. It was built in Rome between A.D. 70 and 80 and could seat 50,000 people.

Interpreting the Visual Record

For what events do you think the Colosseum was used? What type of modern buildings look like this?

Christianity began in the Roman province of Judaea (modern Israel and the West Bank). It then spread through the Roman Empire. Some early Christians were persecuted for refusing to worship the traditional Roman gods. However, in the early A.D. 300s the Roman emperor, Constantine, adopted Christianity. It quickly became the main religion of the empire. The **pope**—the bishop of Rome—is the head of the Roman Catholic Church.

The Renaissance Beginning in the 1300s a new era of learning began in Italy. It was known as the **Renaissance** (re-nuh-SAHNS). In French this word means "rebirth." During the Renaissance, Italians rediscovered the work of ancient Roman and Greek writers. Scholars applied reason and experimented to advance the sciences. Artists pioneered new techniques. Leonardo da Vinci, painter of the *Mona Lisa,* was also a sculptor, engineer, architect, and scientist. Another Italian, Galileo Galilei, perfected the telescope and experimented with gravity.

Christopher Columbus opened up the Americas to European colonization. Although Spain paid for his voyages, Columbus was an Italian from the city of Genoa. The name *America* comes from another Italian explorer, Amerigo Vespucci.

Government Italy was divided into many small states until the late 1800s. Today Italy's central government is a democracy with an elected parliament. Italy has had many changes in leadership in recent years. This has happened because no political party has won a majority of votes in Italian elections. As a result, political parties must form **coalition governments**. A coalition government is one in which several parties join together to run the country. Unfortunately, these coalitions usually do not last long.

✓ **READING CHECK:** *Human Systems* How is the Italian government different from that of the United States?

Leonardo da Vinci painted the *Mona Lisa* about 1503–06.

Interpreting the Visual Record Why do you think Leonardo's painting became famous?

Culture

People from other places have influenced Italian culture. During the Renaissance, many Jews who had been expelled from Spain moved to Italian cities. Jews often had to live in segregated areas called ghettoes. Today immigrants have arrived from former Italian colonies in Africa. Others have come from the eastern Mediterranean and the Balkans.

Religion and Food Some 98 percent of Italians belong to the Roman Catholic Church. The leadership of the church is still based in the Vatican in Rome. Christmas and Easter are major holidays in Italy. Italians also celebrate All Souls' Day on November 2 by cleaning and decorating their relatives' graves.

Italians enjoy a range of regional foods. Recipes are influenced by the history and crops of each area. In the south, Italians eat a Mediterranean diet of olives, bread, and fish. Dishes are flavored with lemons from Greece and spices from Africa. Tomatoes, originally from the Americas, have become an important part of the diet. Some Italian foods, such as pizza, are popular in the United States. Modern pizza originated in Naples. Northern Italians eat more rice, butter, cheeses, and mushrooms than southern Italians.

The Arts The ancient Romans created beautiful glassware and jewelry as well as marble and bronze sculptures. During the Renaissance, Italy again became a center for art, particularly painting and sculpture. Italian artists discovered ways to make their paintings more lifelike. They did this by creating the illusion of three dimensions. Italian writers like Francesco Petrarch and Giovanni Boccaccio wrote some of the most important literature of the Renaissance. More recently, Italian composers have written great operas. Today, Italian designers, actors, and filmmakers are celebrated worldwide.

✓ **READING CHECK:** *Human Systems* What are some examples of Italian culture?

This view of the Pantheon in Rome shows the oculus—the opening at the top. The Pantheon was built as a temple to all Roman gods.

Interpreting the Visual Record Why did the Romans need to design buildings that let in light?

In Rome people attend mass in St. Peter's Square, Vatican City. Vatican City is an independent state within Rome.

Interpreting the Visual Record How does a plaza, or open area, help create a sense of community?

Switzerland
Austria
France
Italy
Rome

Italy Today

Italy is slightly smaller than Florida and Georgia combined, with a population of about 57 million. A shared language, the Roman Catholic Church, and strong family ties continue to bind Italians together.

Economy After its defeat in World War II, Italy rebuilt its industries in the north. Rich soil and plenty of water make the north Italy's "breadbasket," or wheat growing area. Italy's most valuable crop is grapes. Although grapes are grown throughout the country, northern Italy produces the best crops. These grapes help make Italy the world's largest producer of wine. Tourists are also important to Italy's economy. They visit northern and central Italy to see ancient ruins and Renaissance art. Southern Italy remains poorer with lower crop yields. Industrialization there also lags behind the north. Tourist resorts, however, are growing in the south and promise to help the economy.

Cities The northern cities of Milan, Turin, and Genoa are important industrial centers. Their location near the center of Europe helps companies sell products to foreign customers. Also in the north are two popular tourist sites. One is Venice, which is famous for its romantic canals and beautiful buildings. The other is Florence, a center of art and culture. Rome, the capital, is located in central Italy. Naples, the largest city in southern Italy, is a major manufacturing center and port.

✓ READING CHECK: *Environment and Society* What geographic factors influence Italy's economy?

Italy

Country	Population/ Growth Rate	Life Expectancy	Literacy Rate	Per Capita GDP
Italy	57,679,825 / .07%	76, male 83, female	98%	$22,100
United States	281,421,906 / 0.9%	74, male 80, female	97%	$36,200

Sources: Central Intelligence Agency, *The World Factbook 2001*; U.S. Census Bureau

Interpreting the Chart What is the difference in the growth rate of Italy and the United States?

Section 3 Review

go.hrw.com Homework Practice Online
Keyword: SJ3 HP18

Define and explain: pope, Renaissance, coalition governments

Working with Sketch Maps On the map you created in Section 2, label Florence, Genoa, Milan, Naples, Rome, and Turin. Why are they important?

Reading for the Main Idea

1. *Human Systems* What were some of the important contributions of the Romans?
2. *Human Systems* What are some art forms for which Italy is well known?

Critical Thinking

3. **Finding the Main Idea** Which of Italy's physical features encourage trade? Which geographical features make trading difficult?
4. **Analyzing Information** Why is the northern part of Italy known as the country's "breadbasket"?

Organizing What You Know

5. **Finding the Main Idea** Copy the following graphic organizer. Use it to describe the movement of goods and ideas to and from Italy during the early days of trade and exploration.

[ ] ⇨ Italy ⇨ [ ]

CHAPTER 19 Reviewing What You Know

Building Vocabulary

On a separate sheet of paper, write sentences to define each of the following words.

1. navigable
2. loess
3. medieval
4. impressionism
5. Reformation
6. Holocaust
7. chancellor
8. cosmopolitan
9. cantons
10. nationalism

Reviewing the Main Ideas

1. *Places and Regions* What is the climate of west-central Europe like?
2. *Human Systems* What were the effects of religious conflicts on Germany?
3. *Places and Regions* What energy resources are available to the countries of this region?
4. *Human Systems* Name five artists from west-central Europe who have made notable contributions to culture.
5. *Human Systems* What international organizations have created ties between countries of west-central Europe since World War II?

Understanding Environment and Society

Cleaning up Pollution

Create a presentation on East German industries' pollution of the environment. Include a chart, graph, database, model, or map showing patterns of pollutants, as well as the German government's clean-up effort. Consider the following:

- Pollution in the former East Germany.
- Pollution today.
- Costs of stricter environmental laws.

Write a five-question quiz, with answers about your presentation to challenge fellow students.

Thinking Critically

1. **Drawing Inferences and Conclusions** What geographic features have encouraged travel and trade in west-central Europe? What geographic features have hindered travel and trade?
2. **Finding the Main Idea** How have the people of Switzerland altered their environment?
3. **Analyzing Information** What landform regions give France natural borders? Which French borders do not coincide with physical features?
4. **Drawing Inferences and Conclusions** Why might Brussels, Belgium, be called the capital of Europe?
5. **Comparing** What demographic factors are shared by all countries of west-central Europe today? How do they reflect levels of economic development?

Building Social Studies Skills

Map ACTIVITY

On a separate sheet of paper, match the letters on the map with their correct labels.

Northern European Plain
Pyrenees
Alps
Seine River
Rhine River
Danube River
North Sea
Mediterranean Sea
Paris
Berlin

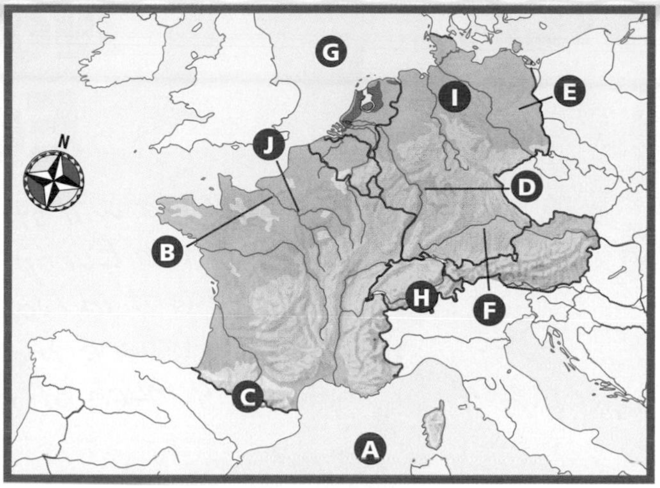

N
A
B
C
D
E
F
G
H
I
J

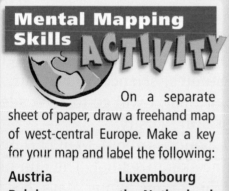

Mental Mapping Skills ACTIVITY

On a separate sheet of paper, draw a freehand map of west-central Europe. Make a key for your map and label the following:

Austria
Belgium
France
Germany
Luxembourg
the Netherlands
North Sea
Switzerland

WRITING ACTIVITY

Imagine you are taking a boat tour down the Rhine River. You will travel from Basel, Switzerland, to Rotterdam, the Netherlands. Keep a journal describing the places you see and the stops you make. Be sure to use standard grammar, spelling, sentence structure, and punctuation.

Alternative Assessment

Portfolio ACTIVITY

Learning About Your Local Geography

Agricultural Products Some countries in west-central Europe are major exporters of agricultural products. Research the agricultural products of your state. Draw a map that shows important products and areas they are produced.

internet connect

Internet Activity: go.hrw.com
KEYWORD: SJ3 GT19

Choose a topic to explore about west-central Europe:

- Tour the land and rivers of Europe.
- Travel back in time to the Middle Ages.
- Visit Belgian and Dutch schools.

CHAPTER 20

Northern Europe

Now we will study the countries of northern Europe. First we meet Lars, a student in Norway. He lives in a place where the Sun does not rise during much of the winter.

Jeg bor i midnattssolens land.

Hi! My name is Lars. I am 13, and I live in Tromsø, one of the northernmost cities in Europe. I am in my seventh year at school. In school we study Norwegian, plus English, French or German, social studies, science, music, art, and cooking. If I do well in junior high, I will go to an academic high school and prepare for a university.

Usually I walk to school, which is about 3 km (1.9 miles) away. In the winter, everyone skis to school. The Sun never shines on many winter days because we live north of the Arctic Circle. On January 20, when the Sun appears again for just a few minutes, we celebrate Sun Day.

In the summer the Sun never sets. This is my favorite time of the year. It still can be cold then. Last summer the temperature was mostly around 6° or 7°C (about 43° or 44°F).

◄ Translation: I live in the Land of the Midnight Sun.

Section 1 Physical Geography

Read to Discover

1. What are the region's major physical features?
2. What are the region's most important natural resources?
3. What climates are found in northern Europe?

Define

fjords
lochs
North Atlantic Drift

Locate

British Isles
English Channel
North Sea
Great Britain
Ireland
Iceland
Greenland
Scandinavian Peninsula
Jutland Peninsula
Kjølen Mountains
Northwest Highlands
Shannon River
Baltic Sea

WHY IT MATTERS

An important physical feature of Northern Europe is the North Sea. Use CNNfyi.com or other **current events** sources to learn more about America's dependence on oil. Record your findings in your journal.

A Viking ship post

Northern Europe: Physical-Political

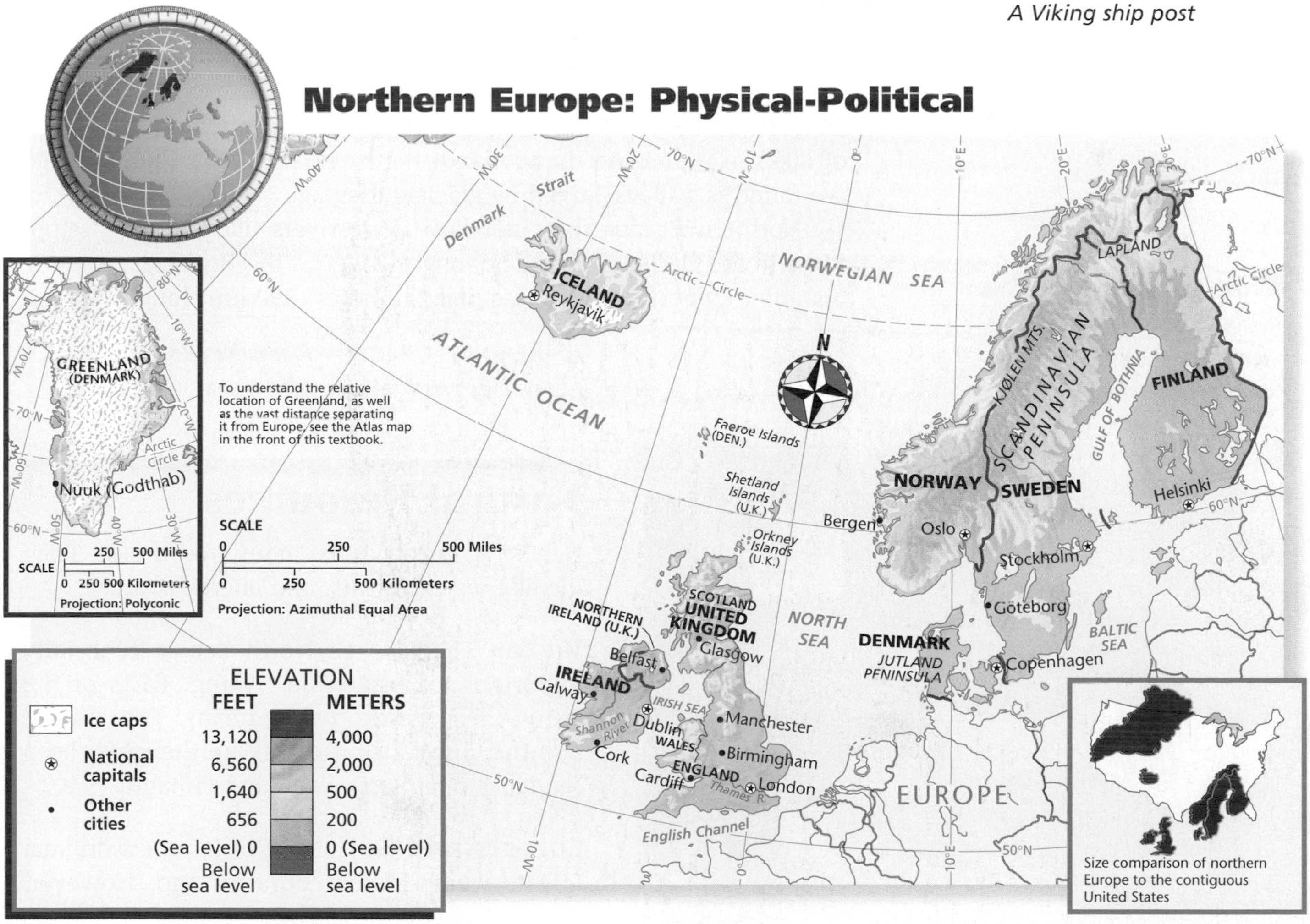

Denmark Strait
ICELAND
Reykjavik
Arctic Circle
NORWEGIAN SEA
ATLANTIC OCEAN
N
Faeroe Islands (DEN.)
Shetland Islands (U.K.)
Orkney Islands (U.K.)
LAPLAND
FINLAND
KJØLEN MTS.
SCANDINAVIAN PENINSULA
GULF OF BOTHNIA
NORWAY
SWEDEN
Helsinki
Bergen
Oslo
Stockholm
Göteborg
BALTIC SEA
DENMARK
JUTLAND PENINSULA
Copenhagen
NORTH SEA
SCOTLAND
UNITED KINGDOM
Glasgow
NORTHERN IRELAND (U.K.)
Belfast
IRELAND
Galway
Shannon River
Cork
IRISH SEA
Dublin
WALES
Manchester
Birmingham
ENGLAND
Cardiff
London
Thames R.
English Channel
EUROPE
70°N
60°N
50°N
40°W
30°W
20°W
10°W
0°
10°E
20°E
30°E
GREENLAND (DENMARK)
Arctic Circle
Nuuk (Godthab)
SCALE
0 250 500 Miles
0 250 500 Kilometers
Projection: Polyconic
To understand the relative location of Greenland, as well as the vast distance separating it from Europe, see the Atlas map in the front of this textbook.
SCALE
0 250 500 Miles
0 250 500 Kilometers
Projection: Azimuthal Equal Area
ELEVATION
FEET METERS
Ice caps
National capitals
Other cities
13,120 4,000
6,560 2,000
1,640 500
656 200
(Sea level) 0 0 (Sea level)
Below sea level Below sea level
Size comparison of northern Europe to the contiguous United States

internet connect

GO TO: go.hrw.com
KEYWORD: SJ3 CH20
FOR: Web sites about northern Europe

Physical Features

Northern Europe includes several large islands and peninsulas. The British Isles lie across the English Channel and North Sea from the rest of Europe. They include the islands of Great Britain and Ireland and are divided between the United Kingdom and the Republic of Ireland. This region also includes the islands of Iceland and Greenland. Greenland is the world's largest island.

To the east are the Scandinavian and Jutland Peninsulas. Denmark occupies the Jutland Peninsula and nearby islands. The Scandinavian Peninsula is divided between Norway and Sweden. Finland lies farther east. These countries plus Iceland make up Scandinavia.

Our Amazing Planet

Scotland's Loch Ness contains more fresh water than all the lakes in England and Wales combined. It is deeper, on average, than the nearby North Sea.

Landforms The rolling hills of Ireland, the highlands of Great Britain, and the Kjølen (CHUH-luhn) Mountains of Scandinavia are part of Europe's Northwest Highlands region. This is a region of very old, eroded hills and low mountains.

Southeastern Great Britain and southern Scandinavia are lowland regions. Much of Iceland is mountainous and volcanic. More than 10 percent of it is covered by glaciers. Greenland is mostly covered by a thick ice cap.

Coasts Northern Europe has long, jagged coastlines. The coastline of Norway includes many **fjords** (fee-AWRDS). Fjords are narrow, deep inlets of the sea set between high, rocky cliffs. Ice-age glaciers carved the fjords out of coastal mountains.

Lakes and Rivers Melting ice-age glaciers left behind thousands of lakes in the region. In Scotland, the lakes are called **lochs**. Lochs are found in valleys carved by glaciers long ago.

Northern Europe does not have long rivers like the Mississippi River in the United States. The longest river in the British Isles is the Shannon River in Ireland. It is just 240 miles (390 km) long.

✓ **READING CHECK:** *Places and Regions* What are the physical features of the region?

Fjords like this one shelter many harbors in Norway.

Interpreting the Visual Record
How are fjords created?

Norway
Sweden
Finland

Natural Resources

Northern Europe has many resources. They include water, forests, and energy sources.

Water The ice-free North Sea is especially important for trade and fishing. Parts of the Baltic Sea freeze over during the winter months. Special ships break up the ice to keep sea lanes open to Sweden and Finland.

Forests and Soil Most of Europe's original forests were cleared centuries ago. However,

Sweden and Finland still have large, coniferous forests that produce timber. The region's farmers grow many kinds of cool-climate crops.

Energy Beneath the North Sea are rich oil and natural gas reserves. Nearly all of the oil reserves are controlled by the nearby United Kingdom and Norway. However, these reserves cannot satisfy all of the region's needs. Most countries import oil and natural gas from southwest Asia, Africa, and Russia. Some, such as Iceland, use geothermal and hydroelectric power.

✓ **READING CHECK:** *Environment and Society* In what way has technology allowed people in the region to keep the North Sea open during the winter?

Climate

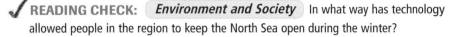

Despite its northern location, much of the region has a marine west coast climate. Westerly winds blow over a warm ocean current called the **North Atlantic Drift**. These winds bring mild temperatures and rain to the British Isles and coastal areas. Atlantic storms often bring even more rain. Snow and frosts may occur in winter.

Central Sweden and southern Finland have a humid continental climate. This area has four true seasons. Far to the north are subarctic and tundra climates. In the forested subarctic regions, winters are long and cold with short days. Long days fill the short summers. In the tundra region it is cold all year. Only small plants such as grass and moss grow there.

✓ **READING CHECK:** *Places and Regions* What are the region's climates?

BUILD on WHAT You Know

Do you remember what you learned about ocean currents? See Chapter 3 to review.

go.hrw.com Homework Practice Online
Keyword: SJ3 HP20

Section 1 Review

Define and explain: fjords, lochs, North Atlantic Drift

Working with Sketch Maps On an outline map that you draw or that your teacher provides, label the following: British Isles, English Channel, North Sea, Great Britain, Ireland, Iceland, Greenland, Scandinavian Peninsula, Jutland Peninsula, Kjølen Mountains, Northwest Highlands, Shannon River, and Baltic Sea. In the margin, write a short caption explaining how the North Atlantic Drift affects the region's climates.

Reading for the Main Idea

1. *Places and Regions* Which parts of northern Europe are highland regions? Which parts are lowland regions?
2. *Places and Regions* What major climate types are found in northern Europe?

Critical Thinking

3. **Finding the Main Idea** How has ice shaped the region's physical geography?
4. **Making Generalizations and Predictions** Think about what you have learned about global warming. How might warmer temperatures affect the climates and people of northern Europe?

Organizing What You Know

5. **Summarizing** Copy the following graphic organizer. Use it to describe the region's important natural resources.

Water	Forests and soil	Energy

Section 2 The United Kingdom

Read to Discover

1. What are some important events in the history of the United Kingdom?
2. What are the people and culture of the country like?
3. What is the United Kingdom like today?

Define

textiles
constitutional monarchy
glen

Locate

England
Scotland
Wales
Northern Ireland
Irish Sea
London
Birmingham
Manchester
Glasgow
Cardiff
Belfast

WHY IT MATTERS

The United States has been heavily influenced by the British people. Use CNNfyi.com or other **current events** sources to find out about present-day ties between the United States and Great Britain. Record your findings in your journal.

British crown

United Kingdom
Ireland
Stonehenge
Belgium
France

Early peoples of the British Isles built Stonehenge in stages from about 3100 B.C. to about 1800 B.C.

History

Most of the British are descended from people who came to the British Isles long ago. The Celts (KELTS) are thought by some scholars to have come to the islands around 450 B.C. Mountain areas of Wales, Scotland, and Ireland have remained mostly Celtic.

Later, from the A.D. 400s to 1000s, new groups of people came. The Angles and Saxons came from northern Germany and Denmark. The Vikings came from Scandinavia. Last to arrive in Britain were the Normans from northern France. They conquered England in 1066. English as spoken today reflects these migrations. It combines elements from the Anglo-Saxon and Norman French languages.

A Global Power England became a world power in the late 1500s. Surrounded by water, the country developed a powerful navy that protected trade routes. In the 1600s the English began establishing colonies around the world. By the early 1800s they had also united England, Scotland, Wales, and Ireland into one kingdom. From London the United Kingdom built a vast British Empire. By 1900 the empire covered nearly one fourth of the world's land area.

This beautiful Anglo-Saxon shoulder clasp from about A.D. 630 held together pieces of clothing.

The United Kingdom also became an economic power in the 1700s and 1800s. It was the cradle of the Industrial Revolution, which began in the last half of the 1700s. Large supplies of coal and iron and a large labor force helped industries grow. The country also developed a good transportation network of rivers, canals, and railroads. Three of the early industries were **textiles**, or cloth products, shipbuilding, iron, and later steel. Coal powered these industries. Birmingham, Manchester, and other cities grew up near Britain's coal fields.

Queen Elizabeth I (1533–1603) ruled England as it became a world power in the late 1500s.

Decline of Empire

World wars and economic competition from other countries weakened the United Kingdom in the 1900s. All but parts of northern Ireland became independent in 1921. By the 1970s most British colonies also had gained independence. Most now make up the British Commonwealth of Nations. Members of the Commonwealth meet to discuss economic, scientific, and business matters.

The United Kingdom still plays an important role in world affairs. It is a leading member of the United Nations (UN), the European Union (EU), and the North Atlantic Treaty Organization (NATO).

The Government

The United Kingdom's form of government is called a **constitutional monarchy**. That is, it has a monarch—a king or queen—but a parliament makes the country's laws. The monarch is the head of state but has largely ceremonial duties. Parliament chooses a prime minister to lead the national government.

In recent years the national government has given people in Scotland and Wales more control over local affairs. Some people think Scotland might one day seek independence.

✓ **READING CHECK:** *Human Systems* How are former British colonies linked today?

The British government is seated in London, the capital. The Tower Bridge over the River Thames [TEMZ] is one of the city's many famous historical sites.

Interpreting the Visual Record
Why do you think London became a large city?

United Kingdom
Ireland
London
Belgium
France

Ireland

Country	Population/ Growth Rate	Life Expectancy	Literacy Rate	Per Capita GDP
Ireland	3,840,838 / 1.1%	74, male; 80, female	98%	$21,600
United States	281,421,906 / 0.9%	74, male; 80, female	97%	$36,200

Sources: Central Intelligence Agency, *The World Factbook 2001;* U.S. Census Bureau

Interpreting the Chart How does life expectancy in Ireland compare with that of the United States?

Economy Until recently, Ireland was mostly an agricultural country. This was true even though much of the country is either rocky or boggy. A **bog** is soft ground that is soaked with water. For centuries, **peat** dug from bogs has been used for fuel. Peat is made up of dead plants, usually mosses.

Today Ireland is an industrial country. Irish workers produce processed foods, textiles, chemicals, machinery, crystal, and computers. Finance, tourism, and other service industries are also important.

How did this change come about? Ireland's low taxes, well-educated workers, and membership in the European Union have attracted many foreign companies. Those foreign companies include many from the United States. These companies see Ireland as a door to millions of customers throughout the EU. In fact, goods from their Irish factories are exported to markets in the rest of Europe and countries in other regions.

Cities Many factories have been built around Dublin. Dublin is Ireland's capital and largest city. It is a center for education, banking, and shipping. Nearly 1 million people live there. Housing prices rapidly increased in the 1990s as people moved there for work.

Other cities lie mainly along the coast. These cities include the seaports of Cork and Galway. They have old castles, churches, and other historical sites that are popular among tourists.

✓ **READING CHECK:** *Human Systems* What important economic changes have occurred in Ireland and why?

go.hrw.com Homework Practice Online
Keyword: SJ3 HP20

Section 3 Review

Define and explain: famine, bog, peat

Working with Sketch Maps On the map you created in Section 2, label Ireland, Dublin, Cork, and Galway. In the margin explain the importance of Dublin to the Republic of Ireland.

Reading for the Main Idea

1. *Human Systems* What were two of the reasons many Irish moved to the United States and other countries in the 1800s?
2. *Human Systems* What are some important reasons why the economy in Ireland has grown so much in recent years?

Critical Thinking

3. **Drawing Inferences and Conclusions** Why do you think the Irish fought against British rule?
4. **Drawing Inferences and Conclusions** Why do you suppose housing prices rapidly increased in Dublin in the 1990s?

Organizing What You Know

5. **Comparing/Contrasting** Copy the following graphic organizer. Use it to compare and contrast the history, culture, and governments of the Republic of Ireland and the United Kingdom.

Ireland	United Kingdom
Conquered by England in the 1100s	Created vast world empire

Section 4 Scandinavia

Read to Discover

1. What are the people and culture of Scandinavia like?
2. What are some important features of each of the region's countries, plus Greenland, and Lapland?

Define

neutral
uninhabitable
geysers

Locate

Oslo
Bergen
Stockholm
Göteborg
Copenhagen
Nuuk (Godthab)
Reykjavik
Gulf of Bothnia
Gulf of Finland
Helsinki
Lapland

Why It Matters

Much of the fish Americans eat comes from the nations of Scandinavia. Use CNNfyi.com or other **current events** sources to learn more about the economic importance of these nations. Record your findings in your journal.

Smoked salmon, a popular food in Scandinavia

People and Culture

Scandinavia once was home to fierce, warlike Vikings. Today the countries of Norway, Sweden, Denmark, Iceland, and Finland are peaceful and prosperous.

The people of the region enjoy high standards of living. They have good health care and long life spans. Each government provides expensive social programs and services. These programs are paid for by high taxes.

The people and cultures in the countries of Scandinavia are similar in many ways. For example, the region's national languages, except for Finnish, are closely related. In addition, most people in Scandinavia are Lutheran Protestant. All of the Scandinavian countries have democratic governments.

✓ **READING CHECK:** *Human Systems* How are the people and cultures of Scandinavia similar?

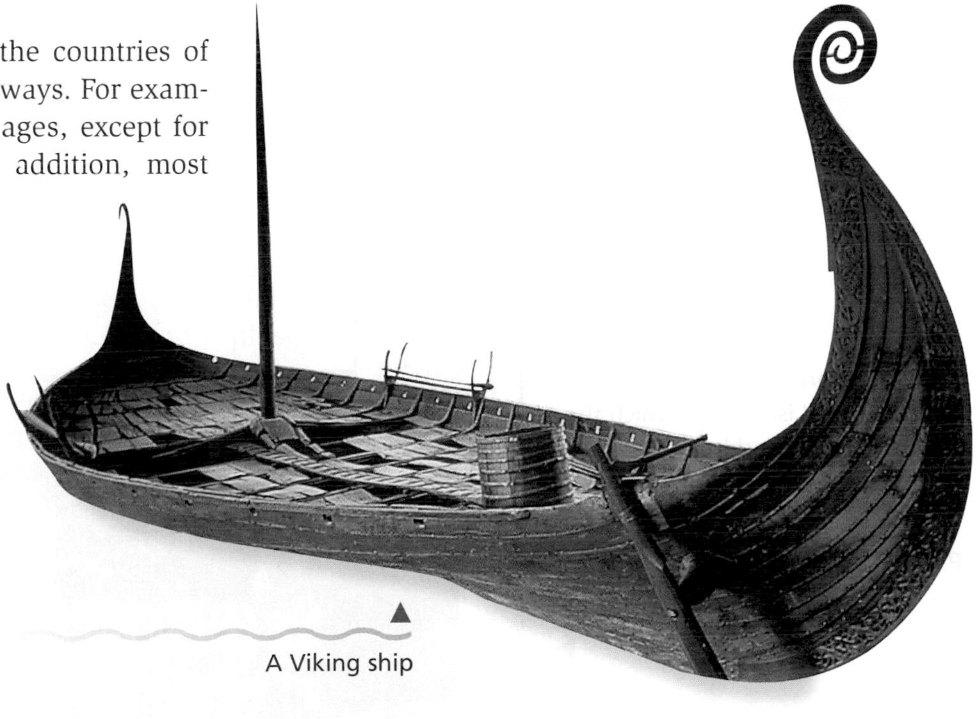

A Viking ship

CHAPTER 20 Reviewing What You Know

Building Vocabulary

On a separate sheet of paper, write sentences to define each of the following words.

1. fjords
2. lochs
3. North Atlantic Drift
4. constitutional monarchy
5. famine
6. bog
7. peat
8. neutral
9. uninhabitable
10. geysers

Reviewing the Main Ideas

1. *Places and Regions* What islands make up the British Isles? What bodies of water surround the British Isles?
2. *Places and Regions* What are the four main climates in northern Europe?
3. *Places and Regions* What large North Atlantic island is a territory of Denmark?
4. *Human Systems* What happened to the British Empire?
5. *Human Systems* What are the two major religions in Northern Ireland? What do these religions have to do with violence in Northern Ireland?

Understanding Environment and Society

Resource Use

Prepare a presentation, along with a map, graph, chart, model, or database, on the distribution of oil and natural gas in the North Sea. You may want to think about the following:

- How oil and natural gas are recovered there.
- How countries divided up the North Sea's oil and natural gas.

Write a five-question quiz, with answers, about your presentation to challenge fellow students.

Thinking Critically

1. **Drawing Inferences and Conclusions** Why do you think British literature, art, and music have been popular around the world?
2. **Drawing Inferences and Conclusions** Why do you think industrial cities like Birmingham and Manchester in Great Britain grew up near coal deposits?
3. **Drawing Inferences and Conclusions** Why do you think most Irish speak English rather than Gaelic?
4. **Making Generalizations and Predictions** How do you think Scandinavians have adapted to life in these very cold environments?
5. **Finding the Main Idea** Why are climates in the British Isles milder than in much of Scandinavia?

Building Social Studies Skills

Map Activity

On a separate sheet of paper, match the letters on the map with their correct labels.

London	**Oslo**
Manchester	**Stockholm**
Belfast	**Copenhagen**
Dublin	**Reykjavik**
Cork	**Helsinki**

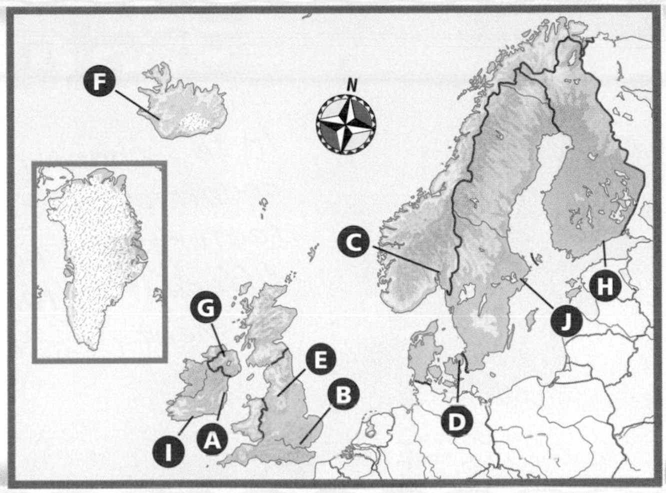

N
F
C
G
E
B
H
J
D
I
A

Mental Mapping Skills Activity

On a separate sheet of paper, draw a freehand map of northern Europe. Make a key for your map and label the following:

Baltic Sea	**Ireland**
Denmark	**Norway**
Finland	**Scandinavian Peninsula**
Great Britain	
Iceland	**Sweden**

Writing Activity

Use print resources to find out more about the Vikings and how they lived in their cold climate. Write a short story set in a Viking village or on a Viking voyage. Describe daily life in the village or on the voyage. Include a bibliography showing references you used. Be sure to use standard grammar, spelling, sentence structure, and punctuation.

Alternative Assessment

Portfolio Activity

Learning About Your Local Geography

Research Project Northern Europe's social programs are supported by taxes. Research the taxes that people in your area must pay. Interview residents, asking their feelings about taxes.

internet connect

Internet Activity: go.hrw.com
KEYWORD: SJ3 GT20

Choose a topic to explore northern Europe:

- Explore the islands and fjords on the Scandinavian coast.
- Visit historic palaces in the United Kingdom.
- Investigate the history of skiing.

CHAPTER 21

Eastern Europe

In this chapter you will learn about countries that share common physical features but have developed very different cultures. First, however, we meet Marta, a Hungarian student.

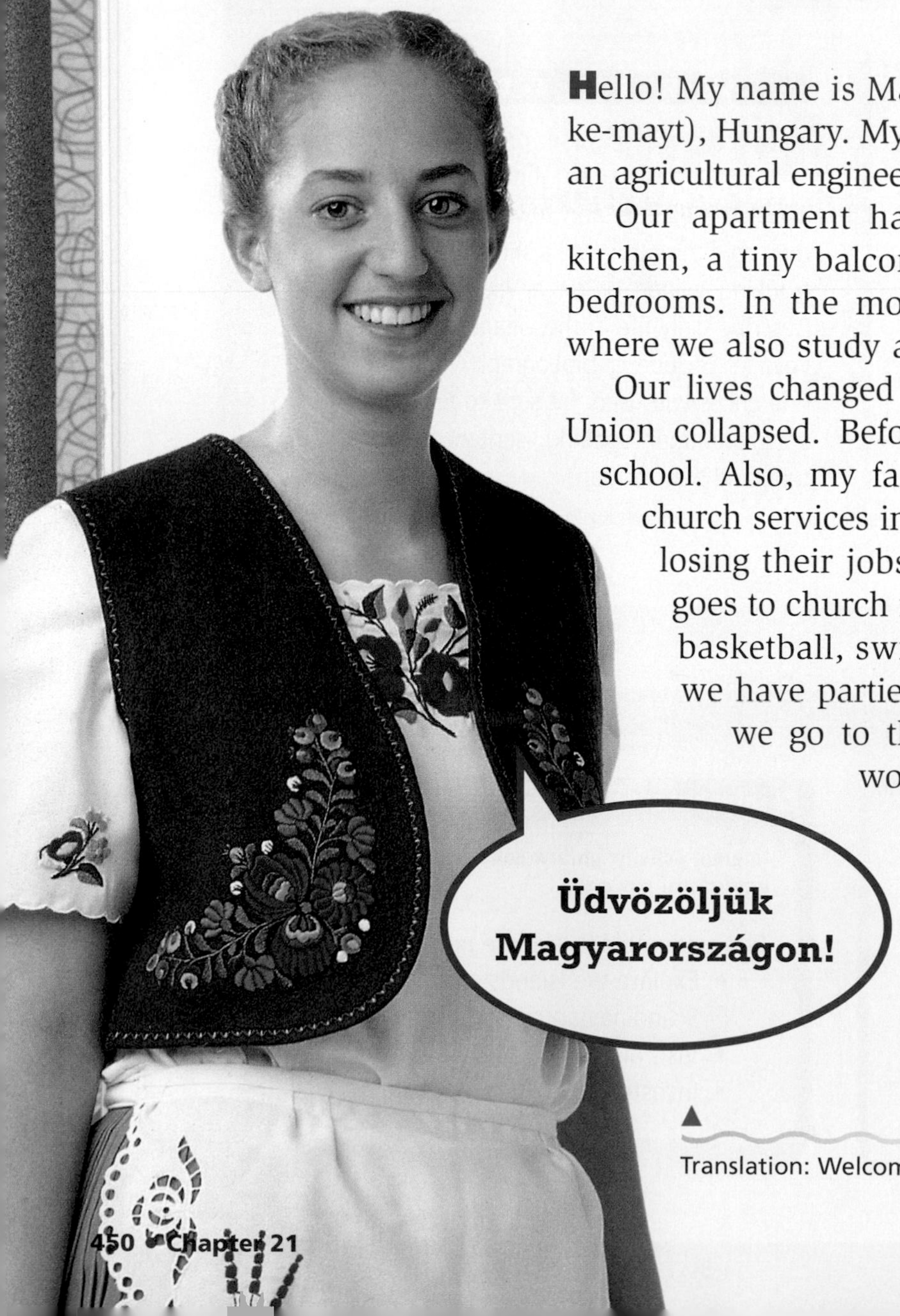
Üdvözöljük Magyarországon!

Hello! My name is Marta, and I am from Kecskemét (KECH-ke-mayt), Hungary. My mother is a secretary, and my father is an agricultural engineer. I am in my last year of high school.

Our apartment has no living or dining room, just a kitchen, a tiny balcony, a bathroom, a hallway, and two bedrooms. In the morning, we eat in my parents' room, where we also study and talk during the day.

Our lives changed very much in 1991 when the Soviet Union collapsed. Before this, we had to study Russian in school. Also, my family is Catholic, but we had to have church services in secret. My parents would have risked losing their jobs if anyone found out. Now everyone goes to church freely. My favorite sports in school are basketball, swimming, and fencing. On Friday night we have parties organized by the school. Sometimes we go to the movies. In the summer, I used to work picking cherries. Now I work in a factory processing chickens.

▲ Translation: Welcome to Hungary!

Section 1 Physical Geography

Read to Discover

1. What are the major physical features of Eastern Europe?
2. What climates and natural resources does this region have?

Define

oil shale
lignite
amber

Locate

Baltic Sea
Adriatic Sea
Black Sea
Danube River
Dinaric Alps
Balkan Mountains
Carpathian Mountains

Amber

WHY IT MATTERS

The Danube and its tributaries are important transportation links in Eastern Europe. The rivers also help spread pollution. Use CNNfyi.com or other **current events** sources to find examples of pollution problems facing the region's rivers. Record your findings in your journal.

Eastern Europe: Physical-Political

ELEVATION
FEET
METERS
13,120
4,000
6,560
2,000
1,640
500
656
200
(Sea level) 0
0 (Sea level)
Below sea level
Below sea level
National capitals
Other cities
N
BALTIC SEA
ESTONIA
Tallinn
LATVIA
Riga
LITHUANIA
Vilnius
NORTHERN EUROPEAN PLAIN
Vistula River
Warsaw
POLAND
Prague
CZECH REPUBLIC
EUROPE
Danube River
CARPATHIAN MOUNTAINS
SLOVAKIA
Bratislava
MOLDOVA
Chisinau
Budapest
HUNGARY
GREAT HUNGARIAN PLAIN
Drava River
Ljubljana
SLOVENIA
Zagreb
CROATIA
ROMANIA
TRANSYLVANIAN ALPS
Belgrade
Bucharest
DINARIC ALPS
BOSNIA AND HERZEGOVINA
Sarajevo
SERBIA
BALKAN MOUNTAINS
Danube River
BLACK SEA
ADRIATIC SEA
YUGOSLAVIA
MONTENEGRO
Kosovo
Sofia
BULGARIA
Skopje
Tiranë
MACEDONIA
ALBANIA
AEGEAN SEA
55°N
50°N
45°N
40°N
5°E
10°E
15°E
20°E
25°E
30°E
35°E
SCALE
0
200
400 Miles
0
200
400 Kilometers
Projection: Azimuthal Equal Area
Size comparison of Eastern Europe to the contiguous United States

▲ This Polish teenager wears traditional dress during a local festival.

Lithuania Lithuania is the largest and southernmost Baltic country. Its capital is Vilnius (VIL-nee-uhs). Lithuania's population has the smallest percentage of ethnic minorities. More than 80 percent of the population is Lithuanian. Nearly 9 percent is Russian, while 7 percent is Polish. Lithuania has ancient ties to Poland. For more than 200 years, until 1795, they were one country. Roman Catholicism is the main religion in both Lithuania and Poland today. As in the other Baltic countries, agriculture and production of basic consumer goods are important parts of Lithuania's economy.

Poland Poland is northeastern Europe's largest and most populous country. The total population of Poland is about the same as that of Spain. The country was divided among its neighbors in the 1700s. Poland regained its independence shortly after World War I. After World War II the Soviet Union established a Communist government to rule the country.

In 1989 the Communists finally allowed free elections. Many businesses now are owned by people in the private sector rather than by the government. The country has also strengthened its ties with Western countries. In 1999 Poland, the Czech Republic, and Hungary joined the North Atlantic Treaty Organization (NATO).

Warsaw, the capital, has long been the cultural, political, and historical center of Polish life. More than 2 million people live in the urban area. The city lies on the Vistula River in central Poland. This location has made Warsaw the center of the national transportation and communications networks as well.

Prague's Charles Bridge is lined with historical statues.
Interpreting the Visual Record **How does this bridge compare to other bridges you have seen?** ▼

Germany
Poland
Prague
Czech Republic
Slovakia
Austria
Hungary

The Former Czechoslovakia Czechoslovakia became an independent country after World War I. Until that time, its lands had been part of the Austro-Hungarian Empire. Then shortly before World War II, it fell under German rule. After the war the Communists, with the support of the Soviet Union, gained control of the government. As in Poland, the Communists lost power in 1989. In 1993 Czechoslovakia peacefully split into two countries. The western part became the Czech Republic. The eastern part became Slovakia. This peaceful split helped the Czechs and Slovaks avoid the ethnic problems that have troubled other countries in the region.

The Czech Republic The Czech Republic experienced economic growth in the early 1990s. Most of the country's businesses are completely or in part privately owned. However, some Czechs worry that the government remains too involved in the economy. As in Poland, a variety of political parties compete in free elections. Czech lands have coal and other important mineral resources that are used in industry. Much of the country's industry is located in and around Prague, the capital. The city is located on the Vltava River. More than 1.2 million people live there. Prague has beautiful medieval buildings. It also has one of Europe's oldest universities.

Slovakia Slovakia is more rugged and rural, with incomes lower than in the Czech Republic. The move toward a freer political system has been slow. However, progress has been made. Bratislava (BRAH-tyee-slah-vah), the capital, is located on the Danube River. The city is the country's most important industrial area and cultural center. Many rural Slovaks move to Bratislava looking for better-paying jobs. Most of the country's population is Slovak. However, ethnic Hungarians account for more than 10 percent of Slovakia's population.

Hungary Hungary separated from the Austro-Hungarian Empire at the end of World War I. Following World War II, a Communist government came to power. A revolt against the government was put down by the Soviet Union in 1956. The Communists ruled until 1989.

Today the country has close ties with the rest of Europe. In fact, most of Hungary's trade is with members of the European Union. During the Communist era, the government experimented with giving some businesses the freedom to act on their own. For example, it allowed local farm managers to make key business decisions. These managers kept farming methods modern, chose their crops, and marketed their products. Today, farm products from Hungary's fertile plains are important exports. Much of the country's manufacturing is located in and around the capital, Budapest (BOO-duh-pest). Budapest is Hungary's largest city. Nearly 20 percent of the population lives there.

✓ **READING CHECK:** *Human Systems* How have the governments and economies of the region been affected by recent history?

Czech Republic
Slovakia
Austria
Budapest
Hungary
Croatia
Romania

▲ The Danube River flows through Budapest, Hungary.

Interpreting the Visual Record **Why might Hungary's capital have grown up along a river?**

go.hrw.com **Homework Practice Online**
Keyword: SJ3 HP21

Section 2 Review

Define and explain: Indo-European

Working with Sketch Maps On the map you drew in Section 1, label the countries of the region, Prague, Tallinn, Riga, Warsaw, Vistula River, Bratislava, and Budapest.

Reading for the Main Idea

1. *Human Systems* How did invasions and migrations help shape the region?
2. *Places and Regions* What has the region contributed to the arts?

Critical Thinking

3. **Drawing Inferences and Conclusions** How did the Soviet Union influence the region?
4. **Summarizing** What social changes have taken place here since the early 1990s?

Organizing What You Know

5. **Sequencing** Copy the following graphic organizer. Use it to show the history of the Baltics since 1900.

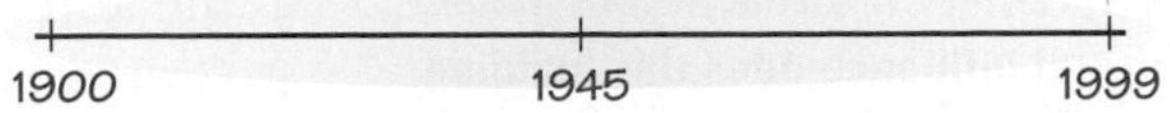

1900
1945
1999

Section 3 The Countries of Southeastern Europe

Read to Discover

1. How did Southeastern Europe's early history help shape its modern societies?
2. How does culture both link and divide the region?
3. How has the region's past contributed to current conflicts?

Define

Roma

Locate

Bulgaria
Romania
Croatia
Slovenia
Serbia
Bosnia and Herzegovina
Albania
Yugoslavia
Kosovo
Montenegro
Macedonia
Belgrade
Podgorica
Sarajevo
Zagreb
Ljubljana
Skopje
Bucharest
Moldova
Chişinău
Sofia
Tiranë

WHY IT MATTERS

Bosnia and the other republics of the former Yugoslavia have experienced ethnic violence since independence. Use CNNfyi.com or other **current events** sources to check on current conditions in the region. Record your findings in your journal.

Dolls in traditional Croatian dress

History

Along with neighboring Greece, this was the first region of Europe to adopt agriculture. From here farming moved up the Danube River valley into central and western Europe. Early farmers and metalworkers in the south may have spoken languages related to Albanian. Albanian is an Indo-European language.

Yugoslavia
Albania
Macedonia
Apollonia
Italy
Greece

These ancient ruins in southern Albania date to the 500s B.C.

Interpreting the Visual Record What cultural influence does this building show?

Early History Around 750–600 B.C. the ancient Greeks founded colonies on the Black Sea coast. The area they settled is now Bulgaria and Romania. Later, the Romans conquered most of the area from the Adriatic Sea to the Danube River and across into Romania. When the Roman Empire divided into west and east, much of the Balkans and Greece became part of the Eastern Roman Empire. This eastern region eventually became known as the Byzantine Empire. Under Byzantine rule, many people of the Balkans became Orthodox Christians.

Kingdoms and Empires Many of today's southeastern European countries first appear as kingdoms between A.D. 800 and 1400. The Ottoman Turks conquered the region and ruled until the 1800s. The Ottomans, who were Muslims, tolerated other religious faiths. However, many peoples, such as the Bosnians and Albanians, converted to Islam. As the Ottoman Empire began to weaken in the late 1800s, the Austro-Hungarians took control of Croatia and Slovenia. They imposed Roman Catholicism.

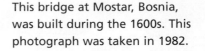

This bridge at Mostar, Bosnia, was built during the 1600s. This photograph was taken in 1982.

Croatia
Bosnia and Herzegovina
Mostar
Yugoslavia

This photograph shows Mostar after civil war in the 1990s.

Interpreting the Visual Record **What differences can you find in the two photos?**

Slav Nationalism The Russians, meanwhile, were fighting the Turks for control of the Black Sea. The Russians encouraged Slavs in the Balkans to revolt against the Turks. The Russians appealed to Slavic nationalism—to the Slav's sense of loyalty to their country. The Serbs did revolt in 1815 and became self-governing in 1817. By 1878 Bulgaria and Romania were also self-governing.

The Austro-Hungarians responded to Slavic nationalism by occupying additional territories. Those territories included the regions of Bosnia and Herzegovina. To stop the Serbs from expanding to the Adriatic coast, European powers made Albania an independent kingdom.

In August 1914 a Serb nationalist shot and killed the heir to the Austro-Hungarian throne. Austria declared war on Serbia. Russia came to Serbia's defense. These actions sparked World War I. All of Europe's great powers became involved. The United States entered the war in 1917.

Creation of Yugoslavia At the end of World War I Austria-Hungary was broken apart. Austria was reduced to a small territory. Hungary became a separate country but lost its eastern province to Romania. Romania also gained additional lands from Russia. Albania remained independent. The peace settlement created Yugoslavia. *Yugoslavia* means "land of the southern Slavs." Yugoslavia brought the region's Serbs, Bosnians, Croatians, Macedonians, Montenegrins, and Slovenes together into one country. Each ethnic group had its own republic within Yugoslavia. Some Bosnians and other people in Serbia were Muslims. Most Serbs were Orthodox Christians, and the Slovenes and Croats were Roman Catholics. These ethnic and religious differences created problems that eventually led to civil war in the 1990s.

✓ **READING CHECK:** *Human Systems* How is southeastern Europe's religious and ethnic makeup a reflection of its past?

Hungary
Romania
Bosnia and Herzegovina
Serbia
Yugoslavia
Montenegro
Pristina
Bulgaria
Albania

Ethnic Albanians worship at a mosque in Pristina, Serbia.

Culture

The Balkans are the most diverse region of Europe in terms of language, ethnicity, and religion. It is the largest European region to have once been ruled by a Muslim power. It has also been a zone of conflict between eastern and western Christianity. The three main Indo-European language branches—Romance (from Latin), Germanic, and Slavic—are all found here, as well as other branches like Albanian. Non-Indo-European languages like Hungarian and Turkish are also spoken here.

Balkan diets combine the foods of the Hungarians and the Slavs with those of the Mediterranean Greeks, Turks, and Italians. In Greek and Turkish cuisines, yogurt and soft cheeses are an important part of most meals, as are fresh fruits, nuts, and vegetables. Roast goat or lamb are the favorite meats for a celebration.

In the Balkans Bosnian and ethnic Albanian Muslims celebrate the feasts of Islam. Christian holidays—Christmas and Easter—are celebrated on one day by Catholics and on another by Orthodox Christians. Holidays in memory of ancient battles and modern liberation days are sources of conflict between ethnic groups.

✓ **READING CHECK:** *Places and Regions* Why is religion an important issue in southeastern Europe?

Our Amazing Planet

The Danube Delta, on the Romanian coast of the Black Sea, is part of a unique ecosystem. Most of the Romanian caviar-producing sturgeon are caught in these waters. Caviar is made from the salted eggs from three types of sturgeon fish. Caviar is considered a delicacy and can cost as much as $50 per ounce.

Southeastern Europe Today

Like other southeastern European countries, Yugoslavia was occupied by Germany in World War II. A Communist government under Josip Broz Tito took over after the war. Tito's strong central government prevented ethnic conflict. After Tito died in 1980, Yugoslavia's Communist government held the republics together. Then in 1991 the republics of Slovenia, Croatia, Bosnia and Herzegovina, and Macedonia began to break away. Years of bloody civil war followed. Today the region struggles with the violence and with rebuilding economies left weak by years of Communist-government control.

Yugoslavia The republics of Serbia and Montenegro remain united and have kept the name of Yugoslavia. Belgrade is the capital of both Serbia and Yugoslavia. It is located on the Danube River. The capital of Montenegro is Podgorica (PAWD-gawr-eet-sah). The Serbian government supported ethnic Serbs fighting in civil wars in Croatia and in Bosnia and Herzegovina in the early 1990s. Tensions between ethnic groups also have been a problem within Serbia. About 65 percent of the people in Serbia and Montenegro are Orthodox Christians. In the southern Serbian province of Kosovo, the majority of people are ethnic Albanian and Muslim. Many of the Albanians want independence. Conflict between Serbs and Albanians led to civil war in the late 1990s. In 1999 the United States, other Western countries, and Russia sent troops to keep the peace.

Bosnia and Herzegovina Bosnia and Herzegovina generally are referred to as Bosnia. Some 40 percent of Bosnians are Muslims, but large numbers of Roman Catholic Croats and Orthodox Christian Serbs also live there. Following independence, a bloody civil war broke out between these groups as they struggled for control of territory. During the fighting the once beautiful capital of Sarajevo (sar-uh-YAY-voh) was heavily damaged.

Croatia Croatia's capital is Zagreb (ZAH-greb). Most of the people of Croatia are Roman Catholic. In the early 1990s, Serbs made up about 12 percent of the population. In 1991 the ethnic Serbs living in Croatia claimed part of the country for Serbia. This resulted in heavy fighting. By the end of 1995 an agreement was reached and a sense of stability returned to the country. Many Serbs left the country.

Slovenia Slovenia is a former Austrian territory. It looks to Western European countries for much of its trade. Most people in Slovenia are Roman Catholic, and few ethnic minorities live there. Partly because of the small number of ethnic minorities, little fighting occurred after Slovenia declared independence from Yugoslavia. The major center of industry is Ljubljana (lee-oo-blee-AH-nuh), the country's capital.

These Muslim refugees are walking to Travnik, Bosnia, with the assistance of UN troops from Britain in the 1990s.

Interpreting the Visual Record What effect might the movement of refugees have on a region?

Croatia
Travnik
Bosnia and Herzegovina
Yugoslavia

Slovenia's capital, Ljubljana, lies on the Sava River.

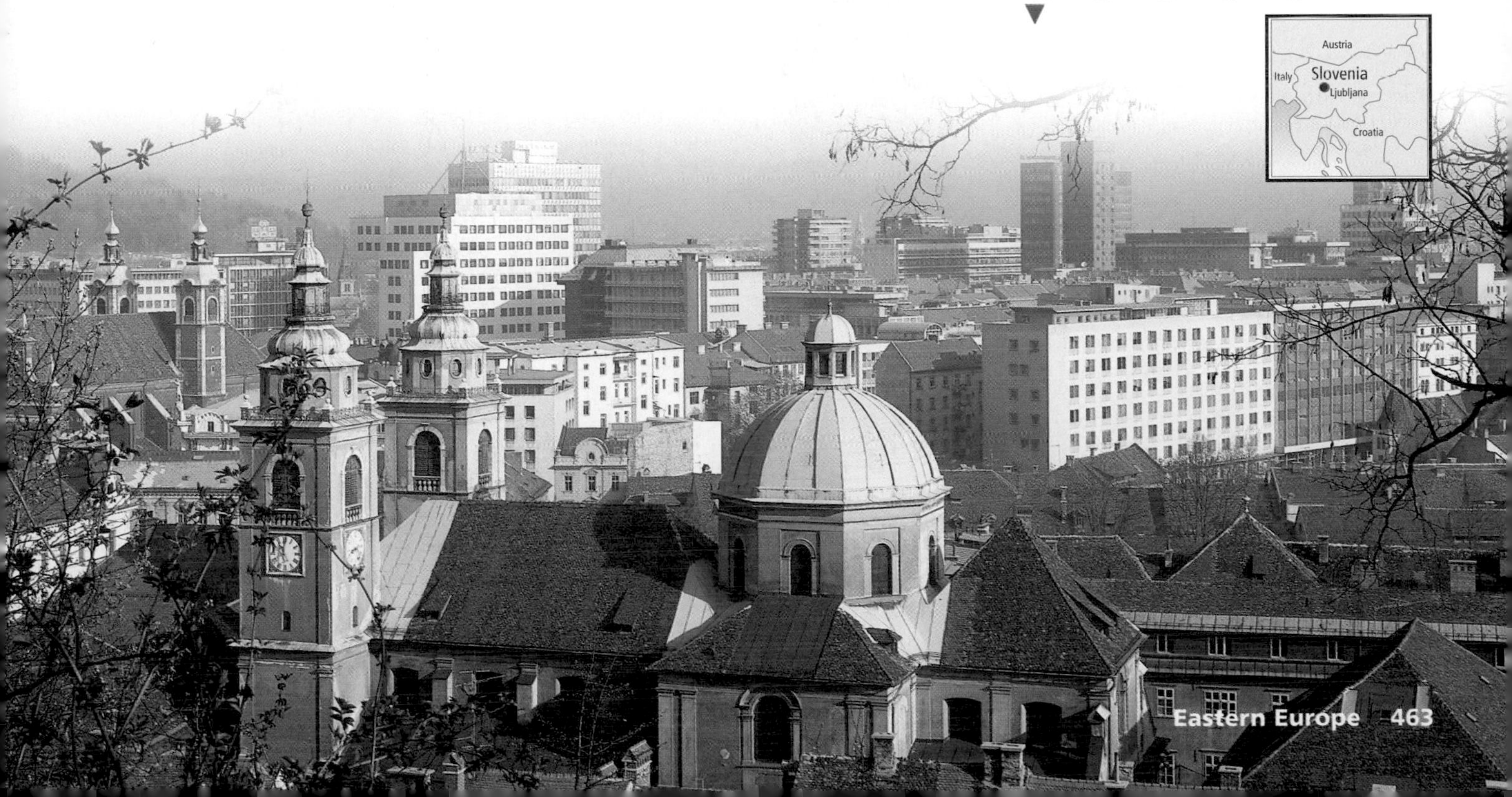

Austria
Italy
Slovenia
Ljubljana
Croatia

Ethnic Groups in Macedonia

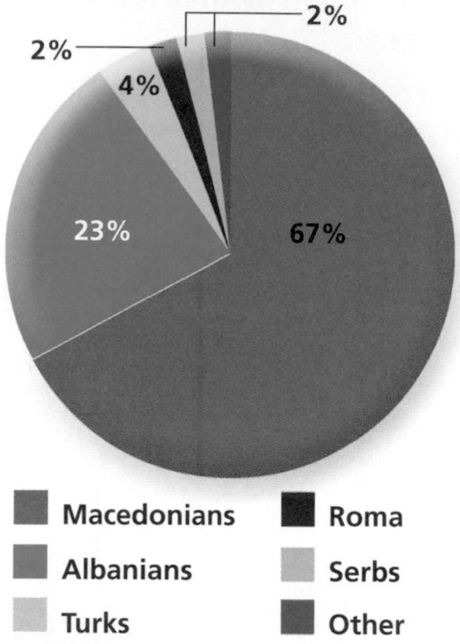
2%
2%
4%
23%
67%
Macedonians
Roma
Albanians
Serbs
Turks
Other

Source: Central Intelligence Agency, *The World Factbook 2001*

In 2001 ethnic Albanian rebels launched months of fighting in hopes of gaining more rights for Macedonia's Albanian minority.

Interpreting the Chart What percentage of Macedonia's people are Albanian?

Macedonia When Macedonia declared its independence from Yugoslavia, Greece immediately objected to the country's new name. Macedonia is also the name of a province in northern Greece that has historical ties to the republic. Greece feared that Macedonia might try to take over the province.

Greece responded by refusing to trade with Macedonia until the mid-1990s. This slowed Macedonia's movement from the command—or government-controlled—economy it had under Communist rule to a market economy in which consumers help to determine what is to be produced by buying or not buying certain goods and services. Despite its rocky start, in recent years Macedonia has made progress in establishing free markets.

Romania A Communist government took power in Romania at the end of World War II. Then in 1989 the Communist government was overthrown during bloody fighting. Change, however, has been slow. Bucharest, the capital, is the biggest industrial center. Today more people work in agriculture than in any other part of the economy. Nearly 90 percent of the country's population is ethnic Romanian. **Roma**, or Gypsies as they were once known, make up almost 2 percent of the population. They are descended from people who may have lived in northern India and began migrating centuries ago. Most of the rest of Romania's population are ethnic Hungarian.

Moldova Throughout history control of Moldova has shifted many times. It has been dominated by Turks, Polish princes, Austria, Hungary, Russia, and Romania. Not surprisingly, the country's population reflects this diverse past. Moldova declared its independence in

Turkish Roma girls

Ukraine
Moldova
Romania
Danube River delta
Yugoslavia
Bulgaria

1991 from the Soviet Union. However, the country suffers from difficult economic and political problems. About 40 percent of the country's labor force works in agriculture. Chişinău (kee-shee-NOW), the major industrial center of the country, is also Moldova's capital.

Bulgaria Mountainous Bulgaria has progressed slowly since the fall of communism. However, a market economy is growing gradually, and the people have more freedoms. Most industries are located near Sofia (SOH-fee-uh), the capital and largest city. About 9 percent of Bulgaria's people are ethnic Turks.

Albania Albania is one of Europe's poorest countries. The capital, Tiranë (ti-RAH-nuh), has a population of about 270,000. About 70 percent of Albanians are Muslim. Albania's Communist government feuded with the Communist governments in the Soviet Union and, later, in China. As a result, Albania became isolated. Since the fall of its harsh Communist government in the 1990s, the country has tried to move toward both democracy and a free market system.

READING CHECK: *Human Systems* What problems does the region face, and how are they reflections of its Communist past?

Southeastern Europe

Country	Population/ Growth Rate	Life Expectancy	Literacy Rate	Per Capita GDP
Albania	3,510,484 / 0.9%	69, male 75, female	93%	$3,000
Bosnia and Herzegovina	3,922,205 / 1.4%	69, male 74, female	not available	$1,700
Bulgaria	7,707,495 / −1.1%	68, male 75, female	98%	$6,200
Croatia	4,334,142 / 1.5%	70, male 78, female	97%	$5,800
Macedonia	2,046,209 / 0.4%	72, male 76, female	not available	$4,400
Moldova	4,431,570 / 0.05%	60, male 69, female	96%	$2,500
Romania	22,364,022 / −0.2%	66, male 74, female	97%	$5,900
Yugoslavia (Serbia and Montenegro)	10,677,290 / −0.3%	70, male 76, female	93%	$2,300
United States	281,421,906 / 0.9%	74, male 80, female	97%	$36,200

Sources: Central Intelligence Agency, *The World Factbook 2001*; U.S. Census Bureau

Interpreting the Chart Based on the table, which southeastern European country has the highest level of economic development?

go.hrw.com **Homework Practice Online**
Keyword: SJ3 HP21

Section 3 Review

Define and explain: Roma

Working with Sketch Maps On the map you drew in Section 2, label the region's countries and their capitals. They are listed at the beginning of the section. In a box in the margin, identify the countries that once made up Yugoslavia.

Reading for the Main Idea

1. *Human Systems* How has the region's history influenced its religious and ethnic makeup?
2. *Human Systems* What events and factors have contributed to problems in Bosnia and other countries in the region since independence?

Critical Thinking

3. **Summarizing** How was Yugoslavia created?
4. **Analyzing Information** How are the region's governments and economies changing?

Organizing What You Know

5. **Categorizing** Copy the following graphic organizer. Use it to identify languages, foods, and celebrations in the region.

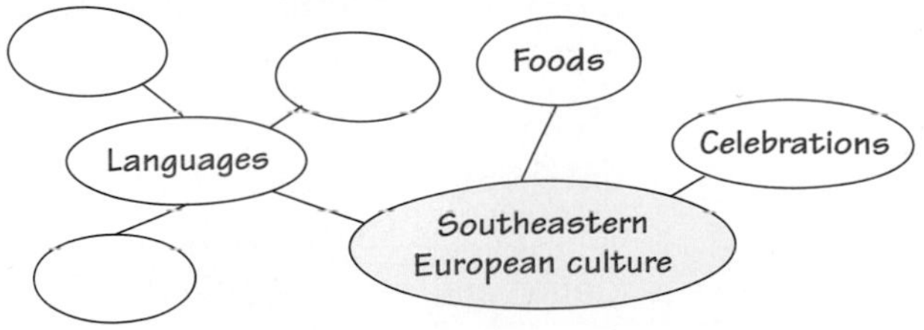
Foods
Languages
Celebrations
Southeastern European culture

CHAPTER 21

Reviewing What You Know

Building Vocabulary

On a separate sheet of paper, write sentences to define each of the following words.

1. oil shale
2. lignite
3. amber
4. Indo-European
5. Roma

Reviewing the Main Ideas

1. *Places and Regions* What are the major landforms of Eastern Europe?
2. *Human Systems* What groups influenced the culture of Eastern Europe? How can these influences be seen in modern society?
3. *Environment and Society* What were some environmental effects of Communist economic policies in Eastern Europe?
4. *Human Systems* What political and economic systems were most common in Eastern Europe before the 1990s? How and why have these systems changed?
5. *Human Systems* List the countries that broke away from Yugoslavia in the early 1990s. What are the greatest sources of tension in these countries?

Understanding Environment and Society

Economic Geography

During the Communist era, the Council for Economic Assistance, or COMECON, played an important role in planning the economies of countries in the region. Create a presentation comparing the practices of this organization to the practices now in place in the region. Consider the following:

- How COMECON organized the distribution of goods and services.
- How countries in the region now organize distribution.

Thinking Critically

1. **Drawing Inferences and Conclusions** How has Eastern Europe's location influenced the diets of the region's people?
2. **Analyzing Information** What is Eastern Europe's most important river for transportation and trade? How can you tell that the river is important to economic development?
3. **Identifying Cause and Effect** What geographic factors help make Warsaw the transportation and communication center of Poland? Imagine that Warsaw is located along the Baltic coast of Poland or near the German border. How might Warsaw have developed differently?
4. **Comparing/Contrasting** Compare and contrast the breakups of Yugoslavia and Czechoslovakia.
5. **Summarizing** How has political change affected the economies of Eastern European countries?

Building Social Studies Skills

Map ACTIVITY

On a separate sheet of paper, match the letters on the map with their correct labels.

Baltic Sea
Adriatic Sea
Black Sea
Danube River
Dinaric Alps
Balkan Mountains
Carpathian Mountains

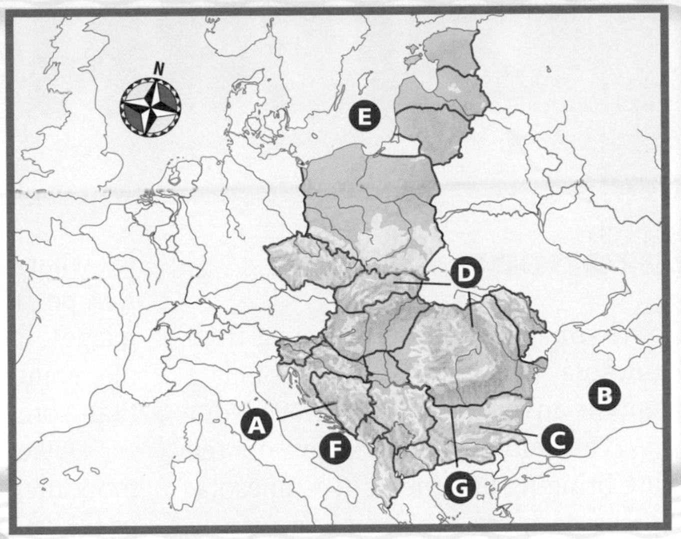

N
A
B
C
D
E
F
G

Mental Mapping Skills ACTIVITY

Using the chapter map or a globe as a guide, draw a freehand map of Eastern Europe and label the following:

Bosnia and Herzegovina
Croatia
Czech Republic
Estonia
Hungary
Macedonia
Poland
Yugoslavia

WRITING ACTIVITY

Imagine that you are a teenager living in Romania and want to write a family memoir of life in Romania. Include accounts of life for your grandparents under strict Soviet rule and life for your parents during the Soviet Union's breakup. Also describe your life in free Romania. Be sure to use standard grammar, spelling, sentence structure, and punctuation.

Alternative Assessment

Portfolio ACTIVITY

Learning About Your Local Geography

Cooperative Project Ask international agencies or search the Internet for help in contacting a boy or girl in Eastern Europe. As a group, write a letter to the teen, telling about your daily lives.

internet connect

Internet Activity: go.hrw.com
KEYWORD: SJ3 GT21

go.hrw.com

Choose a topic to explore Eastern Europe:

- Investigate the conflicts in the Balkans.
- Take a virtual tour of Eastern Europe.
- Learn about Baltic amber.

FOCUS ON GOVERNMENT

The European Union

What if . . . ? Imagine you are traveling from Texas to Minnesota. You have to go through a border checkpoint in Oklahoma to prove your Texas identity. The guard charges a tax on the cookies you are bringing to a friend in Minnesota. Buying gas presents more problems. You try to pay with Texas dollars, but the attendant just looks at you. You discover that they speak "Kansonian" in Kansas and use Kansas coins. All this would make traveling from one place to another much more difficult.

The European Union Fortunately, that was just an imaginary situation. However, it is similar to what might happen while traveling across Europe. European countries have different languages, currencies, laws, and cultures. For example, someone from France has different customs than someone from Ireland.

However, many Europeans also share common interests. For example, they are interested in peace in the region. They also have a common interest in Europe's economic success.

A shared belief in economic and political cooperation has resulted in the creation of the European Union (EU). The EU has 15 countries that are members. They are: Austria, Belgium, Denmark, Finland, France, Germany, Great Britain, Greece, Ireland, Italy, Luxembourg, the Netherlands, Portugal, Spain, and Sweden.

The Eurostar train carries passengers from London to Paris. These two cities are only about 200 miles (322 km) apart. However, they have different cultures and ways of life.

eurostar
3202

The Beginnings of a Unified Europe Proposals for an economically integrated Europe first came about in the 1950s. After World War II, the countries of Europe had many economic problems. A plan was made to unify the coal and steel production of some countries. In 1957 France, Germany, Italy, Belgium, the Netherlands, and Luxembourg formed the European Economic Community (EEC). The name was later shortened to simply the European Community (EC). The goal of the EC was to combine each country's economy into a single market. Having one market would make trading among them easier. Eventually, more countries became interested in joining the EC. In 1973 Britain, Denmark, and Ireland joined. In the 1980s Greece, Portugal, and Spain joined.

ATLANTIC OCEAN
FINLAND
SWEDEN
DENMARK
UNITED KINGDOM
IRELAND
NETHERLANDS
GERMANY
BELGIUM
LUXEMBOURG
AUSTRIA
FRANCE
PORTUGAL
SPAIN
ITALY
GREECE
MEDITERRANEAN SEA
The European Union (EU)

The 15 EU countries produce a wide range of exports and are one of the world's richest markets.

20
EURO CENT
5
012345678900
5 EURO
5 EURO

The flag of the EU features 12 gold stars on a blue background. The EU's currency, the euro, replaced the currencies of most EU countries.

In the early 1990s, a meeting was held in Maastricht, the Netherlands, to discuss the future of the EC. This resulted in the Maastricht Treaty. The treaty officially changed the EC's name from the European Community to the European Union (EU).

The Future Some people believe the EU is laying the foundation for a greater sense of European identity. A European Court of Justice has been set up to enforce EU rules. According to some experts, this is helping to build common European beliefs, responsibilities, and rights.

When the European Union was first established, each country had its own form of money. For example, France used the franc. Italy used the lira. Portugal used the escudo. On January 1, 2002, the euro became a common form of money for most EU countries. With the exception of Denmark, Sweden, and the United Kingdom, the euro replaced the currencies of member countries. Another goal of the EU is to extend membership to other countries.

The EU has resulted in many important changes in Europe. Cooperation between member countries has increased. Trade has also increased. EU members have adopted a common currency and common economic laws. The EU is creating a more unified Europe. Some people even believe that the EU might someday lead to a "United States of Europe."

Understanding What You Read

1. What was the first step toward European economic unity?
2. What is the euro? How will it affect the other currencies of the EU countries?

GeoSkills

INNERES EINER STADT

This illustration shows a German medieval city in the 1400s.

Building Skills for Life: Analyzing Settlement Patterns

There are many different kinds of human settlements. Some people live in villages where they farm and raise animals. Others live in small towns or cities and work in factories or offices. Geographers analyze these settlement patterns. They are interested in how settlements affect people's lives.

All settlements are unique. Even neighboring villages are different. One village might have better soil than its neighbors. Another village might be closer to a main road or highway. Geographers are interested in the unique qualities of human settlements.

Geographers also study different types of settlements. For example, many European settlements could be considered medieval cities. Medieval cities are about 500–1,500 years old. They usually have walls around them and buildings made of stone and wood. Medieval cities also have tall churches and narrow, winding streets.

Analyzing settlement patterns is important. It helps us learn about people and environments. For example, the architecture of a city might give us clues about the culture, history, and technology of the people who live there.

You can ask questions about individual villages, towns, and cities to learn about settlement patterns. What kinds of activities are going on? How are the streets arranged? What kinds of transportation do people use? You can also ask questions about groups of settlements. How are they connected? Do they trade with each other? Are some settlements bigger or older than others? Why is this so?

PRACTICING THE SKILL

1. How do you think a city, a town, and a village are different from each other? Write down your own definition of each word on a piece of paper. Then look them up in a dictionary and write down the dictionary's definition. Were your definitions different?
2. Analyze the settlement where you live. How old is it? How many people live there? What kinds of jobs do people have? How is it connected to other settlements? How is it unique?
3. Besides medieval cities, what other types of cities can you think of? Make a list of three other possible types.

HANDS ON GEOGRAPHY

One type of settlement is called a planned city. A planned city is carefully designed before it is built. Each part fits into an overall plan. For example, the size and arrangement of streets and buildings might be planned.

There are many planned cities in the world. Some examples are Brasília, Brazil; Chandigarh, India; and Washington, D.C. Many other cities have certain parts that are planned, such as individual neighborhoods. These neighborhoods are sometimes called planned communities.

Suppose you were asked to plan a city. How would you do it? On a separate sheet of paper, create your own planned city. These guidelines will help you get started.

1. First, decide what the physical environment will be like. Is the city on the coast, on a river, or somewhere else? Are there hills, lakes, or other physical features in the area?
2. Decide what to include in your city. Most cities have a downtown, different neighborhoods, and roads or highways that connect areas together. Many cities also have parks, museums, and an airport.
3. Plan the arrangement of your city. Where will the roads and highways go? Will the airport be close to downtown? Try to arrange the different parts of your city so that they fit together logically.
4. Draw a map of your planned city. Be sure to include a title, scale, and orientation.

Some people think the city plan for Brasília looks like a bird, a bow and arrow, or an airplane. **Interpreting the Visual Record What do you notice about the arrangement of Brasília's streets?**

Lab Report

1. How was your plan influenced by the physical environment you chose?
2. How do you think planned cities are different from cities that are not planned?
3. What problems might people have when they try to plan an entire city?

UNIT 6

Russia and Northern Eurasia

CHAPTER 22
Russia

CHAPTER 23
Ukraine, Belarus, and the Caucasus

CHAPTER 24
Central Asia

Dancers in Russian national dress

St. Basil's Cathedral, Moscow, Russia

Church overlooking the Black Sea, Ukraine

NOTES FROM THE field

Journalists in Russia

Journalists Gary Matoso and Lisa Dickey traveled more than 5,000 miles across Russia. They wrote this account of their visit with Buyanto Tsydypov. He is a Buryat farmer who lives in the Lake Baikal area. The Buryats are one of Russia's many minority ethnic groups.* WHAT DO YOU THINK? *If you visited a Buryat family, what would you like to see or ask?

Buryat people, Lake Baikal area, Russia

"You came to us like thunder out of the clear blue sky," said our host. The surprise of our visit did not, however, keep him from greeting us warmly.

Buyanto brought us to a special place of prayer. High on a hillside, a yellow wooden frame holds a row of tall, narrow sticks. On the end of each stick, Buddhist prayer cloths flutter in the biting autumn wind.

In times of trouble and thanks, Buryats come to tie their prayer cloths—called *khimorin*—to the sticks and make their offerings to the gods. Buyanto builds a small fire. He unfolds an aqua-blue *khimorin* to show the drawings.

"All around are the Buddhist gods," he says, "and at the bottom we have written our names and the names of others we are praying for."

He fans the flames slowly with the cloth, purifying it with sacred smoke. After a time he moves to the top of the hill where he ties the *khimorin* to one of the sticks.

Understanding Primary Sources

1. How do you know that Buyanto Tsydypov was surprised to meet the two American journalists?
2. What is a *khimorin*?

Brown bear

Russia and Northern Eurasia

Elevation Profile

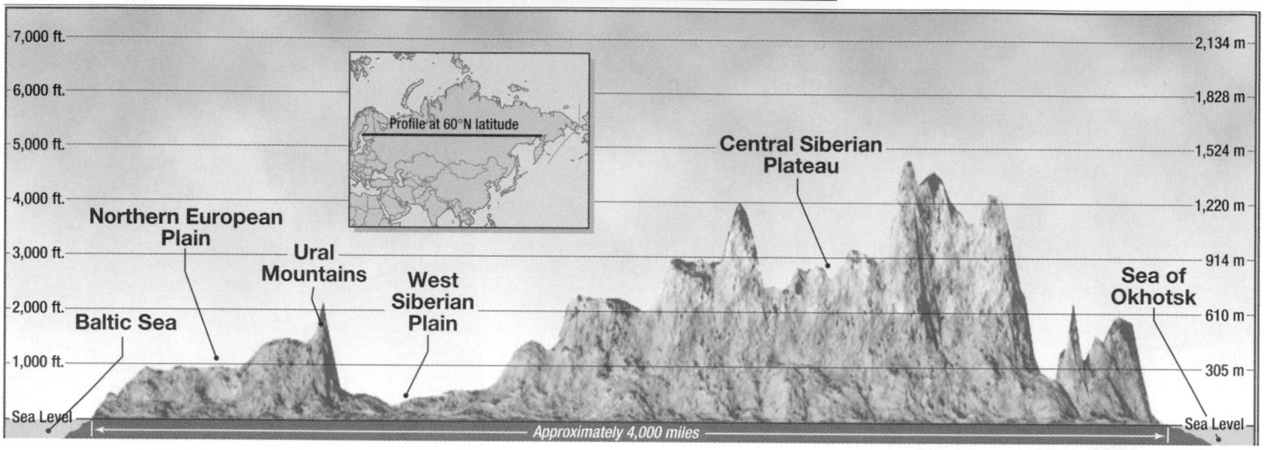
7,000 ft.
6,000 ft.
5,000 ft.
4,000 ft.
3,000 ft.
2,000 ft.
1,000 ft.
Sea Level
2,134 m
1,828 m
1,524 m
1,220 m
914 m
610 m
305 m
Sea Level
Profile at 60°N latitude
Northern European Plain
Ural Mountains
West Siberian Plain
Baltic Sea
Central Siberian Plateau
Sea of Okhotsk
Approximately 4,000 miles

The United States and Russia and Northern Eurasia
Comparing Sizes

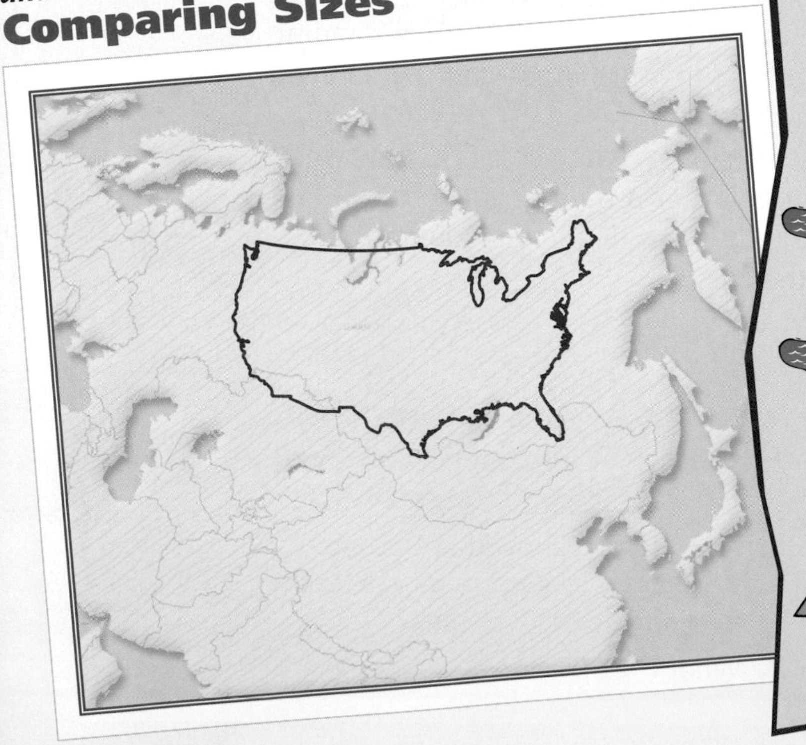

GEOSTATS:

Russia

World's largest country in area: 6,659,328 sq. mi. (17,075,200 sq km)

World's sixth-largest population: 145,470,197 (July 2001 estimate)

World's largest lake: Caspian Sea—143,244 sq. mi. (371,002 sq km)

World's deepest lake: Lake Baikal—5,715 ft. (1,742 m)

Largest number of time zones: 11

Highest mountain in Europe: Mount Elbrus—18,510 ft. (5,642 m)

Russia and Northern Eurasia: Physical

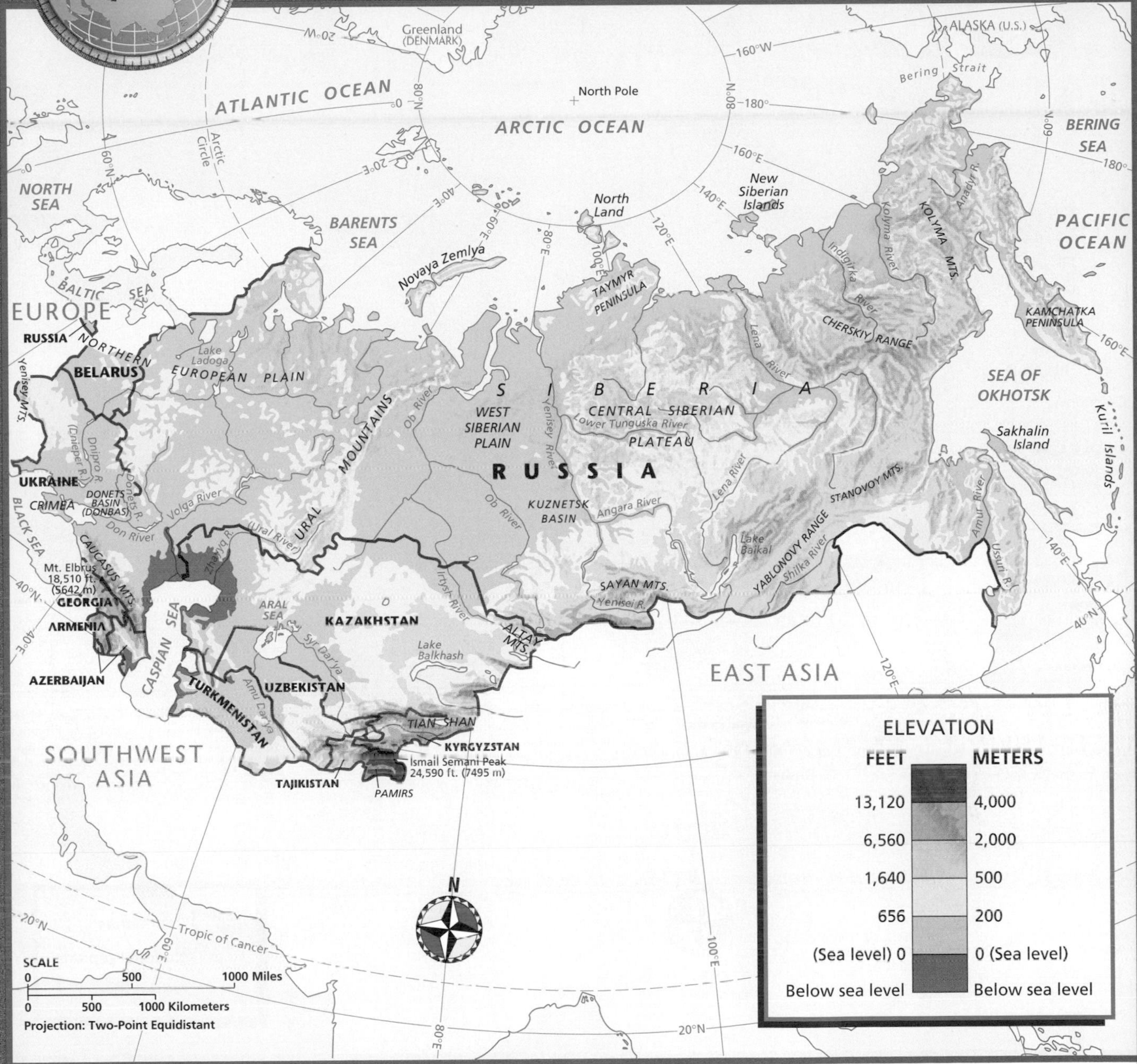

Greenland (DENMARK)
ALASKA (U.S.)
ATLANTIC OCEAN
North Pole
ARCTIC OCEAN
Bering Strait
BERING SEA
Arctic Circle
NORTH SEA
BARENTS SEA
North Land
New Siberian Islands
PACIFIC OCEAN
Novaya Zemlya
TAYMYR PENINSULA
KOLYMA MTS.
Kolyma River
Anadyr R.
Indigirka River
CHERSKIY RANGE
KAMCHATKA PENINSULA
BALTIC SEA
EUROPE
RUSSIA
NORTHERN EUROPEAN PLAIN
Lake Ladoga
BELARUS
Yenisey MTS.
S I B E R I A
WEST SIBERIAN PLAIN
CENTRAL SIBERIAN PLATEAU
Lower Tunguska River
Lena River
SEA OF OKHOTSK
Sakhalin Island
Kuril Islands
URAL MOUNTAINS
Ob River
Yenisey River
RUSSIA
UKRAINE
CRIMEA
Dnieper R.
Dnipro R.
Donets R.
DONETS BASIN (DONBAS)
Volga River
Don River
BLACK SEA
KUZNETSK BASIN
Angara River
STANOVOY MTS.
Amur River
Lake Baikal
YABLONOVY RANGE
Shilka River
Ussuri R.
Ural River
Zhayyq R.
CAUCASUS MTS.
Mt. Elbrus 18,510 ft. (5642 m)
GEORGIA
ARMENIA
AZERBAIJAN
CASPIAN SEA
ARAL SEA
KAZAKHSTAN
Irtysh River
SAYAN MTS.
Yenisei R.
ALTAY MTS.
Syr Dar'ya
Lake Balkhash
Amu Darya
TURKMENISTAN
UZBEKISTAN
TIAN SHAN
KYRGYZSTAN
Ismail Semani Peak 24,590 ft. (7495 m)
TAJIKISTAN
PAMIRS
EAST ASIA
SOUTHWEST ASIA
Tropic of Cancer
ELEVATION
FEET
METERS
13,120
4,000
6,560
2,000
1,640
500
656
200
(Sea level) 0
0 (Sea level)
Below sea level
Below sea level
N
SCALE
0 500 1000 Miles
0 500 1000 Kilometers
Projection: Two-Point Equidistant

1. Places and Regions In what general direction do the great rivers of Siberia flow?

2. Places and Regions Which countries have areas that are below sea level?

Critical Thinking

3. **Drawing Inferences and Conclusions** Russia has often been invaded by other countries. Which part of Russia might be easy to invade? Why do you think this area would be a good invasion route?

4. **Comparing** Northern Russia appears to have many good harbors. Compare this map to the **climate map** of the region. Why have few harbors been developed on Russia's north coast?

Russia and Northern Eurasia: Political

ATLANTIC OCEAN
ARCTIC OCEAN
North Pole
Greenland (DENMARK)
ALASKA (U.S.)
BERING SEA
PACIFIC OCEAN
NORTH SEA
BARENTS SEA
BALTIC SEA
SEA OF OKHOTSK
BLACK SEA
CASPIAN SEA
EUROPE
RUSSIA
St. Petersburg
Minsk
BELARUS
Moscow
Chernobyl
Kiev
Nizhniy Novgorod
UKRAINE
Kharkiv
R U S S I A
Samara
Yekaterinburg
Novosibirsk
GEORGIA
T'bilisi
ARMENIA
Yerevan
Baku
AZERBAIJAN
Astana
KAZAKHSTAN
UZBEKISTAN
TURKMENISTAN
Ashgabat
Tashkent
Bishkek
Almaty
KYRGYZSTAN
TAJIKISTAN
Dushanbe
EAST ASIA
SOUTHWEST ASIA
Vladivostok
Arctic Circle
Tropic of Cancer
N
SCALE
0 500 1000 Miles
0 500 1000 Kilometers
Projection: Two-Point Equidistant
Boundaries
National capitals
Other cities

1. *Places and Regions* Compare this map to the **physical map** of the region. Do any physical features define a border between Russia and the countries of Europe?

Critical Thinking

2. **Analyzing Information** About how far apart are Russia and the Alaskan mainland? the Russian mainland and the North Pole?

3. **Analyzing Information** Which borders separating the countries south and southeast of Russia appear to follow natural features?

4. **Drawing Inferences and Conclusions** Compare this map to the **physical** and **climate maps** of the region. Why do you think the boundary between Kazakhstan and northwestern Uzbekistan is two straight lines?

Russia and Northern Eurasia: Climate

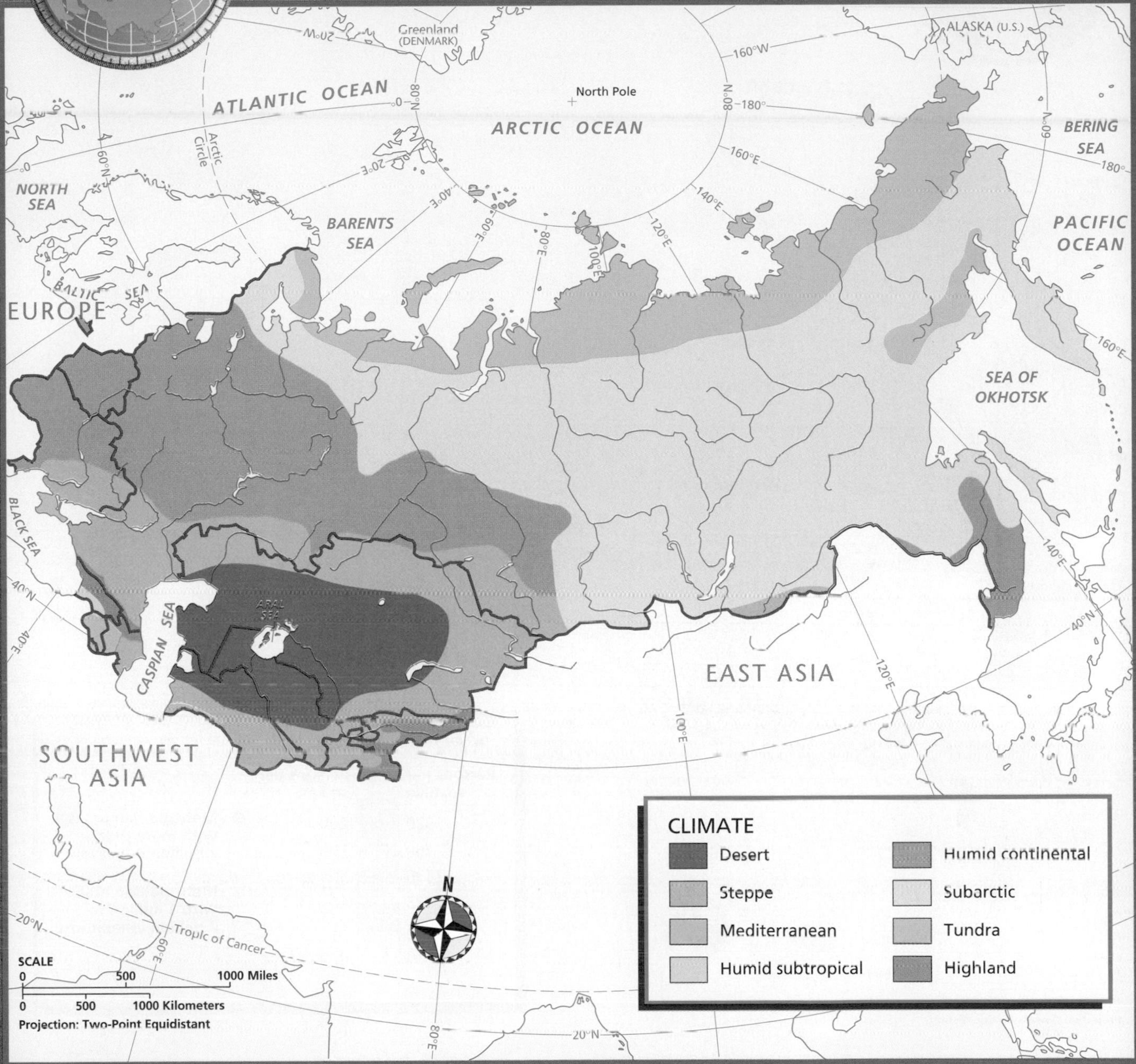

Greenland (DENMARK)
ALASKA (U.S.)
North Pole
ATLANTIC OCEAN
ARCTIC OCEAN
BERING SEA
NORTH SEA
BARENTS SEA
PACIFIC OCEAN
BALTIC SEA
EUROPE
SEA OF OKHOTSK
BLACK SEA
ARAL SEA
CASPIAN SEA
EAST ASIA
SOUTHWEST ASIA
Arctic Circle
Tropic of Cancer
20°W
0°
20°E
40°E
60°E
80°E
100°E
120°E
140°E
160°E
180°
160°W
80°N
60°N
40°N
20°N
N
CLIMATE
Desert
Steppe
Mediterranean
Humid subtropical
Humid continental
Subarctic
Tundra
Highland
SCALE
0 500 1000 Miles
0 500 1000 Kilometers
Projection: Two-Point Equidistant

1. *Places and Regions* Compare this map to the **political map**. Which is the only country that has a humid subtropical climate?
2. *Physical Systems* Which climate types stretch across Russia from Europe to the Pacific?
3. *Places and Regions* Compare this map to the **political map**. Which country has only a humid continental climate?

Critical Thinking

4. **Drawing Inferences and Conclusions** Compare this map to the **land use and resources map**. Why do you think nomadic herding is common east of the Caspian Sea?
5. **Comparing** Compare this to the **political map**. In which countries would you expect to find the highest mountains? Why?

Russia and Northern Eurasia: Population

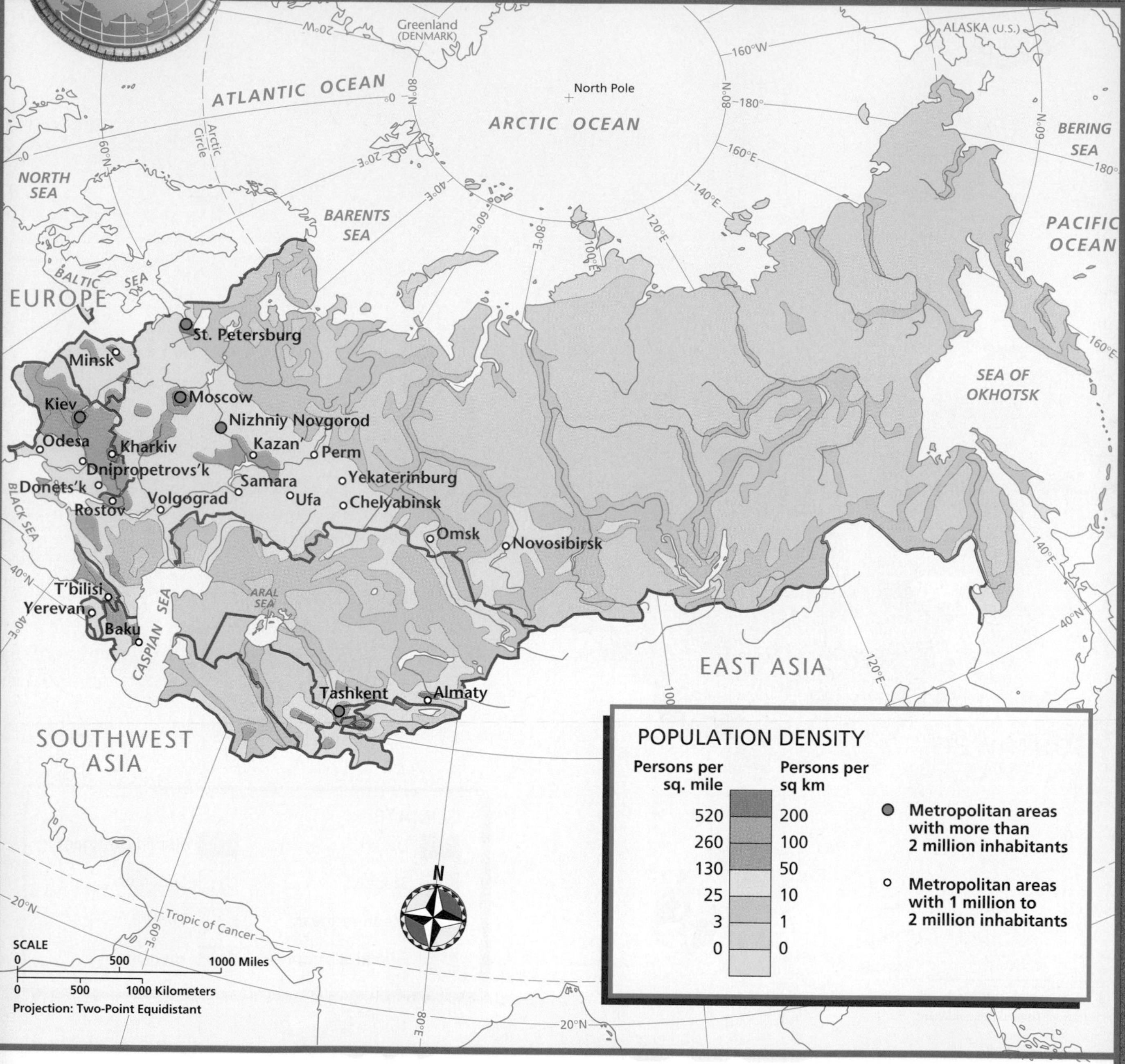

Greenland (DENMARK)
ALASKA (U.S.)
North Pole
ATLANTIC OCEAN
ARCTIC OCEAN
BERING SEA
PACIFIC OCEAN
NORTH SEA
BARENTS SEA
BALTIC SEA
EUROPE
SEA OF OKHOTSK
Arctic Circle
St. Petersburg
Minsk
Moscow
Kiev
Nizhniy Novgorod
Odesa
Kharkiv
Kazan'
Perm
Dnipropetrovs'k
Donets'k
Samara
Yekaterinburg
Ufa
Chelyabinsk
Rostov
Volgograd
BLACK SEA
Omsk
Novosibirsk
T'bilisi
Yerevan
Baku
ARAL SEA
CASPIAN SEA
EAST ASIA
Tashkent
Almaty
SOUTHWEST ASIA
Tropic of Cancer
N
SCALE
0
500
1000 Miles
0
500
1000 Kilometers
Projection: Two-Point Equidistant
POPULATION DENSITY
Persons per sq. mile
Persons per sq km
520
260
130
25
3
0
200
100
50
10
1
0
Metropolitan areas with more than 2 million inhabitants
Metropolitan areas with 1 million to 2 million inhabitants

1. *Places and Regions* Which countries have a large area with more than 260 people per square mile and cities of more than 2 million people?
2. *Places and Regions* Which country has areas in the north where no one lives?

Critical Thinking

3. **Making Generalizations and Predictions** What can you assume about landforms and farming in western Russia just by looking at the **population map**? Check the **physical** and **land use and resources maps** to be sure.
4. **Analyzing Information** Use the map on this page to create a chart, graph, database, or model of population centers in Russia and northern Eurasia.

Russia and Northern Eurasia: Land Use and Resources

UNIT 6 ATLAS

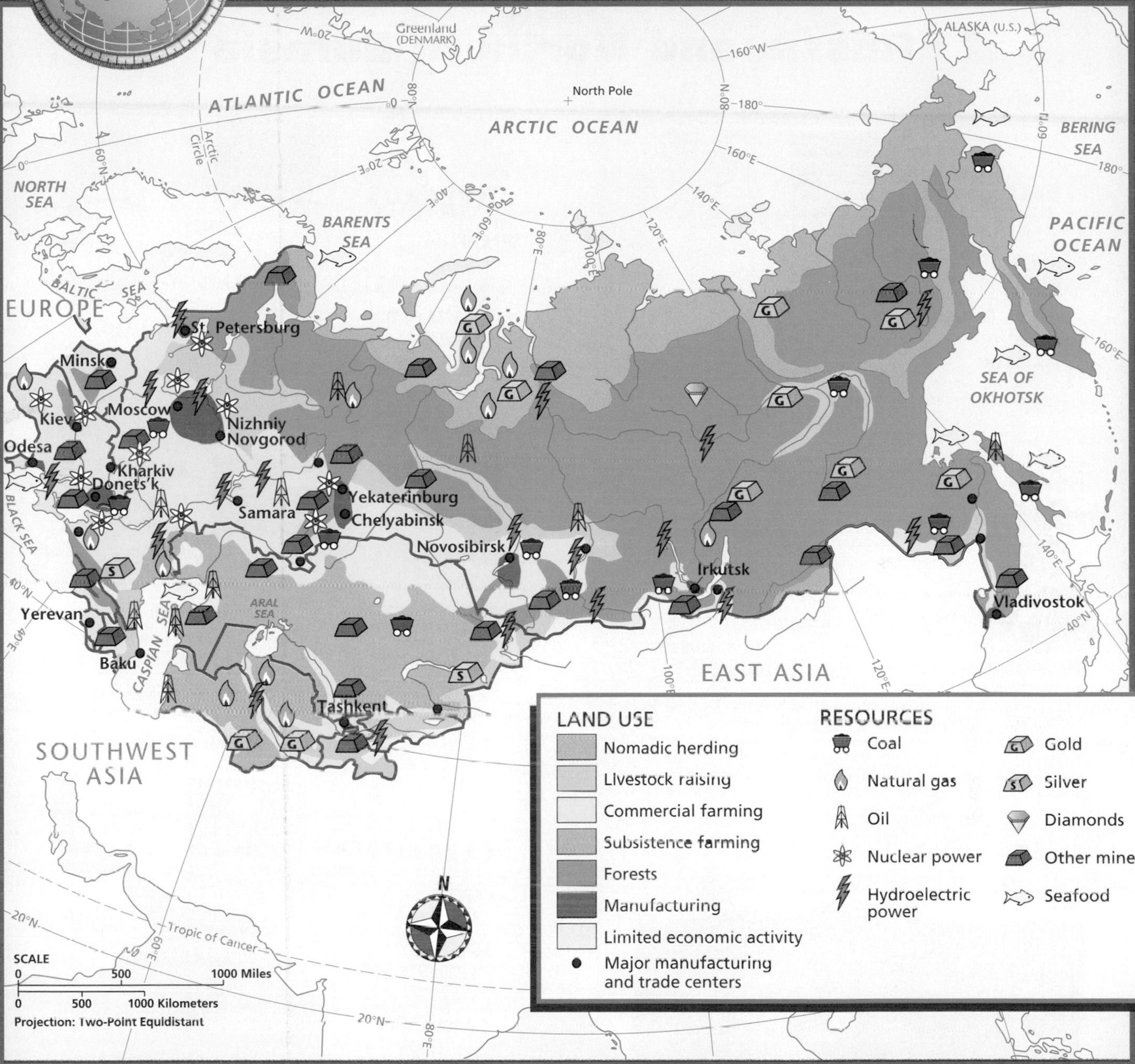

Greenland (DENMARK)
ALASKA (U.S.)
ATLANTIC OCEAN
North Pole
ARCTIC OCEAN
BERING SEA
NORTH SEA
BARENTS SEA
PACIFIC OCEAN
BALTIC SEA
EUROPE
SEA OF OKHOTSK
Arctic Circle
St. Petersburg
Minsk
Moscow
Kiev
Nizhniy Novgorod
Odesa
Kharkiv
Donets'k
Samara
Yekaterinburg
Chelyabinsk
Novosibirsk
Irkutsk
Vladivostok
BLACK SEA
Yerevan
Baku
CASPIAN SEA
ARAL SEA
Tashkent
EAST ASIA
SOUTHWEST ASIA
Tropic of Cancer
LAND USE
Nomadic herding
Livestock raising
Commercial farming
Subsistence farming
Forests
Manufacturing
Limited economic activity
Major manufacturing and trade centers
RESOURCES
Coal
Natural gas
Oil
Nuclear power
Hydroelectric power
Gold
Silver
Diamonds
Other minerals
Seafood
SCALE
0 500 1000 Miles
0 500 1000 Kilometers
Projection: Two-Point Equidistant
N

1. *Places and Regions* Where are most oil reserves in the region located?

2. *Places and Regions* Where are most gold mines in the region located?

3. *Places and Regions* Which country has diamonds? Which countries in the region have silver deposits?

Critical Thinking

4. **Comparing** Compare this to the **physical map**. Which waterways might be used to transport mineral resources mined near Irkutsk to manufacturing and trade centers?

5. **Analyzing Information** Use the map on this page to create a chart, graph, database, or model of economic activities in the region.

Fast Facts

Russia and Northern Eurasia

Armenia

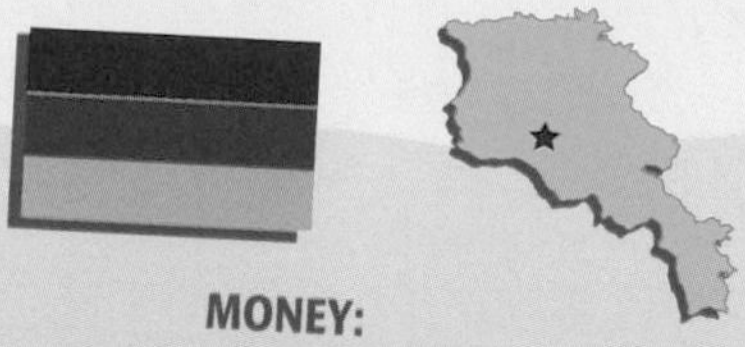

CAPITAL:
Yerevan

AREA:
11,506 sq. mi. (29,800 sq km)

POPULATION:
3,336,100

MONEY:
dram (AMD)

LANGUAGES:
Armenian, Russian

UNEMPLOYMENT:
20 percent

Belarus

CAPITAL:
Minsk

AREA:
80,154 sq. mi.
(207,600 sq km)

POPULATION:
10,350,194

MONEY:
Belarusian rubel (BYB/BYR)

LANGUAGES:
Byelorussian, Russian

UNEMPLOYMENT:
2.1 percent (and many underemployed workers)

Azerbaijan

CAPITAL:
Baku

AREA:
33,436 sq. mi.
(86,600 sq km)

POPULATION:
7,771,092

MONEY:
manat (AZM)

LANGUAGES:
Azeri, Russian, Armenian

UNEMPLOYMENT:
20 percent

Georgia

CAPITAL:
T'bilisi

AREA:
26,911 sq. mi.
(69,700 sq km)

POPULATION:
4,989,285

MONEY:
lari (GEL)

LANGUAGES:
Georgian (official), Russian, Armenian, Azeri

UNEMPLOYMENT:
14.9 percent

Geese flock to this pasture in Ukraine

Kazakhstan

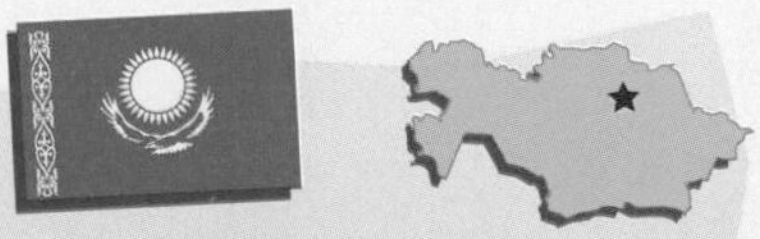

CAPITAL:
Astana

AREA:
1,049,150 sq. mi.
(2,717,300 sq km)

POPULATION:
16,731,303

MONEY:
tenge (KZT)

LANGUAGES:
Kazakh, Russian

UNEMPLOYMENT:
13.7 percent

Kyrgyzstan

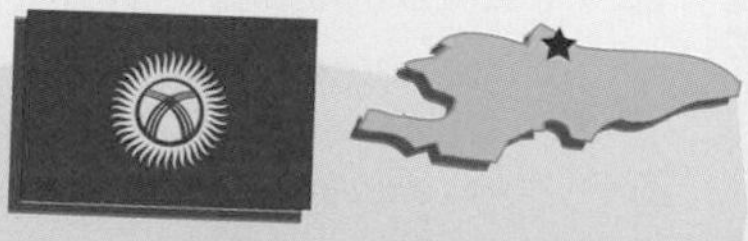

CAPITAL:
Bishkek

AREA:
76,641 sq. mi.
(198,500 sq km)

POPULATION:
4,753,003

MONEY:
Kyrgyzstani som (KGS)

LANGUAGES:
Kirghiz, Russian

UNEMPLOYMENT:
6 percent

Countries not drawn to scale.

Mosque in Uzbekistan

UKRAINE

CAPITAL: Kiev

AREA: 233,089 sq. mi. (603,700 sq km)

POPULATION: 48,760,474

MONEY: hryvna

LANGUAGES: Ukranian, Russian, Romanian, Polish, Hungarian

UNEMPLOYMENT: 4.3 percent officially registered (and many unregistered or underemployed)

RUSSIA

CAPITAL: Moscow

AREA: 6,592,735 sq. mi. (17,075,200 sq km)

POPULATION: 145,470,197

MONEY: Russian ruble (RUR)

LANGUAGES: Russian

UNEMPLOYMENT: 10.5 percent (and many underemployed workers)

UZBEKISTAN

CAPITAL: Tashkent

AREA: 172,741 sq. mi. (447,400 sq km)

POPULATION: 25,155,064

MONEY: Uzbekistani sum (UZS)

LANGUAGES: Uzbek, Russian, Tajik

UNEMPLOYMENT: 10 percent (and many underemployed)

TAJIKISTAN

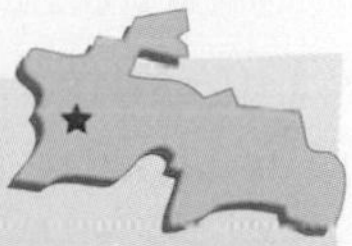

CAPITAL: Dushanbe

AREA: 55,251 sq. mi. (143,100 sq km)

POPULATION: 6,578,681

MONEY: somoni (SM)

LANGUAGES: Tajik (official), Russian

UNEMPLOYMENT: 5.7 percent (and many underemployed workers)

internet connect

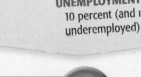

COUNTRY STATISTICS
GO TO: go.hrw.com
KEYWORD: SJ3 FACTSU6
FOR: more facts about Russia and northern Eurasia

TURKMENISTAN

CAPITAL: Ashgabat

AREA: 188,455 sq. mi. (488,100 sq km)

POPULATION: 4,603,244

MONEY: Turkmen manat (TMM)

LANGUAGES: Turkmen, Uzbek, Russian

UNEMPLOYMENT: data not available

Sources: Central Intelligence Agency, *The World Factbook 2001; The World Almanac and Book of Facts 2001;* pop. figures are 2001 estimates.

CHAPTER 22

Russia

Now we will learn about Russia. First we will meet Polina, who lives in Moscow, the capital. She is in the eleventh grade at State School 637 and will graduate in the spring.

P*rivyet!* (Hi!) My name is Polina and I am 17. I live in an apartment in Moscow with my mother and father. Our apartment has two rooms. Every day except Sunday I wake up at 7:00 A.M., have some bread and cheese with tea, and take the subway to school. At the end of eighth grade, we had to choose whether to study science or humanities. I chose humanities. My favorite subjects are history, literature, and English—my history teacher is great!

We have about five or six classes with a 15-minute break between each one. During the breaks, I often eat a snack like *pirozhki*, a small meat pie, at the school snack bar. I go home at 2:00 P.M. for lunch (meat, potatoes, and a salad of cooked vegetables and mayonnaise) and a nap. When I wake up, I go out with my friends to a park. Sometimes my parents and I join my uncle, aunt, and grandmother for Sunday dinner. My uncle makes my favorite dishes, like meat salad with mayonnaise. I love ice cream, too!

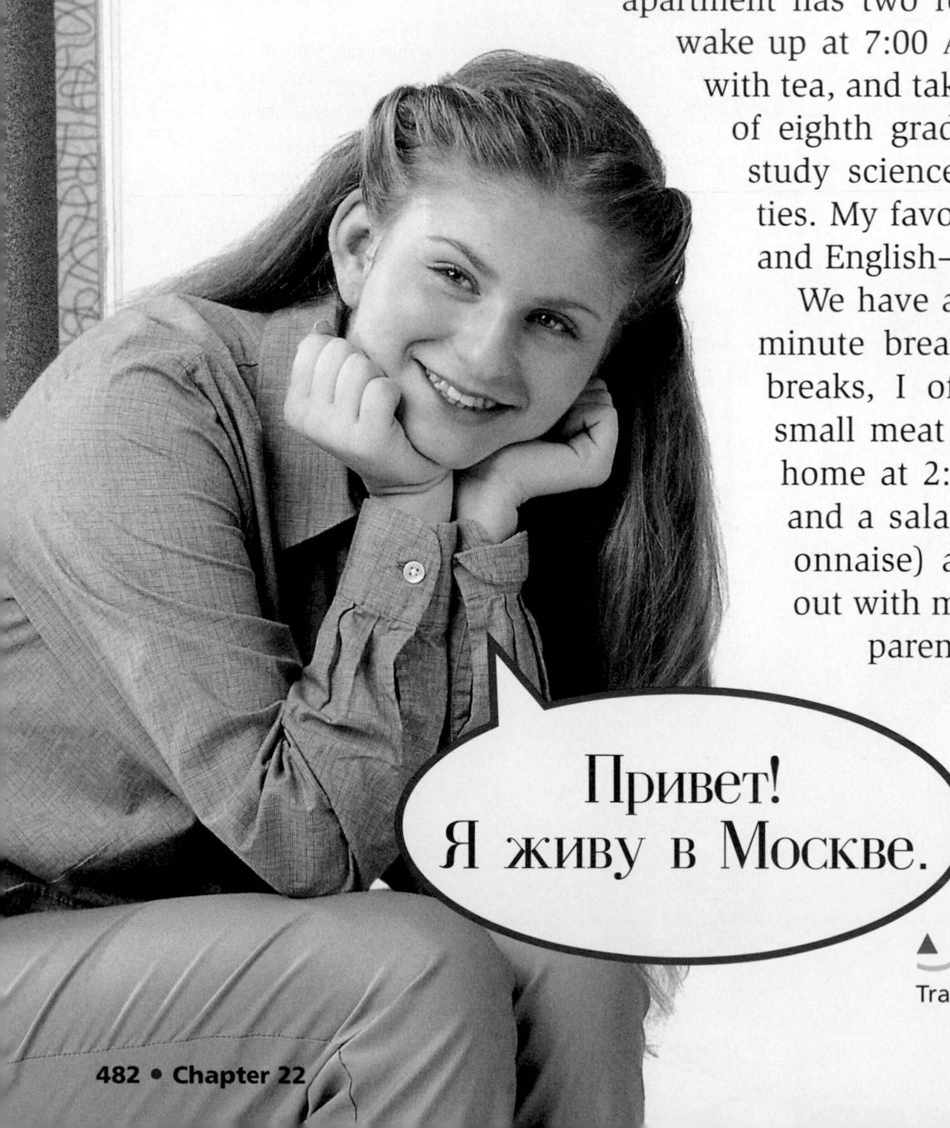
Привет!
Я живу в Москве.

▲ Translation: Hi! I live in Moscow.

Section 1 Physical Geography

Read to Discover

1. What are the physical features of Russia?
2. What climates and vegetation are found in Russia?
3. What natural resources does Russia have?

Define

taiga
steppe

Locate

Arctic Ocean
Caucasus Mountains
Caspian Sea
Ural Mountains
West Siberian Plain
Central Siberian Plateau
Kamchatka Peninsula
Kuril Islands
Volga River
Baltic Sea

Why It Matters

Like many nations, Russia is concerned about environmental issues. Use CNNfyi.com and other **current events** sources to investigate environmental concerns there. Record your findings in your journal.

A Siberian sable

Russia: Physical-Political

ARCTIC OCEAN
North Pole
NORTH SEA
BARENTS SEA
BERING SEA
Bering Strait
Murmansk
Novaya Zemlya
Kaliningrad
RUSSIA
BALTIC SEA
St. Petersburg (Leningrad)
Lake Ladoga
NORTHERN EUROPEAN PLAIN
Moscow
Nizhniy Novgorod (Gorky)
Kazan'
Dnepr R. (Dnieper R.)
Don R.
URAL MOUNTAINS
Ob River
Yenisey R.
S I B E R I A
WEST SIBERIAN PLAIN
CENTRAL SIBERIAN PLATEAU
Lena River
RUSSIA
Yekaterinburg (Sverdlovsk)
Chelyabinsk
Magnitogorsk
KUZNETSK BASIN
Trans-Siberian Railroad
Baikal-Amur Mainline
Lake Baikal
Novosibirsk
Amur R.
Ussuri R.
Khabarovsk
Vladivostok
BLACK SEA
Volgograd (Stalingrad)
Volga River
Astrakhan
CAUCASUS MTS.
Mt. Elbrus 18,510 ft. (5642 m)
CASPIAN SEA
KAMCHATKA PENINSULA
PACIFIC OCEAN
SEA OF OKHOTSK
Sakhalin Island
Kuril Islands
SEA OF JAPAN
Arctic Circle
ELEVATION
FEET METERS
13,120 4,000
6,560 2,000
1,640 500
656 200
(Sea level) 0 0 (Sea level)
Below sea level Below sea level
National capital
Other cities
SCALE
0 500 1000 Miles
0 500 1000 Kilometers
Projection: Two-Point Equidistant
Size comparison of Russia to the contiguous United States

internet connect

GO TO: go.hrw.com
KEYWORD: SJ3 CH22
FOR: Web sites about Russia

Physical Features

Russia was by far the largest republic of what was called the Union of Soviet Socialist Republics, or the Soviet Union. Russia is the largest country in the world. It stretches 6,000 miles (9,654 km), from Eastern Europe to the Bering Sea and Pacific Ocean.

A train chugs through the cold Siberian countryside.

Interpreting the Visual Record What does this photograph tell you about the physical features and climate of Siberia?

The Land Much of western, or European, Russia is part of the Northern European Plain. This is the country's heartland, where most Russians live. To the north are the Barents Sea and the Arctic Ocean. Far to the south are the Caucasus (KAW-kuh-suhs) Mountains. There Europe's highest peak, Mount Elbrus, rises to 18,510 feet (5,642 m). The Caucasus Mountains stretch from the Black Sea to the Caspian (KAS-pee-uhn) Sea. The Caspian is the largest inland body of water in the world.

East of the Northern European Plain is a long range of eroded low mountains and hills. These are called the Ural (YOOHR-uhl) Mountains. The Urals divide Europe from Asia. They stretch from the Arctic coast in the north to Kazakhstan in the south. The highest peak in the Urals rises to just 6,214 feet (1,894 m).

East of the Urals lies a vast region known as Siberia. Much of Siberia is divided between the West Siberian Plain and the Central Siberian Plateau. The West Siberian Plain is a large, flat area with many marshes. The Central Siberian Plateau lies to the east. It is a land of elevated plains and valleys.

A series of high mountain ranges runs through southern and eastern Siberia. The Kamchatka (kuhm-CHAHT-kuh) Peninsula, Sakhalin (sah-kah-LEEN) Island, and the Kuril (KYOOHR-eel) Islands surround the Sea of Okhotsk (uh-KAWTSK). These are in the Russian Far East. The rugged Kamchatka Peninsula and the Kurils have active volcanoes. Earthquakes and volcanic eruptions are common. The Kurils separate the Sea of Okhotsk from the Pacific Ocean.

Our Amazing Planet

The coldest temperature ever recorded outside of Antarctica in the last 100 years was noted on February 6, 1933, in eastern Siberia: –90° F (–68°C).

Rivers Some of the world's longest rivers flow through Russia. These include the Volga (VAHL-guh) and Don Rivers in European Russia. The Ob (AWB), Yenisey (yi-ni-SAY), Lena (LEE-nuh), and Amur (ah-MOOHR) Rivers are located in Siberia and the Russian Far East. The Amur forms part of Russia's border with China.

The Volga is Europe's longest river. Its course and length make it an important transportation route. It flows southward for 2,293 miles (3,689 km) across the Northern European Plain to the Caspian Sea. Barges can travel by canal from the Volga to the Don River. The Don empties into the Black Sea. Canals also connect the Volga to rivers that drain into the Baltic Sea far to the northwest.

In Siberia, the Ob, Yenisey, and Lena Rivers all flow thousands of miles northward. Eventually, they reach Russia's Arctic coast. These and other Siberian rivers that drain into the Arctic Ocean freeze in winter. In spring, these rivers thaw first in the south. Downstream in the north, however, the rivers remain frozen much longer. As a result, ice jams there block water from the melting ice and snow. This causes annual floods in areas along the rivers.

✓ **READING CHECK:** *Places and Regions* What are the major physical features of Russia?

Climate and Vegetation

Nearly all of Russia is located at high northern latitudes. The country has tundra, subarctic, humid continental, and steppe climates. Because there are no high mountain barriers, cold Arctic winds sweep across much of the country in winter. Winters are long and cold. Ice blocks most seaports until spring. However, the winters are surprisingly dry in much of Russia. This is because the interior is far from ocean moisture.

Winters are particularly severe throughout Siberia. Temperatures often drop below –40°F (–40°C). Although they are short, Siberian summers can be hot. Temperatures can rise to 100°F (38°C).

Vegetation varies with climates from north to south. Very cold temperatures and permafrost in the far north keep trees from taking root. Mosses, wildflowers, and other tundra vegetation grow there.

The vast **taiga** (TY-guh), a forest of mostly evergreen trees, grows south of the tundra. The trees there include spruce, fir, and pine. In European Russia and in the Far East are deciduous forests. Many temperate forests in European Russia have been cleared for farms and cities.

Wide grasslands known as the **steppe** (STEP) stretch from Ukraine across southern Russia to Kazakhstan. Much of the steppe is used for growing crops and grazing livestock.

✓ **READING CHECK:** *Physical Systems* How does Russia's location affect its climate?

BUILD on WHAT You Know

Do you remember what you learned about tundra climates? See Chapter 3 to review.

Camels graze on open land in southern Siberia near Mongolia.

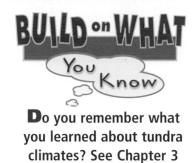

Russia
China
India

A blast furnace is used to process nickel in Siberia. Nickel is just one of Russia's many natural resources.

Resources

Russia has enormous energy, mineral, and forest resources. However, those resources have been poorly managed. For example, much of the forest west of the Urals has been cut down. Now wood products must be brought long distances from Siberia. Still, the taiga provides a vast supply of trees for wood and paper pulp.

Russia has long been a major oil producer. However, many of its oil deposits are far from cities, markets, and ports. Coal is also plentiful. More than a dozen metals are available in large quantities. Russia also is a major diamond producer. Many valuable mineral deposits in remote Siberia have not yet been mined.

✓ **READING CHECK:** *Places and Regions* How might the location of its oil deposits prevent Russia from taking full advantage of this resource?

go.hrw.com **Homework Practice Online** Keyword: SJ3 HP22

Section 1 Review

Define and explain: taiga, steppe

Working with Sketch Maps On a map of Russia that you sketch or that your teacher provides, label the following: Arctic Ocean, Caucasus Mountains, Caspian Sea, Ural Mountains, West Siberian Plain, Central Siberian Plateau, Kamchatka Peninsula, Kuril Islands, Volga River, and Baltic Sea.

Reading for the Main Idea

1. *Places and Regions* What low mountain range in central Russia divides Europe from Asia?
2. *Places and Regions* How is the Volga River linked to the Baltic and Black Seas?
3. *Environment and Society* What are winters like in much of Russia? How might they affect people?

Critical Thinking

4. **Making Generalizations and Predictions** How might Russia's natural resources make the country more prosperous?

Organizing What You Know

5. **Categorizing** Copy the following graphic organizer. Use it to list the climates, vegetation, and resources of Russia.

Climates	Vegetation	Resources

Section 2 History and Culture

Read to Discover

1. What was Russia's early history like?
2. How did the Russian Empire grow and then fall?
3. What was the Soviet Union?
4. What is Russia like today?

Define

czar
abdicated
allies
superpowers
Cold War
consumer goods

Locate

Moscow

Russian caviar, blini *(pancakes), and smoked salmon*

WHY IT MATTERS

Russia is well known for its ballet companies. Use CNNfyi.com or other **current events** sources to discover more about Russia's culture and its international recognition in the field of dance and other arts. Record your findings in your journal.

Early Russia

The roots of the Russian nation lie deep in the grassy plains of the steppe. For thousands of years, people moved across the steppe bringing new languages, religions, and ways of life.

Early Migrations Slavic peoples have lived in Russia for thousands of years. In the A.D. 800s, Viking traders from Scandinavia helped shape the first Russian state among the Slavs. These Vikings called themselves Rus (ROOS). The word *Russia* comes from their name. The state they created was centered on Kiev. Today Kiev is the capital of Ukraine.

In the following centuries, missionaries from southeastern Europe brought Orthodox Christianity and a form of the Greek alphabet to Russia. Today the Russian language is written in this Cyrillic alphabet.

Mongols After about 200 years, Kiev's power began to decline. In the 1200s, Mongol invaders called Tatars swept out of Central Asia across the steppe. The Mongols conquered Kiev and added much of the region to their vast empire.

The Mongols demanded taxes but ruled the region through local leaders. Over time, these local leaders established various states. The strongest of these was Muscovy, north of Kiev. Its chief city was Moscow.

✓ **READING CHECK:** *Human Systems* What was the effect of Viking traders on Russia?

This painting from the mid-1400s shows a battle between soldiers of two early Russian states.

History of Russian Expansion

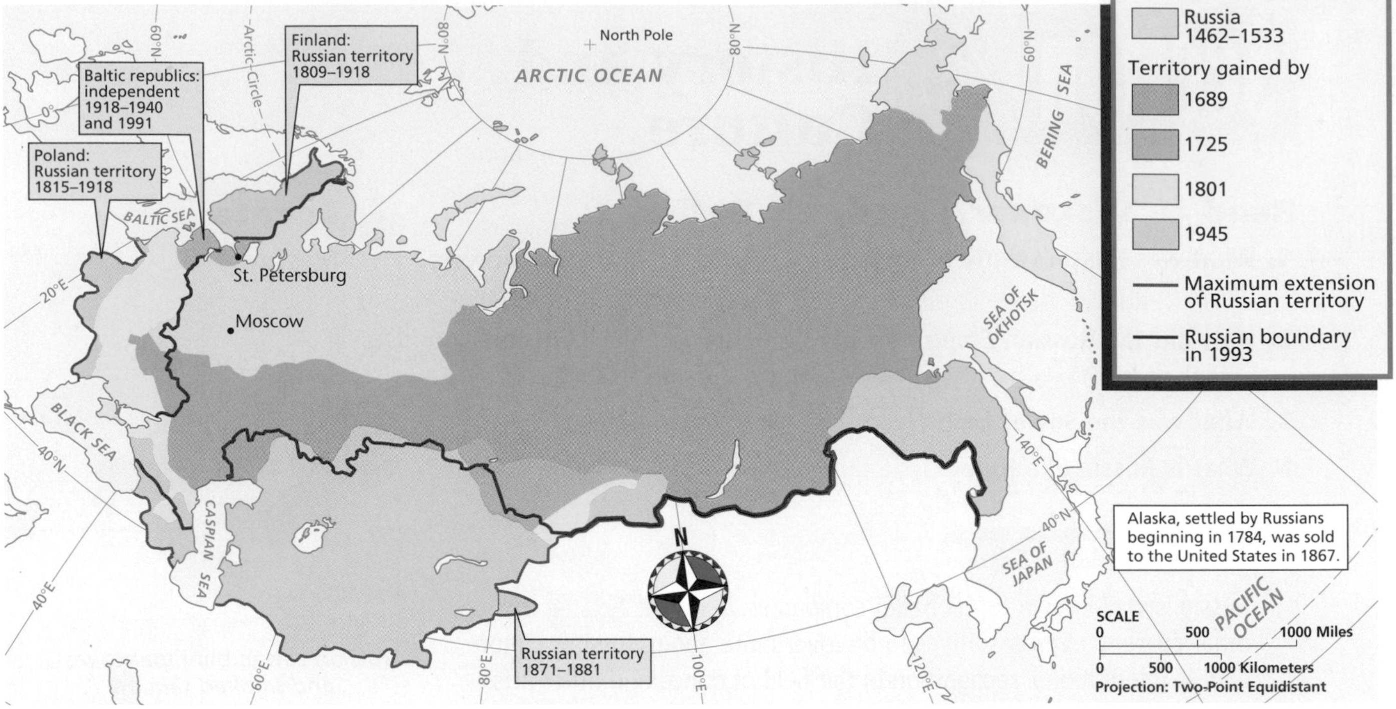

North Pole
ARCTIC OCEAN
Finland: Russian territory 1809–1918
Baltic republics: independent 1918–1940 and 1991
Poland: Russian territory 1815–1918
Arctic Circle
BALTIC SEA
St. Petersburg
Moscow
BLACK SEA
CASPIAN SEA
SEA OF OKHOTSK
BERING SEA
SEA OF JAPAN
PACIFIC OCEAN
Russian territory 1871–1881
Alaska, settled by Russians beginning in 1784, was sold to the United States in 1867.
Russia 1462–1533
Territory gained by
1689
1725
1801
1945
Maximum extension of Russian territory
Russian boundary in 1993
SCALE
0 500 1000 Miles
0 500 1000 Kilometers
Projection: Two-Point Equidistant
N

The colors in this map show land taken by the Russian Empire and the Soviet Union over time.

Interpreting the Map When was the period of Russia's greatest expansion?

The Russian Empire

In the 1400s Muscovy won control over parts of Russia from the Mongols. In 1547 Muscovy's ruler, Ivan IV—known as Ivan the Terrible—crowned himself **czar** (ZAHR) of all Russia. The word *czar* comes from the Latin word *Caesar* and means "emperor."

Expansion Over more than 300 years, czars like Peter the Great (1672–1725) expanded the Russian empire. By the early 1700s the empire stretched from the Baltic to the Pacific.

Russian fur traders crossed the Bering Strait in the 1700s and 1800s. They established colonies along the North American west coast. Those colonies stretched from coastal Alaska to California. Russia sold Alaska to the United States in 1867. Around the same time, Russia expanded into Central Asia.

Decline The Russian Empire's power began to decline in the late 1800s. Industry grew slowly, so Russia remained largely agricultural. Most people were poor farmers. Far fewer were the rich, factory workers, or craftspeople. Food shortages, economic problems, and defeat in war further weakened the empire in the early 1900s.

In 1917, during World War I, the czar **abdicated**, or gave up his throne. Later in 1917 the Bolshevik Party, led by Vladimir Lenin, overthrew the government. This event is known as the Russian Revolution.

✓ **READING CHECK:** *Human Systems* What conflict brought a change of government to Russia?

Ivan the Terrible became grand prince of Moscow in 1533. He was just three years old. He ruled Russia from 1547 to his death in 1584.

The Soviet Union

The Bolsheviks, or Communists, established the Soviet Union in 1922. Most of the various territories of the Russian Empire became republics within the Soviet Union.

Under Lenin and his successor, Joseph Stalin, the Communists took over all industries and farms. Religious practices were discouraged. The Communists outlawed all other political parties. Many opponents were imprisoned, forced to leave the country, or even killed.

The Soviet leaders established a command economy, in which industries were controlled by the government. At first these industries grew dramatically. However, over time the lack of competition made them inefficient and wasteful. The quality of many products was poor. Government-run farms failed to produce enough food to feed the population. By the late 1950s the Soviet Union had to import large amounts of grain.

Cold War The Soviet Union in the 1950s was still recovering from World War II. The country had been a major battleground in the war. The United States and the Soviet Union had been **allies**, or friends, in the fight against Germany. After the war the two **superpowers**, or powerful countries, became rivals. This bitter rivalry became known as the **Cold War**. The Cold War lasted from the 1940s to the early 1990s. The Soviet Union and the United States built huge military forces, including nuclear weapons. The two countries never formally went to war with each other. However, they supported allies in small wars around the world.

Collapse of the Soviet Union The costs of the Cold War eventually became too much for the Soviet Union. The Soviet government spent more and more money on military goods. **Consumer goods** became expensive and in short supply. Consumer goods are products used at home and in everyday life. The last Soviet leader, Mikhail Gorbachev, tried to bring about changes to help the economy. He also promoted a policy allowing more open discussion of the country's problems. However, the various Soviet republics pushed for independence. Finally, in 1991 the Soviet Union collapsed. The huge country split into 15 republics.

In late 1991 Russia and most of the other former Soviet republics formed the Commonwealth of Independent States, or CIS. The CIS does not have a strong central government. Instead, it provides a way for the former Soviet republics to address shared problems.

✓ **READING CHECK:** ***Human Systems*** What was the Cold War, and how did it eventually cause the Soviet Union's collapse?

St. Petersburg
Russia
China
India

Tourists can visit the czar's Summer Palace in St. Petersburg.

Interpreting the Visual Record How do you think the rich lifestyle of the czars helped the Bolsheviks gain support?

A man lights candles in front of portraits of the last czar, Nicholas II, and his wife. Russians are divided over what kind of government their country should have today.

Interpreting the Visual Record Why do you think some Russians might wish to have a czar again?

St. Petersburg
Russia
China
India

Connecting to Literature

Aunt Rimma's Treat

The former Soviet Union was composed of many republics, which are now independent countries. Nina Gabrielyan's The Lilac Dressing Gown *is told from the point of view of an Armenian girl living in Moscow before the Soviet breakup.*

Aunt Rimma. . . came to visit and gave me a pink caramel which I, naturally, popped straight in my mouth. "Don't swallow it," Aunt Rimma says in an odd sort of voice. "You're not supposed to swallow it, only chew it." "Why," I ask, puzzled by her solemn tone. "It's chewing gum," she says with pride in her eyes. "Chewing gum?" I don't know what she means. "American chewing gum," Aunt Rimma explains. "Mentor's sister sent it to us from America." "Oh, from America? Is that where the capitalists are? What is she doing there?" "She's living there," says Aunt Rimma, condescending to my foolishness.

But I am not as foolish as I used to be. I know that Armenians live in Armenia. Our country is very big and includes many republics: Armenia, Georgia, Azerbaijan, Tajikistan, Uzbekistan, Ukraine, Belorussia [Belarus], the Caucasus and Transcaucasia. All this together is the Soviet Union. Americans . . . live in America. Clearly, Mentor's sister cannot possibly be American. . . . Rimma goes on boasting: "Oh! the underwear they have there! . . . And the children's clothes!"

I begin to feel a bit envious. . . . Nobody in our house has anyone living in America, but Aunt Rimma does. My envy becomes unbearable. So I decide to slay our boastful neighbor on the spot: "Well we have cockroaches! This big! Lots and lots of them!'"

Analyzing Primary Sources

1. How does the Armenian girl's frame of reference affect her view of the United States?
2. What does Aunt Rimma seem to think the United States is like?

Russia Today

Russia has been making a transition from communism to democracy and a free market economy since 1991. Change has been slow, and the country faces difficult challenges.

People and Religion More than 146 million people live in Russia today. More than 80 percent are ethnic Russians. The largest of Russia's many minority groups are Ukrainians and Tatars. These Tatars are the descendants of the early Mongol invaders of Russia.

In the past, the government encouraged ethnic Russians to settle in areas of Russia far from Moscow. They were encouraged to move to places where other ethnic groups were in the majority. Today, many non-Russian peoples in those areas resent the domination of ethnic Russians. Some non-Russians want independence from Moscow. At times this has led to violence and even war, as in Chechnya in southern Russia.

Russia

Country	Population/ Growth Rate	Life Expectancy	Literacy Rate	Per Capita GDP
Russia	145,470,197 / –0.4%	62, male 73, female	98%	$7,700
United States	281,421,906 / 0.9%	74, male 80, female	97%	$36,200

Sources: Central Intelligence Agency, *The World Factbook 2001;* U.S. Census Bureau

Interpreting the Chart How many times greater is the U.S. population than the Russian population?

Since 1991 a greater degree of religious expression has been allowed in Russia. Russian Orthodox Christianity is becoming popular again. Cathedrals have been repaired, and their onion-shaped domes have been covered in gold leaf and brilliant colors. Muslims around the Caspian Sea and the southern Urals are reviving Islamic practices.

Food and Festivals Bread is an important part of the Russian diet. It is eaten with every meal. It may be a rich, dark bread made from rye and wheat flour or a firm white bread. As in other northern countries, the growing season is short and winter is long. Therefore, the diet includes many canned and preserved foods, such as sausages, smoked fish, cheese, and vegetable and fruit preserves.

Black caviar, one of the world's most expensive delicacies, comes from Russia. The fish eggs that make up black caviar come from sturgeon. Sturgeon are fish found in the Caspian Sea.

The anniversary of the 1917 Russian Revolution was an important holiday during the Soviet era. Today the Orthodox Christian holidays of Christmas and Easter are again becoming popular in Russia. Special holiday foods include milk puddings and cheesecakes.

The Arts and Sciences Russia has given the world great works of art, literature, and music. For example, you might know *The Nutcracker,* a ballet danced to music composed by Peter Tchaikovsky (1840–93). It is a popular production in many countries.

St. Petersburg
Russia
China
India

Ballet dancers perform Peter Tchaikovsky's *Swan Lake* at the Mariinsky Theater in St. Petersburg.

Many Russian writers are known for how they capture the emotions of characters in their works. Some writers, such as Aleksandr Solzhenitsyn (1918–), have written about Russia under communism.

Russian scientists also have made important contributions to their professions. For example, in 1957 the Soviet Union launched *Sputnik.* It was the first artificial satellite in space. Today U.S. and Russian engineers are working together on space projects. These include building a large space station and planning for a mission to Mars.

Government Like the U.S. government, the Russian Federation is governed by an elected president and a legislature called the Federal Assembly. The Federal Assembly includes representatives of regions and republics within the Federation. Non-Russians are numerous or in the majority in many of those regions and republics.

The government faces tough challenges. One is improving the country's struggling economy. Many government-owned companies have been sold to the private sector. However, financial problems and corruption have made people cautious about investing in those companies.

Corruption is a serious problem. A few people have used their connections with powerful government officials to become rich. In addition, many Russians avoid paying taxes. This means the government has less money for salaries and services. Agreement on solutions to these problems has been hard.

✓ **READING CHECK:** *Human Systems* What are the people and culture of Russia like today?

Republics of the Russian Federation

Adygea	Karachay-Cherkessia
Alania	Karelia
Bashkortostan	Khakassia
Buryatia	Komi
Chechnya	Mari El
Chuvashia	Mordvinia
Dagestan	Sakha
Gorno-Altay	Tatarstan
Ingushetia	Tuva
Kabardino-Balkaria	Udmurtia
Kalmykia	

go.hrw.com Homework Practice Online
Keyword: SJ3 HP22

Section 2 Review

Define and explain: czar, abdicated, allies, superpowers, Cold War, consumer goods

Working with Sketch Maps On the map you created in Section 1, label Moscow. In the margin, explain the role Kiev played in Russia's early history.

Reading for the Main Idea

1. *Places and Regions* How did Russia get its name?
2. *Human Systems* What was the Bolshevik Party?
3. *Places and Regions* What are some of the challenges that Russia faces today?

Critical Thinking

4. **Comparing** Compare the factors that led to the decline of the Russian Empire and the Soviet Union. List the factors for each.

Organizing What You Know

5. **Summarizing** Copy the following graphic organizer. Use it to identify important features of Russia's ethnic population, religion, food, and arts and sciences.

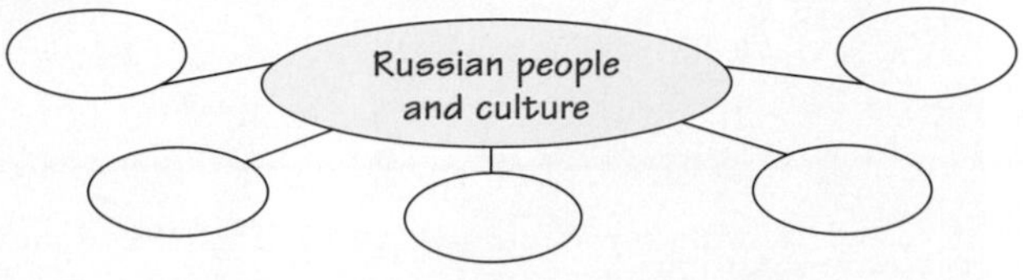
Russian people and culture

Section 3 The Russian Heartland

Read to Discover

1. Why is European Russia considered the country's heartland?
2. What are the characteristics of the four regions of European Russia?

Define

light industry
heavy industry
smelters

Locate

St. Petersburg
Nizhniy Novgorod
Astrakhan
Yekaterinburg
Chelyabinsk
Magnitogorsk

WHY IT MATTERS

Following the fall of Communism, some Russian cities' landscapes began to change. In the larger cities like Moscow there are newer buildings and more restaurants. Use CNNfyi.com or other **current events** sources to find information about Moscow and other large Russian cities. Record your findings in your journal.

Jeweled box made by Peter Carl Fabergé

The Heartland

The European section of Russia is the country's heartland. The Russian nation expanded outward from there. It is home to the bulk of the Russian population. The national capital and large industrial cities are also located there.

The plains of European Russia make up the country's most productive farming region. Farmers focus mainly on growing grains and raising livestock. Small gardens near cities provide fresh fruits and vegetables for summer markets.

The Russian heartland can be divided into four major regions. These four are the Moscow region, the St. Petersburg region, the Volga region, and the Urals region.

✓ **READING CHECK:** *Places and Regions* Why is European Russia the country's heartland?

The Moscow Region

Moscow is Russia's capital and largest city. More than 9 million people live there. In addition to being Russia's political center, Moscow is the country's center for transportation and communication. Roads, railroads, and air routes link the capital to all points in Russia.

At Moscow's heart is the Kremlin. The Kremlin's red brick walls and towers were built in the late 1400s. The government offices, beautiful palaces, and gold-domed churches within its walls are popular tourist attractions.

Twenty towers, like the one in the lower left, are spaced along the Kremlin's walls.

Interpreting the Visual Record What was the advantage of locating government buildings and palaces within the walls of one central location?

Moscow
Russia
China
India

Moscow
Russia
China
India

Vendors sell religious art and other crafts at a sidewalk market in Moscow.

Interpreting the Visual Record **What do the items in this market suggest about the status of religion in Russia since the communist era?**

Moscow is part of a huge industrial area. This area also includes the city of Nizhniy Novgorod, called Gorky during the communist era. About one third of Russia's population lives in this region.

The Soviet government encouraged the development of **light industry**, rather than **heavy industry**, around Moscow. Light industry focuses on the production of lightweight goods, such as clothing. Heavy industry usually involves manufacturing based on metals. It causes more pollution than light industry. The region also has advanced-technology and electronics industries.

The St. Petersburg Region

Northwest of Moscow is St. Petersburg, Russia's second-largest city and a major Baltic seaport. More than 5 million people live there. St. Petersburg was Russia's capital and home to the czars for more than 200 years. This changed in 1918. Palaces and other grand buildings constructed under the czars are tourist attractions today. St. Petersburg was known as Leningrad during the communist era. Much of the city was heavily damaged during World War II.

The surrounding area has few natural resources. Still, St. Petersburg's harbor, canals, and rail connections make the city a major center for trade. Important universities and research institutions are located there. The region also has important industries.

The Mariinsky Theater of Opera and Ballet is one of St. Petersburg's most beautiful buildings. It was called the Kirov during the communist era.

St. Petersburg
Russia
China
India

✓ **READING CHECK:** *Human Systems*
Why are Moscow and St. Petersburg such large cities?

The Volga Region

The Volga region stretches along the middle part of the Volga River. The Volga is often more like a chain of lakes. It is a major shipping route for goods produced in the region. Hydroelectric power plants and nearby deposits of coal and oil are important sources of energy.

During World War II, many factories were moved to the Volga region. This was done to keep them safe from German invaders. Today the region is famous for its factories that produce goods such as motor vehicles, chemicals, and food products. Russian caviar comes from a fishery based at the old city of Astrakhan on the Caspian Sea.

Russia
China
India

A fisher gathers sturgeon in a small shipboard pool in the Volga region. The eggs for making caviar are taken from the female sturgeon. Then the fish is released back into the water.

The Urals Region

Mining has long been important in the Ural Mountains region. Nearly every important mineral except oil has been discovered there. Copper and iron **smelters** are still important. Smelters are factories that process copper, iron, and other metal ores.

Many large cities in the Urals started as commercial centers for mining districts. The Soviet government also moved factories to the region during World War II. Important cities include Yekaterinburg (yi-kah-ti-reem-BOOHRK) (formerly Sverdlovsk), Chelyabinsk (chel-YAH-buhnsk), and Magnitogorsk (muhg-nee-tuh-GAWRSK). Now these cities manufacture machinery and metal goods.

✓ **READING CHECK:** *Places and Regions* What industries are important in the Volga and Urals regions?

Section 3 Review

go.hrw.com Homework Practice Online Keyword: SJ3 HP22

Define and explain: light industry, heavy industry, smelters

Working with Sketch Maps On the map you created in Section 2, label St. Petersburg, Nizhniy Novgorod, Astrakhan, Yekaterinburg, Chelyabinsk, and Magnitogorsk. In the margin of your map, write a short caption explaining the significance of Moscow and St. Petersburg.

Reading for the Main Idea

1. *Places and Regions* Why might so many people settle in Russia's heartland?
2. *Places and Regions* Where did the Soviet government move factories during World War II?

Critical Thinking

3. **Drawing Inferences and Conclusions** Why do you think the Soviet government encouraged the development of light industry around Moscow?
4. **Finding the Main Idea** What role has the region's physical geography played in the development of European Russia's economy?

Organizing What You Know

5. **Contrasting** Use this graphic organizer to identify European Russia's four regions. Write one feature that makes each region different from the other three.

European Russia

Section 4 Siberia

Read to Discover

1. What is the human geography of Siberia like?
2. What are the economic features of the region?
3. How has Lake Baikal been threatened by pollution?

Define

habitation fog

Locate

Siberia
Trans-Siberian Railroad
Baikal-Amur Mainline
Kuznetsk Basin
Ob River
Yenisey River
Novosibirsk
Lake Baikal

Russian matryoshka *nesting doll*

Why It Matters

It takes more than a week by train to cross Russia. The Trans-Siberian Railroad and the Baikal-Amur Mainline let travelers see more of the country. Use CNNfyi.com or other **current events** sources to learn more about these rail systems. Record your findings in your journal.

A Sleeping Land

East of European Russia, across the Ural Mountains, is Siberia. Siberia is enormous. It covers more than 5 million square miles (12.95 million sq. km) of northern Asia. It extends all the way to the Pacific Ocean. That is nearly 1.5 times the area of the United States! To the north of Siberia is the Arctic Ocean. To the south are the Central Asian countries, Mongolia, and China.

Many people think of Siberia as simply a vast, frozen wasteland. In fact, in the Tatar language, *Siberia* means "Sleeping Land." In many ways, this image is accurate. Siberian winters are long, dark, and severe. Often there is little snow, but the land is frozen for months. During winter, **habitation fog** hangs over cities. A habitation fog is a fog caused by fumes and smoke from cities. During the cold Siberian winter, this fog is trapped over cities.

Siberia has lured Russian adventurers for more than 400 years. It continues to do so today. This vast region has a great wealth of natural resources. Developing those resources may be a key to transforming Russia into an economic success.

Reindeer graze around a winter camp in northern Siberia.

Interpreting the Visual Record What climate does this area appear to have, tundra or subarctic?

Russia
China
India

People Siberia is sparsely populated. In fact, large areas have no human population at all. Most of the people live in cities in western and southern parts of the region.

Ethnic Russians make up most of the population. However, minority groups have lived there since long before Russians began to expand into Siberia.

Settlements Russian settlement in Siberia generally follows the route of the Trans-Siberian Railroad. Construction of this railway started in 1891. When it was completed, it linked Moscow and Vladivostok, a port on the Sea of Japan.

Russia's Trans-Siberian Railroad is the longest single rail line in the world. It is more than 5,700 miles (9,171 km) long. For many Siberian towns, the railroad provides the only transportation link to the outside world. Another important railway is the Baikal-Amur Mainline (BAM), which crosses many mountain ranges and rivers in eastern Siberia.

Moscow
Russia
China
India

The Omsk (AWMSK) Cathedral in Omsk, Siberia, provides an example of Russian architecture. Omsk was founded in the early 1700s.

✓ **READING CHECK:** *Places and Regions* Where is Russian settlement located in Siberia, and why do you think this is the case?

Siberia's Economy

The Soviet government built the Baikal-Amur Mainline so that raw materials from Siberia could be easily transported to other places. Abundant natural resources form the foundation of Siberia's economy. They are also important to the development of Russia's struggling economy. Siberia's natural resources include timber, mineral ores, diamonds, and coal, oil, and natural gas deposits.

Although Siberia has rich natural resources, it contains a small percentage of Russia's industry. The harsh climate and difficult terrain have discouraged settlement. Many people would rather live in European Russia, even though wages may be higher in Siberia.

Lumbering and mining are the most important Siberian industries. Large coal deposits are mined in the Kuznetsk Basin, or the Kuzbas. The Kuzbas is located in southwestern Siberia between the Ob and Yenisey Rivers. It is one of Siberia's most important industrial regions.

Siberia's largest city, Novosibirsk, is located near the Kuznetsk Basin. The city's name means "New Siberia." About 1.5 million people live there. It is located about halfway between Moscow and Vladivostok on the Trans-Siberian Railroad. Novosibirsk is Siberia's manufacturing and transportation center.

A worker repairs an oil rig in Siberia.
Interpreting the Visual Record How is this worker protected from the cold Siberian climate?

✓ **READING CHECK:** *Environment and Society* How do Siberia's natural resources influence the economies of Siberia and Russia?

The scenery around Lake Baikal is breathtaking. The lake is seven times as deep as the Grand Canyon.

Interpreting the Visual Record
How would pollution affect this lake and the plants and animals that live there?

Russia
Lake Baikal
China
India

Lake Baikal

Some people have worried that economic development in Siberia threatens the region's natural environment. One focus of concern has been Lake Baikal (by-KAHL), the "Jewel of Siberia."

Baikal is located north of Mongolia. It is the world's deepest lake. In fact, it holds as much water as all of North America's Great Lakes. The scenic lake and its surrounding area are home to many kinds of plants and animals. Some, such as the world's only freshwater seal, are endangered.

For decades people have worried about pollution from a nearby paper factory and other development. They feared that pollution threatened the species that live in and around the lake. In recent years scientists and others have proposed plans that allow some economic development while protecting the environment.

✔ **READING CHECK:** *Environment and Society* How has human activity affected Lake Baikal?

Our Amazing Planet

Lake Baikal covers less area than do three of the Great Lakes: Superior, Huron, and Michigan. Still, Baikal is so deep that it contains about one fifth of all the world's freshwater!

Section 4 Review

go.hrw.com **Homework Practice Online**
Keyword: SJ3 HP22

Define and explain: habitation fog

Working with Sketch Maps On the map you created in Section 3, label Siberia, Trans-Siberian Railroad, Baikal-Amur Mainline, Kuznetsk Basin, Ob River, Yenisey River, Novosibirsk, and Lake Baikal.

Reading for the Main Idea

1. *Places and Regions* What are the boundaries of Siberia?
2. *Human Systems* Where do most people in Siberia live? Why?
3. *Places and Regions* Why does this huge region with many natural resources have little industry?

Critical Thinking

4. **Making Generalizations and Predictions** Do you think Russians should be more concerned about rapid economic development or protecting the environment? Why?

Organizing What You Know

5. **Categorizing** Use this organizer to list the region's resources and industries that use them.

Natural Resources	⇨	Major Industries

Section 5 The Russian Far East

Read to Discover

1. How does the Russian Far East's climate affect agriculture in the region?
2. What are the major resources and cities of the region?
3. What island regions are part of the Russian Far East?

Define

icebreakers

Locate

Sea of Okhotsk
Sea of Japan
Amur River
Khabarovsk
Vladivostok
Sakhalin Island

A Russian figurine

WHY IT MATTERS

Because of conflict over the Kuril Islands, Russia and Japan did not sign a peace agreement to end World War II. Use CNNfyi.com or other **current events** sources to find information on this controversy and other political concerns. Record your findings in your journal.

Agriculture

Off the eastern coast of Siberia are the Sea of Okhotsk and the Sea of Japan. Their coastal areas and islands make up a region known as the Russian Far East.

The Russian Far East has a less severe climate than the rest of Siberia. Summer weather is mild enough for some successful farming. Farms produce many goods, including wheat, sugar beets, sunflowers, meat, and dairy products. However, the region cannot produce enough food for itself. As a result, food must also be imported.

Fishing and hunting are important in the region. There are many kinds of animals, including deer, seals, rare Siberian tigers, and sables. Sable fur is used to make expensive clothing.

✓ **READING CHECK:** *Environment and Society* How does scarcity of food affect the Russian Far East?

The Siberian tiger is endangered. The few remaining of these large cats roam parts of the Russian Far East. They are also found in northern China and on the Korean Peninsula.

Economy

Like the rest of Siberia, the Russian Far East has a wealth of natural resources. These resources have supported the growth of industrial cities and ports in the region.

BUILD on WHAT You Know

Do you remember what you learned about plate tectonics? See Chapter 2 to review.

Resources Much of the Russian Far East remains forested. The region's minerals are only beginning to be developed. Lumbering, machine manufacturing, woodworking, and metalworking are the major industries there.

The region also has important energy resources, including coal and oil. Another resource is geothermal energy. This resource is available because of the region's tectonic activity. Two active volcanic mountain ranges run the length of the Kamchatka Peninsula. Russia's first geothermal electric-power station was built on this peninsula.

Cities Industry and the Trans-Siberian Railroad aided the growth of cities in the Russian Far East. Two of those cities are Khabarovsk (kuh-BAHR-uhfsk) and Vladivostok (vla-duh-vuh-STAHK).

More than 600,000 people live in Khabarovsk, which was founded in 1858. It is located where the Trans-Siberian Railroad crosses the Amur River. This location makes Khabarovsk ideal for processing forest and mineral resources from the region.

Vladivostok is slightly larger than Khabarovsk. *Vladivostok* means "Lord of the East" in Russian. The city was established in 1860 on the coast of the Sea of Japan. Today it lies at the eastern end of the Trans-Siberian Railroad.

Vladivostok is a major naval base and the home port for a large fishing fleet. **Icebreakers** must keep the city's harbor open in winter. An icebreaker is a ship that can break up the ice of frozen waterways. This allows other ships to pass through them.

Historical monuments and old architecture compete for attention in Vladivostok.

Russia
Vladivostok
China
India
ГАСТРОНОМ

The Soviet Union considered Vladivostok very important for defense. The city was therefore closed to foreign contacts until the early 1990s. Today it is an important link with China, Japan, the United States, and the rest of the Pacific region.

✓ **READING CHECK:** *Environment and Society* How do the natural resources of the Russian Far East affect its economy?

Kuril Islands
Russia
China
India

▲ An old volcano created Crater Bay in the Kuril Islands. The great beauty of the islands is matched by the terrible power of earthquakes and volcanic eruptions in the area.

Interpreting the Visual Record What do you think happened to the volcano that formed Crater Bay?

Islands

The Russian Far East includes two island areas. Sakhalin is a large island that lies off the eastern coast of Siberia. To the south is the Japanese island of Hokkaido. The Kuril Islands are much smaller. They stretch in an arc from Hokkaido to the Kamchatka Peninsula.

Sakhalin has oil and mineral resources. The waters around the Kurils are important for commercial fishing.

Russia and Japan have argued over who owns these islands since the 1850s. At times they have been divided between Japan and Russia or the Soviet Union. The Soviet Union took control of the islands after World War II. Japan still claims rights to the southernmost islands.

Like other Pacific regions, Sakhalin and the Kurils sometimes experience earthquakes and volcanic eruptions. An earthquake in 1995 caused severe damage on Sakhalin Island, killing nearly 2,000 people.

✓ **READING CHECK:** *Environment and Society* How does the environment of the Kuril Islands and Sakhalin affect people?

Section 5 Review

go.hrw.com **Homework Practice Online** Keyword: SJ3 HP22

Define and explain: icebreakers

Working with Sketch Maps On the map you created in Section 4, label the Sea of Okhotsk, the Sea of Japan, the Amur River, Khabarovsk, Vladivostok, and Sakhalin Island. In the margin, explain which countries dispute possession of Sakhalin Island and the Kuril Islands.

Reading for the Main Idea

1. *Places and Regions* How does the climate of the Russian Far East compare to the climate throughout the rest of Siberia?
2. *Places and Regions* What are the region's major crops and energy resources?

Critical Thinking

3. **Drawing Inferences and Conclusions** In what ways do you think Vladivostok is "Lord of the East" in Russia today?
4. **Drawing Inferences and Conclusions** Why do you think Sakhalin and the Kuril Islands have been the subject of dispute between Russia and Japan?

Organizing What You Know

5. **Finding the Main Idea** Copy the following graphic organizer. Use it to explain how the location of each city has played a role in its development.

Khabarovsk	Vladivostok

CHAPTER 22 Reviewing What You Know

Building Vocabulary

On a separate sheet of paper, write sentences to define each of the following words.

1. taiga
2. steppe
3. czar
4. abdicated
5. allies
6. superpower
7. Cold War
8. consumer goods
9. light industry
10. heavy industry
11. smelters
12. habitation fog
13. icebreakers

Reviewing the Main Ideas

1. *Places and Regions* What are the major physical features of Russia? Where in Siberia are large coal deposits?
2. *Places and Regions* What landform separates Europe from Asia?
3. *Human Systems* How is Russia's government organized, and how does it compare with that of the United States?
4. *Places and Regions* What four major regions make up European Russia?
5. *Places and Regions* Where were Russian factories relocated during World War II and why?

Understanding Environment and Society

Resource Use

The grasslands of the steppe are one of Russia's most valuable agricultural resources. Create a presentation on farming in the steppe. You may want to consider the following:

- The crops that are grown in the Russian steppe.
- The kinds of livestock raised in the region.
- How the climate limits agriculture in the steppe.

Thinking Critically

1. **Finding the Main Idea** In what ways might Siberia be important to making Russia an economic success?
2. **Contrasting** What kind of economic system did the Soviet Union have, and how did it differ from that of the United States?
3. **Drawing Inferences and Conclusions** Why is transportation an issue for Russia? What have Russians done to ease transportation between European Russia and the Russian Far East?
4. **Analyzing Information** How does Vladivostok's location make it an important link between Russia and the Pacific world?
5. **Identifying Cause and Effect** What problems existed in the Russian Empire and the Soviet Union in the 1900s, and what was their effect?

Building Social Studies Skills

Map ACTIVITY

On a separate sheet of paper, match the letters on the map with their correct labels.

Arctic Ocean
Caucasus Mountains
Caspian Sea
West Siberian Plain
Central Siberian Plateau
Kamchatka Peninsula
Volga River
Moscow
St. Petersburg
Vladivostok

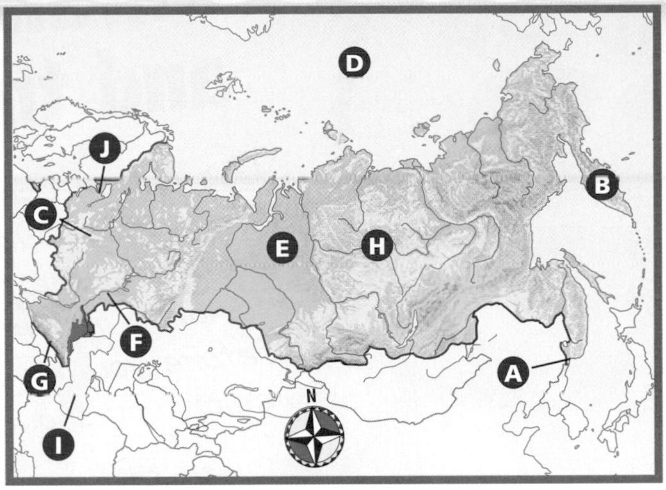
D
J
B
C
E
H
F
A
G
N
I

Mental Mapping Skills ACTIVITY

On a separate sheet of paper, draw a freehand map of Russia and label the following:

Baltic Sea
Kuril Islands
Lake Baikal
Sakhalin Island
Siberia
Ural Mountains

WRITING ACTIVITY

Imagine that you are a tour guide on a trip by train from St. Petersburg to Vladivostok. Use the chapter map or a classroom globe to write a one-page description of some of the places people would see along the train's route. How far would you travel? Be sure to use standard grammar, spelling, sentence structure, and punctuation.

Alternative Assessment

Portfolio ACTIVITY

Learning About Your Local Geography

Youth Organizations The Baikal-Amur Mainline (BAM) was built partly by youth organizations. Make a list of some projects of youth organizations in your community.

internet connect

Internet Activity: go.hrw.com
KEYWORD: SJ3 GT22

Choose a topic to explore about Russia:

- Take a trip on the Trans-Siberian Railroad.
- Examine the breakup of the Soviet Union.
- View the cultural treasures of Russia.

CHAPTER 23

Ukraine, Belarus, and the Caucasus

This region consists of plains in the north and mountains in the south. Both of these physical features made this area important to ancient invaders. Before you learn the history of this region, you should meet Ana.

Hi! I am a senior in high school in the city of T'bilisi, Georgia. I live with my parents and my younger sister. I go to school from 9:00 A.M. to 2:00 P.M. and study foreign languages—English and Spanish. I hope to be a journalist. In school the teachers decide which classes everyone must take.

After school I do my homework as fast as possible and then get together with my friends. I come home in the early evening and listen to music, read, or watch television.

We also have great food. My favorite dish is baked chicken with nuts. If you came to Georgia, I would take you to the mountains, to the seaside, and to some hot springs. We might also go to a festival where you could see Georgians in the country's national dress. Women wear a long red or purple robe with a white head scarf. Men wear a black suit or robe with gold embroidery.

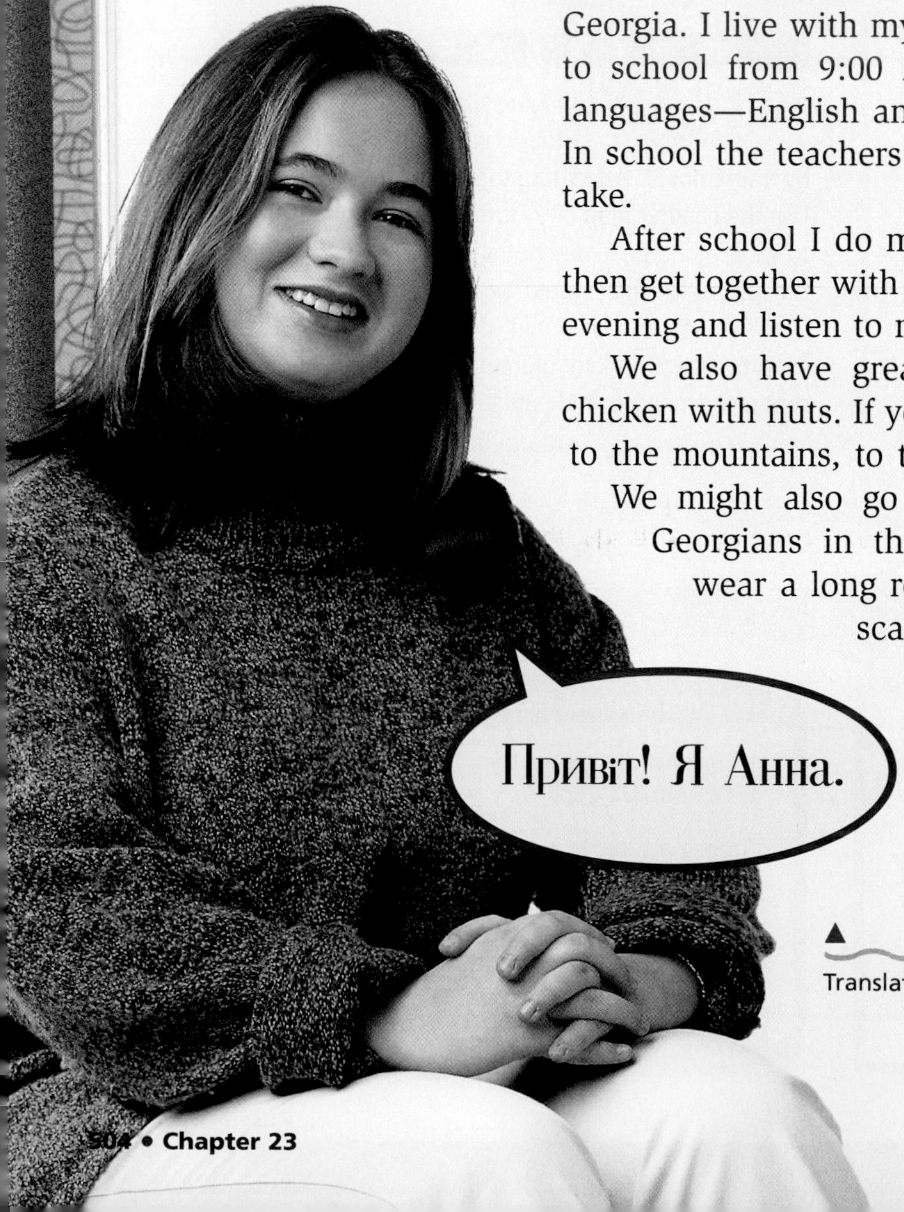
Привіт! Я Анна.

Translation: Hi! I am Ana.

Section 1 Physical Geography

Read to Discover

1. What are the region's major physical features?
2. What climate types and natural resources are found in the region?

Define

nature reserves

Locate

Black Sea
Caucasus Mountains
Caspian Sea
Pripyat Marshes
Carpathian Mountains
Crimean Peninsula
Sea of Azov
Mount Elbrus
Dnieper River
Donets Basin

Why It Matters

Ukraine is trying to create a nature reserve to protect its natural environment. Use CNNfyi.com or other **current events** sources to find information about how other countries are trying to protect their environments. Record your findings in your journal.

A gold pig from Kiev

Ukraine, Belarus, and the Caucasus: Physical-Political

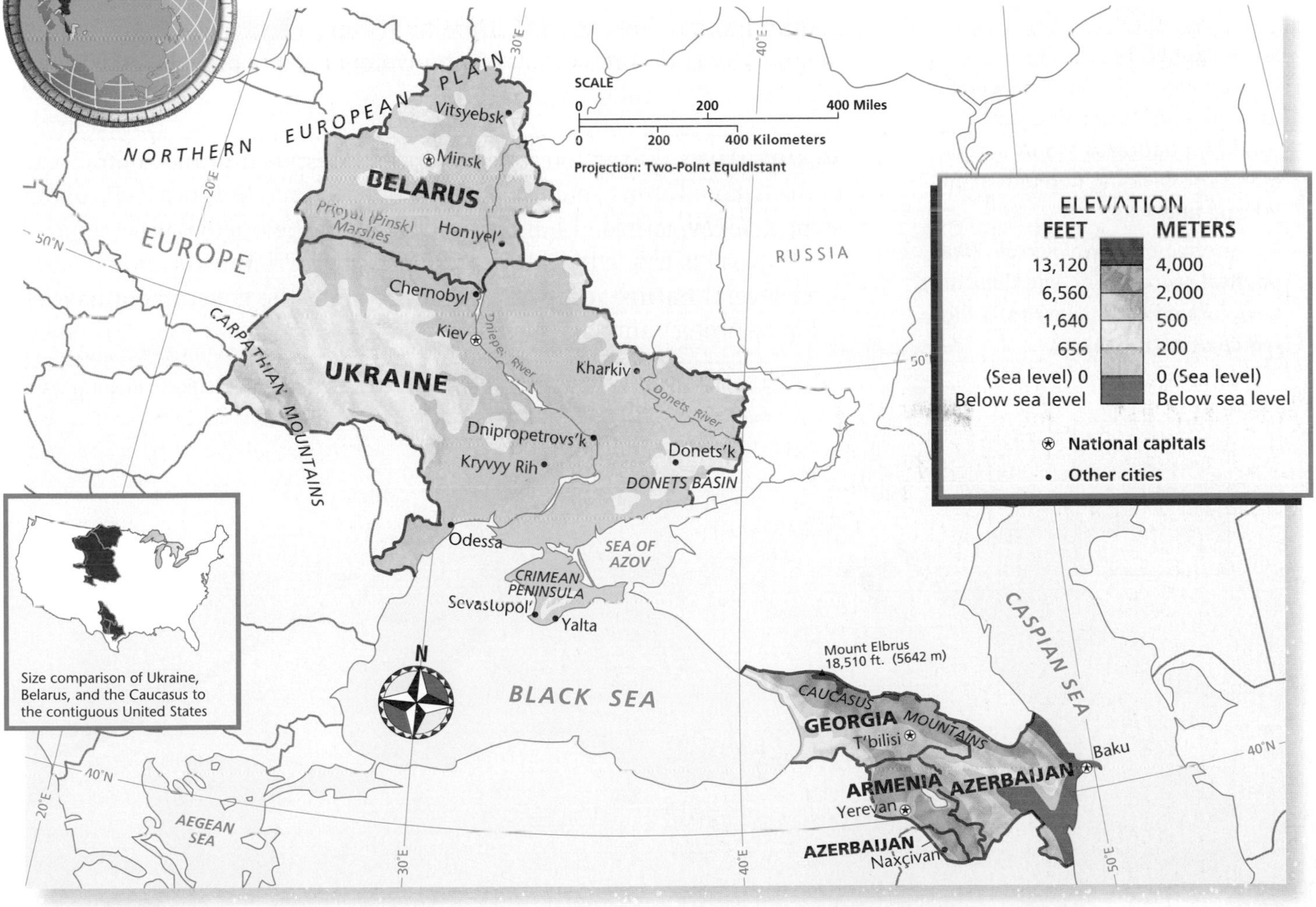

NORTHERN EUROPEAN PLAIN
EUROPE
Vitsyebsk
Minsk
BELARUS
Pripyat (Pinsk) Marshes
Homyel'
Chernobyl
Kiev
Dnieper River
UKRAINE
CARPATHIAN MOUNTAINS
Kharkiv
Donets River
Dnipropetrovs'k
Kryvyy Rih
Donets'k
DONETS BASIN
Odessa
SEA OF AZOV
CRIMEAN PENINSULA
Sevastopol'
Yalta
BLACK SEA
AEGEAN SEA
RUSSIA
CASPIAN SEA
Mount Elbrus 18,510 ft. (5642 m)
CAUCASUS MOUNTAINS
GEORGIA
T'bilisi
ARMENIA
Yerevan
AZERBAIJAN
Baku
AZERBAIJAN
Naxçivan
SCALE
0 200 400 Miles
0 200 400 Kilometers
Projection: Two-Point Equidistant
ELEVATION
FEET METERS
13,120 4,000
6,560 2,000
1,640 500
656 200
(Sea level) 0 0 (Sea level)
Below sea level Below sea level
National capitals
Other cities
N
50°N
40°N
20°E
30°E
40°E
50°E
Size comparison of Ukraine, Belarus, and the Caucasus to the contiguous United States

internet connect

GO TO: go.hrw.com
KEYWORD: SJ3 CH23
FOR: Web sites about Ukraine, Belarus, and the Caucasus

Physical Features

The countries of Ukraine (yoo-KRAYN) and Belarus (byay-luh-ROOS) border western Russia. Belarus is landlocked. Ukraine lies on the Black Sea. Georgia, Armenia (ahr-MEE-nee-uh), and Azerbaijan (a-zuhr-by-JAHN) lie in a rugged region called the Caucasus (KAW-kuh-suhs). It is named for the area's Caucasus Mountains. The Caucasus region is located between the Black Sea and the Caspian Sea.

Landforms Most of Ukraine and Belarus lie in a region of plains. The Northern European Plain sweeps across northern Belarus. The Pripyat (PRI-pyuht) Marshes, also called the Pinsk Marshes, are found in the south. The Carpathian Mountains run through part of western Ukraine. The Crimean (kry-MEE-uhn) Peninsula lies in southern Ukraine. The southern Crimean is very rugged and has high mountains. It separates the Black Sea from the Sea of Azov (uh-ZAWF).

In the north along the Caucasus's border with Russia is a wide mountain range. The region's and Europe's highest peak, Mount Elbrus (el-BROOS), is located here. As you can see on the chapter map, the land drops below sea level along the shore of the Caspian Sea. South of the Caucasus is a rugged, mountainous plateau. Earthquakes often occur in this region.

Rivers One of Europe's major rivers, the Dnieper (NEE-puhr), flows south through Belarus and Ukraine. Ships can travel much of its length. Dams and reservoirs on the Dnieper River provide hydroelectric power and water for irrigation.

Vegetation Mixed forests were once widespread in the central part of the region. Farther south, the forests opened onto the grasslands of the steppe. Today, farmland has replaced much of the original vegetation.

Ukraine is trying to preserve its natural environments and has created several **nature reserves**. These are areas the government has set aside to protect animals, plants, soil, and water.

✓ **READING CHECK:** *Places and Regions* What are the region's major physical features?

Snow-capped Mount Elbrus is located along the border between Georgia and Russia. The surrounding Caucasus Mountains lie along the dividing line between Europe and Asia.

Interpreting the Visual Record What physical processes do you think may have formed the mountains in this region of earthquakes?

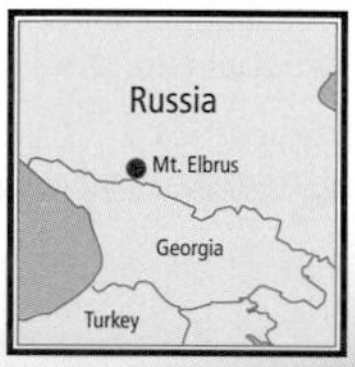
Russia
Mt. Elbrus
Georgia
Turkey

Climate

Like much of western Russia, the northern two thirds of Ukraine and Belarus have a humid continental climate. Winters are cold. Summers are warm but short. Southern Ukraine has a steppe climate. Unlike the rest of the country, the Crimean Peninsula has a Mediterranean climate. There are several different climates in the Caucasus. Georgia's coast has a mild climate similar to the Carolinas in the United States. Azerbaijan contains mainly a steppe climate. Because it is so mountainous, Armenia's climate changes with elevation.

✓ **READING CHECK:** *Places and Regions* What climate types are found in this area?

BUILD on WHAT You Know

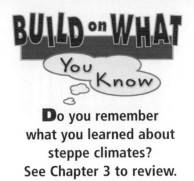

Do you remember what you learned about steppe climates? See Chapter 3 to review.

Resources

Rich farmlands are Ukraine's greatest natural resource. Farming is also important in Belarus. Lowland areas of the Caucasus have rich soil and good conditions for farming.

The Donets (duh-NYETS) Basin in southeastern Ukraine is a rich coal-mining area. Kryvyy Rih (kri-VI RIK) is the site of a huge open-pit iron-ore mine. The region's most important mineral resources are Azerbaijan's large and valuable oil and gas deposits. These are found under the shallow Caspian Sea. Copper, manganese, iron, and other metals are also present in the Caucasus.

✓ **READING CHECK:** *Environment and Society* How have this region's natural resources affected economic development?

Section 1 Review

go.hrw.com **Homework Practice Online** Keyword: SJ3 HP23

Define and explain: nature reserves

Working with Sketch Maps On a map of Europe that you draw or that your teacher provides, label the following: Black Sea, Caucasus Mountains, Caspian Sea, Pripyat Marshes, Carpathian Mountains, Crimean Peninsula, Sea of Azov, Mount Elbrus, Dnieper River, and Donets Basin. Where in the region is a major coal-mining area?

Reading for the Main Idea

1. *Places and Regions* What three seas are found in this region?
2. *Places and Regions* What creates variation in Armenia's climate?

Critical Thinking

3. **Drawing Inferences and Conclusions** Why has so much farming developed in Ukraine, Belarus, and the Caucasus?
4. **Drawing Inferences and Conclusions** How do you think heavy mining in this region could create pollution?

Organizing What You Know

5. **Categorizing** Copy the following graphic organizer. Use it to describe the region's physical features, climates, and resources.

	Physical features	Climate	Resources
Belarus			
Caucasus			
Ukraine			

Section 2 Ukraine and Belarus

Read to Discover

1. Which groups have influenced the history of Ukraine and Belarus?
2. What are some important economic features and environmental concerns of Ukraine?
3. How has the economy of Belarus developed?

Define

serfs
Cossacks
soviet

Locate

Ukraine
Belarus
Kiev
Chernobyl
Minsk

WHY IT MATTERS

Energy created by nuclear power plants is important to the United States, Ukraine, and Belarus. Go to CNNfyi.com or other **current events** sources to find information about nuclear energy. Record your findings in your journal.

A hand-painted Ukrainian egg

гео·
гра·
фия

▲ These are the syllables for the Russian word for geography, written in the Cyrillic alphabet.

History and Government

About 600 B.C. the Greeks established trading colonies along the coast of the Black Sea. Much later—during the A.D. 400s—the Slavs began to move into what is now Ukraine and Belarus. Today, most people in this region speak closely related Slavic languages.

Vikings and Christians In the 800s Vikings took the city of Kiev. Located on the Dnieper River, it became the capital of the Vikings' trading empire. Today, this old city is Ukraine's capital. In the 900s the Byzantine, or Greek Orthodox, Church sent missionaries to teach the Ukrainians and Belorussians about Christianity. These missionaries introduced the Cyrillic alphabet.

St. Sophia Cathedral in Kiev was built in the 1000s. It was one of the earliest Orthodox cathedrals in this area. Religious images decorate the dome's interior. ◄

Mongols and Cossacks A grandson of Genghis Khan led the Mongol horsemen that conquered Ukraine in the 1200s. They destroyed most of the towns and cities there, including Kiev.

Later, northern Ukraine and Belarus came under the control of Lithuanians and Poles. Under foreign rule, Ukrainian and Belorussian **serfs** suffered. Serfs were people who were bound to the land and worked for a lord. In return, the lords provided the serfs with military protection and other services. Some Russian and Ukrainian serfs left the farms and formed bands of nomadic horsemen. Known as **Cossacks**, they lived on the Ukrainian frontier.

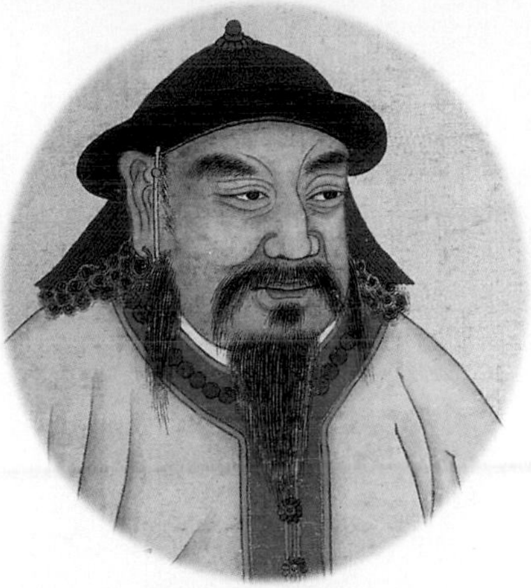

This watercolor on rice paper depicts Kublai Khan. He was the founder of the vast Mongol empire in the 1200s. The Mongols conquered large areas of Asia and Europe, including Ukraine.

The Russian Empire North and east of Belarus, a new state arose around Moscow. This Russian kingdom of Muscovy won independence from the Mongols in the late 1400s. The new state set out to expand its borders. By the 1800s all of modern Belarus and Ukraine were under Moscow's rule. Now the Cossacks served the armies of the Russian czar. However, conditions did not improve for the Ukrainian and Belorussian serfs and peasants.

Soviet Republics The Russian Revolution ended the rule of the czars in 1917. Ukraine and Belarus became republics of the Soviet Union in 1922. Although each had its own governing **soviet**, or council, Communist leaders in Moscow made all major decisions.

Ukraine was especially important as the Soviet Union's richest farming region. On the other hand, Belarus became a major industrial center. It produced heavy machinery for the Soviet Union. While Ukraine and Belarus were part of the Soviet Union, the Ukrainian and Belorussian languages were discouraged. Practicing a religion was also discouraged.

After World War II economic development continued in Ukraine and Belarus. Factories and power plants were built with little concern for the safety of nearby residents.

Belarus
Russia
Kiev
Ukraine
Romania

Kiev remained an important cultural and industrial center during the Soviet era. Parts of the city were destroyed during World War II and had to be rebuilt. Today tree-lined streets greet shoppers in the central city.

Belarus
Russia
Ukraine
Romania
Yalta

Near the end of World War II, Soviet, American, and British leaders met at Livadia Palace in Yalta, Ukraine. There they planned the defeat and occupation of Germany.

End of Soviet Rule When the Soviet Union collapsed in 1991, Belarus and Ukraine declared independence. Each now has a president and a prime minister. Both countries still have economic problems. Ukraine has also had disagreements with Russia over control of the Crimean Peninsula and the Black Sea naval fleet.

✓ **READING CHECK:** *Human Systems* Which groups have influenced the history of Ukraine and Belarus?

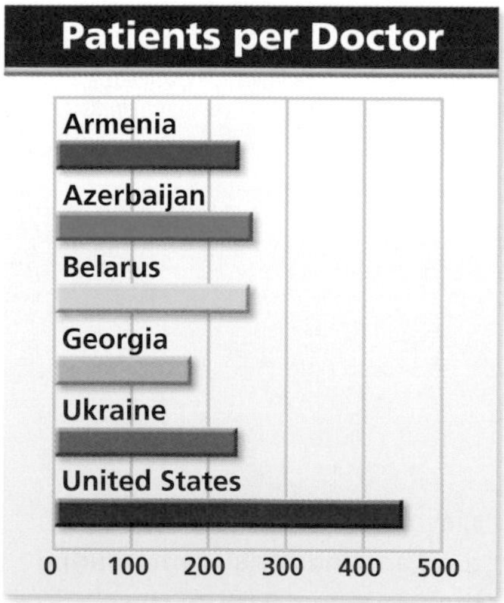
Patients per Doctor
Armenia
Azerbaijan
Belarus
Georgia
Ukraine
United States
0
100
200
300
400
500

Source: *The World Book Encyclopedia of People and Places*

Interpreting the Graph **In what country is the number of patients per doctor greatest?**

Ukraine

Ethnic Ukrainians make up about 75 percent of Ukraine's population. The largest minority group in the country is Russian. There are other ties between Ukraine and Russia. For example, the Ukrainian and Russian languages are closely related. In addition, both countries use the Cyrillic alphabet.

Economy Ukraine has a good climate for growing crops and some of the world's richest soil. As a result, agriculture is important to its economy. Ukraine is the world's largest producer of sugar beets. Ukraine's food-processing industry makes sugar from the sugar beets. Farmers also grow fruits, potatoes, vegetables, and wheat. Grain is made into flour for baked goods and pasta. Livestock is also raised. Ukraine is one of the world's top steel producers. Ukrainian factories make automobiles, railroad cars, ships, and trucks.

CONNECTING TO Science

A combine used during July harvest

Wheat: From Field to Consumer

Wheat is one of Ukraine's most important farm products. The illustration below shows how wheat is processed for use by consumers.

- The head of the wheat plant contains the wheat kernels, wrapped in husks. The kernel includes the bran or seed coat, the endosperm, and the germ from which new wheat plants grow.
- Whole wheat flour contains all the parts of the kernel. White flour is produced by grinding only the endosperm. Vitamins are added to some white flour to replace vitamins found in the bran and germ.
- People use wheat to make breads, pastas, and breakfast foods. Wheat by-products are used in many other foods.

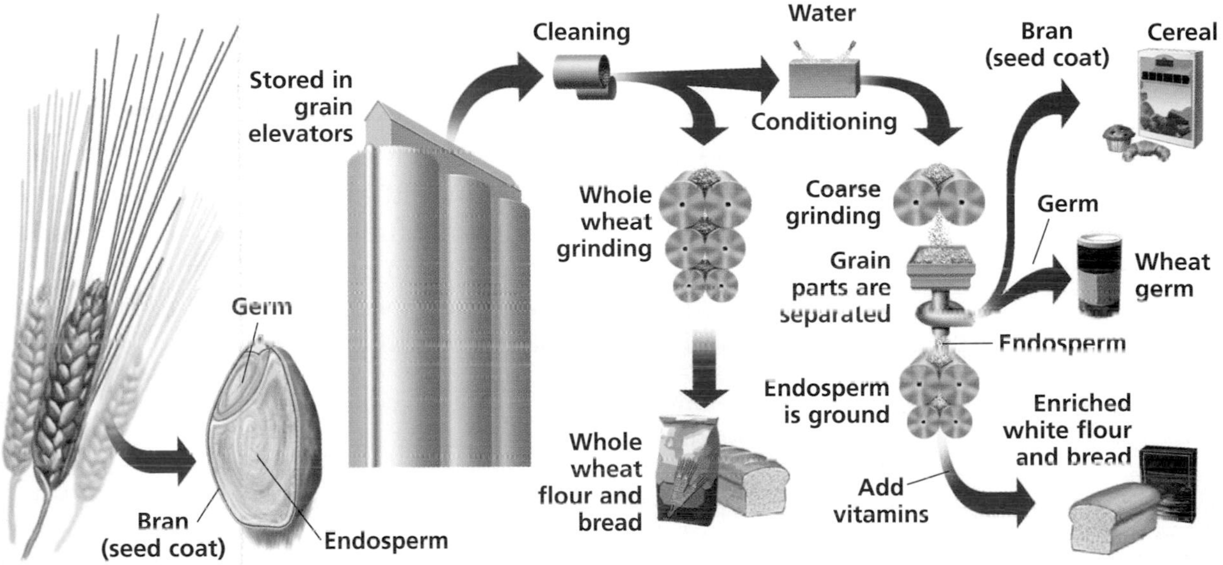
Germ
Bran
(seed coat)
Endosperm
Stored in
grain
elevators
Cleaning
Water
Conditioning
Whole
wheat
grinding
Whole
wheat
flour and
bread
Coarse
grinding
Grain
parts are
separated
Endosperm
Endosperm
is ground
Add
vitamins
Bran
(seed coat)
Cereal
Germ
Wheat
germ
Enriched
white flour
and bread

Environment During the Soviet period, Ukraine experienced rapid industrial growth. There were few pollution controls, however. In 1986 at the town of Chernobyl, the world's worst nuclear-reactor disaster occurred. Radiation spread across Ukraine and parts of northern Europe. People near the accident died. Others are still suffering from cancer. Many Ukrainians now want to reduce their country's dependence on nuclear power. This has been hard because the country has not developed enough alternative sources of power.

✓ **READING CHECK:** *Environment and Society* How has the scarcity of alternative sources of power affected Ukraine?

Belarus and Ukraine

Country	Population/ Growth Rate	Life Expectancy	Literacy Rate	Per Capita GDP
Belarus	10,350,194 / −0.2%	62, male; 75, female	98%	$7,500
Ukraine	48,760,474 / −0.9%	61, male; 72, female	98%	$3,850
United States	281,421,906 / 0.9%	73, male; 80, female	97%	$36,200

Sources: Central Intelligence Agency, *The World Factbook 2001;* U.S. Census Bureau

Interpreting the Chart How does life expectancy in the region compare to that of the United States? Why do you think this is the case?

Belarus

The people of Belarus are known as Belorussians, which means "white Russians." Ethnically they are closely related to Russians. Their language is also very similar to Russian.

Culture Ethnic Belorussians make up about 75 percent of the country's population. Russians are the second-largest ethnic group. Both Belorussian and Russian are official languages. Belorussian also uses the Cyrillic alphabet. Minsk, the capital of Belarus, is the administrative center of the Commonwealth of Independent States.

Economy Belarus has faced many difficulties. Fighting in World War II destroyed most of the agriculture and industry in the country. Belarus also received the worst of the radiation fallout from the Chernobyl nuclear disaster, which contaminated the country's farm products and water. Many people developed health problems as a result. Another problem has been slow economic progress since the collapse of the Soviet Union. Belarus has resisted economic changes made by other former Soviet republics.

There are various resources in Belarus, however. The country has a large reserve of potash, which is used for fertilizer. Belarus leads the world in the production of peat, a source of fuel found in the damp marshes. Mining and manufacturing are important to the economy. Flax, one of the country's main crops, is grown for fiber and seed. Cattle and pigs are also raised. Nearly one third of Belarus is covered by forests that produce wood and paper products.

✓ **READING CHECK:** *Human Systems* How has the economy of Belarus developed?

Section 2 Review

go.hrw.com Homework Practice Online
Keyword: SJ3 HP23

Define and explain: serfs, Cossacks, soviet

Working with Sketch Maps On your map from Section 1, label Ukraine, Belarus, Kiev, Chernobyl, and Minsk.

Reading for the Main Idea

1. *Human Systems* What contributions were made by early groups that settled in this region?
2. *Human Systems* What ethnic groups and languages are found in this region today?

Critical Thinking

3. **Finding the Main Idea** How did the end of Soviet rule affect Ukraine and Belarus?
4. **Summarizing** How has the nuclear disaster at Chernobyl affected the region?

Organizing What You Know

5. **Sequencing** Copy the time line below. Use it to trace the region's history from the A.D. 900s to today.

A.D. 900 ———————————— Today

Section 3 The Caucasus

Read to Discover

1. What groups influenced the early history and culture of the Caucasus?
2. What is the economy of Georgia like?
3. What is Armenia like today?
4. What is Azerbaijan like today?

Define

homogeneous
agrarian

Locate

Georgia
Armenia
Azerbaijan

WHY IT MATTERS

Each of the countries in this section has been involved in a war since the collapse of the Soviet Union in 1991. Use CNNfyi.com or other **current events** sources to find information about the reasons for this unrest. Record your findings in your journal.

Cover of The Knight in Panther's Skin

History

In the 500s B.C. the Caucasus region was controlled by the Persian Empire. Later it was brought under the influence of the Byzantine Empire and was introduced to Christianity. About A.D. 650, Muslim invaders cut the region off from Christian Europe. By the late 1400s other Muslims, the Ottoman Turks, ruled a vast empire to the south and west. Much of Armenia eventually came under the rule of that empire.

Modern Era During the 1800s Russia took over eastern Armenia, much of Azerbaijan, and Georgia. The Ottoman Turks continued to rule western Armenia. Many Armenians spread throughout the Ottoman Empire. However, they were not treated well. Their desire for more independence led to the massacre of thousands of Armenians. Hundreds of thousands died while being forced to leave Turkey during World War I. Some fled to Russian Armenia.

After the war Armenia, Azerbaijan, and Georgia were briefly independent. By 1922 they had become part of the Soviet Union. They again became independent when the Soviet Union collapsed in 1991.

This wall painting is one of many at the ancient Erebuni Citadel in Yerevan, Armenia's capital. The fortress was probably built in the 800s B.C. by one of Armenia's earliest peoples, the Urartians.

This Georgian family's breakfast includes local specialties such as *khachapuri*—bread made with goat cheese.

Interpreting the Visual Record
What other agricultural products do you see on the table?

Government Each country has an elected parliament, president, and prime minister. In the early 1990s there was civil war in Georgia. Armenia and Azerbaijan were also involved in a war during this time. Ethnic minorities in each country want independence. Disagreements about oil and gas rights may cause more regional conflicts in the future.

✓ **READING CHECK:** *Human Systems* How has conflict among cultures been a problem in this region?

Georgia

Georgia is a small country located between the high Caucasus Mountains and the Black Sea. It has a population of about 5 million. About 70 percent of the people are ethnic Georgians. The official language, Georgian, has its own alphabet. This alphabet was used as early as A.D. 400.

As in all the former Soviet republics, independence and economic reforms have been difficult. Georgia has also suffered from civil war. By the late 1990s the conflicts were fewer but not resolved.

Georgia has little good farmland. Tea and citrus fruits are the major crops. Vineyards are an important part of Georgian agriculture. Fish, livestock, and poultry contribute to the economy. Tourism on the Black Sea has also helped the economy. Because its only energy resource is hydropower, Georgia imports most of its energy supplies.

✓ **READING CHECK:** *Human Systems* In what way has scarcity of energy resources affected Georgia's economy?

Armenia

Armenia is a little smaller than Maryland. It lies just east of Turkey. It has fewer than 4 million people and is not as diverse as other countries

Georgia
Armenia
Agartsya Monastery
Azerbaijan
Turkey
Iran

The Orthodox Christian Agartsya Monastery was built in Armenia in the 1200s.

Interpreting the Visual Record
Why do you think this building's exterior is so well preserved?

in the Caucasus. Almost all the people are Armenian, belong to the Armenian Orthodox Church, and speak Armenian.

Armenia's progress toward economic reform has not been easy. In 1988 a massive earthquake destroyed nearly one third of its industry. Armenia's industry today is varied. It includes mining and the production of carpets, clothing, and footwear.

Agriculture accounts for about 40 percent of Armenia's gross domestic product. High-quality grapes and fruits are important. Beef and dairy cattle and sheep are raised on mountain pastures.

✓ **READING CHECK:** *Environment and Society* How did the 1998 earthquake affect the people of Armenia?

The Caucasus

Country	Population/ Growth Rate	Life Expectancy	Literacy Rate	Per Capita GDP
Armenia	3,336,100 −0.2%	62, male 71, female	99%	$3,000
Azerbaijan	7,771,092 0.3%	59, male 68, female	97%	$3,000
Georgia	4,989,285 −0.6%	61, male 68, female	99%	$4,600
United States	281,421,906 0.9%	74, male 80, female	97%	$36,200

Sources: Central Intelligence Agency, *The World Factbook 2001;* U.S. Census Bureau

Interpreting the Chart **Which countries have the lowest per capita GDP in the region? Why might this be the case?**

Azerbaijan

Azerbaijan has nearly 8 million people. Its population is becoming ethnically more **homogeneous**, or the same. The Azeri, who speak a Turkic language, make up about 90 percent of the population.

Azerbaijan has few industries except for oil production. It is mostly an **agrarian** society. An agrarian society is organized around farming. The country's main resources are cotton, natural gas, and oil. Baku, the national capital, is the center of a large oil-refining industry. Oil is the most important part of Azerbaijan's economy. Fishing is also important because of the sturgeon of the Caspian Sea.

✓ **READING CHECK:** *Human Systems* What are some cultural traits of the people of Azerbaijan?

go.hrw.com Homework Practice Online
Keyword: SJ3 HP23

Section 3 Review

Define and explain: homogeneous, agrarian

Working with Sketch Maps On the map you created for Section 2, label Georgia, Armenia, and Azerbaijan. How has the location of this region helped and hindered its growth?

Reading for the Main Idea

1. *Human Systems* Which groups influenced the early history of the Caucasus?
2. *Human Systems* Which country controlled the Caucasus during most of the 1900s?

Critical Thinking

3. **Analyzing Information** Why has economic reform been difficult in Armenia?
4. **Finding the Main Idea** How is Azerbaijan's economy organized?

Organizing What You Know

5. **Comparing/Contrasting** Copy the following graphic organizer. Use it to show the similarities and differences among the countries of the Caucasus region.

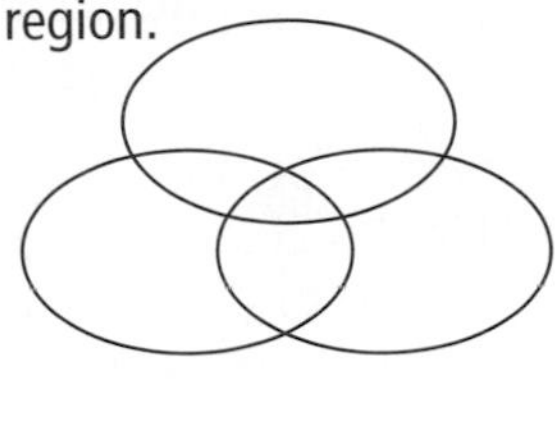

CHAPTER 23

Reviewing What You Know

Building Vocabulary

On a separate sheet of paper, write sentences to define each of the following words.

1. nature reserves
2. serfs
3. Cossacks
4. soviet
5. homogeneous
6. agrarian

Reviewing the Main Ideas

1. *Human Systems* Which industries have traditionally been very important to the economies of the countries covered in this chapter?
2. *Human Systems* What is the relative location of Kiev? Which group of people founded Kiev?
3. *Human Systems* What peoples were apparently the first to settle in Belarus and Ukraine?
4. *Environment and Society* How did industrialization under Soviet rule affect these regions?
5. *Environment and Society* What effect did the earthquake in 1988 have on Armenia's economy?

Understanding Environment and Society

Resource Use

Prepare a chart and presentation on oil and natural gas production in the Caucasus. In preparing your presentation, consider the following:

- When and where oil and natural gas were discovered.
- The importance of oil and natural gas production to the former Soviet Union.
- How oil is transported from there to international markets today.

When you have finished your chart and presentation, write a five-question quiz, with answers, about your chart to challenge fellow students.

Thinking Critically

1. **Drawing Inferences and Conclusions** How might ethnic diversity affect relations among countries?
2. **Analyzing Information** How did the location of Ukraine and Belarus contribute to their devastation during World War II?
3. **Analyzing Information** Of the countries covered in this chapter, which do you think was the most important to the former Soviet Union? Why do you think this was so?
4. **Summarizing** Why did the countries of the Caucasus develop so differently from Russia, Ukraine, and Belarus?
5. **Finding the Main Idea** Why are the economies of each of the Caucasus countries so different from one another?

Building Social Studies Skills

Map Activity

On a separate sheet of paper, match the letters on the map with their correct labels.

Caucasus Mountains
Pripyat Marshes
Carpathian Mountains
Crimean Peninsula
Mount Elbrus
Donets Basin
Chernobyl

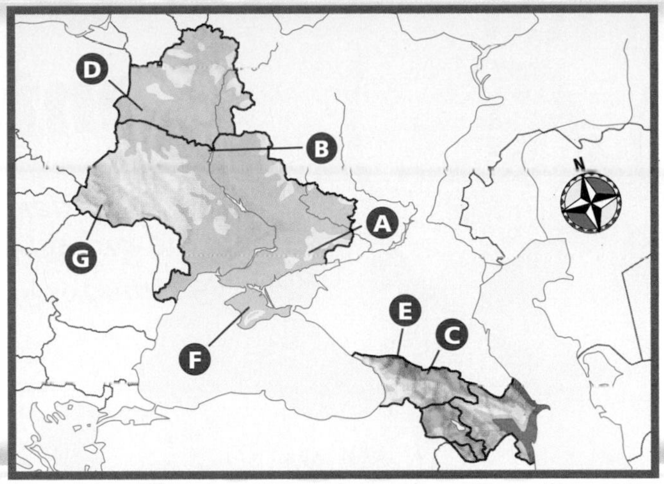
D
B
A
G
E
C
F
N

Mental Mapping Skills Activity

On a separate sheet of paper, draw a freehand map of Ukraine, Belarus, and the Caucasus. Include Russia and Turkey for location reference. Make a map key and label the following:

Armenia
Azerbaijan
Belarus
Black Sea
Caspian Sea
Dnieper River
Georgia
Russia
Turkey
Ukraine

Writing Activity

Choose one of the countries covered in this chapter to research. Write a report about your chosen country's struggle to establish stability since 1991. Include information about the country's government and economic reforms. Describe the social, political, and economic problems the country has faced. Be sure to use standard grammar, sentence structure, spelling, and punctuation.

Alternative Assessment

Portfolio Activity

Learning About Your Local Geography

Cooperative Project What is an important crop in your region of the United States? Work with a partner to create an illustrated flowchart that shows how this crop is made ready for consumers.

internet connect

Internet Activity: go.hrw.com
KEYWORD: SJ3 GT23

Choose a topic to explore about Ukraine, Belarus, and the Caucasus.

- Trek through the Caucasus Mountains.
- Design Ukrainian Easter eggs.
- Investigate the Chernobyl disaster.

CHAPTER 24

Central Asia

Leila is a student from Central Asia, a region of grasslands, scorching deserts, and high mountains.

S*alam!* (Hi!)—we also say "privyet," which is "hi" in Russian. My name is Leila, and I am 16. I live in Turkmenabat, the "city of Turkmen," with my parents, my three older brothers, and my younger sister. My oldest brother's wife also lives with us. My father is a professor of British studies at Turkmenabat University and my mother teaches cooking and sewing at the high school. Our house is on a canal with lots of trees. It is surrounded by a high wall, and has a balcony and an open roof where we can go if we want to be outdoors in privacy.

I am in the ninth and last year at School Number Five. The school has about 2,000 students in nine grades from kindergarten to high school. We go to school six days a week and study 18 different subjects. There is no choice of courses. I could have gone to a Russian school, but my parents chose a Turkmen one. At school, we line up by class and do 5 minutes of exercises before classes start. Each class has 25 boys and girls who stay together from kindergarten through high school. We are like a second family.

Salam!
Men Türkmenistanda ýaşaýaryn.

Translation: Hello, I live in Turkmenistan.

Section 1 Physical Geography

Read to Discover

1. What are the main landforms and climates of Central Asia?

2. What resources are important to Central Asia?

Define

landlocked

oasis

Locate

Pamirs

Tian Shan

Aral Sea

Kara-Kum

Kyzyl Kum

Syr Dar'ya

Amu Dar'ya

Fergana Valley

WHY IT MATTERS

The countries of Uzbekistan, Kazakhstan, and Turkmenistan have large oil and natural gas reserves. Use CNNfyi.com or other **current events** sources to find examples of efforts to develop these resources. Record your findings in your journal.

A Bactrian camel and rider

Central Asia: Physical-Political

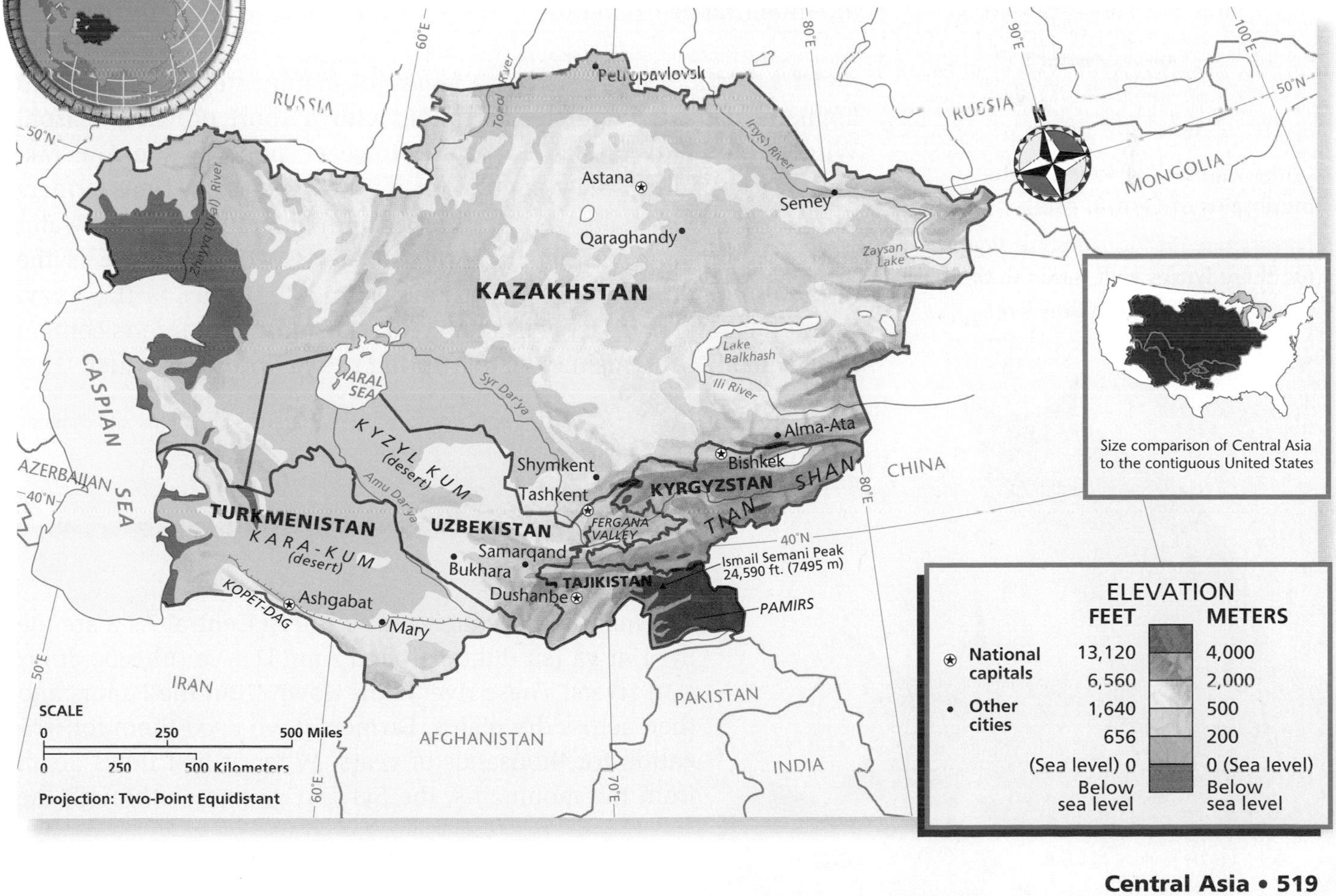

RUSSIA
MONGOLIA
CHINA
KAZAKHSTAN
UZBEKISTAN
TURKMENISTAN
KYRGYZSTAN
TAJIKISTAN
AZERBAIJAN
IRAN
AFGHANISTAN
PAKISTAN
INDIA
CASPIAN SEA
ARAL SEA
Petropavlovsk
Astana
Qaraghandy
Semey
Zaysan Lake
Lake Balkhash
Ili River
Irtysh River
Tobol River
Zhayyq (Ural) River
Syr Dar'ya
Amu Dar'ya
KYZYL KUM (desert)
KARA-KUM (desert)
KOPET-DAG
TIAN SHAN
PAMIRS
FERGANA VALLEY
Alma-Ata
Bishkek
Shymkent
Tashkent
Samarqand
Bukhara
Dushanbe
Ashgabat
Mary
Ismail Semani Peak 24,590 ft. (7495 m)
50°N
40°N
50°E
60°E
70°E
80°E
90°E
100°E
N
Size comparison of Central Asia to the contiguous United States
SCALE
0 250 500 Miles
0 250 500 Kilometers
Projection: Two-Point Equidistant
ELEVATION
FEET METERS
13,120 4,000
6,560 2,000
1,640 500
656 200
(Sea level) 0 0 (Sea level)
Below sea level Below sea level
National capitals
Other cities

Mountain climbers make camp before attempting to scale a peak in the Pamirs.

Our Amazing Planet

With temperatures above 122°F (50°C), it is not surprising that the creatures that live in the Kara-Kum are a tough group. Over a thousand species live there, including cobras, scorpions, tarantulas, and monitor lizards. These lizards can grow to more than 5 feet (1.5m) long.

Landforms and Climate

This huge, **landlocked** region is to the east of the Caspian Sea. Landlocked means the region does not border an ocean. The region lies north of the Pamirs (puh-MIRZ) and Tian Shan (TYEN SHAHN) mountain ranges.

Diverse Landforms As the name suggests, Central Asia lies in the middle of the largest continent. Plains and low plateaus cover much of this area. Around the Caspian Sea the land is as low as 95 feet (29 m) below sea level. However, the region includes high mountain ranges along the borders with China and Afghanistan.

Arid Lands Central Asia is a region of mainly steppe, desert, and highland climates. Summers are hot, with a short growing season. Winters are cold. Rainfall is sparse. However, north of the Aral (AR-uhl) Sea rainfall is heavy enough for steppe vegetation. Here farmers can grow crops using rain, rather than irrigation, as their water source. South and east of the Aral Sea lie two deserts. One is the Kara-Kum (kahr-uh-KOOM) in Turkmenistan. The other is the Kyzyl Kum (ki-ZIL KOOM) in Uzbekistan and Kazakhstan. Both deserts contain several **oasis** settlements where a spring or well provides water.

✓ **READING CHECK:** ***Places and Regions*** What are the landforms and climates of Central Asia?

Resources

The main water sources in southern Central Asia are the Syr Dar'ya (sir duhr-YAH) and Amu Dar'ya (uh-MOO duhr-YAH) rivers. These rivers flow down from the Pamirs and then across dry plains. Farmers have used them for irrigation for thousands of years. When it first flows down from the mountains, the Syr Dar'ya passes through the

Lynxes can still be found in the mountains of Central Asia.

Interpreting the Visual Record **How are these lynxes well suited to the environment in which they live?**

Fergana Valley. This large valley is divided among Uzbekistan, Kyrgyzstan, and Tajikistan. As the river flows toward the Aral Sea, irrigated fields line its banks.

During the Soviet period, the region's population grew rapidly. Also, the Soviets encouraged farmers to grow cotton. This crop grows well in Central Asia's sunny climate. However, growing cotton uses a lot of water. Increased use of water has caused the Aral Sea to shrink.

> **internet connect**
> GO TO: go.hrw.com
> KEYWORD: SJ3 CH24
> FOR: Web sites about Central Asia

A Dying Sea Today, almost no water from the Syr Dar'ya or Amu Dar'ya reaches the Aral Sea. The rivers' waters are used up by human activity. The effect on the Aral Sea has been devastating. It has lost more than 60 percent of its water since 1960. Its level has dropped 50 feet (15 m) and is still dropping. Towns that were once fishing ports are now dozens of miles from the shore. Winds sweep the dry seafloor, blowing dust, salt, and pesticides hundreds of miles.

This boat sits rusting on what was once part of the Aral Sea. The sea's once thriving fishing industry has been destroyed.

Russia
Aral Sea
Kazakhstan
Uzbekistan
Turkmenistan
Iran

Mineral Resources The Central Asian countries' best economic opportunity is in their fossil fuels. Uzbekistan, Kazakhstan, and Turkmenistan all have huge oil and natural gas reserves. However, transporting the oil and gas to other countries is a problem. Economic and political turmoil in some surrounding countries has made it difficult to build pipelines.

Several Central Asian countries are also rich in other minerals. They have deposits of gold, copper, uranium, zinc, and lead. Kazakhstan has vast amounts of coal. Rivers in Kyrgyzstan and Tajikistan could be used to create hydroelectric power.

✓ **READING CHECK:** *Environment and Society* How has human activity affected the Aral Sea?

Section 1 Review

> go.hrw.com **Homework Practice Online**
> Keyword: SJ3 HP24

Define and explain: landlocked, oasis

Working with Sketch Maps On a map of Central Asia that you draw or that your teacher provides, label the following: Pamirs, Tian Shan, Aral Sea, Kara-Kum, Kyzyl Kum, Syr Dar'ya, Amu Dar'ya, and Fergana Valley.

Reading for the Main Idea

1. *Environment and Society* What has caused the drying up of the Aral Sea?
2. *Places and Regions* What mineral resources does Central Asia have?

Critical Thinking

3. **Analyzing Information** Why did the Soviets encourage Central Asian farmers to grow cotton?
4. **Finding the Main Idea** What factors make it hard for the Central Asian countries to export oil and gas?

Organizing What You Know

5. **Sequencing** Copy the following graphic organizer. Use it to describe the courses of the Syr Dar'ya and Amu Dar'ya, including human activities that use water.

Melting snows in the Pamirs ⇨ [ ] ⇨ Aral Sea

Section 2

History and Culture

Read to Discover

1. How did trade and invasions affect the history of Central Asia?
2. What are political and economic conditions like in Central Asia today?

Define

nomads
caravans

WHY IT MATTERS

Even though the Soviet Union has collapsed, traces of its influence remain in Central Asia, particularly in government. Use CNNfyi.com or other **current events** sources to find examples of political events in these countries. Record your findings in your journal.

An ancient Kyrgyz stone figure

History

For centuries, Central Asians have made a living by raising horses, cattle, sheep, and goats. Many of these herders lived as **nomads**, people who often move from place to place. Other people became farmers around rivers and oases.

Trade At one time, the best land route between China and the eastern Mediterranean ran through Central Asia. Merchants traveled in large groups, called **caravans**, for protection. The goods they carried included silk and spices. As a result, this route came to be called the Silk Road. Cities along the road became centers of wealth and culture.

Central Asia's situation changed after Europeans discovered they could sail to East Asia through the Indian Ocean. As a result, trade through Central Asia declined. The region became isolated and poor.

Bukhara, in Uzbekistan, was once a powerful and wealthy trading center of Central Asia.

Interpreting the Visual Record

What architectural features can you see that distinguish Bukhara as an Islamic city?

Kazakhstan
Uzbekistan
Bukhara
Turkmenistan
Iran
Afghanistan

CONNECTING TO History

Silk processing in modern Uzbekistan

The Silk Road

The Silk Road stretched 5,000 miles (8,000 km) across Central Asia from China to the Mediterranean Sea. Along this route passed merchants, armies, and diplomats. These people forged links between East and West.

The facts of the Silk Road are still wrapped in mystery. Chinese trade and military expeditions probably began moving into Central Asia in the 100s B.C. Chinese trade goods soon were making their way to eastern Mediterranean ports.

Over the next several centuries, trade in silk, spices, jewels, and other luxury goods increased. Great caravans of camels and oxcarts traveled the Silk Road in both directions. They crossed the harsh deserts and mountains of Central Asia. Cities like Samarqand and Bukhara grew rich from the trade. In the process, ideas and technology also moved between Europe and Asia.

Travel along the Silk Road was hazardous. Bandits often robbed the caravans. Some travelers lost their way in the desert and died. In addition, religious and political turmoil occasionally disrupted travel.

Understanding What You Read

1. What was the Silk Road?
2. Why was the Silk Road important?

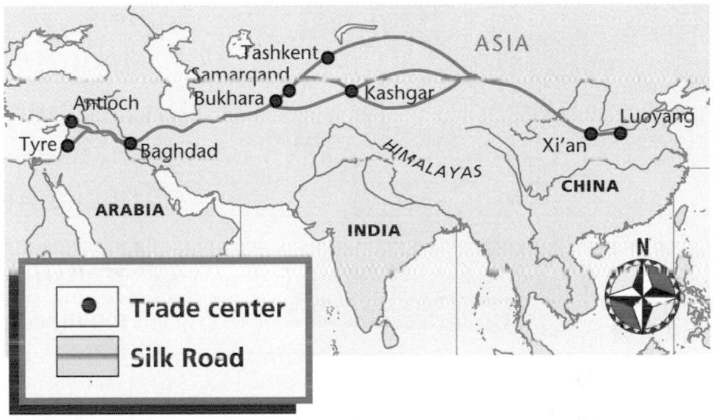
ASIA
Tashkent
Samarqand
Bukhara
Kashgar
Antioch
Tyre
Baghdad
HIMALAYAS
Xi'an
Luoyang
CHINA
ARABIA
INDIA
N
Trade center
Silk Road

Invasions and the Soviet Era About A.D. 500, Turkic-speaking nomads from northern Asia spread through Central Asia. In the 700s Arab armies took over much of the region, bringing Islam. In the 1200s the armies of Mongol leaders conquered Central Asia. Later, another Turkic people, the Uzbeks, took over parts of the region. In the 1800s the Russian Empire conquered Central Asia.

After the Russian Revolution, the Soviet government set up five republics in Central Asia. The Soviets encouraged ethnic Russians to move to this area and made the nomads settle on collective ranches or farms. Religion was discouraged. Russian became the language of government and business. The government set up schools and hospitals. Women were allowed to work outside the home.

✓ **READING CHECK:** *Human Systems* What type of government system did the five republics set up by the Soviet Union have?

BUILD on WHAT You Know

Do you remember what you learned about acculturation? See Chapter 5 to review.

A Kyrgyz teacher conducts class.

Interpreting the Visual Record

How is this class similar to yours?

Central Asia Today

The five republics became independent countries when the Soviet Union broke up in 1991. All have strong economic ties to Russia. Ethnic Russians still live in every country in the region. However, all five countries are switching from the Cyrillic alphabet to the Latin alphabet. The Cyrillic alphabet had been imposed on them by the Soviet Union. The Latin alphabet is used in most Western European languages, including English, and in Turkey.

Government All of these new countries have declared themselves to be democracies. However, they are not very free or democratic. Each is ruled by a strong central government that limits opposition and criticism.

Economy Some of the Central Asian countries have oil and gas reserves that may someday make them rich. For now, though, all are suffering economic hardship. Causes of the hardships include outdated equipment, lack of funds, and poor transportation links.

Farming is important in the Central Asian economies. Crops include cotton, wheat, barley, fruits, vegetables, almonds, tobacco, and rice. Central Asians raise cattle, sheep, horses, goats, and camels. They also raise silkworms to make silk thread.

Industry in Central Asia includes food processing, wool textiles, mining, and oil drilling. Oil-rich Turkmenistan and Kazakhstan also process oil into other products. Kazakhstan and Uzbekistan make heavy equipment such as tractors.

✓ **READING CHECK:** *Human Systems* How do political freedoms in the region compare to those of the United States?

go.hrw.com Homework Practice Online Keyword: SJ3 HP24

Section 2 Review

Define and explain: nomads, caravans

Working with Sketch Maps On the map you created in Section 1, draw and label the five Central Asian countries.

Reading for the Main Idea

1. *Environment and Society* How have the people of Central Asia made a living over the centuries?
2. *Human Systems* What are four groups that invaded Central Asia?
3. *Human Systems* How did Soviet rule change Central Asia?

Critical Thinking

4. **Drawing Inferences and Conclusions** What does the switch to the Latin alphabet suggest about the Central Asian countries?

Organizing What You Know

5. **Categorizing** Copy the following graphic organizer. Use it to categorize economic activities in Central Asia. Place the following items in the chart: making cloth, growing crops, mining metals, making food products, raising livestock, making chemicals from oil, drilling for oil, and manufacturing tractors.

Primary industries	Secondary industries

Section 3 The Countries of Central Asia

Read to Discover

1. What are some important aspects of culture in Kazakhstan?
2. How does Kyrgyz culture reflect nomadic traditions?
3. Why have politics in Tajikistan in recent years been marked by violence?
4. What are two important art forms in Turkmenistan?
5. How is Uzbekistan's population significant?

Define

yurt
mosques

Locate

Tashkent
Samarqand

A warrior's armor from Kazakhstan

WHY IT MATTERS

Since the collapse of the Soviet Union, religious freedom is more common in Central Asia. Use CNNfyi.com or other **current events** sources to find examples of religious and ethnic differences in the countries of Central Asia. Record your findings in your journal.

Kazakhstan

Of the Central Asian nations, Kazakhstan was the first to be conquered by Russia. Russian influence remains strong there. About one third of Kazakhstan's people are ethnic Russians. Kazakh and Russian are both official languages. Many ethnic Kazakhs grow up speaking Russian at home and have to learn Kazakh in school.

Kazakhstanis celebrate the New Year twice—on January 1 and again on Nauruz, the start of the Persian calendar's year. Nauruz falls on the spring equinox.

Food in Central Asia combines influences from Southwest Asia and China. Rice, yogurt, and grilled meat are common ingredients. One Kazakh specialty is smoked horsemeat sausage with cold noodles.

✓ **READING CHECK:** *Human Systems* How has Kazakhstan been influenced by Russia?

A woman in Uzbekistan grills meat on skewers.

Kyrgyzstan

Kyrgyzstan has many mountains, and the people live mostly in valleys. People in the southern part of the country generally share cultural ties with Uzbekistan. People in northern areas are more linked to nomadic cultures and to Kazakhstan.

Ethnic Makeup of Kazakhstan and Uzbekistan

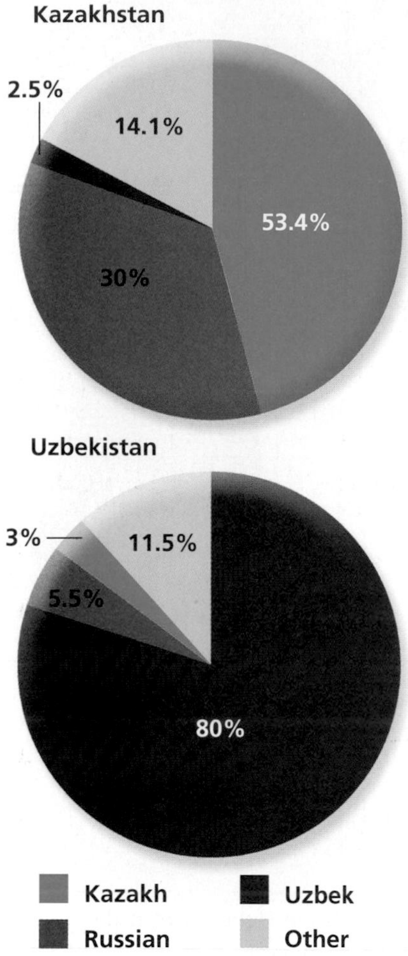
Kazakhstan
2.5%
14.1%
53.4%
30%
Uzbekistan
3%
11.5%
5.5%
80%
Kazakh
Uzbek
Russian
Other

Source: Central Intelligence Agency, *The World Factbook 2001*

Interpreting the Chart How does the number of Russians in Kazakhstan compare to that in Uzbekistan?

The word *kyrgyz* means "forty clans." Clan membership is still important in Krygyz social, political, and economic life. Many Kyrgyz men wear black and white felt hats that show their clan status.

Nomadic traditions are still important to many Kyrgyz. The **yurt** is a movable round house of wool felt mats over a wood frame. Today the yurt is a symbol of the nomadic heritage. Even people who live in cities may put up yurts for weddings and funerals.

✓ **READING CHECK:** *Human Systems* In what ways do the Kyrgyz continue traditions of their past?

Tajikistan

In the mid-1990s Tajikistan experienced a civil war. The Soviet-style government fought against a mixed group of reformers, some of whom demanded democracy. Others called for government by Islamic law. A peace agreement was signed in 1996, but tensions remain high.

The other major Central Asian languages are related to Turkish. However, the Tajik language is related to Persian. Tajiks consider the great literature written in Persian to be part of their cultural heritage.

✓ **READING CHECK:** *Human Systems* What has happened in politics in recent years in Tajikistan?

Turkmenistan

The major first language of Turkmenistan is Turkmen. In 1993 Turkmenistan adopted English, rather than Russian, as its second official language. However, some schools teach in Russian, Uzbek, or Kazakh.

Islam has experienced a revival in Central Asia since the breakup of the Soviet Union. Many new **mosques**, or Islamic houses of worship, are being built and old ones are being restored. Donations from other Islamic countries, such as Saudi Arabia and Iran, have helped

Kazakhstan
Ashgabat
Uzbekistan
Turkmenistan
Iran
Afghanistan

Turkoman women display carpets. Central Asian carpets are famous for their imaginative patterns, bright colors, and expert artistry.

Interpreting the Visual Record Why were carpets suited to the nomadic way of life?

these efforts. The government of Turkmenistan supports this revival and has ordered schools to teach Islamic principles. However, like the other states in the region, Turkmenistan's government views Islam with some caution. It does not want Islam to become a political movement.

Historically, the nomadic life required that all possessions be portable. Decorative carpets were the essential furniture of a nomad's home. They are still perhaps the most famous artistic craft of Turkmenistan. Like others in Central Asia, the people of Turkmenistan also have an ancient tradition of poetry.

✓ **READING CHECK:** *Human Systems* What are two forms of art in Turkmenistan, and how do they reflect its cultural traditions?

Central Asia

Country	Population/ Growth Rate	Life Expectancy	Literacy Rate	Per Capita GDP
Kazakhstan	16,731,303 .03%	58, male 69, female	98%	$5,000
Kyrgyzstan	4,753,003 1.4%	59, male 68, female	97%	$2,700
Tajikistan	6,578,681 2.1%	61, male 67, female	98%	$1,140
Turkmenistan	4,603,244 1.9%	57, male 65, female	98%	$4,300
Uzbekistan	25,155,064 1.6%	60, male 68, female	99%	$2,400
United States	281,421,906 0.9%	74, male 80, female	97%	$36,200

Sources: Central Intelligence Agency, *The World Factbook 2001;* U.S. Census Bureau

Interpreting the Chart **Which country has the lowest per capita GDP in the region?**

Uzbekistan

Uzbekistan has the largest population of the Central Asian countries—about 24 million people. Uzbek is the official language. People are required to study Uzbek to be eligible for citizenship.

Tashkent and Samarqand are ancient Silk Road cities in Uzbekistan. They are famous for their mosques and Islamic monuments. Uzbeks are also known for their art of embroidering fabric with gold.

✓ **READING CHECK:** *Human Systems* What is one of an Uzbekistan citizen's responsibilities?

Section 3 Review

go.hrw.com **Homework Practice Online** Keyword: SJ3 HP24

Define and explain: yurt, mosques

Working with Sketch Maps On the map you created in Section 2, label Tashkent and Samarqand.

Reading for the Main Idea

1. *Places and Regions* In which Central Asian nation is the influence of Russia strongest? Why is this true?
2. *Human Systems* What were the two sides in Tajikistan's civil war fighting for?
3. *Human Systems* What is the role of Islam in the region today?

Critical Thinking

4. **Finding the Main Idea** What are two customs or artistic crafts of modern Central Asia that are connected to the nomadic lifestyle?

Organizing What You Know

5. **Contrasting** Copy the following graphic organizer. Use it to describe the conditions in Central Asia during the Soviet era and today.

	Soviet era	Today
Type of government		
Official language		
Alphabet		
Government attitude toward Islam		

CASE STUDY

KAZAKHS: PASTORAL NOMADS OF CENTRAL ASIA

Nomads are people who move around from place to place during the year. Nomads usually move when the seasons change so that they will have enough food to eat. Herding, hunting, gathering, and fishing are all ways that different nomadic groups get their food.

Nomads that herd animals are called pastoral nomads. Their way of life depends on the seasonal movement of their herds. Pastoral nomads may herd cattle, horses, sheep, goats, yaks, reindeer, camels, or other animals. Instead of keeping their animals inside fenced pastures, pastoral nomads let them graze on open fields. However, they must make sure the animals do not overgraze and damage the pastureland. To do this, they keep their animals moving throughout the year. Some pastoral nomads live in steppe or desert environments. These nomads often have to move their animals very long distances between winter and summer pastures.

The Kazakhs of Central Asia are an example of a pastoral nomadic group. They have herded horses, sheep, goats, and cattle for hundreds of years. Because they move so much, the Kazakhs do not have permanent homes. They bring their homes with them when they travel to new places.

A Kazakh nomad keeps a watchful eye over a herd of horses.

Yurts are carefully stitched together by hand. When it is time to move to new pastures, they are carried from place to place on horseback or on small wagons.

The Kazakhs live in tent-like structures called yurts. Yurts are circular structures made of bent poles covered with thick felt. Yurts can be easily taken apart and moved. They are perfect homes for the Kazakhs' nomadic lifestyle.

During the year, a Kazakh family may move its herds of sheep, horses, and cattle as far as 500 miles (805 km). For one Kazakh family, each year is divided into four different parts. The family spends the first part of the year in winter grazing areas. Then, in early spring, they move to areas with fresh grass shoots. When these spring grasses are gone, the family moves their animals to summer pastures. In the fall, the animals are kept for six weeks in autumn pastures. Finally, the herds are taken back to their winter pastures. Each year, the cycle is repeated.

The nomadic lifestyle of the Kazakhs has changed, however. In the early 1800s people from Russia and eastern Europe began to move into the region. These people were farmers. They started planting crops in areas that the Kazakhs used for pasture. This made it more difficult for the Kazakhs to move their animals during the year. Later, when Kazakhstan was part of the Soviet Union, government officials encouraged the Kazakhs to settle in villages and cities. Many Kazakhs still move their animals during the year. However, tending crops has also become an important way to get food.

Seasonal Movement of a Kazakh Family

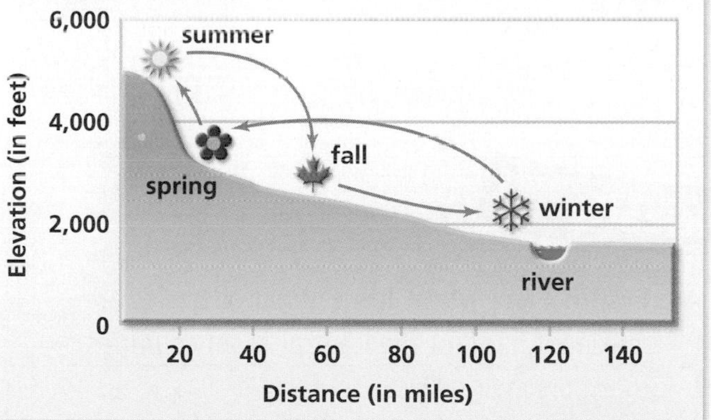

6,000
4,000
2,000
0
Elevation (in feet)
summer
spring
fall
winter
river
20
40
60
80
100
120
140
Distance (in miles)

During the year, a Kazakh family may move its herds to several different pasture areas as the seasons change.

Interpreting the Graph **Why do you think animals are moved to higher elevations during the summer and to lower elevations during the winter?**

Understanding What You Read

1. Why do some pastoral nomads have to travel such great distances?
2. How has the nomadic lifestyle of the Kazakhs changed during the last 100 years?

CHAPTER 24

Reviewing What You Know

Building Vocabulary

On a separate sheet of paper, write sentences to define each of the following words.

1. landlocked
2. oasis
3. nomads
4. caravans
5. yurt
6. mosques

Reviewing the Main Ideas

1. *Places and Regions* What types of climates are most common in Central Asia?
2. *Environment and Society* What problems have resulted from the shrinking of the Aral Sea?
3. *Human Systems* How did Soviet rule change Central Asians' way of life?
4. *Human Systems* What kinds of ties do the Central Asian countries have to Russia today?
5. *Places and Regions* What are the various languages spoken in Central Asia?

Understanding Environment and Society

Aral Sea in Danger

The rapid disappearance of the Aral Sea is a serious concern in Central Asia. Research and create a presentation on the Aral Sea. You may want to think about the following:

- Actions that could be taken to preserve the Aral Sea.
- What could be done to help slow the dropping of the sea's water level.
- Possible consequences if the level of the Aral Sea continues to drop.

Include a bibliography of the sources you used.

Thinking Critically

1. **Summarizing** How have politics influenced language and the alphabet used in Central Asia?
2. **Finding the Main Idea** How do the artistic crafts of Central Asia reflect the nomadic lifestyle?
3. **Analyzing Information** Why did the Soviets encourage cotton farming in the region? What were the environmental consequences?
4. **Finding the Main Idea** What obstacles are making it hard for the Central Asian countries to export their oil?
5. **Summarizing** What are some reasons the Central Asian countries have experienced slow economic growth since independence? How are they trying to improve the situation?

Building Social Studies Skills

Map ACTIVITY

On a separate sheet of paper, match the letters on the map with their correct labels.

Caspian Sea	**Kara-Kum**
Pamirs	**Kyzyl Kum**
Tian Shan	**Tashkent**
Aral Sea	**Samarqand**

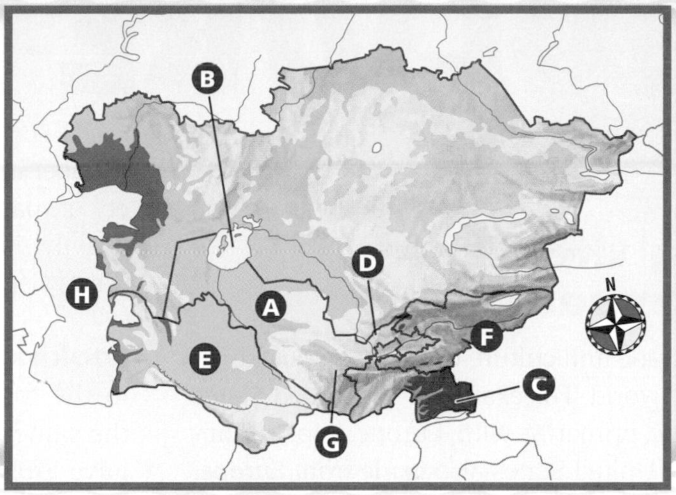

A
B
C
D
E
F
G
H
N

Mental Mapping Skills ACTIVITY

On a separate sheet of paper, draw a freehand map of Central Asia. Make a key for your map and label the following:

Amu Dar'ya	**Syr Dar'ya**
Aral Sea	**Tajikistan**
Kazakhstan	**Turkmenistan**
Kyrgyzstan	**Uzbekistan**

WRITING ACTIVITY

Imagine that you are a caravan trader traveling along the Silk Road during the 1200s. Write a journal entry describing your journey from the Mediterranean Sea through Central Asia. Be sure to use standard grammar, spelling, sentence structure, and punctuation.

Alternative Assessment

Portfolio ACTIVITY

Learning About Your Local Geography

History The Mongol conqueror Genghis Khan is a hero to many Central Asians. Use biographies or interviews with residents to find out about a person who is special to your area. Report your findings.

internet connect

go.hrw.com

Internet Activity: go.hrw.com
KEYWORD: SJ3 GT24

Choose a topic to explore about Central Asia:

- Study the climate of Central Asia.
- Travel along the historic Silk Road.
- Learn about nomads and caravans.

FOCUS ON CULTURE

Facing the Past and Present

Patterns of trade and culture can change quickly in our modern world. For example, the United States used to trade primarily with Europe. Most immigrants to the United States also came from Europe. Today, the American connection to Europe has faded. The United States now trades more with Japan and other Pacific Rim countries than with Europe. New ideas, new technology, and immigrants to the United States come from all around the world.

Central Asia Since the breakup of the Soviet Union, similar changes have taken place in Central Asia. In the past, Central Asia had many ties to the Soviet Union. For example, the economies of the two regions were linked. Central Asia exported cotton and oil to Russia and to countries in Eastern Europe. In exchange, Central Asia received a variety of manufactured goods. The Soviet Union also heavily influenced the culture of Central Asia. Many Central Asians learned to speak Russian.

Looking South Today, Central Asia's links to the former Soviet Union have weakened. At the same time, its ancient ties to Southwest Asia have grown stronger. The Silk Road once linked Central Asian cities to Southwest Asian ports on the Mediterranean. Now the peoples of Central Asia are looking southward once again. New links are forming between Central Asia and Turkey. Many people in Central Asia are traditionally Turkic in culture and language. Turkey's business leaders are working to expand their industries in Central Asia. Also, regular air travel from Turkey to cities in Central Asia is now possible as well.

Religion also links both Central Asia and Southwest Asia. Islam was first introduced into Central Asia in the A.D. 700s. It eventually became the region's dominant religion. However, Islam declined during the Soviet era. Missionaries from Arab countries and Iran are now working to strengthen this connection. Iran is also spending millions of dollars to build roads and rail lines to Central Asia.

◄ These children are learning about Islam in Dushanbe, Tajikistan. Although the former Communist government discouraged the practice of religion, today Islam flourishes in the independent Central Asian republics.

Language Groups of Southwest and Central Asia

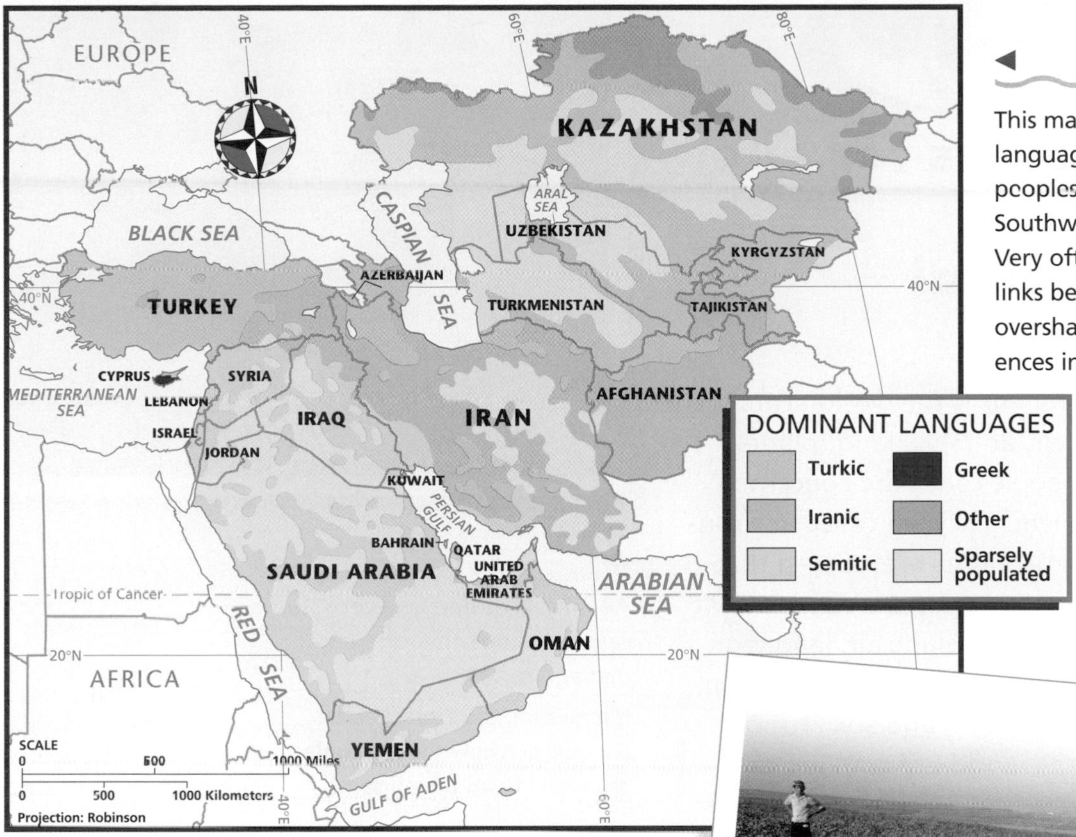

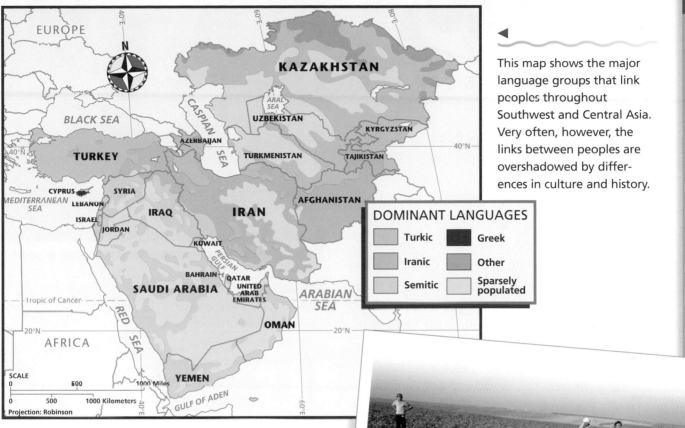

EUROPE
KAZAKHSTAN
ARAL SEA
CASPIAN SEA
UZBEKISTAN
BLACK SEA
KYRGYZSTAN
AZERBAIJAN
TURKEY
TURKMENISTAN
TAJIKISTAN
CYPRUS
SYRIA
MEDITERRANEAN SEA
LEBANON
IRAQ
IRAN
AFGHANISTAN
ISRAEL
JORDAN
KUWAIT
PERSIAN GULF
BAHRAIN
QATAR
UNITED ARAB EMIRATES
SAUDI ARABIA
ARABIAN SEA
Tropic of Cancer
RED SEA
OMAN
AFRICA
YEMEN
GULF OF ADEN
SCALE
Projection: Robinson
DOMINANT LANGUAGES
Turkic
Greek
Iranic
Other
Semitic
Sparsely populated

This map shows the major language groups that link peoples throughout Southwest and Central Asia. Very often, however, the links between peoples are overshadowed by differences in culture and history.

Many people in Central and Southwest Asia grow cotton, such as here in Uzbekistan.

Central Asia and Southwest Asia share a similar climate, environment, and way of life. Both regions are dry, and water conservation and irrigation are important. Many people in both regions grow cotton and herd animals. In addition, both Central Asia and Southwest Asia are dealing with changes caused by the growing influence of Western culture. Some people are worried that compact discs, videotapes, and satellite television from the West threaten traditional beliefs and ways of life. Shared fears of cultural loss may bring Central Asia and Southwest Asia closer together.

Defining the Region As the world changes, geographers must reexamine this and other regions of the world. Will geographers decide to include the countries of Central Asia in the region of Southwest Asia? Will Russia regain control of Central Asia? The geographers are watching and waiting.

Understanding What You Read

1. What ties did Central Asia have to the Soviet Union in the past?
2. Why are ties between Central Asia and Southwest Asia growing today?

GeoSKILLS

Building Skills for Life: Addressing Environmental Problems

The natural environment is the world around us. It includes the air, animals, land, plants, and water. Many people today are concerned about the environment. They are called environmentalists. Environmentalists are worried that human activities are damaging the environment. Environmental problems include air, land, and water pollution, global warming, deforestation, plant and animal extinction, and soil erosion.

People all over the world are working to solve these environmental problems. The governments of many countries are trying to work together to protect the environment. International organizations like the United Nations are also addressing environmental issues.

An oil spill in northwestern Russia caused serious environmental damage in 1995.

Interpreting the Visual Record
Can you see how these people are cleaning up the oil spill?

PRACTICING

THE SKILL

1. **Gather Information.** Create a plan to present to the city council for solving a local environmental problem. Select a problem and research it using databases or other reference materials. How does it affect people's lives and your community's culture or economy?
2. **List and Consider Options.** After reviewing the information, list and consider options for solving this environmental problem.
3. **Consider Advantages and Disadvantages.** Now consider the advantages and disadvantages of taking each option. Ask yourself questions like, "How will solving this environmental problem affect business in the area?" Record your answers.
4. **Choose, Implement, and Evaluate a Solution.** After considering the advantages and disadvantages, you should create your plan. Be sure to make your proposal clear. You will need to explain the reasoning behind the choices you made in your plan.

HANDS ON GEOGRAPHY

The countries of the former Soviet Union face some of the worst environmental problems in the world. For more than 50 years, the region's environment was polluted with nuclear waste and toxic chemicals. Today, environmental problems in this region include air, land, and water pollution.

One place that was seriously polluted was the Russian city of Chelyabinsk. Some people have called Chelyabinsk the most polluted place on Earth. The passage below describes some of the environmental problems in Chelyabinsk. Read the passage and then answer the Lab Report questions.

Chelyabinsk was one of the former Soviet Union's main military production centers. A factory near Chelyabinsk produced nuclear weapons. Over the years, nuclear waste from this factory polluted a very large area. A huge amount of nuclear waste was dumped into the Techa River. Many people in the region used this river as their main source of water. They also ate fish from the river.

In the 1950s many deaths and health problems resulted from pollution in the Techa River. Because it was so polluted, the Soviet government evacuated 22 villages along the river. In 1957 a nuclear accident in the region released twice as much radiation as the Chernobyl accident in 1986. However, the accident near Chelyabinsk was kept secret. About 10,000 people were evacuated. The severe environmental problems in the Chelyabinsk region led to dramatic increases in birth defects and cancer rates.

The village of Mitlino was evacuated after a nuclear accident in 1957.

Lab Report

1. How did environmental problems near Chelyabinsk affect people who lived in the region?
2. What might be done to address environmental problems in the Chelyabinsk region?
3. How can a geographical perspective help to solve these problems?

GAZETTEER

Phonetic Respelling and Pronunciation Guide

Many of the key terms in this textbook have been respelled to help you pronounce them. The letter combinations used in the respelling throughout the narrative are explained in this phonetic respelling and pronunciation guide. The guide is adapted from *Webster's Tenth New College Dictionary*, *Merriam-Webster's New Geographical Dictionary*, and *Merriam-Webster's New Biographical Dictionary*.

MARK	AS IN	RESPELLING	EXAMPLE
a	alphabet	a	*AL-fuh-bet
ā	Asia	ay	AY-zhuh
ä	cart, top	ah	KAHRT, TAHP
e	let, ten	e	LET, TEN
ē	even, leaf	ee	EE-vuhn, LEEF
i	it, tip, British	i	IT, TIP, BRIT-ish
ī	site, buy, Ohio	y	SYT, BY, oh-HY-oh
	iris	eye	EYE-ris
k	card	k	KAHRD
ō	over, rainbow	oh	OH-vuhr, RAYN-boh
u̇	book, wood	ooh	BOOHK, WOOHD
ȯ	all, orchid	aw	AWL, AWR-kid
ȯi	foil, coin	oy	FOYL, KOYN
au̇	out	ow	OWT
ə	cup, butter	uh	KUHP, BUHT-uhr
ü	rule, food	oo	ROOL, FOOD
yü	few	yoo	FYOO
zh	vision	zh	VIZH-uhn

**A syllable printed in small capital letters receives heavier emphasis than the other syllable(s) in a word.*

A

Acapulco (17°N 100°W) city on the southwestern coast of Mexico, 293
Adriatic Sea sea between Italy and the Balkan Peninsula, 117, 451
Aegean (ee-JEE-uhn) **Sea** sea between Greece and Turkey, 114, 117, 393
Africa second-largest continent; surrounded by the Atlantic Ocean, Indian Ocean, and Mediterranean Sea, A2–A3
Albania country in Eastern Europe on the Adriatic Sea, 451
Alberta province in Canada, 261
Aleutian Islands volcanic islands extending from Alaska into the Pacific Ocean, 217
Alps major mountain system in south-central Europe, 117
Altiplano broad, high plateau in Peru and Bolivia, 361
Amazon River major river in South America, 343
Amsterdam (52°N 5°E) capital of the Netherlands, 411
Amu Dar'ya (uh-MOO duhr-YAH) river in Central Asia that drains into the Aral Sea, 519
Amur (ah-MOOHR) **River** river in northeast Asia forming part of the border between Russia and China, 483
Andes (AN-deez) great mountain range in South America, 111, 343
Andorra European microstate in the Pyrenees mountains, A15
Andorra la Vella (43°N 2°E) capital of Andorra, A15
Antarctica continent around the South Pole, A22
Antarctic Circle line of latitude located at 66.5° south of the equator; parallel beyond which no sunlight shines on the June solstice (first day of winter in the Southern Hemisphere), A4–A5, A22
Antigua and Barbuda island country in the Caribbean, 311
Antwerp (51°N 4°E) major port city in Belgium, 411
Apennines (A-puh-nynz) mountain range in Italy, 393
Appalachian Mountains mountain system in eastern North America, 217, 235
Aral (AR-uhl) **Sea** inland sea between Kazakhstan and Uzbekistan, 519
Arctic Circle line of latitude located at 66.5° north of the equator; the parallel beyond which no sunlight shines on the December solstice (first day of winter in the Northern Hemisphere), A4–A5, A22
Arctic Ocean ocean north of the Arctic Circle; world's fourth-largest ocean, A2–A3
Argentina second-largest country in South America, 343
Armenia country in the Caucasus region of Asia; former Soviet republic, 505
Ashgabat (formerly Ashkhabad) (40°N 58°E) capital of Turkmenistan, 519
Asia world's largest continent; located between Europe and the Pacific Ocean, A3
Astana (51°N 71°E) capital of Kazakhstan, 519
Astrakhan (46°N 48°E) old port city on the Volga River in Russia, 483
Asunción (25°S 58°W) capital of Paraguay, 343
Atacama Desert desert in northern Chile, 361
Athens (38°N 24°E) capital and largest city in Greece, 117

Atlanta (34°N 84°W) capital and largest city in the U.S. state of Georgia, 217, 240

Atlantic Ocean ocean between the continents of North and South America and the continents of Europe and Africa; world's second-largest ocean, A2

Australia only country occupying an entire continent, located between the Indian Ocean and the Pacific Ocean, A3

Austria country in west-central Europe south of Germany, 411

Azerbaijan country in the Caucasus region of Asia; former Soviet republic, 505

B

Bahamas island country in the Atlantic Ocean southwest of Florida, 311

Baja California peninsula in northwestern Mexico, 293

Baku (40°N 50°E) capital of Azerbaijan, 505

Balkan Mountains mountain range that rises in Bulgaria, 451

Baltic Sea body of water east of the North Sea and Scandinavia, 431

Baltimore (39°N 77°W) city in Maryland on the western shore of Chesapeake Bay, 217, 235

Barbados island country in the Caribbean, 311

Barcelona (41°N 2°E) Mediterranean port city and Spain's second-largest city, 393

Basel (48°N 8°E) city in northern Switzerland on the Rhine River, 411

Basseterre (17°N 63°W) capital of St. Kitts and Nevis, 311

Bay of Biscay body of water off the western coast of France and the northern coast of Spain, 411

Belarus country located north of Ukraine; former Soviet republic, 505

Belém (1°S 48°W) port city in northern Brazil, 343

Belfast (55°N 6°W) capital and largest city of Northern Ireland, 431

Belgium country between France and Germany in west-central Europe, 411

Belgrade (45°N 21°E) capital of Serbia and Yugoslavia on the Danube River, 451

Belize country in Central America bordering Mexico and Guatemala, 311

Belmopan (17°N 89°W) capital of Belize, 311

Bergen (60°N 5°E) seaport city in southwestern Norway, 431

Berkshire Hills hilly region of western Massachusetts, 235

Berlin (53°N 13°E) capital of Germany, 411

Bern (47°N 7°E) capital of Switzerland, 411

Birmingham (52°N 2°W) major manufacturing center of south-central Great Britain, 431

Bishkek (43°N 75°E) capital of Kyrgyzstan, 519

Black Sea sea between Europe and Asia, A14, 107, 114

Blue Ridge Mountains southern region of the Appalachians, 240

Bogotá (5°N 74°W) capital and largest city of Colombia, 327

Bolivia landlocked South American country, 361

Bonn (51°N 7°E) city in western Germany; replaced by Berlin as the capital of reunified Germany, 411

Bosnia and Herzegovina country in Eastern Europe between Serbia and Croatia, 451

Boston (42°N 71°W) capital and largest city of Massachusetts, 217

Brasília (16°S 48°W) capital of Brazil, 343

Bratislava (48°N 17°E) capital of Slovakia, 451

Brazil largest country in South America, 343

Brazilian Highlands regions of old, eroded mountains in southeastern Brazil, 343

Brazilian Plateau area of upland plains in southern Brazil, 343

Bridgetown (13°N 60°W) capital of Barbados, 311

British Columbia province on the Pacific coast of Canada, 261

British Isles island group consisting of Great Britain and Ireland, A15

Brittany region in northwestern France, 411

Brussels (51°N 4°E) capital of Belgium, 411

Bucharest (44°N 26°E) capital of Romania, 451

Budapest (48°N 19°E) capital of Hungary, 451

Buenos Aires (34°S 59°W) capital of Argentina, 343

Bulgaria country on the Balkan Peninsula in Eastern Europe, 451

C

Calgary (51°N 114°W) city in the western Canadian province of Alberta, 261

Callao (kah-YAH-oh) (12°S 77°W) port city in Peru, 361

Campeche (20°N 91°W) city in Mexico on the west coast of the Yucatán Peninsula, 293

Canada country occupying most of northern North America, 261

Canadian Shield major landform region in central Canada along Hudson Bay, 261

Cancún (21°N 87°W) resort city in Mexico on the Yucatán Peninsula, 293

Cantabrian (kan-TAY-bree-uhn) **Mountains** mountains in northwestern Spain, 393

Cape Cod peninsula off the coast of southern New England, 235

Cape Horn (56°S 67°W) cape in southern Chile; southernmost point of South America, 361

Caracas (kuh-RAHK-uhs) (11°N 67°W) capital of Venezuela, 327

Cardiff (52°N 3°W) capital and largest city of Wales, 431

Caribbean Sea arm of the Atlantic Ocean between North and South America, A10, 311

Carpathian Mountains mountain system in Eastern Europe, 451

Cascade Range mountain range in the Northwestern United States, 217, 253

Caspian Sea large inland salt lake between Europe and Asia, A16, 483

Castries (14°N 61°W) capital of St. Lucia, 311

Cauca River river in western Colombia, 327

Caucasus Mountains mountain range between the Black Sea and the Caspian Sea, 483

Cayenne (5°N 52°W) capital of French Guiana, 327

Central America narrow southern portion of the North American continent, 311

Central Siberian Plateau upland plains and valleys between the Yenisey and Lena Rivers in Russia, 483

Central Valley narrow plain between the Sierra Nevada and Coast Ranges, 253

Chelyabinsk (chel-YAH-buhnsk) (55°N 61°E) manufacturing city in the Urals region of Russia, 483

Chernobyl (51°N 30°E) city in north-central Ukraine; site of a major nuclear accident in 1986, 505

Chesapeake Bay largest estuary on the Atlantic Coast, 235

Chicago (42°N 88°W) major city on Lake Michigan in northern Illinois, 217, 244

Chile country in South America, 361

China country in East Asia; most populous country in the world, 139

Chisinau (formerly Kishinev) (47°N 29°E) capital of Moldova, 451
Ciudad Juárez (syoo-thahth HWAHR-es) (32°N 106°W) city in northern Mexico near El Paso, 293
Coastal Plain North American landform region stretching along the Atlantic Ocean and Gulf of Mexico, 217
Coast Ranges rugged coastline along the Pacific, 253
Cologne (51°N 7°E) manufacturing and commercial city along the Rhine River in Germany, 411
Colombia country in northern South America, 327
Colorado Plateau uplifted area of horizontal rock layers in the western United States, 217
Columbia Basin region of dry basins and mountains east of the Cascades, 253
Columbia River river that drains the Columbia Basin in the northwestern United States, 217
Copenhagen (56°N 12°E) seaport and capital of Denmark, 431
Córdoba (30°S 64°W) large city in Argentina northwest of Buenos Aires, 343
Cork (52°N 8°W) seaport city in southern Ireland, 431
Costa Rica country in Central America, 311
Crater Lake lake in Oregon; deepest in the United States, 253
Crete largest of the islands of Greece, 114
Crimean Peninsula peninsula in Ukraine that juts southward into the Black Sea, 505
Croatia Eastern European country and former Yugoslav republic, 451
Cuba country and largest island in Caribbean, 311
Cumberland Plateau landform in the Coastal Plain area of the South, 240
Cuzco (14°S 72°W) city southwest of Lima, Peru; former capital of the Inca Empire, 361
Czech Republic Eastern European country and the western part of the former country in Czechoslovakia, 451

D

Dallas (33°N 97°W) city in Northern Texas, 240
Danube River major river in Europe that flows into the Black Sea in Romania, 411
Death Valley east of the Sierra Nevada; the lowest point in all of North America, 253
Denmark country in northern Europe, 431
Detroit (42°N 83°W) major industrial city in Michigan, 217, 247
Devil's Island (5°N 53°W) French island off the coast of French Guiana in South America, 327
Dinaric Alps mountains extending inland from the Adriatic coast to the Balkan Peninsula, 451
Dnieper River major river in Ukraine, 505
Dominica Caribbean island country, 311
Dominican Republic country occupying the eastern part of Hispaniola in the Caribbean, 311
Donets Basin industrial region in eastern Ukraine, 505
Douro River river on the Iberian Peninsula that flows into the Atlantic Ocean in Portugal, 393
Dublin (53°N 6°W) capital of the republic of Ireland, 431
Dushanbe (39°N 69°E) capital of Tajikistan, 519

E

Ebro River river in Spain that flows into the Mediterranean Sea, 393
Ecuador country in western South America, 361
Edmonton (54°N 113°W) provincial capital of Alberta, Canada, 261
Egypt country in North Africa located east of Libya, 107
El Salvador country on the Pacific side of Central America, 311
England southern part of Great Britain and part of the United Kingdom in northern Europe, 431
English Channel channel separating Great Britain from the European continent, 411
equator the imaginary line of latitude that lies halfway between the North and South Poles and circles the globe, A4–A5
Essen (51°N 7°E) industrial city in western Germany, 411
Estonia country located on the Baltic Sea; former Soviet republic, 451
Euphrates River major river in southwestern Asia, 107
Europe continent between the Ural Mountains and the Atlantic Ocean, A3
Everglades large wetland area in Florida, 240

F

Fergana Valley fertile valley in Uzbekistan, Kyrgyzstan, and Tajikistan, 519
Finland country in northern Europe located between Sweden, Norway, and Russia, 431
Flanders northern coastal part of Belgium where Dutch is the dominant language, 411
Florence (44°N 11°E) city on the Arno River in central Italy, 393
France country in west-central Europe, 411
Frankfurt (50°N 9°E) main city of Germany's Rhineland region, 411
French Guiana French territory in northern South America, 327

G

Galway (53°N 9°W) city in western Ireland, 431
Geneva (46°N 6°E) city in southwestern Switzerland, 411
Genoa (44°N 10°E) seaport city in northwestern Italy, 393
Georgetown (8°N 58°W) capital of Guyana, 327
Georgia (Eurasia) country in the Caucasus region; former Soviet republic, 505
Germany country in west-central Europe located between Poland and the Benelux countries, 411
Glasgow (56°N 4°W) city in Scotland, United Kingdom, 431
Göteberg (58°N 12°E) seaport city in southwestern Sweden, 431
Gran Chaco (grahn CHAH-koh) dry plains region in Paraguay, Bolivia, and northern Argentina, 343
Great Basin dry region in the western United States, 217
Great Bear Lake lake in the Northwest Territories of Canada, 261
Great Britain major island of the United Kingdom, 431
Greater Antilles larger islands of the West Indies in the Caribbean Sea, 311
Great Lakes largest freshwater lake system in the world; located in North America, 217
Great Plains plains region in the central United States, 217, 248
Great Slave Lake lake in the Northwest Territories of Canada, 261
Great Smoky Mountains southern mountain range in the Appalachians, 240

Greece country in southern Europe located at the southern end of the Balkan Peninsula, 114, 393
Greenland self-governing province of Denmark between the North Atlantic and Arctic Oceans, 431
Green Mountains major range of the Appalachian Mountains in Vermont, 235
Grenada Caribbean island country, 311
Guadalajara (21°N 103°W) industrial city in west-central Mexico, 293
Guadalquivir (gwah-thahl-kee-VEER) **River** important river in southern Spain, 393
Guatemala most populous country in Central America, 311
Guatemala City (15°N 91°W) capital of Guatemala, 311
Guayaquil (gwy-ah-KEEL) (2°S 80°W) port city in Ecuador, 361
Guiana Highlands elevated region in northeastern South America, 327
Gulf of Bothnia part of the Baltic Sea west of Finland, 431
Gulf of California part of the Pacific Ocean east of Baja California, Mexico, 293
Gulf of Mexico gulf of the Atlantic Ocean between Florida, Texas, and Mexico, 293
Gulf of St. Lawrence gulf between New Brunswick and Newfoundland Island in North America, 261
Guyana (gy-AH-nuh) country in South America, 327

H

Haiti country occupying the western third of the Caribbean island of Hispaniola, 311
Halifax (45°N 64°W) provincial capital of Nova Scotia, Canada, 261
Hamburg (54°N 10°E) seaport on the Elbe River in northwestern Germany, 411
Havana (23°N 82°W) capital of Cuba, 311
Hawaii U.S. Pacific state consisting of a chain of eight large islands and more than 100 smaller islands, 253
Helsinki (60°N 25°E) capital of Finland, 431
Hispaniola large Caribbean island divided into the countries of Haiti and the Dominican Republic, 311
Honduras country in Central America, 311
Houston (30°N 95°W) major port and largest city in Texas, 217, 240
Hudson Bay large bay in Canada, 261
Hungary country in Eastern Europe between Romania and Austria, 451

I

Iberian Peninsula peninsula in southwestern Europe occupied by Spain and Portugal, 393
Iceland island country between the North Atlantic and Arctic Oceans, 431
India country in South Asia, 139
Indian Ocean world's third-largest ocean; located east of Africa, south of Asia, west of Australia, and north of Antarctica, A3
Interior Plains vast area between the Appalachians and the Rocky Mountains in North America, 217, 219, 244
Iquitos (4°S 73°W) city in northeastern Peru on the Amazon River, 361
Ireland country west of Great Britain in the British Isles, 431
Irish Sea sea between Great Britain and Ireland, 431
Israel country in southwestern Asia, A5
Italy country in southern Europe, 393

J

Jamaica island country in the Caribbean Sea, 311
Japan country in East Asia consisting of four major islands and more than 3,000 smaller islands, A17
Jerusalem (32°N 35°E) capital of Israel, A5
Jutland Peninsula peninsula in northern Europe made up of Denmark and part of northern Germany, 431

K

Kamchatka Peninsula peninsula along Russia's northeastern coast, 483
Kara-Kum (kahr-uh-KOOM) desert region in Turkmenistan, 519
Kazakhstan country in Central Asia; former Soviet republic, 519
Khabarovsk (kuh-BAHR-uhfsk) (49°N 135°E) city in southeastern Russia on the Amur River, 483
Kiev (50°N 31°E) capital of Ukraine, 505
Kingston (18°N 77°W) capital of Jamaica, 311
Kingstown (13°N 61°W) capital of St. Vincent and the Grenadines, 311
Kjølen (CHUHL-uhn) **Mountains** mountain range in the Scandinavian Peninsula, 431
Korea peninsula on the east coast of Asia, A17
Kosovo province in southern Serbia, 451
Kourou (5°N 53°W) city in French Guiana, 327
Kuril (KYOOHR-eel) **Islands** Russian islands northeast of the island of Hokkaido, Japan, 483
Kuznetsk Basin (Kuzbas) industrial region in central Russia, 483
Kyrgyzstan (kir-gi-STAN) country in Central Asia; former Soviet republic, 519
Kyzyl Kum (ki-zil KOOM) desert region in Uzbekistan and Kazakhstan, 519

L

Labrador region in the territory of Newfoundland, Canada, 261
Lake Baikal (by-KAHL) world's deepest freshwater lake; located north of the Gobi in Russia, 483
Lake Maracaibo (mah-rah-KY-buh) extension of the Gulf of Venezuela in South America, 327
Lake Nicaragua lake in southwestern Nicaragua, 311
Lake Poopó (poh-oh-POH) lake in western Bolivia, 361
Lake Titicaca lake between Bolivia and Peru at an elevation of 12,500 feet (3,810 m), 361
La Paz (17°S 68°W) administrative capital and principal industrial city of Bolivia with an elevation of 12,001 feet (3,658 m); highest capital in the world, 361
Lapland region extending across northern Finland, Sweden, and Norway, 431
Las Vegas (36°N 115°W) city in southern Nevada, 217, 248
Latvia country on the Baltic Sea; former Soviet republic, 451
Lesser Antilles chain of volcanic islands in the eastern Caribbean Sea, 311
Liechtenstein microstate in west-central Europe located between Switzerland and Austria, 411
Lima (12°S 77°W) capital of Peru, 361
Lisbon (39°N 9°W) capital and largest city of Portugal, 393
Lithuania European country on the Baltic Sea; former Soviet republic, 451

Ljubljana (lee-oo-blee-AH-nuh) (46°N 14°E) capital of Slovenia, 451
London (52°N 0°) capital of the United Kingdom, 431
Longfellow Mountains major range of the Appalachian Mountains in Maine, 235
Los Angeles, California (34°N 118°W) major city in California, 253
Luxembourg small European country bordered by France, Germany, and Belgium, 411
Luxembourg (50°N 7°E) capital of Luxembourg, 411

M

Macedonia Balkan country; former Yugoslav republic, 451
Machu Picchu (13°S 73°W) ancient Inca city in the Andes of Peru, 361
Madrid (40°N 4°W) capital of Spain, 393
Magdalena River river in Colombia that flows into the Caribbean Sea, 327
Magnitogorsk (53°N 59°E) manufacturing city of the Urals region of Russia, 483
Malta island country in southern Europe located in the Mediterranean Sea between Sicily and North Africa, 384
Managua (12°N 86°W) capital of Nicaragua, 311
Manaus (3°S 60°W) city in Brazil on the Amazon River, 343
Manchester (53°N 2°W) major commercial city in west-central Great Britain, 431
Manitoba prairie province in central Canada, 261
Marseille (43°N 5°E) seaport in France on the Mediterranean Sea, 411
Martha's Vineyard island off the coast of southern New England, 235
Mato Grosso Plateau highland region in southwestern Brazil, 343
Mazatlán (23°N 106°W) seaport city in western Mexico, 293
Mediterranean Sea sea surrounded by Europe, Asia, and Africa, 114, 117
Mexican Plateau large, high plateau in central Mexico, 293
Mexico country in North America, 293
Mexico City (19°N 99°W) capital of Mexico, 293
Miami (26°N 80°W) city in southern Florida, 217, 240
Milan (45°N 9°E) city in northern Italy, 393
Minsk (54°N 28°E) capital of Belarus, 505
Mississippi Delta low swampy area of the Mississippi formed by a buildup of sediment, 240
Mississippi River major river in the central United States, 217
Moldova Eastern European country located between Romania and Ukraine; former Soviet republic, 451
Monaco (44°N 8°E) European microstate bordered by France, 411
Montenegro See Yugoslavia.
Monterrey (26°N 100°W) major industrial center in northeastern Mexico, 293
Montevideo (mawn-tay-bee-THAY-oh) (35°S 56°W) capital of Uruguay, 343
Montreal (46°N 74°W) financial and industrial city in Quebec, Canada, 261
Moscow (56°N 38°E) capital of Russia, 483
Mount Elbrus (43°N 42°E) highest European peak (18,510 ft.; 5,642 m); located in the Caucasus Mountains, 505
Mount Orizaba (19°N 97°W) volcanic mountain (18,700 ft.; 5,700m) southeast of Mexico City; highest point in Mexico, 293
Mount Whitney highest peak in the 48 contiguous United States, 253
Munich (MYOO-nik) (48°N 12°E) major city and manufacturing center in southern Germany, 411

N

Nantucket island off the coast of southern New England, 235
Naples (41°N 14°E) major seaport in southern Italy, 393
Nassau (25°N 77°W) capital of the Bahamas, 311
Netherlands country in west-central Europe, 411
New Brunswick province in eastern Canada, 261
Newfoundland eastern province in Canada including Labrador and the island of Newfoundland, 261
New Orleans (30°N 90°W) major Gulf port city in Louisiana located on the Mississippi River, 217, 240
New York Middle Atlantic state in the northeastern United States, 217, 235
Nicaragua country in Central America, 311
Nice (44°N 7°E) city in the southeastern coast in France, 411
Nile River world's longest river (4,187 miles; 6,737 km); flows into the Mediterranean Sea in Egypt, 107
Nizhniy Novgorod (Gorky), Russia (56°N 44°E) city on the Volga River east of Moscow, 483
North America continent including Canada, the United States, Mexico, Central America, and the Caribbean Islands, A2
Northern European Plain broad coastal plain from the Atlantic coast of France into Russia, 411
Northern Ireland the six northern counties of Ireland that remain part of the United Kingdom; also called Ulster, 431
North Pole the northern point of Earth's axis, A22
North Sea major sea between Great Britain, Denmark, and the Scandinavian Peninsula, 411
Northwest Highlands region of rugged hills and low mountains in Europe, including parts of the British Isles, northwestern France, the Iberian Peninsula, and the Scandinavian Peninsula, 383
Northwest Territories division of a northern region of Canada, 261
Norway European country located on the Scandinavian Peninsula, 431
Nova Scotia province in eastern Canada, 261
Novosibirsk (55°N 83°E) industrial center in Siberia, Russia, 483
Nunavut Native American territory of northern Canada, 261
Nuuk (Godthab) (64°N 52°W) capital of Greenland, 431

O

Ob River large river system that drains Russia and Siberia, 483
Okefenokee Swamp large wetland area in Florida, 240
Ontario province in central Canada, 261
Orinoco River major river system in South America, 327
Oslo (60°N 11°E) capital of Norway, 431
Ottawa (45°N 76°W) capital of Canada; located in Ontario, 261
Ozark Plateau rugged, hilly region located mainly in Arkansas, 240

P

Pacific Ocean Earth's largest ocean; located between North and South America and Asia and Australia, A2–A3
Pamirs mountain area mainly in Tajikistan in Central Asia, 519
Panama country in Central America, 311
Panama Canal canal allowing shipping between the Pacific Ocean and the Caribbean Sea; located in central Panama, 311
Panama City (9°N 80°W) capital of Panama, 311
Paraguay country in South America, 343
Paraguay River river that divides Paraguay into two separate regions, 343
Paramaribo (6°N 55°W) capital of Suriname in South America, 327
Paraná River major river system in southeastern South America, 343
Paris (49°N 2°E) capital of France, 411
Patagonia arid region of dry plains and windswept plateaus in southern Argentina, 343
Pearl Harbor U.S. naval base in Hawaii; attacked by Japan in 1941, 253
Peloponnesus (pe-luh-puh-NEE-suhs) peninsula forming the southern part of the mainland of Greece, 393
Peru country in South America, 361
Philadelphia (40°N 75°W) important port and industrial center in Pennsylvania in the northeastern United States, 217, 235
Phoenix (34°N 112°W) capital of Arizona, 217, 248
Podgorica (PAWD-gawr-ett-sah) capital of Montenegro, 462
Poland country in Eastern Europe located east of Germany, 451
Po River river in northern Italy, 393
Port-au-Prince (pohr-toh-PRINS) (19°N 72°W) capital of Haiti, 311
Portland (46°N 123°W) seaport and largest city in Oregon, 217, 253
Port-of-Spain (11°N 61°W) capital of Trinidad and Tobago, 311
Portugal country in southern Europe located on the Iberian Peninsula, 393
Prague (50°N 14°E) capital of the Czech Republic, 451
Prince Edward Island province in eastern Canada, 261
Pripyat (Pinsk) Marshes (PRI-pyuht) marshlands in southern Belarus and northwest Ukraine, 505
Puerto Rico U.S. commonwealth in the Greater Antilles in the Caribbean Sea, 311
Puget Sound lowland area of Washington state, 253
Pyrenees (PIR-uh-neez) mountain range along the border of France and Spain, 411

Q

Quebec province in eastern Canada, 261
Quebec (47°N 71°W) provincial capital of Quebec, Canada, 261
Quito (0° 79°W) capital of Ecuador, 361

R

Red Sea sea between the Arabian Peninsula and northeastern Africa, 107
Reykjavik (RAYK-yuh-veek) (64°N 22°W) capital of Iceland, 431
Rhine River major river in Western Europe, 411
Riga (57°N 24°E) capital of Latvia, 451
Río Bravo Mexican name for the river between Texas and Mexico, 293
Rio de Janeiro (23°S 43°W) major port in southeastern Brazil, 343
Río de la Plata estuary between Argentina and Uruguay in South America, 343
Rocky Mountains major mountain range in western North America, 217
Romania country in Eastern Europe, 451
Rome (42°N 13°E) capital of Italy, 393
Rosario (roh-SAHR-ee-oh) (33°S 61°W) city in eastern Argentina, 343
Roseau (15°N 61°W) capital of Dominica in the Caribbean, 311
Russia world's largest country, stretching from Europe and the Baltic Sea to eastern Asia and the coast of the Bering Sea, 483

S

St. George's (12°N 62°W) capital of Grenada in the Caribbean Sea, 311
St. John's (17°N 62°W) capital of Antigua and Barbuda in the Caribbean Sea, 311
St. Kitts and Nevis Caribbean country in the Lesser Antilles, 311
St. Lawrence River major river linking the Great Lakes with the Gulf of St. Lawrence and the Atlantic Ocean in southeastern Canada, 261
St. Lucia Caribbean country in the Lesser Antilles, 311
St. Petersburg (formerly Leningrad; called Petrograd 1914 to 1924) (60°N 30°E) Russia's second largest city and former capital, 483
St. Vincent and the Grenadines Caribbean country in the Lesser Antilles, 311
Sakhalin Island Russian island north of Japan, 483
Salvador (13°S 38°W) seaport city of eastern Brazil, 343
Salzburg state of central Austria, 411
Samarqand (40°N 67°E) city in southeastern Uzbekistan, 519
San Andreas Fault point in California where the Pacific and North American Plates meet, 253
San Diego (33°N 117°W) California's third largest urban area, 217
San Francisco (38°N 122°W) California's second largest urban area, 217
San José (10°N 84°W) capital of Costa Rica, 311
San Juan (19°N 66°W) capital of Puerto Rico, 311
San Marino microstate in southern Europe surrounded by Italy, 393
San Salvador (14°N 89°W) capital of El Salvador, 311
Santa Cruz (18°S 63°W) city in south central Bolivia, 361
Santiago (33°S 71°W) capital of Chile, 361
Santo Domingo (19°N 70°W) capital of the Dominican Republic, 311
São Francisco River river in eastern Brazil, 343
São Paulo (24°S 47°W) Brazil's largest city, 343
Sarajevo (sar-uh-YAY-voh) (44°N 18°E) capital of Bosnia and Herzegovina, 451
Saskatchewan province in central Canada, 261
Scandinavian Peninsula peninsula of northern Europe occupied by Norway and Sweden, 431
Scotland northern part of the island of Great Britain, 431

GLOSSARY

Phonetic Respelling and Pronunciation Guide

Many of the key terms in this textbook have been respelled to help you pronounce them. The letter combinations used in the respelling throughout the narrative are explained in this phonetic respelling and pronunciation guide. The guide is adapted from *Webster's Tenth New College Dictionary, Merriam-Webster's New Geographical Dictionary,* and *Merriam-Webster's New Biographical Dictionary.*

MARK	AS IN	RESPELLING	EXAMPLE
a	alphabet	a	*AL-fuh-bet
ā	Asia	ay	AY-zhuh
ä	cart, top	ah	KAHRT, TAHP
e	let, ten	e	LET, TEN
ē	even, leaf	ee	EE-vuhn, LEEF
i	it, tip, British	i	IT, TIP, BRIT-ish
ī	site, buy, Ohio	y	SYT, BY, oh-HY-oh
	iris	eye	EYE-ris
k	card	k	KAHRD
ō	over, rainbow	oh	OH-vuhr, RAYN-boh
u̇	book, wood	ooh	BOOHK, WOOHD
ȯ	all, orchid	aw	AWL, AWR-kid
ȯi	foil, coin	oy	FOYL, KOYN
au̇	out	ow	OWT
ə	cup, butter	uh	KUHP, BUHT-uhr
ü	rule, food	oo	ROOL, FOOD
yü	few	yoo	FYOO
zh	vision	zh	VIZH-uhn

*A syllable printed in small capital letters receives heavier emphasis than the other syllable(s) in a word.

A

abdicated Gave up the throne, **488**
abolitionist Someone who wants to end slavery, **227**
absolute authority Monarch's power to make all the governing decisions, **141**
absolute location The exact spot on Earth where something is found, often stated in latitude and longitude, **7**
acculturation The process of cultural changes that result from long-term contact with another society, **77**
acid rain A type of polluted rain, produced when pollution from smokestacks combines with water vapor, **64**
Age of Exploration A period when Europeans were eager to find new and shorter sea routes so that they could trade with India and China, **138**
aggression Warlike action, such as an invasion or an attack, **187**
agrarian A society organized around farming, **515**
air pressure The weight of the air, measured by a barometer, **39**
alliance A formal agreement or treaty among nations formed to advance common interests or causes, **152**
allies Friendly countries that support one another against enemies, **489**
alluvial fan A fan-shaped landform created by deposits of sediment at the base of a mountain, **32**
amber Fossilized tree sap, **453**
Antarctic Circle The line of latitude located at 66.5° south of the equator, **20**
anti-Semitism Hatred of Jews, **190**
aqueducts Artificial channels for carrying water, **62, 120**
aquifers Underground, water-bearing layers of rock, sand, or gravel, **62**
archipelago (ahr-kuh-PE-luh-goh) A large group of islands, **312**
Arctic Circle The line of latitude located at 66.5° north of the equator, **20**
arid Dry with little rainfall, **46**
armistice An agreement to stop fighting, **176**
arms race Competition to create and have more advanced weapons, **194**
atmosphere The layer of gases that surrounds Earth, **22**
axis An imaginary line that runs from the North Pole through Earth's center to the South Pole, **19**

B

badlands Rugged areas of soft rock that have been eroded by wind and water into small gullies and have little vegetation or soil, **249**

balance of power A way of keeping peace when no one nation or group of nations is more powerful than the others, **157**
bankrupt Having no money, **179**
barrier islands Long, narrow, sandy islands separated from the mainland, **241**
basins Regions surrounded by mountains or other higher land, **219**
bauxite The most important aluminum ore, **313**
bloc A group of nations united under a common idea or for a common purpose, **193**
bog Soft ground that is soaked with water, **442**

C

cacao (kuh-KOW) A small tree on which cocoa beans grow, **316**
caldera A large depression formed after a major eruption and collapse of a volcanic mountain, **255**
calypso A type of music with origins in Trinidad and Tobago, **320**
cantons Political and administrative districts in Switzerland, **425**
capital The money and tools needed to make a product, **160**
capitalism Economic system in which private individuals control the factors of production, **163**
caravans Groups of people who travel together for protection, **522**
cardamom A spice used in Asian foods, **317**
carrying capacity The maximum number of a species that can be supported by an area, **89**
cartography The art and science of mapmaking, **13**
cash crops Crops produced primarily to sell rather than for the farmer to eat, **305**
cassava (kuh-SAH-vuh) A tropical plant with starchy roots, **332**
cathedrals Huge churches sometimes decorated with elaborate stained-glass windows, **128**
caudillos (kow-THEE-yohs) Military leaders who ruled Venezuela in the 1800s and 1900s, **335**
center-pivot irrigation A method of irrigation which uses long sprinkler systems mounted on huge wheels which rotate slowly, irrigating the area within a circle, **251**
chancellor Germany's head of government, or prime minister, **419**
chinampas (chuh-NAM-puhs) The name the Aztecs gave to raised fields on which they grew crops, **298**
chinooks Strong, dry winds that blow from the Rocky Mountains onto the Great Plains in the United States during drought periods, **250**
chivalry A code of behavior including bravery, fairness, loyalty, and integrity, **127**
city-states Self-governing cities, such as those of ancient Greece, **116, 396**
civilians People who are not in the military, **191**
civil war A conflict between two or more groups within a country, **317**
civilization A highly complex culture with growing cities and economic activity, **80**
clergy Officials of the church, including the priests, bishops, and pope, **128**
climate The weather conditions in an area over a long period of time, **37**
climatology The field of tracking Earth's larger atmospheric systems, **13**
cloud forest A high-elevation, very wet tropical forest where low clouds are common, **313**
coalition governments Governments in which several political parties join together to run a country, **401**
Cold War The rivalry between the United States and the Soviet Union that lasted from the 1940s to the early 1990s, **489**
collective farms Large farms owned and controlled by the central government, **181**
colony Territory controlled by people from a foreign land, **139**
command economy An economy in which the government owns most of the industries and makes most of the economic decisions, **85**
commercial agriculture A type of farming in which farmers produce food for sale, **80**
commonwealth A self-governing territory associated with another country, **323**
communism An economic and political system in which the government owns or controls almost all of the means of production, industries, wages, and prices, **85, 192**
condensation The process by which water changes from a gas into tiny liquid droplets, **24**
conquistadores (kahn-kees-tuh-DAWR-ez) Spanish conquerors during the era of colonization in the Americas, **299**
constitution A document that outlines basic laws that govern a nation, **142**
constitutional monarchy A government with a monarch as head of state and a parliament or other legislature that makes the laws, **435**
consumer goods Products used at home and in everyday life, **489**
contiguous Units, such as states, that connect to or border each other, **218**
Continental Divide The crest of the Rocky Mountains that divides North America's rivers into those that flow eastward and those that flow westward, **219**
continental shelf The gently sloping underwater land surrounding each continent, **25**
continents Earth's large landmasses, **29**
cooperatives Organizations owned by their members and operated for their mutual benefit, **321**
cordillera (kawr-duhl-YER-uh) A mountain system made up of parallel ranges, **328**
core The inner, solid part of Earth, **28**
cork The bark stripped from a certain type of oak tree and often used as stoppers and insulation, **407**

Corn Belt The corn-growing region in the Midwest from central Ohio to central Nebraska, **245**
cosmopolitan Having many foreign influences, **424**
Cossacks Nomadic horsemen who once lived on the Ukrainian frontier, **509**
Counter-Reformation Attempt by the Catholic Church, following the Reformation, to return the Church to an emphasis on spiritual matters, **136**
coup (KOO) A sudden overthrow of a government by a small group of people, **369**
creoles American-born descendents of Europeans in Spanish South America, **368**
crop rotation A system of growing different crops on the same land over a period of years, **59**
Crusades A long series of battles starting in 1096 between the Christians of Europe and the Muslims to gain control of Palestine, **128**
crust The outer, solid layer of Earth, **28**
culture A learned system of shared beliefs and ways of doing things that guide a person's daily behavior, **75**
culture region Area of the world in which people share certain culture traits, **75**
culture traits Elements of culture, **75**
currents Giant streams of ocean water that move from warm to cold or from cold to warm areas, **41**
czar (ZAHR) Emperor of the Russian Empire, **488**

D

Dairy Belt Area including Wisconsin and most of Minnesota and Michigan which produces milk, cheese, and dairy products, **245**
deforestation The destruction or loss of forest area, **61**
deltas Landforms created by the deposits of sediment at the mouths of rivers, **32**
democracy A political system in which a country's people elect their leaders and rule by majority, **86**
desalinization The process in which the salt is taken out of seawater, **63**
desertification The long-term process of losing soil fertility and plant life, **60**
developed countries Industrialized countries that have strong secondary, tertiary, and quaternary industries, **84**
developing countries Countries in different stages of moving toward development, **84**
dialect A variation of a language, **406**
dictator One who rules a country with complete authority, **180, 316**
diffusion The movement of ideas or behaviors from one cultural region to another, **9**
direct democracy Government in which citizens take part in making all decisions, **116**
diversify To produce a variety of things, **242**
division of labor Organization of society in which each person performs a specific job, **106**
domestication The growing of a plant or taming of an animal by a people for their own use, **79**
dominion A territory or area of influence, **266**
droughts Periods when little rain falls and crops are damaged, **245**

E

earthquakes Sudden, violent movement along a fracture in the Earth's crust, **29**
ecology The study of connections among different forms of life, **51**
economic nationalism Putting the economic interests of one's own country above the interests of other countries, **186**
ecosystem All of the plants and animals in an area together with the nonliving parts of their environment, **54**
ecotourism The process of using an area's natural environment to attract tourists, **318**
ejidos (e-HEE-thohs) Lands owned and worked by groups of Mexican Indians, **300**
El Dorado (el duh-RAH-doh) "The Golden One," a legend of the early Chibcha people of Colombia, **330**
El Niño An ocean and weather pattern in the Pacific Ocean in which ocean waters become warmer, **364**
Emancipation Proclamation Lincoln's document that freed the slaves, **227**
emigrate Leave one's country to move to another, **166**
empire A system in which a central power controls a number of territories, **299**
encomienda A system in which Spanish monarchs gave land to Spanish colonists in the Americas; landowners could force Indians living there to work the land, **351**
Enlightenment An era of new ideas from the mid-1600s through the 1700s, **147**
entrepreneurs People who use their money and talents to start a business, **85**
epidemic Widespread outbreak, often referring to a disease, **299**
equinoxes The two days of the year when the Sun's rays strike the equator directly, **21**
erosion The movement by water, ice, or wind of rocky materials to another location, **32**
estuary A partially enclosed body of water where salty seawater and freshwater mix, **238, 345**
ethnic groups Cultural groups of people who share learned beliefs and practices, **75**
evaporation The process by which heated water becomes water vapor and rises into the air, **24**
extinct Something that dies out completely; is no longer present, **51**

F

factors of production The natural resources, money, labor, and capital needed for business operation, **85, 160**

factory A large building to house workers and their equipment, **160**

famine A great shortage of food, **440**

fascism A political movement that puts the needs of the nation above the needs of the individual, **180**

fault A fractured surface in Earth's crust where a mass of rock is in motion, **31**

favelas (fah-VE-lahs) Huge slums that surround some Brazilian cities, **349**

feudalism A system after the 900s under which most of Europe was organized and governed by local leaders based on land and service, **127**

fief A grant of land, **127**

fjords (fee-AWRDS) Narrow, deep inlets of the sea set between high, rocky cliffs, **432**

floodplain A landform of level ground built by sediment deposited by a river or stream, **32**

food chain A series of organisms in which energy is passed along, **51**

fossil fuels Nonrenewable resources formed from the remains of ancient plants and animals, **68**

free enterprise An economic system in which people, not government, decide what to make, sell, or buy, **85**

front The unstable weather where a large amount of warm air meets a large amount of cold air, **40**

frontier Unsettled land, **224**

G

gauchos (GOW-chohz) Argentine cowboys, **351**

genocide The planned killing of a race of people, **190**

geography The study of Earth's physical and cultural features, **3**

geothermal energy A renewable energy resource produced from the heat of Earth's interior, **70**

geysers Hot springs that shoot hot water and steam into the air, **446**

glaciers Large, slow-moving sheets or rivers of ice, **33**

glen A Scottish term for a valley, **437**

global warming A slow increase in Earth's average temperature, **64**

globalization Process in which connections around the world increase and cultures around the world share similar practices, **199**

Good Neighbor Policy Franklin D. Roosevelt's plan for the United States to cooperate with Latin American countries without interfering with their governments, **185**

Great Depression Period after the Stock Market crashed in 1929 when worldwide business slowed down, banks closed, prices and wages dropped, and many people were out of work, **179**

greenhouse effect The process by which Earth's atmosphere traps heat, **38**

gross domestic product The value of all goods and services produced within a country, **83**

gross national product The value of all goods and services that a country produces in one year within or outside the country, **83**

groundwater The water from rainfall, rivers, lakes, and melting snow that seeps into the ground, **25**

guerrilla An armed person who takes part in irregular warfare, such as raids, **321**

H

habitation fog A fog caused by fumes and smoke trapped over Siberian cities by very cold weather, **496**

haciendas (hah see-EN-duhs) Huge farmlands granted by the Spanish monarch to favored people in Spain's colonies, **300**

heavy industry Industry that usually involves manufacturing based on metals, **494**

hieroglyphics A form of ancient writing that uses pictures and symbols, **112**

history A written record of human civilization, **107**

Holocaust The mass murder of millions of Jews and other people by the Nazis in World War II, **190, 419**

hominid An early human like creature, **103**

homogeneous Sharing the same characteristics, such as ethnicity, **515**

human geography The study of people, past or present, **11**

humanists Scholars of the Renaissance who studied history, poetry, grammar, and other subjects taught in ancient Greece and Rome, **132**

humus Decayed plant and animal matter, **55**

hurricanes Tropical storms that bring violent winds, heavy rain, and high seas, **48**

hydroelectric power A renewable energy resource produced from dams that harness the energy of falling water to power generators, **70**

I

icebreakers Ships that can break up the ice of frozen waterways, allowing other ships to pass through them, **500**

impressionism A form of art that developed in France in the late 1800s and early 1900s, **417**

indentured servants People who agree to work for a certain period of time, often in exchange for travel expenses, **337**

indigo (IN-di-goh) A plant used to make a deep blue dye, **334**

individualism A belief in the political and economic independence of individuals, **148**

Indo-European A language family that includes many languages of Europe, such as Germanic, Baltic, and Slavic languages, **454**

Industrial Revolution Period that lasted through the 1700s and 1800s when advances in industry, business, transportation, and communications changed people's lives in almost every way, **159**
inflation The rise in prices that occurs when currency loses its buying power, **304**
Inuit North American Eskimos, **273**
irrigation A system of bringing water from rivers to fields through ditches and canals to water crops, **105**
isthmus A neck of land connecting two larger land areas, **28**

J

junta (HOOHN-tuh) A small group of military officers who rule a country after seizing power, **373**

K

knight A nobleman who serves as a professional warrior, **127**

L

land bridges Strips of dry land between continents caused by sea levels dropping, **104**
landforms The shapes of land on Earth's surface, **28**
landlocked Completely surrounded by land, with no direct access to the ocean, **356, 520**
lava Magma that has broken through the crust to Earth's surface, **29**
levees Large walls, usually made of dirt, built along rivers to prevent flooding, **10**
light industry Industry that focuses on the production of lightweight goods, such as clothing, **494**
lignite A soft form of coal, **453**
limited government Government in which government leaders are held accountable by citizens through their constitutions and democratic processes, **86**
limited monarchy Monarchy in which the powers of the king were limited by law, **141**
literacy The ability to read and write, **166**
Llaneros (lah-NE-rohs) Cowboys of the Venezuelan Llanos, **336**
Llanos (LAH-nohs) A plains region in eastern Columbia and western Venezuela, **328**
lochs Scottish lakes located in valleys carved by glaciers, **432**
loess (LES) Fine, windblown soil that is good for farming, **413**
Loyalists Colonists loyal to Great Britain, **152**

M

magma Melted rock in the upper mantle of Earth, **28**
mainland A region or country's main landmass, **394**
manors Large farm estates developed by nobles, **128**
mantle The liquid layer that surrounds Earth's core, **28**
maquiladoras (mah-kee-lah-DORH-ahs) Foreign-owned factories located along Mexico's northern border with the United States, **307**
maritime On or near the sea, such as Canada's Maritime Provinces, **270**
market economy An economy in which consumers help determine what is to be produced by buying or not buying certain goods and services, **85**
mass production System of producing large numbers of identical items, **163**
medieval Refers to the period from the collapse of the Roman Empire to about 1500, **415**
megalopolis A string of cities that have grown together, **236**
mercantilism Economic theory using colonies to increase a nation's wealth by gaining access to labor and natural resources, **139**
Mercosur A trade organization that includes Argentina, Brazil, Paraguay, Uruguay, and two associate members (Bolivia and Chile), **354**
merengue The national music and dance of the Dominican Republic, **320**
mestizos (me-STEE-zohs) People of mixed European and American Indian ancestry, **300**
metallic minerals Shiny minerals, like gold and iron, that can conduct heat and electricity, **65**
meteorology The field of forecasting and reporting rainfall, temperatures, and other atmospheric conditions, **13**
Métis (may-TEES) People of mixed European and Canadian Indian ancestry in Canada, **267**
middle class Class of skilled workers between the upper class and poor and unskilled workers, **129, 164**
migrated To move from one region or climate to another, **110**
militarism Use of strong armies and the threat of force to gain power, **173**
minerals Inorganic substances that make up Earth's crust, occur naturally, are solids in crystalline form, and have a definite chemical composition, **65**
missions Spanish church outposts established during the colonial era, particularly in the Americas, **300**
monarchy A territory ruled by a king who has total power to govern, **141**
monsoon The seasonal shift of air flow and rainfall, which brings alternating wet and dry seasons, **45**
Moors Muslim North Africans, **405**
moraine A ridge of rocks, gravel, and sand piled up by a glacier, **237**
mosaics (moh-ZAY-iks) Pictures created from tiny pieces of colored stone, **398**
mosques Islamic houses of worship, **526**

mulattoes (muh-LA-tohs) People of mixed European and African ancestry, **300**
multicultural A mixture of different cultures within the same country or community, **75**

N

national parks Large scenic areas of natural beauty preserved by the United States government for public use, **252**
nationalism The demand for self-rule and a strong feeling of loyalty to one's nation, **169, 426**
NATO North Atlantic Treaty Organization, a military alliance of various European countries, the United States, and Canada, **194, 415**
nature reserves Areas a government has set aside to protect animals, plants, soil, and water, **506**
navigable Water routes that are deep enough and wide enough to be used by ships, **412**
neutral Not taking a side in a dispute or conflict, **444**
New Deal Franklin D. Roosevelt's program to help end the Great Depression, **179**
newsprint Cheap paper used mainly for newspapers, **263**
nobles People who were born into wealthy, powerful families, **127**
nomads People who often move from place to place, **104, 522**
nonmetallic minerals Minerals that lack the characteristics of metal, **66**
nonrenewable resources Resources, such as coal and oil, that cannot be replaced by Earth's natural processes or that are replaced very slowly, **65**
North Atlantic Drift A warm ocean current that brings mild temperatures and rain to parts of northern Europe, **433**
nutrients Substances promoting growth, **52**

O

oasis A place in the desert where a spring or well provides water, **520**
oil shale Layered rock that yields oil when heated, **453**
oppression Cruel and unjust use of power against others, **154**
orbit The path an object makes around a central object, such as a planet around the Sun, **17**
ozone A form of oxygen in the atmosphere that helps protect Earth from harmful solar radiation, **22**

P

Pampas A wide, grassy plains region in central Argentina, **344**
Pangaea (pan-GEE-uh) Earth's single, original supercontinent from which today's continents were separated, **31**
pardos Venezuelans of mixed African, European, and South American Indian ancestry, **336**
Parliament An English assembly made up of nobles, clergy, and common people which had the power to pass and enforce laws, **141**
partition To divide a land area into smaller parts, **195**
Patriots Colonists who wanted independence from British rule, **152**
peat Matter made from dead plants, usually mosses, **442**
peninsula Land bordered by water on three sides, **28**
permafrost The layer of soil that stays frozen all year in tundra climate regions, **49**
perspective Point of view based on a person's experience and personal understanding, **3**
Peru Current A cold ocean current off the coast of western South America, **363**
petroleum An oily liquid that can be refined into gasoline and other fuels and oils, **68**
photosynthesis The process by which plants convert sunlight into chemical energy, **51**
physical geography The study of Earth's natural landscape and physical systems, including the atmosphere, **11**
pidgin languages Simple languages that help people who speak different languages understand each other, **337**
pioneers Settlers who lead the way into new areas, **225**
plain A nearly flat area on Earth's surface, **28**
plantains A type of banana used in cooking, **322**
plantations Large farms that grow mainly one crop to sell, **223**
plant communities Groups of plants that live in the same area, **53**
plant succession The gradual process by which one group of plants replaces another, **54**
plateau An elevated flatland on Earth's surface, **28**
plate tectonics The theory that Earth's surface is divided into several major, slowly moving plates or pieces, **28**
police state A country in which the government has total control over the people using the police, **180**
pope The bishop of Rome and the head of the Roman Catholic Church, **401**
popular sovereignty Governmental principle based on just laws and on a government created by and subject to the will of the people, **149**
population density The average number of people living within a square mile or square kilometer, **81**
potash A mineral used to make fertilizer, **263**
precipitation The process by which water falls back to Earth, **24**
prehistory A time before written records, **103**
primary industries Economic activities that directly involve natural resources or raw materials, such as farming and mining, **83**
Protestants Christians who broke away from the Catholic Church during the Reformation, **135**
provinces Administrative divisions of a country, **266**

Pueblo A group of North American Indians who built houses with adobe, **111**
pulp Softened wood fibers used to make paper, **263**
Puritan Member of a group of Protestants who rebelled against the Church of England, **141**

Q

quaternary industries Economic activities that include specialized skills or knowledge and work mostly with information, **83**
Quechua (KE-chuh-wuh) The language of South America's Inca; still spoken in the region, **370**
quinoa (KEEN-wah) A native plant of South America's Andean region that yields nutritious seeds, **365**
quipu (KEE-poo) Complicated system of knots tied on strings of various colors, used by the Inca of South America to record information, **113, 366**

R

race A group of people who share inherited physical or biological traits, **76**
rain shadow The dry area on the leeward side of a mountain or mountain range, **44**
ratified An approval (of the Constitution by the states), **225**
reactionaries People who want to return to an earlier political system, **158**
reason Logical thinking, **148**
refineries Factories where crude oil is processed, **68**
reforestation The planting of trees in places where forests have been cut down, **61**
reform Making something better by removing its faults, **168**
Reformation A movement in Europe to reform Christianity in the 1500s, **135, 418**
refugees People who flee to another country, usually for economic or political reasons, **321**
reggae A type of music with origins in Jamaica, **320**
regionalism The stronger connection to one's region than to one's country, **269**
Reign of Terror Period from 1789 to 1794 when thousands of people died at the guillotine in France, **156**
relative location The position of a place in relation to another place, **7**
Renaissance (re-nuh-SAHNS) French word meaning "rebirth" and referring to a new era of learning that began in Europe in the 1300s, **131, 401**
renewable resources Resources, such as soils and forests, that can be replaced by Earth's natural processes, **59**
republic Government in which voters elect leaders to run the state, **118**
Restoration The reign of Charles II in English history in which the monarchy was restored to power, **142**
revolution One complete orbit around the Sun, **19**
revolutionaries Rebels demanding self-rule, **184**
Roma An ethnic group also known as Gypsies who are descended from people who may have migrated from India to Europe long ago, **464**
rotation One complete spin of Earth on its axis, **19**
rural An area of open land that is often used for farming, **4**

S

Santería A religion, with origins in Cuba, that mixes West African religions and traditions with those of Roman Catholicism, **320**
satellite A body that orbits a larger body, **18**
scarcity Situation that occurs when demand is greater than supply, **87**
Scientific Revolution The period during the 1500s and 1600s when mathematics and scientific instruments were used to learn more about the natural world, **137**
secede To separate from, **227**
secondary industries Economic activities that change raw materials created by primary industries into finished products, **83**
second-growth forests The trees that cover an area after the original forest has been cut, **238**
secularism Playing down the importance of religion, **148**
sediment Small bits of mud, sand, or gravel which collect at the river's mouth, **241**
selvas The thick tropical rain forests of eastern Ecuador, eastern Peru, and northern Bolivia, **363**
semiarid Relatively dry with small amounts of rain, **62**
serfs People who were bound to the land and worked for a lord, **128, 509**
sinkholes A steep-sided depression formed when the roof of a cave collapses, **294**
sirocco (suh-RAH-koh) A hot, dry wind from North Africa that blows across the Mediterranean to Europe, **395**
slash-and-burn agriculture A type of agriculture in which forests are cut and burned to clear land for planting, **307**
smelters Factories that process metal ores, **495**
smog A mixture of smoke, chemicals, and fog, **306**
social contract Idea that government should be based on an agreement made by the people, **149**
soil exhaustion The loss of soil nutrients needed by plants, **346**
solar energy A renewable energy resource produced from the Sun's heat and light, **71**
solar system The Sun and the objects that move about it, including planets, moons, and asteroids, **17**
solstice The days when the Sun's vertical rays are farthest from the equator, **21**
soviet A council of Communists who governed republics and other places in the Soviet Union, **509**

spatial perspective Point of view based on looking at where something is and why it is there, **3**
steppe (STEP) A wide, flat grasslands region that stretches from Ukraine across southern Russia to Kazakhstan, **485**
steppe climate A dry climate type generally found between desert and wet climate regions, **46**
stock market An organization through which shares of stock in companies are bought and sold, **178**
strait A narrow passageway that connects two large bodies of water, **362**
strip mining A kind of coal mining in parts of the Great Plains which strips away soil and rock, **252**
subduction The movement of one of Earth's heavier tectonic plates underneath a lighter tectonic plate, **29**
subregions Small areas of a region, **8**
subsistence agriculture A type of farming in which farmers grow just enough food to provide for themselves and their own families, **80**
suburbs Areas just outside or near a city, **167**
suffragettes Women who fought for all women's right to vote, **168**
superpowers Powerful countries, **489**
symbol A word, shape, color, flag, or other sign that stands for something else, **77**

T

taiga (TY-guh) A forest of evergreen trees growing south of the tundra of Russia, **485**
tepees Tents that are usually made of animal skins, **110**
tepuís (tay-PWEEZ) Layers of sandstone that have resisted erosion atop plateaus in the Guiana Highlands, **328**
terraces Horizontal ridges built into the slopes of steep hillsides to prevent soil loss and aid farming, **60**
tertiary industries Economic activities that handle goods that are ready to be sold to consumers, **83**
textiles Cloth products, **435**
traditional economy Economy based on custom and tradition, **85**
tributary Any smaller stream or river that flows into a larger stream or river, **25**
Tropic of Cancer The line of latitude that is 23.5° north of the equator, **21**
Tropic of Capricorn The line of latitude that is 23.5° south of the equator, **21**
tundra climate A cold region with low rainfall, lying generally between subarctic and polar climate regions, **49**
typhoons Tropical storms that bring violent winds, heavy rain, and high seas, **48**

U

U-boats German submarines from World War I, **174**
uninhabitable Not capable of supporting human settlement, **446**
unlimited governments Governments that have total control over their citizens, **86**
urban An area that contains a city, **4**

V

vassals People who held land from a feudal lord and received protection in return for service to the lord, especially in battle, **127**
vernacular Everyday speech which varies from place to place, **130**
viceroy The governor of a colony, **368**

W

water cycle The circulation of water from Earth's surface to the atmosphere and back, **23**
water vapor The gaseous form of water, **23**
weather The condition of the atmosphere at a given place and time, **37**
weathering The process of breaking rocks into smaller pieces through heat, water, or other means, **31**
wetlands Land areas that are flooded for at least part of the year, **241**
Wheat Belt The wheat-growing area in the United States which stretches across the Dakotas, Montana, Nebraska, Kansas, Oklahoma, Colorado, and Texas, **251**
working class Unskilled and semi-skilled workers with low-paying jobs, **165**

Y

yurt A movable round house of wool felt mats over a wood frame, **526**

SPANISH GLOSSARY

Phonetic Respelling and Pronunciation Guide

Many of the key terms in this textbook have been respelled to help you pronounce them. The letter combinations used in the respelling throughout the narrative are explained in this phonetic respelling and pronunciation guide. The guide is adapted from *Webster's Tenth New College Dictionary, Merriam-Webster's New Geographical Dictionary,* and *Merriam-Webster's New Biographical Dictionary.*

MARK	AS IN	RESPELLING	EXAMPLE
a	alphabet	a	*AL-fuh-bet
ā	Asia	ay	AY-zhuh
ä	cart, top	ah	KAHRT, TAHP
e	let, ten	e	LET, TEN
ē	even, leaf	ee	EE-vuhn, LEEF
i	it, tip, British	i	IT, TIP, BRIT-ish
ī	site, buy, Ohio	y	SYT, BY, oh-HY-oh
	iris	eye	EYE-ris
k	card	k	KAHRD
ō	over, rainbow	oh	OH-vuhr, RAYN-boh
u̇	book, wood	ooh	BOOHK, WOOHD
ȯ	all, orchid	aw	AWL, AWR-kid
ȯi	foil, coin	oy	FOYL, KOYN
au̇	out	ow	OWT
ə	cup, butter	uh	KUHP, BUHT-uhr
ü	rule, food	oo	ROOL, FOOD
yü	few	yoo	FYOO
zh	vision	zh	VIZH-uhn

**A syllable printed in small capital letters receives heavier emphasis than the other syllable(s) in a word.*

A

abdicated/abdicar Renunciar al trono, **488**
abolitionist/abolicionista Persona que desea terminar con la esclavitud, **227**
absolute authority/autoridad absoluta Poder de un rey o reina para tomar todas las decisiones de gobierno, **141**
absolute location/posición exacta Lugar exacto de la tierra donde se localiza un punto, por lo general definido en términos de latitud y longitud, **7**
acculturation/aculturación Proceso de asimilación de una cultura a largo plazo por el contacto con otra sociedad, **77**
acid rain/lluvia ácida Tipo de lluvia contaminada que se produce cuando partículas de contaminación del aire se combinan con el vapor de agua de la atmósfera, **64**
Age of Exploration/Edad de la exploración Periodo en que los europeos estaban ansiosos por hallar rutas nuevas y más cortas para comerciar con la India y China, **138**
aggression/agresión Acción militar, **187**
agrarian/agrario Sociedad basada en la agricultura, **515**
air pressure/presión atmosférica Peso del aire, se mide con un barómetro, **39**
alliance/alianza Acuerdo entre diferentes países para respaldarse los temas de interès y las causas, **152**
allies/aliados Países que se apoyan entre sí para defenderse de sus enemigos, **489**
alluvial fan/abanico aluvial Accidente geográfico en forma de abanico que se origina por la acumulación de sedimentos en la base de una montaña, **32**
amber/ámbar Savia de árbol fosilizada, **453**
Antarctic Circle/círculo antártico Meridiano localizado a 66.5° al sur del ecuador, **20**
anti-Semitism/antisemitismo Sentimiento de rechazo hacia los judíos, **190**
aqueducts/acueductos Canales artificiales usados para transportar agua, **62, 120**
aquifers/acuíferos Capas subterráneas de roca, arena y grava en las que se almacena el agua, **62**
archipelago/archpiélago Grupo grande de islas, **312**
Arctic Circle/círculo ártico Meridiano localizado a 66.5° al norte del ecuador, **20**
arid/árido Territorio done la lluvia es muy escasa, **46**
armistice/armisticio Tregua, **176**
arms race/carrera armamentista Competencia entre países para producir y tener armas más avanzadas, **194**
atmosphere/atmósfera Capa de gases que rodea a la tierra, **22**
axis/eje Línea imaginaria que corre del polo norte al polo sur, pasando por el centro de la Tierra, **19**

B

badlands/tierras de baldío Terrenos irregulares de roca blanda y escasa vegetación o poco suelo, **249**
balance of power/equilibrio de poder Condición que surge cuando varios países o alianzas mantienen niveles tan similares de poder evitar guerras, **157**
bankrupt/bancarrota Sin dinero, **179**

barrier islands/islas de barrera Islas costeras formadas por depósitos de arema arrastrada por las mareas y las corrientes de aguas poco profundas, **241**
basins/cuencas Regiones rodeadas por montañas u otras tierras altas, **219**
bauxite/bauxita El mineral con contenido de aluminio más importante, **313**
bloc/bloque Grupo de naciones unidas por una idea o un propósito común, **193**
bog/ciénaga Tierra suave, humedecida por el agua, **442**

C

cacao/cacas Árbol pequeño que produce los granos de cacao, **316**
caldera/caldera Depresión grande formada por la erupción y explosión de un volcán, **255**
calypso/calipso Tipo de música originado en Trinidad y Tobago, **320**
cantons/cantones Distritos políticos y administrativos de Suiza, **425**
capital/capital Dinero ganado, ahorrado e invertido para conseguir ganancias, **160**
capitalism/capitalismo Sistema económico en el que los negocios, las industrias y los recursos son de propiedad privada, **163**
caravans/caravanas Grupos de personas que viajan juntas por razones de seguridad, **522**
cardamom/cardamomo Especia que se usa en Asia para condimentar alimentos, **317**
carrying capacity/capacidad de carga Número máximo de especies que puede haber en una zona determinada, **89**
cartography/cartografía Arte y ciencia de la elaboración de mapas, **13**
cash crops/cultivos para la venta Cultivos producidos para su venta y no para consumo del agricultor, **305**
cassava/mandioca Planta tropical de raíces almidonades, **332**
cathedrals/catedrales Iglesias grandes, **128**
caudillos/caudillos Líderes militares que gobernaron Venezuela en los siglos XIX y XX, **335**
center-pivot irrigation/irrigación de pivote central Tipo de riego que usa aspersores montadios en grandes ruedas giratorias, **251**
chancellor/canciller jefe de gobierno o primer ministro alemán, **419**
***chinampas*/chinampas** Nombre dado por los aztecas a los campos elevados que usaban como tierras de cultivo, **298**
chinooks/chinooks Vientos cálidos y fuertes que soplan de las montañas Rocosas hacia las Grandes Planicies, **250**
chivalry/caballerosidad Código o sistema medieval de cavellería, **127**
city-states/ciudades estado Ciudades con un sistema de autogobierno, como en la antigua Grecia, **116, 396**
civilians/paisanos Los que no pertenecen a los militares, **191**
civil war/guerra civil conflicto entre dos o más grupos dentro de un país, **317**
civilization/civilización Cultura altamente compleja con grandes ciudades y abundante actividad económica, **80**
clergy/clérigo Oficiante de la Iglesia, **128**
climate/clima condiciones meteorológicas registradas en un periodo largo, **37**
climatology/climatología Registro de los sistemas atmosféricos de la Tierra, **13**
cloud forest/bosque nuboso Bosque tropical de gran elevación y humedad donde los bancos de nubes son muy comunes, **313**
coalition governments/gobiernos de coalición Gobiernos en los que la administración del país es regida por varios partidos políticos a la vez, **401**
Cold War/guerra fría Rivalidad entre Estados Unidos y la Unión Soviética que se extendió de la década de 1940 a la década de 1990, **489**
collective farms/fincas colectivas Tierras mancomunadas en grandes fincas, donde las personas trabajan juntas como un grupo, **181**
colony/colonia Territorio controlado por personas de otro país, **139**
command economy/economía autoritaria Economía en la que el gobierno es propietario de la mayor parte de las industrias y toma la mayoría de las decisiones en materia de economía, **85**
commercial agriculture/agricultura comercial Tipo de agricultura cuya producción es exclusiva para la venta, **80**
commonwealth/mancomunidad Territorio autogobernado que mantiene una sociedad con otro país, **323**
communism/comunismo Sistema politica y económico en el cual los gobiernos poseen los medios de producción y controlan el planeamiento de la economia, **85, 180, 192**
condensation/condensación Proceso mediante el cual el agua cambia de estado gaseoso y forma pequeñas gotas, **24**
conquistadores/conquistadores Españoles que participaron en la colonización de América, **299**
constitution/constitución Documento que contiene las leyes y principios básicos que gobiernan una nación, **142**
constitutional monarchy/monarquía constitucional Gobierno que cuenta con un monarca como jefe de estado y un parlamento o grupo legislador similar para la aprobación de leyes, **435**
consumer goods/bienes de consumo Productos usados en la vida cotidiana, **489**
contiguous/contiguo Unidades de territorio (como los estados) que colindan entre sí, **218**
Continental Divide/divisoria continental Cordillera que divide los ríos de Estados Unidos en dos partes: los que fluyen al este y los que fluyen al oeste, **219**
continental shelf/plataforma continental zona costera de pendiente suave que bordea a todos los continentes, **25**
continents/continentes Grandes masas de territorio sobre la Tierra, **29**
cooperatives/cooperativas Organizaciones creadas por los propietarios de una empresa y operados para beneficio propio, **321**
cordillera/cordillera Sistema montañoso de cordilleras paralelas, **328**
core/núcleo Parte sólida del interior de la Tierra, **28**
cork/corcho Corteza extraída de cierto tipo de roble, usada principalmente como material de bloqueo y aislante, **407**
Corn Belt/región maicera Región del medio oeste de Estados Unidos, de Ohio a Iowa, cuya actividad agrícola se basa en el cultivo del maíz, **245**
cosmopolitan/cosmopolita Que tiene influencia de muchas culturas, **424**
Cossacks/cosacos Arrieros nómadas que habitaban en la región fronteriza de Ucrania, **509**
Counter-Reformation/Contrareforma Intento de la Iglesia Católica, luego de la Reforma, por devolver a la Iglesia a un énfasis en asuntos espirituales, **136**

coup/golpe de estado Ataque repentino de un grupo reducido de personas para derrocar a un gobierno, **369**
creoles/criollos Personas de descendencia europea nacidas en la América colonial, **368**
crop rotation/rotación de cultivos Sistema agrícola en el que se siembran productos differentes en periodos específicos, **59**
Crusades/Cruzadas Expediciones hecas por los cristianos para recuperar la Tierra Santa de los musulmanes, **128**
crust/coteza Capa sólida de la superficie de la Tierra, **28**
culture/cultura Sistema de creencias y costumbres comunes que guía la conducta cotidiana de las personas, **75**
culture region/región cultural Región del mundo en la que se comparten ciertos rasgos culturales, **75**
culture traits/rasgos culturales Características de una cultura, **75**
currents/corrientes Enormes corrientes del océano que transportan agua tibia a las regiones frías y viceversa, **41**
czar/zar Emperador ruso, **488**

D

Dairy Belt/región lechera Región del medio oeste de Estados Unidos, al norte de la franja del maíz, donde la elaboración de productos lácteos es una importante actividad económica, **245**
deforestation/deforestación Destrucción o pérdida de un área boscosa, **61**
deltas/deltas Formaciones creadas por la acumulación de sedimentos en las desembocadura de los ríos, **32**
democracy/democracia Sistema político en el que l a población elige a sus líderes mediante el voto de mayoría, **86**
desalinization/desalinización Proceso mediante el cual se extrae la sal del agua de mar, **63**
desertification/desertificación Proceso a largo plazo en el que el suelo pierde su fertilidad y vegetación, **60**
developed countries/países desarrollados Países industrializados que cuentan con industrias primarias, secundarias, terciarias y cuaternarias, **84**
developing countries/países en vaís de desarrollo países que se encuentran en alguna etapa de su proceso de desarrollo, **84**
dialect/dialecto Variación de un idioma, **406**
dictator/dictadore Persona que ejercen total autoridad sobre un gobierno, **180, 316**
diffusion/difusión Extensión de ideas o conducta de una región cultura a otra, **9**
direct democracy/democracia directa Forma de democracia en la que todos los ciudadanos participan directamente en la toma de decisiones, **116**
diversify/diversificar En la agircultura, se refiere a la siembra de varios productos y uno solo, **242**
division of labor/división de labores Caracterísra de las civilizaciones en la cual diferentes personas realizan diferentes trabajos, **106**
domestication/domesticación Cuidado de una planta o animal para uso personal, **79**
dominion/dominio Territorio en el que se ejerce una influencia, **266**
droughts/sequías Periodos en los que los cultivos sufren daños debido a la escasez de lluvia, **245**

E

earthquakes/terremotos Movimientos repentinos y fuertes que se producen en las fisuras de la superficie de la tierra, **29**
ecology/ecología Estudio de las relacions entre las diversas formas de vida del planeta, **51**
economic nationalism/nacionalismo económico Política económica que usa una nación para tratar de mejorar su economía, por medio de limites en el comercio, **186**
ecosystem/ecosistema Conjunto de plantas y animales que habitan una región, junto con los elementos no vivos de ese entorno, **54**
ecotourism/ecoturismo Uso de regiones naturales para atraer visitantes, **318**
ejidos/ejidos Territorios de cultivo propiedad de los indígenas de México, **300**
El Dorado/El Dorado leyenda que habla de los chibchas, antiguos habitantes de Colombia, **330**
El Niño/El Niño Patrón oceánico y climatológico del océano Pacífico que elevó la temperatura del agua en dicho océano, **364**
Emancipation Proclamation/Proclama de Emancipación Decreto emitido por el presidente Abraham Lincoln en 1863 que acabó efectivamente con la esclavitud, a final de la Guerra Civil, **227**
emigrate/emigrar Dejar un país para ir a otro, **166**
empire/imperio Sistema cuyo gobierno central controla diversos territorios, **299**
encomienda/encomienda Sistema mediante el cual los monarcas españoles cedían territorios de América a los colonizadores de su país, quienes obligaban a los indígenas de esas dichas tierras a trabajar para ganarse el susteno, **351**
Enlightenment/Ilustración Período en los años 1700, cuando los filósofos creían que podían aplicar el método cientifico y el uso de la razón para explicar de manera lógica la naturaleza humana, **147**
entrepeneurs/empresarios Personas que usan su dinero y su talento para iniciar un negocio, **85**
epidemic/epidemia Expansión vasta, por general de una enfermedad, **299**
equinoxes/equinoccios Los dos días del año en que los rayos de sol caen directamente sobre el ecuador, **21**
erosion/erosión Desplazamiento de agua, hielo, viento o minerales a otro lugar, **32**
estuary/estuario Cuerpo de agua parcialmente cerrado en el que el agua de mar se combina con ague dulce, **238, 345**
ethnic groups/grupos étnicos Grupos culturales que comparten creencias y prácticas comunes, **75**
evaporation/evaporación Proceso mediante el cual el agua se convierte en vapor y se eleva en el aire, **24**
extinct/extinto Que deja de existir por completo, **51**

F

factors of production/factores de producción Los recursos naturales, el dinero, el trabajo y los empresarios que se necesitan para las operaciones de negocios, **85, 160**
factory/factoría Fábrica o conjunto de fábricas donde se elabora o produce algún producto, **160**
famine/hambruna Gran escasez de alimeno, **440**

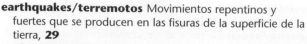

fascism/fascismo Teoría politica que demanda la creación de un gobierno fuerte encabezado por un solo individuo donde el estado sea más importante que el individuo, **180**

fault/falla Fractura de la superficie de la tierra que causa el movimiento de grandes masas de rocas, **31**

favelas/favelas Grandes poblaciones localizadas en los alrededores de algunas ciudades brasileñas, **349**

feudalism/feudalismo Sistema de gobierno local basado en la concesión de tierras como pago por lealtad, ayuda militar y otros servicios, **127**

fief/feudo Concesión de tierras de un amo a su vasayo, **127**

fjords/fiordos Grietas estrechas y profundas localizadas entre altos acantilados donde se acumula el agua de mar, **432**

floodplain/llanura aluvial Especie de plataforma a nivel de la tierra, formada por la acumulación de los sedimentos de una corriente de agua, **32**

food chain/cadena alimenticia Serie de organismos que proveen alimento y energía unos o otros, **51**

fossil fuels/combustibles fósiles Recursos no renovables formados por restos muy antiguos de plantas y animales, **68**

free enterprise/libre empresa Sistema económico en el que las personas, y no el gobierno, deciden qué productos fabrican, venden y compran, **85**

front/frente Inestabilidad climatológica en la que una gran masa de aire tibio choca con una gran masa de aire frío, **40**

frontier/región fronteriza Terreno despoblado, **224**

G

gauchos/gauchos Arrieros argentinos, **351**

genocide/genocidio Aniquilamiento intencional de un pueblo, **190**

geography/geografía Estudio de las características físicas y culturales de la Tierra, **3**

geothermal energy/energía geotérmica Fuente energética no removable producida por el calor del interior de la tierra, **70**

geysers/géiseres Manantiales que lanzan chorros de agua caliente y vapor a gran altura, **446**

glaciers/glaciares Grandes bloques de hielo que se desplazan con lenitud sobre el agua, **33**

glen/glen Término de origen escocés que se sinónimo de valle, **437**

global warming/calentamiento global Aumento lento y constante de la temperatura de la Tierra, **64**

globalization/globalización Proceso mediante el que as comunicaciones alrededor del mundo se han incrementado haciendo a las culturas más parecidas, **199**

Good Neighbor Policy/Política de Buen Vecino Política esta dounidense durante los año 30, que promulga la cooperación entre las naciones de América Latina, **185**

Great Depression/Gran Depresión Depresión mundial a principios de los años 1930, cuando los salarios cayeron, la actividad comercial bajó y hubo mucho desempleo, **179**

greenhouse effect/efecto invernadero Proceso mediante el cual la atmósfera terrestre atrapa el calor de su superficie, **38**

gross domestic product/producto interno bruto Valor de todos los bienes y servicios producidos en un país, **83**

gross national product/producto nacional bruto Valor de todos los bienes y servicios producidos en un año por un país, dentro o fuera de sus límites, **83**

groundwater/agua subterránea Agua de lluva, ríos, lagos y nieve derretida que se filtra al subsuelo, **25**

guerrilla/guerrillero Persona armada que participa en una lucha armada irregular (los ataques sorpresa, por ejemplo), **321**

H

habitation fog/humo residente Especie de niebla producida por el humo atrapado en la atmósfera de las cuidades siberianas debido al intenso frío, **496**

haciendas/haciendas Granjas de gran tamaño cedidas por los monarcas españoles a los colonizadores de América, **300**

heavy industry/industra pesada Industria basada en la manufactura de metales, **494**

hieroglyphics Forma antigua de escritura con imágenes y símbolos usados para registrar información, **112**

history/historia Registro escrito de la civilización humana, **107**

Holocaust/haulocausto Asesinato masivo de millones de judíos y personas de otros grupos a manos. de los nazis durante la Segunda Guerra Mundial, **190, 419**

hominid/homínido Primera criatura similares al hombre, **103**

homogeneous/homogéneo Agrupamiento que comparte ciertas características, como el origin étnico, **515**

human geography/geografía humana estudio del pasado y presente de la humanidad, **11**

humanists/humanistas Filósofos del Renacimiento que hacían énfasis en la individualidad, los logros personales y la razón, **132**

humus/humus Materia vegetal o animal en descomposición, **55**

hurricanes/huracanes Tormentas tropicales con intensos vientos, fuertes lluvias y altas mareas, **48**

hydroelectric power/energía hidroeléctrica Fuente energética renovable producida en generadores impulsados por caídas de agua, **70**

I

icebreakers/rompehielos Barcos que rompen la capa de hielo que se forma en la superficie de algunos cuerpos de agua para permitir el paso de otras embarcaciones, **500**

impressionism/impresionismo Forma de arte desarrollada en Francia a finales del siglo XIX y principios del siglo XX, **417**

indentured servants/trabajadores por contrato Personas que trabajan por un tiempo determinado, en la mayoría de los casos a cambio de gastos de viaje, **337**

indigo/índigo Planta que se usa para fabricar un tinte de color azul oscuro, **334**

individualism/individualismo Creencia en la independencia económica y política de los individuos, **148**

Indo-European/Indoeuropeo Familia que incluye muchos idiomas europeos como el germánico, el báltico y los dialectos eslavos, **454**

Industrial Revolution/Revolución Industrial Cambios producidos a principios de los años 1700, cuando las maquinarias empezaban a hacer mucho del trabajo que las personas tenían que hacer antes, **159**

inflation/inflación Aumento de los precios que ocurre cuando la moneda de un país pierde poder adquisitivo, **304**

Inuit/inuit Tribu esquimal de América del norte, **273**
irrigation/riego Proceso mediante el cual el agua se hace llegar a los cultivos de manera artificial, **105**
isthmus/istmo Franja de tierra que conecta dos áreas de mayor tamaño, **28**

J

junta/junta Grupo de oficiales militares que asumen el control de un país al derrocar al poder anterior, **373**

K

knight/caballero Guerrero profesional noble, **127**

L

land bridges/puentes de terreno Franjas de terreno seco que conecta grandes masas de tierra, **104**
landforms/accidentes geográficos Forma de la tierra en differentes partes de la superficie, **28**
landlocked/sin salida al mar Zona rodeada de agua por completo y sin acceso directo al océano, **356, 520**
lava/lava Magma que emerge del interior de la tierra por un orificio de la corteza, **29**
levees/diques Paredes altas, por lo general de tierra, que se construyen a la orilla de un río para prevenir inundaciones, **10**
light industry/indutria ligera Industria que se enfoca en la manufactura de objetos ligeros como la ropa, **494**
lignite/lignita Tipo de carbón suave, **453**
limited government/gobierno limitado Gobierno en el que los ciudadanos hacen responables a los dirigentes por medio de la constitución y los procesos democráticos, **86**
limited monarchy/monarquía limitada Sistema de gobierno dirigido por una reina o un rey que no tiene el control absoluto de un país, **141**
literacy/alfabetismo Capacidad de leer y escribir, **166**
***Llaneros*/llaneros** Vaqueros de los llanos de Venezuela, **336**
Llanos/llanos Planicies localizadas al este de Colombia y al oeste de Venezuela, **328**
lochs/lagos Lagos escoceses enclavados en valles labrados por los glaciales, **432**
loess/limo Suelo fino de arenisca, excelente para la agricultura, **413**
Loyalists/Loyalistas, Leales Colonistas americanos que se oponían a independización de Intalterra, **152**

M

magma/magma Roca fundida que se localiza en el manto superior de la tierra, **28**
mainland/región continental Región donde se localiza la mayor porción de terreno de un país, **394**
mantle/manto Capa líquida que rodea al centro de la Tierra, **28**
maquiladoras/maquiladoras Fábricas extranjeras establecidas en la frontera de México con Estados Unidos, **307**
maritime/marítimo En o cerca del mar, como las provincias marítimas de Canada, **270**
market economy/economía de mercado Tipo de economía en la qué los consumidores ayudan a determinar qué productos se fabrican al comprar o rechazar ciertos bienes y servicios, **85**
mass production/producción en serie Sistema de producción de grandes cantidades de productos idénticos, **163**
medieval/medieval Periodo de colapso del imperio romano, aproximadamente en el año 1,500 de nuestra era, **415**
megalopolis/megalópolis Enorme zona urbana que abarca una serie de ciudades que se han desarrollado juntas, **236**
mercantilism/mercantilismo Creación y conservación de riquezas mediante un control minucioso de intercambios comerciales, **139**
Mercosur/Mercosur Organización comercial en la que participan Argentina, Brasil, Paraguay, Uruguay y dos países asociados (Bolivia y Chile), **354**
merengue/merengue Tipo de música y baile nacional en la República Dominicana, **320**
mestizos/mestizos Personas cuyo origen combina las razas europeas y las razas indígenas de América, **300**
metallic minerals/minerales metálicos Minerales brillantes, como el oro y el hierro, que conducen el calor y la electricidad, **65**
meteorology/meteorología Predicción y registro de lluvias, temperaturas y otras condiciones atmosféricas, **13**
Métis/Métis Personas cuyo origin combina las razas europeas y las razas indígenas de Canadá, **267**
middle class/clase media Clase formada por comerciantes, patronos de pequeña y mediana industria y profesiones liberales. Está entre la clase noble y la clase campesina en la Edad Media, **129, 164**
migrated/migrar Trasladarse de un lugar a otro, **110**
militarism/militarismo Uso de armamento pesado y amenazas para obtener poder, **173**
minerals/minerales Sustancias inorgánicas que conforman la corteza de la tierra; en su medio natural, aparecen en forma cristalina y tienen una composición química definida, **65**
missions/misiones Puestos españoles de evangelización establecidos en la época colonial, especialmente en América, **300**
monarchy/monarquía Sistema de gobierno dirigido por un rey o una reina, **141**
monsoon/monzón Cambio de corrientes aire y lluvias que produce temporadas alternadas de humedad y sequía, **45**
Moors/moros Musulmanes del norte de África, **405**
moraine/morena Cresta de rocas, grava y arena levantada por un glaciar, **237**
mosaics/mosaicos Imágenes creadas con pequeños fragmentos de piedras coloreadas, **398**
mosques/mezquitas Casas de adoración islámica, **526**
mulattoes/mulatos Personas cuyo origen combina las razas europeas y las razas indígenas de África, **300**
multicultural/multicultural Mezcla de culturas en un mismo país o comunidad, **75**

N

nationalism/nacionalismo Demanda de autogo-bierno y fuerte sentimiento de lealtad hacia una nación, **167, 426**
national parks/parques nacionales Terreno escénico grande preservado por un gobierno para uso público, **252**

NATO/OTAN (Organización del Tratado del Atlántico Norte); alianza militar formada por varios países europeos, Estados Unidos y Canadá, **194, 415**

nature reserves/reservas naturales Zonas asignadas por el gobierno para la protección de animales, plantas, suelo y agua, **506**

navigable/navegable Rutas acuáticas de profundidad suficiente para la navegación de barcos, **412**

neutral/neutral Que no toma ningún partido en una disputa o conflicto, **444**

New Deal/New Deal Pragrama del presidente Franklin D. Roosevelt en el que el gobierno federal estableció un amplio programa de obras públicas para crear empleo y conceder dinero a cada estado para sus necesidades, **179**

newsprint/papel periódico Papel económico usado para imprimir publicaciones periódicas, **263**

nobles/nobles Personas que nacen entre familias ricas y poderosas, **127**

nomads/nómadas Personas que se mudan frecuentemente de un lugar a otro, **104, 522**

nonmetallic minerals/minerales no metálicos Minerales que no tienen las características de los metales, **66**

nonrenewable resources/recursos no renova-bles Recursos, como el carbón mineral y petróleo, que no pueden reemplazarse a corto plazo por medios naturales, **65**

North Atlantic Drift/Corriente del Atlántico Norte corriente de aguas tibias que aumenta la temperatura y genera lluvias en el norte de Europa, **433**

nutrients/nutrientes sustancias que favorecen el crecimiento, **52**

O

oasis/oasis Lugar del desierto donde un manantial proporciona una fuente natural de agua, **520**

oil shale/pizarra petrolífera Capa de roca que al calentarse produce petróleo, **453**

oppression/opresión Uso de poder cruel e injusto contra otros, **154**

orbit/órbita Trayectoria que sigue un objeto que gira alrededor de otro objeto (como la Tierra alrededor del Sol), **17**

ozone/ozono Forma del oxígeno en la atmósfera que ayuda a proteger a la Tierra de los daños que produce la radiación solar, **22**

P

Pampas/pampas Región extensa cubierta de hierba en la zona central de Argentina, **344**

Pangaea/Pangaea Supercontinente original y único del que se separaron los continentes actuales, **31**

***pardos*/pardos** Venezolanos descendientes de la unión entre africanos, europeos e indígenas sudamericanos, **336**

Parliament/Parlamento Órgano británico de legislación, **141**

partition/repartir Separar un terreno formando grupos más pequeños, **195**

Patriots/Patriotas Colonistas americanos que favorecieron con la independencia de Inglaterra, **152**

peat/turba Sustancia formada por plantas muertas, por lo general musgos, **442**

peninsula/península Tierra rodeada de agua en tres lados, **28**

permafrost/permafrost Capa de suelo que permanece congelada todo el año en las regiones con clima de la tundra, **49**

perspective/perspectiva Punto de vista basado en la experiencia y la comprensión de una persona, **3**

Peru Current/corriente de Perú Corriente oceánica fría del litoral oeste de América del Sur, **363**

petroleum/petróleo Líquido graso que al refinarse produce gasolina y otros combustibles y aceites, **68**

photosynthesis/fotosíntesis Proceso por el que las plantas convierten la luz solar en energía quimica, **51**

physical geography/geografía física Estudio del paisaje natural y los sistemas físicos de la Tierra, entre ellos la atmósfera, **11**

pidgin languages/lenguas francas Lenguajes sencillos que ayuden a entenderse a personas que hablan idiomas diferentes, **337**

pioneers/pioneros Primeras personas que llegan a poblar una región, **225**

plain/planicie Área casi plana de la superficie terrestre, **28**

plantains/banano Tipo de plátano que se usa para cocinar, **322**

plantations/plantaciones Granjas muy grandes en las que se produce un solo tipo de cultivo para vender, **223**

plant communities/comunidades de plantas Grupos de plantas que viven en la misma zona, **53**

plant succession/sucesión de plantas Proceso gradual por el que un grupo de plantas reemplaza a otro, **54**

plateau/meseta Terreno plano y elevado sobre la superficie terrestre, **28**

plate tectonics/tectónica de placas Teoría de que la superficie terrestre está dividida en varias placas enormes que se mueven lentamente, **28**

police state/estado totalitario País en que el gobierno tiene un control total sobre la vida de las personas, **180**

pope/papa Obisco de Roma y líder de la Iglesia católica romana, **401**

popular sovereignty/soberanía popular Principio gubernamental basado en leyes justas, y en un gobierno creado y sujeto a la voluntad del pueblo, **149**

population density/densidad de población Número promedio de personas que viven en una milla cuadrada o un kilómetro cuadrado, **81**

potash/potasa Mineral que se usa para hacer fertilizantes, **263**

precipitation/precipitación Proceso por el que el agua vuelve de regreso a la Tierra, **24**

prehistory/prehistoria Tiempo antiguo del que no se conservan registros escritos, **103**

primary industries/industrias primarias Actividades económicas que involucran directamente recursos naturales o materia prima, tales como la agricultura y la minería, **83**

Protestants/protestantes Reformistas que protestaban por la realización de ciertas prácticas de la Iglesia Católica, **135**

provinces/provincias Divisiones administrativas de un país, **266**

pueblo/pueblo grupo de personas que vivian en asientamentos permanentes en el suroests de Estados Unidos, **111**

pulp/pulpa Fibras reblandecidas de madera para hacer papel, **263**

Puritan/Puritano Persona que aspiraban a una doctrina más pura que la propuesta por la Iglesia Católica Inglesa, **141**

Q

quaternary industries/industrias cuaternarias Actividades económicas que abarca destrezas o conocimiento especializados, y trabajan generalmente con la información, **83**

Quechua/quechua Idioma de los incas de América del Sur; todavía se habla en esta región, **370**

quinoa/quinua Planta nativa de la región sudamericana de los Andes que da semillas muy nutritivas, **365**

quipu/quipu Complicado sistema de cuerdas de varios colores con nudos, que usaron los incas de América del Sur para registrar información, **113, 366**

R

race/raza Grupo de personas que comparten características físicas o biológicas heredades, **76**

rain shadow/barrera montañosa Área seca en el sotavento de una montaña o de una cordillera, **44**

ratified/ratificado Aprobado formalmente, **225**

reactionaries/reaccionarios Extremistas que se oponen al cambio, y desean deshacer ciertos cambios, **158**

reason/razón Razonamiento lógico, **148**

refineries/refinerías Fábricas donde se procesa el petróleo crudo, **68**

reforestation/reforestación Plantación de árboles donde los bosques han sido talados, **61**

reform/reformar Mejorar algo reparando sus errores, **168**

Reformation/Reforma Movimiento europeo del siglo XVI para reformar el cristianismo, **135, 418**

refugees/refugiados Personas que han escapado a otro país, generalmente por razones económicas o políticas, **321**

reggae/reggae Tipo de música que tiene sus orígenes en Jamaica, **320**

regionalism/regionalismo Conexión más fuerte con la región a la que se pertenece que con el propio país, **269**

Reign of Terror/Régimen de Terror Período durante la Revolución Francesca cuando la Convención Nacional trabajó para suprimir toda oposición, **156**

relative location/ubicación relativa Posición de un lugar en relación con otro, **7**

Renaissance/Renaissance Palabra francesa que significa "renacimiento" y se refiere a una nueva era de conocimiento que empieza en Europa en el 1300s, **131, 401**

renewable resources/recursos renovables Recursos, como el suelo y los bosques, que pueden reemplazarse por medio de procesos naturales de la Tierra, **59**

republic/república Forma de gobierno representativo en que la soberania reside en el pueblo, **118**

Restoration/Restauración Período en que reinó Carlos II de Inglaterra, cuando la monarquía fué restablecida, **142**

revolution/revolución Una vuelta completa alrededor del Sol, **19**

revolutionaries/revolucionarios Rebeldes que demandan un gobierno propio, **184**

Roma/Roma Grupo étnico, también conocido como gitanos, que pudo haber migrado de la India a Europa hace mucho tiempo, **464**

rotation/rotación Una vuelta completa de la Tierra sobre su propio eje, **19**

rural/rural Área de terreno abierto que se usa para la agricultura, **4**

S

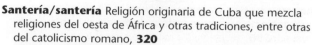

Santería/santería Religión originaria de Cuba que mezcla religiones del oesta de África y otras tradiciones, entre otras del catolicismo romano, **320**

satellite/satélite cuerpo que da vueltas al rededor de un cuerpo grande, **18**

scarcity/escasez Situación que resulta cuando la demanda es mayor que la oferta, **87**

Scientific Revolution/Revolución Cientifica Transformación de pensamiento ocurrido durante 1500 y 1600, causada por la observación cientifica, la experimantación, y el cuestionamiento de las opiniones tradicionales, **137**

secede/separar Dividir un país para formar otro, **227**

secondary industries/industrias secundarias Actividades económicas que convierten en productos terminados la materia prima que producen las industrias primarias, **83**

second-growth forests/bosques reforestados Árboles que cubren una región después de que el bosque original ha sido talado, **238**

secularism/secularismo Énfasis en asuntos no religiosos, **148**

sediment/sedimento Pequeñas partículas de rocas fragmentadas, **241**

***selvas*/selvas** Bosques tropicales exuberantes del oeste de Ecuador y Perú, y del norte de Bolivia, **363**

semiarid/semiárido Terreno relativamente seco, con lluvias escasas, **62**

serfs/siervos Personas que estaban atados a una tierra y trabajaban para un señor, **128, 509**

sinkholes/sumideros Agujero profundo de pendiente empinada que se forma cuando el techo de una cueva se hunde, **294**

sirocco/siroco Viento seco y caliente del norte de África que viaja por el mar Mediterráneo hacia Europa, **395**

slash-and-burn agriculture/agricultura de corte y quema Tipo de agricultura en que los bosques se talan y se queman para limpiar el terreno y plantarlo, **307**

smelters/fundidoras Fábricas que procesan menas de metal, **495**

smog/smog Mezcla de humo, sustancias químicas y niebla, **306**

social contract/contrato social Idea de que el gobierno se basa en un acuerdo entre las personas, **149**

soil exhaustion/agotamiento del suelo Pérdida de los nutrientes del suelo que necesitan las plantas, **346**

solar energy/energía solar Recurso de energía renovable que produce a luz y el calo r del Sol, **71**

solar system/sistema solar El Sol y los cuerpos celestes que se mueven en trono a él, entre otros los planetas, las lunas y los asteroides, **17**

solstice/solsticio Días en que los rayos verticales del Sol están más lejos del ecuador, **21**

soviet/soviet supremo Consejo comunista que gobernó la república y otras regiones de la Unión Soviética, **509**

spatial perspective/perspectiva espacial Punto de vista basado o visto en relación con el lugar en que se encuentra un objeto, así como la razón por la que está ahí, **3**

steppe/estepa Gran llanura de pastos altos que se extiende desde Ucrania, pasa por el sur de Rusia y llega hasta Kazajistán, **485**

steppe climate/clima estepario Tipo de clima, generalmente seco, que se encuentra entre las regiones de climas desértico y húmedo, **46**

stock market/mercado de valores Organización mediante la cual se venden y se compran partes de compañías, **178**
strait/estrecho Paso angosto que une dos grandes cuerpos de agua, **362**
strip mining/minería a cielo abierto Tipo de minería en que se retiran la tierra y las rocas para extraer carbón y otros recursos que están bajo la superficie terrestre, **252**
subduction/subducción Movimiento en el que una placa tectónica terrestre más gruesa se sumerge debajo de una más delgada, **29**
subregions/subregiones Áreas pequeñas de una región, **8**
subsistence agriculture/agricultura de subsistencia Tipo de agricultura en que los campesinos siembran sólo lo necesario para mantenerse a ellos mismos y a sus familias, **80**
suburbs/suburbios Áreas residenciales en las afueras de la ciudad, **167**
suffragettes/sufragistas Mujeres que lucharon por el derecho de las mujeres de votar, **168**
superpowers/superpotencias Países poderosos, **489**
symbol/símbolo Palabra, forma, color, estadarte o cualquier otra cosa que se use en representación de algo, **77**

T

taiga/taiga Bosque de árboles siempre verdes que existen en el sur de la tundra en Rusia, **485**
tepees/tepees Tiendas de forma cónica, hechas de piel de búfalo, **110**
tepuís/tepuís Capas de roca arenisca resistentes a la erosión en las mesetas de los altiplanos de las Guyanas, **328**
terraces/terrazas Crestas horizontales que se construyen sobre las laderas de las colinas para prevenir la pérdida de suelo y favorecer la agricultura, **60**
tertiary industries/industrias terciarias Actividades económicas que trabajan con productos listos para vender a los consumidores, **83**
textiles/textiles Productos para fabricar ropa, **435**
traditional economy/economía tradicional Economía basada en las costumbres y las tradiciones, **85**
tributary/tributario Cualquier corriente pequeña o río que fluye hacia un río o una corriente más grande, **25**
Tropic of Cancer/Trópico de Cáncer Línea de latitud que está a 23.5 grados al norte del ecuador, **21**
Tropic of Capricorn/Trópico de Capricornio Línea de latitud que está a 23.5 grados al sur del ecuador, **21**
tundra climate/clima de la tundra Región fría de lluvias escasas, que por lo genera se encuentra entre los climas de las regiones subártica y polar, **49**
typhoons/tifones Tormentas tropicales de vientos violentos, fuertes lluvias y altas marejadas, **48**

U

U-boats/U-boats Submarinos alemanes usados en la Primer Guerra Mundial, **174**
uninhabitable/inhabitable Que no es propicio para el establecimiento de seres humanos, **446**
unlimited governments/gobiernos ilimitados Gobiernos que tienen un control total sobre sus ciudadanos, **86**
urban/urbano Área en que se encuentra una ciudad, **4**

V

vassals/vassalos Personas a la que un amo le concedía tierras, como pago por sus servicios, **127**
vernacular/vernácular Lenguaje doméstico, natino, propio de un país, **130**
viceroy/virrey Gobernador de una colonia, **368**

W

water cycle/ciclo del agua Circulación del agua del la superficie de la Tierra a la atmósfera y su regreso, **23**
water vapor/vapor de agua Estado gaseoso del agua, **23**
weather/tiempo Condiciones de la atmósfera en un tiempo y un lugar determinados, **37**
weathering/desgaste Proceso de desintegración de las rocas en pedazos pequeños por la acción del calor, el agua y otros medios, **31**
wetlands/terreno pantanoso Paisaje cubierto de agua al menos una parte del año, **241**
Wheat Belt/región triguera Zona de la región de las Grandes Planicies en Estados Unidos en la que la actividad principal es el cultivo del trigo, **251**
working class/clase trabajadora Personas capacitadas y poco capacitadas con empleos de salarios bajos, **165**

Y

yurt/yurta Tienda redonda y portátil de lana tejida que se coloca sobre una armazón de madera, **526**

INDEX

S indicates Skills Handbook | *g indicates graphic* | *m indicates map* | *p indicates photograph*

A

B

D

G

H

P

Q

R

S

ACKNOWLEDGMENTS

For permission to reprint copyrighted material, grateful acknowledgment is made to the following sources:

Casa Juan Diego: Adapted from *Immigrants Risk All: Cry for Argentina* by Ana Maria from *Houston Catholic Worker*, July/August 1997, accessed February 2, 2000, at http://www.cjd.org/stories/risk.html.

Doubleday, a division of Random House, Inc.; electronic format by permission of Harold Ober Associates Incorporated: From "Marriage Is a Private Affair" from *Girls at War and Other Stories* by Chinua Achebe. Copyright © 1972, 1973 by Chinua Achebe.

FocalPoint f/8: From "October 5—Galtai" from "Daily Chronicles" and from "Buddhist Prayer Ceremony" from "Road Stories" by Gary Matoso and Lisa Dickey from *The Russian Chronicles* from *FocalPoint f/8*, accessed October 14, 1999, at http://www.f8.com/FP/Russia.

Glas Publishers (Russia): From "The Lilac Dressing Gown" by Nina Gabrielyan, translated by Joanne Turnbull from *A Will and a Way: New Russian Writing*, edited by Natasha Perova and Arch Tait. Copyright © 1996 by Glas: New Russian Writing.

Sandy Wiseman: From "Photo-Journey Through a Costa Rican Rainforest" by Sandy Wiseman from *EcoFuture™ PlanetKeepers*, accessed October 14, 1999, at http://www.ecofuture.org/ecofuture/pk/pkar9512.html. Copyright © 1999 by Sandy Wiseman.

SOURCES CITED:

From "The Aztecs in 1519" from *The Discovery and Conquest of Mexico* by Bernal Díaz. Published by Routledge and Kegan Paul, London, 1938.

ART CREDITS

Abbreviated as follows: (t) top, (b) bottom, (l) left, (r) right, (c) center.

Unit flags of United States created by One Mile Up, Inc. Unit flags of Canadian provinces created by EyeWire, Inc. Other flags, country silhouettes, feature maps and atlas maps created by MapQuest.com., Inc. All other illustrations, unless otherwise noted, contributed by Holt, Rinehart and Winston.

Study Skills: Page S2, MapQuest.com, Inc.; S3, MapQuest.com, Inc.; S4 (cl, bl), MapQuest.com, Inc.; S5, MapQuest.com, Inc.; S6 (tr), MapQuest.com, Inc.; S7, MapQuest.com, Inc.; S8 (tr), MapQuest.com, Inc.; S9, MapQuest.com, Inc.; S10 (tc, br), Leslie Kell; S11 (cr), Leslie Kell; S11 (b), Ortelius Design; S12 (b), Leslie Kell; S12 (tr), Rosa + Wesley; S13, Uhl Studios, Inc.; S14 (br), MapQuest.com, Inc.; S15 (bl), MapQuest.com, Inc.

Chapter 1: Page 5 (cl), MapQuest.com, Inc.; 6 (bl), MapQuest.com, Inc.; 7 (tl, tr), MapQuest.com, Inc.; 8 (l, bc), MapQuest.com, Inc.; 9 (tr), MapQuest.com, Inc.; 10 (tc), MapQuest.com, Inc.; 11 (bc), MapQuest.com, Inc.; 15 (tr), MapQuest.com, Inc.

Chapter 2: Page 17 (b), Uhl Studios, Inc.; 18 (b), Uhl Studios, Inc.; 19 (bl), Uhl Studios, Inc.; 20 (b), Uhl Studios, Inc.; 22 (tl), Robert Hynes; 23 (cr), MapQuest.com, Inc.; 24 (tr), Uhl Studios, Inc.; 25 (tr, br), Uhl Studios, Inc.; 26 (b), MapQuest.com, Inc.; 28 (b), Uhl Studios, Inc.; 29 (tl), MapQuest.com, Inc.; 29 (c, br), Uhl Studios, Inc.; 31 (tr), MapQuest.com, Inc.; 32 (tr), Ortelius Design; 35 (tr), MapQuest.com, Inc.

Chapter 3: Page 38 (tl), Uhl Studios, Inc.; 38 (cl), MapQuest.com, Inc.; 39 (bl), MapQuest.com, Inc.; 40 (tr), Uhl Studios, Inc.; 42 (cr), Rosa + Wesley; 42 (b), MapQuest.com, Inc.; 43 (t), Rosa + Wesley; 45 (tl), Uhl Studios, Inc.; 46 (br), MapQuest.com, Inc.; 47 (all), MapQuest.com, Inc.; 48 (tl, bc), MapQuest.com, Inc.; 49 (tr), MapQuest.com, Inc.; 50 (tl), MapQuest.com, Inc.; 52 (tr), Robert Hynes; 55 (tr), Uhl Studios, Inc.; 57 (tr), MapQuest.com, Inc.

Chapter 4: Page 60 (tc), MapQuest.com, Inc.; 62 (bl), MapQuest.com, Inc.; 63 (tr, br), MapQuest.com, Inc.; 65 (br), Leslie Kell; 67 (t), MapQuest.com, Inc.; 69 (tl, br), MapQuest.com, Inc.; 70 (tl), MapQuest.com, Inc.; 73 (tr), MapQuest.com, Inc.

Chapter 5: Page 76 (t, bl), MapQuest.com, Inc.; 77 (tr), MapQuest.com, Inc.; 78 (bl), MapQuest.com, Inc.; 81 (cr), MapQuest.com, Inc.; 83 (br) MapQuest.com, Inc.; 86 (c), Rosa + Wesley; 88 (cl), MapQuest.com, Inc.; 89 (tc), MapQuest.com, Inc.; 91 (tr), MapQuest.com, Inc.; 93 (tl), MapQuest.com, Inc.; 98 (t, bl), Ortelius Design.

Chapter 6: Page 106 (t) MapQuest.com, Inc.; 107 (b) MapQuest.com, Inc.; 109 (b) MapQuest.com, Inc.; 111 (b) MapQuest.com, Inc.; 112 (t) Nenad Jakesevic; 114 (b) MapQuest.com, Inc.; 117 (br) MapQuest.com, Inc.; 119 (b) MapQuest.com, Inc.; 123 (tr) MapQuest.com, Inc.

Chapter 7: Page 126 (br) MapQuest.com, Inc.; 128 (cl) Nenad Jakesevic; 138–139 (tr) MapQuest.com, Inc.; 145 (tr) MapQuest.com, Inc.

Chapter 8: Page 153 MapQuest.com, Inc.; 171 MapQuest.com, Inc.; 171 MapQuest.com, Inc.

Chapter 9: Page 174 MapQuest.com, Inc.; 175 (tr) Craig Attebery; 193 (bl) MapQuest.com, Inc.; 197 MapQuest.com, Inc.; 201 (tr) MapQuest.com, Inc.; 203 (tr) MapQuest.com, Inc.; 208 (bl), Ortelius Design; 208 (t), Ortelius Design; 209 (all), MapQuest.com, Inc.; 210 (all), MapQuest.com, Inc.; 211 (all), MapQuest.com, Inc.; 212 (all), MapQuest.com, Inc.; 213 (all), MapQuest.com, Inc.

Chapter 10: Page 217 (b), MapQuest.com, Inc.; 219 (t), MapQuest.com, Inc.; 219 (br), MapQuest.com, Inc.; 220 (bl), MapQuest.com, Inc.; 224 (bl) MapQuest.com, Inc.; 226 (tr) MapQuest.com, Inc.; 233 (tr) MapQuest.com, Inc.; 233 MapQuest.com, Inc.

Chapter 11: Page 237 MapQuest.com, Inc.; 238 Phototake; 239 MapQuest.com, Inc.; 240 (b) MapQuest.com, Inc.; 243 MapQuest.com, Inc.; 244 MapQuest.com, Inc.; 246 (tr) The John Edwards Group; 246 (b) MapQuest.com, Inc.; 247 MapQuest.com, Inc.; 248 (b) MapQuest.com, Inc.; 249 MapQuest.com, Inc.; 249 MapQuest.com, Inc.; 250 MapQuest.com, Inc.; 253 (b) MapQuest.com, Inc.; 255 MapQuest.com, Inc.; 255 MapQuest.com, Inc.; 257 MapQuest.com, Inc.; 259 (tr) MapQuest.com, Inc.; 259 MapQuest.com, Inc.

Chapter 12: Page 261 (b), MapQuest.com, Inc.; 262 (cl), MapQuest.com, Inc.; 263 (tr), MapQuest.com, Inc.; 266 (tr), MapQuest.com, Inc.; 266 (tl), Leslie Kell; 266 (bl), MapQuest.com, Inc.; 267 (cr), MapQuest.com, Inc.; 267 (br), Rosa + Wesley; 268 (cl), MapQuest.com, Inc.; 270 (tl), MapQuest.com, Inc.; 272 (tl), MapQuest.com, Inc.; 275 (tr), MapQuest.com, Inc.; 277 (tr), MapQuest.com, Inc.; 182 (t, bl), Ortelius Design.

Chapter 13: Page 293 (b), MapQuest.com, Inc.; 295 (tc), MapQuest.com, Inc.; 295 (t,br), MapQuest.com, Inc.; 298 (br), MapQuest.com, Inc.; 300 (bl), MapQuest.com, Inc.; 302 (tr), Leslie Kell; 303 (t), MapQuest.com, Inc.; 304 (cl), Rosa + Wesley; 305 (bl); MapQuest.com; 306 (bl), MapQuest.com, Inc.; 309 (tr), MapQuest.com, Inc.

Chapter 14: Page 311 (b), MapQuest.com, Inc.; 312 (bl), MapQuest.com, Inc.; 314 (cl), MapQuest.com, Inc.; 315 (cr), MapQuest.com, Inc.; 317 (br), Leslie Kell; 318 (tl), Rosa + Wesley; 319 (br), MapQuest.com, Inc.; 320 (tl), Rosa + Wesley; 321 (tr, bl), MapQuest.com, Inc.; 323 (tr), MapQuest.com, Inc.; 325 (tr), MapQuest.com, Inc.

Chapter 15: Page 327 (b), MapQuest.com, Inc.; 328 (b), Uhl Studios, Inc.; 330 (bc), MapQuest.com, Inc.; 331 (tr), Rosa + Wesley; 331 (cr), MapQuest.com, Inc.; 333 (tc), MapQuest.com, Inc.; 333 (cr), Leslie Kell; 335 (bl), MapQuest.com, Inc.; 335 (br), MapQuest.com, Inc.; 336 (cl), Rosa + Wesley; 337 (cr), MapQuest.com, Inc.; 338 (tl), Rosa + Wesley; 338 (bc), MapQuest.com, Inc.; 339 (tl), MapQuest.com, Inc.; 341 (tr), MapQuest.com, Inc.

Chapter 16: Page 343 (b), MapQuest.com, Inc.; 344 (bl), MapQuest.com, Inc.; 349 (tr), MapQuest.com, Inc.; 349 (br), Rosa + Wesley; 350 (tl), Leslie Kell; 352 (tl,br), MapQuest.com, Inc.; 354 (tc), MapQuest.com, Inc.; 354 (cl), Rosa + Wesley; 355 (c), MapQuest.com, Inc.; 356 (tc), MapQuest.com, Inc.; 356 (bl), Rosa + Wesley; 359 (tr), MapQuest.com, Inc.

Chapter 17: Page 361 (b), MapQuest.com, Inc.; 363 (cr), MapQuest.com, Inc.; 366 (tl), MapQuest.com, Inc.; 368 (tl), MapQuest.com, Inc.; 370 (bl), MapQuest.com, Inc.; 371 (tr), MapQuest.com, Inc.; 372 (tl), Rosa + Wesley; 373 (tr), Leslie Kell; 375 (tr), MapQuest.com, Inc.; 380 (t, bl), Ortelius Design.

Chapter 18: Page 393 (b), MapQuest.com, Inc.; 394 (bl), MapQuest.com, Inc.; 395 (tr), MapQuest.com, Inc.; 395 (cr), Leslie Kell; 396 (br), MapQuest.com, Inc.; 397 (tc), MapQuest.com, Inc.; 399 (tr), Rosa + Wesley; 400 (cl), MapQuest.com, Inc.; 401 (tc), MapQuest.com, Inc.; 402 (bl), MapQuest.com, Inc.; 403 (tr), Rosa + Wesley; 405 (br), MapQuest.com, Inc.; 405 (c), MapQuest.com, Inc.; 406 (tl), Rosa + Wesley; 407 (tl), MapQuest.com, Inc.; 409 (tr), MapQuest.com, Inc.

Chapter 19: Page 411 (b), MapQuest.com, Inc.; 412 (tl, bc), MapQuest.com, Inc.; 413 (tr), MapQuest.com, Inc.; 416 (cr), MapQuest.com, Inc.; 417 (cl), Rosa + Wesley; 418 (bl), MapQuest.com, Inc.; 419 (cr), MapQuest.com, Inc.; 420 (tl), Leslie Kell; 420 (c), MapQuest.com, Inc.; 421 (cr), Rosa + Wesley; 422 (cl), MapQuest.com, Inc.; 424 (cl), Rosa + Wesley; 426 (tl), MapQuest.com, Inc.; 427 (cr), Rosa + Wesley; 429 (tr), MapQuest.com, Inc.

Chapter 20: Page 431 (b), MapQuest.com, Inc.; 432 (bl), MapQuest.com, Inc.; 434 (cl), MapQuest.com, Inc.; 435 (c), MapQuest.com, Inc.; 436 (bl), Rosa + Wesley; 439, Nenad Jakesevic; 437 (cr), Leslie Kell; 440 (bl), MapQuest.com, Inc.; 442 (tl), Rosa + Wesley; 442 (cl), MapQuest.com, Inc.; 443 (br), Rosa + Wesley; 445 (tl, bc), MapQuest.com, Inc.; 436 (tl), MapQuest.com, Inc.; 437 (cr), MapQuest.com, Inc.; 439 (tr), MapQuest.com, Inc.

Chapter 21: Page 441 (b), MapQuest.com, Inc.; 442 (bl), MapQuest.com, Inc.; 443 (tr), MapQuest.com, Inc.; 446 (tl), Rosa + Wesley; 446 (cl), MapQuest.com, Inc.; 448 (bc), MapQuest.com, Inc.; 449 (tr), MapQuest.com, Inc.; 450 (bl), MapQuest.com, Inc.; 451 (cr), MapQuest.com, Inc.; 452 (tc), MapQuest.com, Inc.; 453 (tr, cr), MapQuest.com, Inc.; 456 (tl), Leslie Kell; 456 (bl), MapQuest.com, Inc.; 455 (tr), Rosa + Wesley; 457 (tr), MapQuest.com, Inc.; 459 (tl), MapQuest.com, Inc.; 474 (t, bl), Ortelius Design.

Chapter 22: Page 483 (b), MapQuest.com, Inc.; 485 (br), MapQuest.com, Inc.; 488 (t), MapQuest.com, Inc.; 489 (tr, bc), MapQuest.com, Inc.; 491 (tr, cr), Rosa + Wesley; 491 (br), MapQuest.com, Inc.; 494 (br), MapQuest.com, Inc.; 494 (tl, bl), MapQuest.com, Inc.; 495 (tr), MapQuest.com, Inc.; 496 (bl), MapQuest.com, Inc.; 497 (tl), MapQuest.com, Inc.; 498 (tl), MapQuest.com, Inc.; 500 (bl), MapQuest.com, Inc.; 501 (tr), MapQuest.com, Inc.; 503 (tr), MapQuest.com, Inc.

Chapter 23: Page 505 (b), MapQuest.com, Inc.; 506 (bl), MapQuest.com, Inc.; 509 (bl), MapQuest.com, Inc.; 510 (tl), MapQuest.com, Inc.; 511 (c), Uhl Studios, Inc.; 512 (tl), Leslie Kell; 512 (cl), Rosa + Wesley; 514 (bc), MapQuest.com, Inc.; 515 (tr), Rosa + Wesley; 517 (tr), MapQuest.com, Inc.

Chapter 24: Page 519 (b), MapQuest.com, Inc.; 521 (cr), MapQuest.com, Inc.; 522 (cl), MapQuest.com, Inc.; 523 (cr), MapQuest.com, Inc.; 524 (l), Leslie Kell; 526 (bc), MapQuest.com, Inc.; 527 (tr), Rosa + Wesley; 529 (cr), Leslie Kell; 531 (tr), MapQuest.com, Inc.; 533 (t), MapQuest.com, Inc.

PHOTO CREDITS

Cover and Title Page: (child image) AlaskaStock Images; (bkgd) Image Copyright © 2003 PhotoDisc, Inc./HRW

Table of Contents: iv (bl), © SuperStock; v (tl) "S. Sherbell/SABA Press Photos, Inc."; vi (bl) "Walters Art Gallery, Baltimore, Courtesy of Robert Forbes Collection"; vi © From the Collections of Henry Ford Museum and Greenfield Village; vii (tl) "Bob Daemmrich/The Image Works, Woodstock, NY"; vii (br), © Marc Muench/CORBIS; viii (tl), © Nazima Kowall/CORBIS; viii (br) Stone/Richard A. Cooke III; ix (bl) HRW Photo; ix (tr), © Stone/Chad Ehlers; x (tl), © The Stock Market/Don Mason; x (br), © Leo de Wys/Siegfried Tauquer; xi (b), © Index Stock Photography; xi (tl), © The Stock Market/H. P. Merten; xi (tr); © Claus Meyer/Black Star/PNI; xii (tl), © Travelpix/FPG International LLC; xii (cl), AKG Photo, London; xii (b) Steve Raymer/NGS Image Collection; xiii (l), © The State Russian Museum/CORBIS; xiv (tl) Alain Le Garsml/Panos Pictures; xiv (b), Gianni Dagli Orti/CORBIS; xv (br) "Image Copyright © 2002 PhotoDisc, Inc./HRW"; xviii (b), © Matt Glass/CORBIS-Sygma; xxiii, CORBIS Images/HRW; xxiv (tl), David Young-Wolf/PNI; xxiv (b), Klaus Lahnstein/Getty Images; S2–S15 (background), DeLorme Mapping; S20 (b), © Nik Wheeler/CORBIS; S21 (cl), Jeffrey Aaronson/Network Aspen; S21 (c), Index Stock Imagery, Inc.; S21 (tr), Amit Bhargava/Newsmakers/Getty Images; S22 (l), Norman Owen Tomalin/Bruce Coleman, Inc.; S22 (cl), © Fritz Polking/Peter Arnold, Inc.; S22 (tl), Larry Kolvoord Photography; S22 (tr), Runk/Schoenberger/Grant Heilman Photography; S22 (tr), Wolfgang Kaehler Photography; S27 (b), Rosenback/ZEFA/Index Stock Imagery, Inc.; **Unit 1**: 1 (b), Photo © Transdia/Panoramic Images, Chicago 1998; 1 (cl), © Joe Viesti/The Viesti Collection; 1 (tr), Francois Gohier/Photo Researchers, Inc.; 1 (t), © Norbert Wu/www.norbertwu.com; 1 (br), Steven David Miller/Animals Animals/Earth Scenes; **Chapter 1**: 2 (cl), © Stone/ Philip & Karen Smith; 2 (bl), Sam Dudgeon/HRW Photo; 2 (tr), CORBIS; 2 (c), © Joseph Sohm; ChromoSohm Inc./CORBIS; 3 (bl), © Stone/Ken McVey; 3 (tr), British Library, London, Great Britain/ Art Resource, NY; 4, Luca Turi/AP/Wide World Photos; 5 (cl), The Stock Market/Jose Fuste Raga; 5 (cr), NASA; 6 (cl), Robert Caputo/Aurora; 6 (tr), © Stone/Robert Frerck; 7–8 © Bob Daemmrich; 8 (b), K.D. Frankel/Bilderberg/Aurora; 9 (t,br), © Wolfgang Kaehler; 10, © Nik Wheeler/CORBIS; 11 (cr), © Ilene Perlman/Stock, Boston; 11 (tr), © Archivo Iconografico S.A./CORBIS; 13 (cr), © Chris Rainier/CORBIS; **Chapter 2**: 16 (c), © Roger Ressmeyer/CORBIS; 16 (tl), Digital Stock Corp./HRW; 16 (t), Steve Winter/Black Star; 16 (cl), T.A. Wiewandt/DRK Photo; 16 (bl), Scala/Art Resource, NY; 17, Monticello. Photo: Edward Owen; 19, © Stone/Earth Imaging; 20 (tl), courtesy of NASA, Marshall Space Flight Center; 21 (t,b), Global Hydrology and Climate Center, NASA Marshall Space Flight Center.; 23 (t), Image copyright ©2002 PhotoDisc, Inc.; 23 (b), © Gerald French/FPG International LLC; 24, © Tom Bean/CORBIS; 26 (t), © Norbert Wu/www.norbertwu.com; 26 (b), Boll/Liaison Agency; 27, © Ed Kashi; 28, © Gary Braasch/CORBIS; 30, © Stone/Andrew Rafkind; 31, © Galen Rowell/CORBIS; 32, © Yann Arhtus-Bertrand/CORBIS; **Chapter 3**: 36 (c), © Stone/ Glenn Christianson; 36 (tr), © Stone/A. Witte/C. Mahaney; 36 (br), © Stone/Brian Stablyk; 36 (b), © 1999 Michael DeYoung/AlaskaStock.com; 36 (tl), Corbis Images; 37, Thomas A. Wiewandt, Ph.D., Wild Horizons; 38, © Layne Kennedy/CORBIS; 39, © Chinch Gryniewicz; Ecoscene/CORBIS; 40, © SuperStock; 41, © Flip Nicklin/Minden Pictures; 43 (cr), NASA; 44 (bl), Image copyright ©1998 PhotoDisc, Inc./HRW; 44 (t), Paul Seheult; Eye Ubiquitous/CORBIS; 45 (br), © Stone/Martin Puddy; 46 © Laurence Parent; 48 (tl), © Gail Mooney/CORBIS; 48 (b), © DiMaggio/Kalish/ Peter Arnold, Inc.; 49, © Darrell Gulin/CORBIS; 50, © Galen Rowell/CORBIS; 51 (c), © Darrell Gulin/CORBIS; 51 (t), Image Copyright ©2002 PhotoDisc, Inc.; 53 (t), Robert Maier; 54 (tl), © E & P Bauer/Bruce Coleman, Inc.; 54 (tr), © Scott T. Smith/CORBIS; 54 (bl), © F. Krahmer/Bruce Coleman, Inc.; 54 (br), © Gary Braasch/CORBIS; 55, Photo by William E. Ferguson © William E. Ferguson; **Chapter 4**: 58 (cl), © Philip James Corwin/CORBIS; 58 (bl), Aaron Chang/The Stock Market; 58 (cr), © Morton Beebe/ Corbis; 58 (t), Mike Huser/DRK Photo; 59 (b), Larry Lefever/ Grant Heilman Photography; 59 (t), Coronado Rodney Jones/HRW Photo; 60, © Michael Busselle/CORBIS; 61, © Kevin Schafer; 62 (bl), © Tom Carroll/FPG International LLC; 62 (t), © Mark Reinstein/FPG International LLC; 63 (t), Grant Heilman/Grant Heilman Photography; 63 (br), Steven Burr Williams/Liaison International; 64 (all), NASA, Goddard Space Flight Center; 65, Image Copyright © 2002 PhotoDisc, Inc./HRW; 66 (t), Sam Dudgeon/HRW Photo; 66 (b), Dr. Bode; 68 (b), © Stone/Mike Abrahams; 68 (t), © Stone/Vince Streano; 69, © Ernest

54 (bl), © F. Krahmer/Bruce Coleman, Inc.; 54 (br), © Gary Braasch/CORBIS; 55, Photo by William E. Ferguson © William E. Ferguson; **Chapter 4**: 58 (cl), © Philip James Corwin/CORBIS; 58 (bl), Aaron Chang/The Stock Market; 58 (cr), © Morton Beebe/Corbis; 58 (t), Mike Huser/DRK Photo; 59 (b), Larry Lefever/Grant Heilman Photography; 59 (t), Coronado Rodney Jones/HRW Photo; 60, © Michael Busselle/CORBIS; 61, © Kevin Schafer; 62 (bl), © Tom Carroll/FPG International LLC; 62 (t), © Mark Reinstein/FPG International LLC; 63 (tr), Grant Heilman/Grant Heilman Photography; 63 (br), Steven Burr Williams/Liaison International; 64 (all), NASA, Goddard Space Flight Center; 65, Image Copyright ©2002 PhotoDisc, Inc./HRW; 66 (t), Sam Dudgeon/HRW Photo; 66 (b), Dr. Bode; 68 (b), © Stone/Mike Abrahams; 68 (t), © Stone/Vince Streano; 69, © Ernest Manewal/FPG International LLC; 70 (b), © Telegraph Colour Library/FPG International LLC; 71, Mark Burnett/Photo Researchers, Inc.; **Chapter 5**: 74 (t), © Gerald Brimacombe/International Stock Photography; 74 (cr), © Bob Firth/International Stock Photography; 74 (b), © Ahu Tongariki/Bruce Coleman, Inc.; 74 (c), © Wally McNamee/CORBIS; 75 (b), © Bob Daemmrich/Stock, Boston; 75 (t), © Galen Rowell/CORBIS; 76, © Bohdam Hrynewch/Stock, Boston/PNI; 77 (b), © Stone/Ron Sherman; 77 (t), © Stone/Rich La Salle; 78 (b), Bruno Barbey/Magnum Photos; 78 (t), S. Sherbell/SABA Press Photos, Inc.; 79, © Werner Forman/CORBIS; 80, © Eric and David Hosking/CORBIS; 81 (b), © Rich Iwasaki/AllStock/PNI; 81 (t), © Stone/Bob Thomas; 83 (t), © Digital Vision; 84 (tl), © Michelle Gabel/The Image Works, Woodstock, NY; 84 (t), © Richard Hamilton Smith/CORBIS; 84 (bl), Henry Friedman; 84 br), © Stephen Frisch/Stock, Boston/PNI; 85, Carolyn Schaefer/SCHAE/Bruce Coleman, Inc.; 87 (b), © Joanna B. Pinneo/Aurora; 87 (t), © Joel W. Rogers/CORBIS; 88, © Pramod Mistry/The Image Works, Woodstock, NY; 89 (t), © Ed Kashi; 92–93 (all), Andrew Miles/HRW; **Unit 2:** 96–97 (all), York Archeological Trust; 98, (tl) © Pix 2000/FPG International; 98, (tr) © the British Museum/The Art Archive; 98, (c) © Private Collection, Milan/Canali Photobank, Milan/SuperStock; 98, (bl) © George Grigoriou/Stone; 99, (tr) Eirik Irgens Johnsen/University Museum of National Antiquities, Oslo, Norway; 99, (tl) © Archivo Iconografico, S.A./CORBIS; 99, (bl) © The Pierpont Morgan Library/Art Resource, NY; 99, (br) © Nimatallah/Art Resource, NY; 99, (cr) © Dagli Orti/Russian Historical Museum, Moscow/the Art Archive; 100, (c) © Dagli Orti/Musée du Chateau de Versailles/the Art Archive; 100, (bl) © Robert Harding Picture Library; 100, (tl) © Victoria & Albert Museum, London/Bridgeman Art Library; 100, (tr) © Museo del Prado, Madrid/the Art Archive; 100, (br) © Philip Mould, Historical Portraits Ltd, London, UK/Bridgeman Art Library; 101, (tr) © Hulton Archive by Getty Images; 101, (bl) © Culver Pictures; 101, (tl) © Sovfoto/Eastfoto; 101, (br) © AFP/CORBIS; **Chapter 6:** 102 (cr) Gianni Dagli Orti/Corbis; 102 (b) Hulton-Deutsch Collection/Corbis; 102 (tr) Sheridan/Ancient Art & Architecture Collection; 102 (cl) "Dagli Orti/Musée du Louvre, Paris/The Art Archive"; 103 (b) "Dr. Owen Lovejoy and students, Kent State University. Photo © 1985 David L. Brill"; 103 (t) Nik Wheeler/Corbis; 104 (t) "Courtesy Mammoth Site Museum, Hot Springs, SD"; 104 (b) Gianni Dagli Orti/Corbis; 105 Paul Almasy/Corbis; 106 (b) "Martha Avery/Asian Art & Archaeology, Inc./Corbis"; 108 Zafer Kizilkaya/Atlas Geographic; 109 (t) Jose Fuste Raga/Corbis Stock Market; 110 (b) Wild Country/Corbis; 110 (t) HRW Photo; 112 (b) "Werner Forman Archive/National Museum of Anthropology, Mexico City/Art Resource, NY"; 114 (t) "Ashmolean Museum, Oxford, UK/Bridgeman Art Library"; 115 (t) "National Archaeological Museum, Athens, Greece/Bridgeman Art Library"; 116 (t) Gian Berto Vanni/Art Resource; 116 (b) Phyllis Picardi/Stock South/PictureQuest; 117 (tr) "Art Resource, NY"; 118 (b) VCG/FPG International; 120 (t) Jose Fuste Raga/Corbis Stock Market; 120 (b) "Gene Plaisted, OSC/The Crosiers"; **Chapter 7:** 124 (tr) Sheridan/Ancient Art & Architecture Collection; 124 (b) Gail Mooney/Corbis; 124 (cl) "Bibliothèque Nationale, Paris/AKG London"; 124 © "Erich Lessing/Art Resource, NY"; 125 (t) AKG London; 125 (b) Robert W. Madden/Paris/AKG London; 126 (tl) AKG London; 127 (t) Bettmann Corbis; 127 (br) "Bibliothèque Nationale, Paris/AKG London"; 128 (t) Bridgeman Art Library/SuperStock; 128 (br) "The Pierpont Morgan Library/Art Resource, NY"; 129 (t) "Musée de la Tapisserie, Bayeux, France/Bridgeman Art Library"; 129 (b) "Giraudon/Art Resource, NY"; 130 (tl) "Bibliothèque Royale de Belgique, Brussels, Belgium/Bridgeman Art Library"; 130 (b) "Archivo Iconografico, S.A./Corbis"; 131 (t) "British Library, London/Bridgeman Art Library, London/SuperStock"; 131 (b) "Dagli Orti/Galleria degli Uffizi, Florence/The Art Archive"; 132 (t) Ali Meyer/Bridgeman Art Library; 132 (br) "Kunsthistorisches Museum, Vienna, Austria/Bridgeman Art Library"; 132 © Bettmann/Corbis; 133 © "The Pierpont Morgan Library/Art Resource, NY"; 133 (t) "Erich Lessing/Art Resource, NY"; 133 (br) "Art Resource, NY"; 134 (b) Gary Yeowell/Stone; 134 (tl) "Giraudon/Art Resource, NY"; 135 (tr) "Scala/Art Resource, NY"; 135 (br) "Belvoir Castle, Leicestershire/Bridgeman Art Library"; 136 (tl) Bridgeman Art Library; 137 (t) "Scala/Art Resource, NY"; 137 (b) "New York Historical Society, New York, USA/Bridgeman Art Library"; 138 (bl) Réunion des Musées Nationaux/Bridgeman Art Library; 139 (cr) David Parker/Science Photo Library/Photo Researchers; 140 (cl) Museum of the City of New York/Corbis; 141 (t) "Palace of Versailles, France/Lauros-Giraudon, Paris/SuperStock"; 141 (b) "National Portrait Gallery, London/SuperStock"; 142 (t) Bridgeman Art Library; 142 (bl) "Dreweatt Neate Fine Art Auctioneers, Newbury/Bridgeman Art Library"; 143 (tr); **Chapter 8:** 146 (tr) Sheridan/Ancient Art & Architecture Collection; 146 (br) Lee Snider/Corbis; 146 (cl) SuperStock; 146, Dietrich Stock Photos, Inc"; 147 (t) David Muench/Corbis; 147 (b) Stock Montage/SuperStock; 148 (b) "Louvre, Bibliothèque, Paris, France/Erich Lessing/Art Resource, NY"; 148 (tl) "Tate Gallery, London/Art Resource, NY"; 149 (cr) Giraudon/Bridgeman; 149 (bl) "Erich Lessing/Art Resource, NY"; 150, The Granger Collection, New York; 151 (t) Colonial Willimasburg Foundation; 151 (b) Stock Montage; 152 (bl) SuperStock; 152 (tl) The Granger Collection, New York; 153 (bl) Christie's Images/SuperStock; 154 (b) "AKG, Berlin/SuperStock"; 155 (t) "Dagli Orti/Musée de l'Affiche, Paris/The Art Archive"; 155 (b) "Dagli Orti/Musée Carnavalet, Paris/The Art Archive"; 156 (tl) "Dagli Orti/Musée Carnavalet, Paris/The Art Archive"; 156 (bl) Dagli Orti/Musée de Versailles/The Art Archive; 157 (tr) "Erich Lessing/Art Resource, NY"; 158, Bettman/CORBIS; 159 (b) Stock Montage; 159 (tr) CORBIS/Hulton-Deutsch Collection Limited; 160 (b) "Steidle Collection, College of Earth and Mineral Sciences, Pennsylvania State University/Steidle Art Collection/SuperStock"; 161 (tr) AKG London; 162 (bl) The Art Archive; 162 (tl) Palubniak Studios; 163 (t) From the Collections of Henry Ford Museum and Greenfield Village; 164 (t) Hulton Archive by Getty Images; 164 (bl) "Gernsheim Collection, Harry Ransom Humanities Research Center, The University of Texas at Austin"; 165 (b) John D. Cunningham/Visuals Unlimited; 165 (tr) Culver Pictures; 166 © "New York Journal, Jan 5, 1896, Courtesy OldNews, Inc. & New York World, 1883, Courtesy OldNews, Inc."; 166 (b), Winslow Homer, American, 1836–1910, Croquet Scene, oil on canvas, 1866, $15\frac{7}{8} \times 26\frac{1}{16}$ in, Friends of American Art Collection, 1942.35, photograph © 1998, The Art Institute of Chicago, All Rights Reserved; 167 (tr) "Erich Lessing/Art Resource, NY, (frame) Image Farm"; 168 (t) Hulton-Deutsch Collection/Corbis; 168 (b), Gianni Dagli Orti/CORBIS; 169 (tr) AKG Berlin/SuperStock; **Chapter 9:** 172 (cl), Franklin D. Roosevelt Library; 172 (tr) Sheridan/Ancient Art & Architecture Collection; 172 (br) SuperStock; 173 (b), Culver Pictures; 173 (t) AKG London; 175 (br) Culver Pictures; 176 (bl) Bettmann/Corbis; 177 (cr) Brown Brothers; 178 (b) AP/Wide World Photos; 178 (tr); 179 (t) Brown Brothers; 180 (tl) AKG London; 180 (bl) AKG London; 181 (cr) AKG London; 182 (cl) Historical Picture Archive/Corbis; 182 (tr) Wolfgang Kaehler/Corbis; 183 (br) Bettmann/Corbis; 183 © Robert Frerck/Woodfin Camp & Associates; 184 (tl) Bettmann/Corbis; 184 (bl) Culver Pictures; 185 (br) Brown Brothers; 186 (cl) Kal Muller/Woodfin Camp & Associates; 187 (t) AKG London; 187 (bl) "Giraudon/Art Resource, NY"; 188 (tl) UPI/Bettmann/Corbis; 188 (br) Bilderdienst Suddeutscher Verlag; 189 (tl) AKG London; 189 (br) "American Stock/Hulton Archive by Getty Images, Hulton Archive by Getty Images"; 190 (tl) Loomis Dean/TimePix; 190 (bl) "Bruno P. Zehnder/Peter Arnold, Inc"; 192 (cl) AP/Wide World Photos; 192 (t) "PhotoDisc, Inc."; 193 (tr) AP/Wide World Photos; 194 (tl) Corbis; 194 (bl) Getty News Services; 195 (cr) Hanan Isachar/Corbis; 195 (t) Bruno Barbey/Magnum/PictureQuest; 196 © AKG London; 197 (tr) Magnus Bartlet/Woodfin Camp & Associates; 197 (bl) Mario Corvetto/Evergreen Photo Alliance; 198 (cl) Novosti/Science Photo Library/Photo Researchers; 198 (br) David Young-Wolff/PhotoEdit; 198 (tl) Bob Daemmrich/Corbis Sygma; 199 (tr), © European Communities; 202 (bl) Stuart Ramson/AP/Wide World Photos; 202 (tr) Mark Wilson/Getty Images; 203 (tr) Galen Rowell/Mountain Light Photography; 204; 205 (cr) "Scala/Art Resource, NY"; 205 (tl) Francis G. Mayer/Corbis; 205 (cl) "Royal Holloway and Bedford New College, Surrey, UK/Bridgeman Art Library"; **Unit 3:** 206 (t), SuperStock; 206 (bl), © Walter Bibikow/FPG International LLC; 206–207 (bc), Lawrence Migdale; 207 (cr), © Stone/Zigy Kaluzny; 207 (br), Alan Nelson/Animals Animals/Earth Scenes; **Chapter 10:** 216 (cl) The Granger Collection, New York; 216 (r), SuperStock; 217, SuperStock; 218, SuperStock; 219, (c) Robert Frerck/Odyssey/Chicago; 220 (br), Image Copyright © 2002 PhotoDisc, Inc./HRW; 220 (cl), Jay Malonson/AP; 220 (bl), Jim Schwabel/Southern Stock/PNI; 220 (cr), SuperStock; 222 (tl) "Christie's Images, New York/SuperStock"; 222 (cl) Steve Vidler/Nawrocki Stock Photo; 223 (tr) Bettmann/Corbis; 223 (b) "The Metropolitan Museum of Art, Gift of Edgar William and Bernice Chrysler Garbish, 1963."; 224 (tl) Stock Montage; 225 (tr) Bettman/Corbis; 226 (b); 227 (t) Francis G. Mayer/Corbis; 227 (b); 228 (t) "Gianni Dagli Orti/Corbis, (b) Bettmann/Corbis"; 228 (br) Andrew Russell/Culver Pictures; 228 (cl) Seneca Falls Historical Society; 229 (t) AP/Wide World Photos; 230 (tr), Mark Wilson/Getty Images; 230 (cl), AP Photo/Daniel Hulshizer; 231 (tl), AFP Photo/Lucy Nicholson; 231 (tr), HRW Photo; 231 (r), Matthew McDermott/Corbis Sygma; 231 (bl), Adrin Snider/Daily Press/Corbis Sygma; **Chapter 11:** 234 Steve Ewert Photography; 236 (b), © Stone/Jake Rajs; 237 (t), © Ace Photo Agency/Phototake; 238 (tl) Michael Sullivan/TexaStock; 239 (tl) John Ficara/Woodfin Camp & Associates; 240 (tl) CORBIS/Robert Holmes; 241 (tr) Jeff Greenberg/Photo Researchers; 242 (bl) Stone/Bruce Hands; 243 (cl) D. Donne Bryant/DDB Stock; 244 (tr) David R. Frazier Photolibrary; 247 (tr) Donald Johnson/The Stock Market; 248 (tr) R. Manley/SuperStock; 249 (bl) James Randkley/Tony Stone Images; 249 (tr) "Dan Abernathy/ProFiles West, Inc."; 250 (bl) Jim Brandenberg/Minden Pictures; 250 (tl) LarryUlrich/DRKPhoto; 251 (tr) "Cotton Coulson/Woodfin Camp & Associates, Inc."; 251 (bl) "Charles R. Belinky/Photo Researchers, Inc."; 253 (tr) "Joe Sohm/The Image Works, Woodstock, NY"; 254 (bl) Kevin Schaefer/Tony Stone Images; 255 (tl) SuperStock; 255 (br) Greg Vaughn/Pacific Stock; 256 (br) Tom & Pat Leeson/DRK Photo; 256 (tl), © 2003 Galen Rowell/Mountain Light Photography; 257 (cr) Charles A. Mauzy/Tony Stone Images; **Chapter 12:** 260, Steve Ewert Photography; 261, Eric Beggs/HRW Photo; 262, © Carr Clifton/Minden Pictures; 263 (c), © Stone/Gordon Fisher; 263 (t), © Walter Bibikow/The Viesti Collection; 264 (t), © Richard Pasley/The Viesti Collection; 264 (c), Henry E. Huntington Library and Art Gallery; 265, © Bill Terry/The Viesti Collection, Inc.; 266, © Stone/Bob Herger; 267, © Robert Winslow/The Viesti Collection; 268, © Mark E. Gibson; 269 (b), © Nazima Kowall/CORBIS; 269 (t), © Ron Watts/CORBIS; 270, © Nik Wheeler/CORBIS; 271, Sam Dudgeon/HRW Photo; 272 (b), © Stone/George Hunter; 272 (t), © Stone/Cosmo Condine; 273, © Stone/Art Wolfe; 276, Bettmann/CORBIS; 279 (all), © Landiscor Aerial Information; **Unit 4:** 280–281, (c), Cliff Hollenbeck/International Stock Photography; 280 (b), Francois Gohier/Photo Researchers, Inc.; 280 (t), George Holton /Photo Researchers, Inc.; 281 (cr), Stephen J. Krasemann/Nature Conservancy/Photo Researchers, Inc.; 281 (b), C.K. Lorenz/Photo Researchers, Inc.; 291, Steve Ewert Photography; **Chapter 13:** 292, Steve Ewert Photography; 293, © Russel Gordon/Odyssey/Chicago; 294 (t), © Robert Frerck/Odyssey/Chicago; 294 (cl), © Stone/George Lepp; 294 (b), Image copyright ©2002 PhotoDisc, Inc.; 295, © Robert Frerck/Odyssey/Chicago; 297 (t), Boltin Picture Library; 297 (b), Dallas and John Heaton/Corbis; 298 (b), © Stone/Richard A. Cooke III; 298 (t), The Bodleian Library, Oxford, MS Arch. Selden A. 1, fol 37R; 299, Reproduced from the collections of The Library of Congress; 300, © Robert Frerck/Odyssey/Chicago; 301 (t), © Danny Lehman/CORBIS; 302, Alex S. MacLean/Landslides; 303, © Bob Daemmrich; 304, © StockFood America/Eising; 305 (b), © Danny Lehman/CORBIS; 305 (t), © Jan Butchofsky-Houser/CORBIS; 306, John Neubauer; 307, © Stone/David Hiser; **Chapter 14:** 310, Steve Ewert Photography; 311, Image Copyright © 2002 PhotoDisc, Inc./HRW; 312, Bruce Dale/NGS Image Collection; 314 (t), © SuperStock; 314 (c), © Frank Staub; 314 (inset), © 1995 Kevin Shafer; 315, © Robert Frerck/Odyssey/Chicago; 316, Ancient Art and Architecture Collection Ltd.; 317, © Robert Frerck/Odyssey/Chicago; 319 (t), Ken Karp/HRW Photo; 319 (c), © Carol Lee; 321 (t), © Stone/Doug Armand; 321 (b), © Jose Azel/Aurora; 322 (all), Image Copyright ©2002 PhotoDisc, Inc./HRW; 323, © The Stock Market/Terry Eggers 1998; **Chapter 15:** 326, Steve Ewert Photography; 327, © Kevin Schafer & Martha Hill; 329, © Kevin Schaeffer; 330 (b), © The Stock Market/Patrick Rouillard/Latin Stock; 330 (t), © Robert Frerck/Odyssey/Chicago; 331, © Dave G. Houser/CORBIS; 332, © Gianni Dagli Orti/CORBIS; 333, © Jeremy Horner/CORBIS; 334 (b), © The Stock Market/James Marshall; 334 (t), © FoodPix; 334 (c), AKG Photo, London; 336, © Kevin Schafer/CORBIS; 337 (t), © Adam Woolfitt/CORBIS; 337 (b), Chip and Rosa Marie Peterson; 338, © Nicole Duplaix/CORBIS; 339 (t), © B.Barbey/Magnum Photos; **Chapter 16:** 342, Steve Ewert Photography; 343, © Gerry Ellis/ENP Images; 344, © Stone/Robert Van Der Hilst; 345, © Gail Shumway/FPG International LLC; 346, © Carlos Humberto T.D.C./Contact Press Images/PNI; 347 (b), © Archivo Iconografico, S.A./CORBIS; 347 (t), © Marlen Raabe/CORBIS; 348, David Leah/Allsport; 349, © Stone/Chad Ehlers; 351 (t), © Barnabas Bosshart/CORBIS; 351 (b), Sepp Seitz/Woodfin Camp & Associates; 352 (br), © Stone/Robert Frerck; 353, © Yann Arthus-Bertrand/CORBIS; 354, © Johnny Stockshooter/International Stock Photography; 355 (t), Chip and Rosa Marie Peterson; 355 (b), © The Stock Market/RAGA; 356 (cl), © Paul Crum/Photo Researchers, Inc.; 356 (t), © Daniel Rivademar/Odyssey/Chicago; 357, © Alex Webb/Magnum; **Chapter 17**: 360, Steve Ewert Photography; 361, © Kevin Schafer; 362, © Stone/William J. Hebert; 363, © Robert Frerck/Odyssey/Chicago; 364, Mireille Vautier/Woodfin/PNI; 365 (bl), © The Stock Market/Don Mason; 365 (br), © The Stock Market/Don Mason; 367–368, © Robert Frerck/Odyssey/Chicago; 369, © Vera A. Lentz/Black Star/PNI; 370 (t), Marty Granger/Edge Video Productions/HRW; 370 (b), © Kevin Schafer; 371 (b), © Index Stock Photography and/or Garry Adams; 371 (t), © Robert Frerck/Odyssey/Chicago; 372, © Daniel Rivademar/Odyssey/Chicago; 376, © David Muench/CORBIS; 377, © Frank Blackburn/CORBIS; **Unit 5:** 380–381 (c), SuperStock; 380 (t), © E. Nagele/FPG International LLC; 380 (bl), Alfredo Venturi/Mastorfilo; 381 (t), FPG International LLC; 381 (br), Robert Maier/Animals Animals/Earth Scenes; **Chapter 18**: 392, Steve Ewert Photography; 393, © Robert Frerck/Odyssey/Chicago; 394, Photo © Earl Bronsteen 1/Panoramic Images, Chicago 1998; 395, © Gary Braasch/CORBIS; 396 (b), © Travelpix/FPG International LLC; 398 (t), Museo Archeologico Nazionale, Naples, Italy/Bridgeman Art Library; 397 (b), © Joe Viesti/The Viesti Collection; 397 (t), © Leo de Wys/Steve Vidler; 398 (bl), SEF/Art Resource, New York; 398 (br), © Araldo de Luca/CORBIS; 400 (l), © Archivo Iconografico, S.A./C; 400 (r), Christie's Images Ltd.; 401 (b), © Gianni Dagli Orti/CORBIS; 401 (t), © Louis Goldman/FPG International LLC; 402 (b), © Leo de Wys/Siegfried Tauquer; 402 (t), © Bill Staley/FPG International LLC; 404 (t,b), © Index Stock Photography; 405, © Jean Kugler/FPG International LLC; 406 (b), © Robert Frerck/Odyssey/Chicago; 407 (t), © Sitki Tarlan/Panoramic Images, Chicago 1998; 407 (b), © Charles O'Rear/CORBIS; **Chapter 19**: 410, Steve Ewert Photography; 411, © Stone/Hideo Kurihara; 412 (b), © Leo de Wys/John Miller; 412 (t), © Leo de Wys/J. Messerschmidt; 413, © The Stock Market/H. P. Merten; 414 (t), Image Copyright ©2002 PhotoDisc, Inc./HRW; 416 (l), Castres, Musee Goya /Art Resource, NY; 415 (b), Scala/Art Resource; 415 (t), The Art Archive; 416 (lc), © Joe Viesti/The Viesti Collection; 416 (r), © Leo de Wys/Mike Busselle; 416 (tl), Pierre Witt/Rapho/Liaison Agency; 418 (b), © Wolfgang Kaehler; 418 (t), © 1999 Ron Kimball/Ron Kimball Photography; 419 (inset), Archive Photos; 419 (cr), AKG Photo, London; 419 (t), CORBIS-Bettmann; 420, © Leo de Wys/Fridmar Damm; 422 (l), © Leo de Wys/Siegfried Tauqueur; 422 (t), Image Copyright ©2002 PhotoDisc, Inc./HRW; 423 (t), © Wolfgang Kaehler; 423 (b), © Steve Vidler/Nawrocki Stock Photo; 425 (t) Image Copyright ©2002 PhotoDisc, Inc./HRW; 425 (b), © Ken Ross/FPG International LLC; 426 (b), © G. Wagner/The Viesti Collection; 426 (t), © Stone/Siegfried Layda; **Chapter 20**: 430, Steve Ewert Photography; 431, © Werner Forman/CORBIS; 432, © Walter Bibikow/The Viesti Collection; 434 (b), British Museum, London, UK/Bridgeman Art Library; 434 (t), Bridgeman Art Library; 434 (c), © Yann Arthus-Bertrand/CORBIS; 435 (b), © Stone/Ed Pritchard; 435 (t), Private Collection/Bridgeman Art Library; 436 (b), © Jim Richardson; 436 (t), Popperfoto/Archive Photos; 438 © Historical Picture Archive/CORBIS, 439 U.S. National Library of Medicine, National Institutes of Health; 440 (t), Image Copyright ©2002 PhotoDisc, Inc./HRW; 440–441, b Joe Englander/Viesti Collection; 441 (r), © Becky Luigart-Stayner/CORBIS; 443 (t), Susan Marie Anderson/Foodpix; 443 (b), © Index Stock Photography; 444 (b), © Walter Bibikow/FPG International LLC; 445 (t), © Index Stock Photography and/or Zefa 1999; 446, © The Stock Market/Tom Stewart; 447, © Bryan & Cherry Alexander; **Chapter 21**: 450, Steve Ewert Photography; 451 (t), © Dr. Paul A. Zahl, Nat'l Audubon Society Collection/Photo Researchers; 452 (b), Robert Tixador/Figaro/Liaison Agency; 453, V. Leloup/Figaro/Liaison Agency; 454 (b), © Paul Almasy/CORBIS; 454 (t), © Archivo Iconografico, S.A./CORBIS; 455 (b), Aldo Pavan/Liaison Agency; 456, © David Bartruff/FPG International LLC; 457 (t), Image Copyright © 2002 PhotoDisc, Inc./HRW; 458 (b), © Fergus O'Brien/FPG International LLC; 458 (t), © Travelpix/FPG International LLC; 459, © Garbor Feher/CORBIS-Sygma; 460 (t), © Jonathan Blair/CORBIS; 460 (l), © Francoise de Mulder/CORBIS; 461 (b), Krpan Jasmin/Liaison Agency; 461 (t), © Michael S. Yamashita/CORBIS; 462, Marleen Daniels/Liaison Agency; 463 (b), Francis Li/Liaison Agency; 463 (t), © Patrick Chauvel/CORBIS-Sygma; 464, © Matt Glass/CORBIS-Sygma; 468, © Bill Ross/CORBIS; 469 (tr), © European Communities; **Unit 6:** 472 (bl), © SuperStock; 472 (br), © Ed Kashi; 472–473 (c), Mark Wadlow/Russia and Eastern Images; 473 (t), Bruce Coleman Inc.; 473 (br), Gerard Lacz/Peter Arnold, Inc.; 480, Robert S. Semeniuk/Black Star; 481 (t), © Gérard Degeorge/CORBIS; 481, Steve Ewert Photography; **Chapter 22**: 482 Steve Ewert Photography; 483, © Itar-Tass/Sovfoto/Eastfoto; 484, © Tass/Sovfoto/Eastfoto; 485, © Bryan & Cherry Alexander; 486, © Hans J. Burkard/Bilderberg/Aurora; 486, CORBIS-Bettmann; 487 (t), © StockFood America/Eising; 487 (b), Battle of the Novgorodians with the Suzdalians, Novgorod School, mid 15th century (tempera and gold on panel)/Tretyakov Gallery, Moscow, Russia/Bridgeman Art Library, London/New York; 489 (b), © Steve Raymer/CORBIS; 489 (t), © Steve Raymer/CORBIS; 490 (t), © Wally McNamee/CORBIS; 491, © Steve Raymer/CORBIS; 493 (b), © Vladimir Pcholkin/FPG International LLC; 493 (t), © Adam Woolfitt/CORBIS; 494 (b), © Steve Raymer/CORBIS; 494 (t), © Steve McCurry/Magnum; 495, © Claus Meyer/Black Star/PNI; 496 (t), Image Copyright ©2002 PhotoDisc, Inc./HRW; 498 (b), 497 (b), © Bryan & Cherry Alexander; 497 (t), Sovfoto/Eastfoto; 498, © Dean Conger/CORBIS; 499 (b), © Planet Earth Pictures/FPG International LLC; 499 (t), © The State Russian Museum/CORBIS; 500, © Wolfgang Kaehler/CORBIS; 501, © Michael S. Yamashita/CORBIS; **Chapter 23**: 504, Steve Ewert Photography; 505, Sisse Brimberg/NGS Image Collection; 506, © Dean Conger/CORBIS; 508 (t), Image Copyright © 2002 PhotoDisc, Inc./HRW; 508 (b), AKG Photo, London; 509 (b), Steve Raymer/NGS Image Collection; 509 (t), AKG Photo, London; 510, Steve Raymer/NGS Image Collection; 511 © Randall Hyman; 513 (b), © Charles Lenars/CORBIS; 513 (t), © Dean Conger/CORBIS; 382 (b), © Sovfoto/Eastfoto; 514 (t), Stephanie Maze, USA; **Chapter 24**: 518, Brian Vikander/Vikander Photography; 519, © Wolfgang Kaehler/CORBIS; 520 b), © Hans Reinhard/Bruce Coleman Inc.; 520 t), © Tass/Sovfoto/Eastfoto; 521, © Yann Arthus-Bertrand/CORBIS; 522 (b), © K.M. Westermann/CORBIS; 522 (t), © David Samuel Robbins/CORBIS; 523, © Wolfgang Kaehler/CORBIS; 524, © Nevada Wier/CORBIS; 525 (b), © Wolfgang Kaehler/CORBIS; 525 (t), © David S. Robbins/CORBIS; 526, © Dean Conger/CORBIS; 528, Alain Le Garsml/Panos Pictures; 529, Chris Stowers/Panos Pictures; 532, © 1990 Abbas/Magnum Photos; 533 (c), Marc Garanger/CORBIS; 534, BIOS/M. Gunther/Peter Arnold, Inc.; 535, Sovfoto/ Eastfoto;